CliffsNotes®

SAT*

CliffsNotes®

SAT*

by
BTPS Testing

Contributing Authors

Joy Mondragon-Gilmore, M.S.

Bernard V. Zandy, M.S.

Jean Eggenschwiler, B.A.

Ron Podrasky, M.S.

Contributing Authors/Consultants

Angel Acosta, B.S.

Pitt Gilmore, B.A.

Robin Hall, M.S.

Mary Ellen Lepionka, M.A.

Kurt S. Lowry, M.Ed., M.A.

Deena Mondragon, B.A.

Joy Peterson, Ph.D.

Howard Zager, M.A.

Mark Zegarelli, B.A.

WILEY

John Wiley & Sons, Inc.

About the Author

BTPS Testing has presented text preparation workshops at the California State Universities for over 35 years. The faculty at BTPS Testing have authored more than 30 national best-selling test preparation books including CliffsNotes preparation guides for the CSET, GRE, CBEST, PPST, RICA, and ACT. Each year the authors of this study guide conduct lectures to thousands of students preparing for the SAT and many other college-level exams.

Author's Acknowledgments

We would like to thank Suzanne Snyder for her many hours of editing the original manuscript, and Christina Stambaugh of Wiley for her assistance and careful attention to the production process. We would also like to thank Pitt Gilmore for his extraordinary patience and support in organizing the manuscript.

Editorial

Acquisition Editor: Greg Tubach

Project Editor: Suzanne Snyder

Copy Editor: Beth Adelman

Technical Editors: Tom Page, Robert Caughey, Mary Jane Sterling

Composition

Proofreader: Melissa D. Buddendeck

John Wiley & Sons, Inc., Composition Services

CliffsNotes® SAT

Published by:
John Wiley & Sons, Inc.
111 River Street
Hoboken, NJ 07030-5774
www.wiley.com

Library of Congress Control Number: 2012930546
ISBN: 978-1-118-05758-2 (pbk)
ISBN: 978-1-118-21250-9 (ebk); 978-1-118-20793-2 (ebk); 978-1-118-20792-5 (ebk)

Printed in the United States of America

10 9 8 7 6 5 4 3 2 1

Table of Contents

PART III: MATH SKILLS REVIEW

This book is dedicated to the memory of
Jerry Bobrow, Ph.D.
Educator and Author

*His wisdom, insight, and humor continue to give
strength to those who knew him.*

Preface

Get the competitive advantage on your SAT score and start your path toward college success today. *CliffsNotes SAT* is a comprehensive study guide that gives you an edge by providing you with maximum benefit in a reasonable amount of time. This book is not meant to be a substitute for formal high school classroom experience, but provides you with important learning tools to improve your reading, writing, and math skills. The skills and concepts presented will help you reach your test-taking potential, and will also help you with future learning opportunities. Using this study guide helps you evaluate and analyze your strengths while providing valuable instructional tools to overcome your weaknesses. The enhanced strategies outlined in this book are designed to deepen your understanding of the test format, question types, and practice problems.

In keeping with the fine tradition of CliffsNotes, this guide was developed by leading educators in the field of test preparation and college entrance preparation. The authors of this text have been successfully teaching thousands of high school students to prepare for the SAT for more than 30 years. The materials, strategies, and techniques presented in this guide have been researched, tested, and evaluated in SAT preparation classes at leading California universities and school districts.

Navigating This Book

This guide is designed to provide you with important information and the tools necessary for comprehensive and successful preparation. As you work through this book, try to follow the recommended sequence of topics within each chapter and make detailed notes on the pages of the book to highlight important facts and concepts. Each chapter presents subject matter material in a structured format to enhance your learning. Many of the sample problems are arranged by level of difficulty. Start in sequence with the easy problems first; then work your way up through the difficult problems as you progress through the book.

After reading the introductory material, begin with the diagnostic exam to assess your strengths and weaknesses. The diagnostic exam will help you pinpoint any areas that may require more preparation time. Focus on specific areas to further develop your skills and awareness of SAT exam questions. Then continue to work through subsequent chapters by examining the comprehensive analysis and review of each exam area, including question types, step-by-step instructions for solving problems, and up-to-date examples.

Once you have taken the diagnostic test and studied the exam areas, this guide provides you with extensive practice opportunities, including four full-length model practice exams. All four practice tests include answers with thorough explanations and sample essay responses. Finally, the last part of this book includes a checklist on page 535 as a reminder of "things to do" before you take your exam.

Overview of This Book

- **Introduction: An Overview of the SAT:** This is a general description of the SAT, exam format, scoring, frequently asked questions, general strategies, and general tips.
- **Part I—Diagnostic Exam:** An introductory diagnostic exam acquaints you with SAT question types, evaluates your areas of improvement, and provides you with a baseline starting point.
- **Part II—Review of Exam Areas:** These review chapters focus on the abilities tested in critical reading, writing, and mathematics, along with the basic skills you'll need, skills and concepts tested, directions, suggested strategies with samples, and additional tips.
- **Part III—Math Skills Review:** This is an intensive review of the basics of arithmetic, algebra, geometry, and data analysis. Each review area offers illustrated sample problems and practice exercises. Important symbols, terminology and equivalents are also included.
- **Part IV—Four Full-Length Practice Exams:** The practice exams include answers and in-depth explanations. The practice exams are followed by analysis worksheets to assist you in evaluating your progress.

Creating Your Customized Study Plan

There are as many "best" ways to study for the SAT as there are people who take the exam. Understanding your unique learning abilities and applying this understanding to a customized study plan will aid in your success on the SAT. Simply, the goal of preparation is to either increase your overall score as much as possible or to achieve scores that are relevant to specific college admission requirements. Before you can begin your preparation, start by exploring desired college programs to gather information and set your goals. Know the scores that you need for success *before* preparing your unique plans.

Start your preparation for the SAT with an *action plan* that recognizes your test-taking strengths and weaknesses, and that you can personally develop and execute. There are many pathways to learning that make use of different learning styles. This is why we have included hundreds of sample or practice problems with step-by-step explanations that are designed to enhance your learning style. While creating your customized study plan, it is recommended that you:

- Assess your strengths and weaknesses.
- Start with a general plan and move to a specific plan.
- Be time-wise.

Assess Your Strengths and Weaknesses

The universal first step in assessing your strengths and weaknesses is to discover where you're at right now. By starting with the practice diagnostic exam in Chapter 1, you will better understand the areas in which you need to improve. If time is of the essence, consider at least working through a range of sample questions to get a sense of your starting point. Then compare your results with the scores you would like to have. The areas that require the most growth are those on which you want to focus the majority of your limited study time. Starting with a look at the improvement you need is also a good way to guesstimate how much overall time you should devote to studying. Then set goals for your study time and be willing to frequently adapt and revise your goals as you evaluate your progress.

Start with a General Overview and Move to a Specific Plan

Even after you've defined the areas that need work, increasing your scores might still not be as simple as studying for a set time each day (though that's a good start!). Again, you know yourself best. Most people find it useful to start by learning general principles and skills that are widely applicable to many problems, and progressing to memorizing important facts and concepts. For example, you should start your *general* math review with basic arithmetic (fractions, percents, decimals, and so on), and then move to a *specific* plan to tackle certain types of basic arithmetic problems (mixed fractions, converting percents to decimals, and so on). Again, start general and move to more specific problems and concepts. As you progress in your preparation, moving from a general plan to a specific plan, you will notice that you may frequently revise and modify your plan to adapt to newly learned concepts.

Be Time Wise

Your study plan depends on the total amount of time until the exam date. If the exam is tomorrow, focus on understanding procedure and instructions (and gathering the necessary identification and a map to the test site). If the exam is four months from now, you can start with training skills and expect that an understanding of exam procedures will materialize as you work your way methodically through this guide. If you have the time, don't forget to check your progress along the way! Every time you take a practice exam, you might need to revise how you prioritize your study time—just remember to keep your college goals in mind!

An Overview of the SAT

The SAT Reasoning Test is the most commonly administered and evaluated college entrance test in the United States. Universities and colleges use SAT test results along with high school performance records to predict academic performance and to assess readiness for college coursework. The test places emphasis on the skills learned in high school and asks you to critically respond to multiple-choice questions in three subject areas: critical reading, writing, and mathematics; and to write one essay in response to a question prompt.

Learning the skills that prepare you for the SAT begin with strategic planning and preparation. This is why you should begin your preparation immediately by contacting the university admissions office for more information about specific minimum score requirements, application deadlines, the weighted value of each test section (i.e. the written essay may not carry the same value as multiple-choice questions), and other admission requirements.

Test Format

SAT Format		
Content	**Question Type**	**Number of Questions**
Critical Reading	Sentence completions Critical reading passages: extended reasoning, literal comprehension and vocabulary-in-context. (*questions intermingled*)	Approximately 19 questions Approximately 48 questions **Time: 3 sections, timed separately (two 25-minute sections and one 20-minute section) = 70 minutes.** **Approximately 67 questions**
Writing	Essay	1 essay **Time: 25 minutes for one written essay**
	Identifying sentence errors Improving sentences Improving paragraphs (*questions intermingled*)	Approximately 18 questions Approximately 25 questions Approximately 6 questions **Time: 2 sections, timed separately (one 25-minute section and one 10-minute section) = 35 minutes.** **Approximately 49 questions**
Mathematics	Numbers and operations Algebra and functions Geometry and measurement Data analysis, statistics, and probability (*questions intermingled*)	Approximately 11–14 questions Approximately 19–22 questions Approximately 14–16 questions Approximately 5–8 questions **Time: 3 sections, timed separately (two 25-minute sections and one 20-minute section) = 70 minutes.** **Approximately 54 questions**
*Unscored Variable Section	Reading, Writing, or Mathematics (unidentified unscored questions)	**25 minutes**
Total Questions		**Approximately 170 multiple-choice questions that count toward your score. Plus approximately 30 variable questions that are unscored.** **1 Essay Writing Task**
Total Testing Time		**Approximately 3 hours and 45 minutes**

TIP: Structure, scoring, and the order of sections are subject to change. Visit www.collegeboard.com for updated exam information.

Variable Section

The SAT has unidentified variable questions that make up an *unscored* section of the exam. These variable questions may appear in any order after the Essay Writing section. They *will not count* toward your SAT score. The variable questions are multiple-choice questions that will either be reading, writing, or mathematics questions. Variable questions are designed for research to make sure that scores compare to other versions of the SAT. It is impossible to differentiate variable questions from scored questions, so don't waste valuable time trying to guess which questions are variable. Just answer all questions and move along as quickly as possible.

Scoring

Scores on the SAT will be reported for three separate measures: critical reading, writing, and mathematics. Sections are scored for multiple-choice and numeric entry questions, including one written essay. The overall score is based on three factors:

- The number of questions answered
- The number of questions answered correctly (1 point each, or approximately 10-scaled points each)
- The number of questions answered incorrectly (one-quarter point is deducted for each incorrect answer)

Note that incorrect answers on math numeric entry questions are not subtracted from your score.

Scaled Scores		
Measure	**Type of Questions**	**Scaled Score**
Critical Reading	Multiple-Choice	200–800
Writing—Multiple Choice **Writing—Essay**	Multiple-Choice Essay	*200–800 Score 1–6 by two readers (total score 2–12) A score of 0 (zero) is unlikely unless an essay is blank, off topic, or written in pen. *Note: The writing, multiple-choice, and essay scores are combined to make up a scaled score of 200–800.
Mathematics	Multiple-Choice	200–800
Total of Three Scaled Scores		600–2400

Multiple-Choice Questions

- Critical Reading
- Writing
- Mathematics

The score for **multiple-choice questions** is based on the number of questions you answer correctly. Keep in mind that except for the math numeric-entry questions, there is a one-quarter point penalty for each incorrect answer. If you are faced with a question that requires additional information or that is impossible to answer, simply leave the question blank. Do not guess unless you can eliminate at least three of the answer choices. Each question computes a *raw score* (1-point increments) that is based on the number of questions you answer correctly. The raw score is equated and converted into a *scaled score* (approximately 10-point increments) from 200 to 800 for each section. The "equating" process takes into account test variations and disparities among different tests. The scaled score also helps to determine your percentile rank, which many colleges use to compare your score results with other applicants. The *average score is 500* on each section of the SAT, denoting that 50 percent of students score above and 50 percent of students score below 500. Remember that scores are based upon the number of questions you answer correctly, minus any penalty points.

Essay Writing Section

In the **essay writing section**, one essay is scored holistically and receives a score from two independent readers that ranges from 1 to 6 (0 for a blank paper) based on the rubric below. Holistic scoring means that readers look at the *overall quality* of each essay. If there is a discrepancy of more than one point (on a 6-point scale) in the assigned scores from the two readers, a third reader will read and evaluate the essay. SAT readers are typically high school or college English teachers with many years of experience and training. After the readers assign a score for each essay, the two essay scores are added together, averaged, and then rounded up to produce a single final score that represents both essay responses. Note that the essay score is converted to about 30% of the total writing section scaled score of 200-800. The general scoring guidelines in the following table provide you with a brief analysis of criteria for the essay score. For more information about the essay scoring criteria, read Chapter 3, "Writing Overview."

SAT Essay Scoring Guide
Score 6 – Convincing and Persuasive Essay
You will receive a score of 6 if the response
❏ demonstrates the ability to reason and put together evidence to present a clear and insightful essay that responds directly to the task
❏ provides well-developed examples and supporting details
❏ is clearly written with only a few minor errors
❏ presents an organized, focused essay that uses transitions to connect ideas
❏ uses well-chosen vocabulary and varied sentence structure types to convey meaning
❏ demonstrates correct usage of the conventions of standard written English
Score 5 – Thoughtful and Well-Developed Essay
You will receive a score of 5 if the response
❏ presents a reasonably clear, well-thought-out essay that responds directly to the task, but has occasional errors and lapses in quality
❏ provides reasonable and logical supporting details for examples
❏ presents a generally well-organized essay with coherence and a progression of connected ideas
❏ uses appropriate vocabulary and sentence variety to convey meaning
❏ demonstrates a good command of the correct usage of the conventions of standard written English
Score 4 – Competent
You will receive a score of 4 if the response
❏ presents a realistic, clear position that responds to the task
❏ demonstrates competence by covering the task at hand and provides reasonably logical supporting details for examples
❏ has adequate organization and development
❏ uses language to convey meaning with adequate clarity
❏ demonstrates some variety in sentence structure and some errors in the conventions of standard written English
Score 3 – Marginally Adequate
You will receive a score of 3 if the response
❏ shows limited competence, and is vague or limited in responding to the specific prompt
❏ uses weak, irrelevant, or inconsistent examples for support
❏ lacks focus or is poorly organized
❏ has language deficiences that interfere with communication
❏ demonstrates frequent errors in grammar, diction, and sentence structure

continued

Score 2 – Inadequate

You will receive a score of 2 if the response

❏ has a significant weakness in responding to the task and demonstrates weak critical thinking

❏ provides limited or inappropriate examples for support

❏ lacks focus and is poorly organized

❏ demonstrates limited language skills with incorrect word choices

❏ contains serious errors in grammar, diction, and sentence structure

Score 1 – Severely Flawed

You will receive a score of 1 if the response

❏ fails to understand the task or issue

❏ provides little or no evidence or support

❏ lacks organization and development

❏ has severe language deficiencies that prevent communication

❏ is extremely brief or short

❏ contains serious errors in grammar, diction, and sentence structure that interfere with the meaning

Frequently Asked Questions

Q. Where do I apply to take the SAT?

A. The SAT is administered by the College Board, http://sat.collegeboard.org, P.O. Box 8056, Mount Vernon, IL 62864-0208, (866) 756-7346 or for students with disabilities (609) 771-7137.

Q. What are the types of SAT tests?

A. There are two types of SAT tests: SAT and SAT Subjects Test. The focus of this book is the standard SAT. It is a reasoning test that assesses general critical reading, writing, and mathematics. The SAT is the more commonly required test for college admission. If you want to get a preview of what the test administration experience will be like, go to the College Board website, *Test Day Simulator,* www.collegeboard.com/register/sattest-day-simulator.

Q. What is the SAT Subjects Test?

A. The Subjects Test is content based and measures your proficiency in specific subject areas. There are 20 subject tests in 5 general areas: English, history, languages, mathematics, and science. If you are uncertain about which test to take, visit the SAT website for more information about college requirements at http://collegesearch.collegeboard.com/search/index.jsp and click on "college quickfinder" for university recommendations.

Q. Can I take the SAT more than once?

A. Yes. It is common for students to take the test more than once.

Q. When should I take the SAT?

A. It is popular for first-time test-takers to take the SAT during the spring of their junior year, and then again in the fall of their senior year. Statistically, the chances are that you will improve your score by your senior year, but check with your high school college advisor (or counseling office) for specific recommendations based upon your personal student profile. Visit the College Board website, www.collegeboard.org, for more information regarding your statistical chances of increasing successive test scores.

If you are a junior and have the time to develop your academic skills related to the SAT, visit the College Board website at SAT® Skills Insight™, http://sat.collegeboard.org/practice/sat-skills-insight for a free online tool that helps you to identify areas of academic improvement and provides you with suggestions to meet your SAT goals.

Q. What materials may I bring to the SAT?

A. Bring your admission ticket, positive identification (driver's license, government-issued I.D., or passport), a watch, three or four sharpened No. 2 pencils (no pens and no mechanical pencils), a good eraser, and an approved calculator. You may not bring scratch paper or books. You may do your figuring in the margins of the test booklet or in the space provided.

Q. If necessary, may I cancel my score?

A. Yes. You may cancel your score on the day of the test by notifying the test center supervisor, and completing and signing a cancellation form *before* leaving the test center. If you decide to cancel your score *after* you leave the test center, your request must be received **in writing** no later than 11:59 p.m. (EST) on the Wednesday after your test date. Fax the **signed** request form to (610) 290-8978, or send it by overnight mail to SAT Program, Score Cancellation, 1425 Lower Ferry Road, Ewing, NJ 08618. See specific instructions for canceling your score on the SAT website. Your score report will record your cancellation, along with any completed test scores.

Q. Should I guess on the SAT?

A. There is a penalty for answering a question incorrectly. However, if you can eliminate two or more of the multiple-choice answers to a question, it is to your advantage to guess. Eliminating two or more answers increases your chance of choosing the right answer. To discourage wild guessing, a quarter of a point is subtracted for every wrong answer, but no points are subtracted if you leave the answer blank. On the grid-in questions, there is no penalty for filling in a wrong answer.

Q. How should I prepare for the test?

A. Understanding and practicing test-taking strategies helps a great deal, especially on the critical reading sections. Subject-matter review is particularly useful for the math section, and a review of basic grammar and usage will be helpful on the writing sections. Reviewing the writing process and practicing timed essay writing will also be helpful. Take advantage of the seven full-length practice tests in this book and the accompanying CD-ROM. In addition, the College Board offers many additional tips, strategies, study guidelines, and online practice at http://sat.collegeboard.org.

Q. How often are the tests administered?

A. The SAT is administered nationwide seven times during the school year, in October, November, December, January, March, May, and June.

Q. Where is the SAT administered?

A. The SAT is administered at hundreds of schools within and outside of the United States. Check online with the College Board or ask your local college testing or placement office. When you register for the test online, you will be prompted to determine which test centers have availability. Registering early will provide you with the best chance to secure your first choice test center. Some special administrations are given in limited locations.

Q. How and when should I register?

A. Registration information is available online. Complete the online registration process or mail your completed registration form to the College Board, www.collegeboard.org. Completing the registration form, plus paying the appropriate fees, completes the registration process. You should register at approximately six weeks prior to the exam date.

Q. Is walk-in registration provided?

A. Yes, on a limited basis. If you are unable to meet regular registration deadlines, you may attempt to register as "standby" on the day of the test. Additional fees are required. You will be admitted only if space remains after preregistered students have been seated.

Q. When will I get my test results?

A. SAT test results are available at www.collegeboard.com approximately three weeks after you take the test.

Taking the SAT: Successful Overall Strategies for Multiple-Choice Questions

There is no right or wrong method of answering questions on the SAT. However, approaching the exam with the knowledge of helpful test-taking strategies can give you the edge you may need to complete the exam with greater ease and confidence.

The multiple-choice questions cover a broad range of topics while considering a variety of question types. To be successful on the exam, you need to recall basic facts and major concepts that are important in critical reading, writing, and math. The facts and concepts on the SAT are often presented in subtle variations of selected answer choices that make it difficult for test-takers to narrow down the correct answer. Additionally, subtle variations in answer choices can distract you from choosing the right answer.

The following information was developed as a guide to introduce general test-taking guidelines, approaches, and strategies that are useful on standardized tests like the SAT. Although this section is limited to general tips and strategies, specific strategies related to *specific subject area question types* are included in each subsequent chapter.

As you practice problems using the strategies outlined in this section, determine if the strategies fit your individual learning style. What may work for some people may not work for others. If it takes you longer to recall a strategy than to solve the problem, it's probably not a good strategy for you to adopt. The goal in offering you strategies is for you to be able to work through problems quickly, accurately, and efficiently. And remember not to get stuck on any one question. Taking your time to answer the most difficult question on the test correctly will result in losing valuable test time, and will not get you the score you deserve. More importantly, remember that there is a penalty for guessing, so be sure that you can eliminate at least two answer choices before making your selection. Otherwise, leave the question blank.

Consider the following guidelines when taking the exam:

- **Manage your time wisely.** When you begin the exam, make a mental note of the time your start and keep track of the time. Never spend more than a minute to a minute and a half on any one question. With sufficient practice, you will almost automatically know when a problem is taking you too long to answer.

- **Read each question carefully.** Do not make a hasty assumption that you know the correct answer without reading the whole question and all the possible answers. It is common to jump to conclusions and select the wrong answer choice after reading only one or two of the answer choices. Note that some of the answer choices only show a "part" of the correct answer. You must look at the entire list of answer choices.

  Another common mistake is to misread a question that includes the words *except* and *not*. These types of questions ask for the opposite to be true in order to select the correct answer. It is helpful to write down brief notes on your test booklet to avoid misreading a question (and therefore answering it incorrectly). Simply write down what you must answer in the question.

- **Fill in the correct answer.** Be very careful that your responses match your intended response. When answering questions quickly, it is common to select the wrong answer choice by mistake. Test-takers who skip questions might make the mistake of continuing to mark their answers in sequence and forget to leave blank the unanswered questions. A good idea is to mark your answer in the test booklet itself (no need to erase later) so that if you do make mistakes in transferring your answer choices to the answer sheet, you can easily correct your errors without having to reconsider the answer choices.

General Approaches for Multiple-Choice Questions

The Elimination Approach

Take advantage of being allowed to mark in your test booklet. When making your answer selection, try to eliminate as many of the answer choices as possible. For example, if you know that answer choice C is incorrect, simply cross it out in your test booklet with a diagonal line. It will just take a few seconds to use this strategy, and will help to keep you from reconsidering impossible answer choices.

Notice that some choices are crossed out with a diagonal line and some choices are marked with question marks, signifying that they may be possible answers. This technique helps you avoid reconsidering those choices you have already eliminated. It also helps you narrow down your possible answers.

> **TIP: The marks you make in your test booklet do not need to be erased, but the marks you make on your answer sheet should always be erased, except for your response marks.**

The Plus-Minus Approach

Many people who take the SAT do not get their best-possible score because they spend too much time on difficult questions, leaving insufficient time to answer the easy questions. Do not let this happen to you. The plus-minus approach will help you categorize problems so that you can focus your attention on problems that you are able to answer quickly. Because every question is worth the same point value, making use of this approach will help you to quickly identify problems that are *solvable, possibly solvable* (+), *and difficult* (–) and be able to move quickly through the test.

Follow these three easy steps:

1. Answer easy questions immediately.
2. Place a "+" next to any problem that seems solvable but is too time-consuming.
3. Place a "–" next to any problem that seems impossible to solve.

Act quickly and don't waste time deciding whether a problem is a "+" or a "–." After working all of the problems you can answer immediately, go back and work your "+" problems. If you finish them, try your "–" problems. Sometimes when you come back to a problem that seemed impossible, you may suddenly realize how to solve it.

Your answer sheet should look something like this after you finish working your easy questions:

  1. Ⓐ ● Ⓒ Ⓓ Ⓔ
+**2.** Ⓐ Ⓑ Ⓒ Ⓓ Ⓔ
  3. Ⓐ Ⓑ ● Ⓓ Ⓔ
−**4.** Ⓐ Ⓑ Ⓒ Ⓓ Ⓔ
+**5.** Ⓐ Ⓑ ● Ⓓ Ⓔ

Guidelines to Identifying Problems		
	Solvable	Answer easy questions immediately. This type of question is answered with little or no difficulty, and requires little or minimal thought.
+	Possibly Solvable	You will recognize this type of question because it appears to be solvable but is overly time consuming. This type of question leaves you feeling, "I can answer this question, but I need more time." A time-consuming question is one that you estimate will take you more than 2 minutes to answer. When you face this type of question, mark a large plus sign (+) on your answer sheet, and then move on to the next question. Go back to this type of question after you have solved all of the solvable problems. Remember that you can only work on one section at a time, but you can move around within a section. Do not proceed to the next section without answering all possible questions within your section.
−	Difficult	The difficult question appears "impossible to solve." When you come to a question that seems impossible to answer, mark a large minus sign (−) on your answer sheet, leave the question blank, and move on to the next question. Don't bother with the "impossible" questions unless you have solved all of the possibly solvable (+) questions first. Rather, spend your time reviewing your work to be sure you didn't make any careless mistakes on the questions you thought were easy to answer. You should only come back to review the difficult-type questions after you have checked your work and have answered the "solvable" and "possibly solvable" questions.

Avoiding Misreads Approach

Due to time constraints, it is common for test-takers to rush through the test and misread a question. Here are some basic techniques to prevent this type of error from occurring.

Watch for questions containing *x* and *y* values in math problems

Sometimes a question may have different answers depending upon what is asked.

For example: If $6y + 3x = 14$, what is the value of y?

The question may instead have asked, "What is the value of x?"

Or: If $3x + x = 20$, what is the value of $x + 2$?

Notice that this question doesn't ask for the value of x, but rather the value of $x + 2$. To help you avoid misreading a question, and therefore answering it incorrectly, simply circle what you must answer in your test booklet. For example, do you have to find x or $x + 2$?

If $6y + 3x = 14$, what is the value of $\boxed{y}$?

If $3x + x = 20$, what is the value of $\boxed{(x+2)}$?

Watch for questions with the negative words EXCEPT and NOT

Negative questions with words like *except* and *not* can be confusing and challenge your thinking processes. You may be asked to choose an answer that is the *exception* from the list of answer choices, or one that is *not correct*.

To help you answer these types of questions, treat the answer choices as true or false statements, and search among the answer choices for the answer that is *false*. There is always only one false answer on the list of answer choices with this type of question. Practice this type of question before your test day so that you can quickly and easily solve these types of problems. Statements like the following are common on the SAT. Notice that the words EXCEPT and NOT change these questions dramatically.

- "All of the following statements are true EXCEPT..."
- "Which of the expressions used in the first paragraph does NOT help develop the main idea?"
- "Which of the following is LEAST LIKELY to be true?"

The Multiple-Multiple-Choice Approach

Some math and verbal questions use a "multiple-multiple-choice" format. The task is to determine which of these statements is accurate or true according to the problem. At first glance, these questions appear more confusing and more difficult than normal five-choice (A, B, C, D, E) multiple-choice problems. Actually, once you understand "multiple-multiple-choice" problem types, they are often *easie*r than comparable standard multiple-choice questions.

I. Statement
II. Statement } Consider each statement as true or false.
III. Statement

A. I and II only
B. II and III only
C. II only } Answer choices A-E vary with each question.
D. III only
E. I, II, and III

Follow these steps to solve multiple-multiple choice problems.

1. Consider each statement (I, II, or III) as *true* or *false* statements.
2. Look at all of the statements and eliminate (cross out with a diagonal line) statements that are *false*.

   I̸. Statement
   II. Statement
   II̸I̸. Statement

3. Look at the remaining statements in the answer choices to determine the correct answer. In the example above, only statement II is true, therefore choice B is the correct answer.

   A. I only
   B. II only
   C. III only
   D. I and II only
   E. I, II and III

In the next example, look for the statement(s) that are *true* to solve the problem.

If x is a positive integer, then which of the following must be true?

   I. $x > 0$

  II. $x = 0$

 III. $x < 1$

  A.   I only

  B.   II only

  C.   III only

  D.   I and II only

  E.   I and III only

You may immediately recognize that x is a positive integer, so it must be a counting number. Note that possible values of x could be 1 or 2 or 3 or 4, and so on. Therefore, statement I, $x > 0$, is always *true*. Knowing that the final answer *must* contain statement I, $x > 2$, you can eliminate (cross out) choices B and C as possible correct answer choices.

  A. I only

  B. II only

  C. III only

  D. I and II only

  E. I and III only

Now that you have determined that statement I is true, look at statement II to determine if it is true or false. Statement II is incorrect, and therefore *false*. If x is positive, x cannot equal zero. Knowing that statement II is false allows you to eliminate answer choice D. Only choices A and E are left as possible correct answers.

Finally, determine if statement III is true or false. Statement III is also false, as x must be 1 or greater; therefore, you can cross out statement III, thus eliminating choice E. The correct answer is A because only statement I is *true*.

General Tips and Helpful Hints

This list provides general advice to review before you begin the following in-depth chapters that introduce you to the question types, subject-matter content, instructional strategies, and practice exercises.

- Set a personal goal. Remember that an average score is about 50 percent right.
- As you approach each chapter, master the basics, and—as your confidence grows—tackle the practice tests.
- Know the general directions for each question type. Memorize them if necessary.
- Answer the question that is asked. Too frequently test-takers jump to conclusions and select incorrect answers because they misread the question.
- When taking the in-book practice tests, be sure to mark your answers in the right place.
- Be careful. Watch out for careless mistakes.
- When taking practice tests, don't make simple mistakes on the easy problems so you can rush to do the difficult ones.
- Know when to skip a question.
- Don't get stuck on any one question.
- Make an educated guess only if you can eliminate two or more answers.
- Don't be afraid to fill in your answer or guess on math grid-in questions.
- Practice using the Plus-Minus and Elimination Approaches. Remember to avoid misreading a question.
- When taking the in-book practice test, get in the habit of erasing any extra marks on your answer sheet.

PART I

DIAGNOSTIC EXAM

Chapter 1

Diagnostic Exam

Answer Sheets

Note: The following answer sheets are for practice and diagnostic purposes only. Math answer sheets for sections 2 and 5 below do not appear in the same format as the actual SAT. After you study the math review chapters and learn how to "grid-in" math answers, you will be ready to answer questions using SAT "grid-in" answer sheets. Practice tests starting on page 258 show the exact format of multiple-choice and grid-in answer sheets.

Section 2

1. _____   8. _____   15. _____
2. _____   9. _____   16. _____
3. _____   10. _____   17. _____
4. _____   11. _____   18. _____
5. _____   12. _____   19. _____
6. _____   13. _____   20. _____
7. _____   14. _____

Section 3

1 Ⓐ Ⓑ Ⓒ Ⓓ Ⓔ	21 Ⓐ Ⓑ Ⓒ Ⓓ Ⓔ
2 Ⓐ Ⓑ Ⓒ Ⓓ Ⓔ	22 Ⓐ Ⓑ Ⓒ Ⓓ Ⓔ
3 Ⓐ Ⓑ Ⓒ Ⓓ Ⓔ	23 Ⓐ Ⓑ Ⓒ Ⓓ Ⓔ
4 Ⓐ Ⓑ Ⓒ Ⓓ Ⓔ	24 Ⓐ Ⓑ Ⓒ Ⓓ Ⓔ
5 Ⓐ Ⓑ Ⓒ Ⓓ Ⓔ	25 Ⓐ Ⓑ Ⓒ Ⓓ Ⓔ
6 Ⓐ Ⓑ Ⓒ Ⓓ Ⓔ	26 Ⓐ Ⓑ Ⓒ Ⓓ Ⓔ
7 Ⓐ Ⓑ Ⓒ Ⓓ Ⓔ	27 Ⓐ Ⓑ Ⓒ Ⓓ Ⓔ
8 Ⓐ Ⓑ Ⓒ Ⓓ Ⓔ	28 Ⓐ Ⓑ Ⓒ Ⓓ Ⓔ
9 Ⓐ Ⓑ Ⓒ Ⓓ Ⓔ	
10 Ⓐ Ⓑ Ⓒ Ⓓ Ⓔ	
11 Ⓐ Ⓑ Ⓒ Ⓓ Ⓔ	
12 Ⓐ Ⓑ Ⓒ Ⓓ Ⓔ	
13 Ⓐ Ⓑ Ⓒ Ⓓ Ⓔ	
14 Ⓐ Ⓑ Ⓒ Ⓓ Ⓔ	
15 Ⓐ Ⓑ Ⓒ Ⓓ Ⓔ	
16 Ⓐ Ⓑ Ⓒ Ⓓ Ⓔ	
17 Ⓐ Ⓑ Ⓒ Ⓓ Ⓔ	
18 Ⓐ Ⓑ Ⓒ Ⓓ Ⓔ	
19 Ⓐ Ⓑ Ⓒ Ⓓ Ⓔ	
20 Ⓐ Ⓑ Ⓒ Ⓓ Ⓔ	

Section 4

1 Ⓐ Ⓑ Ⓒ Ⓓ Ⓔ	21 Ⓐ Ⓑ Ⓒ Ⓓ Ⓔ
2 Ⓐ Ⓑ Ⓒ Ⓓ Ⓔ	22 Ⓐ Ⓑ Ⓒ Ⓓ Ⓔ
3 Ⓐ Ⓑ Ⓒ Ⓓ Ⓔ	23 Ⓐ Ⓑ Ⓒ Ⓓ Ⓔ
4 Ⓐ Ⓑ Ⓒ Ⓓ Ⓔ	24 Ⓐ Ⓑ Ⓒ Ⓓ Ⓔ
5 Ⓐ Ⓑ Ⓒ Ⓓ Ⓔ	25 Ⓐ Ⓑ Ⓒ Ⓓ Ⓔ
6 Ⓐ Ⓑ Ⓒ Ⓓ Ⓔ	
7 Ⓐ Ⓑ Ⓒ Ⓓ Ⓔ	
8 Ⓐ Ⓑ Ⓒ Ⓓ Ⓔ	
9 Ⓐ Ⓑ Ⓒ Ⓓ Ⓔ	
10 Ⓐ Ⓑ Ⓒ Ⓓ Ⓔ	
11 Ⓐ Ⓑ Ⓒ Ⓓ Ⓔ	
12 Ⓐ Ⓑ Ⓒ Ⓓ Ⓔ	
13 Ⓐ Ⓑ Ⓒ Ⓓ Ⓔ	
14 Ⓐ Ⓑ Ⓒ Ⓓ Ⓔ	
15 Ⓐ Ⓑ Ⓒ Ⓓ Ⓔ	
16 Ⓐ Ⓑ Ⓒ Ⓓ Ⓔ	
17 Ⓐ Ⓑ Ⓒ Ⓓ Ⓔ	
18 Ⓐ Ⓑ Ⓒ Ⓓ Ⓔ	
19 Ⓐ Ⓑ Ⓒ Ⓓ Ⓔ	
20 Ⓐ Ⓑ Ⓒ Ⓓ Ⓔ	

CUT HERE

GO ON TO THE NEXT PAGE

Section 5

1. _____   7. _____   13. _____
2. _____   8. _____   14. _____
3. _____   9. _____   15. _____
4. _____   10. _____   16. _____
5. _____   11. _____   17. _____
6. _____   12. _____   18. _____

Section 1: Writing—Essay

Time: 25 minutes
1 Essay Question

You have 25 minutes to plan and write an essay on the topic below. DO NOT WRITE ON ANOTHER TOPIC. AN ESSAY ON ANOTHER TOPIC WILL NOT BE SCORED.

The essay is intended to give you the chance to show your writing skills. Be sure to express your ideas on the topic clearly and effectively. The quality of your writing is much more important than the quantity, but to cover the topic adequately, you may want to write more than one paragraph. Be specific.

Your essay must be written on two lined pages. Two pages should be enough if you write on every line, avoid wide margins, and keep your handwriting a reasonable size. You will not be given any additional paper. On the actual SAT you must

- Only use a pencil. You will receive a score of zero if you use ink.
- Only write on your answer sheet. You will not receive credit for material written in the test book.
- Only write on the topic presented below. An essay that is off-topic will receive a score of zero.
- Write an essay that reflects original work.

Directions: Read the following paragraph and assignment carefully. Then prepare and write a *persuasive* essay. Be sure to support your reasons with specific examples that will make your essay more effective.

We think, sometimes, there's not a dragon left. Not one brave knight, not a single princess gliding through silver forests, enchanting deer and butterflies with her smile.

We think sometimes that ours is an age past frontiers, past adventures. Destiny, it's way over the horizon, glowing shadows galloped past long ago, and gone.

What a pleasure to be wrong. Princesses, knights, enchantments, dragons, mystery and adventure . . . not only are they here-and-now, they're all that ever lived on earth!

—Richard Bach, *The Bridge Across Forever*

> **Assignment:** Are new frontiers to discover just as available today as they were in the past? Write an essay in which you take a position on this question. Use an example or examples from your reading or your personal observation to support or to refute this quote.

ON THE ACTUAL EXAM, THE PROCTOR WILL ANNOUNCE WHEN 25 MINUTES HAVE PASSED. IF YOU FINISH YOUR ESSAY BEFORE 25 MINUTES HAVE PASSED YOU MAY NOT GO ON TO ANY OTHER SECTION OF THE EXAM. THE PROCTOR WILL ANNOUNCE WHEN TO START THE NEXT SECTION.

Section 2: Mathematics

Time: 25 minutes

20 Questions

Directions: Solve each problem in this section by using the information given and your own mathematical calculations, insights, and problem-solving skills. Use the available space on this and the next page for your scratch work and your answer.

For each question, indicate the best answer, using the following notes.

1. All numerical values used are real numbers.
2. Calculators may be used.
3. Some problems may be accompanied by figures or diagrams. These figures are drawn as accurately as possible EXCEPT when it is stated in a specific problem that a figure is not drawn to scale. The figures and diagrams are meant to provide information that is useful in solving the problem or problems. Unless otherwise stated, all figures and diagrams lie on a plane.

Data that Can Be Used for Reference

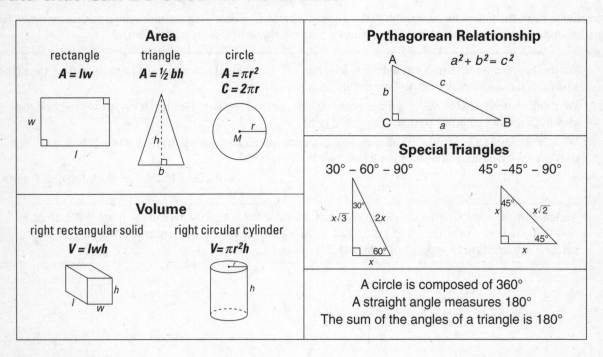

Arithmetic

1. Round 15.3461 to the nearest hundredth.

2. Evaluate: $135 - 56 \div 2^3 + 19 \times 4^2$

3. Subtract: $8\frac{1}{4} - 3\frac{3}{5}$

4. Divide: $5\frac{3}{5} \div 3\frac{1}{2}$

5. Multiply: 5.013×3.4

6. Change $\frac{5}{8}$ to a decimal.

7. Find 37% of 128.

8. Find the simple interest charged on $10,000 borrowed for 5 years at an annual rate of 6%.

9. Find the percent decrease for a product on sale for $60 that regularly sells for $75.

10. The value of $\sqrt{180}$ falls between what two whole numbers?

Algebra

11. Evaluate $z^3 + 2z^2 - 5z - 11$, if $z = -3$.

12. Simplify: $(8a^2 - 4ab + 5b^2) - (5a^2 + 3ab - 7b^2)$

13. Simplify: $(2x - 3)(5x^2 + 9x + 4)$

14. Simplify: $4\sqrt{75} + 8\sqrt{12} - 5\sqrt{27}$

15. Solve for x: $|4x - 11| = 19$

16. Solve for x: $x^2 - 24 = 5x$

17. Solve for x: $\dfrac{3}{2x+5} = \dfrac{5}{3x-2}$

18. Solve for x and y: $3x - 4y = -29$
$$5x + 2y = -5$$

19. Find the slope of a line passing through $(4, -7)$ and $(-8, 1)$.

20. Find the x-intercept(s) for the graph of $y = x^2 + 4x - 12$.

IF YOU FINISH BEFORE TIME IS CALLED, CHECK YOUR WORK ON THIS SECTION ONLY. DO NOT WORK ON ANY OTHER SECTION IN THE TEST.

STOP

Section 3: Critical Reading

Time: 25 minutes

28 Questions

Directions: In this section, choose the best answer for each question and fill in the corresponding circle on the answer sheet.

Each blank in the following sentences indicates that something has been omitted. Consider the lettered words beneath the sentence and choose the word or set of words that best fits the whole sentence.

EXAMPLE:

With a million more people than any other African nation, Nigeria is the most _____ country on the continent.

A. impoverished
B. successful
C. populous
D. developed
E. militant

The correct answer is **C**.

1. By 1812, most of the region now known as the Netherlands had been conquered by the French army and subsequently _____ Napoleon's growing empire.

   A. identified as
   B. separated from
   C. confused with
   D. vanquished by
   E. absorbed into

2. While some of the audience _____, curious to observe whether the understudy could fully _____ a role so unmistakably associated with a particular actor, a significant portion chose to return at a later time when the star would be well enough to perform.

   A. balked . . . play
   B. remained . . . inhabit
   C. cheered . . . botch
   D. lingered . . . refuse
   E. converged . . . distinguish

3. Spurred by the generous _____ promised by the company president, the new sales team worked _____ to meet and surpass its quota for the second quarter.

   A. compensation . . . haphazardly
   B. luxuries . . . passively
   C. incentives . . . diligently
   D. intricacies . . . stalwartly
   E. encumbrances . . . ingenuously

4. The psychiatrist's testimony was interesting and entertaining, but the judge ultimately found it to be _____: it had no true bearing on the case.

   A. immaterial
   B. veritable
   C. damaging
   D. nefarious
   E. obsequious

5. Jerome's parents were _____ by his disruptive behavior at the wedding; he was usually such a _____ boy.

   A. outraged . . . provocative
   B. astonished . . . conscientious
   C. concerned . . . recalcitrant
   D. dissuaded . . . docile
   E encouraged . . . noble

6. Mariah's teacher was _____. He had given her a weeklong extension on her term paper and she had _____ her time to pursue other activities.

   A. livid . . . squandered
   B. exultant . . . hoarded
   C. appreciative . . . invested
   D. vehement . . . volunteered
   E. negligent . . . utilized

7. The book is replete with stunning photographs and _____ descriptions, capturing the _____ beauty of the Amazon forest; all in all, an epicurean feast for the reader.

   A. convoluted . . . infinite
   B. earnest . . . restrained
   C. elaborate . . . solemn
   D. vivid . . . exquisite
   E. belabored . . . intense

8. Principally, pioneers of the Great Plains in the nineteenth century needed to be _____: stalwart, determined, and undeterred by hardship or the threat of danger.

   A. meticulous
   B. indomitable
   C. notorious
   D. rancorous
   E. fraught

GO ON TO THE NEXT PAGE

Directions: Questions follow the passage below. Answer the questions using only the stated or implied information in the passage and in its introduction, if any.

Questions 9–15 are based on the following passage.

Dr. Avi Sadeh at Tel Aviv University is one of a dozen or so experts in the field, frequently collaborating on papers with sleep scholars at Brown University. A couple of years ago, Sadeh
(5) sent 77 fourth-graders and sixth-graders home with randomly-drawn instructions to either go to bed early or stay up later, for three nights. Each child was given an actigraph—a wristwatch-like device that is equivalent to a seismograph for
(10) sleep activity—which allows the researchers to see how much sleep a child is really getting when in bed. Using the actigraph, Sadeh's team learned that the first group managed to get 30 minutes more of true sleep per night. The latter group got
(15) 31 less minutes of true sleep.

After the third night of sleep, a researcher went to the school in the morning to give the children a test of neurobiological functioning. The test, a computerized version of parts of the
(20) Wechsler Intelligence Scale for Children, is highly predictive of current achievement test scores and how teachers rate a child's ability to maintain attention in class.

Sadeh knew that his experiment was a big
(25) risk. "The last situation I wanted to be in was reporting to my grantors, 'Well, I deprived the subjects of an hour sleep, and there was no measurable effect at all, sorry—but can I have some more money for my other experiments?'"

(30) Sadeh needn't have worried. The effect was indeed measurable—and sizeable. The performance gap caused by an hour's difference in sleep was bigger than the intelligence gap between a normal fourth-grader and a normal sixth-grader. Which
(35) is another way of saying that a slightly-sleepy sixth grader will perform in class like a regular fourth-grader. "A loss of one hour of sleep is equivalent to [the loss of] two years of cognitive maturation and development," Sadeh explained.

(40) "Sadeh's work is an outstanding contribution," says Penn State's Dr. Douglas Teti, Professor of Human Development and Family Studies. His opinion is echoed by Brown's Dr. Mary Carskadon, a specialist on the biological systems
(45) that regulate sleep. "Sadeh's research is an important reminder of how fragile children are."

Sadeh's findings are consistent with a number of other researchers' work—all of which points to the large academic consequences of small
(50) sleep differences. Dr. Monique LeBourgeois, also at Brown, studies how sleep affects prekindergarteners. Virtually all young children are allowed to stay up later on weekends. They don't get less sleep, and they're not sleep
(55) deprived—they merely shift their sleep to later at night on Fridays and Saturdays. Yet she has discovered that the sleep shift factor alone is correlated with performance on a standardized IQ test. Every hour of weekend shift costs a child
(60) seven points on the test. Dr. Paul Suratt at the University of Virginia studied the impact of sleep problems on vocabulary test scores taken by elementary school students. He also found a seven-point reduction in scores. Seven points,
(65) Suratt notes, is significant: "Sleep disorders can impair children's IQ as much as lead exposure."

If these findings are accurate, then it should add up over the long term: we should expect to see a correlation between sleep and school
(70) grades. Every study done shows this connection—from a study of second- and third-graders in Chappaqua, New York, to a study of eighth-graders in Chicago.

These correlations really spike in high school,
(75) because that is when there is a steep drop-off in kids' sleep. University of Minnesota's Dr. Kyla Wahlstrom surveyed over 7,000 high schoolers in Minnesota about their sleep habits and grades. Teens who received A's averaged fifteen more
(80) minutes sleep than the B students, who in turn averaged fifteen more minutes of sleep than the C's, and so on. Wahlstrom's data was an almost perfect replication of results from an earlier study of over 3,000 Rhode Island high schoolers
(85) by Brown's Carskadon. Certainly, these are averages, but the consistency of the two studies stands out. Every fifteen minutes counts.

9. In his quote in lines 25–29, Dr. Sadeh is

    A. surprised but pleased to find his theories borne out experimentally.

    B. self-effacing in response to an unforeseen challenge to the basic tenets of his work.

    C. shocked at the disregard that his findings have received despite their obvious promise.

    D. concerned that his results will seem too insignificant to warrant further funding.

    E. confident that financial support for ongoing research will be forthcoming.

10. Which of the following best conveys the meaning of the word "spike" in line 74?

    A. begin

    B. shock

    C. lapse

    D. increase

    E. obliterate

11. Which of the following could NOT be reasonably concluded from the passage?

    A. Even relatively small increments of lost sleep can affect school performance.

    B. Both grades and standardized test scores are affected negatively by a lack of sleep.

    C. Research consistent with Dr. Sadeh's work bolsters his findings, with virtually no evidence for disputing his fundamental ideas.

    D. High-school age children tend to experience more sleep deprivation than younger children.

    E. A shift in sleeping hours with no actual loss of sleep is probably relatively harmless.

12. The intended purpose of the quotation in lines 65–66 is most likely to

    A. restate a theme that occurs throughout the passage.

    B. sum up a sequence of related ideas.

    C. underscore the severity of what has just been stated.

    D. put the reader on alert by making an outrageous claim that cannot be taken seriously.

    E. suggest a specific action that needs to be taken.

13. Lines 67–73 note a correlation that holds across a variety of studies despite differences in

    A. the methods of quantifying the effects of sleep deprivation.

    B. the methods by which sleep deprivation itself is measured.

    C. the performance of the same child when not sleep deprived.

    D. the amount of sleep deprivation.

    E. the ages of the subjects.

14. According to lines 7–14, the specific function of an actigraph is to determine whether

    A. a subject is sleeping.

    B. a sleeping subject is dreaming.

    C. a subject is sleep deprived.

    D. the performance of a sleep deprived subject is impaired.

    E. sleep deprivation correlates with impaired performance.

15. In lines 85–86, the words, "Certainly, these are averages" are meant to

    A. warn the reader about the shaky foundation on which the conclusion that follows is based.

    B. obviate a slight concern that the reader might have before it arises.

    C. surprise the reader by wrapping up the argument with a sudden flourish.

    D. remind the reader of a premise upon which the entire passage is founded.

    E. bring together several previously unrelated ideas to set up the bold statement that follows.

Questions 16–20 are based on the following passage.

"Nothing is perfect." This was one of Mrs. Hopewell's favorite sayings. Another was, "that is life!" And still another, the most important was, "well, other people have their opinions, too." She would make these statements, usually
(5) at the table, in a tone of gentle insistence as if no one held them but her, and the large hulking Joy, whose constant outrage obliterated every expression from her face, would stare just a little
(10) to the side of her, her eyes icy blue, with a look of someone who has achieved blindness by an act of will and means to keep it.

GO ON TO THE NEXT PAGE

When Mrs. Hopewell said to Mrs. Freeman that life was like that, Mrs. Freeman would say,
(15) "I always said so myself." Nothing had been arrived at by anyone that had not first been arrived at by her. She was quicker than Mr. Freeman. When Mrs. Hopewell said to her after they had been on the place a while, "You know, you're the
(20) wheel behind the wheel," and winked, Mrs. Freeman had said, "I know it. I've always been quick. It's some that are quicker than others."

"Everybody is different," Mrs. Hopewell said.

"Yes, most people is," [sic] Mrs. Freeman said.
(25) "It takes all kinds to make the world."

"I always said it did myself."

The girl was used to this kind of dialog for breakfast and more of it for dinner; sometimes they had it for supper too. When they had no
(30) guest they ate in the kitchen because that was easier. Mrs. Freeman always managed to arrive at some point during the meal and to watch them finish it. She would stand in the doorway if it were summer but in the winter she would stand
(35) with one elbow on top of the refrigerator and look down on them, or she would stand by the gas heater, lifting the back of her skirt slightly. Occasionally she would stand against the wall and roll her head from side to side. At no time
(40) was she in any hurry to leave. All this was very trying on Mrs. Hopewell but she was a woman of great patience. She realized that nothing is perfect and that in the Freemans she had good country people and that if, in this day and age,
(45) you get good country people, you had better hang on to them.

She had had plenty of experience with trash. Before the Freemans she had averaged one tenant family a year. The wives of these farmers were
(50) not the kind you would want to be around you for very long. Mrs. Hopewell, who had divorced her husband long ago, needed someone to walk over the fields with her, and when Joy had to be impressed for these services, her remarks were
(55) usually so ugly and her face so glum that Mrs. Hopewell would say, "If you can't come pleasantly, I don't want you at all," to which the girl, standing square and rigid-shouldered with her neck thrust slightly forward, would reply, "If
(60) you want me, here I am—LIKE I AM."

16. Lines 40–46 describe Mrs. Hopewell's principal attitude toward Mrs. Freeman as

  A. direct.
  B. coercive.
  C. forbearing.
  D. distrustful.
  E. subservient.

17. In line 8, the word "obliterated" means

  A. hid.
  B. betrayed.
  C. eliminated.
  D. highlighted.
  E. lifted.

18. In lines 15–17, the author's comment about Mrs. Freeman, "Nothing had been arrived at by anyone that had not first been arrived at by her," means

  A. she believes she knows everything.
  B. she has a basic mistrust of other people.
  C. she is essentially an optimist.
  D. she would prefer to defer to Mrs. Hopewell on most things.
  E. she is a traditionalist by nature.

19. The dialogue between Mrs. Hopewell and Mrs. Freeman in lines 19–26 exemplifies their relationship as fundamentally

  A. superficial.
  B. stormy.
  C. intimate.
  D. professional.
  E. uninhibited.

20. Throughout the passage, the author's tone toward her characters is

  A. harsh and contemptuous.
  B. admiring and respectful.
  C. dry and satirical.
  D. warm and sympathetic.
  E. wavering and inconclusive.

Questions 21–25 are based on the following pair of passages.

Passage 1:

The therapy relationship is unique in several respects. . . . The patient enters therapy in need of help and care. By virtue of this fact, she voluntarily submits herself to an unequal
(5) relationship in which the therapist has superior status and power. . . .

In entering the treatment relationship, the therapist promises to respect the patient's autonomy by remaining disinterested and
(10) neutral. "Disinterested" means that the therapist abstains from using her power over the patient to gratify her own needs. "Neutral" means that the therapist does not take sides in the patient's inner conflicts or try to direct the patient's life
(15) decisions. Constantly reminding herself that the patient is in charge of her own life, the therapist refrains from advancing a personal agenda. The disinterested and neutral stance is an ideal to be striven for, never perfectly attained.

Passage 2:

To the therapist, it is a new venture in relating. He feels, "Here is this other person, my client. . . . I would like to go with him on the fearful journey into himself, into the buried fear, and hate, and
(5) love which he has never been able to let flow in him. I recognize that this is a very human and unpredictable journey for me, as well as for him, and that I may, without even knowing my fear, shrink away within myself, from some of the
(10) feelings he discovers. . . . Most of all I want him to encounter in me a real person. I do not need to be uneasy as to whether my own feelings are 'therapeutic.' What I am and what I feel are good enough to be a basis for therapy, if I can
(15) transparently *be* what I am and what I feel in relationship to him. Then perhaps he can be what he is, openly and without fear."

21. In line 9 of Passage 1, the word "autonomy" means

    A. confidentiality.
    B. mastery.
    C. self-determination.
    D. self-esteem.
    E. solitude.

22. In line 13 of Passage 2, the word "therapeutic" is in quotes to imply that

    A. therapists are in wide disagreement as to what constitutes a therapeutic relationship.
    B. trying too hard to be therapeutic can make a therapist inauthentic, which is counterproductive.
    C. to be truly therapeutic is an ideal that can never be fully realized, however nobly it may be sought after.
    D. a therapeutic relationship is more appropriate for physicians than it is for therapists.
    E. a therapist can only attempt a therapeutic relationship when the client is fully consenting.

23. One point on which the authors of both passages would most likely agree is

    A. if a client or patient does something to anger the therapist, then the therapist should honestly show anger.
    B. a good therapist, like a good scientist, tries to remain as objective as possible.
    C. the relationship between a therapist and a client or patient is not fundamentally different from other types of relationships.
    D. the patient or client, not the therapist, is responsible for the direction that therapy takes.
    E. the therapist should avoid bringing his or her personal life into a therapy session.

24. If the author of Passage 1 were treating an unemployed client named Jack, which of the following actions would she be most likely to take?

    A. Advise Jack to take the first job offered to him, however menial.
    B. Offer Jack a job working in her own office.
    C. Call Jack lazy, hoping to spur him into finding a job sooner.
    D. Push Jack to take a job with a few more responsibilities than he feels ready for.
    E. Refuse to tell Jack which of two job offers to accept.

GO ON TO THE NEXT PAGE

25. The author of Passage 1 would most likely register a concern that Passage 2

    A. disregards the inherent power differential between therapist and patient.
    B. fails to take the therapist's feelings sufficiently into account.
    C. holds the therapist to a standard that is impossibly high.
    D. places the patient rather than the therapist in control of the process of therapy.
    E. unnecessarily complicates the work of therapy.

Questions 26–28 are based on the following passage.

Ernest Hemingway wrote a novel called *The Sun Also Rises*. Promptly upon its publication, Ernest Hemingway was discovered, the Stars and Stripes were reverentially raised over him, eight
(5) hundred and forty-seven book reviewers formed themselves into the word "welcome," and the band played "Hail to the Chief" in three concurrent keys. All of which, I should think, might have made Ernest Hemingway pretty
(10) reasonably sick.

For, a year or so before *The Sun Also Rises*, he had published *In Our Time*, a collection of short pieces. The book caused about as much stir in literary circles as an incompleted dogfight on
(15) upper Riverside Drive. True, there were a few that went about quick and stirred with admiration for this clean, exciting prose, but most of the reviewers dismissed the volume with a tolerant smile and the word "stark."

(20) And besides, *In Our Time* was a book of short stories. That's no way to start off. People don't like that; they feel cheated. Any bookseller will be glad to tell you, in his interesting *argot*, that "short stories don't go." People take up a book
(25) of short stories and say, "Oh, what's this? Just a lot of those short things?" and put it right down again.

Literature, it appears, is here measured by a yard-stick. As soon as *The Sun Also Rises* came
(30) out, Ernest Hemingway was the white-haired boy. He was praised, adored, analyzed, best-sold, argued about, and banned in Boston; all the trimmings were accorded him. People got into feuds about whether or not his story was worth
(35) the telling. . . . They affirmed, and passionately, that the dissolute expatriates in this novel of "a lost generation" were not worth bothering about; and then they devoted most of their time to discussing them. There was a time, and it went
(40) on for weeks, when you could go nowhere without hearing of *The Sun Also Rises*. . . .

Now *The Sun Also Rises* was as "starkly" written as Mr. Hemingway's short stories; it dealt with subjects as "unpleasant." Why it should
(45) have been taken to the slightly damp bosom of the public while the (as it seems to me) superb *In Our Time* should have been disregarded will always be a puzzle to me. As I see it—I knew this conversation would get back to me sooner or
(50) later, preferably sooner—Mr. Hemingway's style, this prose stripped to its firm young bones, is far more effective, far more moving, in the short story than in the novel. He is, to me, the greatest living writer of short stories; he is, also to me,
(55) not the greatest living novelist.

26. Which of the following best sums up the author's description in lines 1–8 of the treatment Ernest Hemingway received after the publication of *The Sun Also Rises*?

    A. He was savaged by the media.
    B. He was lionized by the critics.
    C. He was disregarded by the general public.
    D. He was overlooked by the booksellers.
    E. He was misunderstood by the masses.

27. When the author states, in lines 13–15, "The book caused about as much stir in literary circles as an incompleted dogfight on upper Riverside Drive," she means that it was

    A. unjustly ignored.
    B. vastly overrated.
    C. rightly praised.
    D. considered inflammatory.
    E. outlawed in some communities.

28. In line 33, the word "accorded" means

    A. agreed upon.
    B. lavished upon.
    C. squandered upon.
    D. entrusted to.
    E. cajoled from.

IF YOU FINISH BEFORE TIME IS CALLED, CHECK YOUR WORK ON THIS SECTION ONLY. DO NOT WORK ON ANY OTHER SECTION IN THE TEST.

Section 4: Writing—Multiple Choice

Time: 20 minutes
25 Questions

Directions: In this section, choose the best answer for each question and fill in the corresponding circle on the answer sheet.

The following questions test correctness and effective expression. In selecting the answer, pay attention to grammar, diction, sentence structure, and punctuation. In the following questions, part or all of each sentence is underlined. Answer Choice A repeats the underlined portion of the original sentence, while the next four choices offer alternatives. Choose the answer that best expresses the meaning of the original sentence and at the same time is grammatically correct and stylistically superior. The correct choice should be clear, unambiguous, and concise.

EXAMPLE:

The forecaster predicted <u>rain and the sky was clear</u>.

A. rain and the sky was clear
B. rain but the sky was clear.
C. rain the sky was clear.
D. rain, but the sky was clear.
E. rain being as the sky was clear.

The correct answer is **D.**

1. Between his duties as a military officer and <u>also having responsibilities</u> as a single dad, Sean found that he had little time left for recreational sports.

    A. also having responsibilities
    B. he had responsibilities
    C. his responsibilities
    D. that he was responsible
    E. being responsible

2. Only after discovering that Thomas was missing <u>Charlotte found</u> the letter that he had written to her.

    A. Charlotte found
    B. did Charlotte found
    C. did Charlotte find
    D. that Charlotte found
    E. Charlotte was finding

3. Experience had shown Dr. Vasquez that while medical expertise was essential, <u>it could never entirely replace compassion</u>.

    A. it could never entirely replace compassion
    B. but it could never entirely replace compassion
    C. compassion could never be entirely replaced by it
    D. compassion could never entirely replace it
    E. even so it could never entirely replace compassion

4. Wondering where the time had gone, <u>the clock struck three and Jane hurried out the door</u>.

    A. the clock struck three and Jane hurried out the door
    B. the clock struck three as Jane hurried out the door
    C. out the door hurried Jane as the clock struck three
    D. Jane heard the clock strike three and hurried out the door
    E. hearing the clock strike three, Jane hurried out the door

GO ON TO THE NEXT PAGE

5. Lorenzo was a remarkably dedicated painter <u>and he spent much of his savings on and spent countless hours</u> on the perfection of his craft.

    A. and he spent much of his savings on and spent countless hours
    B. spending much of his savings on and spending countless hours
    C. who spent much of his savings and he spent countless hours
    D. who spent much of his savings and countless hours
    E. he spent much of his savings and countless hours

6. Even if you can secure a bank loan, you will still have the difficult task of finding a landlord <u>willing to agree</u> to a month-to-month lease.

    A. willing to agree
    B. is willing to agree
    C. being willing to agree
    D. is being willing to agree
    E. will be willing to agree

7. <u>She's</u> a little bit nervous and worried about the outcome of the deposition makes sense considering its importance to her future as an attorney.

    A. She's
    B. If she's
    C. When she's
    D. That she's
    E. While she's

8. Here's my advice: <u>I recommend that you be</u> very considerate in all of your future encounters with her entire family.

    A. I recommend that you be
    B. I recommend that you will be
    C. I recommend you being
    D. I recommend that your being
    E. I recommend that you're being

9. Jacob would have been a lot more worried about his standing in the class if the professor <u>wouldn't have graded the tests herself</u>.

    A. wouldn't have graded the tests herself
    B. hadn't have graded the tests herself
    C. hadn't graded the tests herself
    D. didn't grade the tests herself
    E. not having graded the tests herself

10. Expecting an important letter from her daughter, <u>the letter carrier's late arrival worried Ms. Myer</u>.

    A. the letter carrier's late arrival worried Ms. Myer
    B. the late arrival of the letter carrier worried Ms. Myer
    C. the late arrival by the letter carrier worried Ms. Myer
    D. Ms. Myer's late arrival worried the letter carrier
    E. Ms. Myer was worried by the letter carrier's late arrival

11. While getting angry or upset may be common, <u>when one often finds upon reflection</u> that a given situation doesn't merit such a strong reaction.

    A. when one often finds upon reflection
    B. one often finding upon reflection
    C. that upon reflection one often finds
    D. one is upon reflection often finding
    E. one often finds upon reflection

12. Why should she get a full-time job and risk losing her scholarship when <u>only she has to complete one more semester to graduate</u>?

    A. only she has to complete one more semester to graduate
    B. she only has to complete one more semester to graduate
    C. she has to only complete one more semester to graduate
    D. she would have to complete one more semester only to graduate
    E. having to complete only one more semester to graduate

13. <u>Despite its having disadvantages</u> as a year-round home, this cottage is a perfect vacation dwelling for a family like yours.

    A. Despite its having disadvantages
    B. Notwithstanding it has disadvantages
    C. Although it has disadvantages
    D. Even though its disadvantages
    E. While it's having disadvantages

Directions: The following sentences may contain one error of grammar, usage, diction, or idiom. No sentence contains more than one error, and some have no error. If there is an error, it will be underlined and have a letter beneath it. If there is an error, choose the one underlined part that must be changed to correct the sentence. If there is no error, choose E. Sections of the sentence that are not underlined cannot be changed. In selecting your answer, observe the requirements of standard written English.

EXAMPLE:

The film <u>tell the story</u> of a army captain and <u>his wife</u> who <u>try to</u> <u>rebuild their lives</u> after the Iraq War.
      A   B   C   D

<u>No error</u>
  E

The correct answer is **A.**

---

14. <u>Before beginning</u> a project of this magnitude,
    A

    a carpenter <u>is</u> well-advised <u>to create</u> a formal
             B   C

    blueprint of <u>their envisioned outcome</u>.
                 D

    <u>No error</u>
      E

15. <u>With the economy</u> in freefall, the people
      A

    <u>had</u> little recourse but <u>expressing their</u>
     B   C

    <u>discontentment</u> at the polls. <u>No error</u>
        D   E

16. If he expects <u>for one moment</u> that I will
              A

    apologize for the remarks <u>I made</u> <u>to his advisor</u>,
                         B   C

    <u>he would find</u> himself sorely disappointed.
       D

    <u>No error</u>
      E

17. Noreen and her older brother, <u>having promised</u>
                         A

    to trust each other, <u>was</u> now <u>even more</u>
                 B   C

    <u>secretive</u> than <u>they'd ever been</u>. <u>No error</u>
      D   E

18. <u>The three girls went</u> to the movies together,
      A

    and the four of <u>we boys</u> <u>stayed home</u> and
                B   C

    <u>played video games</u>. <u>No error</u>
        D   E

19. In her hurry <u>to leave behind</u> every trace
            A

    of her past, <u>Kara failed to appreciate</u> the
                   B

    pain that <u>she was inflicting upon</u> the people
                 C

    <u>she loved most</u>. <u>No error</u>
       D   E

20. Whenever you drive your car, <u>even when</u>
                       A

    <u>traveling</u> a <u>comparatively</u> short distance,
                 B

    <u>one should</u> always <u>take the precaution of</u>
        C   D

    wearing a seat belt. <u>No error</u>
                 E

21. <u>He told her</u> that <u>there's</u> only two ways to get to
    A   B

    his house, <u>one of which</u> is nearly always <u>faster</u>.
            C   D

    <u>No error</u>
      E

22. Mr. Wright's house is <u>like many other people</u>
                   A

    in this town: <u>essentially sound in structure,</u> but
                 B

    <u>old, weather-beaten, and</u> badly <u>in need of basic</u>
           C   D

    maintenance. <u>No error</u>
             E

GO ON TO THE NEXT PAGE

Directions: The following passage is an early draft of a student essay. Some parts of it need to be revised.

Read the selection carefully and answer the questions that follow. There will be questions about sentence structure, diction, and usage in individual sentences or parts of sentences. Other questions will deal with the whole essay or paragraphs in it and ask you to decide about the organization, development, and appropriate language. Choose the answer that follows the requirements of standard written English and most effectively expresses the intended meanings.

Questions 23–25 are based on the following passage.

(1) When it comes to making and breaking habits, there are all sorts of strategies that don't work. **(2)** One being the all-or-nothing fling. **(3)** You either overdo a new habit or trying to quit an old habit without proper preparation.

(4) For example, have you ever bought an expensive gym membership, hoping it would force yourself to work out on a daily basis? **(5)** This strategy seems sound: if you don't go the gym, you're wasting your money. **(6)** Money is such a precious commodity, not to be squandered, certainly not in times of economic downturn. **(7)** Unfortunately, most people who adopt this strategy put in a good effort at first, but then backslide into inactivity. **(8)** After weeks or months of paying for a membership that they never use, they quit the gym in frustration and failure.

(9) The reason why this type of approach falls apart becomes apparent when you see that making and breaking habits is itself a skill which, like a muscle, can be strengthened. **(10)** Your goal shouldn't be graft to one or two new habits, such as saving money or eating better, into an otherwise chaotic life. **(11)** Instead, become a person who has attained the skill of reliably taking on new habits you want and dropping those that no longer serve you.

23. Which of the following is the best way to revise and combine sentences 2 and 3 (reproduced below)?

One being the all-or-nothing fling. You either overdo a new habit or trying to quit an old habit without proper preparation.

A. One is the all-or-nothing fling, either to overdo a new habit or to try to quit an old habit without proper preparation.

B. One of these would be the all-or-nothing fling, where you either overdo a new habit or try to quit an old habit without proper preparation.

C. One of the worst of these types of strategies is the all-or-nothing fling: either overdoing a new habit or trying to quit an old habit without proper preparation.

D. One such strategy is the all-or-nothing fling: either overdoing a new habit or trying to quit an old habit without proper preparation.

E. One bad habit is the all-or-nothing fling, either overdoing a new habit or trying to quit an old habit without proper preparation.

24. Which sentence can be omitted to improve the flow of the second paragraph?

A. sentence 4
B. sentence 5
C. sentence 6
D. sentence 7
E. sentence 8

25. Which of the following revisions to sentence 9 (reproduced below) is best?

The reason why this type of approach falls apart becomes apparent when you see that making and breaking habits is itself a skill which, like a muscle, can be strengthened.

A. Correct as is

B. Making and breaking habits is like a muscle.

C. Making and breaking habits is a skill which, like a muscle, can be strengthened.

D. The reason why this type of approach falls apart: because making and breaking habits is a skill which, like a muscle, can be strengthened.

E. It becomes apparent why this type of approach fails when you see that making and breaking habits is itself a skill which, like a muscle, can be strengthened.

IF YOU FINISH BEFORE TIME IS CALLED, CHECK YOUR WORK ON THIS SECTION ONLY. DO NOT WORK ON ANY OTHER SECTION IN THE TEST.

Section 5: Mathematics

Time: 25 minutes
18 Questions

Directions: Solve each problem in this section by using the information given and your own mathematical calculations, insights, and problem-solving skills. Use the available space on this and the next two pages for your scratch work and your answer.

For each question, indicate the best answer, using the following notes.

1. All numerical values used are real numbers.

2. Calculators may be used.

3. Some problems may be accompanied by figures or diagrams. These figures are drawn as accurately as possible EXCEPT when it is stated in a specific problem that a figure is not drawn to scale. The figures and diagrams are meant to provide information useful in solving the problem or problems. Unless otherwise stated, all figures and diagrams lie on a plane.

Data that Can Be Used for Reference

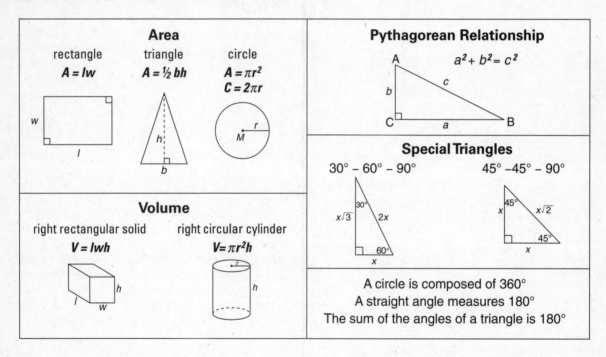

Geometry

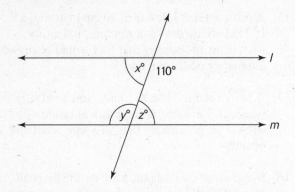

1. If in the figure above, $l \parallel m$, find the value of x, y, and z.

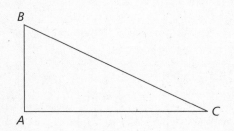

2. In the figure above, $\overline{AB} \perp \overline{AC}$, $AC = 24$, and $BC = 26$. Find AB.

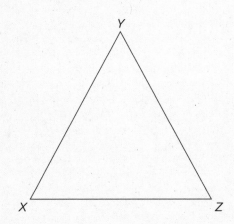

3. In the figure $\triangle XYZ$ above, $XY = YZ$ and $\angle X = 70°$. Find the measure in degrees of $\angle Y$.

4. Find the area of a circle whose circumference is 24π.

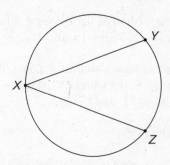

5. If in the figure above $\angle X = 50°$, find the measure in degrees of $\overset{\frown}{YXZ}$.

6. Find the area of a square whose diagonal length is 16.

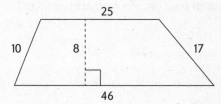

7. In the figure above, find the area of the trapezoid with the indicated dimensions.

8. Find the surface area of a rectangular solid with a length of 24, a width of 15, and a height of 8.

9. What is the volume in cubic inches of a right circular cylinder with a height of 8 inches and a diameter of 10 inches?

GO ON TO THE NEXT PAGE

Data Analysis

10. If 1 mile = 1,760 yards, how many feet are in 4 miles?

11. Find the median of the following quiz scores: 15, 11, 18, 20, 20, 14, 19, and 15.

12. What score must a student get on a fifth exam to average 85, if the scores on the first 4 exams were 86, 91, 73, and 81?

13. Evaluate: $\dfrac{12!}{8! \cdot 4!}$

14. Find the seventh term of a sequence if the first term of the sequence is -3 and each term after the first term is 5 more than twice the preceding term.

15. How many different 4-digit numbers can be formed using the digits 1 through 9, if each digit is used only once in each arrangement?

16. A box contains 7 tickets numbered 1 through 7. If 3 tickets are drawn at random, 1 at a time, what is the probability that they would be drawn alternately odd, even, odd?

17. A bag contains 7 black, 5 pink, and 3 red jelly beans. If 3 jelly beans are drawn at random, what is the probability that all 3 jelly beans will be red?

18. In a class of 30 students, 5 are on the baseball team. If 3 students are chosen at random, what is the probability that none of them are on the baseball team?

IF YOU FINISH BEFORE TIME IS CALLED, CHECK YOUR WORK ON THIS SECTION ONLY. DO NOT WORK ON ANY OTHER SECTION IN THE TEST.

Scoring the Diagnostic Test

The following section will assist you in scoring and analyzing your practice test results. Use the answer key below to score your results, and then carefully review the analysis charts to identify your strengths and weaknesses. Finally, read through the answer explanations starting in the study guide on page 35 to clarify the solutions to the problems.

Answer Key for Diagnostic Test

Section 2: Mathematics

1. 15.35
2. 432
3. $4\frac{13}{20}$
4. $\frac{8}{5}$ or $1\frac{3}{5}$
5. 17.0442

6. 0.625
7. 47.36
8. $3,000
9. 20%
10. 13 and 14

11. -5
12. $3a^2 - 7ab + 12b^2$
13. $10x^3 + 3x^2 - 19x - 12$
14. $21\sqrt{3}$
15. $x = -2$, or $x = \frac{15}{2}$ or $7\frac{1}{2}$

16. $x = -3$, or $x = 8$
17. $x = -31$
18. $x = -3$ and $y = 5$
19. $\frac{-2}{3}$
20. $(-6, 0)$ and $(2, 0)$

Section 3: Critical Reading

1. E
2. B
3. C
4. A
5. B
6. A
7. D

8. B
9. D
10. D
11. E
12. C
13. C
14. A

15. B
16. C
17. C
18. A
19. A
20. C
21. C

22. B
23. D
24. E
25. A
26. B
27. A
28. B

Section 4: Writing—Multiple Choice

1. C
2. C
3. A
4. D
5. D
6. A
7. D

8. A
9. C
10. E
11. E
12. B
13. C
14. D

15. C
16. D
17. B
18. B
19. E
20. C
21. B

22. A
23. D
24. C
25. C

Section 5: Mathematics

1. $x = z = 70$ and $y = 110$
2. 10
3. 40
4. 144π
5. 260
6. 128
7. 284
8. 1344
9. 200π
10. 21,120
11. $\frac{33}{2}$, or $16\frac{1}{2}$
12. 94
13. 495
14. 123
15. 3,024
16. $\frac{6}{35}$
17. $\frac{1}{455}$
18. $\frac{115}{203}$

Charting and Analyzing Your Test Results

The first step in analyzing your results is to chart your answers. Use the charts on the following pages to identify your strengths and areas that need improvement. Complete the process of evaluating your essays and analyzing problems in each area. Reevaluate your results as you look for trends in the types of errors (repeated errors), and look for low scores in *specific* topic areas. This reexamination and analysis is a tremendous asset to help you maximize your best possible score. The answers and explanations following these charts will help you solve these types of problems in the future.

Reviewing the Essay

Refer to the sample essay on page 36 as a reference guide. Have an English teacher, tutor, or someone else with good writing skills read and evaluate your essay using the Essay Checklist below. Have your reader evaluate the complete essay as good, average, or marginal. Note that your paper would actually be scored from 1 to 6 by two trained readers (actual total score 2–12). Since you are trying only for a rough approximation, a strong, average, or weak overall evaluation will give you a general feeling for your score range.

Essay Checklist			
Questions	Strong Response Score 5 or 6	Average Response Score 3 or 4	Weak Response Score 1 or 2
1. Does the essay focus on the topic and respond to the assigned task?			
2. Is the essay organized and well developed?			
3. Does the essay use specific supporting details and examples?			
4. Does the writing use correct grammar, usage, punctuation, and spelling?			
5. Is the handwriting legible?			

Critical Reading Analysis Sheet

Section 3	Possible	Completed	Right	Wrong
Sentence Completions	8			
Long Passages	12			
Paired Passages	5			
Short Passages	3			
Critical Reading Totals	**28**			

Mathematics Analysis Sheet

Section 2	Possible	Completed	Right	Wrong
Math	20			
Section 2 Subtotal	**20**			
Section 5	**Possible**	**Completed**	**Right**	**Wrong**
Math	18			
Section 5 Subtotal	**18**			
Math Totals	**38**			

Writing—Multiple-Choice Analysis Sheet

Section 4	Possible	Completed	Right	Wrong
Improving Sentences	13			
Identifying Sentence Errors	9			
Improving Paragraphs	3			
Writing Totals	**25**			

Diagnostic Test 1: Answers and Explanations

Section 1: Writing—Essay

We think, sometimes, there's not a dragon left. Not one brave knight, not a single princess gliding through silver forests, enchanting deer and butterflies with her smile.

We think sometimes that ours is an age past frontiers, past adventures. Destiny, it's way over the horizon, glowing shadows galloped past long ago, and gone.

What a pleasure to be wrong. Princesses, knights, enchantments, dragons, mystery and adventure . . . not only are they here-and-now, they're all that ever lived on earth!

—Richard Bach, The Bridge Across Forever

Assignment: Are new frontiers to discover just as available today as they were in the past? Write an essay in which you take a position on this question. Use an example or examples from your reading or your personal observation to support or to refute this quote.

Sample Essay

Generally speaking, I agree with the quote: New frontiers are always available for those who are willing to explore.

Great examples immediately spring to mind: Space exploration is only in its infancy, presenting a vast universe to be uncovered. Medical science, too, is a relatively young science, and we are only beginning to utilize the recent mapping of the human genome to cure genetically-based diseases.

Even in our day-to-day experiences, frontiers are always immediately before us. Our relationships with those we love always present us with new challenges and wonderful new sources of joy should we take the time to explore them. And this is only the beginning: The current world population is seven million, and each person is unique and infinitely complex. Every person we pass on the street or in the hallway provides a new frontier to explore, should we take the time to do so.

But the key caviat here is that these frontiers, and many more, are only available to those who are willing to look for them. For those who don't seek them out, the world may well appear to be a flat and dull place, lacking in adventure and its rewards. However, this has always been true, in our century or any other. Frontiers, like dragons, do not appear to those who do not believe in them—and, most important, believe in their own ability to conquer them.

Section 2: Mathematics

Arithmetic

1. **15.35** In the number 15.3461, the 4 is in the hundredths place. Since the number immediately to the right of the hundredths place is 5 or greater, the number is rounded up to 15.35.

2. **432**

$$135 - 56 \div 2^3 + 19 \cdot 4^2 = 135 - 56 \div 8 + 19 \cdot 16$$
$$= 135 - 7 + 304$$
$$= 128 + 304$$
$$= 432$$

3. $4\frac{13}{20}$

$$8\frac{1}{4} = \quad 8\frac{5}{20} = \quad 7\frac{25}{20}$$
$$-3\frac{3}{5} = -3\frac{12}{20} = -3\frac{12}{20}$$
$$\overline{\qquad\qquad\qquad\qquad 4\frac{13}{20}}$$

4. $\frac{8}{5}$ or $1\frac{3}{5}$

$$5\frac{3}{5} \div 3\frac{1}{2} = \frac{28}{5} \div \frac{7}{2}$$
$$= \frac{28}{5} \cdot \frac{2}{7}$$
$$= \frac{8}{5} \text{ or } 1\frac{3}{5}$$

5. **17.0442**

$$\begin{array}{r} 5.013 \\ \times\ 3.4 \\ \hline 20052 \\ \underline{15039} \\ 17.0442 \end{array}$$

6. 0.625

$$\frac{5}{8} = 8\overline{)5.000}$$

$$
\begin{array}{r}
0.625 \\
8\overline{)5.000} \\
\underline{48} \\
20 \\
\underline{16} \\
40 \\
\underline{40} \\
0
\end{array}
$$

7. 47.36

$$37\% \text{ of } 128 = (0.37)(128) =$$

$$
\begin{array}{r}
128 \\
\times\,0.37 \\
\hline
896 \\
\underline{384} \\
47.36
\end{array}
$$

8. \$3,000 The simple interest I on a principal P at an annual rate R for a length of time T is

$$
\begin{aligned}
I &= P \cdot R \cdot T \\
&= (\$10,000)(0.06)(5) \\
&= \$3,000
\end{aligned}
$$

9. 20% The decrease in amount for a product on sale for \$60 that regularly sells for \$75 is \$15. The percent decrease is

$$\frac{\text{decrease amount}}{\text{original price}} = \frac{15}{75} = \frac{1}{5} = 0.2 = 20\%$$

10. 13 and 14

Since $13^2 = 169$ and $14^2 = 196$, $\sqrt{180}$ will fall between 13 and 14.

Algebra

11. –5

If $z = -3$,

$$
\begin{aligned}
z^3 + 2z^2 - 5z - 11 &= (-3)^3 + 2(-3)^2 - 5(-3) - 11 \\
&= (-27) + 2(9) - 5(-3) - 11 \\
&= (-27) + 18 + 15 - 11 \\
&= (-9) + 15 - 11 \\
&= 6 - 11 \\
&= -5
\end{aligned}
$$

12. $3a^2 - 7ab + 12b^2$

$$
\begin{aligned}
&\left(8a^2 - 4ab + 5b^2\right) - \left(5a^2 + 3ab - 7b^2\right) \\
&= 8a^2 - 4ab + 5b^2 - 5a^2 - 3ab + 7b^2 \\
&= 3a^2 - 7ab + 12b^2
\end{aligned}
$$

13. $10x^3 + 3x^2 - 19x - 12$

$$(2x-3)(5x^2+9x+4) = (2x)(5x^2) + (2x)(9x) + (2x)(4) + (-3)(5x^2) + (-3)(9x) + (-3)(4)$$
$$= 10x^3 + 18x^2 + 8x + (-15x^2) + (-27x) + (-12)$$
$$= 10x^3 + 3x^2 - 19x - 12$$

14. $21\sqrt{3}$

$$4\sqrt{75} + 8\sqrt{12} - 5\sqrt{27} = 4\sqrt{25 \cdot 3} + 8\sqrt{4 \cdot 3} - 5\sqrt{9 \cdot 3}$$
$$= 4 \cdot 5\sqrt{3} + 8 \cdot 2\sqrt{3} - 5 \cdot 3\sqrt{3}$$
$$= 20\sqrt{3} + 16\sqrt{3} - 15\sqrt{3}$$
$$= 21\sqrt{3}$$

15. $x = -2$, or $x = \dfrac{15}{2}$ or $7\dfrac{1}{2}$

$$|4x - 11| = 19$$

$4x - 11 = -19$	or $4x - 11 = 19$
$4x - 11 + 11 = -19 + 11$	$4x - 11 + 11 = 19 + 11$
$4x = -8$	$4x = 30$
$\dfrac{4x}{4} = \dfrac{-8}{4}$	$\dfrac{4x}{4} = \dfrac{30}{4}$
$x = -2$	$x = \dfrac{15}{2}$ or $7\dfrac{1}{2}$

16. $x = -3$, or $x = 8$

$$x^2 - 24 = 5x$$
$$x^2 - 24 - 5x = 5x - 5x$$
$$x^2 - 5x - 24 = 0$$
$$(x+3)(x-8) = 0$$

$x + 3 = 0$	or $x - 8 = 0$
$x + 3 - 3 = 0 - 3$	$x - 8 + 8 = 0 + 8$
$x = -3$ or	$x = 8$

17. $x = -31$

$$\frac{3}{2x+5} = \frac{5}{3x-2}$$
$$3(3x-2) = 5(2x+5)$$
$$9x - 6 = 10x + 25$$
$$9x - 6 - 9x = 10x + 25 - 9x$$
$$-6 = x + 25$$
$$-6 - 25 = x + 25 - 25$$
$$-31 = x$$

18. $x = -3$ and $y = 5$

$$3x - 4y = -29 \quad \rightarrow \quad 3x - 4y = -29$$
$$\underline{2(5x + 2y) = 2(-5)} \quad \rightarrow \quad \underline{10x + 4y = -10}$$
$$13x \qquad\quad = -39$$
$$\frac{13x}{13} = \frac{-39}{13}$$
$$x = -3$$

If $x = -3$, then

$$3x - 4y = -29$$
$$3(-3) - 4y = -29$$
$$-9 - 4y = -29$$
$$-9 - 4y + 9 = -29 + 9$$
$$-4y = -20$$
$$\frac{-4y}{-4} = \frac{-20}{-4}$$
$$y = 5$$

19. $\dfrac{-2}{3}$ The slope m of a line passing through the points (x_1, y_1) and (x_2, y_2) is

$$m = \frac{y_1 - y_2}{x_1 - x_2} \quad \text{or} \quad m = \frac{y_2 - y_1}{x_2 - x_1}$$

For the line passing through $(4, -7)$ and $(-8, 1)$,

$$m = \frac{y_1 - y_2}{x_1 - x_2} = \frac{(-7) - 1}{4 - (-8)} = \frac{-8}{12} = \frac{-2}{3}$$

20. **(–6, 0)** and **(2, 0)** The x-intercept(s) for a graph are all points on the graph where $y = 0$. The x-intercept(s) for the graph of $y = x^2 + 4x - 12$ are

$$x^2 + 4x - 12 = 0$$
$$(x + 6)(x - 2) = 0$$

$$x + 6 = 0 \qquad\qquad x - 2 = 0$$
$$x + 6 - 6 = 0 - 6 \qquad\qquad x - 2 + 2 = 0 + 2$$
$$x = -6 \qquad \text{or} \qquad x = 2$$

Hence, the x-intercepts are $(-6, 0)$ and $(2, 0)$.

Section 3: Critical Reading

Sentence Completions

1. **E.** The sentence contains the word "subsequently," which indicates a flow of time from an earlier to a later event. The earlier event is the conquest of the region by the French army, and the later event relates to Napoleon's growing empire. Choice A is incorrect because although the region was conquered, it would not be identified with the empire as a whole. Eliminate Choice B because the region was conquered, so it would be connected with the empire rather than separated from it. Choice C is wrong because a conquered region would not be confused with the empire that conquered it. Choice D can be eliminated because the region was already conquered, so it could not subsequently be vanquished. After the region was conquered, it was absorbed into (became part of) the growing empire. The correct answer is E.

2. **B.** The sentence contrasts two parts of the audience. The first blank tells what the curious part of the audience did, and the second blank implies that they wanted to see whether the understudy would do a good job. At the end of the sentence, in contrast, the rest of the audience left the theater because they wanted to see the star rather than the understudy. Choice A is wrong because the part of the audience that was curious would not have balked (complained). Eliminate Choice C because a cheering audience wouldn't hope for the actor to botch (mishandle) his performance. Choice D is incorrect because the understudy has already agreed to perform, so he is not in a position to refuse. Choice E can be eliminated because neither word makes much sense in context. The curious portion of the audience remained to see whether the understudy could inhabit (embody) the role. The correct answer is B.

3. **C.** The two blanks are both positive words. The first blank describes something generous and the second describes how the team worked in response to the first. Choice A is incorrect because "haphazardly" (messily) is a negative word. Similarly, Choice B can also be eliminated because "passively" (lazily) is a negative word. Choice D is wrong because the word "intricacies" (details) doesn't make much sense in the context of the sentence. Eliminate Choice E because "encumbrances" (difficulties) is a negative word. The employer offered generous incentives (motivations), so the sales team worked diligently (thoroughly) to meet its quota. The correct answer is C.

4. **A.** The word "but" indicates a contrast between the first part of the sentence and the second. The testimony is described with positive words in the first part, so the blank is a negative word. The colon in the sentence implies that the words that follow are a restatement of the blank. Choice B is wrong because "veritable" (true) is a positive word. Eliminate Choice C because damaging testimony would have bearing on a court case. Choice C is incorrect because "nefarious" (evil) is out of context with the sentence. Similarly, Choice E can be eliminated because "obsequious" (flattering) is also out of context. Even though the testimony was interesting and entertaining, it was immaterial (irrelevant); that is, it had no true bearing on the case. The correct answer is A.

5. **B.** The first blank is a negative word describing Jerome's parents' reaction to his behavior. In contrast, the second blank is a positive word describing Jerome's usual behavior. Choice A is wrong because "provocative" (challenging) is a negative word. Similarly, Choice C can be eliminated because "recalcitrant" (unruly) is also a negative word. Choice D is incorrect because the word "dissuaded" (persuaded against taking an action) is out of place in the sentence. Rule out Choice E because "encouraged" is a positive word. Jerome's parents were astonished (surprised) by his bad behavior because most of the time he was conscientious (thoughtful). The correct answer is B.

6. **A.** The second part of the sentence implies a contrast between the teacher's generous act and Mariah's response, so the second blank is a negative word. Thus, the first blank, which describes the teacher's reaction to her behavior, is also a negative word. Rule out Choice B because "exultant" (celebratory) is a positive word. Similarly, Choice C is wrong because "appreciative" is also a positive word. Choice D is wrong because "vehement" (passionate about something) is out of place in the sentence. Choice E is incorrect because "negligent" (careless) describes a person's behavior rather than describing one person's reaction to another person's behavior. Mariah's teacher was livid (angry) because she squandered (wasted) the time he had given her instead of writing her paper. The correct answer is A.

7. **D.** The sentence describes the book and the Amazon forest as uniformly positive, "replete with stunning photographs" and "an epicurean feast." Therefore, the two blanks are both strongly positive words. Choice A is wrong because "convoluted" (drawn out) is a negative word. Rule out Choice B because the words "earnest" (sincere) and "restrained" (calm) are mildly positive at best. Choice C can be ruled out because the word "solemn" (somber) is negative. Choice E is incorrect because the word "belabored" (overdone) is negative. The book is full of beautiful photographs and vivid (colorful) descriptions, capturing the exquisite (superb) beauty of the forest. The correct answer is D.

8. **B.** The colon implies that the blank is defined by what follows, so this word means strong, forceful, and not easily discouraged. Choice A is wrong because "meticulous" means attentive to detail. Rule out Choice C because "notorious" implies famous with a negative connotation. Choice D is incorrect because "rancorous" means vengeful. Choice E can be discarded because "fraught" means plagued. Choice B, "indomitable," means unconquerable. The correct answer is B.

Long Reading Passages

9. **D.** Choice A is wrong because Sadeh is talking about the time before he had the results to his experiment. Choice B is incorrect because, although Sadeh is self-effacing (not taking himself too seriously), this is not in response to an outside challenge. Rule out Choice C because, again, he is talking about the time before the results were in. Eliminate Choice E because he is not confident that financial support will follow. Sadeh's quote tells us that was worried before the results came in that the effect of one hour of sleep deprivation would have no significant effect. The correct answer is D.

10. **D.** Choice A is wrong because the effect of sleep deprivation begins before high school. Choice B is incorrect because "shock" requires a direct object—someone or something that is receiving a shock—which is absent from the sentence. Choice C can be ruled out because the effect doesn't lapse (disappear) in high school, but gets worse. Eliminate Choice E because "obliterate" also requires a direct object—something that is being obliterated. The effect of sleep deprivation increases in high school because of the steep drop-off in sleep among teenagers. The correct answer is D.

11. **E.** Choice A is incorrect because increments of sleep loss as small as 15 minutes can affect a student's grades. Choice B is wrong because Sadeh used the Wechsler Scale, which predicts achievement test scores, and other experiments tracked student grades. Eliminate Choice C because the passage includes only results that are consistent with Sadeh's findings. Rule out Choice D because high school students sleep less than younger children. Lines 59–60 discuss the result that sleep shift can cause the loss of seven IQ points. The correct answer is E.

12. **C.** Rule out Choice A because the theme of the passage does not concern lead exposure. Choice B is incorrect because the quotation does not in any way sum up previous ideas. Choice D is wrong because the effect of the quote is to strengthen rather than weaken the argument being made. Choice E can be ruled out because the quote merely states a fact rather than stating a suggestion. The quote equates the effect of sleep loss, which appears relatively harmless, with lead exposure, which is known to be severely dangerous. The correct answer is C.

13. **C.** Choice A is wrong because lines 67–73 make no mention of how effects of sleep deprivation are quantified. Similarly, rule out Choice B because these lines do not refer to how sleep deprivation is measured. Choice C is also incorrect because no mention is made of how the children perform when they are not sleep deprived. Eliminate Choice D because the amount of sleep deprivation is not mentioned here. In lines 67–73, the focus is the correlation between sleep and school grades, with specific mention made of two studies in different locations and with subjects of different ages in different grade levels. Any of these distinctions would be correct, but only the ages of the subjects is among the choices. The correct answer is C.

14. **A.** Rule out Choice B because no mention is made of whether a subject is dreaming. Choice C is wrong because, by itself, an actigraph doesn't measure sleep deprivation. Choice D is incorrect because testing, not an actigraph, is used to determine a subject's performance. Eliminate Choice E because showing whether sleep deprivation correlates with impaired performance requires statistical analysis. An actigraph is "a wristwatch-like device that's equivalent to a seismograph for sleep activity"—that is, it merely provides raw data on whether a subject is sleeping. The correct answer is A.

15. **B.** Choice A is incorrect because the conclusions of numerous studies all support each other, so they are not built on a shaky foundation. Eliminate Choice C because the words quoted in lines 85–86 do not particularly surprise the reader. Choice D is wrong because these words do not refer the reader back to a premise. Similarly, rule out Choice E because they do not bring together previously unrelated ideas. The words, "Certainly, these are averages" acknowledge simply that even when a study is conclusive, statistics aren't meant to account for every child in every possible situation, addressing a possible reader concern. The correct answer is B.

16. **C.** Rule out Choice A because Mrs. Hopewell is not being direct—Mrs. Freeman annoys her, but she says nothing. Choice B is wrong because Mrs. Hopewell isn't coercive (bullying), but somewhat passive instead. Eliminate Choice D because Mrs. Hopewell has no concerns about Mrs. Freeman's motives. Choice E is incorrect because Mrs. Hopewell clearly places herself on at least an equal footing with Mrs. Freeman, who works for her. Mrs. Hopewell feels slightly annoyed by Mrs. Freeman but resolves to be forbearing (patient) to maintain the relationship. The correct answer is C.

17. **C.** Choice A is incorrect because the effect of Joy's outrage is more forceful than merely hiding her facial expressions. Choice B is wrong because the word "betrayed" doesn't make sense just before the word "from." Similarly, Choice D can be ruled out because the word "highlighted" doesn't make sense before the word "from." Rule out Choice E because, again, in the context of Joy's outrage the word "lifted" is not forceful enough. In this context, the word "obliterated" means eliminated. The correct answer is C.

18. **A.** Choice B is incorrect because there is no evidence that Mrs. Freeman mistrusts people. Choice C is wrong because the author's comment has nothing to do with whether Mrs. Freeman is an optimist. Choice D can be ruled out because the comment underscores that Mrs. Freeman is not at all deferential (willing to take a back seat) to Mrs. Hopewell. Eliminate Choice E because the comment has nothing particularly to do with whether Mrs. Freeman is a traditionalist. The author's comment means that Mrs. Freeman is unwilling to admit that someone else may have a thought that hasn't already occurred to her. The correct answer is A.

19. **A.** Rule out Choice B because the dialogue is friendly and shows the two women to be in agreement. Choice C is wrong because while the dialogue is friendly, neither woman either reveals personal information or shows a deep attachment to the other. Choice D is incorrect because, while Mrs. Freeman works for Mrs. Hopewell, this aspect of the relationship is irrelevant in the dialogue. Choice E can be ruled out because neither woman is tremendously uninhibited (expressive) in the dialogue. The dialogue shows the two women sharing clichés back and forth, remaining on the surface with neither interested in deepening the relationship. The correct answer is A.

20. **C.** Eliminate Choice A because, while the author shows her characters' flaws and idiosyncrasies, she lets them speak for themselves and is never insulting toward them. Choice B is wrong because the author never shrinks from showing us the seamy side of all three characters. Choice D is incorrect because the author maintains distance from her characters, showing their actions without attempting to feel the emotions behind them. Rule out Choice E because the author solidly builds her sketch of the characters, continuing to fill in details without changing her mind about any of them. The author's tone quietly highlights the humor in the situation without overtly calling attention to it. And each character is drawn a little larger than life, which is an earmark of satire. The correct answer is C.

Paired Passages

21. **C.** Choice A is wrong because Passage 1 makes no mention of confidentiality (maintaining the patient's privacy). Rule out Choice B because "mastery" means to get good at doing something, which is out of context. Choice D is incorrect because the self-esteem of the patient is not mentioned in Passage 1. Similarly, eliminate Choice E because the patient's solitude is also not an issue. The author clarifies her meaning in lines 15–16: "the patient is in charge of her own life"—that is, the patient is self-determined. The correct answer is C.

22. **B.** Rule out Choice A because, while therapists are in disagreement about what constitutes a therapeutic relationship, this is not at issue in Passage 2. Choice C is wrong because what constitutes an ideal therapeutic relationship is a concern for the author of Passage 1, but not Passage 2. Choice D is incorrect because neither passage makes any mention of the distinction between physicians and therapists. Choice E is also wrong because the author of Passage 2 is focused on his own conduct rather than that of his client. Finding his own authenticity with a client to be important if the client is to open up, the author rejects presenting himself as anything less than real. The correct answer is B.

23. **D.** Rule out Choice A because the therapist displaying anger might constitute an abuse of power, which the author of Passage 1 would not condone. Choice B is wrong because the author of Passage 2 would consider scientific objectivity to be an obstacle between the client and therapist. Choice C is incorrect because the author of Passage 1 states that the therapy relationship is unique. Eliminate Choice E because the author of Passage 2 would find the dictum not to bring his personal life into therapy too artificial. Both authors agree that the therapist is in service to the patient or client, who is in charge of the therapy. The correct answer is D.

24. **E.** Rule out Choice A because to offer advice would be out of keeping with patient autonomy. Similarly, Choice B is wrong because a therapist hiring a client would disturb patient autonomy. Choice C is incorrect because the therapist would be misusing her power to manipulate a patient. Rule out Choice D because this,

too, is an abuse of power that threatens autonomy. In Passage 1, neutrality dictates that the therapist "does not take sides in the patient's inner conflicts or try to dictate the patient's life decisions." The correct answer is E.

25. **A.** Eliminate Choice B because the author of Passage 1 is concerned solely about the patient's feelings rather than those of the therapist. Similarly, rule out Choice C because the author of Passage 1 herself holds the therapist to a high standard. Choice D is wrong because both authors underscore the importance of patient control of the therapy. Choice E is incorrect because, again, the author of Passage 1 concerns herself with the patient's experience rather than that of the therapist. Passage 1 focuses on the power that a patient inevitably entrusts to a therapist, and the therapist's responsibility to use it wisely. The author of Passage 2 does not address this issue. The correct answer is A.

Short Reading Passage

26. **B.** Choice A is wrong because Hemingway wasn't savaged (abused) by the media. Choice C is incorrect because his novel was widely read rather than disregarded. Rule out Choice D because his novel sold very well. Eliminate Choice E because the author says nothing about his being misunderstood. The author describes how the critics treated Ernest Hemingway like royalty. The correct answer is B.

27. **A.** Choice B can be ruled out because the book was underrated rather than overrated. Choice C is wrong because the book was not praised. Choice D is wrong because the subject matter of the book of short stories, unlike that of the novel, was not considered controversial. Similarly, eliminate Choice E because it was the novel, not the book of stories, that was banned in Boston. Despite its quality, the book had no great impact on the literary community. The correct answer is A.

28. **B.** Choice A is incorrect because the words "agreed upon" are out of place in the context. Choice C is wrong because "squandered" means wasted, which is out of keeping with Hemingway's status as a valued author. Rule out Choice D because the word "entrusted" carries a connotation that is out of keeping with the sense of excess implied in the sentence. Eliminate Choice E because Hemingway received things, whereas "cajoled from" (coaxed from) implies that he gave things. In keeping with his status as a lionized celebrity, all the trimmings were lavished (poured) upon him. The correct answer is B.

Section 4: Writing—Multiple Choice

Improving Sentences

1. **C.** The correlative conjunction "Between . . . and . . . " requires parallel construction to match the noun phrase "his duties as a military officer." Choice A includes the word "also" and a noun phrase beginning with the gerund "having," both of which are awkward. Choice B is an independent clause—including subject, verb, and direct object—which does not fit grammatically. Choice D is a dependent clause, which fails to adhere to the parallel construction required. Choice E is a noun phrase beginning with a gerund, which is awkward. Choice C is a noun phrase that begins with the word "his," which matches the parallel construction, so this is the best answer. The correct answer is C.

2. **C.** When the subordinating conjunction "only" begins a sentence, the main verb of the sentence requires an auxiliary or a modal verb such as "did," "would," or "could." Choice A can be ruled out because it's missing this verb. Choice B is wrong because it contains the auxiliary verb "did" but incorrectly follows it with the past tense verb "found." Eliminate Choice D because it doesn't include an auxiliary or a modal verb. Similarly, Choice E is incorrect because it lacks this verb. Choice C is right because it includes this construction with an auxiliary verb used properly. The correct answer is C.

3. **A.** The dependent clause beginning with "that" has two subclauses, coordinated by the conjunction "while." Choice B is wrong because it begins with the unnecessary conjunction "but." Choice C is incorrect because it uses unnecessary passive construction that disturbs the flow of the sentence. Choice D is wrong because it changes the meaning of the sentence, stating that compassion could never replace expertise, rather than the reverse. Choice E can be ruled out because it begins with the unnecessary words "even so." Choice A is a clause with no unnecessary words, providing a proper balance to the clause "medical expertise was essential." The correct answer is A.

4. **D.** The participial phrase, "Wondering where the time had gone," is a dangling modifier that requires the immediate mention of the noun it is modifying, "Jane." Choice A is incorrect because it begins with a noun, "the clock," which isn't the noun being modified. Choice B is wrong for the same reason. Choice C also fails to begin with the noun being modified. Choice E is incorrect because it begins with an additional participial clause before mentioning the noun "Jane," making the sentence unnecessarily awkward. Choice D mentions the noun "Jane" and then goes on to properly complete the sentence. The correct answer is D.

5. **D.** Choice A is wrong because, as it stands, the sentence suffers from the awkward repetition of words such as "and," "spent," and "on." Rule out Choice B because it fails to solve any of these problems. Choice C introduces the word "he" as an additional subject, compounding the problem. Choice E eliminates the first "and" but fails to make the clause dependent, which turns the sentence into a run-on. Choice D eliminates the first "and" while properly subordinating the clause that follows, streamlining the sentence by eliminating awkward repetition. The correct answer is D.

6. **A.** Rule out Choice B because it introduces the unnecessary verb "is." Choice C is wrong because the introduction of the word "being" changes the phrase either to a gerund phrase or a dangling participial clause, neither of which be a modifier. Choice D is incorrect because, again, the introduction of the verb "is" is grammatically incorrect for this context. Similarly, Choice E is wrong because the verb "will be" is improperly introduced into the sentence. In Choice A, the phrase "willing to agree" is a participial phrase that properly modifies "landlord." The correct answer is A.

7. **D.** Choice A is wrong because, as it stands, the subject of the sentence is "she," which makes the later part of the sentence ungrammatical. The correction requires changing the main verb of the sentence to "makes." As a result, everything that precedes this word—two clauses connected by the conjunction "and"—is the subject of the sentence. This construction must be subordinated properly in a way that allows the first part of the sentence to stand as the subject. Choice B fails to do this, turning the first part of the sentence into a subordinate clause that cannot be used as a subject. Choices C and E fail for the same reason. Choice D introduces the word "that" and turns the entire first part of the sentence into a noun, which becomes the subject of the sentence. The correct answer is D.

8. **A.** Choice B incorrectly provides the future tense verb "will be" rather than the subjunctive verb. Choice C is wrong because, by removing the word "that," the construction now requires a direct object noun such as "your being" rather than "you being." Choice D is incorrect because the word "that" requires the subjunctive, but the words "your being" introduces a noun phrase instead. Choice E can be ruled out because the verb "are being" is not subjunctive. In Choice A, the construction "I recommend that . . ." subjoins the clause that immediately follows, requiring both a subject, "you," and a subjunctive verb, "be." The correct answer is A.

9. **C.** Choice A is wrong because the word "if" cannot be followed by the verb "would have." Choice B is incorrect because the construction "hadn't have" is incorrect in any context. Choice D is incorrect because Jacob's concern is already completed in the present ("would have been"), so the professor graded the papers at an even earlier time. Choice E is a noun phrase, which is completely out of context. Choice C places the grading of the papers properly before Jacob's worry. The correct answer is C.

10. **E.** The participial phrase that begins the sentence requires that the noun that it modifies (Ms. Myer) be mentioned immediately after the comma. Rule out Choice A because "the letter carrier" is the wrong noun. Choice B is wrong because "the late arrival of the letter carrier" is also the wrong noun. Similarly, Choice C is wrong because "the late arrival by the letter carrier" is also the wrong noun. Choice D is incorrect because it states that Ms. Myer rather than the letter carrier arrived late. Choice E is correct; the introduction of passive construction ("was worried by") is slightly weak, but preferable to all other choices because it makes Ms. Myer the subject of the sentence. The correct answer is E.

11. **E.** The first part of the sentence has no verb, and the last part of the sentence is subordinated with "that," so the underlined portion of the sentence is the main clause, which contains the subject and verb of the sentence. Choice A is wrong because the word "when" subordinates the clause that follows. Choice B can be ruled out because it contains no verb. Choice C is incorrect because the word "that" subordinates the clause that follows. Choice D is wrong because the verb "is finding" is split up awkwardly, and the word "often" requires a present tense verb rather than a present progressive verb. Choice E is right because it is a straightforward main clause, with a subject ("one") and verb ("finds"). The correct answer is E.

12. **B.** Choice A is wrong because the adverb "only," which the verb modifies "has," is misplaced before the subject "she." Choice C is incorrect because the modifier "only" is again misplaced, this time splitting the infinitive "to complete." You can rule out Choice D because the modifier "only" is again misplaced, and the verb "would have" alters the meaning of the sentence to imply that her graduation upon completing one more semesters is uncertain. Eliminate Choice E because it doesn't contain a verb. In Choice B, the modifier "only" is placed correctly before the verb "has." The correct answer is B.

13. **C.** Choice A is incorrect because the word "having" makes the construction awkward—the sentence would be better without it. Choice B is wrong because "notwithstanding" cannot be followed by an independent clause. Choice D can be ruled out because "even though" must be followed by a clause rather than a phrase. Choice E is wrong because it uses the present progressive ("is having") rather than the present tense ("has"). Choice C changes the first part of the sentence from a phrase to a subordinate clause, but does so in a way that uses proper grammar and maintains the meaning of the sentence. The correct answer is C.

Identifying Sentence Errors

14. **D.** The subject of the sentence is "a carpenter," which is singular. The word "their" in the phrase "their envisioned outcome" refers to a plural subject. Choice A properly opens the phrase that begins the sentence. Choice B is an appropriate third-person singular verb. Choice C is an infinitive verb that attaches appropriately to the words that precede it. The correct answer is D.

15. **C.** In this context, the use of the gerund "expressing" is incorrect; instead, the infinitive "to express" is proper. Choice A is an appropriate use of a prepositional phrase. Choice B is a proper use of a past tense verb that agrees with the subject, "the people." Choice D is an appropriate use of the possessive adjective "their" that agrees with the subject. The correct answer is C.

16. **D.** The verb "will apologize" is in the future tense, so the verb "would find" is wrong and should be "will find." The sentence uses multiple tenses, with "If he expects" in the present tense, the time in which the sentence occurs. Choice A is the correct use of a prepositional phrase. Choice B is the correct use of a past tense verb, indicating the time when the remarks were made. Choice C is another correct use of a prepositional phrase. The correct answer is D.

17. **B.** The subject of the sentence, "Noreen and her older brother," is plural, but the verb "was" is singular. Choice A is the appropriate use of a participial phrase. Choice C is the correct use of an adjectival phrase. Choice D is a clause whose subject is plural, in proper agreement with the subject of the sentence. The correct answer is B.

18. **B.** The sentence is built from two independent clauses joined with the first "and." The subject of the second clause should be "the four of us boys"—the subject pronoun "we" is never placed directly after the word "of." Choice A is the correct use of a subject and a past tense verb. Choice C is a correct past tense verb and modifier. Choice D is a correct past tense verb and a direct object. The correct answer is B.

19. **E.** Choice A is a correct use of an infinitive verb and modifier. Choice B includes the subject and verb of the sentence. Choice C includes the subject and verb of a dependent clause that begins with the word "that." Choice D is another dependent clause. The correct answer is E.

20. **C.** The sentence begins with a dependent clause whose subject is "you," so the subject of the sentence should also be "you" rather than "one." Choice A correctly begins a modifying phrase. Choice B is an appropriate use of an adverb. Choice D correctly includes part of the verb and part of the direct object of the sentence. The correct answer is C.

21. **B.** The dependent clause beginning with the word "that" has a plural predicate noun, "two ways," so the subject and verb of the sentence should be in agreement: "there are" rather than "there's." Choice A is correct, including the subject, verb, and indirect object of the sentence. Choice C correctly refers to one of the ways to the subject's house. Choice D is an appropriate use of a comparative adjective modifying "one" (of the two ways). The correct answer is B.

22. **A.** The subject of the sentence is "Mr. Wright's house," and the adjective phrase "like many other people" incorrectly describes the house as a person. Choice B is an adjective phrase that appropriately describes the house. Choice C contains two adjectives that further describe the house, with punctuation and the word "and" used appropriately. Choice D also includes most of an adjective phrase that correctly modifies the house. The correct answer is A.

Improving Paragraphs

23. **D.** Choice A is incorrect because the use of the infinitives "to overdo" and "to quit" is awkward. Eliminate Choice B because "where" is used weakly to describe a situation rather than a location. Choice C can be ruled out because "One of the worst of these types of strategies" is unnecessarily wordy and awkward. Choice E is wrong because using "One bad habit" to refer to a bad strategy is a confusing word choice, given that the topic itself is habits. In Choice D, the words "such strategy" refer back to sentence 1, acknowledging the repetition of the word "strategy." The use of the colon clearly marks where the description of the strategy ends and the examples begin. The correct answer is D.

24. **C.** Choice A is wrong because omitting sentence 4 would make sentence 5 confusing. Rule out Choice B because without sentence 5, there is no transition from sentence 4, which discusses gym memberships, and sentence 6, which focuses on the importance of money. Choice D is incorrect because sentence 7 provides points out the flaw in the strategy under discussion in this paragraph; without it, the paragraph as a whole makes no sense. Eliminate Choice E because sentence 8 wraps up the argument and makes the point that the paragraph is trying to make. Sentence 6 is an unnecessary argument about the importance of money, which should already be obvious to the reader. The correct answer is C.

25. **C.** Choice A is incorrect because the sentence as it stands is unnecessarily wordy. Rule out Choice B because this sentence is unnecessarily terse and unclear. Choice D is a wrong because the colon followed by the word "because" is redundant and awkward. Eliminate Choice E because it is just as wordy as the original sentence. Choice C introduces the paragraph by identifying making and breaking habits as a skill and comparing it to a muscle. While it skips a transition from the previous paragraph, the reader's flow is not unduly interrupted. The correct answer is C.

Section 5: Mathematics

Geometry

1. $x = z = 70$ and $y = 110$

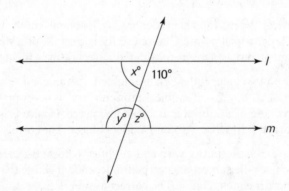

Since $l \parallel m$, alternate interior angles are equal, so $y = 110°$ and $x = z$. Also $x = 70° = z$ since x and the $110°$ angle are supplementary angles.

2. **10** Since $\overline{AB} \perp \overline{AC}$, $\triangle ABC$ is a right triangle and by the Pythagorean Theorem,

$$(AB)^2 + (AC)^2 = (BC)^2$$
$$(AB)^2 + (24)^2 = (26)^2$$
$$(AB)^2 + 576 = 676$$
$$(AB)^2 + 576 - 576 = 676 - 576$$
$$(AB)^2 = 100$$
$$AB = \sqrt{100} = 10$$

3. **40**

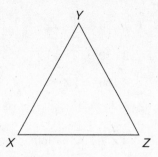

Because $XY = YZ$, $\triangle XYZ$ is an isosceles triangle and $\angle X = \angle Z = 70°$. Because the sum of the interior angles of a triangle is $180°$,

$$\angle X + \angle Y + \angle Z = 180°$$
$$70° + \angle Y + 70° = 180°$$
$$\angle Y + 140° = 180°$$
$$\angle Y + 140° - 140° = 180° - 140°$$
$$\angle Y = 40°$$

4. **144π** The circumference C of a circle with diameter d is

$$C = \pi d$$
$$24\pi = \pi d$$
$$\frac{24\pi}{\pi} = \frac{\pi d}{\pi}$$
$$24 = d$$

The radius r of a circle with a diameter d is

$$r = \frac{1}{2}d$$
$$= \frac{1}{2}(24)$$
$$r = 12$$

The area A of a circle with radius r is

$$A = \pi r^2$$
$$= \pi(12)^2$$
$$= 144\pi$$

5. **260**

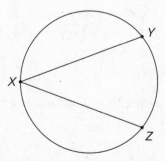

The measure in degrees of inscribed $\angle X$ is half the measure of its intercepted arc $\overset{\frown}{YZ}$.

$$\angle X = \frac{1}{2}\widehat{YZ}$$

$$50° = \frac{1}{2} \cdot \widehat{YZ}$$

$$2 \cdot 50° = 2 \cdot \frac{1}{2}\widehat{YZ}$$

$$100° = \widehat{YZ}$$

Since the degree measure of a circle is 360°,

$$\widehat{YZ} + \widehat{YXZ} = 360°$$

$$100° + \widehat{YXZ} = 360°$$

$$100° + \widehat{YXZ} - 100° = 360° - 100°$$

$$\widehat{YXZ} = 260°$$

6. **128** Since the diagonals d of a square are equal and perpendicular, the area A of a square is

$$A = \frac{1}{2}d \cdot d = \frac{1}{2}d^2$$

$$= \frac{1}{2}(16)^2$$

$$= \frac{1}{2}(256)$$

$$= 128$$

7. **284**

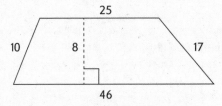

The area A of a trapezoid with bases B and b, and height h is

$$A = \frac{1}{2}h(B+b)$$

$$= \frac{1}{2}(8)(46+25)$$

$$= (4)(71)$$

$$= 284$$

8. **1344** The surface area A of a rectangular solid with length l, width w, and height h is

$$A = 2lh + 2wh + 2lw$$

$$= 2(24)(8) + 2(15)(8) + 2(24)(15)$$

$$= 384 + 240 + 720$$

$$= 1344$$

9. **200π** The volume V of a right circular cylinder with radius r and height h is

$$V = \pi r^2 h$$

$$= \pi(5)^2(8)$$

$$= \pi(25)(8)$$

$$= 200\pi$$

Data Analysis

10. 21,120

Since 1 mile = 1,760 yards, the number of yards in 4 miles is $4 \times 1,760 = 7,040$ yards. Since 1 yard = 3 feet, the number of feet in 4 miles is $3 \times 7,040 = 21,120$ feet.

11. $\frac{33}{2}$, **or** $16\frac{1}{2}$ The median of a set of numbers is the middle number with the numbers arranged in order from smallest to largest (or largest to smallest). Since there is an even number of items in the data, the median is the average of the two middle numbers. For the numbers 11, 14, 15, 15, 18, 19, 20, 20, the two middle numbers are 15 and 18, and the median is

$$\frac{15+18}{2} = \frac{33}{2} \text{ or } 16\frac{1}{2}$$

12. 94 The average of 5 test scores is determined by dividing the sum of the 5 scores by 5. Let $x =$ the fifth test score. For the 5 test scores to average 85,

$$\frac{x+86+91+73+81}{5} = 85$$

$$\frac{x+331}{5} = 85$$

$$\frac{x+331}{5} \cdot 5 = 85 \cdot 5$$

$$x+331 = 425$$

$$x = 94$$

13. 495

$$\frac{12!}{8! \cdot 4!} = \frac{12 \cdot 11 \cdot 10 \cdot 9 \cdot \cancel{8!}}{\cancel{8!} \cdot 4!}$$

$$= \frac{12 \cdot 11 \cdot 10 \cdot 9}{4 \cdot 3 \cdot 2 \cdot 1}$$

$$= 495$$

14. 123

Let $s_n = nth$ term of the sequence.

$s_1 = -3$

$s_2 = 2(-3)+5 = -6+5 = -1$

$s_3 = 2(-1)+5 = -2+5 = 3$

$s_4 = 2(3)+5 = 6+5 = 11$

$s_5 = 2(11)+5 = 22+5 = 27$

$s_6 = 2(27)+5 = 54+5 = 59$

$s_7 = 2(59)+5 = 118+5 = 123$

15. 3,024 Because the order of the numbers chosen is important, this is a permutation of n digits taken r at a time.

$$P(n, r) = \frac{n!}{(n-r)!}$$

$$P(9, 4) = \frac{9!}{5!}$$

$$= \frac{9 \cdot 8 \cdot 7 \cdot 6 \cdot \cancel{5!}}{\cancel{5!}}$$

$$= 9 \cdot 8 \cdot 7 \cdot 6$$

$$= 3024$$

16. $\frac{6}{35}$

Since there are 4 odd numbers in the numbers 1 through 7, the probability that the first ticket chosen will be odd is $\frac{4}{7}$.

Since there are 3 even numbers in the remaining 6 numbers, the probability that the second ticket chosen will be even is $\frac{3}{6} = \frac{1}{2}$.

Since there are 3 odd numbers in the remaining 5 numbers, the probability that the third ticket chosen will be odd is $\frac{3}{5}$.

Hence, the probability P that the tickets drawn will be alternately odd, even, and odd is

$$P = \frac{4}{7} \cdot \frac{1}{2} \cdot \frac{3}{5} = \frac{12}{70} = \frac{6}{35}$$

17. $\frac{1}{455}$

Since there are 3 red jelly beans out of a total of 15 jelly beans, the probability that the first jelly bean drawn will be red is $\frac{3}{15} = \frac{1}{5}$.

Since there are 2 red jelly beans in the remaining 14 jelly beans, the probability that the second jelly bean drawn will be red is $\frac{2}{14} = \frac{1}{7}$.

Since there is 1 red jelly bean in the remaining 13 jelly beans, the probability that the third jelly bean drawn will be red is $\frac{1}{13}$.

Hence, the probability P that all three jelly beans will be red is:

$$P = \frac{1}{5} \cdot \frac{1}{7} \cdot \frac{1}{13} = \frac{1}{455}$$

18. $\frac{115}{203}$

Since there are 25 students who are not on the baseball team out of a total of 30 students, the probability that the first student chosen is not on the baseball team is $\frac{25}{30} = \frac{5}{6}$.

Since there are 24 students of the remaining 29 who are not on the baseball team, the probability that the second student chosen is not on the baseball team is $\frac{24}{29}$.

Since there are 23 students of the remaining 28 students who are not on the baseball team, the probability that the third student chosen is not on the baseball team is $\frac{23}{28}$.

Hence, the probability P that three students chosen at random are not on the baseball team is:

$$P = \frac{5}{6} \cdot \frac{24}{29} \cdot \frac{23}{28} = \frac{2760}{4872} = \frac{115}{203}$$

PART II

REVIEW OF EXAM AREAS

Chapter 2

Critical Reading Overview

The purpose of the critical reading section on the SAT is to assess your readiness for college-level reading material. Good reading skills and your knowledge of both the rhetorical (effective expression) and conventions (grammar, punctuation, word usage, verb forms, and structural and style devices) of standard written English will help you succeed on this section. Accordingly, we have created instructional models to help your *reading skills development* and *vocabulary skills development*. These models will enhance your ability to think critically about written text passages and apply your existing knowledge and skills to the questions on the critical reading section of the SAT.

At first glance, this section may appear very complex because there are so many variables and considerations. However, with a disciplined approach and application of the strategies suggested in this chapter, as well as a careful examination of the question types and answer choices, you can improve your performance on this section of the SAT. Research suggests that a degree of familiarity with test format and types of questions is a proven factor for test-taking success. As you go through this chapter, you should notice a significant increase in your comfort level with the exam questions. You should also notice an improvement in your *consistent* ability to answer questions with greater ease and proficiency.

Introduction to Critical Reading

Critical reading questions are organized and presented in two different *question type formats:* sentence completions and passage-based reading questions. In this chapter, you will review each of these question types, as well as learn how to apply specific strategies to successfully respond to each type of question. Several sample problems will provide plenty of practice to help you reinforce your skills and your approach to these types of questions and problems. Each section of this chapter is designed to help you improve your *reading* and *reasoning abilities*, and to help you develop a greater *understanding of word meanings*. You are encouraged to pace yourself and familiarize yourself with the question types by completing all the practice exercises in each section. At the end of this chapter, you'll find a reference study list of common prefixes, suffixes, and root words to help you determine full or partial word meanings. This will help you expand your working vocabulary.

After you review the concepts and strategies for each type of question, you will be ready to practice what you have learned. Repeated practice is the key to your success on the SAT. The final chapters of this study guide include four full-length practice tests with complete explanations and illustrations, and the accompanying CD-ROM has three more. Apply the rules, concepts, and strategies you learn in this chapter to the practice tests, and review the strategies and questions regularly before your test to maximize your test-taking performance.

Reading Development

It is important to keep in mind that the entire SAT is a reading test; even the math sections require reading skills. As you develop and apply the reading skills presented in this section, what you learn will help you on the entire SAT. You will also develop skills that will help you successfully navigate your future college academic course work. Effective reading improves your thinking abilities and will open up many future learning possibilities and opportunities in life.

To start reading development, it is sometimes helpful to think about related models in other academic disciplines, such as mathematics. To solve math problems, you must develop a mental system for *symbol interpretation*. If you do not understand how to use or interpret various math symbols (decimal point, division sign, multiplication sign, fraction line, greater than, less than, etc.) correctly, you will not understand the problem and you will not be able to find the right answer. Reading is similar to math in this way, except that *words* provide us with the symbols to interpret, rather than numbers. Simply put, our goal in this chapter is to teach you how to identify, interpret, and use word symbols in each of the two question type formats to help you successfully respond to the test.

The most basic approach to tackling passage-based reading questions is to try to understand the author's main idea and purpose for writing the passage. From there, you will be asked to respond to various other questions about *stated* (explicit) and *inferred* (implicit) information, meanings, arguments, and intentions.

Keep in mind that improved reading comprehension is not about moving your eyes across a page more quickly, but about forming a mental framework to help you conceptualize words into ideas and information. Many skilled readers, because of time constraints, approach the passages by quickly "reading between the lines." Critical reading is the conscious process of "thinking about reading" and actively engaging in the reading passage and the questions. For you to attain a higher score, you must think like a detective to search, locate, and extract information in its context so you can accurately respond to the questions.

Successful readers like you will use a variety of strategies to gain an understanding of the reading passages; these will enable you to visualize, pick out details, predict, decode, and summarize the text. Be confident in your ability to learn reading development skills and be patient with yourself as you work through the strategies presented. Remember, repeated practice is the key to your success in critical reading. As you work through the practice tests, pay careful attention to our explanations. These provide you with clues about the thinking patterns of the test to help you determine the correct answer choice.

Vocabulary Development

As students prepare for the verbal section of the SAT, they often spend an inordinate amount of time learning new vocabulary words. Some students bank hundreds of hours trying to memorize new vocabulary words with little guarantee that these memorized words will appear on the SAT. As you begin working on vocabulary development skills, we suggest you learn new techniques to expand your vocabulary instead. Also be mindful of the time you spend memorizing words. Do not let this part of the test interfere with your overall test preparation and study time. Keep in mind that vocabulary and word meanings are just a part of the overall SAT exam.

At the end of this chapter, starting on page 78, there are three resources to help you improve your vocabulary:

- Memory improvement mnemonic devices teach you how to store, retrieve, and recall words.
- Resources for power vocabulary words.
- A list of commonly used prefixes, suffixes, and roots will help you decipher the meaning of words by breaking them down into their base parts.

The principles and methods of vocabulary improvement included in this chapter have been successfully researched and developed over many years. You can apply these vocabulary development techniques to most verbal sections of the exam. Remember, there is no guarantee that the words you study will actually appear on the SAT. But regardless of the question type, if you can expand your knowledge of vocabulary strategies you can improve your overall performance on the verbal portion of the exam.

The following table provides a brief description of the two critical reading sections.

Format of Critical Reading	
Sections	**Number of Questions**
Sentence completions evaluate your understanding of word meanings and the logic you use to identify words in the context of a sentence. There are two basic types of sentence completion questions: vocabulary in context of the sentence, and logic of word meanings in the context of a complex sentence.	Approximately 19 questions (28%)
Passage-based reading (short, long, and paired passages) tests your ability to understand, interpret, and analyze reading passages on a variety of topics. Passages vary in style and subject matter. Questions are drawn from single paragraphs (short passages), longer articles/editorials (long passages), or two related paragraphs (paired passages). You will be asked to evaluate, reason, draw inferences, or determine the meaning of information presented in the passages. There are three basic types of passage-based reading questions: reasoning, reading comprehension, and vocabulary in context.	Approximately 48 questions (72%)
Total critical reading section—the total allotted time for these sections is 70 minutes (two 25-minute sections and one 20-minute section).	Approximately 67 questions *Plus experimental questions

*Experimental questions—The SAT has an experimental, unidentified section that is an unscored section of the exam. The experimental section may appear on your SAT in any section and it may be critical reading or mathematics questions or problems, but it will not count toward your SAT score. You will not know which section is experimental. Experimental questions are used to test future SAT questions. Don't spend valuable time trying to guess which questions are experimental. It is impossible to differentiate experimental questions from scored questions, so it is best to just answer all the questions you can to the best of your ability.

Overview of the Sentence Completions

Sentence completion questions are designed to test your knowledge of vocabulary and sentence structure. Questions assess how well you understand vocabulary within the context of a sentence and how well you use contextual clues. You will be asked to choose the best one or two words to complete the sentence.

Skills and Concepts Tested

Sentence-completion question types test your ability to complete sentences with a word or words that retain(s) the *meaning* of the sentence. The answer you choose should be *structurally* and *stylistically* correct. This requires you to understand word meanings and context clues, and to be able to discriminate word choices by using these context clues. To perform well, you need to think logically and evaluate *subtle differences* in word choices. Words that have subtle differences may be similar, but are not interchangeable. Your knowledge of vocabulary and standard written English should help you create coherent and structurally cohesive sentences.

Directions

In each sentence completion question, you will be presented with a sentence that has one or two blanks, indicating that something has been omitted, or left out of the sentence. The directions will tell you to select the best answer from among the choices labeled A, B, C, D, or E that appear beneath the sentence. Choose the word or set of words that, when inserted in the sentence, best fit the meaning of the sentence as a whole. Fill in the corresponding circle on your answer sheet.

General Strategies for Sentence Completions

Sentence completion questions are divided into two basic types: *vocabulary in the context of the sentence*, and *logic of word meanings in the context of a sentence*. Specific question types, along with general approaches, strategies, and exercises, are described in detail in this section. Before you review specific strategies, consider these general strategies that apply to all sentence completion questions.

1. **Questions appear in order of difficulty,** and all questions are worth the same number of points regardless of the level of difficulty. Unlike the passage-based reading questions, these questions are graduated in difficulty. This means that the easiest questions appear at the beginning and the more difficult questions follow, with the most difficult questions appearing toward the end of the section. With this type of section, it is to your advantage to work problems in the order in which they appear because all questions have the same point value but the earlier ones are easier.

2. **Manage your time wisely.** At first glance you might calculate that you have about *1 minute per question* to read and answer all of the questions. When you begin the exam, make a mental note of the starting time and keep track of the time. Never spend more than a minute on any one question. Remember, there are approximately 19 sentence completion questions, but you will have only 70 minutes to complete the entire critical reading section that contains approximately 67 questions. Because passage-based reading questions are more time consuming, you should work through sentence completion questions quickly so that you will have time to focus on the passage-based reading questions. Some questions are easier than others, some will take less than a minute and others will take slightly longer than a minute. With sufficient practice, you will almost automatically know when a problem is taking too much time and when it is time to select an answer or leave it blank and proceed to the next question.

3. **Use the process of elimination strategy** whenever possible to eliminate one or more answer choices. Be sure to read all of the answer choices carefully and try to eliminate obvious wrong answers as soon as you recognize them. Use the elimination strategy on page 7. If you get stuck on any one question, either take an educated guess by eliminating some of the other choices, or leave it blank and proceed to the next question. The elimination strategy is a very valuable technique for the entire test, but particularly for the critical reading section. Remember, there is a fraction of a point taken off for wrong answers to discourage wild guessing.

4. **Be on the alert for the "attractive distracter" answer choice.** Watch out for answers that look good but are not the best answer choice. The attractive distracter usually appears in this section as a choice that contains a subtle variation in meaning from the correct answer, thus making it more difficult for you to select the correct answer. Attractive distracters are carefully written to be *close to the best answer,* but there is never more than one right answer. The best answer is always the only correct answer choice. When you narrow your choice down to two answers, one is probably the attractive distracter. If this happens, read the question again and select the answer that fits the best *word meaning* for the blank(s) provided in the question.

5. **Use only the information that is directly stated (or implied or inferred)** in the sentence to answer the questions. Base your answer on what you read in the sentence provided. The sentence must support your answer. Do not apply any outside knowledge that you may have about the subject.

6. **Read the sentence actively and always read the entire sentence.** As you read the sentence, circle or underline key words and the main points, or any other items you feel are important (for example, structural trigger words that signal a transition). If the sentence contains two blanks, remember that *both* of the words must fit the sentence. Do not make a hasty assumption that you know the correct answer without reading the whole question and all the possible answers. The hurried test-taker commonly selects an incorrect answer by jumping to a conclusion after reading only one part of the answer choices. Some of the answer choices may only show a part of the correct answer. Remember, *both* words in a two-word answer choice must fit for that answer choice to be the correct answer!

7. **Skip questions only if necessary.** When you encounter a question that contains vocabulary words that are difficult for you to understand, you may choose to skip the question and come back to it later if time permits. Keep in mind that because questions are arranged by order of difficulty, the *plus-minus strategy* discussed on page 7 is *not* typically an effective strategy to use for this type of question. Also, be sure to mark your answer sheet correctly if you skip a question. Test-takers who skip questions might make the mistake of continuing to mark their answers in sequence and forget to leave blank the unanswered questions. A good idea is to mark your answer in the test booklet itself (no need to erase later) so that if you do make mistakes in transferring your answer choices to the answer sheet, you can easily correct your errors without having to reconsider the answer choices.

Suggested Specific Strategies

The Sentence Completions section tests your ability to recognize what is *implied* or *inferred* in a sentence and to select the word or words that best complete the sentence and fit with the meaning. Every question has a built-in context clue to help you to select the correct answer. Context clues are clear and straightforward and leave no room for guesswork. The goal is to recognize the clues so you can answer the questions correctly.

Below are six basic approaches that will help you strategize and plan your course of action as you answer this type of question. The sample exercises in the practice section that follows will help you practice these skills and look for clues to answer questions more quickly and efficiently. With repeated practice, the clues should become more apparent more quickly, thus saving you time on the actual SAT.

Six Basic Approaches to Sentence-Completion Questions

1. **Paraphrase the sentence in your own words.**

   After reading the sentence and before reading the answer choices, think of a word or words that you might insert to complete the sentence. Then look for the answer choice that is synonymous with your selection. Mentally reread the complete sentence with your selected answer to make sure that the sentence reads logically. Practice problems 1 and 5 that follow this section provide examples of this approach.

2. **Look for the answer that fits the meaning of the sentence.**

   The correct answer is always on the list provided. There may be more than one answer that appears to be close to the correct choice, but there is never more than one right answer. In cases where several choices might fit, select the one that fits the meaning of the sentence more exactly. Select only the best answer choice. Practice problems 2, 7, 8, 12, 13, and 19 that follow this section provide examples of this approach.

3. **Use logic and context clues.**

   After you select an answer choice, be sure that there is a logical relationship between the answer you have chosen and the sentence. Focus on finding and understanding the context clues in each sentence. For example, "Her _____ was never doubted for a minute because of her reputation for integrity and credibility." The context clues "integrity" and "credibility" should lead you to an answer choice such as *honesty, veracity, authenticity, or reliability.* Context clues are included to guide you and direct you toward the correct answer choice, even if you don't know the vocabulary. Do not be distracted by sentences that include complicated or unfamiliar vocabulary words. Instead, look for the structural trigger words and context clues in the sentence that can to lead you to the definition or the meaning of other words and help you find the correct answer choice. Practice problems 4, 5, 15, 17, 18, and 23 that follow this section provide examples of this approach.

4. **Work backward.**

   Some questions have one blank space to be completed and some have two blank spaces. The work backward strategy is effective for questions that have two blank spaces. If there are several choices that fit the first blank space, try filling in the second blank space first. Sometimes the SAT is designed so that all of the five choices can fit in the first blank space, but the second blank contains the discriminating answer. The answer to the second blank space will determine which of the five choices is the right answer. Practice problems 3 and 5 that follow this section provide examples of this approach.

5. **Look for structural triggers (transitional words).**

   Transition words, signal words, and qualifiers are collectively referred to as *structural triggers.* Look for structural trigger words and phrases that either continue or alter the flow of a sentence or its ideas. Structural trigger words can help lead to missing words. The following table shows a list of commonly used structural words for your reference. These are the words or phrases that signal a change in direction or the relationship (connection) between the first and second blank. Structural triggers can help you understand the meaning of a sentence with both one blank and two blank spaces. Common structural trigger words are: *but, although, on the other hand, however, despite, rather than,* and *instead.* Practice problems 9, 10, 14, 20, and 22 that follow this section provide examples of this approach.

6. **Watch for positive and negative words.**

Use positive or negative connotations of words in the sentence to help narrow down your answer choices and to eliminate inaccurate ones. A positive connotation suggests something affirmative and a negative connotation is the opposite. The contrast of positive and negative words can change the direction and logic of the sentence. For example, if someone says, "Have you had a good day?" the positive suggestion is that they hope your day was good. If the same question was stated in a neutral way, without a positive or a negative slant, it might be, "How was your day?" You should be looking for an answer with words that have the same direction or connotation as the rest of the sentence. Practice problems 6, 11, 12, 16, and 21 that follow this section provide examples of this approach.

Structural Triggers that Communicate a Transition, Signal Word, or Qualifier in a Sentence	
Operation	**Words used to continue or contrast similar ideas**
Adding an idea	in addition, furthermore, also
Illustrating or demonstrating	in other words, for instance, for example
Showing cause and effect	accordingly, consequently, because, as a result
Yielding a point	granted that, although true
Emphasizing a point	above all, certainly, without a doubt
Comparing or equating	similarly, likewise
Showing a contrast or limitation	however, although, but, nevertheless, in spite of, on the other hand
Showing order	first, second, in conclusion, next, finally
Showing relationships in space	nearby, in the distance, on the right
Summarizing	in summary, briefly, in other words, in the final analysis, in conclusion
Showing relationships in time	before, previously, formerly, afterward, subsequently

Practice Sentence-Completion Questions

Now that you have reviewed the strategies, you can practice on your own. Questions are grouped roughly into sets by their graduated level of difficulty, just as they might appear on the actual SAT. Questions appear in three categories: easy to moderate, average, and above average to difficult. The answers and explanations that follow the questions will include strategies to help you understand how to solve the problems.

Easy to Moderate

1. Money _____ to a political campaign should be used for political purposes and nothing else.

    A. attracted
    B. forwarded
    C. contributed
    D. ascribed
    E. channeled

2. The news report was _____, causing a(n) _____ reaction among the people directly involved.

    A. unfair … happy
    B. innocuous … insignificant
    C. unkind … joyous
    D. scandalous … spurious
    E. uplifting … depressing

3. Beatriz was _____ oriented and liked to be sure that she had more than enough supplies on hand; likewise she took _____ notes during any lecture she attended.

   A. task ... sketchy
   B. specifically ... adequate
   C. precision ... minimal
   D. detail ... copious
   E. object ... general

4. Devon continuously spoke in _____, using exaggerated and extreme examples to try to hold the attention of his lunchtime audience.

   A. analogies
   B. generalizations
   C. superlatives
   D. comparisons
   E. judgments

5. Kiera talked _____, supporting the rumor he had heard about her being _____.

   A. continuously ... foolish
   B. endlessly ... shy
   C. nonstop ... verbose
   D. emotionally ... smart
   E. eloquently ... beautiful

6. The _____ partnership between former friends resulted in a(n) _____ of their previous style of life.

   A. ongoing ... upset
   B. marred ... destruction
   C. continuous ... ending
   D. happy ... deterioration
   E. failed ... expansion

Average

7. The political _____ thrived on debating each vote cast by the legislators.

   A. candidate
   B. pacifist
   C. moderate
   D. liberal
   E. zealot

8. Shakespeare was a(n) _____ writer, producing an impressive number of 39 plays and nearly 154 poems.

   A. famous
   B. outstanding
   C. prolific
   D. diverse
   E. lazy

9. Can public opinion be influenced so that it _____ rather than encourages the proliferation of the sale of firearms?

   A. redoubles
   B. advances
   C. inverts
   D. impedes
   E. amplifies

10. The critic praised the scenery of the film enthusiastically, but _____ her enthusiasm when she discussed its plot and characterizations.

    A. expanded
    B. established
    C. augmented
    D. declined
    E. tempered

11. The secretary's position in the company was _____ as a result of the _____ of the business.

    A. developed ... maintenance
    B. expendable ... downsizing
    C. limited ... growth
    D. expanding ... failure
    E. updated ... decline

12. The newspaper article declared him a(n) _____ because of his desire to relocate to Canada in spite of his American heritage.

    A. expatriate
    B. traitor
    C. hero
    D. citizen
    E. denizen

13. By carefully looking at the math problem, one could estimate the correct answer because of the _____ information.

   A. consistent
   B. accurate
   C. wrong
   D. improper
   E. intrinsic

14. Continuously, the _____ student's loud commentaries challenged everything the professor taught.

   A. smart
   B. gullible
   C. new
   D. exemplary
   E. vociferous

15. Looking at tales of _____ is a way to shed light on the _____ heritage of a people.

   A. leadership … external
   B. romance … political
   C. yore … cultural
   D. comedy … economic
   E. war … gastronomical

16. The team would _____ the facts outlined in the proposal and then finally achieve _____ on how to proceed with its implementation.

   A. corroborate … consensus
   B. argue … agreement
   C. discuss … conclusion
   D. agree … disagreement
   E. complain … frustration

Above Average to Difficult

17. Realizing that Gloria had a(n) _____ belief system, Simon knew their relationship could _____.

   A. moral … terminate
   B. intelligent … last
   C. emotional … stagnate
   D. exciting … fail
   E. viable … survive

18. The word "oftentimes" is a(n) _____ of the two words "often" and "times" that are closely related in meaning; just as the words "fill it up" are similarly _____.

   A. restatement … unnecessary
   B. illustration … elucidating
   C. contradiction … countervailing
   D. repetition … redundant
   E. stupidity … inane

19. Omir's model behavior, a selfless sense of purpose in serving others, was legendary; his devotion led others to refer to him lovingly as a(n) _____ of excellence in the service of others.

   A. paramour
   B. example
   C. paragon
   D. person
   E. individual

20. No matter what _____ was presented, he would _____ it with a counterpoint.

   A. example … expand
   B. argument … repudiate
   C. point … justify
   D. support … strengthen
   E. comment … develop

21. Although all three courses of the meal were
_____, she felt ill after
_____ massive amounts of food.

   A. tasty ... enjoying
   B. undercooked ... nibbling
   C. delectable ... devouring
   D. ingested ... gobbling
   E. expensive ... gulping

22. The lawyer attempted to _____ the
argument, despite the district attorney's claim
that the district attorney had _____
the truth.

   A. sustain ... presented
   B. present ... unmasked
   C. forward ... disguised
   D. repudiate ... discovered
   E. explain ... supported

23. _____ examples inundated his
lecture in an attempt to mislead the audience.

   A. Good
   B. Spurious
   C. Careful
   D. Multiple
   E. Poor

Answers and Explanations for Practice Sentence-Completion Questions

Easy to Moderate

1. **C.** Circle or underline key words and phrases as you read the question to look for clues to your answer. You may have circled "money" and "political purposes." The approach to this type of question is to restate the sentence in your own words to fill in the blank. After reading the question and before scanning the answer choices, try to mentally fill in the blank with your own word, such as "given" or "donated." Remember that there are often subtle differences in answer choices, but you are looking for the answer that best fits in the context of the sentence. The nearest synonym to "given" or "donated" is "contributed."

2. **B.** When answering questions with two blanks, make sure both words match in the sentence and fit the meaning of the sentence. Circle or underline the key words, "causing" and "reaction." Something caused either a positive or a negative reaction. This means that both blanks must parallel, not contrast, each other. Both words must be either positive or negative. Choices A and C are not possible because they contain first words with negative connotations ("unfair" and "unkind"), but the second words are positive ("happy" and "joyous"). Choice D is not possible because "scandalous" (causing public outrage) does not parallel "spurious" (not genuine). Choice E is not possible because it has a positive first word ("uplifting"), and a negative second word ("depressing"). Choice B shows a relationship between the two words, "innocuous" (inoffensive or harmless) and "insignificant" (minor or inconsequential).

3. **D.** This question requires that you make sure both blanks match in the sentence. After quickly reviewing your answer choices, you may have wondered where to begin. Starting with the second word choices and working backward will help you answer this question. When you feel stumped, work from the second blank first. The only possible choice is "copious" (plentiful or ample). All of the other choices do not reflect evidence that supports someone who is conscientious enough to "have more than enough supplies on hand."

4. **C.** Use logic, reasoning, and the elimination strategy to answer this question. Spend no more than about 30 seconds to answer this type of question. Quickly review the question to look for clues, underline or circle keywords, such as "exaggerated" and "extreme," and then scan your answer choices. The answer should include a word that parallels "highest intensity." The only answer that fits this criterion and matches "exaggerated" or "extreme" in intensity is "superlatives" (something that has the highest quality).

5. **C.** Look for synonyms to answer this type of question. Circle the key words "talked" and "supporting the rumor." Notice that all of the first word choices are reasonable answers. This means your answer depends on the second blank word. You must work backward from the second word and make sure that your selected choice fits the context of the sentence. By highlighting key words in the question, you will be able to quickly search for words that fit the second blank and that are synonymous with "talked" to support the "rumor." Plug each word into the second blank of the question to find the best choice. The only possible synonymous answer that matches "talked" is "verbose" (wordy, talkative, profuse). Reread the complete sentence with your inserted first and second words to make sure the sentence reads logically.

6. **B.** Compare the relationship between the first blank word and the second blank word. The first part of the sentence shows a circumstance that affects the second part of the sentence. The key words that connect the two words are "former friends" and "resulted in." The context for both of these phrases is negative. The "results" are presumed to be negative because the word "former" implies a relationship at odds or estranged. Your answer should have parallel negative words. With this in mind, scan and eliminate the first word choices A, C, and D ("ongoing," "continuous," "happy"), because these are positive first word choices. Choice E can be ruled out because "failed" and "expansion" contradict each other: one word is negative and the other is positive. Now reread the sentence with Choice B, "marred" (damaged, imperfect) and "destruction."

Average

7. **E.** This type of question may present you with many choices that appear similar, but remember there is never more than one correct answer and you must look for evidence to find the *best* answer choice. The approach to use for this type of question is to look for the answer that fits the meaning. Although choices A and D are plausible answers, the *best* choice that matches the enthusiasm of the word "thrived" (to flourish or grow vigorously) is Choice E. "Zealot" is defined as engaging in fanatic, radical, and enthusiastic pursuits. Choice B, "pacifist," does not fit because it means "peacekeeper." Remember to be a detective and look for clues in the sentence, like "thrived," to answer the question. If you answered this question incorrectly, try thinking of other words to complete the sentence, such as "extremist" or "supporter" or "fanatic." This should help you at least eliminate the implausible choices.

8. **C.** The approach to use with this type of question is the same as the sample above: Look for the answer that fits the meaning. Several answers are reasonable choices, but there is only one correct response. Choice E can be eliminated because there is no evidence that supports the idea that Shakespeare was lazy. In fact, evidence proves the opposite because Shakespeare produced an "impressive number" of plays. Although Shakespeare was a famous and outstanding writer, choices A and B, these choices do not match the sizable number of plays and poems he produced. Remember that critical reading questions *do not* require prior knowledge of Shakespeare's background (that he was an outstanding, famous writer). Use only the information provided in the sentence. "Prolific" is defined as "abundant, fertile, and fruitful,"—Choice C. Even if you did not know the definition of "prolific," you might have been able to guess at the answer by knowing the prefix "pro," which means "forward" or "ahead of," to help you eliminate other answer choices that do not fit.

9. **D.** Look for clues that help you determine what you are searching for. In this case, the approach to this type of question is to look for structural trigger words that signal connecting or contrasting ideas. Read the question and circle or underline key words, "influenced" and "rather than encourages the proliferation." The clue here is "rather than encourages." This phrase signals a contrasting answer choice. You need a verb whose object is "proliferation" (the rise or increase in numbers) and that means the opposite of "encourages." To encourage means to give confidence, so you can eliminate choices A, B, and E ("redoubles," "advances," and "amplifies") because they are parallel and positive words. If you take a careful look at the word meanings of choices C and D, "inverts" ("overturn" or "turn upside down") and "impedes" ("obstructs" or "retards"), you should recognize that Choice D, "impedes," is the best fit for the context of the sentence.

10. **E.** Look for structural trigger words to signal whether ideas in the first part and the second part of the sentence are contrasting or similar. Contrasting signal words include "but," "however," "nevertheless," and "despite." In this sentence, the word "but" signals that you need a verb denoting something that contrasts the "enthusiasm" in the first part of the sentence. Choices A, B, and C ("expanded," "established," and "augmented") are not contrasting. The verb "tempered" (moderated, reduced in intensity) is both more suitable in meaning and more idiomatic (natural) than Choice D, "declined."

11. **B.** This is a positive-negative approach type of question. The first word and second word must match and fit in the sentence. Circle or underline the key words, "secretary's position" and "as a result." Something *caused* either a positive or negative *result*. This means that both blanks must match, not contrast with, each other. Choice A is not reasonable because "developed" suggests expanding, but "maintenance" suggests a continuation of the status quo. Choices C, D, and E have opposite and contrasting meanings—"limited" versus "growth," "expanding" versus "failure," and "updated" versus "decline." Choice B is the only probable answer that makes both words fit the sentence.

12. **A.** This type of question requires you to look for the answer that fits the meaning of the sentence. This may be a difficult question if you do not know the meaning of the word "denizen" (resident or habitual visitor). To answer this question, start with information you understand, and then narrow down your choices. After reading the question, you should have circled or underlined several key words that will help you hunt for evidence to support *positive or negative* traits about the man who "desired to relocate to Canada." The phrase "in spite of" signals negative characteristics about the man. Therefore, choices C and D can be eliminated. This leaves you with three possible choices: "expatriate," "traitor," and "denizen." Choice A, "traitor," (spy or conspirator), is incorrect because it implies a harsh, treacherous act. Remember that the SAT requires you to understand subtle differences in word meanings, so extreme answers such as "traitor" will rarely appear on the test as the correct answer. Using the *elimination strategy* should have helped you narrow down your choices, so that you might be able to take an educated guess. "Expatriate" (deportee, renouncing one's own country) fits the context of the sentence.

13. **E.** This is a straightforward problem that requires you to study the answer choices and select the *best* answer choice to *fit the context of the sentence*. The clue provided in the question, "one could estimate the correct answer," gives you information that leads you to the correct answer choice. Choices C and D can be ruled out immediately because these words have opposite meanings to "estimate the correct answer." Choices A, "consistent" (regular, constant, dependable), and B, "accurate" (correct, true, precise) are not the best fit in the context of the sentence. Remember you are looking for the best answer among five choices. "Intrinsic" (inherent, fundamental, basic) is the *best* choice.

14. **E.** This question requires that you look for structural trigger words that *continue* the flow of ideas in the sentence. Structural trigger words are transitional words, signal words, or qualifiers that signal a change (or a connection to) something about the relationship between the first part and the second part of the sentence. Circle or underline the key words "continuously" and "challenged everything," and then plug in the answer choices to see which word reads best. Choice B can be eliminated because "gullible" implies that the student would not question the professor because the student is naïve. Eliminate choice C because a new student could not have been in class long enough to "continuously" question the professor. Choices A and D, "smart" and "exemplary," are reasonable answers because smart students frequently challenge teachers. However, these choices imply the student's knowledge, but do not give evidence to support the student's behavior in class. This type of question depends on your ability to know the definition of choice E, "vociferous," matches "loud." Vociferous means outspoken, noisy, vocal, or clamorous.

15. **C.** *Look for context clues* to find the relationship between the paired word answer choices. Circle or underline the key words "looking at tales," "way to shed light." Review each of the pairs of answer choices. Notice that the first blank word connects to the second blank word. Look for clues in the answer choices and ask yourself, "Does this pair of words have a relationship?" Choice A does not fit the sentence because "external" means outside or outer. Notice that in choices B, D, and E the word pairs have no relationship. Choice C is the best answer, "yore" (in the time long past) and "cultural." Even if you did not know the definition of "yore," you might have been able to make an educated guess by eliminating the answers in which there was no relationship between the two paired words. These choices did not fit the logic of the sentence.

16. **A.** Look again for the relationship between the paired words. This is another example of positive or negative connecting paired words. There is a connecting, not contrasting relationship in *time* between the two parts of the sentence. In other words, there is a cause and effect response. Something would need to happen *before* something else could be achieved. Circle or underline "team would" and "finally achieve." To "achieve" means to accomplish or attain, denoting a positive accomplishment. Therefore, scan the first word choices to look for something positive. Hence, choices B and E, "argue" and "complain," can be ruled out immediately. Choice D can be eliminated because "agree" and "disagreement" are contrasting, not complementary words. By narrowing down your choices to two possible answers, you can then reread the sentence and insert both choices A and D to see which paired words fit the best. "Corroborate" means to confirm, support with evidence, or substantiate, and "consensus" means agreement or compromise.

Above Average to Difficult

17. **E.** This type of question requires you to find a logical relationship between the pair of words *within the context of the sentence.* Both word choices must be examined and inserted into the two blanks for the sentence to read logically. Circle or underline the key words "belief system" and "relationship could." Choice A, "moral," means honest, good, decent. This choice can be eliminated because it is not likely that Simon would terminate a relationship because of Gloria's good belief system. Choice B can be eliminated because belief systems are not intelligent or unintelligent. Belief systems are convictions of one's internalized principles and faith. Although belief systems can be described as "emotional" and "exciting," choices C and D, the second blank words, "stagnate" and "fail," suggest the opposite idea and do not fit the context. "Viable" means capable of surviving or growing; practical and workable.

18. **D.** Look for the logical relationship between the pair of words *within the context of the sentence.* Circle or underline the key words, "closely related" and "similarly." The pair of words in the correct answer choice must fit the meaning of the sentence. Choices C and E can be ruled out immediately because the first words, "contradiction" and "stupidity," do not logically flow with the words that follow after the first blank. You may have considered the first word in choices A and B, "restatement" and "illustration," but if you reread the sentence with the second word choices, "unnecessary" and "elucidating," you will see that the second words do not logically fit in the sentence. "Oftentimes" is a "repetition" of meaning, just as "fill it up" is a "redundant" meaning.

19. **C.** This is a vocabulary-in-context type question and requires that your answer *fit the meaning of the sentence.* After reading the question, you could have circled or underlined the key words, "model behavior" and "excellence." Look for the most logical word that describes Omir's "excellence." If you did not know the meaning of the words "paramour" and "paragon," start with the words that you recognized to narrow down your choices. Choices D and E can be eliminated because they do not logically fit in the sentence. Choice B is a possible answer, but is not the most logical answer. The prefix "para" means beyond, beside, or associated with. The suffix "mour" or "amour" means love, and the suffix "gon" means to parallel or to match. "Paramour" means lover, and "paragon" means shining example of excellence, or matched beyond.

20. **B.** Look for clues to determine how the two words relate to one another. In this case, *look for structural trigger words* to signal a transition. The two blank words should be contrasting because the sentence begins with "no matter what . . . was presented" and ends with "a counterpoint." This tells you that something in the second part of the sentence is going to change. Because most of the first part of the answer choices can fit the sentence, it is more efficient to *work backward* from the second blank. The answer will be determined by the second word that has a contrasting meaning to the first word. Choices A, C, D, and E are incorrect because none of the second word choices (which are all positive) contrast with the first word choices.

21. **C.** You should have circled or underlined the key words "although" and "she felt ill." When the introduction to a sentence with two blanks begins with "although," "despite," or "even though," this signals that you should watch for a contradiction in the second part of the sentence. If the first word is affirmative, then the second word should be contradictory. Just as in the example above, look for pairs of words that contrast or contradict. Notice that all of the first words are plausible choices until you read the second part of the sentence. Choice A presents two parallel words, so this answer can be eliminated. Choice B is not logical, "she felt ill after nibbling." "Nibbling" suggests a small bite. Choice D is incorrect because

"ingested" and "gobbling" have parallel meanings, and Choice E is incorrect because eating expensive food has no relationship to taste. The best answer choice that shows a contrast between the two word blanks is "delectable" (delicious) and "devouring" (to eat greedily).

22. **D.** When reading the question, you should have circled the key words "lawyer attempted" and "despite the district attorney's claim." The *structural trigger word* that changes the meaning in the relationship in the pair of words is "despite." This question is similar to Question 14, except that you should look at the first word blank that contrasts with the second word blank because all of the second word blank choices appear to be plausible. Choice A, "sustain," means to continue or maintain and is parallel to "presented." The word pair that best answers the question and provides contrasting first and second words is Choice D, "repudiate" (reject, recant, disclaim, or disavow) and "discovered."

23. **B.** *Use context clues* to figure out which words should fill in the blanks. The clues in the key words "examples inundated" and "attempt to mislead" help guide you to the correct answer. "Inundated" means to flood or swamp, and "mislead" tells you that you will be looking for an answer choice that attempts to deceive the audience. You can eliminate choices A and C, "good" and "careful," because they are positive "examples." Choice E, "poor," does not fit the sentence because bad "examples" do not typically mislead; rather, "poor" examples tend to be inadequate. Choice D is a possible answer because the audience may be misled by "multiple examples." But Choice B, "spurious" (fake, bogus, inauthentic), is the best answer choice.

Overview of Passage-Based Reading Questions

The passage-based reading section assesses your reasoning and critical thinking skills as you read passages from a wide variety of topics that appear in different styles: short passages, long passages, and paired (two related) passages. Each passage is between 100 and 850 words and is followed by 2 to 15 questions based on the passage's content, structure, or style. There are approximately 48 passage-based questions in total. *Passage-based reading questions account for approximately 72% of your total critical reading score*, so it is important for you to achieve your best possible score on this question type. Take time to learn the reading strategies presented in this section and practice your reading skills regularly before you take your exam.

Skills and Concepts Tested

Reading passage questions will appear in three different styles: extended reasoning passages, literal reading comprehension passages, and vocabulary-in-context. You are not expected to be familiar with the subject matter of the passage or with its specific content, nor will you be expected to have any prior knowledge of the subject. The passages are taken from a wide variety of subjects, including social studies (history, government, economics, politics); humanities (art, music); literature (fiction); and natural sciences (biology, medicine, physics, astronomy, environmental science). Students who have the ability to read actively and to efficiently locate, interpret, and summarize text passages tend to do well on this section, but keep in mind that it is never too late to improve your critical reading performance.

Directions

Each reading passage will be followed by one or more questions based on the passage's content. Some questions may be based on the relationship between the paired passages. After reading the passage, carefully read each question and choose an answer that is based on what is *stated, implied, or inferred* in the passages and in any introductory material that may be provided.

Passage Styles and Question Types

Passage-based reading questions are divided into 3 specific *passage styles* (long, short, and paired passages) and *question types* (literal comprehension, extended reasoning, and vocabulary-in-context). Each passage may contain any of the three question types. Specific question types, along with general and specific strategies, are described in detail in this section.

Passage Styles	Question Types
Long Passages Passages can be expository, narrative, persuasive, or literary and are drawn from social studies, humanities, science, or literature. Long passages are about 450 to 850 words with about 5 to 15 questions.	**Literal Comprehension Questions** This question type assesses your ability to comprehend, literally, specific material presented in a passage. You will be asked to look for material that is directly acquired from and/or stated in the passage and respond to specific questions.
Short Passages Passages can be expository, narrative, persuasive, or literary and drawn from social studies, humanities, science, or literature. Short passages are from 100 to 200 words with two to three questions.	**Extended Reasoning Questions** Sometimes called reasoning questions, this type of question requires that you distinguish fact from opinion to draw inferences about the information presented in the passage. Your ability to read with a critical eye and to evaluate and draw reasonable conclusions about the material presented are important skills for this question type.
Paired (Related) Passages Paired passages consist of two related passages that have common themes or subjects from social studies, humanities, science, or literature. Each passage in a pair relates in some way to the other passage—sometimes supporting, sometimes opposing, or sometimes complementing the views given. In some instances, the two passages are about the same subject but written at different places or time periods (years, decades, or centuries). Specific strategies for paired passages will be detailed on page 70.	**Vocabulary-in-Context Questions** This type of question tests your skills and knowledge of word meanings in the context of a passage. To perform well, you will need to think logically and to understand subtle differences in word choices to create a coherent, meaningful passage.

General Strategies for Passage-Based Reading

Read the following general strategies and helpful hints that apply to all questions, and then review the specific strategies for the particular questions that follow this section.

- Questions do *not* appear in order of difficulty, as they do with sentence completion questions. This means that easy, average, and difficult questions are intermingled, appearing in any order throughout the section. Use the plus-minus strategy on page 7 to help you with this section.

- Test-takers might believe that the shorter passages are easier to read, but this is not necessarily true. All passages require careful consideration and focus.

- Concentrate on using your time efficiently and do not allow the reading comprehension passage and questions to slow your pace. When you begin the exam, make a mental note of the starting time and keep track of the time. Overall, you are given approximately 50 minutes to answer 47 passage-based reading questions. At first glance you might calculate that you have about *1-minute per question* to answer all of the questions, but remember you must factor in the time it takes to read the passages. Never spend more than about 45 seconds on any one question or you will not finish this section. Because some questions are easier than others, some will take less time and others will take slightly longer time. With sufficient practice, you will almost automatically know when a problem is taking too much time.

- All reading passages have line numbers. In questions that mention specific line numbers, you will be able to quickly spot where the information is located. After you spot the location, be sure to read the lines just before and after the line(s) mentioned in the question. The text information that comes before and after the line(s) in the question can be very helpful in putting the information in the proper context and answering the question.

- Develop good reading habits. Reading is a habit that develops through time and practice. Spend about 15 to 20 minutes per day, at least 6 weeks before your exam, reading faster than your normal reading speed. As you read, pay special attention to key words—structural triggers and transitional words. Circle or underline these key words. This process will help stimulate and build pathways to a part of your brain that strengthens cognitive reading development. Developing good reading habits is similar to going to the gym to build and strengthen a muscle in your body. You must frequently practice reading to build your brain "muscles." You can read newspaper editorials, internet news, magazine articles, or book excerpts. Don't get hooked into reading only interesting articles. Try to read material that you might not normally read because you have no interest in the topic. Most likely the passages on the SAT will be ones that you may not normally choose to read.

- Use only the information that is directly stated (implied or inferred) in the passage to answer the questions. Base your answer on what you read in the passage, the introduction to the passage, and any footnotes that follow the passage. The passage *must support your answer.* Do not apply any outside knowledge that you may have about the subject.

- Be on alert for the "attractive distracter" answer choice. Watch out for answers that look good but are not the *best* answer choice. The attractive distracters are usually the most common wrong answers. The facts and concepts presented on the exam are often subtle variations of selected answer choices that make it difficult for test-takers to narrow down the correct answer. Attractive distracters are carefully written to be close to the best answer, but *there is never more than one right answer.* When you narrow your choice down to two answers, one is probably the attractive distracter. If this happens, read the question again and select the answer that fits the *meaning* of the question more exactly. And remember, the answer does not have to be perfect; just the best of five answer choices.

- Negative questions can initially be confusing and challenge your thinking. You may be asked to choose an answer that is *not correct* or is *not true.* Practice this type of question before the day of the test to familiarize yourself with it. For example, negative questions may read, "Which of the following is not true?" or, "Which of the following is least likely to be true?" or, "All of the following are true, except . . .?" To help answer this type of question, treat the answer choices as *true* and *false* statements. Search among the answer choices and select the one that is false. There may be more than one answer that is false, but follow the flow of logic, context clues, and key words to determine which answer is not true, and therefore, is the correct choice.

- Do not allow long reading passages to slow your pace. Think of each passage as a "thought unit." Read the first paragraph, last paragraph, and first and last sentence of the paragraphs in between. This usually helps to provide enough context and information to answer the majority of questions given. As you read, try to move your eyes rapidly down the passage. Sometimes it's useful to read peripherally while scanning for information down the page, rather than reading left to right. It may seem awkward at first, but it will become more natural as you practice.

  When you encounter a long reading passage that contains written material that is extremely difficult to comprehend because you are unfamiliar with the subject matter, you may choose to skip the passage and come back to it later if time permits. Mark that passage with a minus (–) symbol so you can quickly return to the unanswered passage. Be careful to mark your answer sheet correctly if you skip a passage. Test-takers who skip questions might make the mistake of continuing to mark their answers in sequence and forget to leave space for the unanswered questions.

- In the case of paired passages, treat them as two separate passages. Answer the questions for the first passage and then complete the questions for the second passage. If time allows, tackle the questions that relate to both passages.

A Four-Step Approach to Reading Questions

The following strategies are proven techniques that have helped scores of students improve their reading comprehension skills. Understanding SAT reading material is different from passive reading. This type of reading requires a commitment on your behalf to actively participate in the reading process. To be a successful reader, there is a conscious interaction between the *reader*, the *passage,* and the *context* of the passage. Hundreds of prospective college students have come to us who are troubled about "not retaining," "not understanding," and "not being able to concentrate" on unfamiliar written material similar to the passages on the SAT. The purpose of this section is to respond to those concerns.

We have developed a framework for reading strategies that focuses your attention on engaging the written material as you participate in decoding passages and questions. Successful readers use these strategies to challenge their own understanding and enhance their overall comprehension.

As you study the suggested techniques, determine whether the strategies fit with your individual learning style. What may work for some people may not work for you. If it takes you longer to recall a strategy than to solve the problem, it's probably not a good strategy for you to adopt. The goal in offering you strategies is for you to be able to work through problems quickly, accurately, and efficiently. And remember, avoid spending too much time on any one question. Taking a lot of time to answer the most difficult question on the test correctly, while losing valuable test time, won't get you the score you deserve.

Now, let's walk you through step by step specific methods to improve your reading skills. The mnemonic for this method is The Four-R Strategies: Review, Read, Record, and Respond. Apply these strategies to the types of reading questions that follow this table.

Review, Read, Record, and Respond	
Step 1	**Review and preread the questions.** This proven question-driven strategy will remind you to "shop before you read." Prereading the questions before you read the passage will help you to identify what you should focus on in the passage. Circle or underline important words and specific line numbers to give you clues about what to look for in the passage. This can be especially helpful with unfamiliar reading material. One example is to highlight key words and phrases in a question that asks you to locate specific facts presented in the passage. If you're asked to make an inference or to draw a conclusion, circle or underline the words "inference" or "conclusion" to remind you what to look for as you read the passage. Allow your eyes to move quickly over the questions as you highlight the main points and key words. By scanning the questions first, you will understand the gist of what you are being asked, which in turn will help you focus as you read the passage more closely. Remember to read only the questions and not the answer choices during this first step, because the latter will distract you.
Step 2	**Read actively.** Active reading provides the highest level of success when answering SAT questions. As you read through the text passage, practice being a reading detective. Gather clues from the passage to help you answer the questions. Read the passage carefully to try to understand the facts, their meanings, their implications, and their logical sequence of progression. As you become more mindful of the passage's content, you will be directing your attention to clues and can respond with a greater sense of awareness. Use the information about the specific question types to help you know what to look for in the questions and the passages as you read actively.
Step 3	**Record important points from the passage.** Lessons learned from a variety of effective reading programs have shown that surveying the passage, paraphrasing, clarifying, and predicting will improve your reading comprehension. After you preread the question, you should read and actively mark the passage. This strategy helps you form visual representations of the written material. Your written notes on the passage will help trigger your memory and make mental associations to help you remember content from the passages. All students have different learning styles, but this technique helps you focus on the passage's central ideas and avoid distractions during the exam. You may be surprised at the information you can recall when writing down just a few trigger words as you link mental word associations to the context of the reading passage. Writing down key words and phrases within the passage is important, and it is also important to write brief notes in the margins to paraphrase, clarify, and predict important points from the passage. **Paraphrase.** Restating written material in your own words will help you concentrate as you read and untangle difficult passages. Read closely and summarize the content of the passage in your own words. Always look for the main point of the passage and restate it in your own words. When working through sample practice tests in this study guide, gather information to paraphrase by circling key words and phrases. Use these key words and phrases to trigger your memory so that you can summarize and restate the passage. See if you can use your restatement to answer the question, and keep in mind that getting the best answer is your only goal. **Clarify.** Some passages are difficult to understand, but the answer to every question is always stated directly or inferred from the information in the passage. Pay attention to the written material and if there is a word, phrase, or concept that you don't necessarily understand, write a quick note to yourself to seek clarification later. Documenting material that requires further clarification will help you complete the task at hand, and often the answers to your questions may appear later in the passage. **Predict.** Make predictions so that your mind is continuously guessing/anticipating about what is going to come next. For example, in a three-paragraph passage that introduces "winged insects" in the first sentence, you might immediately predict that the passage will be related to a natural science topic.

(continued)

(continued)

Step 4	**Respond to the question.**
	After you have preread the questions, read actively through the passage, and recorded important points in the passage or in the margins by paraphrasing, clarifying, and predicting, it's time to answer the questions. Be sure to carefully read all the answer choices and eliminate obvious wrong answers as soon as you recognize them. Often, you can arrive at the right answer by eliminating other answers. Use the elimination strategy on page 7 to eliminate choices that are not supported by the passage. Watch for key words in the answer choices to help you find the main point given in each choice. If you get stuck on any one question, either make an educated guess by eliminating some of the choices first, or leave the question blank and proceed to the next question. The elimination strategy is a very valuable technique that you can use for the entire test, and it is particularly useful in the passage-based reading section. Only attempt to answer a question if you can eliminate one or more of the answer choices. Remember, there is a penalty for guessing that is designed to discourage wild guessing.

Specific Strategies Related to the Three Types of Questions

Every single answer on the passage-based reading section of the SAT can be found directly in the passage or can be inferred/implied from the passage. If a question asks you for a specific fact or detail, it is a *literal comprehension type question*. If the question asks you for an inference, it is a *reasoning type question*. Use this guide to help you recognize *literal, reasoning,* and *vocabulary-in-context* types of questions.

Question Type	Skills Measured
Literal Comprehension Questions	**Specific skills related to literal reading comprehension questions are** • understanding material that is stated directly in a passage • identifying detailed information that is directly stated in the passage • separating the main idea from the supporting ideas and from the specific facts that are cited • distinguishing between what the passage says directly (explicitly) and what it implies indirectly (implicitly) • understanding how to restate or extract direct information from the passage
Reasoning Questions	**Specific skills related to reasoning questions are** • identifying information that is not directly stated in the passage • drawing reasonable conclusions about information that is implied, inferred, assumed, or suggested from the passage • identifying and understanding the author's main idea, main point, or the purpose of the passage • recognizing the meaning or theme of the passage • evaluating the meaning of a word, phrase, or quotation in the context of the passage and making an inference about its function • recognizing the relevance of the author's opinions, views, or ideas • identifying the author's style, tone, or attitude in specific parts of the passage • distinguishing and identifying comparable thoughts in a passage
Vocabulary-in-Context Questions	**Specific skills related to reasoning questions are** • identifying the meaning of a word or phrase within the context of a passage • recognizing written clues to determine the meaning of a word or a phrase • drawing a logical relationship between the content in the passage and a word • distinguishing negative and positive connotations in the passage's content to discern the meaning of a word or phrase

Question Type One: Literal (Direct) Comprehension Questions

Literal questions ask you for explicit information from the passage; therefore, look for information that is stated directly in the passage to answer literal comprehension questions. In this type of question, you can always find the answer somewhere in the passage. Approach this type of problem as a detective looking for clues to answer the question. Look for specific words, phrases, or facts that are contained in the passage. Remember to actively work back and forth between the passage and the questions. Practice this type of problem first before undertaking other types of questions. After you have a good command of literal types of questions, you will be ready to tackle the slightly more challenging reasoning type questions.

Question Type Two: Reasoning (Inference) Questions

Reasoning-type questions can be slightly more difficult than literal questions. In reasoning questions you will need to make inferences and find a flow of logic to solve the problem as you draw reasonable conclusions from the passage based on information given in the passage that is *not directly stated*. As you search for the answer in the passage, think about being a detective, gathering words and phrases to understand what is not stated. Look for supporting proof and evidence among the author's words and circle or underline these words. "Read between the lines" as you gather supporting evidence and write down key words. Do not over-think this type of question. The answer is never vague and is always based on evidence from the passage. Once you understand what the author is communicating in the passage, your inference should make logical sense. This type of question often asks, "What can be implied?" "What can be inferred?" "What is suggested?" "What is assumed?" or "What is indicated?" After you have gathered information from the passage, read the five answer choices to determine which answer is most plausible based on the evidence you gathered from the passage.

Read the whole passage carefully and look for the author's main idea and overall message. A skilled reader finds different meanings in the same passage after synthesizing ideas presented in the passage. After you read the passage, try to focus on what the author is really saying or what point the author is trying to make. The best way to isolate the main point of the passage is to summarize and condense the author's ideas in your own words. This is done by *paraphrasing* the passage. If you paraphrase the general substance of the passage correctly, you will be able to answer any question that asks for the author's main point, the author's purpose, a summary of the passage, or the meaning of the passage. You will find that through practice, it will become easier to paraphrase the author's main point and distinguish the author's main ideas from the supporting ideas. For example, a question may ask how one sentence functions within a paragraph or how one paragraph relates to the whole passage. This type of question requires you to break down the passage and examine its component parts. In addition to the sample passages and questions in this study guide, try practicing this method regularly with newspaper articles, news articles from the internet, magazine articles, or excerpts from books.

Identify the tone of the passage. This strategy requires you to identify the author's *attitude* and *mood* through the author's writing tone. The overall tone of the passage is communicated through the author's word choices, which help the reader feel a sense of connection with the written material. The words the author uses to describe events, people, or places will give you a clue about what and how the author wants you to feel or think. Pay careful attention to the types of words the author uses in the passage. For example, if you read the word "tentative," you may feel a sense of something unsure, cautious, or hesitant. Look for words that stir up a subtle feeling or emotion while reading the passage. Also look for various punctuation marks and/or italicized words or phrases that convey the author's tone. As you read through the passage, circle or highlight the key words that signal the author's tone and then compare these words with the five answer choices. These types of questions can be as simple as just identifying positive or negative words that set the tone.

Avoid selecting extreme ("all or nothing") word answer choices unless the written material is clearly compelling. The SAT typically evaluates your ability to look for subtle differences in word choices, not for obvious extreme answer choices. For example, if you have narrowed your answer choices to "bleak" and "doubtful," the correct answer most likely is "doubtful." This is true because the word "doubtful" shows a possibility for hope and the word "bleak" is very much without hope.

Question Type Three: Vocabulary-in-Context Questions

Some questions deal with vocabulary in context, that is, with understanding the meaning of a word as it is used in the passage. To help you with vocabulary-in-context questions, pay close attention to the word or phrase in the context of the sentence. Use the context to figure out the meaning of words, even if you're unfamiliar with them. Sometimes you will need to read the sentence just before and after where the word is presented to understand the word's association to the surrounding text. Even if you don't know the meaning of the word, the passage will give you good clues. You can also read the sentence in the passage, leaving the word space blank, and literally plug in each answer to see which answer choice makes the most sense in the sentence. At the end of this section, be sure to review the vocabulary development techniques on page 78.

Passage Styles

Now that you have read about the strategies for the types of questions, you can focus on how to implement these strategies in the passage styles. Remember, there are three styles of passages: long, short, and paired. All of the strategies mentioned earlier apply to all of the passage styles. Here are a few added tips for each passage style.

Short passages are only about 100 words long. After you skim the questions, try to move through these passages quickly by underlining the author's main ideas and the tone of the passage. Practice reading several short excerpts and passages before the day of the test. These passages are straightforward and require efficient, active reading skills.

Long passages can be time consuming and can leave the unsuspecting reader overwhelmed. But if you can become skilled at reading long reading passages, all passages will become easier to tackle.

1. First, look at the title (if given) and the short italicized abstract at the beginning of the passage to get a sense of the author's topic, tone, and main purpose. Determine if the author has a positive or a negative attitude. You may be able to determine the tone of the passage by paying attention to the prefixes and suffixes in the words. Understanding the author's attitude will help you eliminate improbable answer choices.

2. Then, look for specific information within the question and passage before you look for general information. Do this by skimming the questions for literal information related to specific line number references, facts, and details to circle before you read the passage. Long passage-type questions usually include line number(s) to help direct you to relevant information within the passage. After you circle the reference line number(s) in the question, circle the sentence(s) in the passage and make any necessary notes in the margins of the passage. For example, if the question says, "In line 27, the quotation marks around the word 'abnormal' refer to . . . ," you should mark "abnormal" within the passage and quickly write down "line 27" and the words "refers to" in the margins. This will help keep your mind focused on what to look for in line 27. Long passages can contain up to 15 questions, and if you are rushed for time, chances are you will at least be able to complete the direct, specific questions before reading every single word in the passage. If applicable, answer the specific questions first, and be careful about where you fill in the correct answer for the corresponding question on your answer sheet.

3. After you have answered the literal questions that ask for specific information in specific line numbers, it's time to answer the general questions. Remember to read the passage using your well-developed active reading skills. Note that sometimes questions can refer to specific line numbers but also require general information that is related to the entire passage. For example, a question may say, "In the context of the passage, the statement 'It creates a new set of conditions' (line 12) suggests that, . . ." In this case, circle the phrase, "It creates a new set of conditions," and write in the margins "context" and "suggests" to remind you of what you are looking for as you read the entire passage.

In **paired passage-type** questions, you will be given two related passages (paired passages) that have a common theme or subject. Each passage in some way relates to the other passage, and each passage either supports or opposes the views of the other passage. This type of arrangement is typically followed by questions that are set up to *compare and contrast specific points* from the passages. In some instances, the two passages are about the same subject but were written at different times, years, decades, or centuries in different places.

You can use all of the general strategies on page 65 for paired passages. In addition, use the following specific strategies for paired passage questions.

- Note that the first group of questions refers to the first passage; the second group of questions refers to the second passage; and the last group of questions refers to both passages as they relate to each other. A common paired passage question will ask you for the primary purpose of both passages. Always look for the main point of each passage. Use what you know about writing to help you with reading, and locate the topic sentence and the conclusion of each passage. Remember to review/preread the questions that follow each passage before you read the passages.

- Consider reading the first passage and answering the first group of questions. Then read the second passage and answer the second group of questions. Finally, answer the remaining questions that relate to both passages.

- Paired passages will often ask questions related to comparing and contrasting specific and general information within the passages. As you read the passages, use active reading skills to note in the margins important points about how the passages are alike and different. For example, a question that relates to how passages are alike might read, "Which of the following statements is supported by both passages?" Write down "supported" or "alike" in the margins to remind you of what you are looking for in the passage. For a question that relates to how the two passages are different, for example, "Passage 2 is unlike Passage 1 in that Passage 2 . . . ," you might write in the margins "unlike" or "different."

- Use the elimination strategy to rule out implausible answer choices. If a question asks for a statement that supports both passages, for example, watch out for answer choices that are true for one passage but false for the other. This will help you quickly eliminate answer choices that do not supply what the question requires.

Practice Passage-Based Reading Questions

The passages below are followed by questions based on their content; questions following a pair of related passages may also be based on the relationship between the paired passages. Answer the questions based on what is stated or implied in the passages and in any introductory material that may be provided.

Short Passages

Questions 1–2 are based on the following passage.

American faith in democracy, like that in nationalism, is partially traceable to the frontier heritage. That either democratic theory or practice originated in the backwoods is
(5) demonstrably untrue; both were well advanced when the conquest of the West began and both continued to receive stimulation from Europe during the eighteenth and nineteenth centuries. Yet frontier conditions tended to modify
(10) imported institutions along more democratic lines. In primitive communities the wide diffusion of land ownership created a natural demand that those with a stake in society should have a voice in society, while the common level of social and
(15) economic status and the absence of any prior leadership structure encouraged universal participation in government. With self-rule a brutal necessity due to the nonexistence of external controls, and with men and women
(20) accustomed to widespread participation in group affairs through cabin raising, corn husking bees, and the like, it was natural that they should think in terms of political equality. Democratic practices came naturally to frontier groups, and
(25) with them an unswerving faith in democracy as a panacea for all the ills of the nation or the world.

1. In the last sentence of the passage, the best definition for "panacea" is

   A. bandage.
   B. medicine.
   C. cure-all.
   D. elixir.
   E. inspiration.

2. According to the author, one important reason democratic institutions in American frontier society differed from European models was that

   A. Americans distrusted Europeans in general and therefore didn't want to imitate their institutions.
   B. unlike in Europe, the American frontier lacked a history of leadership.
   C. Americans in the westward movement were fierce nationalists, whereas Europeans were not.
   D. Americans had a tradition of strong individualism while Europe relied more on conformity.
   E. on the frontier in America, stronger restrictions were required than the European institutions allowed.

Questions 3–4 are based on the following passage.

Potatoes changed history or rather, the lack of potatoes changed history. The Great Famine in Ireland (1846–1849) was partly the result of a potato fungus that destroyed the major food
(5) source of the Irish and was particularly devastating to the poor. Food relief from the British was inadequate and came too late. Some estimates place the number of deaths at 750,000, with an equal number of the Irish poor
(10) emigrating to Britain, Canada, Australia, and the United States. British economic policy including the policy of *laissez faire,* which argued against state intervention, was partly responsible for the disaster. Among the other culprits were
(15) the nature of Irish land-holdings, destructive farming methods, and a lack of agricultural diversity.

3. The first sentence of the paragraph can best be described as intended to

A. create interest.
B. mislead the reader.
C. provide facts.
D. promote a myth.
E. provide a humorous perspective on an otherwise tragic period.

4. From the passage, one can infer that during the famine, aid from the British came too late because of

A. animosity between Great Britain and Ireland.
B. poor methods of food distribution.
C. inadequate communication about the extent of the disaster.
D. the British policy of laissez faire.
E. the lack of agricultural diversity.

Long Passage

Questions 5–11 are based on the following passage.

Human beings have in recent years discovered that they may have succeeded in achieving a momentous but rather unwanted accomplishment. Because of our numbers and our technology, it
(5) now seems likely that we have begun altering the climate of our planet.

Climatologists are confident that over the past century, the global average temperature has increased about half a degree Celsius. This warming
(10) is thought to be at least partly the result of human activity, such as the burning of fossil fuels in power plants and automobiles. Moreover, because populations, national economies, and the use of technology are all growing, the global average
(15) temperature is expected to continue increasing by an additional 1.0 to 3.5 degrees C by the year 2100.

Such warming is just one of the many consequences that climate change can have. Nevertheless, the ways that warming might affect
(20) the planet's environment—and therefore, life itself—are among the most urgent and compelling research topics in earth and environmental science. Unfortunately, they are also among the most difficult to predict. The
(25) effects of global warming will be complex and vary considerably from place to place. Of particular interest are the changes in regional climate and local weather and especially extreme

events—record temperatures, heat waves, very
(30) heavy rainfall, or drought, for example—which could very well have staggering effects on societies, agriculture, and ecosystems.

Based on studies of how the earth's weather has changed over the past century as global
(35) temperatures edged upward, as well as on sophisticated computer models of climate, it now seems probable that warming will accompany changes in regional weather. For example, longer and more intense heat waves—a likely consequence
(40) of an increase in either the mean temperature or in the variability of daily temperatures—would result in public health threats and even unprecedented levels of mortality, as well as play a role in such costly inconveniences as road
(45) buckling and high cooling loads, the latter possibly leading to electrical brownouts or blackouts.

Climate change would also affect the patterns of rainfall and other precipitation levels, with some areas getting more and others less, resulting
(50) in changing global patterns and occurrences of droughts and floods. Similarly, increased variability and extremes in precipitation can exacerbate existing problems in water quality and sewage treatment and in erosion and urban
(55) storm-water routing, among other problems. Such possibilities underscore the need to understand the consequences of humankind's effect on global climate.

(60) Researchers have two main—and complementary—methods of investigating these climate changes. Detailed meteorological records go back about a century, which coincides with the period during which the global average temperature increased by half a degree. By examining these (65) measurements and records, climatologists are beginning to get a picture of how and where extremes of weather and climate have occurred. It is the relation between these extremes and the overall temperature increase that really interests (70) scientists. This is where another critical research tool—global ocean-atmosphere climate models—comes in. These high-performance computer programs simulate the important processes of the atmosphere and oceans, giving researchers insights (75) into the links between human activities and major weather and climate events.

The combustion of fossil fuels, for example, increases the concentration in the atmosphere of certain greenhouse gases, the fundamental agents (80) of the global warming that may be attributable to humans. These gases, which include carbon dioxide, methane, ozone, halocarbons, and nitrous oxide, let in sunlight but tend to insulate the planet against the loss of heat, not unlike the glass of a (85) greenhouse. Thus, a higher concentration means a warmer climate.

5. Which of the following would be the best title for this passage?

A. The History of Climate
B. Fossil Fuels and Greenhouse Gases
C. Extremes of Climate
D. Global Warming and the Changing Climate
E. Methods of Researching Global Climate

6. Which of the following inferences is NOT supported by information in the passage?

A. Computer models of climate have proved superior to old meteorological records in helping climatologists pinpoint changes.
B. Changes in climate are affected by both natural and human activities.
C. Whatever the changes that occur in North America's climate over the next 200 years, it is unlikely they will be accompanied by cooler average temperatures.
D. Dramatic changes in precipitation could have negative effects, producing both droughts and floods.
E. Increased industrialization in developing countries could lead to increases in the rate of global warming.

7. Which of the following best describes the author's tone in this passage?

A. Alarmist
B. Irate
C. Concerned
D. Accusatory
E. Indifferent

8. The best definition of "exacerbate" in line 53 is

A. worsen.
B. change.
C. cause.
D. complicate.
E. affect.

9. The name "greenhouse gases," first mentioned in line 79, is appropriate because these gases

A. are hot.
B. are produced in controlled circumstances.
C. filter the sun's harmful rays.
D. are highly concentrated.
E. prevent heat loss.

10. If true, which of the following would call into question current theories of global warming?

A. A dramatic increase in world precipitation.
B. A dramatic decrease in world precipitation.
C. An increase in the rate of global warming following the elimination of the use of fossil fuels.
D. Below-normal temperature recordings in Canada for two years.
E. The discovery that average global temperatures were lower 500 years ago than they are today.

11. According to the passage, scientists are most interested in the link between global warming and extreme changes in regional climate because

A. such a link has never been made and cannot be easily explained.
B. establishing the link will prove their current theories about the causes of global warming.
C. it could help explain the effects of natural forces, such as gravitational pull, on climate.
D. finding it will solve the problem of global warming.
E. it could help pinpoint which human activities are involved in climate extremes.

Paired (Related) Passages

Questions 12–16 are based on the following passages.

Passage 1:

The impact of World War II on women cannot easily be measured in the immediate postwar era. Other wars such as the Civil War and World War I had clearly broadened the
(5) boundaries of acceptable behavior for men and women and had hastened changes already in process such as suffrage, but their impact on women's status—their culturally defined roles— remained similarly ambiguous and ephemeral.
(10) The American Revolution had the most powerful symbolic and culturally formative impact on women prior to the twentieth century. That war, concerned with the definition of public life and the citizen, created new republican political
(15) consciousness and practice. Women, like men, found themselves engaged in political struggles and acts despite the solidly masculine military. And male politicians wrestled with the problem of whether women who acted thus were citizens
(20) and, if so, in what sense. The result was the powerful new ideology of republican motherhood that acknowledged women's political engagement but contained it within the ideal of motherhood. Women's political work was the rearing of good
(25) citizens.

The context for women in World War II was vastly different from that of their revolutionary foremothers, though each war was understood to have been fought to preserve liberty and
(30) overthrow tyranny. By the mid-twentieth century public life had come to be defined by the growing activities of the state. Where women during the Revolution had spontaneously organized boycotts and petitions, governmental control of
(35) both media and economy during World War II ensured efficient use of voluntary energies. There was little discussion of the political meaning of women's changed participation in public life, only assurance that it would be temporary.
(40) Women lacked collective, public spaces within which to redefine themselves as a group in relation to society or to critique a social order that simultaneously called on them and restricted their possibilities. Many traditional women's
(45) organizations remained bounded by class and race, unable to achieve a broader vision of women's needs. Millions of women left the labor force [after the war], voluntarily and involuntarily;

the women who stayed represented an increase in
(50) labor force participation consistent with previous trends. In other words, one could argue that the war itself made little difference.

Ideologically, wartime propaganda justified the erosion of gender boundaries "for the
(55) duration" and no more. The intense pressure on women to return to domesticity coincided with the wishes of a younger cohort of women and men to focus on their private lives. This privatization promised a dramatically new level
(60) of isolation within the family as bulldozers began to reshape the landscape in preparation for growing suburbs.

Passage 2:

During World War II the role of women in America changed dramatically, if only briefly. With men going off to war, women on the home front had to take over jobs that were not only
(5) traditionally "men's work" but that also could be described at the time as decidedly unfeminine, such as building ships, tanks, and planes. In 1941 women made up 24 percent of the labor force; by 1946 the number had grown to 36 percent. The
(10) government encouraged women to become part of the war effort, particularly in the defense industry. One poster announced, "If you've used an electric mixer in your kitchen, you can learn to run a drill press!" A famous propaganda
(15) poster showed "Rosie the Riveter," a strong woman in a kerchief with the motto, "We can do it!"

After the war, the jobs that had been temporarily held by women were needed for the
(20) returning soldiers and many women left their jobs—sometimes happily, sometimes not—to return to their homes and take up their places as wives and mothers. But the taste of a new role for women had been whetted. A cartoon in the
(25) Des Moines *Register* in 1943 shows a larger- than-life woman war worker striding along with a paycheck in the back pocket of her overalls, while a tiny man in a housewife's apron stands aside, saying, "But remember. You gotta come
(30) right back as soon as the war is over." Her reply, which she tosses over her shoulder, is "Oh, yeah?"

Surprisingly, according to many commentators, most women did "come right back" after the war to their positions as housewives and mothers.
(35) Their contributions to World War II were lauded,

but the view of a "woman's place" hadn't significantly changed. Society in the late 1940s and the 1950s had high expectations of women as wives, mothers, and housekeepers. The perfect
(40) wife was to support her husband at every turn, the perfect mother was expected to stay home and nurture children, and the perfect homemaker (a term everyone seemed to prefer to "housekeeper") was to have dinner on the table
(45) and the house cleaned by the time her husband arrived home from work. This perfect woman, of course, is an exaggerated stereotype that could probably be found only in television shows like "Father Knows Best" and "Leave It to Beaver."
(50) In fact, signs of change were beginning to appear. In 1950, for example, Harvard Law School admitted women for the first time. The U.S. Census recognized a woman's right to use her maiden name after she was married. And, in
(55) 1955, Rosa Parks violated the stereotype of women and particularly black women by refusing to give up her seat on a bus to a white man, initiating a famous boycott in the South. World War II, while it didn't seem to change the
(60) traditional role of women at once, had sown seeds that would come to life in the following decades.

12. Based on information in the two passages, the authors would agree with which of the following statements?

   A. World War II, while apparently helping women to advance, was a stumbling block.
   B. The volunteer efforts of women during America's wars worked against their being treated as equals in American society.
   C. A women's role after the Revolutionary War and immediately after World War II was primarily domestic.
   D. Women supported men but played a minor role in American wars.
   E. The government was largely responsible for women's slow progress toward equality.

13. The two passages differ in which of the following ways?

   A. Passage 1 credits World War II with changing women's role in society while Passage 2 suggests World War II had little effect on women's role.
   B. Passage 2 gently pokes fun at women while Passage 1 elevates them.
   C. Passage 1 presents two points of view, while Passage 2 presents only one.
   D. The author of Passage 2 uses concrete examples of its points while the author of Passage 1 presents a narrative of general points.
   E. In Passage 1, the author cites facts, while in Passage 2 the author cites opinions only.

14. According to Passage 1, the effect on women of the Revolutionary War and Civil War was to

   A. strengthen their relationships with men.
   B. engage them in political acts.
   C. lead them to form anti-war organizations.
   D. fight for more political power.
   E. make them better mothers.

15. In the parenthetical phrase ("a term everyone seemed to prefer to 'housekeeper'") (Passage 2, lines 43–44) the author is

   A. underlining the idea that a woman was to feel elevated by her role at home.
   B. showing that language was in the process of changing because of the war.
   C. ridiculing the role of women after the war by emphasizing her domestic role.
   D. comparing women unfavorably to the ideals presented in "Father Knows Best" and "Leave It to Beaver."
   E. indicating how women were ashamed of their wartime jobs.

16. Passage 2 makes all of the following points EXCEPT

   A. women were successful performing their defense jobs during World War II.
   B. the U.S. government used methods of propaganda to urge women to join the war effort.
   C. women worked for less pay than men in defense jobs.
   D. the percentage of women in the work force increased significantly during World War II.
   E. one reason women quit working at the end of the war was to make the jobs available to returning soldiers.

Answers and Explanations for Practice Passage-Based Reading Questions

Short Passages

1. **C.** This question asks for the specific definition of "panacea." After prereading the question, you should have circled or underlined "last sentence" and "panacea" to quickly locate this word in the passage. This type of question requires you to be familiar with *vocabulary-in-context*. Even if you are not familiar with the word "panacea," you might figure out the meaning based on the information provided in the sentence. In this case, the author's attitude about democracy is very positive, evidenced by phrases such as "unswerving faith," and as something to remedy the "ills of the nation or the world." Choice B is too general and choices A, D, and E are not appropriate in the context of the passage. The answer choice should be a cure-all for all the ills of the nation or the world.

2. **B.** After prereading the question you should have circled or underlined "American frontier society," "differed," and "European models." This type of question requires you to understand the written material presented directly in the passage. This is a *literal comprehension question type*. Notice that you must read the entire passage to search for differing or contrasting points of view, but you must also read all of the answer choices before you can answer the question. The first strategy for this type of question requires you to pre-read the question to highlight important facts before you read the passage. The second strategy requires you to carefully read all the answer choices after reading the passage. There is only one possible correct answer choice. While some of the answer choices may be true, they are not addressed in the passage.

3. **A.** This question asks for the intent of the first sentence. You should have underlined the key words *"What is the first sentence trying to do?"* Instead of beginning immediately with facts, as in Choice C, the author chooses to create interest by making a surprising statement ("Potatoes changed history. . . ."). The intent is not to mislead, as in Choice B, or to promote a myth, as in Choice D. The most likely wrong answer is E, but nothing in the entire remainder of the paragraph could be viewed from even a remotely humorous perspective. Otherwise, Choice E might have been the correct choice.

4. **D.** First, you should have underlined the words "infer" and "aid came too late because." Remember, inference questions are asking you to *read between the lines*. Focusing on lines 11–12 will give you the answer. The British government didn't intervene in the famine earlier because British economic policy was "hands off," that is, the less intervention by government, the better. The British policy of laissez faire at that time typifies why Choice D is correct. While it is possible that A, B, and C are accurate, none of these can be inferred from the information in the passage. Choice E is not a viable choice.

Long Passage

5. **D.** This question type assesses your ability to understand the author's main idea from information that is not directly stated in the passage. Ask yourself, "What is the author saying?" To look for the *best title*, you must identify the main theme of the passage. The best title is a main-point or main-idea *reasoning type question*. Notice that Choice A is too broad. The passage doesn't actually address the history of climate. Choices B, C, and E, on the other hand, are too narrow and specific. While it's true that all three of these topics are mentioned in passing in the passage, the title should cover the passage as a whole from the author's main point. "Global Warming and the Changing Climate," Choice D, is the best title for the entire passage.

6. **A.** This question asks you which of the answer choices is NOT supported by the passage. The strategy for this type of *reasoning question* calls on your ability to "reverse your thinking" to understand what the question is asking. When prereading the question, you should have circled "inferences NOT supported" to help you focus on the meaning of the question. Choice B, lines 9–12, states that warming is thought to be at least *partly* the result of human activity, suggesting that natural forces are involved as well. Choice C is supported by lines 7–16. Choice D is supported by lines 47–51. Choice E is supported by lines 12–16. Only Choice A is not supported in the passage.

7. **C.** This question type requires you to identify the author's attitude through tone. It is a *reasoning type question.* Tone is communicated in writing by the author's word choices to give you an understanding of what and how the author wants you to feel or think. The author's overall tone in the passage is reflective about the consequences of climate change. Although the author does mention some possible "alarmist" effects, the tone appears sober, composed, and calm, not highly emotional as in Choice A. Nor is the tone "irate" or "accusatory," as in choices B and D. The author presents facts about fossil fuels' role in global warming, but doesn't place blame. Lines 56–58 indicate the author is not *indifferent* to the issue of humans' effect on global climate, therefore Choice E is incorrect. Choice C best describes the author's tone.

8. **A.** The first step for this problem is to preread the question and circle or underline "exacerbate" in line 53. This is a *vocabulary-in-context type question.* As it is used in this sentence, "exacerbate" means to aggravate or irritate or make worse. Notice that the sentence describes problems as already existing "extremes in precipitation." Therefore, Choice C could not be correct. Choices B, D, and E are too mild; none of them includes the concept of an existing problem (such as water quality) becoming *worse* because of variable and extreme precipitation. Choice A is the correct definition of "exacerbate."

9. **E.** This is a *literal comprehension question type.* Choice B is incorrect because even though it is a true statement (a greenhouse is a controlled climate), this information is not in the passage. Nothing in the passage suggests that these gases are hot, Choice A, or that they filter out harmful rays, Choice C. Although it is true that the gases can be highly concentrated, Choice D, a high concentration has nothing to do with the term "greenhouse." Choice E is the most appropriate because it connects prevention of heat loss with global warming.

10. **C.** Use the elimination strategy for this type of question. Because experts believe that the use of fossil fuels is partly responsible, one would expect the elimination of the use of fossil fuels to lead to a *decrease*, not an increase, in the rate of global warming. Therefore, Choice C is the correct answer. Both increases and decreases in precipitation are stated or implied in the passage as consequences of continued global warming. Therefore, choices A and B are incorrect. Two years of decreased temperatures in a particular area wouldn't disprove global warming; its effects vary considerably from place to place, according to the passage. Thus, Choice D can be eliminated. Finally, you can eliminate Choice E because it would support the theory, not call it into question.

11. **E.** In this type of question, you should read all the choices and look for the best answer. It is possible that choices A and B are peripheral reasons for their interest, but not their main reason, and therefore, not the *best* answers. Choice C is not the best answer because scientists are more interested in the effects of human activities than those of natural forces on global warming. Even though it is a step toward a solution, understanding the link would not in itself *solve* the problem of global warming, thus eliminating Choice D. Notice that some of the choices here are possible, but Choice E is the *best* because it is clearly supported in lines 72–76.

Paired (Related) Passages

12. **C.** See Passage 1, lines 20–25; and Passage 2, lines 32–34 and 58–62. Both passages make the point that after the respective wars, women returned to their traditional roles. A and B aren't supported in either passage, and Passage 2 indicates that women didn't play a minor role (D). E is not a point made in either passage. The authors would agree with Choice C, in that women returned to a primarily domestic existence.

13. **D.** The author of Passage 1 makes several general statements about the role of women, but unlike Passage 2, specific examples aren't given. Passage 2 presents several concrete examples: lines 3–7, 14–17, 24–31, 46–49, and 50–58. Choices A, C, and E are inaccurate. Choice B is inaccurate because the tone of Passage 2 does not indicate that the author is poking fun at women in the examples presented, and the author of Passage 1 doesn't elevate women. This choice doesn't recognize the tone of either passage. Choice D is the correct answer.

14. **B.** See lines 15–17. Although the passage states that male politicians adopted a "powerful new ideology of republican motherhood" in which women's work was seen as rearing good citizens, i.e. making them better mothers, Choice E, the effect on women themselves was to engage them in political struggles, Choice B. There is no evidence for choices A or D, nor is Choice C suggested by the passage (nor would it be likely during the Revolutionary War). Choice B is correct.

15. **A.** Choice A is the best answer. "Homemaker" is a euphemism for "housekeeper," and the author references the term to demonstrate society's expectation that a woman's place, at the time, was in the home and that such a role for women was important, elevated beyond that of a "housekeeper." It does not suggest that women were ashamed (Choice E). There is no evidence in the passage for Choice B, nor does the use of the term indicate that women are being unfavorably compared (Choice D) or ridiculed (Choice C).

16. **C.** The only point not made in Passage 2 is that women worked for less pay. Although this was most likely the case, the passage does not state or imply Choice C. All other points are stated in the passage and are, therefore, incorrect choices.

Vocabulary Development

The SAT is written with a complexity of language and a subtlety of word meanings. You will be required to know the obvious and subtle differences in words and their meanings in the context of a sentence or passage. Words are always associated with meanings, and with more than 500,000 words in the English language even famous writers have understood the difficulty of building a rich vocabulary. While some words are used daily, others are used infrequently. The SAT tests your understanding of infrequently used words and their meanings. This is why vocabulary development is an important part of your preparation.

Research has proven that vocabulary growth correlates with increased academic performance and higher SAT scores, yet it requires a commitment to practice and repetition. An increased vocabulary can give you a greater sense of accomplishment and a greater ability to interpret reading passages on the SAT. As you increase your vocabulary skills, you are increasing your odds of building a better score. Searching for words to study and their definitions on the SAT may feel like looking for a needle in a haystack, but if you follow the *word attack skills* outlined in this section, you will find your vocabulary gradually expanding.

The purpose of this section is to give you a distinct learning advantage. This is done by introducing several approaches to improve your vocabulary and increase your knowledge of word meanings. Consider using any combination of the suggested approaches presented in this section. Vocabulary development models are based on improving your memory to manage difficult words, building a solid base of commonly used words, and helping you become familiar with word parts (prefixes, suffixes, and roots).

Memory Improvement

Mnemonic devices help you store, retrieve, and recall words and phrases. The principles and methods of memory improvement using mnemonics have been successfully researched and developed for many years. Memory improvement is based on techniques that integrate your physical senses (seeing, hearing, and touching) with schematic brain structures. In other words, if you can develop an association in your physical body, your brain tends to remember facts and details. You already perform this function all the time when you use your memory to recall events from your past.

Visual Encoding Technique

The most successful mnemonic device is *visually encoding* information so that you can *associate* a word with a mental picture to form a new schematic representation of the word. As you associate a word with a mental picture, the two things interact with one another to form *one mental representation* of the word. For example, if memorizing the word "quandary," which means dilemma or entanglement, you might visualize two pieces of rope tied together (entangled). The trick is to form a visual image that has as much detail and clarity as possible. The more details in your visual image, the greater the possibility you will remember the word. Memory experts also report that associating bizarre visual pictures with words helps in memory retention. For example, you might visualize two snakes entangled together to remember the meaning of "quandary."

The visual picture that you choose to create is unique to your learning style. Trust whatever visual picture comes to mind. Just keep in mind that creating mental pictures has a strong link to memory improvement.

After you have mastered visual encoding, you can expand this method by *chunking* words together that have synonymous word meanings. Begin by looking up all related words for your new word. Let's say you have successfully created a visual representation for the word "quandary." Now that you know this meaning, you can chunk other synonymous words with the same visual picture. So instead of associating just one word, you can expand your vocabulary to four new related words: "quandary," "dilemma," "entanglement," and "predicament."

The process of association is especially helpful to students who are *visual learners.* You know you are a visual learner if you find you do not comprehend class material that was not given to you in written form (books, handouts, computer, or chalkboard). Comments from students who are visual learners typically include, "I couldn't understand what the teacher was talking about until he or she wrote it or projected it on the board."

Auditory Technique

Another successful strategy is to use *rhymes* to trigger your memory. As you associate a new word with a rhymed word, you are creating a mental representation that will aid in your memory recall. For example, the word "quandary" rhymes with "laundry." You might make up a simple phrase to help you remember, "It's such a quandary when I wash the laundry."

These types of word study strategies should help you with very difficult words. Try this method to see if it works for you. It may sound childish, but it works for many test-takers. This technique works especially well if you are an *auditory learner,* meaning that you need to repeat words or phrases to yourself before they sink in. Saying words out loud to yourself is especially helpful for auditory learners.

Writing (Kinesthetic) Technique

Writing is a kinesthetic action that boosts cognitive brain structures. The physical psychomotor action of writing down words is communicated through neurons to the brain to help you remember what is being written. When you come across an unfamiliar word, write it down, along with its meaning. Use index cards to make flash cards to carry with you. Print the word on one side of the card and the definition on the other side of the card. This is an effective way to gain independent practice and differentiate between those words and definitions that need further memorization. The kinesthetic process of writing helps imprint words into your explicit memory.

Power Vocabulary Words

The best way to expand your vocabulary is to read regularly. Read newspaper articles, magazines, journals, internet articles, and books. As mentioned above, when you come across an unfamiliar word, write it down on a flash card or in a vocabulary journal. Try to read material from a wide variety of subject areas to help you with the different topics on the SAT. Repeated exposure to new words is a great tool to develop your vocabulary.

When you come across new words, try to use the words in your personal vocabulary every day, and always remember to use words in context to derive the meaning of a word in question. Words on the SAT are always presented in the context of a sentence or a paragraph. As an example, consider the meaning of the following words in the context of the phrase in which they appear. Notice that the same words have different meanings. "A farmer can *produce produce* for harvesting," "The soldier was *deserted* in the *desert*," "He was too *close* to the window to *close* the door," "I decided to *present* her with a *present* on her birthday." There are hundreds of other examples that could be used here, but the point is for you to always learn the *meaning* of words so that you can apply the words within the context of the sentence or passage.

There are a variety of study materials available that list high-powered SAT vocabulary words. We recommend *Name That Movie! A Painless Vocabulary Builder* (2011) by Brian Leaf, *The Wizard of Oz Vocabulary Builder* (2003) by Mark Phillips or *Tooth and Nail: A Novel Approach to the SAT* (1994) by Charles Elster and Joseph Elliot. These books use vocabulary lists within the context of a story to help you remember the words. As you review these books, use the memory improvement techniques described in the previous section to help you remember new words.

Word Parts

When confronted with a new or unusual word, using your knowledge of common word roots and prefixes to break the word down into its parts will help you understand subtle variations in word meanings. Your knowledge of word parts can noticeably expand your ability to understand the general meaning of words.

English language developed from Latin and Greek origins, and *parts* of their words (prefixes, suffixes, and roots or stems) are shared with many languages. If you have studied other languages, you may have recognized a word or part of a word because of its similarity to a word in English. As a living language, English continues to grow daily, but the basic parts of words remain fairly consistent. One research study showed that when combining 20 prefixes and 14 root words, it is possible to learn as many as 100,000 new words.

The knowledge of word parts can dramatically improve your ability to decode, interpret, and comprehend SAT vocabulary. Most words can be broken down into their base words, and by knowing how to do this, you can skillfully make an educated guess about a word's actual meaning, and therefore eliminate incorrect answer choices.

Prefixes

It is especially helpful to use prefixes to understand positive, negative, and neutral connotations of words. Knowing this, you can quickly assess the author's general *tone* of a reading passage. The table below contains commonly used positive and negative prefixes.

Positive and Negative Prefixes	
Prefixes with Positive Connotations	**Prefixes with Negative Connotations**
ad (to)	a or an (not or without)
ben (well or good)	ab (away from)
con (together)	anti, contra, contro, counter (against)
for (front of)	de (opposite of or away from)
magni (large, great)	dis (not or apart)
omni (all, everywhere)	dys (bad or poor)
pro (forward, in favor of)	hyper (over or too much)
super (greater)	hypo (under or too little)
	in (not), male (ill) mis or miso (badly, wrong, hatred)
	of (very), over (extra)
	sub (under or less than)
	un (not)

Roots

Words are built from base words called *roots*. Root words are the second most important group of word parts, and learning these can help you pinpoint the exact meaning of a word. Unlike prefixes and suffixes, a root word is the core of a word that carries meaning. Words are made from root words and can be modified when adding a prefix at the beginning, or a suffix at the ending.

Suffixes

Suffixes may appear easier to remember than prefixes. Suffixes help to determine the part of speech of a word. For example, the verb "establish" becomes a noun when adding the suffix "ment"—establishment. A suffix can also help determine the correct spelling of a word.

Examples of Word Parts

Here are a few easy examples of how you can combine your knowledge of word parts to understand the meaning of a word.

- Let's look at the word "psychology." "psych" is a root word meaning the mind, and "ology" is a suffix meaning the study of. Psychology is the study of the mind.
- "Biology" means the study of life. "bio" is a root word meaning "life," and "ology" is a suffix meaning the study of.

Now let's look at a sample question that incorporates all word parts:

Wilson readily accepted the offer to run for governor of New Jersey because his position at Princeton University was becoming untenable. What is the *best meaning for untenable*?

A. Unlikely to last for years.
B. Filled with considerably less tension.
C. Difficult to maintain or continue.
D. Filled with achievements that would appeal to voters.
E. Something he did not have a tenacious desire to continue.

Let's break "untenable" into word parts. The prefix "un" means not, the root word "ten" means to have, and "able" is a suffix that means worthiness, or an inclination toward a specified action or state. Therefore, the word *untenable* is not having a specified state or action, Choice C. Many of the answer choices may have appeared plausible, but after a careful look at word parts, you will see that the subtle differences in word meanings can make the difference between answering the question correctly and incorrectly. Notice the "attractive distracter" answer choices. Remember, it's important to look at *all* of the answer choices before making your selection. Choice A appears plausible because at first glance "unlikely" appears similar to "untenable," but there is no evidence in the word parts of "untenable" that points to "lasting for years." Choice B is also plausible because "less ten . . ." is similar to "unten . . .," but there is no part of "untenable" that refers to tension. Choice D does not fit the context of the sentence, and Choice E uses the words "not" and "tenacious" that do not fit the meaning of the sentence. The skilled test-taker should make the connection to the word parts "un," "ten," and "able" and the correct answer, which is C.

Use the following table to help you develop the *skill of combining word parts:* prefixes, suffixes, and roots.

Common Prefixes		
Prefix	**Meaning**	**Examples**
ab-, abs-	away from; off	abhor—to withdraw from in fear or disgust abscond—to run away
ac-, ad-, af-, ag-, an-, ap-, ar-, as-, at-	to	accede—to agree to adapt—to fit to
ambi-	both	ambivalent—having two feelings ambidextrous—able to use both hands with equal skill
amphi-	on both sides; around	amphibian—an animal that lives first in the water then adapts to land life amphitheater—a theater with seats all around

(continued)

continued

Prefix	Meaning	Examples
ante-	before	antebellum—before the Civil War
anti-	against	antifreeze—a substance added to a liquid to prevent freezing
auto-	self	automobile—a self-propelled vehicle
bi-	two	bifocals—glasses with lenses for two focuses
circu-, circum-	around	circumscribe—to draw around circumvent—to manage to get around, especially by clever means.
co-, col-, com-, con-	with; together	combine—to bring together conjoin—to join together co-worker—one who works with
contra-, contro-, counter-	against	contradict—to say the opposite counteract—to act against
de-	away from; down; the opposite of	deactivate—to make inactive decline—to turn down, to drop down depart—to go away from
di-	twice	dioxide—an oxide with two atoms of oxygen in a molecule
dia-	across; through	diagnose—to determine what is wrong through knowledge diagonal—across or through a figure
dis-	apart; not	disperse—to scatter widely dishonest—not honest
dys-	bad; ill	dysfunction—a poor level of functioning
epi-	upon	epitaph—an inscription upon a tombstone (upon burial)
equi-	equal; equally	equitable—fair
ef-, ej-, ex-	out; from	effuse—to pour out eject—to throw out excavate—to hollow out
extra-	outside; beyond	extraordinary—outside the usual
fore-	before; in front of	foresee—to anticipate
geo-	earth	geology—the study of the earth
homo-	same; equal; alike	homonym—a word with the same pronunciation as another word
hyper-	over; too much	hypertension—unusually high tension
hypo-	under; too little	hypodermic—under the skin
ig-, il-, im-, in-, ir-	not	ignoble—not noble illegal—not legal improbable—not probable inactive—not active irreverent—not reverent
il-, im-, in-, ir-	in; into	illuminate—to light up implant—to fix firmly in inject—to put in irradiate—to cast light on
inter-	between; among	interurban—between cities

Prefix	Meaning	Examples
intra-, intro-	within; inside of	intravenous—directly into a vein introvert—one who looks inside oneself
mal-, male-	bad; wrong; ill	malfunction—to fail to function correctly malevolent—wishing harm to others
mis-	wrong; badly	mistreat—to treat badly
mis-, miso-	hatred	misanthrope—one who hates humanity
mono-	one; alone	monologue—a speech by one person
neo-	new	neologism—a new word or a new meaning for an old word
non-	not; the reverse of	nonsense—something that makes no sense
omni-	all; everywhere	omnipresent—present everywhere
pan-	all	pandemic—existing over a whole area
per-	by; through	pervade—to be present throughout
poly-	many	polyglot—speaking or writing several languages
post-	after	postwar—after the war
pro-	forward; going ahead of; supporting	proceed—to go forward proboscis—a snout pro-war—supporting war
re-	again; back	retell—to tell again retroactive—applying to things that have already taken place
se-	apart	secede—to withdraw
semi-	half; partly	semicircle—half a circle semiliterate—able to read and write a little
sub-	under; less than	submarine—underwater subconscious—beneath the consciousness
super-	over; above	superimpose—to put something over something else superstar—a star greater than the others
syl-, sym-, syn-, sys-	with; at the same time	symmetry—balance on both sides of a dividing line synchronize—to make things agree or happen at the same time
tele-	far	telepathy—communication from a distance by thought alone
trans-	across	transcontinental—across the continent
un-	not	unhelpful—not helpful

Common Suffixes

Suffix	Meaning	Examples
-able, -ible, -ble	able to; capable of being	viable—able to live edible—capable of being eaten
-acious, -cious	having the quality of	tenacious—holding firmly to
-al	of; like	nocturnal—of the night
-ance, -ancy	the act of; a state of being	performance—the act of performing truancy—the act of being truant

(continued)

continued

Suffix	Meaning	Examples
-ant, -ent	one who	occupant—one who occupies respondent—one who responds
-ar, -ary	connected with; concerning	ocular—pertaining to the eye beneficiary—one who receives benefits
-ence	the act, fact, or quality of	existence—the quality of being
-er, -or	one who does	teacher—one who teaches visitor—one who visits
-ful	full of; having qualities of	fearful—full of fear masterful—having the qualities of a master
-fy	to make	deify—to make into a god
-ac, -ic	of; like; pertaining to	cryptic—hidden cardiac—pertaining to the heart
-il, -ile	pertaining to	civil—pertaining to citizens infantile—pertaining to infants
-ion	the act or condition of	correction—the act of correcting
-ism	the philosophy, act, or practice of	patriotism—the sentiment of supporting one's country
-ist	one who does, makes, or is occupied with	artist—one who makes art
-ity, -ty, -y	the state or character of	unity—the state of being one novelty—the quality of being novel or new
-ive	containing the nature of; giving or leaning toward	pensive—thoughtful
-less	without; lacking	heartless—cruel; without a heart
-logue	a particular kind of speaking or writing	dialogue—a conversation or interchange
-logy	a kind of speaking; a study or science	eulogy—a speech or writing in praise of someone who is now deceased theology—the study of God and related matters
-ment	the act of; the state of	alignment—the act of aligning retirement—the state of being retired
-ness	the quality of	eagerness—the quality of being eager
-ory	having the nature of; a place or thing for	laudatory—showing praise laboratory—a place where work is done
-ose, -ous	full of; having	dangerous—full of danger verbose—wordy
-ship	the art or skill of; the state or quality of being	leadership—the ability to lead
-some	full of; like	troublesome—full of trouble
-tude	the state or quality of	servitude—slavery or bondage
-y	full of; somewhat; somewhat like	musty—having a stale odor chilly—somewhat cold willowy—like a willow

Common Root Words		
Root	**Meaning**	**Examples**
acr	sharp; bitter	acrid—sharp, bitter
act, ag	to do; to act	activity—action agent—one who does
acu	sharp; keen	acuity—keenness
alt	high	exalt—to raise or lift up
anim	life; mind	animate—to make alive
ann	year	annual—yearly
anthrop	human; humankind	misanthrope—one who hates people anthropology—study of the development of humankind
apt	fit	adapt—to fit to
arch	to rule	patriarch—a father and ruler
aud	to hear	audience—those who hear
bas	low	debase—to make lower
belli	war	bellicose—hostile, warlike
ben, bene	well; good	benevolent—doing or wishing well or good
bio	life	biology—the study of living things
brev	short	abbreviate—to shorten
cad, cas	to fall	cadence—a falling of the voice; the beat, time, or measure of rhythmical motion cascade—a small waterfall
cap, capt, ceit, ceive, cept, cip	to take or hold	captive—one who is caught and held receive—to take
cav	hollow	excavate—to hollow out
cede, ceed, cess	to go; to give in	precede—to go before access—a means of entering or approaching
chrom	color	chromatic—relating to color
chron, chrono	time	synchronize—to make agree in time chronology—the order of events
cid, cis	to cut; to kill	incisive—cutting into, sharp homicide—the killing of one human by another
clin	to lean; to bend	decline—to bend or turn downward
claud, claus, clos, clud, clus	to close; to shut	exclude—to shut out claustrophobia—fear of closed places
cogn, cognit	to know; to learn	cognizant—aware recognition—knowing on sight
cor, cordi	heart	accord—agreement
corp, corpor	body	corporal—bodily
cred, credit	to believe	credible—believable
crypt	hidden	cryptic—with hidden meaning
cum	to heap up	cumulative—increasing by additions
cur	to care	accurate—careful and precise
cours, curr, curs	to run	current—the flow of running water
da, date	to give	date—a given time

(continued)

continued

Root	Meaning	Examples
dem, demo	people	demography—a statistical study of the population
di	day	diary—a daily record
dic, dict	to say	diction—wording; verbal expression indict—to make a formal accusation
doc, doct	to teach	doctrine—something taught
dol	grief; pain	doleful—sorrowful
domin	to rule; to master	dominion—rule; a ruled territory
dorm	to sleep	dormant—sleeping; inactive
duc, duct	to lead	induce—to lead to action aqueduct—a pipe or waterway
dynam	power	dynamite—a powerful explosive
ego	I; the self	egocentric—seeing everything in relation to oneself
eu	good; beautiful	euphonious—having a pleasant sound
fac, fact, fec, fect, fic	to make; to do	facile—easy to do artifact—an object made by humans fiction—something that has been made up
fer, ferr	to carry; to bring or bear	refer—to carry to something or someone else
fid	faith; trust	confide—to tell a trusted person
fin	end; limit	final—coming at the end
force, fort	strong	fortitude—strength enforce—to give strength to
fract, frag	to break	fragment—a part broken from the whole
gen	birth	generate—give birth to
gen, gener	kind; race	general—applying to a whole class or kind gender—classification of words by sex
gnos	to know	agnostic—one who believes people cannot know whether God exists
grad, gress	to step; to go	graduate—to go from one state to another progress—to move forward
gram, graph	writing	graphic—relating to writing telegram—a written message sent over a distance
helio	sun	heliolatry—sun worship
hydro	water	hydrant—a pipe from which one draws water
jac, jact, jec, ject	to throw	trajectory—the path of an object that has been thrown or shot project—to propose; to put forward
junct	to join	junction—a joining
jur	to swear	perjure—to lie under oath
labor	to work	elaborate—work out carefully
lect, leg	to gather; to choose	legion—a large number gathered together elect—to choose
leg	law	legislate—to make laws
liber	book	library—a book collection
liber	free	liberation—freedom

Root	Meaning	Examples
loc	place	dislocate—to displace
locut, loqu	to talk	loquacious—talkative elocution—style of speaking
luc	light	elucidate—to clarify ("throw light on")
magn	great	magnanimous—of noble mind; generous magnate—an important person
man, mani, manu	hand	manipulate—to work with the hands manuscript—a document written by hand
mar	the sea	maritime—having to do with the sea
medi	middle	intermediate—in the middle
mens, meter, metr	to measure	thermometer—an instrument to measure temperature symmetry—similarity of measurement on both sides immense—very large (immeasurable)
micro	very small	microbe—an organism too small to be seen with the naked eye
min, mini	small	minute—very tiny miniature—a small copy of something
miss, mit, mitt	to send	admit—to allow in missile—a projectile
mon, monit	to advise; warn; remind	monument—a plaque, statue, building, set up to commemorate someone or something premonition—an advance warning
mort, morti	to die	mortal—destined to die moribund—dying
mob, mot, mov	to move	remove—to move away emotion—strong (moving) feelings immobile—not movable
mut	to change	immutable—never changing
nat, nasc	born	prenatal—before birth nascent—coming into being; being born
nav	ship	circumnavigate—to sail around
nocturne	night	nocturnal—taking place at night
nomy	law; arranged order	astronomy—the science of the stars
nov, novus	new	innovation—something new
onym	name	anonymous—without a name
oper	to work	operative—capable of working
pac	peace	pacify—to calm
par	equal	disparate—not alike; distinct
pars, part	part	depart—to go away from
part, pater	father	paternal—fatherly patriarch—a father and a ruler
pas, pat, path	feeling; suffering	empathy—"feeling with" another person patient—suffering without complaint passion—strong emotion

(continued)

continued

Root	Meaning	Examples
ped, pede, pod	foot	pedestal—the bottom of a statue or column impede—to hinder podium—a platform on which to stand
pel, puls	to drive	expel—to drive out repulse—to drive back
pend, pens	to hang; to weigh; to pay	pendulous—hanging loosely pensive—thoughtful pension—a payment to a person after a certain age
pet, petit	to seek	impetus—a motive petition—to request
phil, philo	loving	philanthropy—a desire to help humanity philosophy—a love of knowledge
phobia	fear	hydrophobia—fear of water
phon, phone	sound	symphony—harmony of sounds telephone—an instrument for sending sound over a distance
plac	to please	placate—to stop from being angry
polis	city	metropolis—a major city
pon, pos, pose, posit	to place; position	proponent—a person who makes a suggestion or supports a cause
port, portat	to carry	porter—one who carries transportation—a means of carrying
psych, psycho	mind	psychology—the science or study of the mind
quer, quisit	to ask	query—to question inquisition—a questioning
quies	quiet	acquiesce—to agree without protest
radi	ray	irradiate—to shine light on
rap, rapt	to seize	rapine—the act of seizing another's property by force rapture—being seized or carried away by emotion
rid, ris	to laugh	ridiculous—laughable risible—causing laughter
rog, rogate	to ask; to propose	abrogate—to abolish (unpropose); to ignore to treat as nonexistent interrogate—to question
rupt	to break	disrupt—to break up
sat, satis	enough	satiate—to provide with enough or more than enough satisfy—to meet the needs of
schis, schiz	to cut	schism—a split or division schizophrenia—a mental disorder characterized by a separation of the thoughts and emotions
sci	to know	science—knowledge
scop	to watch; to view	telescope—an instrument for seeing things at a distance

Root	Meaning	Examples
scrib, script	to write	describe—to tell or write about transcript—a written copy
sec, sect	to cut	sectile—able to be cut with a knife bisect—to cut in two
sed, sess, sid	to sit	sediment—material that settles to the bottom (in liquid) session—a meeting preside—to have authority
sens, sent	to feel; to think	sentiment—feeling sensitive—responding to stimuli
secu, secut, sequ	to follow	sequence—a specific order consecutive—one following another
solut, solv	to loosen	absolve—to free from guilt solution—the method of working out an answer
soph	wise; wisdom	sophisticate—a worldly wise person
spec, spect, spic	to look; to appear	specimen—an example inspect—to look over perspicacious—having sharp judgment
spir, spirit	to breathe	expire—to exhale; to die spirit—life
sta, stat	to stand	stable—steady stationary—fixed, unmoving
stru, struct	to build	construe—to explain or deduce the meaning structure—a building
suad, suas	to urge	persuasive—having the power to cause something to change dissuade—to change someone's course
sum, sumpt	to take	assume—to take on resumption—taking up again
tact, tang	to touch	tactile—able to be touched or felt intangible—unable to be touched
tempor	time	temporal—lasting only for a time; temporary
tain, ten, tent	to hold	untenable—unable to be held retentive—holding maintain—to keep or keep up
tend, tens	to stretch	extend—to stretch out or draw out tension—tautness
terr	land	territory—a portion of land
the, theo	god	atheist—one who believes there is no God theocracy—rule by God or by persons claiming to represent God
thermo	heat	thermal—having to do with heat
tract	to draw	attract—to draw to
trud, trus	to thrust	protrude—to stick out intrusive—pushing into or upon something
un, uni	one	unanimous—of one opinion uniform—of one form

(continued)

continued

Root	Meaning	Examples
urb	city	suburb—a district near a city
ut, util	to use; useful	utile—the quality of being useful
vac	empty	vacuum—empty space
ven, vent	to come	convene—to meet together advent—an arrival
ver	true	verify—to prove to be true
verd	green	verdant— green
vers, vert	to turn	avert—to turn away
vi, via	way	deviate—to turn off the prescribed way via—by way of
vid, vis	to see	evident—apparent; obvious invisible—unable to be seen
vict, vinc	to conquer	convince—to overcome the doubts of victory—an overcoming
vit, viv	to live	vital—alive vivacious—lively
voc, vocat, voke	to call	vocal—spoken or uttered aloud invoke—to call on vocation—a calling
void	empty	devoid—without
volut, volv	to roll or turn around	evolve—to develop by stages, to unfold
vol	to fly	volatile—vaporizing quickly

Chapter 3

Writing Overview

Research has identified that "writing is the best predictor for academic success" (College Board, 2008) and helps evaluate how well students perform in college. The purpose of the writing section of the SAT is to see how well you can demonstrate your ability to think critically under the constraint of time, while you apply the rules of standard written English to

- Multiple-choice questions (approximately 49 questions—35 minutes for two sections)
- Essay writing (one written essay—25 minutes)

As you make your way through this chapter, notice that we begin by introducing you to the writing section's multiple-choice question types before introducing you to the essay writing section. Many of the concepts you will learn in the multiple-choice section will help you develop and write a successful essay. As you work through the multiple-choice diagnostic quiz, examples, and exercises, you should be able to grasp and identify structurally and grammatically incorrect sentences, so you can compose a strong and persuasive essay.

Multiple-Choice Writing Section

The SAT multiple-choice writing section emphasizes the importance of evaluating and identifying word mechanics, word choices, and grammar in sentences. This study guide targets common grammatical errors to help you perform well on this section of your exam. You do not have to know every rule of standard written English, but with repeated practice you will be able to look for the common patterns of writing errors. Reading and writing go hand in hand, so as you study, use what you know about reading to help you with this portion of the exam.

Multiple-choice writing questions are presented and organized by specific question types. Start your review of this section by familiarizing yourself with each question type, and then study the specific strategies and sample practice problems to apply what you have learned and reviewed. It is very important to carefully review this section, take conscientious notes, and practice diligently. The extra time you spend reviewing this material will provide you with a competitive edge and advance your writing skills so you will be a competent writer. Even if your knowledge of English is strong, you should complete the short diagnostic test and review the list of "Common Writing Errors" to reinforce your understanding of some of the most common grammar and usage mistakes that occur in the English language.

Format and Question Types

A typical exam will have two multiple-choice sections: one 25 minutes and one 10 minutes. Expect three kinds of questions in the multiple-choice writing section.

  I. **Identifying Sentence Errors** (usage): approximately 18 questions (37%)
  II. **Improving Sentences** (sentence correction): approximately 25 questions (51%)
  III. **Improving Paragraphs** (revision-in-context): approximately 6 questions (12%)

I. Identifying Sentence Errors Question Type

The identifying sentence errors question type will ask you to identify word choice errors in sentences. You will be evaluated on how well you understand words used within the context of a sentence and how well you can identify errors in a sentence, based on your ability to apply the rules of standard written English.

Skills and Concepts Tested

Knowledge of basic grammar and usage (how words are used together to form meaning) will help in this section. Review the rules of correct grammar and usage that have been emphasized in your high school English classes. In order to score well in this section, you will need to identify errors that break the rules of standard written English.

The identifying sentence error question type may contain one of the following errors:

- Grammar: rules that govern the structure of how words are organized in a sentence
- Usage: how words are used in a sentence
- Diction: the right choice of word in a sentence
- Idiom: expressions or figures of speech in a sentence

Directions

Sentences may contain one error of grammar, usage, diction, or idiom. No sentence contains more than one error, and some sentences have no error. Each question contains a single complete sentence of fewer than 30 words (and usually fewer than 25), with 4 underlined words or phrases lettered A, B, C, and D. You simply find the part with the error, if there is one, and select the corresponding answer choice. If there is no error, choose E (No Error). Parts of the sentence that are not underlined cannot be changed. In selecting your answer, observe the requirements of standard written English. If you cannot find a clear error in a sentence, do not hesitate to choose E.

Example:

> 1. The reporter asked the first person <u>whom</u> he saw <u>leaving</u> the building whether the paramedics <u>done</u> all
>   A   B   C
>
>   they could to save the victims of the explosion and whether any of them <u>had survived</u>. <u>No error</u>.
>   D   E

First, notice that the answer choices are set up differently than in other question types. The lettered choices (A, B, C, D, and E) in this type of question are just below the answer choices. One of the first four choices may have an error. If there is no error, choose E.

This type of question requires you to know verb tenses. In Choice C, the past tense of "did" is "done," but here the past participle "had done" is needed. Therefore, Choice C contains an error. Choice A, "whom," is a distracting answer choice. The rule is to use "who" for the subject and "whom" for the object of a sentence. In this case, "whom" is used correctly as the object of "he saw." Memorize the rules for "who" and "whom" because this type of problem frequently appears on the SAT.

II. Improving Sentences Question Type

More than 50% of the questions in the multiple-choice writing section will ask you to correct faulty structure and grammar in sentences. These questions evaluate your ability to identify common mistakes in grammar and sentence structure while applying your knowledge of word mechanics.

Skills and Concepts Tested

To be successful with this type of question, you must master the same skills as in the previous question type, Identifying Sentence Errors, and practice recognizing errors in grammar and sentence structure. You will be presented with a sentence that examines the phrasing of correct written expression. The correct answer choice should be clear, unambiguous, and concise. As you read the sentence, focus on one of the following types of errors:

- Grammar: rules that govern the structure of words
- Punctuation: how words are separated by a comma, semicolon, and/or apostrophe

- Diction: the right word choice in a sentence
- Sentence structure: how words are organized in a sentence

Directions

The improving sentences question type tests the correctness of effective written expression. In the questions, part or all of each sentence is underlined. Each question contains five lettered answer choices, A, B, C, D, and E, which offer five possible versions of the underlined part. The parts of the sentence that are not underlined cannot be changed and must be used to determine which of the five answers is the best choice. The first choice, A, repeats the original version of the sentence, while the next four choices make changes.

Sometimes the original sentence is better than the four proposed alternatives. If you find no error and you believe that the original sentence is best, select Choice A. Choose the answer that best expresses the meaning of the original sentence and at the same time is grammatically correct and stylistically superior. The correct choice should be clear, unambiguous, and concise.

Example:

2. According to a recent poll, more people like <u>going to the movies than television</u>.

   A.   going to the movies than television.
   B.   going to the movies than television shows.
   C.   going to the movies than watching television.
   D.   going to the movies then they like television.
   E.   movies then television shows.

This question is an example of *faulty parallelism,* which occurs when two or more related ideas are expressed in different grammatical structures. In the original sentence, "going" must parallel "watching." Choice B also has a problem with faulty parallelism. Choices D and E mistakenly use "then" instead of "than." The correct answer is Choice **C.**

Remember that the first answer, Choice A, reproduces the original underlined version of the sentence. Choice A is similar to "No Error" in the previous question type. If you select Choice A, then you are saying that there is no error in the sentence.

III. Improving Paragraphs Question Type

The improving paragraphs question type will ask you to evaluate and improve upon faulty paragraphs. These questions test your ability to identify, edit, and correct errors in paragraphs by following and applying the guidelines of standard written English. You will be asked to analyze paragraphs on a variety of topics and logically revise incorrect sentences in the context of each paragraph. There are one or two sets of questions based on short samples of student writing. As a rule, each selection contains approximately three paragraphs and consists of approximately 200 to 300 words. There are typically four to seven questions following each passage.

Skills and Concepts Tested

Your ability to apply basic rules of grammar, sentence structure, and usage skills will help you in this section. Another important skill is your ability to identify organization, development, and language in a paragraph or essay. Review the rules of correct grammar and usage that are emphasized in this study guide, and review the elements of a well-written essay on page 121. As you read the essay, focus on the following types of errors:

- Transitions from sentence to sentence
- Organization and development
- Logic and clarity
- Sentence structure, diction, and usage
- Language use and verbosity (passive rather than active voice; using too many words)

Directions

The passages in this section are early drafts of student essays. Portions of the student essays will require revising and editing. Read the selections carefully and answer the questions that follow. Questions may address the whole essay or selected items from paragraphs. Typical questions will ask you to combine two or three sentences, or to identify and correct a usage error. Choose the answer that follows the requirements of standard written English and keep in mind that the best answer is one that will *most effectively express the intended meaning*.

Example:

Question 3 is based on the following passage.

(1) Sometimes one person considers another to be a friend, but in fact the other person doesn't feel the same way about him. (2) This is called an unbalanced relationship. (3) The second person may act in a friendly way, but the friendliness is only in a superficial way on the surface. (4) These unbalanced relationships can be found quite often even in elementary schools.

---

3. Which of the following is the best way to revise and combine sentences 1 and 2 (*reproduced below*)?

Sometimes one person considers another to be a friend, but in fact the other person doesn't feel the same way about him. This is called an unbalanced relationship.

A. In an unbalanced relationship, one person considers another person a friend, but the feeling isn't mutual.

B. When one person considers another person a friend, but the second person doesn't consider the first to be a friend, is an example of an unbalanced relationship.

C. If one person considers another person to be a friend, but that person doesn't consider the first person to be a friend, that is an unbalanced relationship.

D. When one person considers another person a friend, it is an unbalanced relationship if the other person doesn't consider the first person in the same way.

E. A relationship is unbalanced when a person considers another person to be a friend, and yet the other person doesn't consider the first person to be a friend.

Choice A is the most efficient, succinct revision and combination. Choices C, D, and E are too wordy. Choice B is an incorrect construction. The correct answer is **A.**

General Strategies

Multiple-choice question types, along with general approaches, strategies, and exercises, are described in detail in this part of the chapter. Before you review specific question types, consider these general strategies that apply to all multiple-choice writing questions.

- **Focus on the underlined words or underlined part of the sentence.** Read the entire sentence or paragraph actively, and as you read the sentence or paragraph, circle or underline key words and main points. Do not make a hasty assumption that you know the correct answer without reading all the possible answer choices.

- **Always observe the rules of standard written English.** This study guide is consistent with the rules of standard *written* English, which are slightly different from spoken English. As you work through the practice exercises, silently read sentences to yourself to hear how they sound. Take into account that if a sentence "sounds" accurate, it may still be incorrect if it contains one of the common grammatical or structural errors outlined in this chapter. Always remember that the guidelines of standard written English prevail over spoken English.

- **Questions may appear in order of difficulty** but all questions are worth the same number of points regardless of the level of difficulty. Take advantage of your ability to work through problems in the order that they appear.

- **Manage your time wisely.** At first glance you might calculate that you have about *1 minute per question* to read and answer all of the questions. When you begin the exam, make a mental note of the starting time and keep track of the time. Never spend more than a minute on any one question. Problems of the identifying sentence errors type will probably take less time, so try to spend less than a minute on these types of problems to save your time for the more difficult types of problems. With sufficient practice, you will almost automatically know when a question is taking too much time and when it is time to select an answer or leave it blank and proceed to the next question.

- **Use the process of elimination strategy** whenever possible to eliminate one or more answer choices. In the identifying sentence errors question type, watch for errors in the choices and eliminate those choices. Use the elimination strategy outlined in the Introduction on page 7. If you get stuck on any one question, either take an educated guess by eliminating some of the other choices first, or leave it blank and proceed to the next question. Remember that it is better not to answer a question than to take a wild guess, since there is a penalty for wrong answers.

- **Be on alert for the "attractive distracter" answer choice.** Watch out for answers that look good but are not the best answer choice. The attractive distracter usually appears in this section as a choice that contains a subtle variation in meaning from the correct answer choice, thus making it more difficult for you to select the correct answer. Attractive distracters are carefully written to be *close to the best answer,* but there is never more than one right answer. When you narrow down your choice to two answers, one is probably the attractive distracter. If this happens, read the question again and take an educated guess.

- **Skip questions only if necessary,** and be sure to mark your answer sheet correctly if you skip a question. Test-takers who skip questions might make the mistake of continuing to mark their answers in sequence and forget to leave a blank space for the unanswered questions. A good idea is to mark your answer in the test booklet itself (no need to erase later) so that if you do make mistakes in transferring your answer choices to the answer sheet, you can easily correct your errors without having to reconsider the answer choices.

Diagnostic Quiz

Directions: Now that you have reviewed the multiple-choice question types, you can take a short diagnostic quiz. This short essay contains 88 errors that are frequently found in print. You will find errors in grammar, diction, sentence structure, and punctuation. As you read through the essay, circle or underline each error. Time yourself, and spend no more than 10 minutes evaluating the essay. You might be surprised at the results following the essay.

How Good is Your Grasp of English?

WASHINGTON, D.C.—The steps of the nations capital were the sight of an unusual ceremony today as the Vice Chairman addressed the imminent new members of the diplomatic core.

"Its' a pleasure for Sara and myself to welcome you," said Wright, as his wife stood discretely in the background with a navel aid. Dressed in a smart blue surge suit, Mrs. Wright looked like she was enjoying the acclimation of the group. Despite the vary cold whether, which didn't seam to phase them, the dignitaries gave free reign to their applause.

Between thirty to forty diplomats listened with rapped attention, standing stationery like gripped in a vice, under the watchful eyes of the Secret Service men their to guard against incidence.

Hardly never at a loss for words, but looking a bit pail, Wright said he hoped his listeners had become use to the bitter cold, the worse the city has scene in years. "Between you and I, he said, "its become so chilly anymore that I'd try and lay in bed on days like this if it were'nt against my principals. Besides, Sara makes me get up early every morning and test my metal by peddling my exorcise bike."

In a more serious vain, the Vice Chairman then told the tail of a racetrack better who lost al his money and, out of shear hunger, had committed a miner theft. He stole an orange, which he was pealing when arrested. On advise of council the gamboler waved a jury trial and through himself on the mercy of the court. As the culprit stood ringing his hands, the judge hit the sealing: He denied bale, meeting out thirty days in jail, and leveed a fine of one hundred dollars.

"The man took his punishment pretty good," said Wright, "but it was a hard way to learn a lessen we all can prophet from: As we sew, so shall we reap, weather we are individuals or nation's. Let us not reek vengeance on one another, Instead, let us saver the blessings of piece!"

As the teaming crowd began to disburse, the Vice Chairman spied a pare of newlyweds who's bridle party was standing further back in the crowd. A reporter, pouring over his notes, then overhead Wright tell his wife, to who he was whispering, "Like I always say, its alot easier to tie the not than to undue it. I hope they never loose site of that and play it strait. Otherwise, there happiness will just be an allusion and ware off soon. Now I'd like some hot bullion—I feel like I've caught a sleight cold."

Reprinted with permission from *The Goof-Proofer* by Stephen J. Manhard.

This humorous essay is useful in identifying grammatical and sentence structure mistakes. Did you find most of the errors? You should have counted 88 total errors. Below is a list of the errors in the order of their appearance. Corrections are noted in parentheses.

Grammar Diagnostic Quiz Errors			
1. nations (nation's)	20. rapped (rapt)	42. tail (tale)	66. piece (peace)
2. capital (capitol)	21. stationery (stationary)	43. better (bettor)	67. teaming (teeming)
3. sight (site)	22. like (as if, or as though)	44. shear (sheer)	68. disburse (disperse)
4. imminent (eminent)	23. vice (vise)	45. miner (minor)	69. pare (pair)
5. core (corps)	24. their (there)	46. pealing (peeling)	70. who's (whose)
6. Its' (It's)	25. incidence (incidents)	47. advise (advice)	71. bridle (bridal)
7. myself (me)	26. never (ever)	48. council (counsel)	72. further (farther)
8. discretely (discreetly)	27. pail (pale)	49. gamboler (gambler)	73. pouring (poring)
9. navel (naval)	28. use (used)	50. waved (waived)	74. to who (to whom)
10. aid (aide)	29. worse (worst)	51. through (threw)	75. Like (As)
11. surge (serge)	30. scene (seen)	52. ringing (wringing)	76. its (it's)
12. like (as if, or as though)	31. I (me)	53. sealing (ceiling)	77. alot (a lot)
13. acclimation (acclamation)	32. its (it's)	54. bale (bail)	78. not (knot)
14. vary (very)	33. anymore (nowadays, or lately)	55. meeting (meting)	79. undue (undo)
15. whether (weather)	34. try and (try to)	56. leveed (levied)	80. loose (lose)
16. seam (seem)	35. lay (lie)	57. good (well)	81. site (sight)
17. phase (faze)	36. were'nt (weren't)	58. lessen (lesson)	82. strait (straight)
18. reign (rein)	37. principals (principles)	59. prophet (profit)	83. there (their)
19. between . . . to (between . . . and), or (from . . . to)	38. metal (mettle)	60. sew (sow)	84. allusion (illusion)
	39. peddling (pedaling)	61. weather (whether)	85. ware (wear)
	40. exorcise (exercise)	62. nation's (nations)	86. bullion (bouillon)
	41. vain (vein)	63. reek (wreak)	87. like (as if, or as thought)
		64. Instead (;)	88. sleight (slight)
		65. saver (savor)	

Approaches with Samples: Identifying Sentence Errors and Improving Sentences Question Types

The first two multiple-choice writing question types—identifying sentence errors and improving sentences—are discussed in this section. Improving paragraphs question types will be addressed in the next section. Questions in this section are roughly grouped into sets by the type of grammar or structural errors they contain. Common types of errors appear in nine categories: agreement, pronoun, verb tense, parallel structure, diction and idiom, double negatives, dangling and misplaced modifiers, sentence structure, and punctuation.

The following table and subsequent practice exercises provide you with information about grammatical and structural errors that may appear on the SAT. Take your time to study and carefully examine this list of common mistakes. Not all of these errors will appear on the exam or be discussed in this section, but many of them have appeared on previous exams. Some of the grammatical and structural errors may appear more than once (such as verb agreement errors). These types of errors will appear in *both* the identifying sentence errors (usage), and improving sentences (sentence correction) question types.

In this section, you will see both types of questions (labeled "*usage*" or "*sentence correction*"). Apply what you learn from the following table of Common Types of Writing Errors to the practice exercises that follow. In addition, continue your practice by completing the full-length practice tests in this study guide and the accompanying CD-ROM. The extra practice will help you master the material that is covered in this section.

Common Types of Writing Errors		
Type of Error	**Example of Error**	**Corrected Example**
I. Agreement Errors (nouns, verbs, pronouns, adverbs, and adjectives)		
Noun agreement error	France and Italy are a country in Europe.	France and Italy are countries in Europe.
Subject-verb agreement error	The students of English is taking the test.	The students of English are taking the test.
Pronoun agreement error	Jack was late, so we left without them.	Jack was late, so we left without him.
Comparative adjective error	Of the seven swimmers, she is the stronger.	Of the seven swimmers, she is the strongest.
Adjective/adverb error	His writing is carelessly because he writes too rapid.	His writing is careless because he writes too rapidly.
II. Pronoun Errors		
Unclear pronoun reference	Jane, June, and Joan applied, and she got the job.	Jane, June, and Joan applied, and Jane got the job. (Joan or June)
Missing specific pronoun antecedent	Dave ate too fast, which made him sick.	Dave ate too fast so he got sick.
Change of pronoun subjects	One needs a calculator, and you should bring two pens.	One needs a calculator, and one should bring two pens.
Wrong pronoun	She is the judge which sentenced the felon.	She is the judge who sentenced the felon.
III. Verb Tense Errors		
Verb form error	He has brung a bottle of wine.	He has brought a bottle of wine.
Verb tense sequence error	He rang the bell, opened the door, and enters the house.	He rang the bell, opened the door, and entered the house.
Verb tense error	Last week she buys a new car.	Last week she bought a new car.
IV. Parallel Structure Errors		
Parallelism error	He is studying biology, physics, and how to swim.	He is studying biology, physics, and swimming.
Illogical comparison	In California, the sun rises later than New York.	In California, the sun rises later than in New York.
V. Diction and Idiom Errors		
Diction error	He will be relapsed from prison in June.	He will be released from prison in June.
Idiom error: gerund infinitive confusion	I am eager in seeing the film. He is incapable to answer the question.	I am eager to see the film. He is incapable of answering the question.
Idiom error: choice of conjunction	He is as subtle than a fox.	He is as subtle as a fox.
Idiom error: choice of preposition	They are in support to the idea.	They are in support of the idea.
VI. Double Negative Errors		
Double negative	There is hardly no coffee left in the pot.	There is hardly any coffee left in the pot.

continued

Type of Error	Example of Error	Corrected Example
VII. Dangling and Misplaced Modifier Errors		
Misplaced modifier	We saw the boy and his mother in a Batman costume.	We saw the boy in a Batman costume and his mother.
Dangling modifier	Flowing from the mountain top, he drank from the stream.	He drank from the stream that was flowing from the mountain top.
VIII. Sentence Structure Errors		
Sentence fragment	Having three sisters, two of them doctors.	Having three sisters, two of them doctors, made her feel better.
Sentence fragment	Hoping to be elected on either the first or second ballot.	She hoped to be elected on either the first or second ballot.
Fused (or run-on) sentences	She drove off in the Range Rover, Juan watched her leave.	She drove off in the Range Rover. Juan watched her leave.
Wordiness	Because of the fact that he failed to give total and complete attention, he missed the exit.	Because he failed to give complete attention, he missed the exit.
IX. Punctuation Errors		
Comma splice	She has three sisters, two of them are doctors.	She has three sisters, and two of them are doctors.

I. Agreement Errors

Subject-Verb Agreement Errors

Verbs must match the nouns to which they refer. An agreement error is the faulty combination of a *singular* and a *plural* in a sentence. A singular subject must be matched with a singular verb, and a plural subject must be matched with a plural verb. In other words, the *verb must always agree with the subject*. As long as you know whether the subject is singular or plural, you should have no trouble with this type of problem. Verbs ending in *–s* are usually singular, and nouns ending in *–s* are usually plural. Be sure you can identify the subject and the verb of the sentence, and do not let the intervening words distract you. For example:

> The *cyclist pedaled swiftly.* (singular)
> The *cyclists pedal swiftly.* (plural)

Examples:

Directions: Questions 1–2 may contain an error of grammar. No sentence will contain more than one error, and some may have no error. A possible error will be underlined and have a letter beneath it. Choose the one underlined part that must be changed to correct the sentence. If there is no error, choose E.

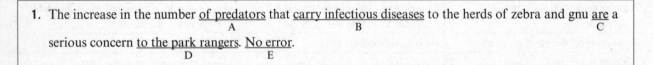

1. The increase in the number <u>of predators</u> that <u>carry infectious diseases</u> to the herds of zebra and gnu <u>are</u> a
                 A   B   C

   serious concern <u>to the park rangers</u>. <u>No error.</u>
                 D   E

The subject of the sentence is the singular noun "increase," and its verb, though widely separated from it, is the plural "are." The sentence should read "the increase . . . is." The correct answer for this *usage* type of problem is **C**.

---

2. The books of Hill Harper <u>tackles</u> the need for positive role models for youth in the black community
A

through <u>affirmations in a colloquial style,</u> <u>quotes from African-American celebrities,</u> and
B   C

<u>examples of personal experiences.</u> <u>No error</u>.
D   E

The subject "books" is a plural. To agree, the verb should be the plural form, "tackle." The correct answer for this *usage* type of problem is **A**.

Pronoun Agreement Errors

Pronouns can be either singular or plural and must agree with the noun, verb, or other pronoun to which they refer. Personal pronouns have distinctive singular and plural forms (he/they, his/their, him/them), and pronoun agreement errors are as common as subject-verb errors. The *number* of a pronoun (that is to say, whether it is singular or plural) is determined by its *antecedent* (the word, phrase, or clause to which it refers). *Pronouns must agree in number with their antecedents*. Watch for a change of pronoun subjects as well. For example, if the pronoun "one" is used in a sentence, then the pronoun "you" should not be used.

Examples:

Directions: Questions 3–4 may contain an error of grammar. No sentence will contain more than one error, and some may have no error. A possible error will be underlined and have a letter beneath it. Choose the one underlined part that must be changed to correct the sentence. If there is no error, choose E.

---

3. The greatest strength of the American political system <u>is</u> each voter's right <u>to determine</u> which way <u>they</u>
A   B   C

<u>will vote</u>. <u>No error</u>.
D   E

The singular "is" agrees with the singular "strength," therefore, there is no error in choice A. Choice C contains an error in agreement. The plural "they" does not agree with the singular "each voter." To answer this question correctly, remember to look for the *number* (singular or plural) of a pronoun. It is always determined by its *antecedent*. The correct answer in this *usage* type of problem is **C**.

---

4. The governor <u>hopes</u> <u>to increase and redistribute</u> tax money, <u>raising</u> the expenditure on education and
A   B   C

<u>equalizing them</u> throughout the state. <u>No error</u>.
D   E

There are no errors in choices A, B, or C, but there is an error of agreement in Choice D. The plural pronoun "them" refers to the singular "expenditure." The corrected sentence would have either "expenditures" and "them" or "expenditure" and "it." The correct answer in this *usage* type of problem is **D**.

Directions: In questions 5–6 part or all of each sentence is underlined. Answer Choice A repeats the underlined portion of the original sentence, while the next four choices offer alternatives. Choose the answer that best expresses the meaning of the original sentence and at the same time is grammatically correct and stylistically superior.

---

5. <u>When one reaches the first plateau, it</u> does not guarantee that you will complete the climb to the summit.

    A.   When one reaches the first plateau, it
    B.   Because one reaches the first plateau, it
    C.   One's reaching the first plateau
    D.   That you have reached the first plateau
    E.   Reaching the first plateau

This sentence contains an inconsistency in the pronouns. The part that cannot be changed uses "you," but the underlined section uses "one." A right answer will either use "you" or eliminate the pronoun altogether. Choices A, B, and C cannot be right, but choices D and E are both grammatically correct. In this case Choice E is preferable because it is more direct. The correct answer in this *sentence correction* type of problem is **E**.

---

6. Weaver's policy allowed a slave to earn cash <u>if they were able to produce</u> more than the average expected output each week.

    A.   if they were able to produce
    B.   if they produced
    C.   if they overproduced
    D.   by producing
    E.   producing

The error in choices A, B, and C is an agreement error; "slave" is singular, but the pronoun in all three is the plural "they." Choice D solves the problem by omitting the pronoun. The original meaning is unclear if the preposition "by" is dropped. The correct answer in this *sentence correction* type of problem is **D**.

II. Pronoun Errors

The *antecedent* of a pronoun (the word to which the pronoun refers) should be clear. In spoken conversation and in informal writing, we often use pronouns that have no single word as their antecedent. For example, "*This* happens all the time." The word "this" is incorrect because it refers to a general idea of the preceding sentence but not to a specific subject. On the SAT, you should immediately regard a pronoun that does not have a specific noun (or word used as a noun) as its antecedent as an error. Note that sentences in which a pronoun could have two or more possible antecedents should be rewritten.

Examples:

Directions: Questions 7–8 may contain an error of grammar. No sentence will contain more than one error, and some may have no error. A possible error will be underlined and have a letter beneath it. Choose the one underlined part that must be changed to correct the sentence. If there is no error, choose E.

---

7. Many historians <u>believe</u> the Obama-McCain election <u>was decided by</u> the grassroots support raised
             A   B

    through the use of social media <u>at which</u> <u>his campaign</u> excelled. <u>No error</u>.
                                    C   D   E

The pronoun error is the ambiguous "his." Notice there are two antecedents, so the reader has no way of knowing whether the antecedent of the pronoun is Obama or McCain. The correct answer in this *usage* type of problem is **D**.

8. <u>In recent years,</u> Anne Perry <u>wrote the Victorian Christmas books</u> *A Christmas Homecoming* and *A*
    A   B

   Christmas Odyssey: A Novel, <u>but it did not</u> attain the <u>popularity of</u> her Victorian crime series involving
                         C   D

   Thomas and Charlotte Pitt. <u>No error.</u>
                            E

This sentence contains two possible antecedents to the singular pronoun "it," *A Christmas Homecoming* and *A Christmas Odyssey: A Novel.* The correct answer in this *usage* type of problem is **C.**

Directions: In questions 9–11 part or all of each sentence is underlined. Answer Choice A repeats the underlined portion of the original sentence, while the next four choices offer alternatives. Choose the answer that best expresses the meaning of the original sentence and at the same time is grammatically correct and stylistically superior.

9. A considerable number of California counties and cities have farmland retention policies, often as part of their general plans, and they call for avoiding the best land and developing other land more efficiently, <u>which is encouraging to agricultural conservationists.</u>

   A.   which is encouraging to agricultural conservationists.
   B.   which is one of the most encouraging practices in agricultural conservation.
   C.   and this is one of agricultural conservation's most encouraging practices.
   D.   and these policies are one of agricultural conservation's most encouraging practices.
   E.   and that appears to be encouraging to agricultural conservationists.

Sentences in which a pronoun has two or more different antecedents should be rewritten. Choice D is incorrect because it is an ambiguous pronoun error. This choice provides a noun as the subject of the clause that replaces the pronouns "which," "this" and "that."

In choices B, C and E the pronouns changing "which" to "this" or "that" do nothing to correct the ambiguity of the pronoun. The correct answer to this *sentence correction* type of problem is **D.**

10. <u>I came in fifteen minutes late which</u> made the whole class difficult to understand.

   A.   I came in fifteen minutes late which
   B.   I came in fifteen minutes late, and this
   C.   I came in fifteen minutes late, and this is what
   D.   By coming in fifteen minutes late, which
   E.   Coming in fifteen minutes late

The pronoun "which" has no specific antecedent here, and the change of "which" to "this" does not correct the problem. Choice E eliminates the pronoun altogether and corrects the sentence. Choice D is a sentence fragment. The correct answer to this *sentence correction* type of problem is **E.**

11. Ending the hope that a single genetic flaw might cause Alzheimer's disease, <u>they say the disorder apparently has multiple causes,</u> as do heart disease and cancer.

   A.   they say the disorder apparently has multiple causes
   B.   they say the disease has multiple apparent causes
   C.   they say that it apparently has multiple causes
   D.   researchers report the disease has many causes, apparent
   E.   researchers report the disorder apparently has multiple causes

The vague "they" is the problem here. They who? Choices D and E replace the inexact pronoun with a specific noun. There is no important difference between "many" and "multiple," but choice E uses "apparently" correctly. The correct answer to this *sentence correction* type of problem is **E.**

Pronoun Case Errors

Pronouns and nouns in English may be used as *subjects* (The *cell phone* is small. *I* am tired.), as *objects* (David watered the *lawn*. David met *him*.), and as *possessors* (*Kyle's* guitar is large. *His* arm is broken.). The function of the pronoun in the sentence determines the case. Nouns and pronouns have a *subjective* case, an *objective* case, and a *possessive case* (see the table below). Since the form of a noun in the subjective case is no different from the form of the same noun in the objective case (The *bat* hit the *ball*. The *ball* hit the *bat*.), errors of case are not a problem with nouns. However, several pronouns have different forms as subjects and objects, and you should be aware of this type of error on the SAT.

Subjective, Possessive, and Objective Pronouns			
	First Person	**Second Person**	**Third Person**
Subjective Case			
Singular	I	you	he, she, it, who
Plural	we	you	they, who
Possessive Case			
Singular	mine	yours	his, hers, whose
Plural	ours	yours	theirs, whose
Objective Case			
Singular	me	you	him, her, it, whom
Plural	us	you	them, whom

Examples:

Directions: Questions 12–13 may contain an error of grammar. No sentence will contain more than one error, and some may have no error. A possible error will be underlined and have a letter beneath it. Choose the one underlined part that must be changed to correct the sentence. If there is no error, choose E.

12. When <u>we were</u> in elementary school, <u>there was</u> a competition <u>between my sister and I</u> that now <u>seems</u>
          A   B   C   D
    ridiculous. <u>No error.</u>
             E

The personal pronoun is the object of the preposition "between," so the phrase should be "between my sister and me." It is easy to see case errors like this when the pronoun immediately follows the preposition (to me, like him, without her), but it is harder when another object intercedes (to David and me, like Meagan and him, with Cristy and her). The correct answer for this *usage* type of problem is **C**.

13. According to the surgeon, the <u>diagnosis of illness</u> <u>was</u> <u>not likely</u> to alarm either <u>she</u> or <u>her husband</u>. <u>No error.</u>
                                      A   B   C   D   E

The object of the infinitive "to alarm" is "she or her husband." The "she" should be the objective case "her." To help you arrive at the correct answer, isolate the phrase "to alarm." You wouldn't say "to alarm she." You would naturally say "to alarm her." The correct answer for this *usage* type of problem is **C**.

III. Verb Tense Errors

A verb is a part of speech that expresses a state of being or action. Verb tenses are formed according to person, number, and tense. The tenses (present, past, and future) of the verbs in a sentence must be logical and consistent. Many of the verb tense errors on the SAT occur in sentences with two verbs, and with past and past participle forms of irregular verbs. Always look carefully at the tenses of the verbs in a sentence and ask yourself, "Does the time scheme make logical sense?" The time scheme will determine the tense. Look carefully at the verbs and the other words in the sentence to establish the time scheme. Adverbs such as "then," "subsequently," "before," "yesterday," and "tomorrow," and prepositional phrases such as "in the last decade" and "in the future" work with the verbs to make the time of the actions clearer.

Directions: Question 14 may contain an error of grammar. No sentence will contain more than one error, and some may have no error. A possible error will be underlined and have a letter beneath it. Choose the one underlined part that must be changed to correct the sentence. If there is no error, choose E.

Examples:

14. When the bell rang, I <u>grabbed</u> my backpack and <u>run</u> as fast as I could to catch the first bus. <u>No error</u>.
                       A   B   C   D   E

The first two verbs ("rang," "grabbed") are in the past tense. To be consistent, "run" should be "ran." The correct answer for this *usage* type of problem is **B**.

Directions: In questions 15–16, part or all of each sentence is underlined. Choice A repeats the underlined portion of the original sentence, while the next four choices offer alternatives. Choose the answer that best expresses the meaning of the original sentence and at the same time is grammatically correct and stylistically superior.

15. Facebook users love to update their status and converse with friends, <u>but frequent changes in their privacy policies are often made by the company, which frustrates users</u>.

    A. but frequent changes in their privacy policies are often made by the company, which frustrates users.
    B. but the company has often made frequent changes to their privacy policies, which frustrates users.
    C. and frequent changes in their privacy policies are often made by the company, which frustrates users.
    D. but the company makes frequent privacy policy changes, which frustrate users.
    E. but frequent changes in their privacy policies have often been made by the company, which frustrates users.

The first clause is in the active voice, present tense form of the verbs "love" and "converse," but in Choice A, the second clause changes the verb "are often made" to the passive voice. Choice B uses the active voice but a different verb tense, "has often made." Choice E again uses the passive voice, "have often been made," and Choice C maintains the change to the passive voice. Choice D is correct because it keeps the verb in the second clause, "makes," in the active voice. The correct answer for the *sentence correction* type of problem is **D**.

16. Combining flavors from America's melting pot with traditional techniques, <u>New American bistro dining include</u> ethnic twists on old standbys and Old World peasant dishes made from luxury American ingredients.

    A. New American bistro dining include
    B. New American bistro dining have included
    C. New American bistros includes
    D. New American bistros include
    E. New American bistro chefs includes

The participle "combining" modifies the plural noun "flavors," so the verb should modify a plural noun. Because "bistros" is plural, "include" should be plural. The correct answer for this *sentence correction* type of problem is **D**.

IV. Parallel Structure Errors

Errors of parallelism occur when two or more linked words or phrases are expressed in different grammatical structures. The basic rule is that when there are two or more linked constructs, they must show the same grammar construction.

Parallel structure errors may include unnecessary shifts in verb tense (past to present, for example) or voice (active to passive, for example). They may also include shifts in pronouns ("you" to "one," for example). Watch for these errors in lists or series. Be especially careful with sentences that use *correlatives* (both . . . and; no . . . but; not only . . . but also; not . . . but; either . . . or; and others). Make sure the construction that follows the second of the correlative conjunctions is the same construction as the one that follows the first.

Examples:

Directions: Questions 17–19 may contain an error of grammar. No sentence will contain more than one error, and some may have no error. A possible error will be underlined and have a letter beneath it. Choose the one underlined part that must be changed to correct the sentence. If there is no error, choose E.

---

17. Miguel <u>enjoyed</u> <u>swimming</u>, <u>weight lifting</u>, and <u>to run</u>. <u>No error</u>.
         A   B   C   D   E

"To run" is incorrect; it should be an "-ing" word ("running") like the other items. The correct answer for this *usage* type of problem is **D.**

---

18. <u>Working at a full-time job</u>, <u>helping to support a family</u>, and <u>a college education</u> added up to a
          A   B   C

<u>tremendous burden</u> for Tom. <u>No error</u>.
     D   E

An error in parallelism occurs with "a college education," which may be corrected by adding an "-ing" word such as "completing." Then the correct parallel phrase would be "completing a college education." The correct answer for this *usage* type of problem is **C.**

---

19. Law school will <u>not only enable</u> one to pass the bar exam, <u>but also teach</u> <u>you</u> to <u>think clearly</u>. <u>No error</u>.
                  A   B   C   D   E

The verbs "enable" and "teach" are correctly parallel, but the pronoun shift from "one" to "you" is an error. The correct answer for this *usage* type of problem is **C.**

Directions: In questions 20–21, part or all of each sentence is underlined. Choice A repeats the underlined portion of the original sentence, while the next four choices offer alternatives. Choose the answer that best expresses the meaning of the original sentence and at the same time is grammatically correct and stylistically superior.

---

20. <u>After he graduated from college, his parents gave him a new car, ten thousand dollars, and sent him on a</u> trip around the world.

  A. After he graduated from college, his parents gave him a new car, ten thousand dollars, and sent him on a

  B. After graduating from college, his parents gave him a new car, ten thousand dollars, and a

  C. After he had graduated from college, his parents gave him a new car, ten thousand dollars, and a

  D. After he had graduated from college, his parents gave him a new car, ten thousand dollars, and sent him on a

  E. After graduating from college, his parents gave him a new car, ten thousand dollars, and sent him on a

---

The problem in the original sentence is parallelism. The verb "gave" begins a series with nouns as objects ("car," "dollars") but the third part of the series ("and sent him on") interrupts the series. Choices B and C correct this error by making "trip" a third object of "gave." Choice B cannot be right, though, because it begins with a dangling participle; it appears that the parents are graduating from college. The correct answer for this *sentence correction* type of problem is **C.**

---

21. Please remind me not only <u>that I must cash a check, but also to have the car washed.</u>

    A. that I must cash a check, but also to have the car washed.
    B. that I must cash a check, but also to wash the car.
    C. to cash a check, but also that the car needs washing.
    D. to cash a check, but also that I must have the car washed.
    E. to cash a check, but also to have the car washed.

The correlative here is "not only . . . but also." Choice E is the only answer that correctly uses a parallel construction ("not only to cash," "but also to have"). The correct answer for this *sentence correction* type of problem is **E.**

V. Diction and Idiom Errors

Diction errors use the wrong word for the meaning intended. These errors in word choice are especially likely to show up on the SAT with a word that looks or sounds very much like another: "sit" and "set," or "retain" and "detain," for example. Diction errors are words you already know, but they are easily mixed up. We have listed some examples below, with their definitions, for your easy reference. In the examples that follow, remember to read *each word* carefully before you answer the question.

Pairs of Commonly Misused Words	
accept (to agree)	except (excluding)
affect (to influence)	effect (noun—a result; verb—to bring about)
afflict (cause suffering to)	inflict (impose)
allude (to mention indirectly)	elude (to physically or mentally escape from)
allusion (reference)	illusion (false or misleading appearance)
between (when there are only two)	among (three or more)
break (noun—a rest; verb—to fracture)	brake (a device to decelerate)
cite (mention as the source)	site (a place)
complement (to make complete or improve)	compliment (to praise or flatter)
elicit (to bring forth or arrive at by reasoning)	illicit (prohibited by law)
farther (more distant)	further (more time or quantity)
imply (to express indirectly)	infer (to conclude from evidence)
its (of it)	it's (it is)
lie (to be in a horizontal position) or lie (to tell something that is not true)	lay (to cause something to be in a certain place, or to produce eggs)
precede (to go before)	proceed (to go on, advance, or continue)
principle (a standard rule)	principal (a head of a school or the initial investment in an account or first in order of importance)
that (refers to an understood thing or place)	which (refers to a specific thing or place) or who (refers to an understood person)
then (at another time or next in order)	than (a comparison of unequal parts)
there (in that place)	their (belonging to them)

Examples:

Directions: Question 22 may contain an error of grammar. No sentence will contain more than one error, and some may have no error. A possible error will be underlined and have a letter beneath it. Choose the one underlined part that must be changed to correct the sentence. If there is no error, choose E.

22. <u>Setting on the porch</u> every evening <u>during the summer</u> soon <u>became a habit</u> to her <u>during the long summers</u>
        A   B   C   D

    in southern Alabama. <u>No error.</u>
                             E

This is an error of diction, or choice of word. The writer has confused "to sit" (an intransitive verb) and "to set" (a verb that takes an object). The correct answer for this *usage* type of problem is **A**.

Directions: In question 23, part or all of each sentence is underlined. Answer Choice A repeats the underlined portion of the original sentence, while the next four choices offer alternatives. Choose the answer that best expresses the meaning of the original sentence and at the same time is grammatically correct and stylistically superior.

23. Although a complete understanding <u>of how slaves in the region that is now called Turkey lived in their day-to-day lives is most likely impossible, a recently-discovered manuscript is providing new evidence</u> of a higher rate of literacy than was previously imagined.

    A. of how slaves in the region that is now called Turkey lived in their day-to-day lives is most likely impossible, a recently-discovered manuscript is providing new evidence

    B. is most likely impossible of how slaves in the region that is now called Turkey lived their day-to-day lives, recently, a manuscript was discovered that provides new evidence

    C. of the day-to-day lives of slaves in the region that is now called Turkey is most likely impossible, a recently-discovered manuscript provides new evidence

    D. of the day-to-day lives of slaves in the region that is now called Turkey is most likely impossible, new evidence is provided in a recently-discovered manuscript

    E. is most likely impossible of the day-to-day lives of slaves in the region that is now called Turkey, a manuscript discovered recently provides new evidence

The phrasing, "lived in their day-to-day lives" is awkward and redundant, therefore, eliminate Choice A. Choice B also redundantly uses the words "lived" and "lives," compounding the awkwardness by splitting up the word "understanding" and "of." Choice D is wrong because it includes the passive construction "is provided." Eliminate choice E because it awkwardly separates the words "understanding" and "of." Choice C removes the redundancy, streamlines the sentence, and avoids the use of passive construction. The correct answer for this *sentence-correction* type of problem is **C**.

VI. Double Negative Errors

A double negative error is the use of two negative words in the same sentence. Double negative words cancel each other out as in the formula below.

Negative + Negative = Positive

Negative + Positive = Negative

Words like "never," "none," "nor," "neither," "rarely," "seldom," " scarcely," "hardly," "no," not," and "barely" are negatives. Some double negative errors are obvious ("I don't play no soccer"), while others are less obvious ("I don't have hardly any clothes"). The last statement should read, "I have hardly any clothes."

Examples:

Directions: Questions 24–25 may contain an error of grammar. No sentence will contain more than one error, and some may have no error. A possible error will be underlined and have a letter beneath it. Choose the one underlined part that must be changed to correct the sentence. If there is no error, choose E.

---

24. Unaffected by <u>neither hunger nor cold,</u> Scott covered up to twenty miles <u>on each of the days</u> that the
                 A   B

    weather <u>permitted him</u> to <u>travel at all</u>. <u>No error.</u>
              C   D   E

The error here is A, a double negative, since "unaffected" and "neither" are both negatives. To correct the sentence, change "unaffected" to "affected" or "neither . . . nor" to "either . . . or." Since "unaffected" is not underlined, Choice A must be changed. The correct answer for this *usage* type of problem is **A.**

---

25. Many psychologists <u>claim that</u> slips of the tongue do not mask <u>no deeply concealed wishes,</u> but are <u>simply</u>
                         A   B   C

    signs of <u>momentary confusion.</u> <u>No error.</u>
              D   E

The error here is the double negative "do not mask . . . no." The correct answer for this *usage* type of problem is **B.**

VII. Dangling and Misplaced Modifier Errors

Misplaced parts are often awkward but not, strictly speaking, grammatical errors. The questions that test for misplaced parts will usually ask you to select the sentence that is not only grammatically correct but also clear and exact, free from awkwardness and ambiguity. This kind of problem typically appears as a sentence correction question type. Watch for sentences that seem odd or have an unnatural word order. Also watch for phrases that have nothing to modify, called *dangling modifiers.*

Examples:

Directions: In questions 26–27, part or all of each sentence is underlined. Answer Choice A repeats the underlined portion of the original sentence, while the next four choices offer alternatives. Choose the answer that best expresses the meaning of the original sentence and at the same time is grammatically correct and stylistically superior.

---

26. Fearing criticism of his book, <u>the publisher had to convince Jim that his story would be well received in order to get his signature on the contract.</u>

    A. the publisher had to convince Jim that his story would be well received in order get his signature on the contract.

    B. the publisher had to demonstrate to Jim that it was worthy of being published in order to get him to sign the contract.

    C. Jim was reluctant to sign the contract until the publisher convinced him that it would be well received.

    D. the publisher had to convince Jim that it would be well received before he agreed to sign the contract.

    E. the publisher had to work hard to convince Jim to sign the book contract.

With a dangling participle, a misplaced modifying phrase for "Jim," the modifying phrase needs to be moved closer to the subject, "Jim" to connect to the person who was worried about criticism of Jim's book. The correct *sentence correction* answer is **C.**

27. <u>Looking at the tiny image on the screen of her iPhone</u>, Mount Rushmore seemed much smaller and farther away than it had only seconds before.

    A. Looking at the tiny image on the screen of her iPhone
    B. With her iPhone in hand
    C. Via the image displayed by the screen of the iPhone she was looking at
    D. When she looked at the tiny image of it on the screen of her iPhone
    E. Against the screen of her iPhone

Literally interpreted, the original sentence seems to say that Mount Rushmore, rather than the woman, was looking at the iPhone screen, because the modifier (*Looking*) modifies *Mount Rushmore* instead of *the woman who was looking at her iPhone*. In other words, the modifier "dangles." Choice D eliminates this dangling modifier in a clear and concise way, unlike Choice C. By beginning the sentence with *When she looked at the tiny image of it*— a clause that modifies *Mount Rushmore*, rather than *the woman*—Choice D makes the remainder of the sentence flow logically. Choices A and B contain dangling modifiers, and Choice E changes the meaning of the sentence. The correct *sentence correction* answer is **D**.

VIII. Sentence Structure Errors

Make sure that the answer you choose makes a complete sentence. Do not assume that a subject and verb automatically make a complete sentence. A complete sentence must form an *independent clause* (a group of words that include a subject, a predicate, and a complete thought). The subject tells what or whom the sentence is about and the predicate tells something about the subject.

Examples:

Directions: In questions 28–29, part or all of each sentence is underlined. Choice A repeats the underlined portion of the original sentence, while the next four choices offer alternatives. Choose the answer that best expresses the meaning of the original sentence and at the same time is grammatically correct and stylistically superior.

28. By the early eleventh century, Muslim scientists <u>knowing the rich medical literature of ancient Greece, as well as</u> arithmetic and algebra.

    A. knowing the rich medical literature of ancient Greece, as well as
    B. knew the rich medical literature of ancient Greece, as well as
    C. know the rich medical literature of ancient Greece, as well as
    D. having learned the rich medical literature of ancient Greece, as well as
    E. having been given knowledge of the rich medical literature of ancient Greece, as well as

As it stands, this is a sentence fragment, with a participle ("knowing") but no main verb. Choice B supplies the missing verb. Choice C eliminates the sentence fragment, but uses the present tense where past tense is required. Choices D and E are just participles in a different tense. The correct *sentence correction* answer is **B**.

29. According to the police lieutenant's testimony as an expert witness, the assailant used a stack of discarded wooden crates to climb up to an open second floor window, <u>and thereby bypassing</u> the building's security system and gaining access to approximately two hundred thousand dollars in Persian rugs.

    A. and thereby bypassing
    B. by which he was bypassing
    C. bypassed
    D. by which he bypassed
    E. thereby bypassing

Choice A is wrong because the word "and" should not be included in this context. Eliminate Choice B because the verb "was bypassing" fails to convey that the testimony refers to a completed action in the past. Choice C is incorrect because the word "bypassed" fails to maintain parallel construction with the word "gaining." Choice D is wrong for the same reason. Choice E economically uses "thereby" to indicate causality and maintains parallel construction with the words "bypassing" and "gaining." The correct *sentence correction* answer is Choice **E**.

IX. Punctuation Errors

Look carefully at the punctuation in each sentence. Before you begin, make sure you know the proper way to use commas and semicolons. Comma errors are the most common type of punctuation error on the SAT.

Use commas

- In a series to separate words, phrases, or clauses: "Mark bought yellow, orange, and green flowers."
- To separate introductory words or phrases: "Yes, I can attend the basketball game."
- To set off nonrestrictive clauses: A nonrestrictive clause contains elements that are not essential to the basic meaning of the sentence. Commas are used to add a phrase (clause) to the sentence. In a way, the commas interrupt the sentence to add extra information. "In 2004, when Facebook was launched, college students were eager to become socially connected."
- To set off parenthetic phrases: A parenthetical phase is an expression that is not part of the main ideas of a sentence. Commas are used on both sides of the phrase to set it off from the sentence. "The invitation, you will be happy to know, is in the mail."
- To set off appositives: An appositive is a noun phrase that is set it off by commas on each side. "Kobe Bryant, the shooting guard for the L.A. Lakers, scored a three-point basket in the first minute of the playoffs."

Examples:

Directions: In questions 30–31, part or all of each sentence is underlined. Choice A repeats the underlined portion of the original sentence, while the next four choices offer alternatives. Choose the answer that best expresses the meaning of the original sentence and at the same time is grammatically correct and stylistically superior.

---

30. Each year about fifty thousand books are <u>published in Great Britain, that is as many as in</u> the four-times-larger United States.

   A.   published in Great Britain, that is as many as in

   B.   published in Great Britain; that is as many as in

   C.   published in Great Britain; as many as in

   D.   published in Great Britain; which is as many as in

   E.   published in Great Britain as many as in

The error in the original sentence is the comma splice—joining the two independent clauses (or complete sentences) with only a comma. Correct the error by using a period, a comma with a conjunction, or, as here, a semicolon. Although C and D use semicolons, they no longer have independent second clauses, while E, which has made the second clause dependent, omits the comma. The correct *sentence correction* answer is **B**.

---

31. George Eliot did not begin to write fiction until she was nearly <u>forty, this</u> late start accounts for the maturity of even her earliest works.

   A.   forty, this

   B.   forty this

   C.   forty, and this

   D.   forty, a

   E.   forty, such a

This is a comma splice. It can be corrected by changing the comma to a semicolon, or by adding a conjunction such as "and." The correct *sentence correction* answer is **C**.

Questions with No Error

About one in five questions on this portion of the exam will have no error.

Example:

Directions: Question 32 may contain an error of grammar. No sentence will contain more than one error, and some may have no error. A possible error will be underlined and have a letter beneath it. Choose the one underlined part that must be changed to correct the sentence. If there is no error, choose E.

---

32. The popularity <u>of many recent films</u> <u>is due</u> <u>not to their</u> sentiment or morality, <u>but to their</u> violence.
                    A   B   C   D

    <u>No error</u>.
     E

There is no error in this sentence. The singular "is" agrees with the singular "popularity," while the phrases "not to their" and "but to their" are correctly parallel. The correct answer for this *usage* type of problem is **E**.

> **TIP: In sentence correction types of problems, read the original sentence very carefully a couple of times. If you cannot spot an error, chances are that there might not be one. Don't be afraid to select Choice E, no error, if the sentence seems correct.**

Questions with More than One Error

Many of the sentence correction questions have several errors. The usual strategy in the answers is to give one choice that maintains both errors, and two others that correct only one of the two mistakes. Sometimes a choice will introduce a new kind of error. This type of problem is not as common, but be sure the answer you choose is grammatically correct and like the original in meaning.

Example

Directions: In question 33, part or all of each sentence is underlined. Choice A repeats the underlined portion of the original sentence, while the next four choices offer alternatives. Choose the answer that best expresses the meaning of the original sentence and at the same time is grammatically correct and stylistically superior.

---

33. The strike cannot be settled until the growers agree to improve healthcare benefits <u>and improving the workers' housing.</u>

    A. and improving the workers' housing.
    B. and improving worker housing as well.
    C. and to improve the workers' housing.
    D. and the workers' housing.
    E. and also to the improvement of the housing of the workers.

The phrases "to improve healthcare benefits" and "improving the workers' housing" are repetitive and not parallel. Choice B is wordy and not parallel. Choice C corrects the parallelism error but not the repetition. Choice E is wordy. Choice D is brief and grammatical. The correct *sentence correction* answer is **D**.

Approaches with Samples: Improving Paragraphs Question Type

The final multiple-choice writing question type (Type III) is improving paragraphs, also called *revision-in-context*. Carefully review this section and apply what you have learned from this section to also help you write, revise, and edit your SAT essay. The answers and explanations that follow each question include strategies to help you understand how to solve the problems.

Revising and Combining Sentences

About one-third or more of the questions may ask you to revise and combine sentences from a student writing sample. Although your revision choices will be influenced by the rest of the paragraph, you can practice this technique with two or three sentences that are not part of a paragraph or essay.

Choppy and Wordy Sentences

The SAT exam will ask you to review sentences that are grammatically correct but structurally incorrect. The organizational flow of structurally incorrect sentences is often choppy or wordy. In sentences that are choppy, you are expected to organize and simplify the sentences so that the reader will not be forced to stop and start when reading. In sentences that are wordy, you are expected to economize the writing and eliminate unnecessary words.

Sentence Structure Errors	
Error	**Example**
Choppy sentences are a series of very short sentences.	"Elizabeth is 20. She is getting married in June. She is designing a dress. It is white."
Wordy sentences use unnecessary words and phrases, and often include words that are redundant.	"Elizabeth is 20, and she is getting married in June, and she is designing a dress, and the dress is white."

A revised version of the structurally incorrect sentences illustrated above might read like this:

"Twenty year-old Elizabeth is designing a white dress for her June wedding."

Combining Sentences Using Coordinating and Subordinating Conjunctions

Another improving paragraphs question type will ask you to combine sentences using conjunctions. To combine sentences, you will need to balance and control the elements in each sentence using *coordinating and subordinating conjunctions*. To coordinate is to make equal; to subordinate is to place in a less important position.

The best way to tackle combining sentences is to first determine the author's points that are emphasized in each sentence. If two points are equally significant, use a *coordinating* conjunction that best expresses this relationship. If one thought is more important, use a *subordinate* conjunction. If you have not already done so in your English classes, practice different ways of combining sentences, especially sentences that seem awkward to you. It will help you with this type of question.

Coordinating Conjunctions that Express Equal Relationships		
and	for	so
but	nor	yet

Subordinating Conjunctions that Express Unequal Relationships		
after	despite	though
although	how	unless
as	if	yet
as . . . as	in order that	until
as if	provided that	when
as long as	since	whenever
as soon as	so . . . as	where
as though	so that	wherever
because	than	whereupon
before	that	while
		why

Sentence-combining questions appear in two types. In the first type, the end of one sentence and part of the beginning of the next sentence will be underlined. You will be asked to select the *best version* among five answer choices. In the second type, the question will ask for the best way to *revise and combine* two or three complete sentences from the passage.

Suggested Approaches with Samples

Following are two sets of improving paragraphs type questions, based on two separate passages from student essays.

Best-Version Questions

Questions 34–37 are based on the following passage.

(1) Is a man or a woman more likely to ask questions? (2) I think it depends on what the circumstances are and on who is around when a time to ask questions comes along. (3) In my family, my mother and I ask more questions than my brother or my father when all our family is together. (4) My father would never ask for directions when we're in the car, and this is when he is not sure of the way. (5) My mother would stop right away to ask, unless she was in an unsafe neighborhood.

(6) My brother tells me that he asks questions in school, and when he is at work after school, he doesn't. (7) It is because he thinks his boss will think he doesn't know his job. (8) He won't ask any questions at all. (9) At work he will ask questions only to his friend, Eddie. (10) Based on my brother and my father, men are more likely to not ask when they don't know something because they think it will hurt their image as able to do things well. (11) Women are more practical and will not drive around not knowing where you are.

---

34. Which of the following is the best version of the underlined portion of sentence 2 (*reproduced below*)?

I think it depends <u>on what the circumstances are and on who is around when a time to ask questions comes along.</u>

- **A.** Leave it as it is.
- **B.** on the circumstances.
- **C.** on what the circumstances are and who is around at the time.
- **D.** on the circumstances and who is around when a time to ask questions comes along,
- **E.** on what the circumstances and the situation are for asking questions.

Since the word "circumstances" really includes "who is around" or "situation," there is no need to say more than what is said in B. All of the other choices are, by comparison, wordy. The correct answer is **B**.

35. Which of the following is the best version of the underlined portion of sentence 4 (*reproduced below*)?

My father would never ask for directions when we're in the car, and this is when he is not sure *of the way.*

- **A.**   Leave it as it is.
- **B.**   car, and at a time when he is not sure
- **C.**   car, even if he is not sure
- **D.**   car, when he may not be sure
- **E.**   car, because he is not sure

This section of the exam is likely to ask a question that depends on the careful choice of the right conjunctions. Here, the use of "even if" is concise and clearly expresses the best conjunction for this sentence. The correct answer is **C.**

Phrases that Follow a Sentence

36. Which of the following phrases should follow, "Based on my brother and my father" in sentence 10?

- **A.**   Leave it as it is.
- **B.**   it is more likely that men
- **C.**   my opinion is that men are more likely
- **D.**   men, unlike women are more likely
- **E.**   men are probably more likely

The problem in this sentence is that the opening phrase is a dangling modifier unless it is followed by something that is "based on. . . ." The writer's opinion, not men, is based on her father and brother. The correct answer is **C.**

Techniques Used by the Writer

37. The writer of this passage uses all of the following EXCEPT

- **A.**   development of a contrast.
- **B.**   employment of specific examples.
- **C.**   chronological organization.
- **D.**   raising and answering a question.
- **E.**   reference to personal opinions.

The writer contrasts men and women, using examples from her family. The passage opens with a question that the rest of the two paragraphs attempts to answer. Sentence 10, for example, is a personal opinion. The passage does not use chronological organization. The correct answer is **C.**

Revising and Combining Sentences

Questions 38–40 are based on the following passage.

(1) Many people think that they have insomnia. (2) If they haven't had eight hours of sleep, they think they have insomnia. (3) There is no evidence to support the common belief that you have to have eight hours of sleep every night. (4) Some people sleep as little as two hours a night. (5) They wake up the next morning, and they feel fine. (6) Some people need only five hours of sleep. (7) Some people must have more than eight hours of sleep to feel refreshed. (8) It is harder to keep track of time in a dark room than in the daylight. (9) It is easy to overestimate how long you have been awake, or underestimate how long you have been asleep.

38. Which of the following is the best way to combine sentences 1 and 2 (reproduced below)?

Many people think that they have insomnia. If they haven't had eight hours of sleep, they think they have insomnia.

A. Many people think that they have insomnia; if they haven't had eight hours of sleep, they think they have insomnia.

B. If they haven't had eight hours of sleep, there are many people who think they have insomnia.

C. Many people haven't had eight hours sleep, and they think they have insomnia.

D. Many people, when they haven't had eight hours sleep, think they have insomnia.

E. Many people who haven't had eight hours of sleep are the ones who think they have insomnia.

When combining sentences, try to consolidate words that are repeated once or twice. Here, the redundant phrase is "they think that they have insomnia." Choice B adds the unneeded "there are," and uses "they" twice. Choice C uses "they" twice, and Choice E adds the wordy "are the ones who." The correct answer is **D.**

39. All of the following pairs of sentences would probably be improved by being combined EXCEPT

A. 1 and 2.

B. 2 and 3.

C. 4 and 5.

D. 6 and 7.

E. 8 and 9.

All of these pairs could be combined except sentences 2 and 3. The correct answer is **B.**

Replacing Sentences

40. Which of the following would be the best replacement for sentences 8 and 9 (reproduced below) to make the conclusion of the paragraph more coherent?

It is harder to keep track of time in a dark room than in the daylight. It is easy to overestimate how long you have been awake or underestimate how long you have been asleep.

A. Because the number of hours asleep is difficult to estimate, many people have slept more than they think, and do not really need more.

B. It is harder to keep track of time in a dark room than in the daylight; it is easy to overestimate how long you have been awake or underestimate how long you have been asleep.

C. Because it is hard to keep track of time in the dark, people cannot really tell how long they have been asleep.

D. Insomniacs cannot really tell how long they have slept.

E. Insomniacs are more likely to overestimate their sleeplessness than to underestimate it.

The paragraph has moved from the varied number of hours of sleep people require to a slightly different topic: the difficulty of determining how long a person has slept. Choices A, D, and E add new information that is not included in the original sentences. Choice B is as wordy and rambling as the original. Choice C is at least more concise and attempts to relate the idea to the difficulty of deciding what insomnia is—the concept underlying the paragraph. The correct answer is **C.**

Essay Writing Section

The essay writing section of the SAT requires every student to compose an original essay on an assigned topic. Our study guide will lead you through the process of developing your ideas to produce an effective essay and to help you learn skills that will improve your essay score.

The essay section can be intimidating for some students, but remember that the essay is just a portion of the entire test. You will probably be applying to several colleges simultaneously, and the essay assignment can reveal how well you write and think under time constraints. Even if your intended college does not give the same weighted value to the essay portion as it does to the multiple-choice portion of the SAT, colleges will be able to view a copy of your essay if they desire. It will benefit you to try to achieve your best-possible results by following the guidelines in this section.

Although there are some people who appear to be natural-born writers, writing skills and concepts can be learned by anyone. Remember that you have already been writing many essays and research papers for your high school classes, and now you will have an additional edge by reviewing and practicing the writing process steps in this section. Your ability to communicate and support your thoughts and ideas in writing in a clear and concise manner will help you with this section of the test, and it will also help you with the multiple-choice writing portion of the exam.

Skills and Concepts Tested

The essay section of the exam tests your ability to carefully read a topic prompt, organize your ideas before you write, and write a clear, well-written essay. Good high school-level writing, reading, and reasoning skills will help you with this portion of the test.

To demonstrate the basic skills necessary to score well on this component of the SAT, your essay must

- Express your ideas clearly
- Be organized into a logical sequence of events
- Use the conventions of English grammar
- Show unity and coherence from paragraph to paragraph
- Provide supporting examples and details

Directions

The essay assignment will be the first section of the test. You will have 25 minutes to plan and write an essay on an assigned topic. The topic prompt will be a short paragraph that features either a single quote or a pair of quotes about an issue. You are asked to discuss this issue and support your ideas with examples from your reading, personal experiences, or observations. *Do not write on another topic* because an essay on another topic will not be scored.

The essay is intended to give you an opportunity to demonstrate your writing skills. Be sure to express your ideas on the topic clearly and effectively. The quality of your writing is much more important than the quantity, but to cover the topic adequately, you may want to write three to five paragraphs. Be specific.

Your essay must be written in *pencil on the two lined pages provided*. You will not be given any additional paper. If you keep your handwriting to a reasonable size, write on every line, and avoid wide margins, you should have enough space to complete your essay.

Scoring

Know your audience. Your essay will be scored by experienced and trained high school and college teachers who teach English, writing, or language arts courses. Two teachers will score your essay on a scale of 1 to 6 (6 is the highest score). The two readers will not know each other's scores. If their scores are more than two points apart, your essay will be scored by a third reader. The combined essay score of 2 to 12 will be scaled and factored in with the writing multiple-choice sections to give an overall writing skills score that ranges from 200 to 800.

Rubric for Analyzing Scores
Score of 6: Convincing and Persuasive Convincing and persuasive essays have only minor errors and are characterized by the following: ❑ Effective and insightful coverage of the tasks required by the exam question ❑ Good organization and development, with relevant supporting details ❑ Command of standard written English, with a range of vocabulary and sentence variety
Score of 5: Thoughtful and Well-Developed Thoughtful and well-developed essays have occasional errors or lapses in quality and are characterized by the following: ❑ Effective coverage of the tasks required by the exam question ❑ Generally good organization and development, with some supporting details ❑ Good handling of standard written English, with some range of vocabulary and sentence variety
Score of 4: Competent Competent essays have occasional errors or lapses in quality and are characterized by the following: ❑ Coverage of the tasks required by the exam question ❑ Adequate organization and development, with some supporting details ❑ Adequate handling of standard written English, but with minimal variety and some grammar or diction errors
Score of 3: Marginally Adequate Marginally adequate papers are characterized by the following: ❑ Failure to fully cover required tasks ❑ Weak organization and/or development ❑ Failure to use relevant supporting detail ❑ Several errors of grammar, diction, and sentence structure
Score of 2: Inadequate Inadequate papers are characterized by the following: ❑ Failure to cover the assignment ❑ Poor organization and development ❑ Lack of supporting detail ❑ Frequent errors of grammar, diction, and sentence structure
Score of 1: Severely Flawed Severely flawed papers are characterized by the following: ❑ Failure to cover the assignment ❑ Very poor organization and development ❑ Errors of grammar, diction, and sentence structure so frequent as to interfere with meaning ❑ Extreme brevity or shortness

Rhetorical versus Conventional English

Essays are scored holistically. This means that *all aspects* of a well-written essay count toward your final score: well-developed ideas, good organization, supporting evidence, and an effective use of grammar and language. The impression that your essay makes upon the readers is important, but keep in mind that the readers who score your essay are on your side. The readers make every effort to focus on your writing strengths. Because of the limited time that is allotted for you to write your essay (25 minutes), scorers take into consideration that even the highest-scoring essay may contain minor errors of grammar or word mechanics. Your final score is mostly based on rhetorical English (what you say and how you say it) and not on conventional English (spelling and punctuation). Remember that your essay is technically a "first draft" and will probably not be errorless, even with a score of 6.

These scoring allowances do not mean you should ignore the rules of standard written English in the finished essay, but remember that they are not as important to your overall score as your ideas and how you have organized them. Essays are expected to be superior in content, organization, and development.

Essay Writing Tips and Strategies

- **Stay focused on the assignment.** There is an old Buddhist saying, "The answer is contained in the question." This is important to remember when taking a standardized test like the SAT. One of the primary reasons students do not perform well on the essay section is that they do not stay focused on the topic and do not respond to the complete assigned task. There is always something in the question that helps to guide your response. Answering each part of the assignment is crucial to providing a complete essay response. A recent question on the SAT asked, "Should sports programs be eliminated from schools because they waste valuable educational funding?" Although many student responses addressed the idea of sports programs being eliminated (or not), few students addressed the funding aspect of the question.

  Because time management is critical to your success on the SAT, the hurried test-taker frequently will read the topic and merely scan the assignment. Too often students neglect to complete all parts of the assignment and their scores are adversely affected as a result. To help you stay focused, circle or underline key words and phrases as you develop your ideas.

  The example below highlights important points in the assigned task. Notice that the assignment requires that you state your position, "Do you agree . . . for or against having a job while in school?" In addition, the assignment requires that you provide specific examples from "reading, personal experiences, or observation." Again, remember to circle or underline key words to keep you focused on the assigned task. (In this example, we have done that for you.)

  > "<u>Work experience is the best teacher</u>," say many sociologists. With this in mind, <u>some parents encourage</u> their high school–aged children to get an after-school or weekend <u>job</u>. <u>Other parents</u> cite the importance of getting good grades and <u>discourage</u> their high school–aged children from getting an after-school or weekend job.
  >
  > **Assignment:** <u>Do you agree</u> with the parents who are <u>for or against</u> having a job while in school? <u>Using an example</u> or examples from your <u>reading, personal experiences, or observations</u>, write an essay to support your position.

- **Write notes in the space provided.** You have 25 minutes to plan and write an essay on one assigned topic. Use the space provided for writing notes to help you organize your thoughts. (These notes will not be read or scored by the people scoring your essay.)

- **Read the paraphrase of the topic.** Some assignments will include a "gloss" or quick paraphrase of the topic's main idea. This "gloss" is meant to assist you if you are not familiar with the quote or topic.

- **Use your time wisely.** Take about 5 or 6 minutes to prewrite and organize your thoughts. Take about 16 to 18 minutes to write your essay and about 3 or 4 minutes to proofread your essay.

- **Write three to five paragraphs.** The general instructions include a sentence that suggests that "you may want to write more than one paragraph." This remark is a polite way of saying if you expect to score well, you *had better* write more than one paragraph. Very short essays usually receive very low scores. Aim for a minimum of three paragraphs.

- **Be specific.** Your readers are looking for specific details, in other words, for concrete evidence of some kind to support your points.

- **Make sure your writing is legible and neat.** Also don't use excessively large writing, don't leave wide margins, and don't skip any lines.

- **Avoid jargon, clichés, and slang.** Traditional, more formal writing is preferred.

- **Carefully consider your voice.** Although personal observation and opinion is acceptable on your essay to develop your point of view, a general rule is to avoid using "I" unless the assignment specifically asks your opinion to support your ideas.

Now that we have covered tips and strategies, let's examine a few approaches to writing a timed essay. The following section will review the three-step writing process, how to develop a five-paragraph essay, how to write a four-paragraph essay, and will provide you with a few sample essays.

The Three-Step Writing Process

For any timed writing task, you should take three steps that lead to the finished product: *prewriting, writing, and proofreading.* One of the biggest mistakes a student can make is beginning to write an essay without first taking the time to plan it. Prewriting is when you plan your essay. The step after this, writing, is simply arranging it in the proper format. It is important to take a few minutes to organize your ideas before you begin to write your essay, and to save a few minutes at the end to proofread your work.

There are a number of strategies you can use to write a successful essay, but if you are able to understand the stages of the writing process, you will gain control over any writing method you select. The step-by-step guidelines that follow will help you plan and compose a well-written essay. As you practice the steps of the writing process, make a note about which strategies work best for you and use them to develop your own preferred writing style.

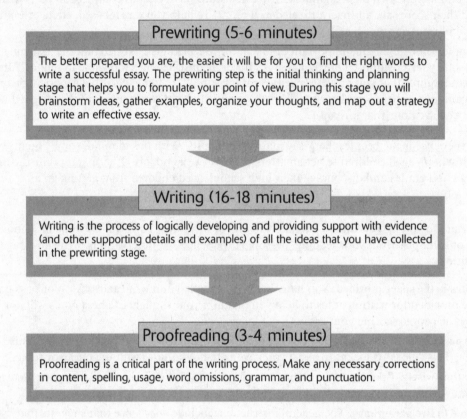

Prewriting (5-6 minutes)

The better prepared you are, the easier it will be for you to find the right words to write a successful essay. The prewriting step is the initial thinking and planning stage that helps you to formulate your point of view. During this stage you will brainstorm ideas, gather examples, organize your thoughts, and map out a strategy to write an effective essay.

Writing (16-18 minutes)

Writing is the process of logically developing and providing support with evidence (and other supporting details and examples) of all the ideas that you have collected in the prewriting stage.

Proofreading (3-4 minutes)

Proofreading is a critical part of the writing process. Make any necessary corrections in content, spelling, usage, word omissions, grammar, and punctuation.

Prewriting

Many students believe that good writers just sit down and miraculously produce an essay. On the contrary, most experienced writers know that effective writing requires an organization and planning process. The prewriting process helps you gather information and ideas as you prepare to write a well-written essay.

Before you begin prewriting, read the topic and the assignment very carefully and circle or underline key words to help you focus on the assigned task. Then reread the assignment. If there are several tasks given, number them or write them down. Let the nature of the assignment determine the structure of your essay.

Developing and organizing information on short notice can be difficult, unless you are ready with an effective technique. Take some time to organize your thoughts on paper before you write your essay by using the following basic prewriting techniques of *brainstorming, clustering,* or *outlining.*

Brainstorming

The technique of creating and accumulating ideas and examples is called *brainstorming*. Brainstorming is an exploration process that allows you to imagine and generate ideas about your topic. Your "imaginings" will help you to compile words and phrases about the essay topic by simply jotting down as many thoughts, ideas, and possibilities as you can remember, invent, or otherwise bring to mind to address the topic. It is important to remember that *all ideas are acceptable* during the brainstorming process and that neatness, order, and spelling do not matter at this point.

After generating as many ideas or examples as you can, evaluate and organize your notes by looking for patterns or themes so you can group your ideas into categories. For example, in the topic, "Work experience is the best teacher," you might have brainstormed the following points:

- increased learning
- skill building
- teaches responsibility

Each one of these three points might be considered a benefit of work experience. Then you might also brainstorm the academic sacrifices of work experience. Grouping together and categorizing your main points can help you develop a strong, coherent essay.

Decide which examples best support your points. Cross out those you do not wish to use, and number those in the order in which you want to address them in your essay response. Add any notes regarding more specific details or new thoughts that come to mind. However, do not worry about developing everything because you will be the only one using these notes. Your time will be better spent developing your chosen points in the actual writing of your essay and not in your notes.

Remember, too, that you can change the order of your main points later. In the brainstorming stage, it is important to just consider each idea and how it might support the central purpose of your essay.

Clustering

Clustering is another prewriting strategy you might use to help you visually organize your thoughts before you write. Clustering begins with a key word related to the topic. Ideas are then *clustered* around the key word and then numbered in the order you will present them. Clustering gives you a way to put all your ideas down on paper before you write, so that you can quickly visualize how they will support your assigned writing task. You do not have to use all of the ideas in your cluster; just cross out any you decide not to use.

It is often helpful to create new clusters from one of the ideas of your original cluster. The connecting ideas in the new clusters are thoughts and ideas that will be written in supporting sentences. They will reveal an important relationship with the original core idea.

As an example, let's again use the topic, "Work experience is the best teacher," to demonstrate clustering.

"Work experience is the best teacher," say many sociologists. With this in mind, some parents encourage their high school–aged children to get an after-school or weekend job. Other parents cite the importance of getting good grades and discourage their high school–aged children from getting an after-school or weekend job.

Assignment: Do you agree with the parents who are for or against having a job while in school? Using an example or examples from your reading, personal experiences, or observations, write an essay to support your position.

After you choose a topic or main idea, start by writing it down and then draw a circle around that topic.

For a few moments, think of all of the elements that the topic brings to mind and connect them to the central topic cluster. Remember that related ideas are written in groups, and their circles are connected to the main ideas with lines. A sample cluster might look like this.

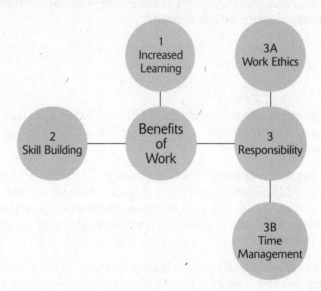

Outlining

Outlining is a traditional form of prewriting that you can use to organize your ideas. Use a simple, informal outline that clearly arranges each main idea and connects supporting details in the form of phrases. Your outline is meant to help you organize your thoughts in a pattern and should be kept simple so you can use it to save time when you write your essay.

Introduction or Main idea/Thesis (1 paragraph)

    Working is beneficial to enhance education

        Learning skills

        Helps to build skills

        Teaches responsibility

Body or Discussion (3 paragraphs)

    Provides increased opportunities for learning skills

    Helps to build real-world skills, abilities, and experiences

    Teaches students responsibility (work ethic and time management)

Conclusion or Summary (1 paragraph)

    Working depends on the student

    Students can gain from their learning experiences

    A universal truth

Notice that this outline is informal but the basic parts—*introduction, body,* and *conclusion*—help you focus and organize your response.

Writing a Five-Paragraph Essay

The five-paragraph essay model is the suggested example to follow when writing your essay. The exception to this rule is if you are presented with a compare-and-contrast topic. Information and a description of the four-paragraph essay model follows this section on page 123.

When writing an essay, it is important to remember to weave the main or unifying idea, or purpose, throughout your essay. Sometimes it is helpful to visualize colors as representing ideas. So for example, if the unifying idea or purpose is a color, say the color black, you might weave or connect the color black into each paragraph as you continue to make the main point of your essay. The table below should help you visualize the organization of a five-paragraph essay.

Five-Paragraph Essay					
Paragraph 1 **Introduction**	**Black** Main idea or purpose (preview)	**Green** Supporting point/details #1 (preview)	**Red** Supporting points/details #2 (preview)	**Blue** Supporting points/details #3 (preview)	**Black** Connect ideas back to the main idea/purpose
Paragraph 2 **Body** Supporting point #1	**Green** Supporting point #1	**Green** Supporting point #1	**Green** Supporting point #1	**Green** Supporting point #1	**Black** Connect ideas back to the main idea/purpose
Paragraph 3 **Body** Supporting point #2	**Red** Supporting point #2	**Red** Supporting point #2	**Red** Supporting point #2	**Red** Supporting point #2	**Black** Connect ideas back to the main idea/purpose
Paragraph 4 **Body** Supporting point #3	**Blue** Supporting point #3	**Blue** Supporting point #3	**Blue** Supporting point #3	**Blue** Supporting point #3	**Black** Connect ideas back to the main ideas/ purpose
Paragraph 5 **Conclusion**	**Black** Main idea or purpose (restate)	**Green** Supporting point/details #1 (restate)	**Red** Supporting point/details #2 (restate)	**Blue** Supporting point/details #3 (restate)	**Black** Connect ideas back to the main idea/purpose

Paragraph One: Introduction

A strong opening paragraph is critical to an effective essay and previews what readers can expect to read about in the entire essay. The purpose of the introduction is to grab hold of the reader's attention while you provide a brief preview of the main points to be discussed in the body of the essay. This is the "hook" that catches the reader's interest in your topic. The first sentence provides a general overview of the assigned topic; the second, third, and fourth sentences focus on what you have chosen to discuss; and the last sentence provides the particulars about the points you intend to develop in your essay. Try to avoid a long introduction and try to keep it about the same length as the conclusion.

Paragraphs Two, Three, and Four: Body

The body provides detailed support of the information presented in your introduction. You should spend more time on the body than on your introduction and conclusion, but keep your writing concise and to the point. In describing a rainstorm, William Faulkner would spend pages and pages providing dozens of details. Ernest Hemingway, on the other hand, just wrote, "It rained." Both are legitimate styles of writing, but on the SAT, it is important to find a middle ground and provide a few supporting details or examples.

Each paragraph begins with a unifying sentence, and then provides supporting evidence with specific examples from your reading, life experience, or observations. Each paragraph elaborates on and provides examples or details of the main points mentioned briefly in paragraph one. In a standard five-paragraph essay, you might consider organizing the body paragraphs as follows to help you avoid ending with the weakest point:

- Paragraph two: most important point or argument
- Paragraph three: third most important point or argument
- Paragraph four: second most important point or argument

Adding some heart and soul to your writing by providing relevant personal experiences or connections can also add a human and personal quality to your essay. It would be appropriate to add this personal touch in the fourth paragraph, just before the conclusion, as the second most important detail. Regardless of what you write, keep your writing concise and to the point.

Students will sometimes digress from their original outline when adding a more personal emotional experience to their essay, so remember to stay focused on your intended topic and to keep it concise.

As you transition from one thought to another, use transition words that signal or show the relationships between ideas and bridge the paragraphs. In particular, use them between paragraphs three and four, and four and five. This is not difficult to accomplish, and good transitions can make a big difference in the way your essay reads. Sequence cues such as "although," "first," "second," "however," "next," "finally," "initially," "since," "subsequently," "therefore," "thus," and "ultimately" help you clarify the hierarchy of the points being made and assist the reader in having a clear understanding of what is being said.

Some examples of transition words and phrases are

- to add ideas: *furthermore, in addition*
- to illustrate or demonstrate: *for example, in other words*
- to show cause and effect: *consequently, instead, regardless, therefore*
- to show contrast, change, opposition, negation, limitation: *conversely, however, on the other hand*
- to emphasize a point: *above all, without a doubt*
- to show order: *first, second, third, next, in conclusion*
- to summarize: *in short, for these reasons*
- to show relationships in time: *before, previously, subsequently, then*

Paragraph Five: Conclusion

Your conclusion should be approximately the same length as your introduction and should summarize the main points from your introduction. The fifth paragraph repeats the three points (in the same order) that were presented in paragraph one. If you follow this order, you will be adding a sense of continuity and structural integrity to your writing. This is the time to briefly clarify any points presented that may need further illumination.

Some readers comment that essays can "start out strong but end up weak." Don't let this happen to you. Be sure to emphasize the importance of the topic in your final paragraph. This is the section where you can add a *universal truth* (search the internet for universal truth topics of interest). Remember that you must allow enough time to prepare and write your conclusion, and keep in mind that you should leave at least 3 to 4 minutes at the end to proofread your essay.

Writing a Four-Paragraph Essay

The four-paragraph essay is an acceptable alternative to the five-paragraph essay and is particularly useful when responding to topics that ask you to make comparisons, as indicated by phrases such as "compare and contrast," "cause and effect," or "pro or con." Notice that these prompts might contain such key words as "and," or "or" in them. If you read an assignment that prompts you to address a topic that includes the word "and," the word "and" should be viewed as a clear signal to you that you must present an essay that addresses both sides of an issue. If you read an assignment that prompts you to address a topic that denotes "or," the word "or" should be viewed as a clear signal to you that you should present only one side of the issue or perspective. If the directions do not ask you to provide a position on two sides of an issue, do not write about both positions. Your essay will actually be scored lower, not higher, if you do not follow the directions. Remember to focus on the assignment.

Follow the format below when writing a four-paragraph essay. Notice that you will write about divergent ideas in two separate paragraphs.

- Paragraph one: introduction
- Paragraph two: body (first position on topic/issue)
- Paragraph three: body (second position on topic/issue)
- Paragraph four: conclusion

Proofreading

You should use the last 3 to 4 minutes to read over your essay and correct errors. If you detect an error, either erase it or simply line it out carefully and insert the correction neatly. Keep in mind, both while you are writing and while you are correcting, that your handwriting must be legible. Pay special attention to words you have left out. Watch the clock! Once the 25-minute time is called, you will be unable to make any more changes.

Practice with a Sample Topic and Essays

Now let's take a close look at a sample topic and two sample essays.

Directions: Read the following paragraph and assignment carefully. Then prepare and write a persuasive essay. Be sure to support your reasons with specific examples that will make your essay more effective.

Assignment: Do you agree with parents who are for or against their children having a job while in school? Using an example or examples from your reading, personal experiences, or observations, write an essay to support your position.

Two Well-Written Essays (with Comments)

The essays on pages 124 and 125 were written by students. The papers are reproduced exactly as they were written, so they contain some mechanical errors and some general writing mistakes. The students wrote the essays in the allotted 25 minutes.

Essay 1

Title: The Benefits of Students Working

This is a good first paragraph. It clearly states the writer's position, and by suggesting that work can develop nonacademic skills, it prepares for the arguments of the next three paragraphs.

Note how the repetition of the word "skills" links the second paragraph with the first.

Paragraph three moves on to another advantage (development of a work ethic). The second sentence explains fully what the writer understands a "work ethic" to be.

The last paragraph is the weakest paragraph of this essay. The writer has argued forcefully in favor of after-school work. There is no reason to weaken the argument with the trite suggestion that it will depend on the individual. What doesn't? In an argument essay like this, it is not necessary (and is usually a waste of time) to pay lip service to the opposing point of view.

There is a great deal of controversy among parents as to whether or not their children should hold a paying job while in high school. Some parents believe that working while in school is a valuable experience; others believe that the importance of good grades **superceeds** any value that a job might offer. **I think that working while in school can be very beneficial to students and provide them with skills that might enhance their "formal" education.**

One of the **skills** is time management. Learning how to balance your activities and obligations is essential as an adult. It is invaluable to know what you can handle and when you are taking on too much. **When I got a job in high school, I began to realize the importance of using my time wisely since I had less of it to throw around.** I think that I gained a lot from having to make those decisions as well as earning my own money.

Another benefit is that students can **develop a work ethic** which can be applied to their academic schooling or any task that they choose to take on. **Understanding the importance of working hard, doing a good job and being responsible are skills that are assets to any endeavor.** Students often develop **confidence** from being counted on to get something done and then rising to that challenge. **Additionally, learning to take pride in your work is really important.** When you care about something your performance often reflects that. Academic success largely depends upon this same kind of pride and confidence.

Ultimately, I believe that whether a child should work while in school **depends on the child.** Some children feel that they can't handle the responsibility while others are willing to try. I think **that students stand to gain a lot from working**, but should be able to **make that choice for themselves** in the end.

A well-chosen word, but misspelled. It should be "supersede."

The writer supports her argument (that part-time work develops the ability to manage time efficiently) by referring to personal experience.

The move to a second point in this paragraph (increased confidence) would be clearer with the addition of a transitional word or phrase (such as "Further" or "Also") to begin the sentence. But, the writer rightly does include a transitional word ("Additionally") at the beginning of the next sentence.

Aside from the last paragraph, this is a very good essay, well-organized, well-supported, and specific. Its word choice, syntax, and mechanics are all thoughtful and well-developed.

Essay 2

Title: Life is Not all Study

Introduction is focused and states position *clearly* and *immediately.*

Some parents want their high school aged children to work part-time, while other parents prefer their children not to work and instead concentrate on studies. **I agree with the parents who want their children to get good grades, although I believe that after school work, sports or other activities are helpful in establishing good study habits** and creating a well-rounded, successful student.

Notice how the paragraph uses words from the counter-argument, "good grades," to support the position that part-time jobs are good because they lead to good grades.

The second paragraph supports the main position of the introduction—again supports the position that jobs can lead to good grades.

Life is not all study any more than it is all play. Students need to learn how to manage their time. They need to learn the organizational skills necessary to do a lot of different tasks in a timely manner. Work, sports, and other activities are necessary to provide a break from continual studying. **They also provide experiences that are essential to education and can lead to understanding and, therefore, better grades.**

Since my older brother was responsible for paying for his own college education, it was necessary for him to work part-time throughout his college years. He had to organize his work hours around class and study hours, so he found **a job in a grocery store** as this gave him the greatest flexibility. He organized his time and was able to work and keep up his grades.

The third paragraph gives supporting details from *experience* as asked for — personal experience *supports* the *position.*

The fourth paragraph shows that not working in part-time jobs doesn't mean that good grades will necessarily follow. Notice the supporting example from the experience and observation of the writer.

He told me that many of his college classmates came from wealthier backgrounds. **They didn't have to work and were able to concentrate full-time on their studies and their grades.** A lot of these kids took study breaks for coffee or beers or just chatting, and didn't organize their time well. **Some did quite poorly in school even though their parents did all they could to help them focus on grades.**

The conclusion:
• again restates the essay topic;
• uses support from observations to again support the original restated position.

From my own observations and experience **I do not feel that after-school or weekend jobs hinder a student from getting good grades.** I feel that these activities can be more helpful than harmful by providing the student with the opportunity to organize their life activities. Whether in high school or in college **a student should be encouraged to engage in many activities and to organize their time so they can succeed in all they do. I plan to get a part-time job during my senior year in high school.**

TIP: Since the question is "what is your opinion," it is quite permissible to write in the first person, "I," and give your opinion without saying "in my opinion" or "I believe" or "my viewpoint is." Be personal and invent supporting examples!

Practice Writing Exercises

Use the strategies and techniques presented on the previous pages to develop and write practice essays. Below the topic is an analysis sheet to help you evaluate your essay.

Topic

Directions: Read the following quotation and assignment carefully. Then prepare and write an essay about the issue presented.

"Genius is one percent inspiration and ninety-nine percent perspiration."—Thomas Edison

Assignment: Edison suggests that the major contributing factor to genius is hard work, as opposed to thoughts and ideas. Do you agree or disagree with Edison? Using an example or examples from your reading or your personal observation, write an essay to support your position.

When you practice, use the following checklist to evaluate your essay on topic two.

Evaluating Your Essay			
Questions	Excellent	Average	Weak
1. Does the essay focus on the topic and complete the assigned task?			
2. Is the essay well organized, well developed, and consistent?			
3. Does the essay provide specific supporting details and examples?			
4. Does the essay use correct grammar, usage, punctuation, and spelling?			
5. Is the handwriting legible?			

Sample Topics for Extra Practice

Here are a few other sample essay topics.

1. If someone wise gave you advice, what would it be?
2. Are we living in the best or the worst of times?
3. How does technology make people happy?
4. Is it ever necessary to be impolite?
5. Discuss a book or movie that changed your point of view.
6. What would be an important value to instill in today's youth?
7. Write a letter about a social issue.
8. To what extent is violence the responsibility of the school?
9. How can we learn from history?
10. How do friends affect your point of view?

Chapter 4

Mathematics Overview

The mathematics section of the SAT is designed to test your ability to *reason* and *think critically* about arithmetic, algebra, geometry, and data analysis. This chapter introduces these math topics and presents strategies with practice questions to help you understand how to solve problems. Use the strategies suggested in this chapter as you work through each of the subsequent topic areas— Chapter 5, "Arithmetic," Chapter 6, "Algebra and Functions," Chapter 7, "Geometry and Measurement," and Chapter 8, "Data Analysis, Statistics, and Probability"—and try to focus your attention on one math chapter at a time. After you have thoroughly reviewed the skills and concepts in each chapter, you will be ready to sharpen your skills by actively working through the four full-length practice tests in this study guide and the three additional tests in the accompanying CD-ROM.

SAT Math Skills and Concepts You Should Know			
Chapter 5 **Arithmetic: Number and Operations Review**	**Chapter 6** **Algebra and Functions Review**	**Chapter 7** **Geometry and Measurement Review**	**Chapter 8** **Data Analysis, Statistics, and Probability Review**
• Number properties: positive and negative integers, odd and even numbers, prime numbers • Applying rules of addition, subtraction, multiplication, and division • Operations with fractions and decimals • Ratios, proportions, percents • Square roots and cube roots • Measurement	• Set theory (union, intersection, elements) • Working with algebraic expressions • Exponents and basic factoring • Solving equations and inequalities • Solving quadratic equations • Rational/fractional equations • Radicals and roots • Direct and inverse variations • Coordinate (analytic) geometry: two-dimension coordinate system—midpoint formula, distance formula • Linear graphs: slope and intercept • Function notation and evaluation	• Geometry terms: point, line, ray, line segment, plane • Angles in figures (polygons) • Triangles: right, isosceles, equilateral, angle measure • Pythagorean Theorem • Special triangles 30°–60°–90°, 45°–45°–90° • Quadrilaterals: trapezoid, parallelogram, rectangle, rhombus, square • Circles: radius, diameter, circumference, area • Volume and surface area of solids	• Basic statistics: mean, median, mode • Factorials, combinations, permutations • Probability • Data interpretation: tables, graphs, charts

Introduction to the Mathematics Section

The mathematics section of the SAT consists of two basic types of questions: *multiple-choice questions* and *student-produced responses* (called *grid-ins*).

The SAT has a total of three math sections (two are 25 minutes long and one is 20 minutes long). There may also be one additional 25-minute experimental math section. The math section has approximately 54 questions that will count toward your score and will generate a scaled math score that ranges from 200 to 800. If you answer approximately 50% of the questions correctly, you should achieve an average SAT score.

- 44 multiple-choice questions
- 10 student-produced response questions (grid-ins)

Questions increase in their level of difficulty within each math section. The easiest questions are at the beginning and the more difficult questions appear toward the end of each section. If a section has two types of questions, usually both types start with easier problems. For example, a section may start with easy multiple-choice questions. The last few multiple-choice questions will be more difficult before you start the grid-ins. The grid-in questions start easy and then gradually become more difficult toward the end of the section.

Skills and Concepts Tested

SAT math questions test your ability to use math insight, simple calculations, or common sense to solve math problems. The basic skills necessary to do well on this section include concepts from high school math classes through second-year algebra and formal geometry. Multiple-choice questions include arithmetic, algebra, geometry, basic statistical concepts, data interpretation, and word problems using problem-solving insight and logic. There are no concepts tested from trigonometry, calculus, or other higher-level mathematics courses.

Using Your Calculator

The SAT allows you to use *approved calculators*, and the College Board recommends that each test-taker bring a calculator to the test. Even though no question will require the use of a calculator (each question can be answered without a calculator), in some instances using a calculator will save you valuable time.

Take advantage of using your personal calculator on the test. With repeated practice, you can learn to use the calculator with greater efficiency. Try not to become too dependent on your calculator, and keep in mind that a calculator will not solve the problem for you. *You must have a basic understanding of the problem first,* before you decide whether you should use your calculator. As you approach a problem, first focus on how to solve that problem and then decide whether the calculator will be helpful. If you use your calculator on every problem, you will use too much time and never finish the test.

You should

- Visit the College Board website for updated information about *approved calculators* sat.collegeboard.com/register/sat-test-day-checklist.
- Make sure you know which calculators are *not approved.* Calculators that have QWERTY keypads (TI-92 Plus or Voyage 200), cell phones, electronic writing pads, iPads, and any other laptop computers are not allowed.
- Make sure you bring a calculator that doesn't make noise or have a paper tape.
- Bring your own calculator on the day of the test because you can't borrow or share one during the exam.
- Bring a calculator on the day of the test even if you don't think you will use it.
- Make sure you are familiar with how the calculator operates. Don't bring a calculator you are not familiar with, and don't buy an advanced calculator for the test.
- Make sure your calculator has new, fresh batteries and is in good working order. Don't bring a calculator that requires an outlet or any other external power source.
- Before doing an operation, check the number that you keyed in on the display to make sure you keyed in the right number. You may want to check each number as you key it in.
- Practice using your calculator on the problems in this study guide to determine the types of problems that require electronic calculations. *Only use your calculator if it is time-effective.*

Mathematics General Directions

Study the following directions *before* the day of your test to save you valuable testing time. As you become more familiar with the instructions, you'll only need to scan the written directions to confirm that no changes have been made to the instructions.

Directions: For each question, indicate the best answer, using the following notes.

- Read the directions for each question type carefully.
- All numerical values used are real numbers.
- Calculators may be used.

- Some problems may be accompanied by figures or diagrams. These figures are drawn as accurately as possible, EXCEPT when it is stated in a specific problem that a figure is *not drawn to scale*. The figures and diagrams are meant to provide information that is useful in solving the problem or problems.

- Unless otherwise stated, all figures and diagrams lie on a plane.

- All scratch work should be done in the test booklet. Get accustomed to doing this because scratch paper is NOT allowed into the testing area.

Question Types

The diagram below shows the possible SAT math topics and corresponding question types. Notice that there are four possible math *topics* AND each topic may be matched to one of two *question types*. For example, you may be given an algebra problem that is presented as a multiple-choice question, or you may be given an algebra problem that is presented as a grid-in (student response) question. It is important to be aware of the two question types, but remember that the focus of your preparation will be to gain a solid understanding of the math topics. Topics for multiple-choice and grid-in questions are straightforward, but some problems can appear as word problems or data interpretation problems.

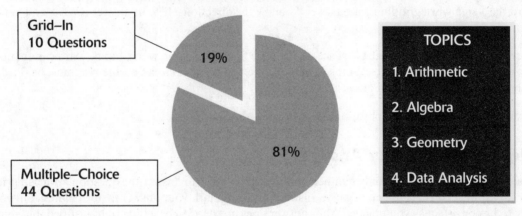

SAT MATH QUESTION TYPES

Grid–In 10 Questions — 19%

Multiple–Choice 44 Questions — 81%

TOPICS
1. Arithmetic
2. Algebra
3. Geometry
4. Data Analysis

Let's take a closer look at the two math question types before approaching strategies for these types of problems.

Multiple-Choice Questions

The multiple-choice question type requires you to solve math problems and then choose *one single answer* that best answers the question.

Solve each problem in this section by using the information given and your own mathematical calculations, insights, and problem-solving skills. Then select the one (best) correct answer of the five given choices, and mark the corresponding circle on your answer sheet. Use the available space on the page for your scratch work. There is a penalty for incorrectly answered multiple-choice questions.

Grid-In Questions

Student-produced response questions (grid-ins) require that you solve the problem and fill in your answer on a special grid answer sheet. Unlike multiple-choice questions, you *will not* be provided with a group of five answer choices. You must solve the problem and then enter your answer by carefully marking the circles in a special grid.

Since you will not be selecting from a group of possible answers, you should be extra careful in checking and double-checking your answers. Your calculator can be useful in checking answers. Keep in mind that answers to grid-in questions are given either full credit or no credit. There is no partial credit. However, *no points are deducted for incorrect answers* in this section only. That is, there is no penalty for guessing or attempting a grid-in question, so at least take an educated guess.

Before you begin working grid-in questions, it is important that you become familiar with the grid-in rules and procedures and learn to grid accurately. Practice this type of question *before* your test day so that you are comfortable with the grid-in procedure. You must first solve the problem, and then you must fill in the grid with the corresponding numerical answer. The final step requires that you write out your numerical answer in the boxes above the grid. This sequence is helpful so that you can visually check to make sure you have completely filled-in (bubbled-in) the answer sheet circles with the correct response. Writing out your answer is optional because the computer will only scan your dark bubble response, but keep in mind that you will not receive credit if you only write out your answer and do not completely fill in the bubble on your answer sheet grid.

There is no penalty for guessing on grid-in questions. Although it may be difficult to get an answer correct by writing in a wild guess, fill in your answer anyway, even if you think it's probably wrong. You have nothing to lose and quite possibly, something to gain. Even though there is no penalty for guessing on grid-in questions, check your work carefully because answer sheets are electronically scored and must match your answer *exactly*.

Some questions will have a note in parentheses that may say, "Disregard the % sign when gridding your answer," or "Disregard the $ sign when gridding your answer." Follow the directions. If your answer is 68%, grid in **68,** or if it's $95, grid in **95.**

Remember that you can use the available space on the page for your scratch work, but be extra careful not to make any marks on the grid. See the examples below and remember that circles on the grid must be filled in completely to receive credit for your answer.

The following examples show the appropriate way to mark the grid.

Sample 1: Gridding Your Answer

Positive numbers (and zero) are the only numbers that you should use to answer the question. You can grid in up to four positive integers. There are no negative answers. You can mark your answer in any column, but you should try to be consistent as you practice. Your answer does not need to be left or right justified, but remember to grid in your answer completely to receive full credit.

No credit will be given if more than one circle in a column is marked.

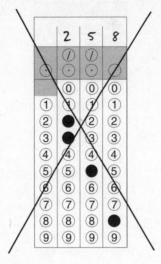

Sample 2: Gridding Decimal Points

Decimal points (.) are located in a shaded row, just above the grid numbers. Make sure to answer what is being asked. If the question asks for a percent and you get an answer of 57%, grid in **57,** not .57. Or if a question asks for dollars and you get an answer of 75 cents, remember that 75 cents is .75 of a dollar. Grid in **.75,** not 75.

If the answer is 3.7, as illustrated in the example below, write in your answer as a visual reminder before filling in the circles. Notice that the decimal point is located in the shaded area just above the numbers.

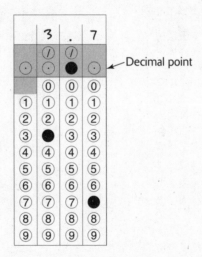

When writing **repeating decimals,** always enter the most complete answer the grid will accommodate. Since the grid is limited to four spaces, .8888 can be gridded as **.888** or **.889.** Gridding as .8, .88, or .89 are not acceptable. The acceptable grid-in answers for $\frac{8}{9}$ in decimal or fraction form are

Sample 3: Gridding Fractions

Fraction bars (/) are located in a shaded row just above the grid numbers. Answers that are mixed numbers such as $3\frac{1}{2}$ or $7\frac{1}{4}$ must be changed to improper fractions $\left(3\frac{1}{2} = \frac{7}{2},\ 7\frac{1}{4} = \frac{29}{4}\right)$ or decimals $\left(3\frac{1}{2} = 3.5,\ 7\frac{1}{4} = 7.25\right)$ before being gridded. Improper fractions or decimals can be gridded, but mixed numbers cannot because the scoring system cannot distinguish between $3\frac{1}{2}$ and $\frac{31}{2}$.

As the example below shows, if your answer is $1\frac{1}{2}$, you can change your answer to 1.5 or $\frac{3}{2}$.

Strategies

Suggested General Strategies

Consider the following list of *general* test-taking strategies when preparing for the SAT. After you have carefully reviewed this section, proceed to the next section emphasizing *specific* strategies that are designed to help you decipher and effectively work through math problems.

1. **Only one answer.** For multiple-choice questions, the correct answer is always in the list provided. Select only one answer because there is never more than one right answer.

2. **Questions appear in order of difficulty** and all questions are worth the same number of points regardless of the level of difficulty. This means the easiest questions appear at the beginning of each section and the more difficult questions follow, with the most difficult questions appearing toward the end of the section. It is to your advantage to work multiple-choice math problems in the order that they appear because all questions have the same point value.

3. **Manage your time wisely.** At first glance you might calculate that you have about *1 minute per* question to read and answer all the questions. When you begin the exam, make a mental note of the starting time and keep track of the time. Don't get stuck on any one problem, and never spend more than a minute on any one question. Some questions are easier than others; some will take less than a minute and others will take slightly more than a minute. With sufficient practice, you will almost automatically know when a problem is taking too much time and when it is time to select an answer or leave it blank and proceed to the next question.

4. **Use the *elimination strategy*** on page 7 whenever possible to eliminate one or more answer choices on multiple-choice questions. Be sure to read all the answer choices carefully and try to eliminate obvious wrong answers as soon as you recognize them. If you get stuck on any one question, either make an educated guess by eliminating some of the other choices first, or leave it blank and proceed to the next question. Remember, there is a penalty for guessing that is designed to discourage wild guessing on multiple-choice questions, but there is *no penalty for guessing* on grid-in questions.

5. **Be on alert for the *attractive distracter* answer choice.** Watch out for answers that look good but are not the best answer choice. The attractive distracter usually appears in this section as a choice that contains a subtle variation in meaning from the correct answer, thus making it more difficult for you to select the correct answer. Attractive distracters are carefully written to be close to the *best* answer, but there is never more than one right answer. When you narrow your choice down to two answers, one is probably the attractive distracter. If this happens, read the question again and select the answer that is the best fit.

6. **Read the question actively and circle or underline what you are looking for on the test booklet to make sure you are answering the right question.** As you read the question, circle or underline key words, numbers, or any other items you feel are important. Do not make a hasty assumption that you know the correct answer without reading the whole question and all the possible answers. The hurried test-taker commonly selects an incorrect answer by jumping to a conclusion after reading only one part of the question. Take advantage of being allowed to mark on the test booklet by always underlining or circling what you are looking for. This will ensure that you are answering the right question.

7. **Skip questions only if necessary (on multiple-choice questions).** When you encounter a question that is difficult for you to solve, you may choose to skip the question and come back to it later if time permits. Remember that with grid-in questions, you should always record an answer because there is no penalty for guessing on this type of question. Be sure to mark your answer sheet correctly if you skip a question. Test-takers who skip questions might make the mistake of continuing to mark their answers in sequence and forget to leave blank the unanswered questions. A good idea is to mark your answer in the test booklet itself (no need to erase later) so that if you do make mistakes in transferring your answer choices to the answer sheet, you can easily correct your errors without having to reconsider the answer choices.

8. **Use your calculator** when necessary, but remember that you should only use your calculator for problems that require more time (square roots, long division, and problems with several digits). If you do not see a fast method but know that you could compute the answer, use your calculator. A calculator is especially useful on the grid-in (student-response) question type because you cannot pick your answer from a list of choices. Your answer must be precise. A calculator will help you double-check your work on the grid-in questions.

9. **Glance at all the choices** before you answer your question. Even if you think you are certain about the correct answer choice, you should at least scan all the answer choices before making your final selection.

Suggested Specific Strategies

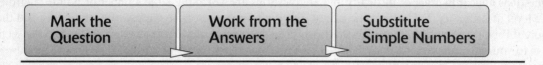

Draw, Mark, or Label the Question

Drawing, marking, or labeling diagrams and word problems as you read the questions can save you valuable time. After reading the question and the possible answer choices, marking and pulling out information from the question can give you a visual picture about what you should look for in the answer.

When information isn't given in the form of a diagram, take advantage of being allowed to write in the test booklet. The example questions and answers on the next page show how to sketch and draw information to organize a visual picture of the question.

Remember to watch for diagrams that **may not be drawn to scale.** You should NOT assume that quantities such as lengths and angle measurements are as they appear in the figure. Diagrams are drawn as accurately as possible, unless a diagram is labeled "not drawn to scale." That label is the tip-off that the diagram could be drawn differently or is out of proportion. In this case, mark the diagram and/or quickly redraw it more accurately.

Work from the Answer Choices and Approximate

If you see a method to quickly solve the problem (under 1 minute), then work the problem. However, if you don't immediately recognize a method or formula, or if a method will take you a great deal of time, **work backward** from the answers. This method will at least eliminate some of the choices and may help lead you to the correct answer. In other questions, using the **approximation** strategy may be all you need to arrive at the correct choice. In other words, if it appears that extensive calculations are going to be necessary to solve a problem, check to see how far apart the choices are and then approximate. It may be useful to look at the answer choices to see how close together or far apart the answers are. This will guide you in determining how close your approximation needs to be to choose the correct answer.

Substitute Simple Numbers

Substituting numbers for variables can often be an aid to understanding a problem. Remember to substitute simple numbers, since you have to do the work. Sometimes you will immediately recognize a simple method to solve a problem. If this is not the case, try a reasonable approach and then check the answers to see which one is most reasonable.

Example Questions

Practice using the strategies described above by reviewing the following multiple-choice questions. The example questions below are arranged by topic area: arithmetic, algebra, geometry, and data analysis. Additional example questions are included for word problems and data interpretation style problems. As you approach the example questions, remember to

- Pull out, circle, or underline what you are looking for.
- Draw, sketch, and mark diagrams.
- Work backward from the answer choices and approximate.
- Substitute simple numbers for variables to understand a problem.
- Use your calculator when appropriate to solve a problem or to check your answer if time permits.
- Make sure your answer is reasonable.
- Jot down your scratch work or calculations in the space provided in your test booklet.

Arithmetic

---

1. If a beaker of liquid is $\frac{3}{7}$ *alcohol* by volume and $\frac{4}{7}$ *water* by volume, what is the ratio of the volume of alcohol to the volume of water in this mixture?

   A. $\frac{3}{7}$

   B. $\frac{4}{7}$

   C. $\frac{3}{4}$

   D. $\frac{4}{3}$

   E. $\frac{7}{4}$

STRATEGY: When pulling out and marking information, write out the numbers and/or letters on your test booklet, putting them into some helpful form and eliminating some of the wording.

Circle or underline key words: $\frac{3}{7}$ *alcohol* and $\frac{4}{7}$ *water*. The first bit of information you pull out should be what you are looking for: the ratio of the volume of alcohol to the volume of water. Rewrite it as *A:W* and then put it into its working form: $\frac{A}{W}$. Next, you should pull out the volumes of each:

$$A = \frac{3}{7} \text{ and } W = \frac{4}{7}$$

Now the answer can be easily figured by inspection or substitution. Using $\left(\frac{3}{7}\right) \div \left(\frac{4}{7}\right)$, invert the second fraction and multiply, $\frac{3}{7} \times \frac{7}{4} = \frac{21}{28} = \frac{3}{4}$. The ratio of the volume of alcohol to the volume of water is 3 to 4. Note: If this problem were a grid-in question, it would be necessary to reduce the answer to its lowest terms since $\frac{21}{28}$ would not fit into the answer grid. The correct answer is **C**.

---

2. What is the approximate value of $\sqrt{1596}$?

   A. 10
   B. 20
   C. 30
   D. 40
   E. 50

STRATEGY: By working with the answer choices first and approximating, the problem can be easily solved.

Remember to approximate when possible. If you know that $10^2 = 100$, it is rather easy to find the squares of the other answer choices. If $2^2 = 4$ then $20^2 = 400$, $3^2 = 9$ and $30^2 = 900$, $4^2 = 16$ and $40^2 = 1,600$, and $5^2 = 25$ and $50^2 = 2,500$. Now, since the question only asks for the approximate value of $\sqrt{1596}$, round it off to $\sqrt{1600}$. Choice **D**, 40, when squared, is the closest approximation to $\sqrt{1596}$. By using a calculator, it is also quite easy to compute square roots.

It is also sometimes useful to start from the middle number and then work forward or backward. Start from Choice C, $30^2 = 900$, which is too small, eliminating choices A and B. Choice D, $40^2 = 1,600$ is the closest approximation to 1,596.

Algebra

---

3. If $\frac{x}{4} + 2 = 22$, what is the value of x?

   A.   40
   B.   80
   C.   100
   D.   120
   E.   160

STRATEGY: If you cannot solve this problem algebraically, it is useful to work from the answer choices. Start with the middle choice, C, $x = 100$.

$$\frac{x}{4} + 2 = 22$$

$$\frac{100}{4} + 2 = 22$$

$$25 + 2 = 22$$

$$27 \neq 22$$

Since 27 is too large, you can immediately eliminate choices D and E (120 and 160) because these choices are also too large. This narrows your choices to A or B. Working backward from C, plug in Choice B, 80, to solve the problem. The correct answer is **B**.

$$\frac{x}{4} + 2 = 22$$

$$\frac{80}{4} + 2 = 22$$

$$20 + 2 = 22$$

$$= 22$$

---

4. If $x > 1$, which of the following decreases as x decreases?

   I. $x + x^2$

   II. $2x^2 - x$

   III. $\frac{1}{x+1}$

   A.   I only
   B.   II only
   C.   III only
   D.   I and II only
   E.   II and III only

STRATEGY: This problem is most easily solved by eliminating answer choices and substituting simple numbers.

Since $x > 1$, start with $x = 3$ then $x = 2$ to see if there is a trend in the answers to the expressions $x + x^2$, $2x^2 - x$, and $\frac{1}{x+1}$. When $x = 3$, $x + x^2 = 3 + (3)^2 = 12$. When $x = 2$, $x + x^2 = 2 + (2)^2 = 6$. So when x decreased, $x + x^2$ decreased. Hence Choice A must be included in the answer, eliminating choices B, C, and E. Test the values of x in II, $2x^2 - x$, to find the answer. When $x = 3$, $2x^2 - x = 2(3)^2 - (3) = 15$. When $x = 2$, $2x^2 - x = 2(2)^2 - (2) = 6$. Therefore, when x decreased, $2x^2 - x$ also decreased. The correct answer is **D**.

Geometry

5. If P lies on $\overparen{ON}$ such that $\overparen{OP} = 2\overparen{PN}$ and Q lies on $\overparen{OP}$ such that $\overparen{OQ} = \overparen{QP}$, what is the ratio of $\overparen{OQ}$ to $\overparen{PN}$?

   A. $\frac{1}{3}$

   B. $\frac{1}{2}$

   C. $\frac{1}{1}$

   D. $\frac{2}{1}$

   E. $\frac{3}{1}$

STRATEGY: Redrawing and marking in diagrams on your scratch paper as you read them can save you valuable time. Marking can also give you insight into how to solve a problem because you will have the complete picture clearly in front of you.

Draw a simple sketch to help visualize the solution.

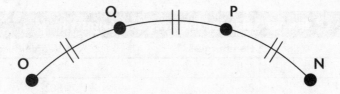

It appears from the sketch that $\overparen{OQ} = \overparen{PN}$, so the ratio (relationship) of $\overparen{OQ}$ to $\overparen{PN}$ is 1 to 1 or $\frac{1}{1}$, which is answer Choice C. Or, you could assign values on $\overparen{ON}$ such that $\overparen{OP} = 2\overparen{PN}$, such as: $\overparen{OP}$ equals 2, and $\overparen{PN}$ equals 1. If Q lies on $\overparen{OP}$ such that $\overparen{OQ} = \overparen{QP}$, then $\overparen{OP}$ is divided in half by point Q. So $\overparen{OQ} = 1$, and $\overparen{QP} = 1$. Therefore, the relationship (ratio) of is 1 to 1. The correct answer is **C**.

Data Analysis

6. There are 12 jelly beans in a bag: 6 red, 3 green, 2 yellow, and 1 orange. What is the probability that 3 randomly selected jelly beans, chosen without replacement, will all be red?

   A. 0.08
   B. 0.09
   C. 0.10
   D. 0.11
   E. 0.12

STRATEGY: Although there is a more "statistical" method of solving using "combinations," it is better to choose methods that use simple arithmetic computations.

This is an example of a problem presented in a word problem format. Six of the 12 jelly beans are red. So, the probability that the first one selected is red is $\frac{6}{12}$. Out of the remaining 11 jelly beans, there are 5 red ones. Thus, the probability that the second selection is red, given that the first selection was red, is $\frac{5}{11}$. Out of the remaining 10 jelly beans, there are 4 red ones. Thus, the probability that the third selection is red, given that the first two selections were red, is $\frac{4}{10}$. Therefore, to find the probability that all three selections were red would be the product of these three probabilities: $\frac{6}{12} \times \frac{5}{11} \times \frac{4}{10} = \frac{1}{11} \approx 0.09$. Note: If this type of problem appears as a grid-in question, remember that the answer must be exact. Be sure to place the decimal point in the right position on the grid. The correct answer is **B**.

Data Interpretation

Data interpretation questions can appear as tables, graphs, or charts. Problems in this format require you to interpret data from a graphic figure to answer the question. Strong arithmetic and data analysis skills will help you with this type of problem. Do not try to memorize the graphic information, but use the strategy of *drawing and marking* the table, chart, or graph as needed to answer the question. To solve this type of problem you should know how to

- Read and understand data that is provided in the graphic figure. Be sure to read *all* the information provided (headings, legends, etc.).
- Interpret, calculate, and apply the information provided in the question.
- Easily recognize and predict trends from the information provided in the graphic figure. With practice, you will learn how to quickly scan a figure to look for obvious differences (high points, low points, or trends).

Tables

Use the table below to answer the question that follows.

Burger Sales for the Week of August 8–14		
Day	**Hamburgers**	**Veggie Burgers**
Sunday	120	92
Monday	85	80
Tuesday	77	70
Wednesday	74	71
Thursday	75	72
Friday	91	88
Saturday	111	112

7. On which day were the most burgers sold (hamburgers and veggie burgers)?

    A. Sunday
    B. Monday
    C. Tuesday
    D. Friday
    E. Saturday

STRATEGY: Working backward from the answer choices is probably the easiest method to solve this type of problem.

To answer this question, you must understand the chart and do some simple computations. Glancing at the columns will help you to quickly narrow your choices to A or E. Perform a simple calculation:

Sunday	$120 + 92 = 212$
Monday	$85 + 80 = 165$
Tuesday	$77 + 70 = 147$
Friday	$91 + 88 = 179$
Saturday	$111 + 112 = 223$

Since 223 is the greatest amount, the correct answer is **E.**

Graphs and Charts

Graph and chart displays may appear in several forms. The three basic types of graphs are circle graphs (pie charts), line graphs, and bar graphs.

Circle Graphs

A circle graph, or pie chart, shows the relationship between the whole circle (100%) and the various slices that represent portions of that 100%. The larger the slice, the higher the percentage.

Use the pie chart below to answer the question that follows.

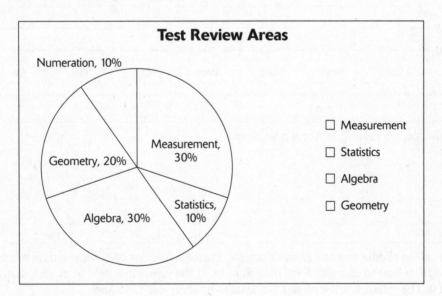

8. According to the test review areas listed, if the test contains 5 numeration problems, then how many algebra problems should be expected?

   A. 10
   B. 15
   C. 20
   D. 30
   E. 25

The format of this question is data interpretation. After reviewing the graph, notice that numeration is 10% and algebra is 30%. This means there should be three times as many algebra problems as there are numeration problems. Use multiplication to solve this problem. If there are five numeration problems, then multiply by 3 to find the solution.

$$5 \times 3 = 15 \text{ algebra problems}$$

The correct answer is **B**.

Line Graphs

Line graphs convert data into points on a grid. These points are then connected to show a relationship among the items, dates, and times. For example, notice the slopes of the lines connecting the points. These lines show increases and decreases. The sharper the slope upward, the greater the *increase*. The sharper the slope downward, the greater the *decrease*. Line graphs can show trends, or changes, in data over a period of time.

Use the line graph below to answer the question that follows.

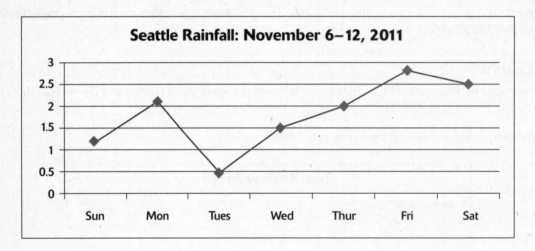

9. What was the median rainfall for the week shown?

   A. 1.2
   B. 1.8
   C. 1.5
   D. 1.65
   E. 2.0

The median value is the middle number. In this example, the median value of the seven days will be the fourth value, when listed from least to greatest. Even though most of the values can only be approximated, the fourth value is exactly 2.0. The values, when written from least to greatest, are as follows:

Tuesday—exactly 0.5	**Thursday—exactly 2.0**	Monday—approximately 2.1
Sunday—approximately 1.2		Saturday—exactly 2.5
Wednesday—exactly 1.5		Friday—approximately 2.8

The correct answer is **E**.

Bar Graphs

Bar graphs convert the information in a chart into separate bars or columns. Some graphs list numbers along one edge, and places, dates, people, or things (individual categories) along another edge. Always try to determine the relationship between the columns in a graph or chart.

Use the following bar graph to answer the question that follows.

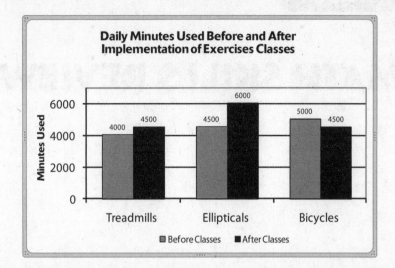

Machine Usage—Exercisers Per Day		
Machine	**Before-Class Implementation**	**After-Class Implementation**
Treadmills	128	120
Ellipticals	180	220
Bicycles	160	150

---

10. Exercisers increased their elliptical minutes per person usage by approximately what percent after exercise classes were implemented?

  A. 8%
  B. 9%
  C. 12%
  D. 22%
  E. 33%

Before exercise classes were implemented, 180 people used the ellipticals for 4,500 minutes, or $\frac{4500}{180} = 25$ minutes per person. After exercise classes were implemented, 220 people used ellipticals for 6,000 minutes, or $\frac{6000}{220} = 27.27$ minutes per person. The percent increase is the actual increase, 2.27, divided by the original amount, or $\frac{2.27}{25} = 0.0908$, or approximately 9%. The correct answer is **B.**

PART III

MATH SKILLS REVIEW

Chapter 5

Arithmetic: Number and Operations Review

SAT arithmetic questions cover basic high school math concepts and skills. Arithmetic is the foundation for *all math concepts* and deals with basic properties of counting (adding, subtracting, multiplying, and dividing). You will need to have a solid understanding of arithmetic *before* you undertake the more advanced topics of algebra, geometry, and data analysis. Some students try to skip this section and move on to algebra and geometry, but it would be prudent for you to at least skim through the topic headings covered in this chapter to help support your understanding of forgotten math concepts.

Earmark this chapter as you review and practice math problems in this study guide. This section contains basic math symbols and references that you may refer to again and again during your SAT preparation. It was compiled so that you can easily have basic math concepts at your fingertips. These basic references will help you save time trying to search for fundamental information necessary to solve problems.

SAT problems include:

- Arithmetic: numbers and operations
- Applying addition, subtraction, multiplication, and division to problem solving
- Arithmetic mean (average), mode, and median
- Ratio and proportion
- Number properties: positive and negative integers, odd and even numbers, prime numbers, factors and multiples, divisibility
- Word problems, solving for: percents, averages, rate, time, distance, interest, price per item
- Number line: order, consecutive numbers, and fractions
- Sequences involving exponential growth
- Sets (union, intersection, elements)

Symbols, Terms, and Sets of Numbers

Common Math Symbols			
=	is equal to	≤	is less than or equal to
≠	is not equal to	⊥	is perpendicular to
≈ or ≐	is approximately equal to	‖	is parallel to
>	is greater than	≅	is congruent to
≥	is greater than or equal to	~	is similar to
<	is less than		

Common Math Terminology: Words that Signal an Operation		
Sum	The answer to an addition problem.	What is the sum of 4 + 17?
Difference or Remainder	The answer to a subtraction problem.	What is the difference between 17 and 4? or What is the remainder if you subtract 4 from 17?
Product	The answer to a multiplication problem.	What is the product of 4 × 17?
Quotient	The answer to a division problem.	What is the quotient of 17 ÷ 4?

Special Sets of Numbers

In completing arithmetic and algebra problems, you will work with several groups of numbers.

Natural or Counting Numbers: {1, 2, 3, 4, 5...}

Whole Numbers: {0, 1, 2, 3, 4...}

Prime Numbers: Prime numbers are all natural numbers greater than 1 that are divisible only by 1 and the number itself. For example, 17 is a prime number because it can be only be divided by 17 and 1. The only even prime number is 2. Zero and 1 *are not* prime numbers. The first ten prime numbers are 2, 3, 5, 7, 11, 13, 17, 19, 23, and 29.

Composite Numbers: Composite numbers are all natural numbers greater than 1 that are not prime. Composite numbers are divisible by more than just 1 and itself. For example, 4, 6, 8, 9 10, 12, 14, 15...

Tip: 1 is neither prime nor composite.

Integers: {...,−3, −2, −1, 0, 1, 2, 3...}

Even Integers: {...,−6, −4, −2, 0, 2, 4, 6...}

Odd Integers: {...,−5, −3, −1, 1, 3...}

Rational Numbers: Rational numbers are all numbers that can be expressed as a fraction in the form $\frac{a}{b}$ where a and b are integers and $b \neq 0$. Rational numbers may also be expressed as a terminating or repeating decimal. All integers are rational numbers.

Irrational Numbers: Irrational numbers are all numbers that cannot be expressed in the form of a fraction $\frac{a}{b}$ where a and b are integers and $b \neq 0$. Some examples of irrational numbers are π, $\sqrt{5}$, and $\sqrt[3]{10}$.

Real Numbers: Real numbers are the combination of all rational numbers and irrational numbers. On the SAT, you should assume all problems use real numbers unless stated otherwise.

Basic Mathematical Properties, Place Value and Expanded Notation

The section above described the different types of *numbers*. As you may recall, numbers on the SAT are *real numbers* (rational and irrational numbers) unless otherwise specified. The numerical value of every real number fits between the numerical values of two other real numbers, and the result of adding or multiplying real numbers is always another real number. This operation is described as a closure property. For example, if you add two even numbers, the answer will always be an even number (8 + 6 = 14). Therefore, the set of even numbers is called "closed." This section helps you understand these basic properties of mathematical operations, makes it easier for you to work with real numbers, and helps you conceptually understand how sets of numbers fit together.

As you work with real numbers, it is also important to understand the *value* of numbers assigned in a place value system (decimal system). To assist you, this section provides you with examples of written numbers in the decimal system in expanded notation and points out the place value of each digit.

Properties of Addition

The **Commutative Property of Addition** shows that the *order* does not affect the sum of two or more numbers:

$$a + b = b + a \qquad\qquad 2 + 3 = 3 + 2$$

Tip: The Commutative Property is not true for subtraction: 2 − 3 ≠ 3 − 2.

The **Associative Property of Addition** shows that grouping does not affect the sum of three or more numbers. Even though the grouping changes, the sum is still equal:

$$(a + b) + c = a + (b + c) \qquad (2 + 3) + 4 = 2 + (3 + 4)$$

Tip: The Associative Property is not true for subtraction: $(2 - 3) - 4 \neq 2 - (3 - 4)$.

The **Additive Identity Property** shows that any number added to 0 is always the original number:

$$a + 0 = 0 + a = a \qquad 5 + 0 = 0 + 5 = 5$$

The **Additive Inverse Property** shows that the sum of any number and its additive inverse (opposite) is 0:

$$a + (-a) = (-a) + a = 0 \qquad 5 + (-5) = (-5) + 5 = 0$$

Properties of Multiplication

The **Commutative Property of Multiplication** shows that order does not affect the product of two or more numbers:

Tip: The Commutative Property is not true for division: $2 \div 3 \neq 3 \div 2$.

$$a \cdot b = b \cdot a \qquad 2 \cdot 3 = 3 \cdot 2$$

The **Associative Property of Multiplication** shows that grouping does not affect the product of three or more numbers:

Tip: The Associative Property is not true for division: $(2 \div 3) \div 4 \neq 2 \div (3 \div 4)$.

$$(a \cdot b) \cdot c = a \cdot (b \cdot c) \qquad (2 \cdot 3) \cdot 4 = 2 \cdot (3 \cdot 4)$$

The **Multiplicative Identity Property** shows the product of 1 and any number is always the original number:

$$a \cdot 1 = 1 \cdot a = a \qquad 2 \cdot 1 = 1 \cdot 2 = 2$$

The **Multiplicative Inverse Property** shows the product of any nonzero number and its multiplicative inverse (reciprocal) is 1:

$$a \cdot \frac{1}{a} = \frac{1}{a} \cdot a = 1 \quad (a \neq 0) \qquad 2 \cdot \frac{1}{2} = \frac{1}{2} \cdot 2 = 1 \quad (2 \neq 0)$$

Tip: 0 is the only real number that does not have a reciprocal.

Other Properties

The **Distributive Property** shows the process of distributing the number on the outside of the parentheses to each term on the inside (multiplication over addition):

$$a \cdot (b + c) = a \cdot b + a \cdot c \qquad 2 \cdot (3 + 4) = 2 \cdot 3 + 2 \cdot 4$$

and

$$a \cdot b + a \cdot c = a \cdot (b + c) \qquad 2 \cdot 3 + 2 \cdot 4 = 2 \cdot (3 + 4)$$

The **Distributive Property** shows the process of multiplication over subtraction

$$a \cdot (b-c) = a \cdot b - a \cdot c \qquad\qquad 2 \cdot (3-4) = 2 \cdot 3 - 2 \cdot 4$$

and

$$a \cdot b - a \cdot c = a \cdot (b-c) \qquad\qquad 2 \cdot 3 - 2 \cdot 4 = 2 \cdot (3-4)$$

Place Value

Each digit in any real number has place value. A general example of place value is

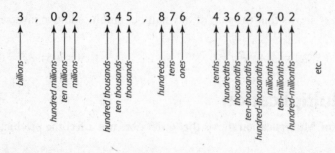

For example, in the number 629.453 the 6 is in the hundreds place, the 2 is in the tens place, the 9 is in the ones place, the 4 is in the tenths place, the 5 is in the hundredths place, and the 3 is in the thousandths place.

Expanded Notation

A number can be expressed in expanded notation to emphasize the place value for each digit. The number 629.453 can be written as

$$600 \quad + \quad 20 \quad + \quad 9 \quad + \quad 0.4 \quad + \quad 0.05 \quad + \quad 0.003$$
$$(6 \times 100) + (2 \times 10) + (9 \times 1) + \left(4 \times \frac{1}{10}\right) + \left(5 \times \frac{1}{100}\right) + \left(3 \times \frac{1}{1000}\right)$$

Using exponents, 629.453 can be written as

$$\left(6 \times 10^2\right) + \left(2 \times 10^1\right) + \left(9 \times 10^0\right) + \left(4 \times 10^{-1}\right) + \left(5 \times 10^{-2}\right) + \left(3 \times 10^{-3}\right)$$

Operations on Real Numbers

Grouping Symbols

Parentheses ( ), brackets [ ], and braces { }, are frequently needed to group numbers in mathematics. Generally parentheses are used first followed by brackets and then braces. Operations inside grouping symbols must be performed before any operations outside the grouping symbols.

Order of Operation Rules

When performing operations on real numbers, the following order rules must be followed

1. Work symbols from the inside out.
2. Exponents and roots in order from left to right.
3. Multiplication and division in order from left to right.
4. Addition and subtraction in order from left to right.

Example:

$$[15+3(10-6)]-8\cdot3=$$

$$[15+3(10-6)]-8\cdot3$$
$$=[15+3(4)]-8\cdot3$$
$$=[15+12]-8\cdot3$$
$$=27-8\cdot3$$
$$=27-24$$
$$=3$$

Rounding-Off Numbers

Rounding-Off Numbers Rules

1. Identify the number in the place value you are rounding off.
2. Look at the digit immediately to the right of this number.
3. If the number to the right is 5, 6, 7, 8 or 9, then increase the indicated place value by 1.
4. If the number to the right is 0, 1, 2, 3 or 4, then the indicated place value remains unchanged.
5. If the number to be rounded is a whole number, all numbers to the right of the indicated place value are zeros.
6. If the number to be rounded is a decimal number, all numbers to the right of the indicated place value are omitted.

Examples:

1. Round 463,856 to the nearest hundred: $463,856 = 463,900$

2. Round 463,856 to the nearest ten thousand: $463,856 = 460,000$

3. Round 13.6249 to the nearest hundredth: $13.6249 = 13.62$

4. Round -42.381 to the nearest tenth: $-42.381 = -42.4$

Addition

Steps to Approach Adding Real Numbers

1. If the two numbers have the same sign, add their absolute values (see Chapter 6, "Algebra and Functions Review" on page 171) and keep the same sign.
2. If the two numbers have different signs, subtract their absolute values and take the sign of the number with the largest absolute number.
3. If the two numbers are opposites, their sum is zero.

Examples:

1. $(-12) + (-10) = -22$

2. $(-25) + 15 = -10$

3. $(-8) + 20 = 12$

4. $13 + (-13) = 0$

Subtraction

Steps to Approach Subtracting Real Numbers

1. To subtract two real numbers, rewrite the subtraction as addition and take the opposite of the number being subtracted.
2. As a formula, this may be written as: $a - b = a +$ (opposite of b).

Examples:

1. $(-10) - 15 = (-10) + (-15) = -25$

2. $16 - (-7) = 16 + 7 = 23$

3. $(-22) - 23 = (-22) + (-23) = -45$

Multiplication

Steps to Approach Multiplying Real Numbers

1. If the two numbers have the same sign, multiply their absolute values and their product is positive.
2. If the two numbers have different signs, multiply their absolute values and their product is negative.
3. If one of the numbers is zero, the product is zero.

Examples:

1. $8(-5) = -40$

2. $(-3) \times (-12) = 36$

3. $(-2)(-3)(-1)(4) = 6(-1)(4) = (-6)(4) = -24$

Division

Steps to Approach Dividing Real Numbers

1. If the two numbers have the same sign, divide their absolute values and their quotient is positive.
2. If the two numbers have different signs, divide their absolute values and their quotient is negative.
3. If the first number is zero and the divisor is any nonzero number, the quotient is zero.

Tip: The divisor cannot be zero since division by zero is undefined.

Examples:

1. $100 \div (-20) = -5$

2. $(-18) \div (-6) = 3$

3. $0 \div (-5) = 0$

Divisibility Rules	
Divisible by	**Rule**
2	Last digit is 0, 2, 4, 6, or 8.
3	The sum of its digits is divisible by 3.
4	Last two-digit number is divisible by 4.
5	Last digit is 0 or 5.
6	Divisible by 2 and 3.
7	No simple rule.
8	Last three digit number is divisible by 8.
9	The sum of its digits is divisible by 9.
10	Last digit is 0.

Examples:

1. 6345 is divisible by 3, 5, and 9, but not divisible by 2, 4, 6, 7, 8, or 10.

2. 10448 is divisible by 2, 4, and 8, but not divisible by 3, 5, 6, 7, 9, or 10.

3. 750 is divisible by 2, 3, 5, 6, and 10, but not divisible by 4, 7, 8, 9.

Fractions

A fraction is the comparison of two quantities a and b, by division written $\frac{a}{b} = a \div b$. The expression above the fraction bar is called the *numerator* and the expression below the fraction bar is called the *denominator*. Since division by zero is undefined, the denominator of a fraction cannot be zero.

Negative Fractions

Fractions that are negative may be written in any of three ways: $-\frac{a}{b} = \frac{-a}{b} = \frac{a}{-b}$.

They are, however, usually expressed with the negative next to the fraction bar $\left(-\frac{a}{b}\right)$.

Proper Fractions, Improper Fractions, and Mixed Numbers

Proper Fraction: A fraction in which the numerator is less than the denominator, such as $\frac{3}{4}$.

Improper Fraction: A fraction in which the numerator is greater than or equal to the denominator, such as $\frac{11}{5}$ or $\frac{6}{6}$.

Mixed Number: A fraction expression that is made of a whole number and a fraction, such as $5\frac{2}{3}$ or $6\frac{1}{4}$.

Simplifying Fractions

Fractions should be expressed in lowest terms by dividing both the numerator and denominator by the largest number that will divide both.

Examples:

1. Simplify $\frac{40}{48}$: $\frac{40}{48} = \frac{40 \div 8}{48 \div 8} = \frac{5}{6}$

2. Simplify $\frac{18}{24}$: $\frac{18}{24} = \frac{18 \div 6}{24 \div 6} = \frac{3}{4}$

Expanding Fractions

Fractions may be expanded by multiplying both the numerator and denominator by the same number to generate an equivalent fraction.

Examples:

1. Expand $\frac{5}{6}$: $\frac{5}{6} = \frac{5 \cdot 4}{6 \cdot 4} = \frac{20}{24}$

2. Expand $\frac{2}{3}$: $\frac{2}{3} = \frac{2 \cdot 10}{3 \cdot 10} = \frac{20}{30}$

Factors and Multiples

Factors

Factors of a number are the whole numbers whose product equals the given number.

Examples:

1. The factors of 15 are 1, 3, 5, and 15 since $1 \times 15 = 15$ and $3 \times 5 = 15$.

2. The factors of 36 are 1, 2, 3, 4, 6, 9, 12, 18, and 36 since $1 \times 36 = 36$, $2 \times 18 = 36$, $3 \times 12 = 36$, $4 \times 9 = 36$, and $6 \times 6 = 36$.

Greatest Common Factor

The Greatest Common Factor (GCF) is the largest factor common of two or more numbers.

Example:

> Find the GCF of 16, 24, and 40.

Since the factors of 16 are 1, 2, 4, 8, and 16, the factors of 24 are 1, 2, 3, 4, 6, 8, 12, and 24, and the factors of 40 are 1, 2, 4, 5, 8, 10, 20, and 40, the GCF is 8. Note that 1, 2, and 4 are common factors of 8, 16, 24, and 40.

Multiples

Multiples of a number are the product of that number and consecutive natural numbers.

Example:

> Multiples of 5 are 5, 10, 15, 20, 25...

Least Common Multiple

The Least Common Multiple (LCM) is the smallest multiple common to two or more numbers.

Example:

> Find the LCM of 6 and 8.

Since the multiples of 6 are 6, 12, 18, 24, 30, and the multiples of 8 are 8, 16, 24, 32, 40..., the LCM of 6 and 8 is 24.

> **Tip: In working with fractions, the Least Common Denominator (LCD) of two or more fractions is the same as the LCM of the denominators.**

Adding and Subtracting Fractions and Mixed Numbers

Adding and Subtracting Fractions

When adding or subtracting fractions, the denominators must be the same. If the denominators are not the same, you must expand each fraction to their LCD, and then add or subtract the numerators and keep the same denominator.

Addition: $\dfrac{a}{c} + \dfrac{b}{c} = \dfrac{a+b}{c}$

Subtraction: $\dfrac{a}{c} - \dfrac{b}{c} = \dfrac{a-b}{c}$

Examples:

> 1. $\dfrac{3}{4} + \dfrac{1}{6} =$

$$\frac{3}{4} + \frac{1}{6} = \frac{9}{12} + \frac{2}{12} = \frac{11}{12}$$

2. $\left(-\dfrac{2}{5}\right)-\left(-\dfrac{1}{3}\right)=$

$$\left(-\dfrac{2}{5}\right)-\left(-\dfrac{1}{3}\right)=\left(-\dfrac{6}{15}\right)+\dfrac{5}{15}=-\dfrac{1}{15}$$

Adding and Subtracting Mixed Numbers

When adding and subtracting mixed numbers, add or subtract the whole numbers and add or subtract the fractions.

Examples:

1. Addition: $\begin{array}{r} 4\dfrac{2}{3} \\ +5\dfrac{3}{4} \\ \hline \end{array}$

$$4\dfrac{2}{3}=4\dfrac{8}{12}$$
$$+5\dfrac{3}{4}=5\dfrac{9}{12}$$
$$\rule{3cm}{0.4pt}$$
$$=9+\dfrac{17}{12}=9+1\dfrac{5}{12}=10\dfrac{5}{12}$$

2. Subtraction: $\begin{array}{r} 8\dfrac{1}{4} \\ -\;3\dfrac{7}{8} \\ \hline \end{array}$

$$8\dfrac{1}{4}=8\dfrac{2}{8}=7\dfrac{10}{8}$$
$$-3\dfrac{7}{8}=3\dfrac{7}{8}=3\dfrac{7}{8}$$
$$\rule{3cm}{0.4pt}$$
$$=4\dfrac{3}{8}$$

Multiplying and Dividing Fractions

Multiplying Fractions

When multiplying fractions, simply multiply the numerators and multiply the denominators. Simplifying may be done before the multiplication, if possible.

$$\dfrac{a}{b}\cdot\dfrac{c}{d}=\dfrac{a\cdot c}{b\cdot d}$$

Examples:

1. $\dfrac{7}{12} \times \dfrac{8}{9} = \dfrac{7}{\cancel{12}_3} \times \dfrac{\cancel{8}^2}{9} = \dfrac{14}{27}$

2. $\left(-3\dfrac{1}{3}\right) \times 5\dfrac{1}{4} = -\dfrac{\cancel{10}^5}{\cancel{3}_1} \times \dfrac{\cancel{21}^7}{\cancel{4}_2} = -\dfrac{35}{2} = -17\dfrac{1}{2}$

Dividing Fractions

When dividing fractions, take the reciprocal of the second fraction and multiply.

$$\dfrac{a}{b} \div \dfrac{c}{d} = \dfrac{a}{b} \cdot \dfrac{d}{c} = \dfrac{a \cdot d}{b \cdot c}$$

Examples:

1. $\dfrac{3}{7} \div \dfrac{9}{14} = \dfrac{\cancel{3}^1}{\cancel{7}_1} \cdot \dfrac{\cancel{14}^2}{\cancel{9}_3} = \dfrac{2}{3}$

2. $4\dfrac{1}{6} \div 1\dfrac{1}{3} = \dfrac{25}{6} \div \dfrac{4}{3} = \dfrac{25}{\cancel{6}_2} \cdot \dfrac{\cancel{3}^1}{4} = \dfrac{25}{8} = 3\dfrac{1}{8}$

Decimals

Converting Decimals to Fractions

When converting decimals to fractions, numbers to the left of the decimal point are whole numbers and numbers to the right of the decimal point may be expressed as fractions determined by their place value.

Examples:

1. Convert .09 to a fraction: $.09 = \dfrac{9}{100}$

2. Convert .048 to a fraction: $.048 = \dfrac{48}{1000} = \dfrac{6}{125}$

3. Convert 8.6 to a fraction: $8.6 = 8\dfrac{6}{10} = 8\dfrac{3}{5}$

Adding and Subtracting Decimals

To add or subtract decimals, line up the decimal points and add or subtract as usual. It is helpful to fill in zeros to the right of the decimal point before adding or subtracting.

Examples:

1. 18.9 + 0.34 + 632.056 =

$$
\begin{array}{r}
18.900 \\
0.340 \\
+632.056 \\
\hline
651.296
\end{array}
$$

2. 93.5 − 18.91 =

$$
\begin{array}{r}
93.50 \\
-18.91 \\
\hline
74.59
\end{array}
$$

Multiplying Decimals

To multiply decimals, multiply as usual and take the sum of the digits to the right of the decimal point in the original numbers. This sum indicates the number of digits to the right of the decimal point in the product.

Example:

13.84 × 4.1 =

$$
\begin{array}{r}
13.84 \quad \text{(2 digits)} \\
\times \ 4.1 \quad \text{(1 digit)} \\
\hline
1384 \\
\underline{5536} \\
56.744 \quad \text{(3 digits)}
\end{array}
$$

Dividing Decimals

When dividing decimals, the divisor should always be a whole number. If the divisor is not a whole number, move the decimal to the right to make it a whole number and then move the decimal the same number of places in the number being divided into.

Example:

> $5.796 \div 0.12 =$

$$0.12\overline{)5.796} =$$

$$\begin{array}{r} 48.3 \\ 12\overline{)579.6} \\ \underline{48} \\ 99 \\ \underline{96} \\ 36 \\ \underline{36} \end{array}$$

Ratios and Proportions

Ratios

A ratio is a comparison of two quantities and is usually expressed as a fraction. The ratio of a to b may be written as $\frac{a}{b}$ or $a:b$.

Examples:

> 1. What is the ratio of 24 to 36? The ratio of 24 to 36 is $\frac{24}{36} = \frac{2}{3}$ or 2:3.

> 2. What is the ratio of 8 to 25? The ratio of 8 to 25 is $\frac{8}{25}$ or 8:25.

Proportion

A proportion is an equality statement between two ratios. If $\frac{a}{b} = \frac{c}{d}$ is a true proportion, then their cross products are equal: $a \cdot d = b \cdot c$.

Example:

> $\frac{24}{36} = \frac{2}{3}$ is a true proportion since $24 \cdot 3 = 36 \cdot 2$.

Percents

A percent is a ratio of a number compared to 100. The symbol for percent is %.

Example:

$$23\% = \frac{23}{100} = 0.23$$

Changing Percents to Decimals

Steps to Change a Percent to a Decimal

To change a percent to a decimal

1. Drop the percent symbol.
2. Shift the decimal point two places to the left, adding zeros if necessary.

Examples:

1. $8\% = 0.08$

2. $73\% = 0.73$

Changing Decimals to Percents

Steps to Change Decimals to Percents

To change a decimal to a percent

1. Shift the decimal point two places to the right.
2. Add the percent symbol.

Examples:

1. $0.37 = 37\%$

2. $3.1 = 310\%$

Changing Percents to Fractions

Steps to Change Percents to Fractions

To change a percent to a fraction

1. Drop the percent symbol.
2. Express as a fraction over 100 and simplify if possible.

Examples:

1. Change 30% to a fraction: $30\% = \dfrac{30}{100} = \dfrac{3}{10}$

2. Change 8% to a fraction: $8\% = \dfrac{8}{100} = \dfrac{2}{25}$

Changing Fractions to Percents

Steps to Change Fractions to Percents

To change a fraction to a percent

1. Convert the fraction to a decimal.
2. Convert the decimal to a percent.

Examples:

1. Change $\dfrac{3}{5}$ to a percent: $\dfrac{3}{5} = 0.6 = 60\%$

2. Change $\dfrac{5}{2}$ to a percent: $\dfrac{5}{2} = 2.5 = 250\%$

Solving Percent Problems

Before trying to solve a percent problem, change the percent to a fraction or decimal depending upon what seems easier. Also keep in mind that the word "of" suggests multiplication.

Examples:

1. What is 13% of 40?

Remember that "of" means to multiply.

To find the percent, eliminate the percent sign and move the decimal two places to the left (add zeros as necessary). Therefore, 13% = 0.13.

$$0.13 \cdot 40 = 5.2$$

2. 42 is 20% of what number?

$$0.2(x) = 42$$
$$x = \frac{42}{0.2}$$
$$x = 210$$

3. 16 is what percent of 64?

$$x(64) = 16$$
$$x = \frac{16}{64} = \frac{1}{4} = 0.25$$
$$x = 25\%$$

Finding Percent Increase or Percent Decrease

To find the percent increase/decrease use the following formula: $\text{Percent Change} = \dfrac{\text{Increase/Decrease}}{\text{Original Amount}}$

Example:

Find the percent decrease from 12 to 8.

$$\text{Percent Decrease} = \frac{\text{Decrease}}{\text{Original Amount}}$$

$$\frac{4}{12} = \frac{1}{3} = 0.33\frac{1}{3}$$

$$= 33\frac{1}{3}\%$$

Square Roots and Cube Roots

Perfect Squares

A perfect square is a product that results from squaring a number (multiplying a number by itself).

It is useful to memorize the perfect squares found by squaring the integers 1 through 15:

1, 4, 9, 16, 25, 36, 49, 64, 81, 100, 121, 144, 169, 196, and 225

Tip: These are also found by squaring the integers (−1) through (−15).

Examples:

1. Why is 49 a perfect square? 49 is a perfect square since $7^2 = 49$ and $(-7)^2 = 49$.

2. Why is 900 a perfect square? 900 is a perfect square since $30^2 = 900$ and $(-30)^2 = 900$.

Perfect Cubes

A perfect cube is a product that results from cubing a number (multiplying a number two times). It would be useful to memorize the perfect cubes found by cubing the integers 1 through 6:

1, 8, 27, 64, 125, and 216

As well as the integers (−1) through (−6):

−1, −8, −27, −64, −125, and −216

Examples:

1. Why is 125 a perfect cube? 125 is a perfect cube since $5^3 = 125$.

2. Why is 8000 a perfect cube? 8000 is a perfect cube since $20^3 = 8000$.

Square Roots

To find the square root of a number, you must find a number that when multiplied by itself yields the original number. The symbol for the square root is $\sqrt{}$.

$$\sqrt{64} = 8$$

$$-\sqrt{121} = -11$$

$\sqrt{-25}$ does not exist. A square root of a negative number is not a real number.

Cube Roots

To find the cube root of a number, you must find a number that when multiplied by itself, twice yields the original number. The symbol for the cube root is $\sqrt[3]{}$.

$$\sqrt[3]{64} = 4$$

$$\sqrt[3]{-125} = -5$$

Simplifying Square Roots and Cube Roots

To simplify square roots, factor the number under the symbol so that one of its factors is the largest perfect square that divides the number. To simplify cube roots, factor the number under the symbol so that one of its factors is the largest perfect cube that divides the number.

Examples:

1. Simplify $\sqrt{40}$: $\sqrt{40} = \sqrt{4 \cdot 10} = \sqrt{4} \cdot \sqrt{10} = 2\sqrt{10}$

2. Simplify $\sqrt[3]{40}$: $\sqrt[3]{40} = \sqrt[3]{8 \cdot 5} = \sqrt[3]{8} \cdot \sqrt[3]{5} = 2\sqrt[3]{5}$

Units of Measure

Measures		
Length	**Volume**	**Time**
12 inches (in.) =1 foot (ft.) 3 feet = 1 yard (yd.) 36 inches = 1 yard 1760 yards =1 mile (mi.) 5280 feet =1 mile	16 ounces (oz.) = 1 pint (pt.) 2 cups = 1 pint 2 pints = 1 quart (qt.) 4 quarts = 1 gallon (gal.)	60 seconds = 1 minute 60 minutes = 1 hour 24 hours = 1 day 7 days = 1 week 365 days = 1 year 52 weeks = 1 year
Weight	**Months of the Year**	
16 ounces (oz.) = 1 pound (lb.) 2000 pounds =1 ton (T)	It is useful to know the number of days in each of the 12 months of the year. 1. February, 28 days (29 days in a leap year). 2. April, June, September, and November—30 days. 3. Remaining seven months, 31 days.	

Converting Units of Measure

Examples:

1. How many inches in 9 yards? Since 1 yard = 36 inches, 9 yards = $9 \times 36 = 324$ inches.

2. How many pounds in 288 ounces? Since 1 pound = 16 ounces, 288 pounds = $288 \div 16 = 18$ pounds.

3. How many ounces in 7 quarts? Since 1 quart = 2 pints, 7 quarts = $7 \times 2 = 14$ pints. Since 1 pint = 16 ounces, 14 pints = $14 \times 16 = 224$ ounces.

Practice Questions: Arithmetic

Now that you have reviewed the strategies, you can practice on your own. Questions are roughly grouped into sets by their graduated level of difficulty just as they might appear on the actual SAT. Questions appear in three categories: easy to moderate, average, and above-average to difficult. The answers and explanations that follow the questions will include strategies to help you understand how to solve the problems.

Easy to Moderate

1. Round 53,614 to the nearest thousand.

2. Evaluate: $14 - (-8) - 19 + (-16)$

3. Evaluate: $(-3)(-2)(-4)(-1)$

4. Rewrite: $8\frac{3}{4}$ as an improper fraction.

5. Multiply: $8\frac{5}{6} \times 4$

6. Add: $6.4 + 4.923 + 8.18$

7. Subtract: $8.05 - 4.639$

8. Find the ratio of 36 inches to 60 inches.

9. Convert 14 yards to inches.

10. Convert 304 ounces to pounds.

Average

11. Express 3674 in expanded notation using exponents.

12. Evaluate: $3 + 8 \div 4 - (2 + 3)^2 + 10 \times 5$

13. List all the prime numbers between 40 and 50.

14. Find the only number between 170 and 180 that is divisible by 6.

15. Add: $\frac{2}{3} + \frac{1}{2} + \frac{3}{8}$

16. Subtract: $8\frac{1}{4} - 2\frac{3}{5}$

17. Divide: $\frac{8}{21} \div \frac{4}{15}$

18. Multiply: 6.8×0.23

19. Convert $\frac{9}{25}$ to a percent.

20. Convert 56% to a fraction in lowest terms.

21. Find: 35% of 93

22. Evaluate: $3^4 - 2^5$

23. Evaluate: $\sqrt{49} \times \sqrt[3]{64}$

24. Simplify: $\sqrt{90}$

25. Simplify: $\sqrt[3]{56}$

26. Divide: $3.428 \div 0.04$

Above Average to Difficult

27. Find the percent decrease from 150 to 120.

28. Approximate $\sqrt{110}$ to the nearest tenth.

Answers and Explanations

Easy to Moderate

1. Start by determining what numeral is in the thousands place, and one place to the right of the thousands place. Since the number immediately to the right of the thousands place is a 6, 53,614 becomes 54,000 when rounded to the nearest thousand.

2. If a minus precedes a parenthesis, change the sign within the parenthesis to its opposite sign and add.

$$14 - (-8) - 19 + (-16)$$
$$= 14 + 8 + (-19) + (-16)$$
$$= 22 + (-19) + (-16)$$
$$= 3 + (-16)$$
$$= -13$$

3. Multiplying two negative numbers together produces a positive product. Multiplying a positive number and a negative number produces a negative number.

$$(-3)(-2)(-4)(-1)$$
$$= (6)(-4)(-1)$$
$$= (-24)(-1)$$
$$= 24$$

4. The whole number 8 is composed of 32 "fourths" ($8 \times 4 = 32$). Add the three additional fourths to this to find the answer $\frac{35}{4}$.

$$8\frac{3}{4} = \frac{(8 \times 4) + 3}{4}$$
$$= \frac{32 + 3}{4}$$
$$= \frac{35}{4}$$

5. First use the method in the previous problem to convert $8\frac{5}{6}$ to the fraction $\frac{53}{6}$. Then, before multiplying $\frac{53}{6}$ by 4, divide both the numerator and denominator by 2. After simplifying the numerator and the denominator, multiply across the top and across the bottom to arrive at $\frac{106}{3}$, and then rewrite to $35\frac{1}{3}$.

$$8\frac{5}{6} \times 4 = \frac{53}{\cancel{6}_3} \times \frac{\cancel{4}^2}{1}$$
$$= \frac{53}{3} \times \frac{2}{1}$$
$$= \frac{106}{3}$$
$$= 35\frac{1}{3}$$

6. Align the decimal points when adding and subtracting.

$$6.4 + 4.923 + 8.18 =$$

$$
\begin{array}{r}
6.400 \\
4.923 \\
+8.180 \\
\hline
19.503
\end{array}
$$

7. Align the decimal points as in the previous example.

$$8.05 - 4.639 = \quad
\begin{array}{r}
8.050 \\
-4.639 \\
\hline
3.411
\end{array}
$$

8. Ratios are a method of comparing a number or variable "to" another number or variable. Ratios are expressed as fractions. The "to" in the sentence identifies the numerator and denominator (or what should be on top and what should be on the bottom) of the fraction. In the ratio of 36 to 60, the "to" indicates that 36 is the numerator and 60 is the denominator. Don't forget to reduce the fraction.

$$= \frac{36 \text{ inches}}{60 \text{ inches}}$$
$$= \frac{36}{60}$$
$$= \frac{6}{10} = \frac{3}{5}$$

9. This measurement conversion problem requires you to know how many inches are in a yard. If 1 foot equals 12 inches, and there are 3 feet in one yard, then $1 \times 12 \times 3 = 36$ inches in a yard. Multiply the number of yards (14) times the number of inches (36) to find your answer.

$$1 \text{ yard} = 36 \text{ inches}$$
$$14 \text{ yards} = (14 \times 36) \text{ inches}$$
$$= 504 \text{ inches}$$

10. This is a converting units of measure type of problem that requires you know how many ounces are in a pound. Since 16 ounces equals 1 pound, divide 304 ounces by 16 ounces.

$$16 \text{ ounces} = 1 \text{ pound}$$
$$304 \text{ ounces} = (304 \div 16) \text{ pounds}$$
$$= 19 \text{ pounds}$$

Average

11. If you don't know expanded notation, this might be a difficult problem to solve. Be sure to memorize place value and expanded notation before you take your test. 3674 expressed in expanded notation:

$$3674 = 3000 + 600 + 70 + 4$$
$$= (3 \times 1000) + (6 \times 100) + (7 \times 10) + (4 \times 1)$$
$$= (3 \times 10^3) + (6 \times 10^2) + (7 \times 10^1) + (4 \times 10^0)$$

12. Remember the acronym PEMDAS to help you follow the order of operation. Start with the parentheses, followed by exponents and square roots as they occur from left to right, multiplication and division as they occur from left to right, and last addition and subtraction as they occur from left to right.

$$3 + 8 \div 4 - (2 + 3)^2 + 10 \times 5$$
$$= 3 + 8 \div 4 - 5^2 + 10 \times 5$$
$$= 3 + 8 \div 4 - 25 + 10 \times 5$$
$$= 3 + 2 - 25 + 50$$
$$= 5 - 25 + 50$$
$$= -20 + 50$$
$$= 30$$

13. The even numbers between 40 and 50 may be eliminated since they are divisible by 2. That leaves 41, 43, 45, 47, and 49. Since 45 is divisible by 5 and 49 is divisible by 7, the only prime numbers between 40 and 50 are 41, 43, and 47.

14. For a number to be divisible by 6, it must be divisible by both 2 and 3. The numbers between 170 and 180 that are divisible by 2 are 172, 174, 176, and 178. The numbers between 170 and 180 that are divisible by 3 are 171, 174, and 177. Hence the only number between 170 and 180 that is divisible by 6 is 174. If you forget the rule for divisibility by 6, you should still be able to reason that only even numbers are possibilities.

15. To add or subtract fractions, all fractions must have the same denominator. The first step is to find the Least Common Denominator. The LCD of $\frac{2}{3}$, $\frac{1}{2}$, and $\frac{3}{8} = 24$

$$\frac{2}{3} + \frac{1}{2} + \frac{3}{8} = \frac{2 \cdot 8}{3 \cdot 8} + \frac{1 \cdot 12}{2 \cdot 12} + \frac{3 \cdot 3}{8 \cdot 3}$$

$$= \frac{16}{24} + \frac{12}{24} + \frac{9}{24}$$

$$= \frac{37}{24}$$

$$= 1\frac{13}{24}$$

16. The LCD of $8\frac{1}{4}$ and $2\frac{3}{5}$ is 20.

$$8\frac{1}{4} = 8\frac{5}{20} = 7 + 1\frac{5}{20} = 7\frac{25}{20}$$

$$\underline{-2\frac{3}{5} = -2\frac{12}{20} = -2\frac{12}{20} = -2\frac{12}{20}}$$

$$= 5\frac{13}{20}$$

17. To divide fractions, multiply by the reciprocal of the second fraction. Reduce if necessary.

$$\frac{8}{21} \div \frac{4}{15} = \frac{\cancel{8}^2}{\cancel{21}_7} \cdot \frac{\cancel{15}^5}{\cancel{4}_1}$$

$$= \frac{2}{7} \cdot \frac{5}{1}$$

$$= \frac{10}{7}$$

$$= 1\frac{3}{7}$$

18. After evaluating this problem using long multiplication, the trick is to correctly place the decimal point. Count the total number of digits in the problem that are to the right of all decimal points. Place the decimal point in the answer so there are an equal number of digits to the right of the decimal point as there were in the problem. The answer has 3 digits to the right of the decimal point.

$$
\begin{array}{r}
6.8 \\
\times 0.23 \\
\hline
204 \\
136 \\
\hline
1.564
\end{array}
$$

19. Find the answer by changing the fraction to a decimal and then to a percent. $\frac{9}{25}$ means 9 divided by 25, and then insert the decimal point accordingly, or .36.

   To find the percent, move the decimal point two places to the right and insert a percent sign.

$$\frac{9}{25} = \frac{x}{100}, \quad \begin{array}{l} 25x = 9 \cdot 100 \\ \frac{25x}{25} = \frac{900}{25} \\ x = 36\% \end{array} \quad \text{or} \quad \begin{array}{l} \overset{.36}{25)9.00} = .36 = 36\% \\ \underline{75} \\ 150 \\ \underline{150} \end{array}$$

20. To convert a percent to a fraction, move the decimal point two places to the left, or write the number as a fraction over 100. $56\% = .56 = \frac{56}{100} = \frac{14}{25}$

21. When you see the word "of," automatically think about multiplying. Change the percent by eliminating the percent sign and moving the decimal two places to the left, and then multiply. 35% of $93 = .35 \times 93 = 32.55$.

22. Remember the acronym PEMDAS to solve this order of operation problem. Simplify the exponents and then subtract: $3^4 - 2^5 = 81 - 32 = 49$

23. Simplify the square root and the cube root and then multiply.

$$\sqrt{49} \times \sqrt[3]{64} = 7 \times 4 = 28$$

24. Factor the largest perfect square of 90, which is 9.

$$\sqrt{90} = \sqrt{9 \cdot 10} = \sqrt{9} \cdot \sqrt{10} = 3\sqrt{10}$$

25. Factor the largest perfect cube of 56, which is 8.

$$\sqrt[3]{56} = \sqrt[3]{8 \cdot 7} = \sqrt[3]{8} \cdot \sqrt[3]{7} = 2\sqrt[3]{7}$$

26. This is a long division problem. When dividing with decimals, move the decimal in the divisor to the right to create a whole number. Then move the decimal in the dividend the same number of spaces to the right and add zeros if necessary. The decimal in the answer should be placed directly above this decimal point.

$$0.04)\overline{3.428} = \begin{array}{l} \overset{85.7}{4)342.8} \\ \underline{32} \\ 22 \\ \underline{20} \\ 28 \\ \underline{28} \end{array}$$

Hence $3.428 \div 0.04 = 85.7$.

Above Average to Difficult

27. A percent compares a part to a whole and in this case the amount of decrease to the original amount:

$$\text{Percent decrease} = \frac{\text{amount of decrease}}{\text{original amount}}$$

The amount of decrease from 150 to 120 = 30 and the original amount is 150.

$$\text{Percent decrease} = \frac{30}{150} = \frac{1}{5} = .20 = 20\%$$

28. Since 110 is not a perfect square, it is necessary to estimate an answer.

$$\sqrt{100} = 10 \text{ and } \sqrt{121} = 11, \, 10 < \sqrt{110} < 11$$

Since 110 is approximately halfway between 100 and 121, $\sqrt{110}$ is approximately halfway between $\sqrt{100}$ and $\sqrt{121}$. Hence a reasonable approximation for $\sqrt{110}$ is 10.5.

Chapter 6

Algebra and Functions Review

Algebra is a branch of mathematics in which you will continue to use the four basic operations of arithmetic: addition, subtraction, multiplication, and division. Before you begin your algebra review, you must have a solid understanding of the basic math skills presented in the previous chapter. In algebra, variables, usually written as letters, are used to represent numbers. The rules that are applied for algebra are basically the same as the rules for arithmetic. The use of variables, numbers, and mathematical symbols allows us to write algebraic expressions instead of more complicated verbal math statements.

Algebraic Basics

Algebra's Implied Multiplication

The operation of multiplication may be expressed in a variety of ways algebraically. For example, the product of 5 times z may be expressed as $5z$ with no symbol to indicate the operation of multiplication. A raised dot or parentheses may also indicate the operation of multiplication. For example, the product of 3 times 8 may be expressed as $3 \cdot 8 = 3(8) = (3)8 = (3)(8) = 3 \times 8$.

Set Theory

Set theory is fundamental for most topics in modern mathematics. Sets are defined as a collection of groups of objects.

Set Theory Terminology		
Term	**Definition**	**Examples**
Set	A set is a collection of objects that are separated by a comma and grouped in braces.	A = {1, 2, 3, 4, 5} B = {a, e, i, o, u}
Element	The objects that make up a set are called elements (or members) of the set. The symbol used for an element is $\in$. ($\notin$ means not an element of the set.)	$4 \in A$ $h \notin B$
Subset	If a set is part of or identical to another set, it is called a subset of the set. The symbol used for subset is $\subset$. *Note: A proper subset $\subset$ cannot be identical to the original set.*	$\{1,4,5\} \subset \{1,2,3,4,5\}$ $\{a,e,i,o,u\} \subset \{a,e,i,o,u\}$
Empty or Null Set	A set with no elements is called the empty set or null set. The symbol used for the empty set is $\varnothing$ or { }.	$\varnothing$ or $\{\ \}$
Finite Set	A set that has a countable number of elements is called a finite set.	{1, 2, 3, 4, 5} is a finite set with 5 elements.
Infinite Set	A set whose elements continue indefinitely is called an infinite set. Note that three dots are used to indicate a set is infinite.	{5, 10, 15, 20, 25, 30…}
Equal Sets	Sets that have exactly the same elements are called equal sets.	{3, 8, 10, 12} = {10, 8, 3, 12}
Equivalent Sets	Sets that have the same number of elements are called equivalent sets.	{1, 2, 3, 4, 5} and {a, e, i, o, u} are equivalent sets.
Union	The union of two or more sets is a set that contains the elements of all the sets. The symbol used for union is $\cup$.	$\{1,2,3,4,5\} \cup \{2,4,6,8\} =$ $\{1,2,3,4,5,6,8\}$
Intersection	The intersection of two or more sets is a set that contains only those elements that are common to the sets. If the sets have no elements in common, then their intersection is the null set. The symbol used for intersection is $\cap$.	$\{1,2,3,4,5\} \cap \{2,4,6,8\} = \{2,4\}$ $\{1,3,5,7\} \cap \{2,4,6,8,10\} = \varnothing$

Algebra Review

The major algebraic topics reviewed in this section are:

- Exponents
- Absolute value
- Algebraic expressions
- Linear equations and inequalities
- Systems of equations
- Polynomials
- Quadratic and polynomial equations
- Rational equations
- Radicals, roots, and solving radical equations
- Variations
- Analytic geometry
- Functions

Solving algebraic equations requires knowledge of relationships between numbers and symbols. This section will define key algebraic terms, introduce important algebraic topics and walk you through step-by-step practice examples. As you review this section, keep in mind that algebraic equations are like a balance scale. When you perform an operation on one side of the equal sign, you must do the same thing on the other side of the equal sign.

Exponents

An exponent is a number written above and to the right of a number or variable. The number or variable the exponent is applied to is called the base.

Positive Integer Exponents

A positive integer exponent indicates the number of times the base is to be used as a factor.

Examples:

1. $2^5 = 2 \cdot 2 \cdot 2 \cdot 2 \cdot 2 = 32$

2. $(-3)^4 = (-3)(-3)(-3)(-3) = 81$

Zero Exponents

Any nonzero number raised to the 0 power is 1. Note that 0^0 is undefined.

Examples:

1. $8^0 = 1$

2. $(-12)^0 = 1$

3. $\left(\dfrac{2}{3}\right)^0 = 1$

Negative Integer Exponents

Any negative integer exponent can be rewritten as a positive integer exponent by changing the base to its reciprocal.

In general, $x^{-n} = \left(\dfrac{1}{x}\right)^n$ or $\dfrac{1}{x^n}$.

Examples:

1. $5^{-2} = \left(\dfrac{1}{5}\right)^2 = \dfrac{1^2}{5^2} = \left(\dfrac{1}{5}\right)\left(\dfrac{1}{5}\right) = \dfrac{1}{25}$

2. $\left(\dfrac{3}{4}\right)^{-3} = \left(\dfrac{4}{3}\right)^3 = \dfrac{4^3}{3^3} = \left(\dfrac{4}{3}\right)\left(\dfrac{4}{3}\right)\left(\dfrac{4}{3}\right) = \dfrac{64}{27}$ or $2\dfrac{10}{27}$

Fractional or Rational Exponents

A fractional exponent may be interpreted in two parts with the numerator indicating the power and the denominator indicating the root to be applied to the base.

In general, $x^{\frac{m}{n}} = \sqrt[n]{x^m} = \left(\sqrt[n]{x}\right)^m$.

It is usually easier to apply the root before evaluating the power.

Examples:

1. $100^{\frac{3}{2}} = \left(\sqrt{100}\right)^3 = 10^3 = 10 \cdot 10 \cdot 10 = 1000$

2. $27^{\frac{4}{3}} = \left(\sqrt[3]{27}\right)^4 = 3^4 = 3 \cdot 3 \cdot 3 \cdot 3 = 81$

Properties of Exponents

There are five basic properties of exponents, all of which apply to positive integer, negative integer, zero, and fractional exponents.

Addition Property

When multiplying exponent expressions with the same base, keep the base the same and add the exponents.

$$x^m \cdot x^n = x^{m+n}$$

Examples:

1. $z^4 \cdot z^{-5} \cdot z^8 = z^{4+(-5)+8} = z^7$

2. $= y^{-6} \cdot y^2 = y^{(-6)+2} = y^{-4} = \dfrac{1}{y^4}$

Subtraction Property:

When dividing exponent expressions with the same base, keep the base the same and subtract the exponents.

$$x^m \div x^n = x^{m-n}$$

Examples:

1. $a^{10} \div a^2 = a^{10-2} = a^8$

2. $x^4 \div x^9 = x^{4-9} = x^{-5} = \dfrac{1}{x^5}$

Power to a Power Property:

When raising an exponent expression to a power, keep the base the same and multiply the exponents.

$$\left(x^m\right)^n = x^{mn}$$

Examples:

1. $(z^4)^3 = z^{4(3)} = z^{12}$

2. $\left(x^3\right)^{-2} = x^{3(-2)} = x^{-6} = \dfrac{1}{x^6}$

Product Rule:

Exponents may be distributed over multiplication.

$$(a \cdot b)^n = a^n \cdot b^n$$

Examples:

1. $\left(x^2 y^3\right)^4 = x^{2 \cdot 4} \cdot y^{3 \cdot 4} = x^8 y^{12}$

2. $\left(5a^5 b^6\right)^2 = 5^2 \cdot a^{5 \cdot 2} \cdot b^{6 \cdot 2} = 25a^{10}b^{12}$

Quotient Rule:

Exponents may be distributed over division.

$$\left(\dfrac{a}{b}\right)^n = \dfrac{a^n}{b^n}$$

Example:

$$\left(\frac{x^2}{y^5}\right)^3 = \frac{x^{2\cdot3}}{y^{5\cdot3}} = \frac{x^6}{y^{15}}$$

Absolute Value

The absolute value of a number x is its distance from zero (disregarding direction), and is denoted $|x|$. Note that the absolute value of a number is always nonnegative.

Examples:

1. $|12| = 12$

2. $|-5| = 5$

3. $|0| = 0$

Operations on Algebraic Expressions

Addition

When adding algebraic expressions, combine like or similar terms. Like terms should have the same variable(s) and the same exponent applied to the variable(s). Like terms are combined by adding or subtracting the numerical coefficients and keeping the variable(s) the same.

Examples:

1. $5ab + 6bc - 2ab - 11bc = 3ab - 5bc$

2. $9x^2y + 10xy^2 + 4x^2y - 3xy^2 = 13x^2y + 7xy^2$

Subtraction

Subtracting algebraic expressions follows the same rule as addition-combine like terms. The signs in each of the terms of the expression that follow the subtraction should be changed and then added.

Examples:

1. $(8x^2 - 2x + 5) - (6x^2 - 7x + 9) = 8x^2 - 2x + 5 - 6x^2 + 7x - 9$
$$= 2x^2 + 5x - 4$$

2. $(3y + 8z - 7) - (12 + 4z - 6y) = 3y + 8z - 7 - 12 - 4z + 6y$
$$= 9y + 4z - 19$$

Multiplication

To multiply algebraic expressions, multiply numerical coefficients and multiply variables applying the addition property of exponents if possible. Also keep in mind that each term in one expression must be multiplied by each term in the other expression. After the multiplication has been performed, look for any like terms to combine.

Examples:

1. $(8y^5)(-5y^4) = -40y^9$

2. $3x^2(5x^2 - 4x + 7) = 15x^4 - 12x^3 + 21x^2$

3. $(4z + 7)(3z - 2) = 12z^2 - 8z + 21z - 14$

$\qquad = 12z^2 + 13z - 14$

Example 3 is a special case that is sometimes referred to as the "FOIL" method. **(F) first, (O) outside, (I) inside, and (L) last terms** are multiplied to get the product.

4. $(4a + 9b)(4a - 9b) = 16a^2 - 36ab + 36ab - 81b^2$

$\qquad = 16a^2 - 81b^2$

Example 4 is a special case that is often referred to **as the product of a sum times a difference** since the terms are the same except for the signs between them.

5. $(2x - 5)(x^2 - 5x + 3) = 2x^3 - 10x^2 + 6x - 5x^2 + 25x - 15$

$\qquad = 2x^3 - 15x^2 + 31x - 15$

Division

To divide algebraic expressions, divide numerical coefficients and divide variables applying the subtraction property of exponents if possible. Note that division of algebraic expressions is somewhat similar to the method used in multiplication of algebraic expressions.

Examples:

1. $(48a^8) \div (-6a^2) = -8a^6$

2. $\dfrac{35x^2 y^5}{5x^6 y^3} = 7x^{-4} y^2 = \dfrac{7y^2}{x^4}$

3. $(14z^5 - 21z^3 + 28z^2) \div 7z^2 = \dfrac{14z^5}{7z^2} - \dfrac{21z^3}{7z^2} + \dfrac{28z^2}{7z^2} = 2z^3 - 3z + 4$

Evaluating Algebraic Expressions

To evaluate an algebraic expression substitute the given values for the variables using parentheses and perform the indicated operations following the order of operation rules.

Examples:

1. Evaluate: $3y^2 + 5y + 23$, if $y = -3$

$$3y^2 + 5y + 23 = 3(-3)^2 + 5(-3) + 23$$
$$= 3(9) - 15 + 23$$
$$= 27 - 15 + 23$$
$$= 35$$

2. Evaluate: $\dfrac{3x - 4y}{2z}$, if $x = -2$, $y = -1$ and $z = 3$

$$\frac{3x - 4y}{2z} = \frac{3(-2) - 4(-1)}{2(3)}$$
$$= \frac{-6 + 4}{6}$$
$$= \frac{-2}{6}$$
$$= -\frac{1}{3}$$

3. Evaluate: $5ab - a^2$, if $a = -3$ and $b = 4$

$$5ab - a^2 = 5(-3)(4) - (-3)^2$$
$$= -60 - 9$$
$$= -69$$

Linear Equations

Solving Linear Equations in One Variable

An equation is like a balance scale. A basic rule to follow to maintain the balance is: The arithmetic operations you perform on one side of the equation must also be performed on the other side of the equation. To solve an equation means to find all values for the variable that make the equation a true statement. An equation consists of a left member and a right member, separated by an equal (=) sign. The goal in solving an equation is to get the variable isolated on one side of the equation and the numerical value on the other side of the equation. Although most linear equations have only one solution, it is important to note that a linear equation may have more than one solution or have no solution.

Examples:

1. Solve: $3y + 49 = 25$

$$3y + 49 - 49 = 25 - 49$$
$$3y = -24$$
$$\frac{3y}{3} = \frac{-24}{3}$$
$$y = -8$$

2. Solve: $\frac{3}{4}z - 17 = -5$

$$\frac{3}{4}z - 17 + 17 = -5 + 17$$

$$\frac{3}{4}z = 12$$

$$\frac{4}{3}\left(\frac{3}{4}z\right) = \frac{4}{3}(12)$$

$$z = \frac{48}{3}$$

$$z = 16$$

3. Solve: $5x - 33 = 7x - 19$

$$5x - 33 - 7x = 7x - 19 - 7x$$

$$-2x - 33 = -19$$

$$-2x - 33 + 33 = -19 + 33$$

$$-2x = 14$$

$$\frac{-2x}{-2} = \frac{14}{-2}$$

$$x = -7$$

4. Solve for x: $3x + 5y = 4z$

$$3x + 5y - 5y = 4z - 5y$$

$$3x = 4z - 5y$$

$$\frac{3x}{3} = \frac{4z - 5y}{3}$$

$$x = \frac{4z - 5y}{3}$$

Absolute Value Linear Equations

Some linear expressions are included inside the absolute value symbol as part of the equation. These are referred to as absolute value linear equations.

Examples:

1. Solve $|3x + 5| = 10$

If $|3x + 5| = 10$, then

$3x + 5 = 10$	or	$3x + 5 = -10$
$3x + 5 - 5 = 10 - 5$		$3x + 5 - 5 = -10 - 5$
$3x = 5$		$3x = -15$
$\frac{3x}{3} = \frac{5}{3}$		$\frac{3x}{3} = \frac{-15}{3}$
$x = \frac{5}{3}$ or $1\frac{2}{3}$		$x = -5$

2. Solve: $|6y + 24| = 0$

$$\text{If } |6y + 24| = 0, \text{ then}$$
$$6y + 24 = 0$$
$$6y + 24 - 24 = 0 - 24$$
$$6y = -24$$
$$\frac{6y}{6} = \frac{-24}{6}$$
$$y = -4$$

3. Solve: $|2z + 11| = -10$

Since the absolute value of a number can never be negative, the absolute value of an algebraic expression cannot equal –10. Hence, this equation has no solution. Note that replacing the variable with any real number will result in an absolute value that is a positive number or zero.

Tip: In general, if the absolute value of a linear expression is equal to a positive number, the equation will have two solutions. If the absolute value of a linear expression is equal to zero, the equation will have only one solution. However, if the absolute value of a linear expression is equal to a negative number, the equation will have no solution.

Solving Systems of Equations in Two Variables

Solving a system of linear equations in two variables requires finding a value for both unknowns. This can be done by using one of two algebraic methods: Elimination Method or Substitution Method.

Elimination Method

1. Arrange the terms in each of the equations so that the variables are on one side of the equation and the constant is on the other side of the equation.
2. Multiply one or both equations by a constant so that the numeral coefficients of one of the variables are opposites of each other.
3. Add the resulting equations to eliminate that variable.
4. Solve the resulting equation for the remaining variable.
5. Substitute this value in either of the two original equations and solve for the second variable.
6. Check your answers by substituting these values in each of the original equations.

Examples:

1. Solve: $5x + 3y = -4$
$3x - 6y = -57$

Multiply both sides of the first equation by 2:

$$2(5x + 3y) = 2(-4) \rightarrow 10x + 6y = -8$$

Leave the second equation as is.

$$3x - 6y = -57 \rightarrow 3x - 6y = -57$$

Add the equations to eliminate the y terms:

$$10x + 6y = -8$$
$$\underline{3x - 6y = -57}$$
$$13x = -65$$
$$\frac{13x}{13} = \frac{-65}{13}$$
$$x = -5$$

Substitute $x = -5$ in the first equation:

$$5x + 3y = -4$$
$$5(-5) + 3y = -4$$
$$-25 + 3y = -4$$
$$-25 + 3y + 25 = -4 + 25$$
$$3y = 21$$
$$\frac{3y}{3} = \frac{21}{3}$$
$$y = 7$$

Hence the solution is $x = -5$ and $y = 7$, which will yield a true statement when these values are substituted for x and y in each of the original equations.

> **2.** Solve: $\quad 2x + 3y = 12$
> $\qquad\quad -2x + 5y = -28$

Since the numerical coefficients of the x variable are opposites, the equations may be added to eliminate the x terms.

$$2x + 3y = 12$$
$$\underline{-2x + 5y = -28}$$
$$8y = -16$$
$$\frac{8y}{8} = \frac{-16}{8}$$
$$y = -2$$

Substitute $y = -2$ in the second equation:

$$-2x + 5y = -28$$
$$-2x + 5(-2) = -28$$
$$-2x - 10 = -28$$
$$-2x - 10 + 10 = -28 + 10$$
$$-2x = -18$$
$$\frac{-2x}{-2} = \frac{-18}{-2}$$
$$x = 9$$

Hence the solution is $x = 9$ and $y = -2$, which will yield a true statement when these values are substituted for x and y in each of the original equations.

Elimination Method Special Cases

There are two special cases that sometimes occur when you solve a system of equations by means of the Elimination Method:

1. If both variables are eliminated when adding the equations and the resulting equation is a true statement $0 = 0$, then the equations are, in fact, the same equations and the system has an infinite number of solutions for each of the variables.

   Solve:

   $$3a - 6b = 15$$
   $$a - 2b = 5$$

   Multiplying both sides of the second equation by -3: $\quad -3(a - 2b) = -3(5) \rightarrow -3a + 6b = -15$

   Leave the first equation as is: $\qquad\qquad\qquad 3a - 6b = 15 \qquad \rightarrow \quad 3a - 6b = 15$

   Adding the equations:
   $$3a - 6b = 15$$
   $$\underline{-3a + 6b = -15}$$
   $$0 = 0$$

   Since both variables are eliminated and the resulting statement $0 = 0$ is true, the system has an infinite number of solutions. Any order pair that satisfies one of the equations will also satisfy the other equation. Graphically, this means that the two equations represent the same straight line.

2. If both variables are eliminated when adding the equations and the resulting equation is a false statement, then the system has no solution.

   Solve:

   $$2x - y = 5$$
   $$-4x + 2y = 7$$

   Multiplying both sides of the first equation by 2: $\quad 2(2x - y) = 2(5) \rightarrow \quad 4x - 2y = 10$

   Leave the second equation as is: $\qquad\qquad\quad -4x + 2y = 7 \quad \rightarrow -4x + 2y = 7$

   Adding the equations:
   $$4x - 2y = 10$$
   $$\underline{-4x + 2y = 7}$$
   $$0 = 17$$

   Since both variables are eliminated and the resulting statement $0 = 17$ is false, the system has no solution. Graphically, this means that the lines are parallel and have no points in common.

Substitution Method

1. Choose one of the equations and solve for one of its variables in terms of the other variable.
2. Substitute this expression for that variable in the other equation.
3. Solve the equation for the remaining variable.
4. Substitute this value in either of the two original equations and solve for the second variable.
5. As with the Elimination Method, if both values are eliminated after substituting and the resulting equation is a true statement, then the equations are the same and the system has an infinite number of solutions for each of the variables. If, on the other hand, the resulting equation is a false statement, then the system has no solution.

Examples:

> **1.** Solve: $x - 2y = 7$
>
> $2x + 3y = 28$

Solving the first equation for x:

$$x - 2y = 7$$
$$x - 2y + 2y = 7 + 2y$$
$$x = 2y + 7$$

Substitute x in the second equation with $2y + 7$:

$$2x + 3y = 28$$
$$2(2y + 7) + 3y = 28$$
$$4y + 14 + 3y = 28$$
$$7y + 14 = 28$$
$$7y + 14 - 14 = 28 - 14$$
$$7y = 14$$
$$\frac{7y}{7} = \frac{14}{7}$$
$$y = 2$$

Substitute $y = 2$ in the first equation:

$$x - 2y = 7$$
$$x - 2(2) = 7$$
$$x - 4 = 7$$
$$x - 4 + 4 = 7 + 4$$
$$x = 11$$

Hence the solution is $x = 11$ and $y = 2$ which will yield a true statement when these values are substituted for x and y in each of the original equations.

> **2.** Solve: $6x + 2y = -12$
>
> $3x + y = 10$

Solve the second equation for y:

$$3x + y = 10$$
$$3x + y - 3x = 10 - 3x$$
$$y = 10 - 3x$$

Substitute y in the first equation with $10 - 3x$:

$$6x + 2y = -12$$
$$6x + 2(10 - 3x) = -12$$
$$6x + 20 - 6x = -12$$
$$20 = -12$$

Since both variables were eliminated and the resulting equation, $20 = -12$ is false, the system has no solution.

Solving Linear Inequalities in One Variable

To solve an inequality means to find all values for the variable that make the inequality a true statement. An inequality consists of a left member and a right member separated by any one of four inequality symbols: $>$, $<$, $\geq$, or $\leq$. The goal in solving an inequality is to get the variable isolated on one side of the inequality symbol and the numerical value on the other side. The method used is basically the same as the method used for solving linear equations: What is done to one side of an inequality must be done to the other side as well. There is a special case that must be observed that requires that the inequality symbol must be reversed when both sides of the inequality are multiplied or divided by a negative number.

Examples:

> **1.** Solve: $4z - 19 < 9$

$$4z - 19 < 9$$
$$4z - 19 + 19 < 9 + 19$$
$$4z < 28$$
$$\frac{4z}{4} < \frac{28}{4}$$
$$z < 7$$

An equivalent solution would be $7 > z$.

> **2.** Solve: $5x + 12 \geq 8x - 15$

$$5x + 12 - 8x \geq 8x - 15 - 8x$$
$$-3x + 12 \geq -15$$
$$-3x + 12 - 12 \geq -15 - 12$$
$$-3x \geq -27$$
$$\frac{-3x}{-3} \leq \frac{-27}{-3} \qquad \text{Inequality is reversed.}$$
$$x \leq 9$$

An equivalent solution would be $9 \geq x$.

Polynomials and Factoring

Special types of algebraic expressions, called polynomials, occur in many algebra problems. Factoring polynomials can often simplify the process of solving what would otherwise appear to be a difficult problem.

Polynomials

A **polynomial** is an algebraic expression made up of two or more terms. Terms are separated by addition or subtraction.

Polynomials are commonly written in descending order with the power of terms decreasing with each successive term. The powers (exponent) in a polynomial is always a whole number. Exponents may also be written in ascending order with the power of terms increasing with each successive term.

Examples:

1. $3y^5 + 4y - 9$

2. $3a + 5b$

3. $x^2 - 6z^2$

Monomials

A **monomial** is an algebraic expression made up of only one term.

Examples:

1. $3x^5$

2. $4a^2b^3c$

Binomials

A **binomial** is a polynomial with exactly two terms.

Examples:

1. $4x + 3y$

2. $6z^4 - 11$

Trinomials

A **trinomial** is a polynomial with exactly three terms.

Examples:

1. $3y^5 + 4y - 9$

2. $8a^2b^2 - 9a^2b + 10ab^2$

Operations on Polynomials: Since polynomials are algebraic expressions, the same rules apply for addition, subtraction, multiplication, and division of polynomials as for algebraic expressions.

Factoring Polynomials

Factoring a polynomial means to find two or more expressions whose product is the given polynomial. This is equivalent to being given the answer to a multiplication problem and trying to determine what was multiplied to get the product.

Factoring Out the Greatest Common Factor

1. Find the Greatest Common Factor (GCF) of each term of the polynomial. The GCF is the largest factor that is common to each term of the polynomial.
2. Divide each term of the polynomial by the GCF to obtain the second factor.

Examples:

1. Factor: $9z^5 - 15z^3$

The GCF of $9z^5$ and $15z^3$ is $3z^3$.

$$\text{Since } \frac{9z^5}{3z^3} = 3z^2 \text{ and } \frac{15z^3}{3z^3} = 5,$$
$$9z^5 - 15z^3 = 3z^3\left(3z^2 - 5\right).$$

2. Factor: $4a^4 + 20a^3 + 2a^2$

The GCF of $4a^4$, $20a^3$, and $2a^2$ is $2a^2$.

$$\text{Since } \frac{4a^4}{2a^2} = 2a^2, \frac{20a^3}{2a^2} = 10a, \text{ and } \frac{2a^2}{2a^2} = 1,$$
$$4a^4 + 20a^3 + 2a^2 = 2a^2\left(2a^2 + 10a + 1\right).$$

Factoring the Difference of Two Squares

This method may be used if the given polynomial is the subtraction of two monomials that are perfect squares.

1. Find the square root of each of the two terms in the polynomial.
2. The factors may be expressed as the product of the sum of the two square roots times the difference of the two square roots from the previous step.

Examples:

1. Factor: $25y^2 - 9$.

Since $25y^2$ and 9 are both perfect squares,

$$25y^2 - 9 = (5y + 3)(5y - 3)$$

The factors may also be written $(5y - 3)(5y + 3)$.

2. Factor: $x^4 - 100z^2$.

Since x^4 and $100z^2$ are both perfect squares, $x^4 - 100z^2 = (x^2 + 10z)(x^2 - 10z)$.

The factors may also written $(x^2 - 10z)(x^2 + 10z)$.

Polynomials that Are the Sum of Two Squares

It is important to note that a polynomial that is the sum of two squares is not factorable since it is a prime polynomial.

Examples:

1. $x^2 + 49$ is not factorable.

2. $9x^2 + 16$ is not factorable.

Tip: Always factor out the greatest common factor, if possible, before considering the difference of two squares or any other factoring technique.

Factoring Trinomials

When factoring trinomials of the form $ax^2 + bx + c$:

1. Check for a greatest common factor and factor it out if possible.
2. Consider all possible factors of the first term, ax^2, and place these factors as the first term in each of the double parentheses of the form ( )( ).
3. Consider all possible factors of the last term, c, and place these factors as the second term in each of the double parentheses.
4. Apply the "FOIL" multiplication method to each of the possible factors to determine which pair of factors will generate the correct middle term, bx.
5. Note that if the last term c is positive, then the last two terms in the double parentheses must both be positive or both be negative. However, if the last term c is negative, then one of the last terms in the double parentheses must be positive and the other must be negative.
6. Remember to check the answer by multiplying the factors to get the original polynomial.

Examples:

1. Factor: $x^2 - 5x + 6$

There are no common factors to pull out and the only factors of x^2 are $(x)(x)$, while the possible factors of +6 are $(1)(6)$, $(-1)(-6)$, $(2)(3)$, and $(-2)(-3)$.

The correct factorization is

$$x^2 - 5x + 6 = (x - 2)(x - 3)$$

2. Factor: $x^2 - 5x - 6$

There are no common factors to pull out and the only factors of x^2 are $(x)(x)$, while the possible factors of –6 are $(-1)(6)$, $(1)(-6)$, $(-2)(3)$, and $(2)(-3)$.

The correct factorization is

$$x^2 - 5x - 6 = (x + 1)(x - 6)$$

> **3.** Factor: $3z^2 + 2z - 21$

There are no common factors to pull out and the only factors of $3z^2$ are $(3z)(z)$, while the possible factors of -21 are $(-1)(21)$, $(1)(-21)$, $(-3)(7)$, and $(3)(-7)$.

The correct factorization is

$$3z^2 + 2z - 21 = (3z - 7)(z + 3)$$

> **4.** Factor: $4y^2 + 9y + 2$

There are no common factors to pull out and the only factors of $4y^2$ are $(2y)(2y)$ and $(4y)(y)$. The possible factors of $+2$ are $(1)(2)$ and $(-1)(-2)$.

The correct factorization is

$$4y^2 + 9y + 2 = (4y + 1)(y + 2)$$

> **5.** Factor: $3x^4 - 6x^3 - 45x^2$

The greatest common factor of the polynomial is $3x^2$, which should be factored out first. This yields

$$3x^4 - 6x^3 - 45x^2 = 3x^2(x^2 - 2x - 15)$$

The only factors of the first term of $x^2 - 2x - 15$ are $(x)(x)$ while the possible factors of -15 are $(1)(-15)$, $(-1)(15)$, $(3)(-5)$, and $(-3)(5)$.

The correct factorization is

$$3x^4 - 6x^3 - 45x^2 = 3x^2(x^2 - 2x - 15)$$
$$= 3x^2(x - 5)(x + 3)$$

> **6.** Factor: $a^2 - 7a - 12$

There are no common factors to pull out and the only factors of a^2 are $(a)(a)$, while the possible factors of -12 are $(1)(-12)$, $(-1)(12)$, $(-2)(6)$, $(2)(-6)$, $(3)(-4)$, and $(-3)(4)$. However, no combination of the factors in the double parentheses form $(\ )(\ )$ will yield a middle term of $-7a$. Hence, this polynomial is not factorable and is a prime polynomial.

Solving Quadratic Equations

A **quadratic equation** is an equation that may be written in the form $ax^2 + bx + c = 0$, where $a \neq 0$.

Tip: The largest exponent on the variable in a quadratic equation is two.

Factoring Method

1. Express the equation in the form $ax^2 + bx + c = 0$.
2. Factor the polynomial.
3. Set each factor equal to zero.
4. Solve each of the resulting equations.
5. Check all answers in the original equation.

Examples:

1. Solve: $x^2 - 12 = 4x$

$$x^2 - 12 = 4x$$
$$x^2 - 12 - 4x = 4x - 4x$$
$$x^2 - 4x - 12 = 0$$
$$(x-6)(x+2) = 0$$
$$x - 6 = 0 \text{ or } x + 2 = 0$$
$$x = 6 \text{ or } x = -2$$

Each answer will check in the original equation.

2. Solve: $2y^2 + 7y + 3 = 0$

$$2y^2 + 7y + 3 = 0$$
$$(2y+1)(y+3) = 0$$
$$2y + 1 = 0 \text{ or } y + 3 = 0$$
$$2y = -1$$
$$y = -\frac{1}{2} \text{ or } y = -3$$

Each answer will check in the original equation.

3. Solve: $4z^2 - 25 = 0$

$$4z^2 - 25 = 0$$
$$(2z+5)(2z-5) = 0$$
$$2z + 5 = 0 \quad \text{ or } \quad 2z - 5 = 0$$
$$2z = -5 \qquad\qquad 2z = 5$$
$$z = -\frac{5}{2} \qquad\qquad z = \frac{5}{2}$$

Each answer will check in the original equation.

4. Solve: $3x^2 - 2x + 8 = 2x^2 + 3x + 8$

Simplify by moving all terms to one side of the equation,

$$3x^2 - 2x + 8 - 2x^2 - 3x - 8 = 2x^2 + 3x + 8 - 2x^2 - 3x - 8$$
$$x^2 - 5x = 0$$
$$x(x-5) = 0$$
$$x - 5 = 0$$
$$x = 0 \text{ or } x = 5$$

Each answer will check in the original equation.

Solving Polynomial Equations that Are Not Necessarily Quadratic Equations

The factoring method may also be used to solve polynomial equations that are not necessarily quadratic equations.

Example:

Solve: $3x^4 - 6x^3 - 45x^2 = 0$

$$3x^4 - 6x^3 - 45x^2 = 0$$
$$3x^2\left(x^2 - 2x - 15\right) = 0$$
$$3x^2(x-5)(x+3) = 0$$
$$3x^2 = 0 \ \ or \ \ x - 5 = 0 \ \ or \ \ x + 3 = 0$$
$$x^2 = 0$$
$$x = 0 \ \ or \ \ x = 5 \ \ or \ \ x = -3$$

Each answer will check in the original equation.

Quadratic Formula Method

The quadratic formula may be used to solve a quadratic equation in the form $ax^2 + bx + c = 0$, $a \neq 0$.

This method is useful when a quadratic expression cannot be factored or when the factors are difficult to determine.

The formula is $x = \dfrac{-b \pm \sqrt{b^2 - 4ac}}{2a}$, where a, b, and c are determined after the equation is written in the form $ax^2 + bx + c = 0$. If the factoring method was used, the answers would be the same as those found using the quadratic formula.

Examples:

1. Solve: $x^2 - 12 = 4x$

$$x^2 - 12 - 4x = 4x - 4x$$
$$x^2 - 4x - 12 = 0 \rightarrow a = 1, \ b = -4, \ c = -12$$
$$x = \frac{-(-4) \pm \sqrt{(-4)^2 - 4(1)(-12)}}{2(1)}$$
$$= \frac{4 \pm \sqrt{16 + 48}}{2}$$
$$= \frac{4 \pm \sqrt{64}}{2}$$
$$= \frac{4 \pm 8}{2}$$
$$x = \frac{4+8}{2} = \frac{12}{2} = 6 \ \ or \ \ x = \frac{4-8}{2} = \frac{-4}{2} = -2$$

2. Solve: $4z^2 - 25 = 0$

$$4z^2 - 25 = 0 \rightarrow a = 4, b = 0, c = -25$$

$$z = \frac{-(0) \pm \sqrt{(0)^2 - 4(4)(-25)}}{2(4)}$$

$$= \frac{\pm\sqrt{400}}{8}$$

$$= \pm\frac{20}{8}$$

$$z = \frac{20}{8} = \frac{5}{2} \quad or \quad z = \frac{-20}{8} = \frac{-5}{2}$$

3. Solve: $x^2 - 5x = 0$

$$x^2 - 5x = 0 \rightarrow a = 1, b = -5, c = 0$$

$$x = \frac{-(-5) \pm \sqrt{(-5)^2 - 4(1)(0)}}{2(1)}$$

$$= \frac{5 \pm \sqrt{25 - 0}}{2}$$

$$= \frac{5 \pm 5}{2}$$

$$x = \frac{5 + 5}{2} = \frac{10}{2} = 5 \quad or \quad x = \frac{5 - 5}{2} = 0$$

Rational/Fractional Equations

A **rational equation** is simply an algebraic expression containing one or more fractional expressions.

The method used in solving rational equations is as follows:

1. Find the Least Common Denominator (LCD) of all fractions in the equation.
2. Eliminate the fractions in the equation by multiplying both sides of the equation by the LCD.
3. Solve the resulting equation.
4. Check all answers in the original equation to avoid answers that make a denominator equal to zero.

Examples:

1. Solve: $=\frac{3x}{2} - \frac{7x}{3} = \frac{5}{6}$

The LCD of 2, 3, and 6 is 6. Multiply both sides of the equation by the LCD,

$$\frac{\cancel{6}^3}{1} \cdot \frac{3x}{\cancel{2}_1} - \frac{\cancel{6}^2}{1} \cdot \frac{7x}{\cancel{3}_1} = \frac{\cancel{6}^1}{1} \cdot \frac{5}{\cancel{6}_1}$$

$$9x - 14x = 5$$

$$-5x = 5$$

$$x = -1$$

2. Solve: $=\dfrac{3}{4x}+\dfrac{2}{x}=\dfrac{2}{3}$

The LCD of $4x$, x, and 3 is $12x$. Multiply both sides of the equation by the LCD.

$$\overset{3}{\dfrac{\cancel{12x}}{1}}\cdot\dfrac{3}{\underset{1}{\cancel{4x}}}+\dfrac{12\cancel{x}}{1}\cdot\dfrac{2}{\underset{1}{\cancel{x}}}=\overset{4}{\dfrac{\cancel{12x}}{1}}\cdot\dfrac{2}{\underset{1}{\cancel{3}}}$$

$$3\cdot3+12\cdot2=4x\cdot2$$

$$9+24=8x$$

$$33=8\text{x}$$

$$x=\dfrac{33}{8}$$

$$x=4\dfrac{1}{8}$$

Radicals and Roots

A **radical** is an indicated root of a number or algebraic expression. The symbol $\sqrt[n]{\ }$ is a radical sign where n is called the index of the radical and the number or expression under the radical sign is the radicand. For square roots, the index 2 is understood and is not indicated as part of the radical sign, written $\sqrt{\ }$. The square root of a number is one of its two equal factors, the cube root of a number is one of its three equal factors, and so on. In general, the nth root of a number x, $\sqrt[n]{x}$ is one of its n equal factors.

Examples:

1. $\sqrt{49}=7$ since $7^2=49$

2. $\sqrt[3]{125}=5$ since $5^3=125$

3. $\sqrt[4]{81}=3$ since $3^4=81$

4. $\sqrt[5]{-32}=-2$ since $(-2)^5=-32$

Note that an even root of a negative number is not a real number but an odd root of a negative number is a real number.

Examples:

1. $\sqrt{-100}$ is not a real number; $(-10)^2=100$, $(n^2\neq\text{negative number})$.

2. $\sqrt[3]{-64}=-4$ since $(-4)^3=-4\cdot-4\cdot-4=-64$

Solving Radical Equations

Radical equations are equations in which a variable expression is included in a radicand.

The method for solving radical equations is as follows:

1. Isolate the radical on one side of the equation.
2. Eliminate the radical by raising both sides of the equation to the nth power where n is the index of the radical.

3. Solve the resulting equation.
4. Check all answers in the original equation.

Examples:

> **1.** Solve: $\sqrt{2x-5}+6=13$

Isolate the radical:

$$\sqrt{2x-5}+6-6=13-6$$
$$\sqrt{2x-5}=7$$

Square both sides to eliminate the radical:

$$\left(\sqrt{2x-5}\right)^2=(7)^2$$
$$2x-5=49$$
$$2x=54$$
$$x=27$$

Check the answer: $x = 27$

$$\sqrt{2x-5}+6=\sqrt{2(27)-5}+6$$
$$=\sqrt{54-5}+6$$
$$=\sqrt{49}+6$$
$$=7+6$$
$$=13$$

> **2.** Solve: $25=21+\sqrt[3]{40-3y}$

Isolate the radical:

$$25-21=21+\sqrt[3]{40-3y}-21$$
$$4=\sqrt[3]{40-3y}$$

Cube both sides to eliminate the radical:

$$(4)^3=\left(\sqrt[3]{40-3y}\right)^3$$
$$64=40-3y$$
$$64-40=40-3y-40$$
$$24=-3y$$
$$y=-8$$

Check the answer: $y = -8$

$$21+\sqrt[3]{40-3y}=21+\sqrt[3]{40-3(-8)}$$
$$=21+\sqrt[3]{40+24}$$
$$=21+\sqrt[3]{64}$$
$$=21+4$$
$$=25$$

3. Solve: $\sqrt{11+2z}+35=30$

Isolate the radical:

$$\sqrt{11+2z}+35-35=30-35$$
$$\sqrt{11+2z}=-5$$

Square both sides to eliminate the radical:

$$\left(\sqrt{11+2z}\right)^2=(-5)^2$$
$$11+2z=25$$
$$11+2z-11=25-11$$
$$2z=14$$
$$z=7$$

Check the answer: $z=7$

$$\sqrt{11+2z}+35=\sqrt{11+2(7)}+35$$
$$=\sqrt{11+14}+35$$
$$=\sqrt{25}+35$$
$$=5+35$$
$$=40\neq30$$

Since $z=7$ does not check, this equation has no solution.

Direct and Inverse Variations

Direct Variation: If a variable y varies directly to a variable x then $y=kx$ or $k=\dfrac{y}{x}$, where k is called the constant of variation. It may be stated that y is directly proportional to x.

Inverse Variation: If a variable y varies inversely to x then $y=\dfrac{k}{x}$ or $k=xy$, where k again is called the constant of variation. It may also be stated that y is inversely proportional to x.

Examples:

1. If y varies directly to x and $y=108$ when $x=27$, find y when $x=9$.

Since y varies directly to x, $y=kx$.

Since $y=108$ when $x=27$:

$$108=27k$$
$$k=4$$

Hence, the constant of variation is $k=4$ and $y=4x$. When $x=9$:

$$y=4x$$
$$y=4(9)$$
$$y=36$$

> **2.** If a varies inversely to z and $a = 18$ when $z = 10$, find z when $a = 15$

Since a varies inversely to z:

$$a = \frac{k}{z}$$

Since $a = 18$ when $z = 10$:

$$18 = \frac{k}{10}$$
$$k = 180$$

Hence, the constant of variation $k = 180$ and $a = \frac{180}{z}$.

When $a = 15$: $a = \frac{k}{z}$.

$$15 = \frac{180}{z}$$
$$15z = 180$$
$$z = 12$$

Analytic Geometry

Rectangular Coordinate System

Frequently in algebra we must work with two variables. Since each point on a number line corresponds to a real number, two perpendicular number lines may be used to identify a pair of real numbers. The number lines are referred to as the coordinate axes, with the horizontal number line called the **x-axis** and the vertical number line called the **y-axis.** The point at which the two axes intersect is called the origin.

For each point in a plane there is a corresponding and unique pair of real numbers x and y, where x refers to the horizontal position of the point and y identifies the vertical position of the point. This unique pair is called the **coordinates** of the point and is represented as the ordered pair (x, y). The coordinates of the origin are $(0,0)$ with any point to the right of the origin having a positive x-coordinate and any point to the left of the origin having a negative x-coordinate. Similarly, any point above the origin is assigned a positive y-coordinate, while any point below the origin is assigned a negative y-coordinate.

The coordinate axes separate the plane into four distinct regions called **quadrants.** The quadrants are numbered as follows:

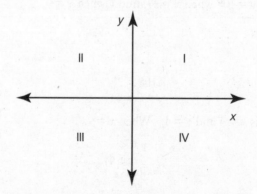

We can generalize about the x and y coordinates in each of the four quadrants as follows:

> In quadrant I, $x > 0$ and $y > 0$.
> In quadrant II, $x < 0$ and $y > 0$.
> In quadrant III, $x < 0$ and $y < 0$.
> In quadrant IV, $x > 0$ and $y < 0$.

Also note that if a point lies on the horizontal *x*-axis, its *y* coordinate is 0, and if a point lies on the vertical *y*-axis, its *x* coordinate is 0.

Example:

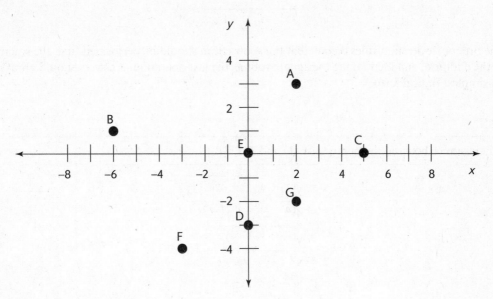

The coordinates of each of the points are:

A (2, 3)	*E* (0, 0)
B (–6, 1)	*F* (–3, –4)
C (5, 0)	*G* (2, –2)
D (0, –3)	

Midpoint Formula

The point *M* that is halfway between two points $A(x_1, y_1)$ and $B(x_2, y_2)$ is called the **midpoint** of segment *AB*. To find the coordinates of *M*, find the average value of the *x*-coordinates and the average value of the *y*-coordinates. The coordinates of the midpoint *M* are

$$\frac{x_1 + x_2}{2}, \frac{y_1 + y_2}{2}$$

Example:

Find the coordinates of the midpoint *M* between *A*(–5, 8) and *B*(11, 3).

$$M\left(\frac{-5+11}{2}, \frac{8+3}{2}\right) = M\left(\frac{6}{2}, \frac{11}{2}\right) = M\left(3, \frac{11}{2}\right)$$

Hence the coordinates of *M* are $\left(3, \frac{11}{2}\right)$.

Distance Formula

The distance d, between two points $A(x_1, y_1)$ and $B(x_2, y_2)$ is the same as the length of the segment AB. The formula for finding the distance between A and B is

$$d = \sqrt{(x_1 - x_2)^2 + (y_1 - y_2)^2}$$

Note that the order of operation rules dictate that the subtraction should be performed first, the squaring second, followed by the addition, and then taking the square root as the last operation. Answers should always be expressed in simplest radical form.

Examples:

1. Find the distance between the points $A(4,-1)$ and $B(7, 3)$:

$$d = \sqrt{(x_1 - x_2)^2 + (y_1 - y_2)^2}$$
$$= \sqrt{(4 - 7)^2 + (-1 - 3)^2}$$
$$= \sqrt{(-3)^2 + (-4)^2}$$
$$= \sqrt{9 + 16}$$
$$= \sqrt{25}$$
$$d = 5$$

2. Find the length of the segment AB where $A(-5,-10)$ and $B(5,-6)$:

$$d = \sqrt{(x_1 - x_2)^2 + (y_1 - y_2)^2}$$
$$= \sqrt{(-5 - 5)^2 + (-10 + 6)^2}$$
$$= \sqrt{(-10)^2 + (-4)^2}$$
$$= \sqrt{100 + 16}$$
$$= \sqrt{116}$$
$$= \sqrt{4 \cdot 29}$$
$$d = 2\sqrt{29}$$

Linear Graphs and Slope of a Line

The graph of an equation in the form $ax + by = c$ where a and b cannot both be zero is a straight line. Note that the largest exponent on x and y is 1 in a linear equation.

The slope of a line m, is defined as the ratio of the vertical change to the horizontal change in moving from one point on a line to any other point on the line. Since the vertical position of a point is determined by the y value, another way to define the slope of a line is as the ratio of the change in y values to the change in x values in moving from one point to any other point on the line.

If $A(x_1, y_1)$ and $B(x_2, y_2)$ are two points on a line, then the slope of the line, is determined by

$$m = \frac{\text{Vertical Change}}{\text{Horizontal Change}}$$

$$m = \frac{y_1 - y_2}{x_1 - x_2} \text{ or } m = \frac{y_2 - y_1}{x_2 - x_1}$$

Note that the order in which the y values are subtracted must be the same as the order in which the x values are subtracted.

Example:

Find the slope of the line passing through $A(-5, 1)$ and $B(7, -7)$.

$$m = \frac{y_1 - y_2}{x_1 - x_2}$$

$$m = \frac{1 - (-7)}{-5 - 7}$$

$$m = \frac{8}{-12} = -\frac{2}{3}$$

Slope-Intercept Form of a Linear Equation

When a linear equation is written in the form $y = mx + b$ with the y variable isolated, it is called the **slope-intercept form** for the equation of a line. The m value is the slope of the line and the b value is the y-coordinate of the point where the line intersects the y-axis, called the **y-intercept.**

Examples:

1. Find the slope and y-intercept of the line with the equation $2x + 3y = 18$.

Solving for y to express the equation in slope-intercept form

$$2x + 3y = 18$$

$$2x + 3y - 2x = 18 - 2x$$

$$3y = -2x + 18$$

$$\frac{3y}{3} = \frac{-2x}{3} + \frac{18}{3}$$

$$y = -\frac{2}{3}x + 6$$

Hence the slope of the line $m = -\frac{2}{3}$ and the y-intercept is the point $(0, 6)$.

2. Find the equation of the line that passes through the points $(-3, 7)$ and $(1, -1)$ and express the answer in slope-intercept form.

The slope of the line using the two given points is

$$m = \frac{y_1 - y_2}{x_1 - x_2}$$

$$m = \frac{7 - (-1)}{-3 - 1}$$

$$m = \frac{8}{-4}$$

$$m = -2$$

Using the slope-intercept form $y = mx + b$, substitute for x and y.

Using the point $(-3, 7)$ and $m = -2$

$$y = mx + b$$

$$7 = -2(-3) + b$$

$$7 = 6 + b$$

$$1 = b$$

The slope-intercept form of the equation $y = mx + b$ is

$$y = -2x + 1$$

Quadratic Graphs

The graph of an equation in the form $y = ax^2 + bx + c$ or $x = ay^2 + by + c$, where $a \neq 0$, is a U-shaped curve called a **parabola.** If $y = ax^2 + bx + c$ with $a > 0$, the parabola will open upward. If $a < 0$, the parabola will open downward. If $x = ay^2 + by + c$ with $a > 0$, the parabola will open to the right. If $a < 0$, the parabola will open to the left.

A critical point on the graph of a parabola is its **vertex** because this is where the U-shaped curve changes direction. If the quadratic equation is of the form $y = ax^2 + bx + c$, then the x-coordinate of the vertex is

$$x = \frac{-b}{2a}$$

The y-coordinate can be determined by substituting this value for x in the original equation. Similarly, if the quadratic equation is of the form $x = ay^2 + by + c$, then the y-coordinate of the vertex is

$$y = \frac{-b}{2a}$$

and the x-coordinate can be determined by substituting this value for y in the original equation.

Example:

Find the vertex of the parabola with the equation $y = 2x^2 + 8x - 3$.

Since the equation is of the form $y = ax^2 + bx + c$, the x coordinate of the vertex is

$$x = \frac{-b}{2a}$$
$$x = \frac{-8}{2(2)}$$
$$x = \frac{-8}{4}$$
$$x = -2$$

Substituting $x = -2$ in the original equation

$$\begin{aligned} y &= 2x^2 + 8x - 3 \\ &= 2(-2)^2 + 8(-2) - 3 \\ &= 2(4) - 16 - 3 \\ &= 8 - 16 - 3 \\ y &= -11 \end{aligned}$$

Hence the vertex of the parabola is the point $(-2, -11)$. Also note that the parabola will open upward from the vertex since $a > 0$.

Functions

A function is a correspondence that assigns each member of a first set to one and only one member of the second set. The first set is called the **domain of the function** and the second set is called the **range of the function.** If a variable y is a function of a variable x, write $y = f(x)$ which is read "y equals f of x" or "y equals f at x."

$y = x^2 + 1$ is a function since any value of x generates one and only on value for y. We may write $y = f(x) = x^2 + 1$.

$x = |y|$ is not a function since one value of x such as $x = 5$, yields two possible values of y, either $y = 5$, or $y = -5$.

Examples:

1. If $f(x) = x^3 - 3x^2 + x + 5$, find $f(2)$.

$$f(2) = (2)^3 - 3(2)^2 + 2 + 5$$
$$= 8 - 12 + 2 + 5$$
$$f(2) = 3$$

2. If $g(x) = 3x - 5$, find $g(-2) - g(2)$.

$$g(-2) = 3(-2) - 5 \quad \text{and} \quad g(2) = 3(2) - 5$$
$$= -6 - 5 \qquad\qquad = 6 - 5$$
$$g(-2) = -11 \qquad\qquad g(2) = 1$$

Hence, $g(-2) - g(2) = -11 - 1 = -12$.

Transformations of Functions

Transformations of a function $f(x)$ change the positions of the graph of $f(x)$ but do not affect the basic shape of the graph. There are three different types of transformations: **Horizontal Shifts, Vertical Shifts,** and **Reflections.** The following represent the basic transformations on the graph of $y = f(x)$:

Basic Transformations on the Graph of y = f(x):	
Reflection about the *x*-axis:	$y = -f(x)$
Reflection about the *y*-axis:	$y = f(-x)$
Reflection about the origin:	$y = -f(-x)$
Horizontal shift *a* units to the right:	$y = f(x-a)$ where $a > 0$
Horizontal shift *a* units to the left:	$y = f(x+a)$ where $a > 0$
Vertical shift *a* units upward:	$y = f(x)+a$ where $a > 0$
Vertical shift *a* units downward:	$y = f(x)-a$ where $a > 0$

Examples:

1. If $f(x) = x^2$, how will the graph of $g(x) = x^2 - 2$ differ from the graph of $f(x)$?

Since $g(x) = f(x) - 2$, the graph of $g(x)$ will be the graph of $f(x)$ shifted vertically down 2 units.

2. If $f(x) = x^3$, how will the graph of $h(x) = (x + 5)^3$ differ from the graph of $f(x)$?

Since $h(x) = f(x + 5)$, the graph of $h(x)$ will be the graph of $f(x)$ shifted horizontally 5 units to the left.

3. If $f(x) = x^4$, how will the graph of $m(x) = -x^4$ differ from the graph of $f(x)$?

Since $m(x) = -f(x)$, the graph of $m(x)$ will be the graph of $f(x)$ reflected about the x–axis.

> **4.** If $f(x) = \sqrt{x}$ how will the graph of $t(x) = \sqrt{x-2} + 3$ differ from the graph of $f(x)$?

Since $t(x) = f(x-2) + 3$, the graph of $t(x)$ will be the graph of $f(x)$ shifted horizontally to the right 2 units and shifted vertically up 3 units.

Practice Questions: Algebra

Now that you have reviewed the strategies, you can practice on your own. The questions are roughly grouped into sets by their level of difficulty, just as they might appear on the actual SAT. The questions are grouped into three categories: easy to moderate, average, and above-average to difficult. The answers and explanations that follow the questions will include strategies to help you understand how to solve the problems.

Easy to Moderate

1. $\{1,3,4,5,8,9\} \cap \{1,3,5,7,9\}$

2. $\{2,4,5,6,9,10\} \cup \{3,5,7,9\}$

3. Factor completely: $24x^5 - 30x^3 + 12x^2$

Average

4. Write an algebraic expression for seven more than twice the number x.

5. Evaluate: $\left(\dfrac{4}{3}\right)^{-3}$

6. Simplify: $(x^5)(x^{-8})(x^{12})$

7. Simplify: $(4x^5y^3)^2$

8. Simplify: $(5y^2 - 9y + 2) + (3y^2 + 4y - 7) + (6y^2 - 11y + 1)$

9. Simplify: $(3x + 5)(4x - 9)$

10. Simplify: $(20x^8 - 8x^6 + 12x^4 + 4x^2) \div 4x^2$

11. Solve for x: $\dfrac{3}{5}x - 4 = 6$

12. Solve for y: $3x + 5y = 8z$

13. Solve for x: $3x + 11 < 6x - 16$

14. Factor completely: $y^2 + 8y - 48$

15. If y varies directly to x, and $y = 6$ when $x = 21$, find y when $x = 28$.

16. Find the midpoint of a line segment whose endpoints are $(-5, 8)$ and $(11, 4)$.

17. Find the y-intercept of the line $4x - 3y - 24 = 0$.

18. Find the slope of the line with the equation $3x + 5y = 15$

19. If $f(x) = x^3 + 2x^2 + 5x + 6$, find $f(-4)$.

20. Simplify: $(z^2 - 5z - 36) \div (z + 4)$

Above Average to Difficult

21. Simplify: $(a^6b^2c^8) \div (a^3b^4c^2)$

22. Expand: $(2z - 3)(z^2 - 5z + 4)$

23. Solve for z: $|4z - 9| = 15$

24. Solve for y: $\sqrt{3y + 4} - 8 = -3$

25. Factor completely: $8z^3 - 72z$

26. Solve for x: $4x^2 - 19 = 30$

27. Find the length of the line segment whose endpoints are $(5, -3)$ and $(10, 7)$.

28. Find the vertex of the parabola with the equation $y = 2x^2 - 8x - 5$

29. If $g(x) = x^2$ and $h(x) = (x + 3)^2 - 4$, how will the graph of $h(x)$ differ from the graph of $g(x)$?

30. Solve for x and y: $3x + 4y = -10, 6x + 8y = 24$

Answers and Explanations

Easy to Moderate

1. The intersection of two sets is the set of elements common to both sets. They are 1, 3, 5, and 9.

Hence, $\{1,3,4,5,8,9\} \cap \{1,3,5,7,9\} = \{1,3,5,9\}$

2. The union of two sets is the set of all elements in the given sets. They are 2, 3, 4, 5, 6, 7, 9, and 10.
Hence, $\{2,4,5,6,9,10\} \cup \{3,5,7,9\} = \{2,3,4,5,6,7,9,10\}$

3. The greatest common factor of all three terms of the polynomial is $6x^2$.

Factoring $6x^2$ out of each term

$24x^5 - 30x^3 + 12x^2 = 6x^2(4x^3 - 5x + 2)$

Average

4. Seven more than twice some number x may be expressed as: $7 + 2x$ or $2x + 7$.

5. $\left(\frac{4}{3}\right)^{-3} = \left(\frac{3}{4}\right)^3 = \left(\frac{3}{4}\right)\left(\frac{3}{4}\right)\left(\frac{3}{4}\right) = \frac{27}{64}$

6. $\left(x^5\right)\left(x^{-8}\right)\left(x^{12}\right) = x^{5+(-8)+12} = x^9$

7. $\left(4x^5y^3\right)^2 = 4^{1\cdot2} \cdot x^{5\cdot2} \cdot y^{3\cdot2}$
$= 16x^{10}y^6$

8. $5y^2 - 9y + 2$

$3y^2 + 4y - 7$

$\underline{+6y^2 - 11y + 1}$

$14y^2 - 16y - 4$

9. $(3x+5)(4x-9) = (3x)(4x) + (3x)(-9) + (5)(4x) + (5)(-9)$

$= 12x^2 - 27x + 20x - 45$

$= 12x^2 - 7x - 45$

10. $(20x^8 - 8x^6 + 12x^4 + 4x^2) \div 4x^2 = \dfrac{20x^8 - 8x^6 + 12x^4 + 4x^2}{4x^2}$

$= \dfrac{20x^8}{4x^2} - \dfrac{8x^6}{2x^2} + \dfrac{12x^4}{4x^2} + \dfrac{4x^2}{4x^2}$

$= 5x^6 - 2x^4 + 3x^2 + 1$

11. $\dfrac{3}{5}x - 4 = 6$

Multiplying both sides of the equation by 5

$5\left(\dfrac{3}{5}x - 4\right) = 5(6)$

$3x - 20 = 30$

$\underline{+20 = +20}$

$3x = 50$

$\dfrac{3x}{3} = \dfrac{50}{3}$

$x = \dfrac{50}{3}$ or $16\dfrac{2}{3}$

12. $\quad 3x + 5y = 8z$

$3x + 5y - 3x = 8z - 3x$

$5y = 8z - 3x$

$\dfrac{5y}{5} = \dfrac{8z - 3x}{5}$

$y = \dfrac{8z - 3x}{5}$ or $y = \dfrac{8}{5}z - \dfrac{3}{5}x$

13. $\quad 3x + 11 < 6x - 16$

$3x + 11 - 6x < 6x - 16 - 6x$

$-3x + 11 < -16$

$-3x + 11 - 11 < -16 - 11$

$-3x < -27$

$\dfrac{-3x}{-3} > \dfrac{-27}{-3}$

$x > 9$

14. There is no common factor in each term of the polynomial so reversing the FOIL method should be used. The only way to factor the first term y^2 is $(y)(y)$, but there are a number of factors of the last term –48. The only pair of factors for –48 that yields a middle term of $+8y$ are $+12$ and -4.

Hence, $y^2 + 8y - 48 = (y + 12)(y - 4)$.

Tip: The answer can be checked by multiplying the two polynomials.

15. If y varies directly to x, $y = kx$ or $k = \dfrac{y}{x}$ where k is the constant of variation. Since $y = 6$ when $x = 21$ we have $k = \dfrac{y}{x} = \dfrac{6}{21} = \dfrac{2}{7}$ and $y = \dfrac{2}{7}x$. Find y if $x = 28$.

$$y = \frac{2}{7}x$$
$$= \frac{2}{7}(28)$$
$$y = 8$$

16. The midpoint, M, between two points (x_1, y_1) and (x_2, y_2) is

$$M = \frac{x_1 + x_2}{2}, \frac{y_1 + y_2}{2} = \left(\frac{-5 + 11}{2}, \frac{8 + 4}{2}\right)$$
$$M = \left(\frac{6}{2}, \frac{12}{2}\right)$$
$$M = (3, 6)$$

17. A linear equation in the form $y = mx + b$ will have a y-intercept at $(0, b)$.

$$4x - 3y - 24 = 0$$
$$4y - 3y - 24 + 24 = 0 + 24$$
$$4x - 3y = 24$$
$$4x - 3y - 4x = 24 - 4x$$
$$-3y = -4x + 24$$
$$\frac{-3y}{-3} = \frac{-4x + 24}{-3}$$
$$y = \frac{-4}{-3}x + \frac{24}{-3}$$
$$y = \frac{4}{3}x - 8$$

Hence the y-intercept is $(0, -8)$.

18. A linear equation of the form $y = mx + b$ will have a slope of m.

$$3x + 5y = 15$$
$$3x + 5y - 3x = 15 - 3x$$
$$5y = -3x + 15$$
$$\frac{5y}{5} = \frac{-3x + 15}{5}$$
$$y = \frac{-3}{5}x + 3$$

Hence the slope of the line is $m = \dfrac{-3}{5}$.

19. If $f(x) = x^3 + 2x^2 + 5x + 6$ then $f(-4)$

$$f(-4) = (-4)^3 + 2(-4)^2 + 5(-4) + 6$$
$$= -64 + 2(16) - 20 + 6$$
$$= -64 + 32 - 20 + 6$$
$$f(-4) = -46$$

20. $\left(z^2 - 5z - 36\right) \div (z + 4) = \dfrac{z^2 - 5z - 36}{z + 4}$

$$= \frac{(z - 9)(z + 4)}{(z + 4)}$$
$$= z - 9$$

Above Average to Difficult

21. $\left(a^6 b^2 c^8\right) \div \left(a^3 b^4 c^2\right) = a^{6-3} \cdot b^{2-4} \cdot c^{8-2}$

$$= a^3 \cdot b^{-2} \cdot c^6$$

$$= a^3 \cdot \frac{1}{b^2} \cdot c^6$$

$$= \frac{a^3 c^6}{b^2}$$

22. $(2z-3)\left(z^2 - 5z + 4\right)$

$$= (2z)\left(z^2\right) + (2z)(-5z) + (2z)(4) + (-3)\left(z^2\right) + (-3)(-5z) + (-3)(4)$$

$$= 2z^3 - 10z^2 + 8z - 3z^2 + 15z - 12$$

$$= 2z^3 - 13z^2 + 23z - 12$$

23. If $|4z = 9| = 15$, then

$$
\begin{array}{ll}
4z - 9 = 15 \quad \text{or} & 4z - 9 = -15 \\
4z - 9 + 9 = 15 + 9 & 4z - 9 + 9 = -15 + 9 \\
4z = 24 & 4z = -6 \\
\dfrac{4z}{4} = \dfrac{24}{4} & \dfrac{4z}{4} = \dfrac{-6}{4} \\
z = 6 \quad \text{or} & z = \dfrac{-3}{2} \text{ or } -1\dfrac{1}{2}
\end{array}
$$

24.

$$\sqrt{3y+4} - 8 = -3$$

$$\sqrt{3y+4} - 8 + 8 = -3 + 8$$

$$\sqrt{3y+4} = 5$$

$$\left(\sqrt{3y+4}\right)^2 = (5)^2$$

$$3y + 4 = 25$$

$$3y + 4 - 4 = 25 - 4$$

$$3y = 21$$

$$\frac{3y}{3} = \frac{21}{3}$$

$$y = 7$$

Check $y = 7$ in the original equation:

$$\sqrt{3y+4} - 8 = -3$$

$$\sqrt{(3)(7)+4} - 8 = -3$$

$$\sqrt{21+4} - 8 = -3$$

$$\sqrt{25} - 8 = -3$$

$$5 - 8 = -3$$

$$-3 = -3$$

25. The greatest common factor of the two terms of the polynomial is $8z$.

Factoring $8z$ out of each term: $\qquad 8z^3 - 72z = 8z(z^2 - 9)$

Since the second factor is the difference of two squares, it may be factored further:

$$8z^3 - 72z = 8z\left(z^2 - 9\right)$$

$$= 8z(z+3)(z-3)$$

26. Set the polynomial equal to zero and write it in descending order:

$$4x^2 - 19 = 30$$
$$4x^2 - 19 - 30 = 30 - 30$$
$$4x^2 - 49 = 0$$

Factor the polynomial completely:

$$4x^2 - 49 = 0$$
$$(2x + 7)(2x - 7) = 0$$

Hence, $2x + 7 = 0$ or $2x - 7 = 0$

$2x + 7 - 7 = 0 - 7$	$2x - 7 + 7 = 0 + 7$
$2x = -7$	$2x = 7$
$\dfrac{2x}{2} = \dfrac{-7}{2}$	$\dfrac{2x}{2} = \dfrac{7}{2}$
$x = \dfrac{-7}{2}$ or $-3\dfrac{1}{2}$ or	$x = \dfrac{7}{2}$ or $3\dfrac{1}{2}$

27. The distance d between two points (x_1, y_1) and (x_2, y_2) is

$$d = \sqrt{(x_1 - x_2)^2 + (y_1 - y_2)^2}$$
$$= \sqrt{(5 - 10)^2 + (-3 - 7)^2}$$
$$= \sqrt{(-5)^2 + (-10)^2}$$
$$= \sqrt{25 + 100}$$
$$= \sqrt{125}$$
$$= \sqrt{25 \cdot 5}$$
$$d = 5\sqrt{5}$$

28. The vertex of a parabola whose equation is $y = ax^2 + bx + c$ can be found by finding the x-coordinate that is $x = \dfrac{-b}{2a}$ and substituting this value in the original equation to find the y-coordinate of the vertex. For the given parabola with the equation

$y = 2x^2 - 8x - 5$, $a = 2$ and $b = -8$

The x-coordinate of the vertex is

$$x = \frac{-b}{2a} = \frac{-(-8)}{2(2)} = \frac{8}{4} = 2$$

The y-coordinate of the vertex is

$$y = 2x^2 - 8x - 5$$
$$= 2(2^2) - 8(2) - 5$$
$$= 2(4) - 16 - 5$$
$$= 8 - 16 - 5$$
$$= -13$$

Hence the vertex of the parabola is $(2, -13)$.

29. If $g(x) = x^2$ and $h(x) = (x + 3)^2 - 4$, the graph of $h(x)$ will be the same as the graph of $g(x)$ shifted horizontally to the left 3 units and shifted vertically downward 4 units.

30. $3x + 4y = -10$

$6x + 8y = 24$

Multiply the first equation by (–2):

$-2(3x + 4y) = -2(-10)$

$6x + 8y = 24$

$-6x - 8y = 20$

$6x + 8y = 24$

Add the two equations:

$0 + 0 = 44$

$0 = 44$

Since both variables were eliminated and the resulting equation $0 = 44$ is a false statement, the system has no solution.

Chapter 7

Geometry and Measurement Review

The word *geometry* literally means "earth measurement," and its concepts have been studied for thousands of years. Ancient Egyptian civilizations applied geometry to build pyramids, and intuitive geometry concepts studied in high school were developed by the Greek mathematician Euclid in about 300 B.C.E. The SAT tests your ability to apply these geometric and measurement concepts to solve problems within the context of math logic. You will be asked to apply your knowledge of mathematical relationships among geometric shapes, angles, and other configurations.

As you approach geometry problems on the SAT, keep in mind that the visual illustrations of geometric figures are *not* necessarily drawn to scale. However, lines shown in the figures are straight and points on the line occur in the order shown. Some shapes may appear larger, while others may appear smaller. When selecting the answer choice, you should always base your answer on geometric logic, and not on estimating or comparing quantities by sight.

Geometry and measurement mathematics topics and concepts include

- Lines, segments, rays, angles, and congruence
- Perimeter, area, and angle measures of polygons
- Triangles: right, isosceles, equilateral, special triangles
- Pythagorean Theorem
- Quadrilaterals: trapezoid, parallelogram, rectangle, rhombus, and square
- Circles: radius, diameter, circumference, and area
- Volume and surface area of solids

Basic Geometry Terms

Point

A *point* is a way of designating a location in space. It has no length, no width, and no depth. It is usually named by an uppercase letter and identified by a dot.

Line (Straight Line)

A *line* is a set of points that continues indefinitely in both directions. A line is always considered to be straight. A line has one dimension, length, but its length cannot be measured. The symbol $\leftrightarrow$ is used to represent a line:

$$\text{Line } AB = \overleftrightarrow{AB} = \overleftrightarrow{BA} = \text{Line } BA$$

Ray

A *ray* is a set of points on a line that has one definite endpoint, called its *vertex,* and continues indefinitely in one direction only. A ray has one dimension, length, but its length cannot be measured. The symbol $\rightarrow$ is used to represent a ray:

$$\text{Ray } AB = \overrightarrow{AB}$$

Note that $\overrightarrow{AB}$ and $\overrightarrow{BA}$ are not the same rays since they do not have the same vertex.

Line Segment

A *line segment* is a set of points on a line that has two distinct endpoints. A line segment has one dimension, length, and its length can be measured. The symbol ‾ is used to represent a line segment:

$$\text{Line segment } AB = \overline{AB} = \overline{BA} = \text{line segment } BA$$

Line segment *AB* is sometimes referred to simply as segment *AB*.

Plane

A *plane* is a flat surface consisting of an infinite number of points. A plane has only two dimensions, length and width, neither of which can be measured.

Angle

An *angle* is formed by the union of two rays with a common endpoint called the *vertex of the angle*. The rays are called the *sides of the angle* and an angle is measured in units called *degrees* (°). The symbol ∠ is used to represent an angle and the vertex letter may be used to identify the angle being referred to. However, if there is more than one angle with the same vertex, three letters may be used to identify the angle, with the vertex as the middle letter.

Example:

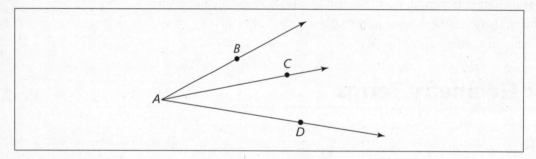

There are three angles in the given figure, each with a vertex at *A*. The two smaller angles are

∠*BAC* = ∠*CAB*, and

∠*CAD* = ∠*DAC*, and the largest angle is

∠*BAD* = ∠*DAB*.

Note that writing ∠*A* would be inconclusive since there are three angles with vertex *A*.

Types of Angles

There are several types of angles: single angles (acute, right, obtuse, and straight) and pairs of angles (adjacent, complementary, supplementary, vertical, alternate interior, and alternate exterior).

Single Angles

- **Acute Angle:** An angle whose measure is between 0° and 90°
- **Right Angle:** An angle whose measure is 90°. If two rays form a right angle, the rays are said to be *perpendicular;* conversely, if two rays are perpendicular the angle formed is a right angle. The symbol for perpendicular is ⊥.

- **Obtuse Angle:** An angle whose measure is between 90° and 180°
- **Straight Angle:** An angle whose measure is 180°

Example:

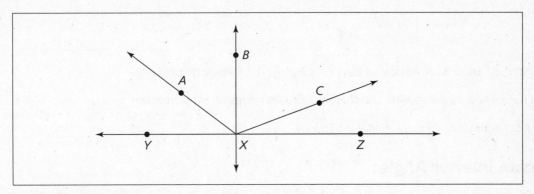

Given the figure with $\overleftrightarrow{YZ} \perp \overleftrightarrow{XB}$

∠AXY, ∠AXB, ∠BXC, and ∠CXZ are acute angles.

∠AXZ and ∠CXY are obtuse angles.

∠BXY and ∠BXZ are right angles.

∠YXZ is a straight angle.

Pairs of Angles

Adjacent Angles

Two angles that have the same vertex share a common side, and do not overlap.

Example:

In the previous figure, ∠AXB and ∠BXC are one pair of adjacent angles.

Complementary Angles

Two angles whose sum is 90°

Example:

In the previous figure, ∠AXY and ∠AXB are one pair of complementary angles.

Supplementary Angles

Two angles whose sum is 180°

Example:

In the previous figure, ∠AXY and ∠AXZ are one pair of supplementary angles.

Vertical Angles

Two angles that have the same vertex and whose sides are opposite rays are called vertical angles. These are sometimes referred to as *opposite angles*. One important property of vertical angles is that they will always be equal.

Example:

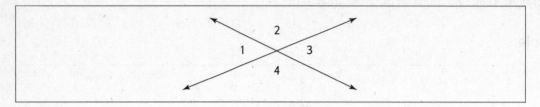

In the figure, ∠1 and ∠3 are vertical angles and ∠2 and ∠4 are vertical angles.

Hence ∠1 ≅ ∠3 and ∠2 ≅ ∠4. Note that there are also four pairs of supplementary angles:

∠1 and ∠2, ∠2 and ∠3, ∠3 and ∠4, and ∠1 and ∠4.

Alternate Interior Angles

If two lines are intersected by a third line called a *transversal,* they form two pairs of alternate interior angles. These angles will be inside the two lines and on alternative sides of the transversal.

Example:

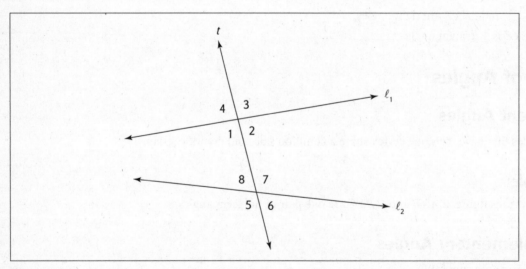

In the figure, ℓ_1 and ℓ_2 are cut by the transversal, t, forming two pairs of alternative interior angles: ∠1 and ∠7, and ∠2 and ∠8.

Alternate Exterior Angles

If two lines are intersected by a third line, then two pairs of alternate exterior angles are formed. These angles will be outside the two lines and on alternate sides of the transversal.

Example:

In the previous figure, two pairs of alternate exterior angles are formed:

∠3 and ∠5, and ∠4 and ∠6.

A special case occurs when the two lines, ℓ_1 and ℓ_2, are parallel and are cut by a transversal. In this situation, each pair of alternate interior angles is equal and each pair of alternate exterior angles is equal.

Example:

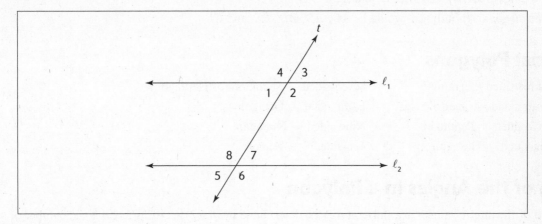

In the figure, $(\ell_1 \parallel \ell_2)$, and are cut by transversal t.

Hence the alternate interior angles are equal: $\angle 1 \cong \angle 7$ and $\angle 2 \cong \angle 8$, and the alternate exterior angles are equal as well: $\angle 3 \cong \angle 5$ and $\angle 4 \cong \angle 6$. It should be noted that if the measure of any one of the angles is given, the measures of the remaining seven angles can be determined. Also note that there are four pairs of vertical angles and eight pairs of supplementary angles in the figure.

In the figure, if $\angle 2 = 140°$, find the measures of the other seven angles.

$$\angle 2 = \angle 8 = \angle 6 = \angle 4 = 140°$$
$$\angle 1 = \angle 7 = \angle 5 = \angle 3 = 40°$$

Polygons

A *polygon* is a closed plane figure made up of line segments that intersect only at their endpoints. The segments are called the sides of the polygon, and any two sides with a common endpoint form an *angle of the polygon*. The endpoint of any side is called a *vertex of the polygon,* and the number of sides, angles, and vertices is always the same in any polygon. A segment whose endpoints are two nonadjacent vertices is called a *diagonal of the polygon*. The minimum number of sides, angles, or vertices of a polygon is three, and there is no maximum number. A *regular polygon* is a polygon in which all sides have the same length and all angles have the same measure.

Example:

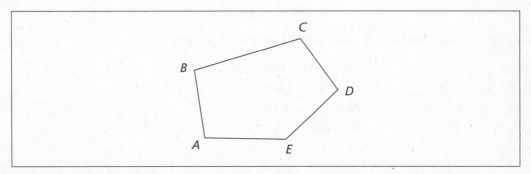

In the figure, polygon *ABCDE* has five vertices, five angles, and five sides.

The vertices are *A, B, C, D*, and *E*.

The angles are $\angle A$, $\angle B$, $\angle C$, $\angle D$, and $\angle E$.

The sides are $\overline{AB}$, $\overline{BC}$, $\overline{CD}$, $\overline{DE}$, and $\overline{AE}$.

The diagonals (not drawn) would be $\overline{AC}$, $\overline{AD}$, $\overline{BD}$, $\overline{BE}$, and $\overline{CE}$.

Special Polygons

Three-sided — Triangle   Seven-sided — Septagon (or Heptagon)

Four-sided — Quadrilateral   Eight-sided — Octagon

Five-sided — Pentagon   Nine-sided — Nonagon

Six-sided — Hexagon   Ten-sided — Decagon

Sum of the Angles in a Polygon

The sum of the interior angles in a polygon may be determined by $(n-2) \times 180°$ where *n* is the number of sides, angles, or vertices in the polygon.

Examples:

1. Find the sum of the interior angles of a triangle.

Since a triangle has three sides, $n = 3$. The sum of its interior angles is

$$(n-2)\cdot 180° = (3-2)\cdot 180°$$
$$= 180°$$

2. A stop sign has the shape of a regular octagon. Find the measure of one of its angles.

Since an octagon has eight sides, $n = 8$. The sum of its interior angles is

$$(n-2)\cdot 180° = (8-2)\cdot 180°$$
$$= 6 \cdot 180°$$
$$= 1,080°$$

Since a regular octagon has all of its angles equal, the measure of any one angle is

$$1,080° \div 8 = 135°$$

The following is a summary of the sum of the interior angles of a polygon:

Triangle — 180°   Septagon (or Heptagon) — 900°

Quadrilateral — 360°   Octagon — 1,080°

Pentagon — 540°   Nonagon — 1,260°

Hexagon — 720°   Decagon — 1,440°

Triangles

A *triangle* is a polygon with three sides, angles, and vertices. The symbol for a triangle is △.

The sum of the interior angles in a triangle is 180°.

If the sides of a triangle have lengths *a, b,* and *c,* then the perimeter *P* is

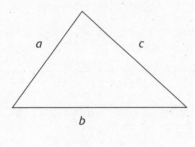

$$P = a + b + c$$

Altitude or Height

A segment drawn from any vertex of a triangle perpendicular to the opposite side or the extension of the opposite side is called an *altitude or height of the triangle.*

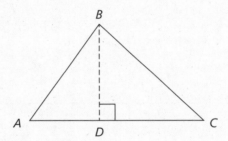

Given △*ABC* with $\overline{BD} \perp \overline{AC}$, $\overline{BD}$ is an altitude or height of △*ABC*. Every triangle has three distinct heights.

Median

A segment drawn from any vertex of a triangle to the midpoint of the opposite side is called a *median of the triangle.*

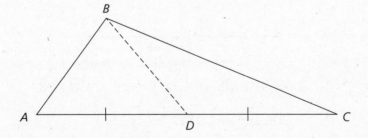

Given △*ABC* with *AD = CD*, $\overline{BD}$ is a median of △*ABC*. Every triangle has three distinct medians.

Angle Bisector

A segment drawn from any vertex of a triangle that bisects the angle at the vertex is called *an angle bisector of the triangle*.

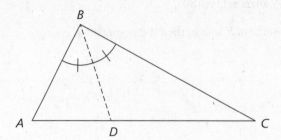

Given $\triangle ABC$ with $\overline{BD}$ bisecting $\angle ABC$, $\overline{BD}$ is an angle bisector of $\triangle ABC$. Every triangle has three distinct angle bisectors.

Area of a Triangle

The formula for the area of a triangle is $A = \frac{1}{2}bh$

Where b is any side of the triangle and h is the altitude or height drawn to that side, called the base.

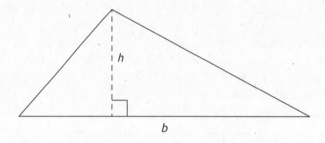

Example:

Find the perimeter P and area of $\triangle XYZ$ where $\overline{YA} = 10$ and $\overline{YA} \perp \overline{XZ}$.

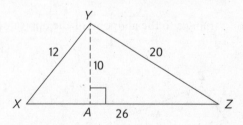

The perimeter P of $\triangle XYZ$ is the sum of the lengths of its sides = 12 + 20 + 26 = 58.

$$\text{The area } A \text{ of } \triangle XYZ = \frac{1}{2}bh$$
$$= \frac{1}{2}(XZ)(YA)$$
$$= \frac{1}{2}(26)(10)$$
$$A = 130$$

Triangle Inequality Theorem

This theorem states that the sum of the lengths of any two sides of a triangle must be greater than the length of the remaining side.

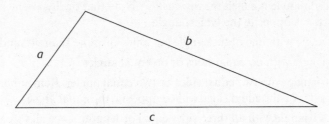

In the figure above,

$$a + b > c$$
$$a + c > b$$
$$b + c > a$$

Exterior Angle Theorem

If one side of a triangle is extended in either direction, an exterior angle is formed. This theorem states that an exterior angle of a triangle is equal to the sum of the two remote interior angles.

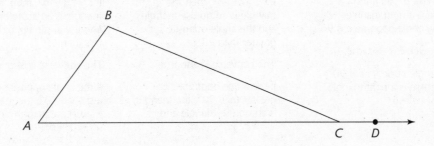

In the figure above, $\angle BCD = \angle ABC + \angle BAC$. Note that every triangle has six exterior angles.

Opposite Angles and Opposite Sides

The largest (or smallest) side of a triangle is opposite its largest (or smallest) angle. Conversely, the largest (or smallest) angle of a triangle is opposite its largest (or smallest) side. If two sides of a triangle are equal, then the angles opposite these sides are equal. Conversely, if two angles of a triangle are equal, then the sides opposite these angles are equal.

Example:

Arrange the sides of the triangle from smallest to largest.

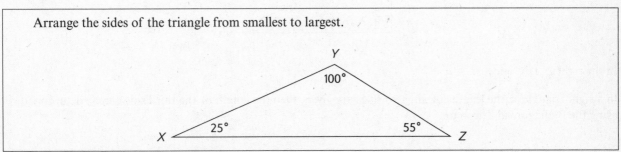

Since $\angle X = 25°$ is the smallest angle of $\triangle XYZ$, the side opposite, $\angle X$, $\overline{YZ}$ is the smallest side of $\triangle XYZ$. The next larger side is $\overline{XY}$, and the largest side of $\triangle XYZ$ is $\overline{XZ}$.

Types of Triangles

- **Acute Triangle:** A triangle in which all three angles are acute angles
- **Right Triangle:** A triangle with one right angle. The two sides that form the right angle are called *legs* and the side opposite the right angle is called the *hypotenuse.* Note that the hypotenuse must be the longest side in a right triangle, since it is opposite the largest angle.
- **Obtuse Triangle:** A triangle with one obtuse angle (an angle of more than 90° and less than 180°)
- **Scalene Triangle:** A triangle with no equal sides or no equal angles
- **Isosceles Triangle:** A triangle with two equal sides or two equal angles. Remember that the equal angles will be opposite the equal sides or the equal sides will be opposite the equal angles.
- **Equilateral Triangle:** A triangle with all three sides equal of length. Since all three angles must also be equal, this is also called an *equiangular triangle,* with each of its angles equal to 60°.

Examples of Common Triangles

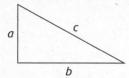
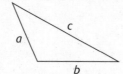

If $c^2 = a^2 + b^2$, then the triangle is a right triangle and the angle opposite c is 90°.

The converse is also true.

If the angle opposite c is 90°, the triangle is a right triangle and $c^2 = a^2 + b^2$.

If $c^2 > a^2 + b^2$, then the triangle is an obtuse triangle and the angle opposite c is greater than 90°.

The converse is also true.

If the angle opposite c is greater than 90°, the triangle is an obtuse triangle and $c^2 > a^2 + b^2$.

If $c^2 < a^2 + b^2$, then the triangle is an acute triangle and the angle opposite c is less than 90°.

The converse is also true.

If the angle opposite c is less than 90°, the triangle is an acute triangle and $c^2 < a^2 + b^2$.

Special Right Triangle Theorems

Pythagorean Theorem

In any right triangle, the sum of the squares of the two legs is equal to the square of the hypotenuse.

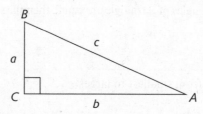

In the right $\triangle ABC$ above: $c^2 = a^2 + b^2$

In a right triangle, if the lengths of any two sides are given, then the length of the third side can be determined using the Pythagorean Theorem.

Examples:

1. In $\triangle XYZ$, $\overline{XY} \perp \overline{XZ}$, $XY = 5$ and $YZ = 13$. Find XZ.

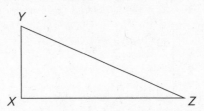

Since $\overline{XY} \perp \overline{XZ}$, $\triangle XYZ$ is a right triangle with legs $\overline{XY}$ and $\overline{XZ}$ and hypotenuse $\overline{YZ}$. Using the Pythagorean Theorem

$$c^2 = a^2 + b^2$$
$$(YZ)^2 = (XY)^2 + (XZ)^2$$
$$13^2 = 5^2 + (XZ)^2$$
$$169 = 25 + (XZ)^2$$
$$(XZ)^2 = 169 - 25$$
$$(XZ)^2 = 144$$
$$XZ = \sqrt{144} = 12$$

2. The legs of a right triangle have lengths of 3 and 9. Find the length of the hypotenuse.

$$c^2 = a^2 + b^2$$
$$c^2 = (3)^2 + (9)^2$$
$$c^2 = 9 + 81$$
$$c^2 = 90$$
$$c = \sqrt{90} = \sqrt{9 \cdot 10}$$
$$c = 3\sqrt{10}$$

Pythagorean Triples

It is useful to note that certain integer values work in the Pythagorean Theorem, and these integers are called *Pythagorean triples*. Any multiples of these triples will also satisfy the Pythagorean Theorem as well.

Examples:

1. 3, 4, 5, and any multiple of these, such as 6, 8, 10 and 9, 12, 15

2. 5, 12, 13, and any multiple of these, such as 10, 24, 26 and 15, 36, 39

3. 8, 15, 17, and any multiple of these, such as 16, 30, 34, and 24, 45, 51

The 30°-60°-90° Right Triangle Theorem

In a right triangle whose acute angles measure 30° and 60°, the leg opposite the 30° angle equals one-half the hypotenuse and the side opposite the 60° angle equals one-half the hypotenuse times the square root of 3.

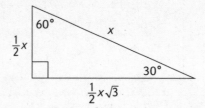

In the triangle above, the hypotenuse has length x, the leg opposite the 30° angle has length $\frac{1}{2}x$, and the leg opposite the 60° angle has length $\frac{1}{2}x\sqrt{3}$. In a 30°-60°-90° right triangle, if the length of any one side is known then the lengths of the remaining two sides can be determined.

Example:

The hypotenuse of a right triangle has length 20 and one of its angles measures 60°. Find the area of the triangle.

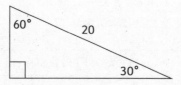

In the right triangle above, since one of its acute angles is 60°, the other acute angle must be 30° and it is a 30°-60° -90° right triangle. The side opposite the 30° angle is $\frac{1}{2} \cdot 20 = 10$. The side opposite the 60° angle is

$$\frac{1}{2}(20)\left(\sqrt{3}\right) = 10\sqrt{3}$$

Since the legs of a right triangle are perpendicular, one leg is a base and the other leg is an altitude or height. Using the area formula for a triangle

$$\begin{aligned} Area &= \frac{1}{2}bh \\ &= \frac{1}{2}\left(10\sqrt{3}\right)(10) \\ &= \frac{1}{2}\left(100\sqrt{3}\right) \\ Area &= 50\sqrt{3} \end{aligned}$$

The 45°-45°-90° Right Triangle Theorem

Also known as the *Isosceles Right Triangle Theorem*, this is a right triangle whose acute angles measure 45°. The hypotenuse equals the length of either leg times the square root of 2. In the triangle below, the legs have length x and the hypotenuse has length $x\sqrt{2}$.

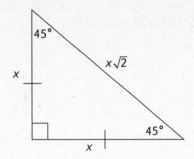

Example:

> If the length of the longest side of an isosceles right triangle is $15\sqrt{2}$, find the lengths of the other two sides.

Since the triangle is an isosceles right triangle, its acute angles measure 45° and the longest side must be the hypotenuse. If the hypotenuse of a 45° -45° -90° right triangle is $15\sqrt{2}$, then the length of each leg is 15.

Quadrilaterals

A *quadrilateral* is a polygon with four sides, angles, and vertices. A quadrilateral has two diagonals.

The sum of the interior angles in a quadrilateral is 360°.

If the sides of a quadrilateral have lengths *a*, *b*, *c*, and *d*, then the perimeter *P* is $P = a + b + c + d$.

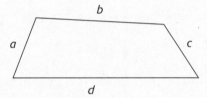

Types of Quadrilaterals

Trapezoid

A *trapezoid* is a quadrilateral with only one pair of parallel sides. The parallel sides are called the *bases of the trapezoid* and the nonparallel sides are called the *legs*. The height or altitude of a trapezoid is a segment perpendicular to the two parallel sides. An *isosceles trapezoid* is a trapezoid in which the legs are equal.

Area of a Trapezoid

The area *A* of a trapezoid is

$A = \frac{1}{2}h(b_1 + b_2)$ where *h* is the height and b_1 and b_2 are the bases of the trapezoid. Consecutive angles between the parallel sides of a trapezoid are *supplementary* (two angles whose sum is 180°).

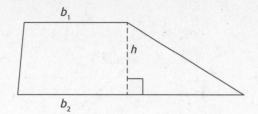

Example:

Find the perimeter and area of the trapezoid.

The perimeter of the trapezoid is the sum of the lengths of its sides:

$$P = 10 + 16 + 17 + 37$$
$$P = 80$$

The area of the trapezoid is

$$A = \frac{1}{2}h(b_1 + b_2)$$
$$= \frac{1}{2}(8)(16 + 37)$$
$$= 4(53)$$
$$A = 212$$

Parallelogram

A *parallelogram* is a quadrilateral with opposite sides that are parallel.

> Opposite sides and opposite angles are equal.
>
> Consecutive angles are supplementary.
>
> The diagonals bisect each other.

Area of a Parallelogram

The area of a parallelogram is $A = b \times h$ where the base, b, is any one side, and the height, h, is the height or altitude to that side.

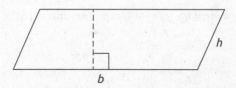

Example:

Find the area of a parallelogram whose sides have lengths of 10 and 16 and a base angle of 30°.

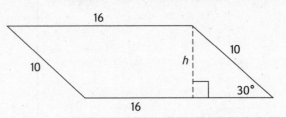

In the figure, the base of the parallelogram is 16 and the height is 5 since the height of the parallelogram is opposite the 30° angle of a 30°-60°-90° triangle whose hypotenuse is 10. The area A is

$$A = b \cdot h$$
$$= (16)(5)$$
$$A = 80$$

Rectangle

A *rectangle* is a parallelogram with four right angles.

Opposite sides are equal.

Consecutive angles are supplementary.

The diagonals are equal and bisect each other.

Area of a Rectangle

The area of a rectangle is

$$A = b \cdot h$$

$A = b \times h$, where b is the base and h is the height or altitude of the rectangle. Another formula that can be used for the area is

$A = \ell w$, where ℓ is the length and w is the width of the rectangle.

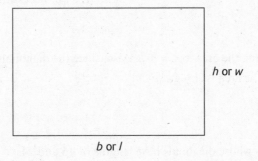

Example:

Find the area of a rectangle with a base length of 15 and a diagonal length of 17.

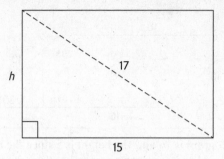

The height, h, can be determined using the Pythagorean Theorem.

$$c^2 = a^2 + b^2$$
$$17^2 = h^2 + 15^2$$
$$289 = h^2 + 225$$
$$h^2 = 289 - 225$$
$$h^2 = 64$$
$$h = \sqrt{64} = 8$$

The area A of the rectangle is

$$A = b \cdot h$$
$$= (15)(8)$$
$$A = 120$$

Rhombus

A *rhombus* is a parallelogram with four equal sides.

Opposite angles are equal.

Consecutive angles are supplementary.

The diagonals bisect each other.

The diagonals bisect the angles of the rhombus.

The diagonals are perpendicular.

It should be noted that the angles of a rhombus are not necessarily equal.

Area of a Rhombus

Since a rhombus is a parallelogram, the area is $A = b \cdot h$. Also, since the diagonals d_1 and d_2 of a rhombus are perpendicular, another formula for the area is $A = \frac{1}{2} d_1 d_2$.

Example:

Find the area of a rhombus whose diagonals have lengths of 15 and 24.

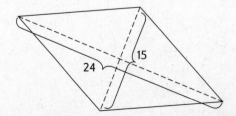

Since the diagonals are perpendicular,

$$A = \frac{1}{2} d_1 d_2$$
$$= \frac{1}{2}(15)(24)$$
$$A = 180$$

Square

A *square* is a rectangle and a rhombus.

> All four sides and angles are equal.
>
> Consecutive angles are supplementary.
>
> The diagonals are equal, perpendicular, bisect each other, and bisect the angles of a square.

Area of a Square

The area of a square is $A = s^2$ where s is the length of one of its four equal sides. Since the diagonals, d, of a square are equal and perpendicular, another formula for the area is

$$A = \frac{1}{2} d \cdot d = \frac{1}{2} d^2$$

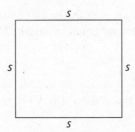

It should be noted that the area formula $A = \frac{1}{2} d_1 d_2$ can be used for any quadrilateral with perpendicular diagonals.

Example:

Find the perimeter of a square with a diagonal length of $25\sqrt{2}$.

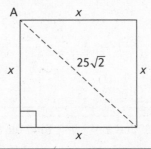

Since the diagonal forms two isosceles right triangles in the square, the two legs of the triangles will have length 25, which is also the length of each side of the square. The perimeter, P, of the square is

$$P = 4 \cdot x = 4 \cdot 25 = 100$$

Summary of the Properties of Quadrilaterals					
Property	Trapezoid	Parallelogram	Rectangle	Rhombus	Square
Four sides, angles, and vertices	✓	✓	✓	✓	✓
Opposite sides are parallel		✓	✓	✓	✓
Opposite sides are equal		✓	✓	✓	✓
Opposite angles are equal		✓	✓	✓	✓
Consecutive angles are supplementary		✓	✓	✓	✓
Diagonals bisect each other	✓	✓	✓	✓	✓
Diagonals bisect the angles				✓	✓
Diagonals are equal			✓		✓
Diagonals are perpendicular				✓	✓
All sides are equal				✓	✓
All angles are equal			✓		✓

Polygons

Congruent Polygons

Two polygons are said to be *congruent* if they are exactly the same shape and size. Their corresponding angles are equal in measure and their corresponding sides are equal in length. The symbol for congruence is ≅.

Examples:

1. In the figures, if quadrilateral $ABCD \cong$ quadrilateral $WXYZ$, then

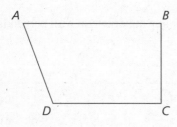

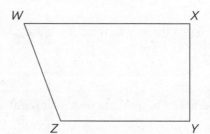

$\angle A = \angle W$ and $\overline{AB} = \overline{WX}$

$\angle B = \angle X$ and $\overline{BC} = \overline{XY}$

$\angle C = \angle Y$ and $\overline{CD} = \overline{YZ}$

$\angle D = \angle Z$ and $\overline{DA} = \overline{ZW}$

2. Given: $\triangle RST \cong \triangle MNQ$ with $\angle M = 53°$ and $\angle N = 98°$. Find the measures of the angles in $\triangle RST$.

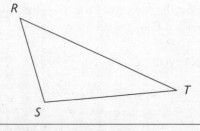

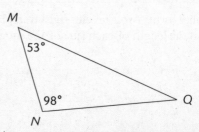

$$\text{In } \triangle MNQ, \angle M + \angle N + \angle Q = 180°$$
$$53° + 98° + \angle Q = 180°$$
$$151° + \angle Q = 180°$$
$$\angle Q = 29°$$

$$\text{Since } \triangle RST \cong \triangle MNQ$$
$$\angle R = \angle M = 53°$$
$$\angle S = \angle N = 98°$$
$$\angle T = \angle Q = 29°$$

Similar Polygons

Two polygons are said to be similar if they have exactly the same shape but are not necessarily the same size. Their corresponding angles are equal in measure and their corresponding sides are proportional in measure. The symbol for similarity is ~.

Examples:

1. In the figures, if quadrilateral $ABCD$ ~ quadrilateral $WXYZ$, then

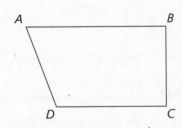 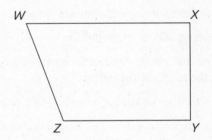

$\angle A \cong \angle W$ and $\dfrac{AB}{WX} = \dfrac{BC}{XY} = \dfrac{CD}{YZ} = \dfrac{DA}{ZW}$

$\angle B \cong \angle X$ or

$\angle C \cong \angle Y$ $\dfrac{WX}{AB} = \dfrac{XY}{BC} = \dfrac{YZ}{CD} = \dfrac{ZW}{DA}$

$\angle D \cong \angle Z$

2. Given: $\triangle DEF$ ~ $\triangle RST$ with $DE = 18$, $EF = 24$, $DF = 30$, and $ST = 16$. Find the perimeter of $\triangle RST$.

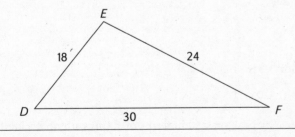 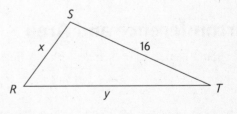

Since $\triangle DEF \sim \triangle RST$, their corresponding sides are proportional:

$$\frac{DE}{RS} = \frac{EF}{ST} = \frac{DF}{RT}$$

$$\frac{DE}{RS} = \frac{EF}{ST} \qquad \text{and} \qquad \frac{EF}{ST} = \frac{DF}{RT}$$

$$\frac{18}{x} = \frac{24}{16} \qquad\qquad\qquad \frac{24}{16} = \frac{30}{y}$$

$$24x = (18)(16) \qquad\qquad 24y = (16)(30)$$

$$24x = 288 \qquad\qquad\qquad 24y = 480$$

$$x = \frac{288}{24} = 12 \qquad\qquad y = \frac{480}{24} = 20$$

Hence the perimeter of $\triangle RST = 16 + 12 + 20 = 48$.

Circles

A *circle* is the set of all points in a plane that are the same distance from a fixed point, called the *center of the circle*.

Basic Terms

Radius: A line segment whose endpoints are the center of a circle and any point on a circle

Chord: A line segment whose endpoints are any two points on a circle

Diameter: A chord that passes through the center of a circle. The diameter of a circle is the longest chord of a circle and is two times the length of the radius.

Circumference: The distance around a circle. The circumference of a circle has a degree measure of 360°.

Arc: A portion of the circumference of a circle consisting of two points on the circle and all points on the circle between the endpoints. The symbol for an arc is $\frown$.

Semicircle: An arc that is equal to one-half the circumference of a circle and has a degree measure of 180°

Minor Arc: An arc whose measure is less than 180°

Major Arc: An arc whose measure is greater than 180°

Tangent: A line that intersects a circle at exactly one point

Secant: A line that intersects a circle at two points

Concentric Circles: Coplanar circles that have the same center

Circumference and Area

The circumference, C, of a circle, with a diameter d and radius r is

$$C = \pi \cdot d \text{ or } C = 2\pi r$$

where $\pi \approx 3.14$ or $\pi \approx \frac{22}{7}$. In many cases, the circumference may be expressed in terms of π (pi) with no decimal or fractional approximation.

The area A of a circle with a radius r is

$$A = \pi r^2$$

where $\pi \approx 3.14$ or $\pi \approx \frac{22}{7}$. As noted with the circumference of a circle, the area may be expressed in terms of π with no decimal or fractional approximation.

Example:

Find the circumference and area of a circle whose diameter is 24 and express each in terms of π.

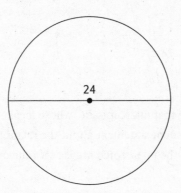

The circumference of the circle is

$$C = \pi d$$
$$= \pi(24)$$
$$C = 24\pi$$

Since the diameter of the circle is 24, the radius is 12 and the area of the circle is

$$A = \pi r^2$$
$$= \pi\left(12^2\right)$$
$$A = 144\pi$$

Special Circle-Related Angles

Central Angle

A *central angle* is an angle whose vertex is the center of a circle. The measure of a central angle is the same as the arc it intercepts on the circle.

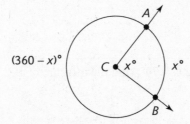

In the circle with center C, $\angle ACB$ is a central angle and the measure of minor arc $\overarc{AB} = x^\circ = \angle ACB$. Note that the measure of the major arc $\overarc{AB} = (360 - x)^\circ$.

Inscribed Angle

An *inscribed angle* is an angle whose vertex is on the circle and whose sides intersect the circle at two other points. The measure of an inscribed angle is one-half the measure of the arc it intercepts on the circle.

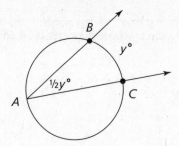

In the circle, $\angle BAC$ is an inscribed angle that intercepts $\overset{\frown}{BC}$ whose measure is $y°$. The measure of the inscribed angle $\angle BAC = \frac{1}{2}\left(\overset{\frown}{BC}\right) = \frac{1}{2}y°$. An equivalent statement about the relationship between an inscribed angle and its intercepted arc is that the measure of the intercepted arc is twice the measure of the inscribed angle.

Secant-Tangent Angle

A *secant-tangent angle* is an angle whose vertex is on the circle, with one side intersecting the circle at another point and the other side having no other points on the circle. The measure of a secant-tangent is one-half the measure of the arc it intercepts on the circle.

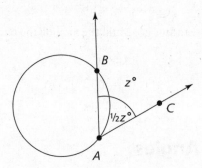

In the circle, $\angle BAC$ is a secant-tangent angle that intercepts $\overset{\frown}{AB}$ whose measure is $z°$. The measure of this secant-tangent angle $\angle BAC = \frac{1}{2}\left(\overset{\frown}{AB}\right) = \frac{1}{2}z°$. It may also be said that the measure of the intercepted arc is twice the measure of the secant-tangent angle.

Examples:

1. If the circle has a center at C and $\angle C = 70°$, find the measure of $\angle YXZ$.

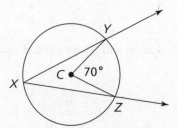

Since $\angle C$ is a central angle, the measure of its intercept arc $\overset{\frown}{YZ} = 70°$. Since $\angle YXZ$ is an inscribed angle, its measure is one-half the measure of its intercept arc $\overset{\frown}{YZ}$.

$$\angle YXZ = \frac{1}{2}\left(\overset{\frown}{YZ}\right)$$
$$= \frac{1}{2}(70°)$$
$$\angle YXZ = 35°$$

---

2. Given a circle with chords $\overline{AB}$, $\overline{AC}$, $\overline{BD}$, and $\overline{CD}$ and $\overset{\frown}{BC} = 110°$, find the measure of $\angle x + \angle y$.

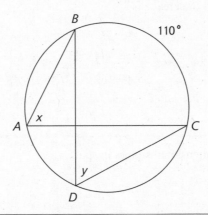

Both $\angle x$ and $\angle y$ are inscribed angles whose measures are one-half the measure of their intercepted arc $\overset{\frown}{BC}$. Hence,

$$\angle x = \frac{1}{2}\left(\overset{\frown}{BC}\right) \qquad \text{and} \qquad \angle y = \frac{1}{2}\left(\overset{\frown}{BC}\right)$$
$$= \frac{1}{2}(110°) \qquad\qquad\qquad = \frac{1}{2}(110°)$$
$$\angle x = 55° \qquad\qquad\qquad\quad \angle y = 55°$$

The sum of $\angle x + \angle y = 55° + 55° = 110°$.

---

3. Given a circle with center C, $RS = 24$ and $ST = 10$, find the area of the circle.

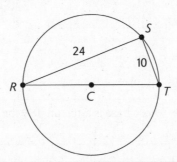

To determine the area of a circle, the radius or diameter must be known. $\angle RST$ is an inscribed angle whose intercepted arc is a semicircle, since $\overline{RT}$ is the diameter of the circle. The measure of the inscribed angle is one-half the measure of its intercepted arc:

$$\angle RST = \frac{1}{2}(180°) = 90°, \text{ and } \triangle RST \text{ is a right triangle.}$$

Using the Pythagorean Theorem

$$(RT)^2 = (RS)^2 + (ST)^2$$
$$= (24)^2 + (10)^2$$
$$= 576 + 100$$
$$(RT)^2 = 676$$
$$RT = \sqrt{676}$$
$$RT = 26, \text{ which is the diameter of the circle.}$$

Hence the radius of the circle is 13 and the area A is

$$A = \pi r^2$$
$$= \pi\left(13^2\right)$$
$$A = 169\pi$$

Solid Geometry

Solid geometry is the study of three-dimensional shapes in space.

Volumes

Volume of a Rectangular Solid (Box)

The volume V of a right rectangular solid with length l, width w, and height h is $V = l \cdot w \cdot h$.

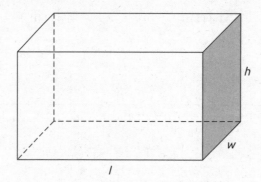

Example:

Find the volume of a cardboard box whose base is a rectangle 9 inches by 12 inches, and whose height is 4 inches.

$$V = l \cdot w \cdot h$$
$$= (12)(9)(4)$$
$$V = 432 \text{ cubic inches}$$

Volume of a Cube

Since the length, width, and height of a cube are all equal, the volume V of a cube whose side has length x is $V = x^3$.

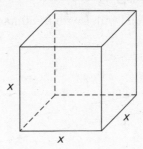

Example:

Find the volume of a cube whose height is 5 feet.

$$V = x^3$$
$$= 5^3$$
$$V = 125 \text{ cubic feet}$$

Volume of a Right Circular Cylinder

The volume V of a right circular cylinder with radius r and height h is $V = \pi r^2 h$.

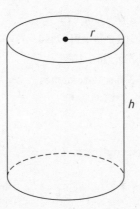

Example:

Find the volume of a beverage can with radius of 2 inches and a height of 8 inches.

$$V = \pi r^2 h$$
$$= \pi\left(2^2\right)(8)$$
$$= \pi(4)(8)$$
$$V = 32\pi \text{ cubic inches}$$

Surface Areas

Surface Area of a Right Rectangular Solid

The surface area SA of a right rectangular solid with length l, width w, and height h is $SA = 2wh + 2lh + 2lw$.

If the rectangular solid is open at the top, then its outside surface area SA is $SA = 2wh + 2lh + lw$.

Since each of the faces of a right rectangular solid is a rectangle, their areas are determined using the area formula for a rectangle.

Example:

> Find the outside surface area of a cardboard box with no top whose base is a rectangle 9 inches by 12 inches and whose height is 4 inches.

$$SA = 2wh + 2lh + lw$$
$$= 2(9)(4) + 2(12)(4) + 1(9)(12)$$
$$= 72 + 96 + 108$$
$$SA = 276 \text{ square inches}$$

Surface Area of a Cube

The surface area SA of a cube whose side has length x is $SA = 6x^2$.

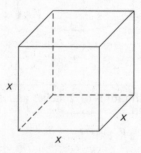

Since each of the six faces is a square whose side has length x, the area of each square is x^2. If the cube has an open top then its outside surface area SA is $SA = 5x^2$.

Example:

Find the surface area of a cube whose height is 5 feet.

$$SA = 6x^2$$
$$= 6(5^2)$$
$$= 6(25)$$
$$SA = 150 \text{ square feet}$$

Surface Area of a Right Circular Cylinder

The surface area SA of a right circular cylinder with radius r and height h is $SA = 2\pi r^2 + 2\pi rh$.

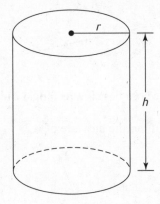

If the cylinder is open at the top then its outside surface area SA is $SA = \pi r^2 + 2\pi rh$.

Example:

Find the surface area of a beverage can with a radius of 2 inches and a height of 8 inches.

$$SA = 2\pi r^2 + 2\pi rh$$
$$= 2\pi \left(2^2\right) + 2\pi (2)(8)$$
$$= 2\pi (4) + 32\pi$$
$$= 8\pi + 32\pi$$
$$SA = 40\pi \text{ square inches}$$

Practice Questions: Geometry

Now that you have reviewed the strategies, you can practice on your own. These questions are roughly grouped into sets by their graduated level of difficulty, just as they might appear on the actual SAT. Questions appear in three categories: easy to moderate, average, and above-average to difficult. The answers and explanations that follow the questions will include strategies to help you understand how to solve the problems.

Easy to Moderate

1. Find the supplement of an angle whose measure is 75°.

2. Find the measure of $\angle BAC$ if $\overrightarrow{AB} \perp \overrightarrow{AC}$.

3. If in $\triangle XYZ$, $\angle X = 58°$ and $\angle Y = 63°$, which side is the longest side of the triangle?

4. In the figure, A is a point on the circle and $\angle A = 40°$. Find the measure of $\overparen{BC}$.

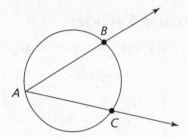

5. Find the volume of a cardboard box whose base is a rectangle 2 feet by 3 feet and whose height is 4 feet.

6. In the figure, $\angle 1 = 27°$ and $\angle 3 = 67°$. Find the measure of $\angle 2$.

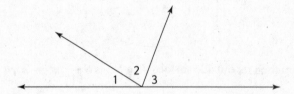

Average

7. In the figure $\ell_1 \parallel \ell_2$ and $\angle 1 = 50°$. Find the measure of $\angle 2$.

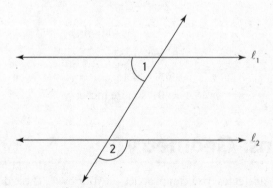

8. In $\triangle ABC$, $\angle A = 53°$ and $\angle C = 91°$. Find the measure of $\angle B$.

9. Find the sum of the measures of the interior angles of a decagon.

10. In $\triangle ABC$, $\angle C$ is a right angle, $AC = 9$, and $AB = 15$. Find BC.

11. An isosceles right triangle has a leg length of 12. Find the length of its hypotenuse.

12. Find the area of the trapezoid *ABCD*.

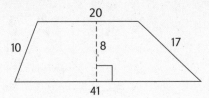

13. Find the area of a rhombus whose diagonals have lengths of 20 and 25.

14. Find the perimeter of a square whose diagonal has a length of $15\sqrt{2}$.

15. Given $\triangle MNQ \sim \triangle RST$ with $\angle N = 51°$ and $\angle Q = 95°$, find the measures of the three angles in $\triangle RST$.

16. Find the area of a circle with a circumference of 18π and express the answer in terms of π.

17. In the circle with center *C*, $\angle C = 90°$. Find the measure of $\angle XYZ$.

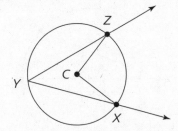

18. Find the outside surface area of a box with square faces and side lengths of 8 inches if the box has no top.

19. Find the volume of a right circular cylinder with a radius of 3 inches and a height of 10 inches and express the answer in terms of π.

20. Find the surface area of a beverage can with a radius of 2 inches and a height of 6 inches and express the answer in terms of π.

21. An angle has a measure that is four times the measure of its complement. Find the measure of the smaller angle.

22. A right triangle has a leg length of 10 and a hypotenuse length of 20. Find the length of its other leg.

Above Average to Difficult

23. A stop sign is a regular octagon. Find the measure of one of its interior angles.

24. Find the area of the given triangle.

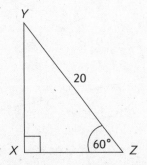

25. In the figure, $AB = BC$ and $\angle A = 55°$. Find the measure of $\angle 1$.

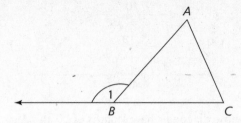

26. Find the area of a parallelogram whose sides have lengths of 20 and 24 and whose base angle is 30°.

27. Find the area of a rectangle with a side length of 16 and a diagonal length of 20.

28. Given $\triangle ABC \sim \triangle XYZ$ with $AB = 16$, $BC = 20$, $AC = 24$, and $XZ = 30$, find the perimeter of $\triangle XYZ$.

29. In the circle with center C, $AX = 24$ and $BX = 18$. Find the area of the circle.

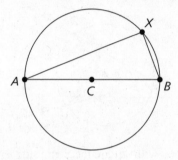

30. Find the area of an equilateral triangle whose sides have a length of 18.

Answers and Explanations

Easy to Moderate

1. Since the sum of two supplementary angles is 180°, the supplement of an angle that measures 75° is $180° - 75° = 105°$.

2. If $\overrightarrow{AB} \perp \overrightarrow{AC}$, the angle formed by the two rays, $\angle BAC$, is a right angle whose measure is 90°.

3. Since $\angle X = 58°$ and $\angle Y = 63°$ in $\triangle XYZ$, $\angle Z = 59°$ for the sum of the angles to equal 180°. In any triangle, the longest side is opposite the largest angle. So the side opposite $\angle Y$ is the longest side $\overline{XZ}$ of the triangle.

4. Since A is a point on the circle, $\angle A$ is an inscribed angle whose measure is one-half the measure of its intercepted arc $\overset{\frown}{BC}$:

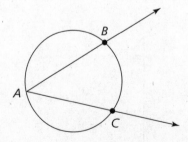

$$\angle A = \tfrac{1}{2}\left(\overset{\frown}{BC}\right)$$

$$40° = \tfrac{1}{2}\left(\overset{\frown}{BC}\right)$$

$$2 \cdot 40° = \cancel{2}^{\,1} \cdot \tfrac{1}{\cancel{2}_{\,1}}\left(\overset{\frown}{BC}\right)$$

$$\overset{\frown}{BC} = 80°$$

5. The volume V of a rectangular solid with length l, width w, and height h is

$$V = l \cdot w \cdot h$$
$$= (3)(2)(4)$$
$$V = 24 \text{ cubic feet}$$

6. Since the three angles $\angle 1$, $\angle 2$, and $\angle 3$ form a straight line, their sum is 180° and

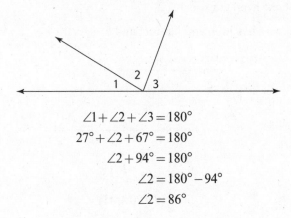

$$\angle 1 + \angle 2 + \angle 3 = 180°$$
$$27° + \angle 2 + 67° = 180°$$
$$\angle 2 + 94° = 180°$$
$$\angle 2 = 180° - 94°$$
$$\angle 2 = 86°$$

Average

7. Since $\ell_1 \parallel \ell_2$ alternate interior angles are equal, $\angle 1 = \angle 3 = 50°$. Since $\angle 2$ and $\angle 3$ form a straight line, they are supplementary:

$$\angle 2 + \angle 3 = 180°$$
$$\angle 2 + 50° = 180°$$
$$\angle 2 = 180° - 50°$$
$$\angle 2 = 130°$$

8. In any triangle, the sum of its interior angles is 180°. In $\triangle ABC$

$$\angle A + \angle B + \angle C = 180°$$
$$53° + \angle B + 91° = 180°$$
$$\angle B + 144° = 180°$$
$$\angle B = 180° - 144°$$
$$\angle B = 36°$$

9. The sum of the interior angles of a polygon with n sides is $(n-2) \times 180°$. Since a decagon is a ten-sided polygon, the sum of its interior angles is $(10-2) \cdot 180° = 8 \cdot 180° = 1,440°$.

10. $\triangle ABC$ is a right triangle since $\angle C$ is a right angle. $\overline{AB}$ is the hypotenuse and $\overline{AC}$ is a leg of the triangle. By the Pythagorean Theorem

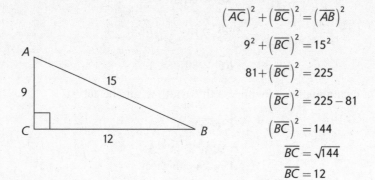

$$\left(\overline{AC}\right)^2 + \left(\overline{BC}\right)^2 = \left(\overline{AB}\right)^2$$

$$9^2 + \left(\overline{BC}\right)^2 = 15^2$$

$$81 + \left(\overline{BC}\right)^2 = 225$$

$$\left(\overline{BC}\right)^2 = 225 - 81$$

$$\left(\overline{BC}\right)^2 = 144$$

$$\overline{BC} = \sqrt{144}$$

$$\overline{BC} = 12$$

11. In an isosceles right triangle, the hypotenuse has a length equal to the leg times $\sqrt{2}$. Since the leg has a length of 12, the length of the hypotenuse is $12\sqrt{2}$.

12. The area A of a trapezoid with height h, and bases b_1 and b_2 is

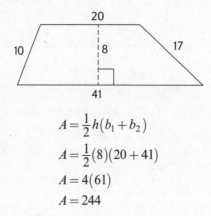

$$A = \frac{1}{2}h(b_1 + b_2)$$

$$A = \frac{1}{2}(8)(20 + 41)$$

$$A = 4(61)$$

$$A = 244$$

13. Since the diagonals d_1 and d_2 of a rhombus are perpendicular, the area A of a rhombus is

$$A = \frac{1}{2}d_1 \cdot d_2$$

$$= \frac{1}{2}(20)(25)$$

$$= (10)(25)$$

$$A = 250$$

14. The perimeter P of a square with side s is

$$P = 4 \cdot s$$

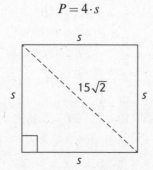

The diagonal of a square forms two isosceles right triangles whose hypotenuse is equal to the length of the legs times $\sqrt{2}$. Since the hypotenuse has a length of $15\sqrt{2}$, the length of the legs are 15, which is the same as the sides of the square. The perimeter P of the square is

$$P = 4 \times s$$
$$= 4 \times (15)$$
$$P = 60$$

15. Since $\triangle MNQ \sim \triangle RST$, the corresponding angles are equal and $\angle M \cong \angle R$, $\angle N \cong \angle S$, and $\angle Q \cong \angle T$.

In $\triangle MNQ$, $\angle N = 51°$ and $\angle Q = 95°$, so $\angle M = 34°$ for the sum of its angles to equal 180°. The measures of the angles in $\triangle RST$ are

$$\angle R = \angle M = 34°$$
$$\angle S = \angle N = 51°$$
$$\angle T = \angle Q = 95°$$

16. The area A of a circle with radius r is $A = \pi r^2$.

The circumference C of a circle with diameter d is $C = \pi d$.

Since the circumference of the circle is 18π

$$C = \pi d$$
$$18\pi = \pi d$$
$$\frac{18\not\pi}{\not\pi} = \frac{\not\pi d}{\not\pi}$$
$$d = 18$$

If the diameter of a circle is 18, its radius r is one-half the diameter: $r = \frac{1}{2}d = \frac{1}{2}(18) = 9$.

The area A of the circle is

$$A = \pi \cdot r^2$$
$$= \pi\left(9^2\right)$$
$$A = 81\pi$$

17. Since C is the center of the circle, $\angle C$ is a central angle whose measure is equal to its intercepted arc: $\angle C = \overset{\frown}{XZ} = 90°$.

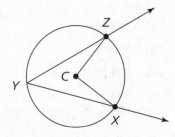

$\angle Y$ is an inscribed angle whose measure is one-half the measure of its intercepted arc $\overset{\frown}{XZ}$

$$\angle Y = \frac{1}{2}\left(\overset{\frown}{XZ}\right)$$
$$= \frac{1}{2}(90°)$$
$$\angle Y = 45°$$

18. Since the box has no top, there are five outside square faces, each with an area $A = s^2$, where s is the length of the sides of the square. The outside surface area SA of the box is

$$SA = 5s^2$$
$$= 5(8^2)$$
$$= 5(64)$$
$$SA = 320 \text{ square inches}$$

19. The volume V of a right circular cylinder with radius r and height h is

$$V = \pi r^2 h$$
$$= \pi(3^2)(10)$$
$$V = 90\pi \text{ cubic inches}$$

20. The surface area SA of a right circular cylinder with radius r and height h is

$$SA = 2\pi r^2 + 2\pi rh$$
$$= 2\pi(2^2) + 2\pi(2)(6)$$
$$= 2\pi(4) + 2\pi(12)$$
$$= 8\pi + 24\pi$$
$$SA = 32\pi \text{ square inches}$$

21. Two angles are complementary if their sum is 90°.

    Let x = the measure of the smaller angle and

    $4x$ = the measure of the larger angle.

$$x + 4x = 90°$$
$$5x = 90°$$
$$\frac{\cancel{5}^1 x}{\cancel{5}^1} = \frac{\cancel{90}^{18°}}{\cancel{5}^1}$$
$$x = 18°$$

22. By the Pythagorean Theorem, if a right triangle has legs with lengths of a and b and a hypotenuse of length c

$$c^2 = a^2 + b^2$$
$$20^2 = 10^2 + b^2$$
$$400 = 100 + b^2$$
$$400 - 100 = 100 + b^2 - 100$$
$$b^2 = 300$$
$$b = \sqrt{300} = \sqrt{100 \cdot 3} = \sqrt{100} \cdot \sqrt{3}$$
$$b = 10\sqrt{3}$$

Above Average to Difficult

23. A regular polygon is a polygon with all sides equal in measure. A regular octagon will have eight equal sides and angles. The sum of the interior angles in any octagon is $(8-2)\cdot 180° = 6\cdot 180° = 1,080°$.

    Since there are eight equal angles in a regular octagon, each interior angle will have a measure of

    $$1,080° \div 8 = 135°$$

24. Since $\angle Z$ is 60° and $\angle X$ is a right angle, $\angle X = 90°$, $\angle Z = 60°$, and $\angle Y = 30°$. In a 30°-60°-90° triangle, the side opposite the 30° angle is one-half the hypotenuse. The side opposite the 60° angle is one-half the hypotenuse times $\sqrt{3}$.

    In $\triangle XYZ$, $XZ = \frac{1}{2}(YZ) = \frac{1}{2}(20) = 10$

    and $XY\,(height) = \frac{1}{2}(YZ)\cdot\sqrt{3} = \frac{1}{2}(20)\cdot\sqrt{3} = 10\sqrt{3}$

    The area A of a triangle with base b and height h is $A = \frac{1}{2}bh$.

    $$\begin{aligned} \text{In } \triangle XYZ, \quad A &= \frac{1}{2}(10)\left(10\sqrt{3}\right) \\ &= 5\left(10\sqrt{3}\right) \\ A &= 50\sqrt{3} \end{aligned}$$

25. Since $AB = BC$, $\triangle ABC$ is an isosceles triangle with $\angle A = \angle C = 55°$. Since $\angle 1$ is an exterior angle of $\triangle ABC$

    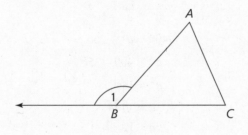

    $$\begin{aligned} \angle 1 &= \angle A + \angle C \\ &= 55° + 55° \\ \angle 1 &= 110° \end{aligned}$$

26. The area A of a parallelogram with base b and height h is $A = bh$.

    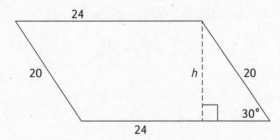

The height is drawn to form a 30°-60°-90° right triangle with a hypotenuse length of 20.

The height h, will have a length equal to one-half the hypotenuse or $\frac{1}{2}(20)=10$. The area A of the parallelogram is

$$A = bh$$
$$= (24)(10)$$
$$A = 240$$

27. The area A of a rectangle with length l and width w is $A = lw$.

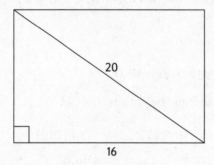

The diagonal of a rectangle forms two congruent right triangles with the diagonal as the hypotenuse and the sides of the rectangle as the legs of the right triangle. By the Pythagorean Theorem

$$c^2 = a^2 + b^2$$
$$20^2 = a^2 + 16^2$$
$$400 = a^2 + 256$$
$$a^2 = 400 - 256$$
$$a^2 = 144$$
$$a = \sqrt{144}$$
$$a = 12$$

The area A of the rectangle is

$$A = l \times w$$
$$= (16)(12)$$
$$A = 192$$

28. Since $\triangle ABC \sim \triangle XYZ$, the corresponding sides are proportional and

$$\frac{AB}{XY} = \frac{BC}{YZ} = \frac{AC}{XZ}$$

$AB = 16 \quad XY = ?$

$BC = 20 \quad YZ = ?$

$AC = 24 \quad XZ = 30$

The perimeter P of $\triangle XYZ$ is: $P = XY + YZ + XZ$.

To find XY	To find YZ

$$\frac{AB}{XY}=\frac{AC}{XZ}$$

$$\frac{16}{XY}=\frac{24}{30}$$

$$24(XY)=16\cdot 30$$

$$24(XY)=480$$

$$XY=\frac{480}{24}$$

$$XY=20$$

$$\frac{BC}{YZ}=\frac{AC}{XZ}$$

$$\frac{20}{YZ}=\frac{24}{30}$$

$$24(YZ)=20\cdot 30$$

$$24(YZ)=600$$

$$YZ=\frac{600}{24}$$

$$YZ=25$$

Hence the perimeter P of $\triangle XYZ$ is

$$P = XY + YZ + XZ$$
$$= 20 + 25 + 30$$
$$P = 75$$

29. Since C is the center of the circle, $\overline{AB}$ is a diameter that divides the circle into two semi-circles whose measure is 180°. $\angle X$ is an inscribed angle whose measure is one-half the measure of its intercepted arc $\overset{\frown}{AB}$.

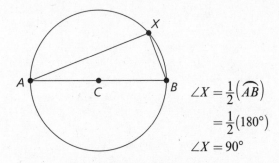

$$\angle X = \frac{1}{2}\left(\overset{\frown}{AB}\right)$$
$$= \frac{1}{2}(180°)$$
$$\angle X = 90°$$

Therefore $\triangle AXB$ is a right triangle with leg lengths of 24 and 18. By the Pythagorean Theorem

$$(AB)^2 = (AX)^2 + (BX)^2$$
$$= (24)^2 + (18)^2$$
$$= 576 + 324$$
$$(AB)^2 = 900$$
$$AB = \sqrt{900}$$
$$AB = 30$$

Hence the circle has a diameter length of 30 and a radius length of 15. The area A of the circle is

$$A = \pi r^2$$
$$= \pi\left(15^2\right)$$
$$A = 225\pi$$

30. An equilateral triangle is also an equiangular triangle whose angles have a measure of 60°. Any height drawn to one of its sides forms two 30°-60°-90° triangles, each with a hypotenuse of 18. The height h is opposite the 60° angle and has a length equal to one-half the hypotenuse times $\sqrt{3}$.

$$h = \frac{1}{2} \cdot (18) \cdot \sqrt{3} = 9\sqrt{3}$$

The area A of the triangle is

$$A = \frac{1}{2}bh$$
$$= \frac{1}{2}(18)\left(9\sqrt{3}\right)$$
$$A = 81\sqrt{3}$$

Chapter 8
Data Analysis, Statistics, and Probability Review

Data analysis, statistics, and probability questions on the SAT require problem-solving skills and the ability to recognize, analyze, and answer variations of data. A solid understanding of arithmetic will help you to solve this type of question. As you make inferences from the information presented, you will be gathering, organizing, and analyzing data. Topics include

- Basic statistics (mean, median, mode, and range)
- Factorials, combinations, and permutations
- Probability

Basic Statistics

Mean

The mean for a set of data is found by adding the numbers in the set of data and then dividing by the total number of items in the set. The mean is also called the average, and for any set of data there is one, and only one, mean.

Median

The median for a set of data is the middle number in the set. Before the median can be determined, each number in the set of data should be ordered from smallest to largest, or from largest to smallest. If the number of items in the data is even, then the median is determined by finding the mean of the two middle numbers. For any set of data there is one, and only one, median.

Mode

The mode for a set of data is the number that occurs most frequently. One difference between the mode, mean, and median is that there may be more than one mode, or no mode for any given set of data.

Range

The range for a set of data is simply the difference between the largest and the smallest numbers of the set.

Examples:

> 1. A student has test scores of 83, 67, 92, 88, and 79 in her math class. Find her mean test score.

The first step in finding the mean is to find the sum of the five test scores.

$$83 + 67 + 92 + 88 + 79 = 409$$

Since there are five test scores, the sum is divided by 5.

$$\frac{409}{5} = 81\frac{4}{5} \text{ or } 81.8$$

If the problem had asked for the answer to be rounded to the nearest whole number, the mean would be 82.

2. What would the student in the previous example need to score on the sixth test to have an average score of 84?

The sum of six test scores required to have an average of 84 is $84 \times 6 = 504$.

Since her first five scores have a sum of 409, her sixth test score must be $504 - 409 = 95$.

The student would need a score of 95 on the sixth test.

3. Find the median for the eight given quiz scores: 6, 9, 8, 7, 10, 10, 7, 5.

The scores should first be arranged in numerical order.

$$5, 6, 7, 7, 8, 9, 10, 10 \text{ or } 10, 10, 9, 8, 7, 7, 6, 5$$

Since there is an even number of scores (8), the median is the average of the two middle scores.

$$\frac{7+8}{2} = \frac{15}{2} = 7\frac{1}{2} \text{ or } 7.5$$

4. Find the mode of the quiz scores given in the previous example.

The mode refers to the score that occurs most frequently. Since there are two quiz scores of 7 and two quiz scores of 10, the mode is 7 and 10.

5. Find the mean, median, and mode of: 2, 5, 5, 5, 5, 6, 11, 11, 11, 13, 14.

$$\text{The mean is: } (2 + 5 + 5 + 5 + 5 + 6 + 11 + 11 + 11 + 13 + 14) \div 11 =$$

$$88 \div 11 = 8$$

$$\text{Mean} = 8$$

The median is the middle number in the set. In the preceding example the median is the sixth number in a set of data with eleven items. Median = 6

The mode is the number that occurs most frequently in the set of data. Mode = 5

Factorials, Combinations, and Permutations

Factorials

Factorials allow us to express the product of a set of decreasing natural numbers without having to write each factor. The symbol used for factorials is ! and the general definition for $n!$ where n is a natural number is

$$n! = n \cdot (n-1) \cdot (n-2) \cdot (n-3) \ldots 3 \cdot 2 \cdot 1$$

By definition, $0! = 1$

Examples:

1. Evaluate: (a) 3! (b) 5! (c) 8!

(a) $3! = 3 \cdot 2 \cdot 1 = 6$

(b) $5! = 5 \cdot 4 \cdot 3 \cdot 2 \cdot 1 = 120$

(c) $8! = 8 \cdot 7 \cdot 6 \cdot 5 \cdot 4 \cdot 3 \cdot 2 \cdot 1 = 40,320$

2. Evaluate: $\frac{8!}{5!}$

$$\text{Since } 8! = 8 \cdot 7 \cdot 6 \cdot (5!)$$

$$\frac{8!}{5!} = \frac{8 \cdot 7 \cdot 6 \cdot (\cancel{5!})}{\cancel{5!}}$$

$$\frac{8!}{5!} = 8 \cdot 7 \cdot 6$$

$$\frac{8!}{5!} = 336$$

3. Evaluate: $\frac{12!}{9! \cdot 3!}$

$$\text{Since } 12! = 12 \cdot 11 \cdot 10 \cdot (9!)$$

$$\frac{12!}{9! \cdot 3!} = \frac{12 \cdot 11 \cdot 10 \cdot (\cancel{9!})}{\cancel{9!} \cdot 3!}$$

$$\frac{12!}{9! \cdot 3!} = \frac{12 \cdot 11 \cdot 10}{3 \cdot 2 \cdot 1}$$

$$\frac{12!}{9! \cdot 3!} = 220$$

4. Simplify: $\frac{(x+2)!}{(x-1)!}$

$$\text{Since } (x+2)! = (x+2)(x+1)(x)(x-1)!$$

$$\frac{(x+2)!}{(x-1)!} = \frac{(x+2)(x+1)(x)(\cancel{x-1)!}}{(\cancel{x-1)!}}$$

$$\frac{(x+2)!}{(x-1)!} = (x+2)(x+1)(x)$$

$$\frac{(x+2)!}{(x-1)!} = x^3 + 3x^2 + 2x$$

Combinations

A selection of *r* objects from a set with a total of *n* objects without regard for the order of the selected objects is called a *combination*. The notation for the number of combinations is: $_nC_r$ or $C(n, r)$.

The total number of ways to select r objects from a set of n objects without regard for the order of the selected objects is

$$_nC_r \text{ or } C(n,r) = \frac{n!}{r! \cdot (n-r)!}$$

Examples:

1. How many different groups of 4 students can be formed by choosing from a total of 10 students?

Since the order of the students selected is not important, this is a combination of 4 students from a set of 10 students. The number of different groups possible is

$$_{10}C_4 \text{ or } C(10,4) =$$
$$= \frac{10!}{4! \cdot (10-4)!}$$
$$= \frac{10!}{4! \cdot 6!}$$
$$= \frac{10 \cdot 9 \cdot 8 \cdot 7 \cdot \cancel{6}!}{4! \cdot \cancel{6}!}$$
$$= \frac{10 \cdot 9 \cdot 8 \cdot 7}{4 \cdot 3 \cdot 2 \cdot 1}$$
$$= 210 \text{ groups}$$

As an example to illustrate the order is not important, note that a group consisting of students A, B, C, and D is the same as a group consisting of students C, D, A, and B.

2. How many different pairs of books may be selected from a shelf containing 12 books?

This is a combination of 2 books from a set of 12 books. The number of different pairs possible is

$$_{12}C_2 = C(12,2)$$
$$= \frac{12!}{2! \cdot (12-2)!}$$
$$= \frac{12!}{2! \cdot 10!}$$
$$= \frac{12 \cdot 11}{2 \cdot 1}$$
$$= 66 \text{ pairs}$$

3. How many different 5-card poker hands are possible from a deck of 52 cards?

This is a combination of 5 cards from a set of 52 cards. The number of different 5-card hands is

$$_{52}C_5 = C(52,5)$$
$$= \frac{52!}{5! \cdot (52-5)!}$$
$$= \frac{52!}{5! \cdot 47!}$$
$$= \frac{52 \cdot 51 \cdot 50 \cdot 49 \cdot 48}{5 \cdot 4 \cdot 3 \cdot 2 \cdot 1}$$
$$= 2,598,960 \text{ hands}$$

> 4. How many 4-person committees may be formed from a group of 5 males and 7 females if each committee must have 2 male and 2 female members?

This is a combination of 2 males from a group of 5 males and a combination of 2 females from a group of 7 females.

The number of different groups of 2 males is

$$_5C_2 = C(5,2) = \frac{5!}{2! \cdot (5-2)!} = \frac{5!}{2! \cdot 3!} = \frac{5 \cdot 4}{2 \cdot 1} = 10$$

The number of different groups of 2 females is

$$_7C_2 = C(7,2) = \frac{7!}{2! \cdot (7-2)!} = \frac{7!}{2! \cdot 5!} = \frac{7 \cdot 6}{2 \cdot 1} = 21$$

Hence, the total number of 2-male, 2-female groups is

$$_5C_2 \cdot {_7C_2} = 10 \cdot 21 = 210 \text{ groups}$$

Permutations

A selection of r objects to be arranged in order from a set with a total of n objects is called a *permutation*. The primary difference between combinations and permutations is that the order is *important* to consider in a permutation, but not in a combination. The notation for the number of permutations is $_nP_r = P(n,r)$. The total number of ways to arrange r objects in order from a set of n objects is:

$$_nP_r = P(n,r) = \frac{n!}{(n-r)!}$$

Examples:

> 1. How many four-letter words can be made from the letters in the word numerical?

This is a permutation of 4 letters from a set of 9 letters where the order is *important*. The number of different four-letter words is

$$
\begin{aligned}
_9P_4 &= P(9,4) \\
&= \frac{9!}{(9-4)!} \\
&= \frac{9!}{5!} \\
&= 9 \cdot 8 \cdot 7 \cdot 6 \\
&= 3024 \text{ four-letter words}
\end{aligned}
$$

> 2. How many different first-, second-, and third-place finishers are possible if there are 8 competitors in the race?

This is a permutation of 3 ordered finishers from a set of 8 competitors. The number of different finishers possible is

$$_8P_3 = P(8,3) = \frac{8!}{(8-3)!} = \frac{8!}{5!} = 8 \cdot 7 \cdot 6 = 336$$

> **3.** Four government offices — finance, health, parks, and safety — are to be filled from a committee composed of 12 members. How many different ways can these offices be filled?

This is a permutation of 4 ordered offices to be filled from a set of 12 committee members. The number of different outcomes is

$$_{12}P_4 = P(12,4) = \frac{12!}{(12-4)!} = \frac{12!}{8!} = 12 \cdot 11 \cdot 10 \cdot 9 = 11{,}880 \text{ outcomes}$$

> **4.** How many numbers between 2000 and 5000 can be formed using the digits 0, 1, 2, 3, 4, 5, 6, 7, 8 and 9 if each digit may not be repeated once it is used?

The first place of the four-digit number may be filled by only one of three numbers, 2, 3, or 4. The remaining nine numbers may be used to fill the other three places, which is a permutation of 3 numbers from a set of 9 numbers. The total number of four-digit numbers possible is

$$3 \cdot _9P_3 = 3 \cdot P(9,3) = 3 \cdot \frac{9!}{(9-3)!} = 3 \cdot \frac{9!}{6!} = 3 \cdot 9 \cdot 8 \cdot 7 = 1512 \text{ four-digit numbers}$$

Probability

The term *probability* is used to indicate the likelihood that a particular outcome will occur. The probability is assigned a measure from 0 to 1, where 0 indicates that the outcome will never happen, while 1 indicates that the outcome is sure to occur. As a formula, the probability p, may be expressed by

$$p = \frac{\text{number of desired outcomes}}{\text{number of possible outcomes}}$$

If p is the probability that an event will occur, then the probability that the same event will not occur is $1 - p$.

Examples:

> **1.** A bag of marbles contains 6 red marbles, 9 blue marbles, and 5 white marbles. If a marble is drawn at random from the bag, what is the probability that the marble will be
>
> (a) red
>
> (b) blue
>
> (c) not white

(a) The probability p that the marble will be red is $p = \dfrac{6}{20} = \dfrac{3}{10}$

(b) The probability p that the marble will be blue is $p = \dfrac{9}{20}$

(c) The probability p that the marble will be white is $p = \dfrac{5}{20} = \dfrac{1}{4}$

Therefore the probability that it will not be white is $1 - p = 1 - \dfrac{1}{4} = \dfrac{3}{4}$

> **2.** In the previous example of 20 marbles in a bag, what is the probability that the first 2 marbles drawn will be blue?

The probability that the first marble will be blue is $\frac{9}{20}$. Since there are 8 blue marbles among the remaining 19 marbles, the probability that the second marble will be blue is $\frac{8}{19}$. The probability p that the first two drawn will be blue is

$$p = \frac{9}{20} \cdot \frac{8}{19} = \frac{18}{95}$$

> **3.** In the previous example with 20 marbles in a bag, what is the probability that 1 marble is red and 1 marble is white?

The probability that the first marble is red is $\frac{6}{20} = \frac{3}{10}$. Since there are 5 white marbles among the remaining 19 marbles, the probability that the second marble is white is $\frac{5}{19}$. The probability p that the first marble drawn is red and the second marble drawn is white is

$$\frac{3}{10} \cdot \frac{5}{19} = \frac{3}{38}$$

Note that the outcome will be the same even if the order of selection is reversed. Since the probability that the first marble is white is $\frac{5}{20} = \frac{1}{4}$ and the probability that the second marble is red is $\frac{6}{19}$, the probability p that the first marble is white and the second marble is red is $\frac{1}{4} \cdot \frac{6}{19} = \frac{3}{38}$. Hence the probability p that one marble is red and one marble is white is

$$p = \frac{3}{38} + \frac{3}{38}$$
$$= \frac{6}{38}$$
$$p = \frac{3}{19}$$

> **4.** A student has 5 raffle tickets left from a total of 50 tickets sold. If there are two winning tickets, what is the probability that the student has exactly one winning ticket?

The probability p_1 of having the first winning ticket but not the second winning ticket is

$$p_1 = \frac{5}{50} \cdot \frac{45}{49} = \frac{9}{98}$$

and the probability p_2 of having the second winning ticket , but not the first winning ticket is

$$p_2 = \frac{45}{50} \cdot \frac{5}{49} = \frac{9}{98}$$

Therefore, the probability p of having exactly one winning ticket is

$$p = \frac{9}{98} + \frac{9}{98} = \frac{18}{98} = \frac{9}{49}$$

5. A box contains nine cards numbered 1 through 9. If three of the cards are drawn, one at a time, what is the probability that they will be alternatively odd, even, odd?

The probability that the first card drawn will be odd is $\frac{5}{9}$ since there are 5 odd numbers and 4 even numbers. The probability that the second card drawn will be even is $\frac{4}{8} = \frac{1}{2}$ and that the third card drawn will be odd is $\frac{4}{7}$. The probability p that they are drawn alternatively odd, even, odd is

$$p = \frac{5}{9} \cdot \frac{1}{2} \cdot \frac{4}{7} = \frac{10}{63}$$

6. In the previous example, what is the probability that the three cards will be drawn alternatively even, odd, even?

The probability that the first card will be even is $\frac{4}{9}$, that the second card will be odd is $\frac{5}{8}$, and that the third card will be even is $\frac{3}{7}$. The probability p that the three cards drawn will be alternatively even, odd, even is

$$p = \frac{4}{9} \cdot \frac{5}{8} \cdot \frac{3}{7} = \frac{5}{42}$$

7. In the previous example, what is the probability that the sum of the first two cards drawn will be an odd number?

For the sum of the first two numbers drawn to be odd, one of the numbers must be odd and the other number must be even. The probability that the first card drawn will be odd is $\frac{5}{9}$ and the probability that the second card drawn will be even is $\frac{4}{8} = \frac{1}{2}$.

Therefore, the probability p_1 that the first card drawn will be even is

$$p_1 = \frac{5}{9} \cdot \frac{1}{2} = \frac{5}{18}$$

The probability is the same if we consider the first card being even (a probability of $\frac{4}{9}$) and the second card being odd (a probability of $\frac{5}{8}$). The probability p_2 is

$$p_2 = \frac{4}{9} \cdot \frac{5}{8} = \frac{5}{18}$$

Therefore, the probability p that the sum of the first two cards will be odd is

$$p = p_1 + p_2 = \frac{5}{18} + \frac{5}{18} = \frac{10}{18} = \frac{5}{9}$$

Note that the probability of the sum of the first two cards drawn will be even is

$$1 - p = 1 - \frac{5}{9} = \frac{4}{9}$$

8. If a number between 1 and 100 is drawn at random, what is the probability that the number will be divisible by 5?

For a number to be divisible by 5, its last digit must be 0 or 5. There are nine numbers that end in 0 between 1 and 100 and ten numbers that end in 5 between 1 and 100. There are 98 numbers between 1 and 100, therefore the probability p that a number chosen at random will be divisible by 5 is

$$p = \frac{9 + 10}{98} = \frac{19}{98}$$

Practice Questions: Data Analysis, Statistics, and Probability

Now that you have reviewed the strategies, you can practice on your own. Questions are roughly grouped into sets by their graduated level of difficulty just as they might appear on the actual SAT. Questions appear in three categories: easy to moderate, average, and above-average to difficult. The answers and explanations that follow the questions will include strategies to help you understand how to solve the problems.

Easy to Moderate

1. Find the mean of: 17, 20, 18, 12, 15, and 18.

2. Find the mode of: 8, 9, 3, 7, 8, 6, and 10.

3. Find the mode of: 18, 20, 13, 16, 18, 19, 17 and 13.

4. Find the mode of: 6, 3, 10, 8, 1, 9, 5, 4, and 7.

5. Evaluate: 8!

Average

6. Find the median of: 53, 81, 75, 84, 61, 83, 43, and 82.

7. A student has test scores of 87, 96, 81, and 93. Find the score needed on the fifth test to attain an average of 90.

8. Evaluate: $\dfrac{15!}{11! \cdot 4!}$

9. How many different 6-letter words can be formed with the first 10 letters of the alphabet?

10. How many 5-person committees can be formed from a total of 8 people?

11. In how many different ways may 6 people be seated in a row?

12. How many four-digit numbers may be formed using the digits 0, 1, 2, 3, 4, 5, 6, 7, 8, and 9 if none of the digits are repeated after once being used?

13. A box contains all 26 letters of the alphabet. What is the probability that if two letters are drawn from the box, they will be vowels (a, e, i, o, u)?

14. Three cards are drawn from a deck of 52 cards. Determine the probability that all three cards are kings.

15. A committee of three is to be chosen from a group consisting of 4 men and 5 women. Determine the probability that all three are men.

16. In a single throw of two dice, determine the probability that they will total 8.

17. A bag contains 8 white marbles, 7 black marbles, and 5 yellow marbles. If one marble is drawn at random, what is the probability that the marble is *not* white?

18. If a coin is tossed four times, what is the probability that all four tosses will be heads?

19. If one card is drawn from a deck of 52 cards, what is the probability that the card will not be a diamond?

Above Average to Difficult

20. Simplify: $\dfrac{(n+1)!}{(n-2)!}$

21. From a group of 8 mathematicians and 6 chemists, a committee of 7 is chosen to include exactly 4 mathematicians. In how many ways can this be accomplished?

22. One bag contains 5 blue marbles and 3 green marbles. A second bag contains 4 blue marbles and 4 green marbles. If one marble is drawn from each bag, determine the probability that both are blue.

23. In the previous problem, determine the probability that one marble is blue and one marble is green.

24. A box contains the numbers 1 through 9 inclusive. If 4 numbers are drawn consecutively, determine the probability that they are alternately even, odd, even, odd.

25. Three students are given a math problem to solve. The probability that the first student can solve the problem is $\dfrac{3}{5}$, that the second student can solve the problem is $\dfrac{4}{7}$, and that the third student can solve the problem is $\dfrac{3}{4}$. If all three students work on the problem, determine the probability that the problem will be solved.

Answers and Explanations

Easy to Moderate

1. The mean or average of 17, 20, 18, 12, 15, and 18 is

$$(17+20+18+12+15+18) \div 6 = 100 \div 6$$
$$= 16\frac{4}{6}$$
$$= 16\frac{2}{3}$$

2. The mode of 8, 9, 3, 7, 8, 6, and 10 is 8 because it is the number that occurs most frequently in the data.

3. The answer is both 13 and 18 because they are the most frequently used numbers in the set of data 18, 20, 13, 16, 18, 19, 17, and 13.

4. There is no mode for 6, 3, 10, 8, 1, 9, 5, 4, and 7 because no number occurs more frequently than any of the other numbers in the data.

5. $8! = 8 \cdot 7 \cdot 6 \cdot 5 \cdot 4 \cdot 3 \cdot 2 \cdot 1 = 40{,}320$

Average

6. Since there are an even number of items in the data, the median is the average of the two middle numbers. Arranging the numbers from smallest to largest yields

$$43, 53, 61, 75, 81, 82, 83, \text{ and } 84.$$

The two middle numbers are 75 and 81 whose average is

$$(75+81) \div 2 = 156 \div 2$$
$$= 78 \text{ the median}$$

7. Let x = the fifth test score. For the average of the 5 test scores to equal 90:

$$(87 + 96 + 81 + 93 + x) \div 5 = 90$$

$$\frac{357 + x}{5} = 90$$

$$\frac{357 + x}{5} \cdot 5 = 90 \cdot 5$$

$$357 + x = 450$$

$$357 + x - 357 = 450 - 357$$

$$x = 93$$

Hence, the student needs a score of 93 on the fifth test.

8.

$$\frac{15!}{11! \cdot 4!} = \frac{15 \cdot 14 \cdot 13 \cdot 12 \cdot \cancel{11!}}{\cancel{11!} \cdot 4!}$$

$$= \frac{15 \cdot \cancel{14}^{7} \cdot 13 \cdot \cancel{12}}{\cancel{4} \cdot \cancel{3} \cdot \cancel{2} \cdot 1}$$

$$= 15 \cdot 7 \cdot 13$$

$$= 1365$$

9. Since the order of the letters is important to consider, this is a permutation of 6 letters from a set of 10 letters.

The number of permutations of n things, taken r at a time: $_nP_r = \dfrac{n!}{(n-r)!}$

The number of different 6-letter words is

$$_{10}P_6 = P(10,6) = \frac{10!}{(10-6)!} = \frac{10!}{4!}$$

$$= \frac{10 \cdot 9 \cdot 8 \cdot 7 \cdot 6 \cdot 5 \cdot \cancel{4!}}{\cancel{4!}}$$

$$= 10 \cdot 9 \cdot 8 \cdot 7 \cdot 6 \cdot 5$$

$$= 151{,}200 \text{ six-letter words.}$$

10. Since the order of the 5 people chosen is not important, this is a combination of 5 people from a set of 8 people.

The number of combinations of n things, taken r at a time: $_nC_r = \dfrac{n!}{r!(n-r)!}$

The number of 5-person committees is

$$_8C_5 = C(8,5) = \frac{8!}{5!(8-5)!}$$

$$= \frac{8!}{5! \cdot 3!}$$

$$= \frac{8 \cdot 7 \cdot 6 \cdot \cancel{5!}}{\cancel{5} \cdot 3!}$$

$$= \frac{8 \cdot 7 \cdot \cancel{6}}{\cancel{3} \cdot \cancel{2} \cdot 1}$$

$$= 8 \cdot 7$$

$$= 56 \text{ five-person committees.}$$

11. Since the order of the people is important to consider, this is a permutation of 6 people from a group of 6 people. The number of different orders is

$$_6P_6 = P(6,6) = \frac{6!}{(6-6)!}$$

$$= \frac{6!}{0!} \, (0! \text{ is defined as being equal to 1})$$

$$= \frac{6 \cdot 5 \cdot 4 \cdot 3 \cdot 2 \cdot 1}{1}$$

$$= 720 \text{ different orders.}$$

12. In a four-digit number, the first digit cannot be zero so there are 9 possible numbers for the thousands place. The remaining three place values will be selected from 9 possible numbers where the order is important, which is a permutation of 3 numbers from a group of 9 numbers. Hence, the number of four-digit numbers possible is:

$$9 \cdot P(9,3) = 9 \cdot \frac{9!}{(9-3)!}$$

$$= 9 \cdot \frac{9 \cdot 8 \cdot 7 \cdot \cancel{6!}}{\cancel{6!}}$$

$$= 9 \cdot 9 \cdot 8 \cdot 7$$

$$= 4,536 \text{ different four-digit numbers}$$

13. The probability that the first letter drawn is a vowel is $\frac{5}{26}$, while the probability that the second letter drawn is a vowel is $\frac{4}{25}$. Hence, the probability p that the first two letters drawn are vowels is

$$p = \frac{5}{26} \cdot \frac{4}{25} = \frac{20}{650} = \frac{2}{65}$$

14. The probability that the first card drawn is a king is $\frac{4}{52}$. The probability that the second card drawn is a king is $\frac{3}{51}$. The probability that the third card drawn is a king is $\frac{2}{50}$. Hence, the probability p that all three cards drawn are kings is

$$p = \frac{4}{52} \cdot \frac{3}{51} \cdot \frac{2}{50}$$

$$p = \frac{1}{5525}$$

15. Since there are a total of 9 people including 4 men, the probability that the first person selected is a man is $\frac{4}{9}$. The probability that the second person selected is a man is $\frac{3}{8}$. The probability that the third person selected is a man is $\frac{2}{7}$. Hence, the probability p that all three people selected are men is:

$$p = \frac{\cancel{4}}{\cancel{9}_3} \cdot \frac{\cancel{3}}{\cancel{8}_2} \cdot \frac{\cancel{2}}{7}$$

$$p = \frac{1}{21}$$

16. Since each die contains the numbers 1 through 6, there are 36 possible outcomes when 2 dice are thrown. There are five ways of throwing a total of 8: 2 and 6, 6 and 2, 3 and 5, 5 and 3, and 4 and 4. The probability p of the two dice having a total of 8 is:

$$p = \frac{5}{36}$$

17. The probability that the marble drawn is white is $\frac{8}{20}$ or $\frac{2}{5}$. The probability p that the marble is *not* white is: 1 minus the probability that the marble is white.

$$p = 1 - \frac{2}{5}$$

$$p = \frac{3}{5}$$

18. Since there are only two possible outcomes (heads or tails) when a coin is tossed, the probability that a toss will result in heads is $\frac{1}{2}$. Hence, the probability p that all four tosses of a coin will be heads is

$$p = \frac{1}{2} \cdot \frac{1}{2} \cdot \frac{1}{2} \cdot \frac{1}{2}$$
$$p = \frac{1}{16}$$

19. Since there are 13 diamonds in a deck of 52 cards, the probability that one card selected from the deck will be a diamond is $\frac{13}{52}$ or $\frac{1}{4}$. The probability p that the card drawn will not be a diamond is 1 minus the probability that it is a diamond.

$$p = 1 - \frac{1}{4}$$
$$p = \frac{3}{4}$$

Above Average to Difficult

20. $\dfrac{(n+1)!}{(n-2)!} = \dfrac{(n+1)(n)(n-1)(n-2)!}{(n-2)!}$

$\qquad = (n+1)(n)(n-1)$

$\qquad = (n^2+n)(n-1)$

$\qquad = n^3 - n$

21. Each committee is formed by selecting 4 mathematicians out of 8, and selecting 3 chemists out of 6 where the order is not important. The number of 7-person committees possible is

$$C(8,4) \cdot C(6,3) = \frac{8!}{4! \cdot 4!} \cdot \frac{6!}{3! \cdot 3!}$$

$$= \frac{\cancel{8} \cdot 7 \cdot \cancel{6}^2 \cdot 5}{\cancel{4} \cdot \cancel{3} \cdot \cancel{2} \cdot 1} \cdot \frac{\cancel{6} \cdot 5 \cdot 4}{\cancel{3} \cdot \cancel{2} \cdot 1}$$

$$= 70 \cdot 20$$

$$= 1400 \text{ seven-person committees}$$

22. The probability that the marble drawn from the first bag will be blue is $\frac{5}{8}$. The probability that the marble drawn from the second bag will be blue is $\frac{4}{8}$ or $\frac{1}{2}$. Hence, the probability p that both marbles will be blue is

$$p = \frac{5}{8} \cdot \frac{1}{2}$$
$$p = \frac{5}{16}$$

23. The desired outcome of drawing one blue marble and one green marble may occur in two different ways:

    a. The marble drawn from the first bag is blue, while the marble drawn from the second bag is green.

    b. The marble drawn from the first bag is green, while the marble drawn from the second bag is blue.

    The probability p_1 that the marble from the first bag is blue and the marble from the second bag is green is $p_1 = \frac{5}{8} \cdot \frac{4}{8} = \frac{20}{64} = \frac{5}{16}$.

    The probability p_2 that the marble from the first bag is green and the marble from the second bag is blue is $p_2 = \frac{3}{8} \cdot \frac{4}{8} = \frac{12}{64} = \frac{3}{16}$.

Hence, the probability p that one marble is blue and one marble is green is

$$p = p_1 + p_2$$
$$= \frac{5}{16} + \frac{3}{16}$$
$$= \frac{8}{16}$$
$$p = \frac{1}{2}$$

24. For the numbers 1 through 9, there are four even numbers and 5 odd numbers. The probability that the first number will be even is $\frac{4}{9}$. The probability that the second number will be odd is $\frac{5}{8}$. The probability that the third number will be even is $\frac{3}{7}$. The probability that the fourth number will be odd is $\frac{4}{6}$ or $\frac{2}{3}$. Hence, the probability p that the four numbers drawn are alternatively even, odd, even, odd is

$$p = \frac{\cancel{4}}{9} \cdot \frac{5}{\cancel{8}_2} \cdot \frac{\cancel{3}}{7} \cdot \frac{\cancel{2}}{\cancel{3}}$$
$$p = \frac{5}{63}$$

25. The only way for the problem to not be solved is for all three students to be unable to solve the problem. The probability that the first student cannot solve it is $1 - \frac{3}{5} = \frac{2}{5}$. The probability that the second student cannot solve it is $1 - \frac{4}{7} = \frac{3}{7}$. The probability that the third student cannot solve it is $1 - \frac{3}{4} = \frac{1}{4}$. The probability that all three students will fail to solve the problem is $\frac{2}{5} \cdot \frac{3}{7} \cdot \frac{1}{4} = \frac{3}{70}$. Hence, the probability p that the problem will be solved is: one minus the probability that it will not be solved.

$$p = 1 - \frac{3}{70}$$
$$p = \frac{67}{70}$$

PART IV

FULL-LENGTH SAT PRACTICE EXAMS

This section contains four simulated full-length practice SAT exams, followed by complete answers, explanations, and analysis techniques. The format, levels of difficulty, question structure, and number of questions are similar to those on the SAT. The number and order of question types may vary.

The SAT is copyrighted and may not be duplicated, and these questions are not taken directly from the actual exams or released sample problems. The sections in these practice exams are labeled by subject for your convenience in reviewing. They are not labeled on the actual SAT.

When you take these exams, try to simulate the test conditions by carefully following the time allotments.

Chapter 9

Practice Exam 1

Section 2

1 Ⓐ Ⓑ Ⓒ Ⓓ Ⓔ
2 Ⓐ Ⓑ Ⓒ Ⓓ Ⓔ
3 Ⓐ Ⓑ Ⓒ Ⓓ Ⓔ
4 Ⓐ Ⓑ Ⓒ Ⓓ Ⓔ
5 Ⓐ Ⓑ Ⓒ Ⓓ Ⓔ
6 Ⓐ Ⓑ Ⓒ Ⓓ Ⓔ
7 Ⓐ Ⓑ Ⓒ Ⓓ Ⓔ
8 Ⓐ Ⓑ Ⓒ Ⓓ Ⓔ
9 Ⓐ Ⓑ Ⓒ Ⓓ Ⓔ
10 Ⓐ Ⓑ Ⓒ Ⓓ Ⓔ
11 Ⓐ Ⓑ Ⓒ Ⓓ Ⓔ
12 Ⓐ Ⓑ Ⓒ Ⓓ Ⓔ
13 Ⓐ Ⓑ Ⓒ Ⓓ Ⓔ
14 Ⓐ Ⓑ Ⓒ Ⓓ Ⓔ
15 Ⓐ Ⓑ Ⓒ Ⓓ Ⓔ
16 Ⓐ Ⓑ Ⓒ Ⓓ Ⓔ
17 Ⓐ Ⓑ Ⓒ Ⓓ Ⓔ
18 Ⓐ Ⓑ Ⓒ Ⓓ Ⓔ
19 Ⓐ Ⓑ Ⓒ Ⓓ Ⓔ
20 Ⓐ Ⓑ Ⓒ Ⓓ Ⓔ

Section 3

1 Ⓐ Ⓑ Ⓒ Ⓓ Ⓔ
2 Ⓐ Ⓑ Ⓒ Ⓓ Ⓔ
3 Ⓐ Ⓑ Ⓒ Ⓓ Ⓔ
4 Ⓐ Ⓑ Ⓒ Ⓓ Ⓔ
5 Ⓐ Ⓑ Ⓒ Ⓓ Ⓔ
6 Ⓐ Ⓑ Ⓒ Ⓓ Ⓔ
7 Ⓐ Ⓑ Ⓒ Ⓓ Ⓔ
8 Ⓐ Ⓑ Ⓒ Ⓓ Ⓔ
9 Ⓐ Ⓑ Ⓒ Ⓓ Ⓔ
10 Ⓐ Ⓑ Ⓒ Ⓓ Ⓔ
11 Ⓐ Ⓑ Ⓒ Ⓓ Ⓔ
12 Ⓐ Ⓑ Ⓒ Ⓓ Ⓔ
13 Ⓐ Ⓑ Ⓒ Ⓓ Ⓔ
14 Ⓐ Ⓑ Ⓒ Ⓓ Ⓔ
15 Ⓐ Ⓑ Ⓒ Ⓓ Ⓔ
16 Ⓐ Ⓑ Ⓒ Ⓓ Ⓔ
17 Ⓐ Ⓑ Ⓒ Ⓓ Ⓔ
18 Ⓐ Ⓑ Ⓒ Ⓓ Ⓔ
19 Ⓐ Ⓑ Ⓒ Ⓓ Ⓔ
20 Ⓐ Ⓑ Ⓒ Ⓓ Ⓔ
21 Ⓐ Ⓑ Ⓒ Ⓓ Ⓔ
22 Ⓐ Ⓑ Ⓒ Ⓓ Ⓔ
23 Ⓐ Ⓑ Ⓒ Ⓓ Ⓔ
24 Ⓐ Ⓑ Ⓒ Ⓓ Ⓔ
25 Ⓐ Ⓑ Ⓒ Ⓓ Ⓔ

Section 4

1 Ⓐ Ⓑ Ⓒ Ⓓ Ⓔ
2 Ⓐ Ⓑ Ⓒ Ⓓ Ⓔ
3 Ⓐ Ⓑ Ⓒ Ⓓ Ⓔ
4 Ⓐ Ⓑ Ⓒ Ⓓ Ⓔ
5 Ⓐ Ⓑ Ⓒ Ⓓ Ⓔ
6 Ⓐ Ⓑ Ⓒ Ⓓ Ⓔ
7 Ⓐ Ⓑ Ⓒ Ⓓ Ⓔ
8 Ⓐ Ⓑ Ⓒ Ⓓ Ⓔ

9.

10.

11.

12.

13.

14.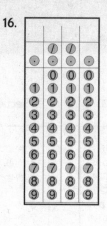

15.

16.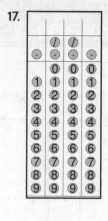

17.

18.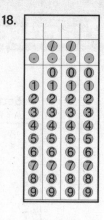

Section 5

1 Ⓐ Ⓑ Ⓒ Ⓓ Ⓔ
2 Ⓐ Ⓑ Ⓒ Ⓓ Ⓔ
3 Ⓐ Ⓑ Ⓒ Ⓓ Ⓔ
4 Ⓐ Ⓑ Ⓒ Ⓓ Ⓔ
5 Ⓐ Ⓑ Ⓒ Ⓓ Ⓔ
6 Ⓐ Ⓑ Ⓒ Ⓓ Ⓔ
7 Ⓐ Ⓑ Ⓒ Ⓓ Ⓔ
8 Ⓐ Ⓑ Ⓒ Ⓓ Ⓔ
9 Ⓐ Ⓑ Ⓒ Ⓓ Ⓔ
10 Ⓐ Ⓑ Ⓒ Ⓓ Ⓔ
11 Ⓐ Ⓑ Ⓒ Ⓓ Ⓔ
12 Ⓐ Ⓑ Ⓒ Ⓓ Ⓔ
13 Ⓐ Ⓑ Ⓒ Ⓓ Ⓔ
14 Ⓐ Ⓑ Ⓒ Ⓓ Ⓔ
15 Ⓐ Ⓑ Ⓒ Ⓓ Ⓔ
16 Ⓐ Ⓑ Ⓒ Ⓓ Ⓔ
17 Ⓐ Ⓑ Ⓒ Ⓓ Ⓔ
18 Ⓐ Ⓑ Ⓒ Ⓓ Ⓔ
19 Ⓐ Ⓑ Ⓒ Ⓓ Ⓔ
20 Ⓐ Ⓑ Ⓒ Ⓓ Ⓔ
21 Ⓐ Ⓑ Ⓒ Ⓓ Ⓔ
22 Ⓐ Ⓑ Ⓒ Ⓓ Ⓔ
23 Ⓐ Ⓑ Ⓒ Ⓓ Ⓔ
24 Ⓐ Ⓑ Ⓒ Ⓓ Ⓔ
25 Ⓐ Ⓑ Ⓒ Ⓓ Ⓔ
26 Ⓐ Ⓑ Ⓒ Ⓓ Ⓔ
27 Ⓐ Ⓑ Ⓒ Ⓓ Ⓔ
28 Ⓐ Ⓑ Ⓒ Ⓓ Ⓔ
29 Ⓐ Ⓑ Ⓒ Ⓓ Ⓔ
30 Ⓐ Ⓑ Ⓒ Ⓓ Ⓔ
31 Ⓐ Ⓑ Ⓒ Ⓓ Ⓔ
32 Ⓐ Ⓑ Ⓒ Ⓓ Ⓔ
33 Ⓐ Ⓑ Ⓒ Ⓓ Ⓔ
34 Ⓐ Ⓑ Ⓒ Ⓓ Ⓔ
35 Ⓐ Ⓑ Ⓒ Ⓓ Ⓔ

Section 6

1 Ⓐ Ⓑ Ⓒ Ⓓ Ⓔ
2 Ⓐ Ⓑ Ⓒ Ⓓ Ⓔ
3 Ⓐ Ⓑ Ⓒ Ⓓ Ⓔ
4 Ⓐ Ⓑ Ⓒ Ⓓ Ⓔ
5 Ⓐ Ⓑ Ⓒ Ⓓ Ⓔ
6 Ⓐ Ⓑ Ⓒ Ⓓ Ⓔ
7 Ⓐ Ⓑ Ⓒ Ⓓ Ⓔ
8 Ⓐ Ⓑ Ⓒ Ⓓ Ⓔ
9 Ⓐ Ⓑ Ⓒ Ⓓ Ⓔ
10 Ⓐ Ⓑ Ⓒ Ⓓ Ⓔ
11 Ⓐ Ⓑ Ⓒ Ⓓ Ⓔ
12 Ⓐ Ⓑ Ⓒ Ⓓ Ⓔ
13 Ⓐ Ⓑ Ⓒ Ⓓ Ⓔ
14 Ⓐ Ⓑ Ⓒ Ⓓ Ⓔ
15 Ⓐ Ⓑ Ⓒ Ⓓ Ⓔ
16 Ⓐ Ⓑ Ⓒ Ⓓ Ⓔ
17 Ⓐ Ⓑ Ⓒ Ⓓ Ⓔ
18 Ⓐ Ⓑ Ⓒ Ⓓ Ⓔ
19 Ⓐ Ⓑ Ⓒ Ⓓ Ⓔ
20 Ⓐ Ⓑ Ⓒ Ⓓ Ⓔ
21 Ⓐ Ⓑ Ⓒ Ⓓ Ⓔ
22 Ⓐ Ⓑ Ⓒ Ⓓ Ⓔ
23 Ⓐ Ⓑ Ⓒ Ⓓ Ⓔ
24 Ⓐ Ⓑ Ⓒ Ⓓ Ⓔ

Section 7

1 Ⓐ Ⓑ Ⓒ Ⓓ Ⓔ
2 Ⓐ Ⓑ Ⓒ Ⓓ Ⓔ
3 Ⓐ Ⓑ Ⓒ Ⓓ Ⓔ
4 Ⓐ Ⓑ Ⓒ Ⓓ Ⓔ
5 Ⓐ Ⓑ Ⓒ Ⓓ Ⓔ
6 Ⓐ Ⓑ Ⓒ Ⓓ Ⓔ
7 Ⓐ Ⓑ Ⓒ Ⓓ Ⓔ
8 Ⓐ Ⓑ Ⓒ Ⓓ Ⓔ
9 Ⓐ Ⓑ Ⓒ Ⓓ Ⓔ
10 Ⓐ Ⓑ Ⓒ Ⓓ Ⓔ
11 Ⓐ Ⓑ Ⓒ Ⓓ Ⓔ
12 Ⓐ Ⓑ Ⓒ Ⓓ Ⓔ
13 Ⓐ Ⓑ Ⓒ Ⓓ Ⓔ
14 Ⓐ Ⓑ Ⓒ Ⓓ Ⓔ
15 Ⓐ Ⓑ Ⓒ Ⓓ Ⓔ
16 Ⓐ Ⓑ Ⓒ Ⓓ Ⓔ

Section 8

1 Ⓐ Ⓑ Ⓒ Ⓓ Ⓔ
2 Ⓐ Ⓑ Ⓒ Ⓓ Ⓔ
3 Ⓐ Ⓑ Ⓒ Ⓓ Ⓔ
4 Ⓐ Ⓑ Ⓒ Ⓓ Ⓔ
5 Ⓐ Ⓑ Ⓒ Ⓓ Ⓔ
6 Ⓐ Ⓑ Ⓒ Ⓓ Ⓔ
7 Ⓐ Ⓑ Ⓒ Ⓓ Ⓔ
8 Ⓐ Ⓑ Ⓒ Ⓓ Ⓔ
9 Ⓐ Ⓑ Ⓒ Ⓓ Ⓔ
10 Ⓐ Ⓑ Ⓒ Ⓓ Ⓔ
11 Ⓐ Ⓑ Ⓒ Ⓓ Ⓔ
12 Ⓐ Ⓑ Ⓒ Ⓓ Ⓔ
13 Ⓐ Ⓑ Ⓒ Ⓓ Ⓔ
14 Ⓐ Ⓑ Ⓒ Ⓓ Ⓔ
15 Ⓐ Ⓑ Ⓒ Ⓓ Ⓔ
16 Ⓐ Ⓑ Ⓒ Ⓓ Ⓔ
17 Ⓐ Ⓑ Ⓒ Ⓓ Ⓔ
18 Ⓐ Ⓑ Ⓒ Ⓓ Ⓔ
19 Ⓐ Ⓑ Ⓒ Ⓓ Ⓔ
20 Ⓐ Ⓑ Ⓒ Ⓓ Ⓔ

Section 9

1 Ⓐ Ⓑ Ⓒ Ⓓ Ⓔ
2 Ⓐ Ⓑ Ⓒ Ⓓ Ⓔ
3 Ⓐ Ⓑ Ⓒ Ⓓ Ⓔ
4 Ⓐ Ⓑ Ⓒ Ⓓ Ⓔ
5 Ⓐ Ⓑ Ⓒ Ⓓ Ⓔ
6 Ⓐ Ⓑ Ⓒ Ⓓ Ⓔ
7 Ⓐ Ⓑ Ⓒ Ⓓ Ⓔ
8 Ⓐ Ⓑ Ⓒ Ⓓ Ⓔ
9 Ⓐ Ⓑ Ⓒ Ⓓ Ⓔ
10 Ⓐ Ⓑ Ⓒ Ⓓ Ⓔ
11 Ⓐ Ⓑ Ⓒ Ⓓ Ⓔ
12 Ⓐ Ⓑ Ⓒ Ⓓ Ⓔ
13 Ⓐ Ⓑ Ⓒ Ⓓ Ⓔ
14 Ⓐ Ⓑ Ⓒ Ⓓ Ⓔ

CUT HERE

Section 1: Writing—Essay

Time: 25 minutes

1 Essay Question

You have 25 minutes to plan and write an essay on the topic below. DO NOT WRITE ON ANOTHER TOPIC. AN ESSAY ON ANOTHER TOPIC WILL NOT BE SCORED.

The essay is intended to give you the chance to show your writing skills. Be sure to express your ideas on the topic clearly and effectively. The quality of your writing is much more important than the quantity, but to cover the topic adequately you may want to write more than one paragraph. Be specific.

Your essay must be written on two lined pages. Two pages should be enough if you write on every line, avoid wide margins, and keep your handwriting a reasonable size. You will not be given any additional paper. On the actual SAT you must

- Only use a pencil. You will receive a score of zero if you use ink.
- Only write on your answer sheet. You will not receive credit for material written in the test book.
- Only write on the topic presented below. An essay that is off-topic will receive a score of zero.
- Write an essay that reflects original work.

Directions: Read the following paragraph and assignment carefully. Then prepare and write a persuasive essay. Be sure to support your reasons with specific examples that will make your essay more effective.

"Work experience is the best teacher," say many sociologists. With this in mind, some parents encourage their high school-age children to get an after-school or weekend job. Other parents cite the importance of getting good grades to discourage their high school-age children from getting an after-school or weekend job.

Assignment: Do you agree with the parents who are for or against having a job while in school? Use an example or examples from your reading, personal experiences, or observations to write an essay to support your position.

ON THE ACTUAL EXAM, THE PROCTOR WILL ANNOUNCE WHEN 25 MINUTES HAVE PASSED. IF YOU FINISH YOUR ESSAY BEFORE 25 MINUTES HAVE PASSED, YOU MAY NOT GO ON TO ANY OTHER SECTION OF THE EXAM. THE PROCTOR WILL ANNOUNCE WHEN TO START THE NEXT SECTION.

Section 2: Mathematics

Time: 25 minutes
20 Questions

Directions: Solve each problem in this section by using the information given and your own mathematical calculations, insights, and problem-solving skills. Then select the one correct answer of the five choices given and mark the corresponding circle on your answer sheet. Use the available space on the page for your scratch work.

For each question, indicate the best answer, using the following notes.

1. All numerical values used are real numbers.
2. Calculators may be used.
3. Some problems may be accompanied by figures or diagrams. These figures are drawn as accurately as possible EXCEPT when it is stated in a specific problem that a figure is not drawn to scale. The figures and diagrams are meant to provide information useful in solving the problem or problems. Unless otherwise stated, all figures and diagrams lie on a plane.

Data that Can Be Used for Reference

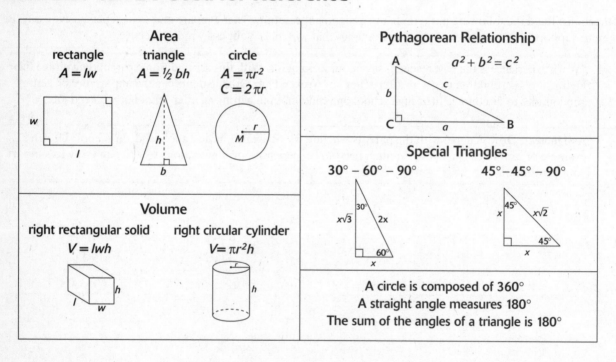

1. The total price of 4 equally priced markers is $6.40. If 10 or more markers are purchased, the cost per marker is decreased by $0.25 for the entire order. How much will 12 of these markers cost?

   A. $13.50
   B. $16.20
   C. $18.20
   D. $19.20
   E. $22.20

2. Which of the follow linear equations contains the points (–3, 6), (0, 4), (6, 0), and (9, –2)?

   A. $2x + y = 0$
   B. $y - 2x = 12$
   C. $2x + 3y = 12$
   D. $x + 3y = 15$
   E. $x + y = 3$

GO ON TO THE NEXT PAGE

3. If y is inversely proportional to x and $y = 12$ when $x = 5$, what is the value of x when $y = 15$?

   A. $\frac{3}{4}$
   B. 3
   C. 4
   D. 8
   E. 60

4. If $3a + c = 5b$ and $3a + 5b + c = 80$, what is the value of b?

   A. 8
   B. 10
   C. 15
   D. 20
   E. It cannot be determined from the information given.

5. If $\frac{z-2}{z+4} = \frac{13}{15}$, then $z =$

   A. 11
   B. 13
   C. 15
   D. 41
   E. 81

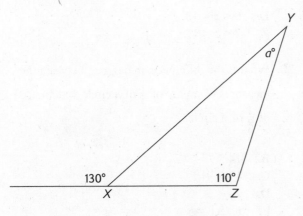

(Note: Figure not drawn to scale.)

6. In the above $\triangle XYZ$, what is the value of a?

   A. 10
   B. 20
   C. 30
   D. 50
   E. 70

7. If the average of x, $2x +1$, and $2x +7$ is 16, what is the value of x?

   A. $1\frac{3}{5}$
   B. 8
   C. 12
   D. 16
   E. 48

8. The perimeter of square $ABCD$ is 4 times the perimeter of equilateral triangle XYZ. If the perimeter of $\triangle XYZ$ is 13, what is the length of one side of square $ABCD$?

   A. $3\frac{1}{4}$
   B. $6\frac{1}{2}$
   C. 13
   D. 26
   E. 42

9. If $y^2 + 5y + k = y^2 - 3$, what is k in terms of y?

   A. $2y^2 + 5y - 3$
   B. $2y^2 + 5y + 3$
   C. $5y + 3$
   D. $5y - 3$
   E. $-5y - 3$

10. How many integers between 10 and 50 are multiples of 3 but not multiples of 6?

   A. 3
   B. 4
   C. 5
   D. 6
   E. 7

11. If x is a positive integer, what is the smallest value of x for which $\sqrt{\frac{6x}{5}}$ is an integer?

   A. 5
   B. 6
   C. 25
   D. 30
   E. 36

GO ON TO THE NEXT PAGE

12. If m is an odd integer, which of the following must be an odd integer?

    A. m^2
    B. $(m - 1)^2$
    C. $5m - 1$
    D. $(m + 1)^3$
    E. $2m + 4$

13. If the hypotenuse of an isosceles right triangle has a length of 16 units, what is the area, in square units, of the triangle?

    A. 32
    B. 64
    C. 128
    D. 256
    E. It cannot be determined from the information given.

14. Find all values of x where the graph of $y = x^2 + 5x - 24$ intersects the x-axis.

    A. $-8, -3$
    B. $-8, 3$
    C. $-3, 8$
    D. $3, 8$
    E. The graph does not intersect the x-axis.

15. If $f(x) = x^2$, which of the following functions would have a graph that is the same as the graph of $f(x)$ moved horizontally to the right 5 units?

    A. $g(x) = x^2 - 5$
    B. $g(x) = x^2 + 5$
    C. $g(x) = (x - 5)^2$
    D. $g(x) = (x + 5)^2$
    E. $g(x) = 5x^2$

16. If $16^{x+1} = 32^{x-3}$, then $x =$

    A. -5
    B. 5
    C. 6
    D. 7
    E. 19

17. How many different words of 4 letters each can be formed from the word "chemistry" if each letter is used no more than one time? Hint: the words do not have to have meaning.

    A. 24
    B. 256
    C. 729
    D. 3024
    E. 6561

18. If b and c are constants and $x^2 + bx + 18$ is equivalent to $(x + 1)(x + c)$, what is the value of b?

    A. 9
    B. 11
    C. 18
    D. 19
    E. It cannot be determined from the information given.

19. A triangle has sides of length 5, 12, and z. Which of the following must be true of z?

    A. $z < 5$
    B. $z > 12$
    C. $z > 17$
    D. $8 < z < 18$
    E. $7 < z < 17$

20. What is the difference, in degrees, between the measures of an arc of $\frac{1}{5}$ of a circle and an arc of $\frac{1}{8}$ of a circle?

    A. 27
    B. 14.5
    C. 13.5
    D. 13
    E. 6.75

IF YOU FINISH BEFORE TIME IS CALLED, CHECK YOUR WORK ON THIS SECTION ONLY. DO NOT WORK ON ANY OTHER SECTION IN THE TEST.

STOP

Section 3: Critical Reading

Time: 25 minutes

25 Questions

Directions: In this section, choose the best answer for each question and fill in the corresponding circle on the answer sheet.

Each blank in the following sentences indicates that something has been omitted. Consider the lettered words beneath the sentence and choose the word or set of words that best fits the whole sentence.

EXAMPLE:

With a million more people than any other African nation, Nigeria is the most _____ country on the continent.

    A. impoverished

    B. successful

    C. populous

    D. developed

    E. militant

The correct answer is **C.**

1. The attentive audience was expecting to hear _____ approaches to the energy issue, but instead they were subjected to well-worn _____.

    A. meritorious . . . discussions

    B. innovative . . . platitudes.

    C. unrealistic . . . attitudes.

    D. scholarly . . . fallacies.

    E. specialized . . . pedantry.

2. Although the new governor was considered something of a _____, he believed in maintaining _____ when it came to plans for the inauguration.

    A. malcontent . . . peace

    B. miscreant . . . control

    C. maverick . . . protocol

    D. dissident . . . composure

    E. narcissist . . . generosity

3. Despite offering very few _____, the hotel served our purpose because of its excellent location and low rates.

    A. amenities

    B. reservations

    C. plaudits

    D. bargains

    E. advertisements

4. The _____ between the two groups made it impossible to carry on a _____ discussion about how to move forward with the plans for the youth center.

    A. apathy . . . heated

    B. enmity . . . fruitful

    C. consensus . . . logical

    D. provocation . . . mature

    E. collaboration . . . harmonious

GO ON TO THE NEXT PAGE

5. As a result of her lawsuit, the business owner agreed to find a position for Elizabeth that was _____ her education and skills rather than _____ her to a menial job.

   A. superior to . . . reduce
   B. relevant to . . . sentence
   C. commensurate with . . . assign
   D. accountable to . . . demote
   E. compatible with . . . elevate

6. The commentator insisted that her off-camera _____ was not intended to have a _____ effect on the young man's career.

   A. belief . . . noxious
   B. diatribe . . . pernicious
   C. photograph . . . pathetic
   D. musings . . . felicitous
   E. evaluation . . . lugubrious

7. We were annoyed by the spokesperson's _____ when he tried to present the president's stand on budget cuts.

   A. equivocation
   B. relentlessness
   C. directness
   D. succinctness
   E. equanimity

8. Mrs. Doolittle was willing to forgive her husband's little _____ because he was an honest, good-hearted man.

   A. harangues
   B. minions
   C. misappropriations
   D. libels
   E. foibles

GO ON TO THE NEXT PAGE

Directions: Questions follow each of the passages below. Answer the questions using only the stated or implied information in each passage and in its introduction, if any.

Questions 9–13 are based on the following pair of passages.

Passage 1:

The impact of World War II on women cannot easily be measured in the immediate postwar era. Other wars such as the Civil War and World War I had clearly broadened the boundaries of
(5) acceptable behavior for men and women and had hastened changes already in process such as suffrage, but their impact on women's status— their culturally defined roles—remained similarly ambiguous and ephemeral. The American
(10) Revolution had the most powerful symbolic and culturally formative impact on women prior to the twentieth century. That war, concerned with the definition of public life and the citizen, created new republican political consciousness
(15) and practice. Women, like men, found themselves engaged in political struggles and acts despite the solidly masculine military. And male politicians wrestled with the problem of whether women who acted thus were citizens and, if so, in what
(20) sense. The result was the powerful new ideology of republican motherhood that acknowledged women's political engagement but contained it within the ideal of motherhood. Women's political work was the rearing of good citizens.
(25) The context for women in World War II was vastly different from that of their revolutionary foremothers, though each war was understood to have been fought to preserve liberty and overthrow tyranny. By the mid-twentieth century public life
(30) had come to be defined by the growing activities of the state. Where women during the Revolution had spontaneously organized boycotts and petitions, governmental control of both media and economy during World War II ensured
(35) efficient use of voluntary energies. There was little discussion of the political meaning of women's changed participation in public life, only assurance that it would be temporary. Women lacked collective, public spaces within which to redefine
(40) themselves as a group in relation to society or to critique a social order that simultaneously called on them and restricted their possibilities. Many traditional women's organizations remained bounded by class and race, unable to achieve a
(45) broader vision of women's needs.

Millions of women left the labor force [after the war], voluntarily and involuntarily; the women who stayed represented an increase in labor force participation consistent with previous trends. In
(50) other words, one could argue that the war itself made little difference.

Ideologically, wartime propaganda justified the erosion of gender boundaries "for the duration" and no more. The intense pressure on women to
(55) return to domesticity coincided with the wishes of a younger cohort of women and men to focus on their private lives. This privatization promised a dramatically new level of isolation within the family as bulldozers began to reshape the
(60) landscape in preparation for growing suburbs.

Passage 2:

During World War II the role of women in America changed dramatically, if only briefly. With men going off to war, women on the home front had to take over jobs that were not only
(5) traditionally "men's work" but that also could be described at the time as decidedly unfeminine, such as building ships, tanks, and planes. In 1941 women made up 24 percent of the labor force; by 1946 the number had grown to 36 percent. The
(10) government encouraged women to become part of the war effort, particularly in the defense industry. One poster announced, "If you've used an electric mixer in your kitchen, you can learn to run a drill press!" A famous propaganda poster
(15) showed "Rosie the Riveter," a strong woman in a kerchief with the motto, "We can do it!"

After the war, the jobs that had been temporarily held by women were needed for the returning soldiers and many women left their jobs—
(20) sometimes happily, sometimes not—to return to their homes and take up their places as wives and mothers. But the taste of a new role for women had been whetted. A cartoon in the *Des Moines Register* in 1943 shows a larger-than-life female
(25) war worker with a paycheck in the back pocket of her overalls, while a tiny man in a housewife's apron stands aside, saying, "But remember. You gotta come right back as soon as the war is over."

GO ON TO THE NEXT PAGE

Her reply, which she tosses over her shoulder, is
(30) "Oh, yeah?"

Surprisingly, according to many commentators, most women did "come right back" after the war to their positions as housewives and mothers. Their contributions to World War II were lauded,
(35) but the view of a "woman's place" hadn't significantly changed. Society in the late 1940s and the 1950s had high expectations of women as wives, mothers, and housekeepers. The perfect wife was to support her husband at every turn,
(40) the perfect mother was expected to stay home and nurture children, and the perfect homemaker (a term everyone seemed to prefer to "housekeeper") was to have dinner on the table and the house cleaned by the time her husband
(45) arrived home from work.

This perfect woman, of course, is an exaggerated stereotype that could probably be found only in television shows like *Father Knows Best* and *Leave it to Beaver*. In fact, signs
(50) of change were beginning to appear. In 1950, for example, Harvard Law School admitted women for the first time. The U.S. Census recognized a woman's right to use her maiden name after she was married. And, in 1955, Rosa Parks violated
(55) the stereotype of women and particularly black women by refusing to give up her seat on a bus to a white man, initiating a famous boycott in the South. World War II, while it didn't seem to change the traditional role of women at once, had
(60) sown seeds that would come to life in the following decades.

9. Based on information in the two passages, the authors would agree with which of the following statements?

A. World War II, while apparently helping women to advance, was in fact a stumbling block.
B. The volunteer efforts of women during America's wars worked against their being treated as equals in postwar American society.
C. A woman's role after the Revolutionary War and immediately after World War II was primarily domestic.
D. Women supported men but played a minor role in American wars.
E. The government was largely responsible for women's slow progress toward equality.

10. The two passages differ in which of the following ways?

A. Passage 1 credits World War II with changing women's role in society while Passage 2 suggests World War II had little effect on women's role.
B. Passage 2 gently pokes fun at women while Passage 1 elevates them.
C. Passage 1 presents two points of view, while Passage 2 presents only one.
D. The author of Passage 2 uses concrete examples to illustrate its points, while the author of Passage 1 presents a narrative of general points.
E. In Passage 1, the author cites facts, while in Passage 2, the author cites opinions only.

11. According to Passage 1, the effect on women of the Revolutionary War and Civil War was to

A. strengthen their relationships with men.
B. engage them in political acts.
C. lead them to form anti-war organizations.
D. fight for more political power.
E. make them better mothers.

12. According to Passage 2, in the parenthetical phrase ("a term everyone seemed to prefer to 'housekeeper'") (lines 42–43) the author is

A. underlining the idea that a woman was to feel elevated by her role at home.
B. showing that language was in the process of changing because of the war.
C. ridiculing the role of women after the war by emphasizing her domestic role.
D. comparing women unfavorably to the ideals presented in *Father Knows Best* and *Leave it to Beaver*.
E. indicating how women were ashamed of their wartime jobs.

GO ON TO THE NEXT PAGE

13. Passage 2 makes all of the following points EXCEPT

  A. women were successful performing their defense jobs during World War II.

  B. the U.S. government used methods of propaganda to urge women to join the war effort.

  C. women worked for less pay than men in defense jobs.

  D. the percentage of women in the work force increased significantly during World War II.

  E. one reason women quit working at the end of the war was to make the jobs available to returning soldiers.

Questions 14–25 are based on the following passage.

Passage 3:

Over the past decade geneticists have proved that all people alive today are descendants of a relatively small number of individuals who walked out of Africa some 60,000 years ago and
(5) carried the human spirit and imagination to every corner of the habitable world. Our shared heritage implies that all cultures share essentially the same potential, drawing on similar reserves of raw genius. Whether they exercise this intellectual
(10) capacity to produce stunning works of technological innovation (as has been the great achievement of the West) or to maintain an incredibly elaborate network of kin relationships (a primary concern of the Aborigines of
(15) Australia) is simply a matter of choice and orientation, adaptive benefits and cultural priorities. Each of the planet's cultures is a unique answer to the question of what it means to be human. And together they make up our repertoire
(20) for dealing with the challenges that will confront us as a species in the millennia to come.

But these global voices are being silenced at a frightening rate. They key indicator of this decline in cultural diversity is language loss. A language,
(25) of course, is not merely a set of grammatical rules or a vocabulary. It is the vehicle by which the soul of each particular culture comes into the material world. Each one is an old-growth forest of the mind. Linguists agree, however, that 50 percent
(30) of the world's 7,000 languages are endangered. Every fortnight an elder dies and carries with him or her into the grave the last syllables of an ancient tongue. Within a generation or two, then, we may be witnessing the loss of fully half of

(35) humanity's social, cultural and intellectual legacy. This is the hidden backdrop of our age.

People often ask why it matters if these exotic cultures and their belief systems and rituals disappear. What does a family in New York care
(40) if some distant tribe in Africa is extinguished? In truth it probably matters little, no more than the loss of New York would directly affect a tribe in Africa. I would argue that the loss of either way of life does matter to humanity as a whole.

(45) Consider the achievements of the Polynesians. Ten centuries before Christ—at a time when European sailors, incapable of measuring longitude and fearful of the open ocean, hugged the shores of continents—the Polynesians set sail
(50) across the Pacific, a diaspora that would eventually bring them to every island from Hawaii to Rapa Nui, the Marquesas to New Zealand. They had no written word. They only knew where they were by remembering how they had got
(55) there. Over the length of a long voyage the navigator had to remember every shift of wind, every change of current and speed, every impression from sea, sky and cloud. Even today Polynesian sailors, with whom I have voyaged,
(60) readily name 250 stars in the night sky. Their navigators can sense the presence of distant atolls of islands beyond the visible horizon by watching the reverberation of waves across the hull of their vessels, knowing that every island group had its
(65) own reflective pattern that can be read with the ease with which a forensic scientist reads a fingerprint. In the darkness they can discern five distinct ocean swells, distinguishing those caused by local weather disturbances from the deep
(70) currents that pulsate across the Pacific and can be followed as readily as a terrestrial explorer would follow a river to the sea.

There are many such examples of ancient wisdom. Among the Barasana people of the
(75) northwest Amazon in Colombia, for whom all the elements of the natural world are inextricably linked, complex mythologies about the land and its plants and animals have given rise to highly effective land-management practices that serve as
(80) a model for how humans can live in the Amazon basin without destroying its forests. The Buddhists of Tibet spend their lives preparing for a moment that we spend most of our lives pretending does not exist: death. Surely their science of the mind—
(85) informed by 2,500 years of empirical observation— has something meaningful to contribute to the human patrimony.

GO ON TO THE NEXT PAGE

14. The author of Passage 3 makes which of the following assumptions in paragraph one?

    A. The key to a culture's survival is adaptability.
    B. The importance of kinship is universal.
    C. Initially, cultures essentially share the same potential.
    D. The West has proven its intellectual superiority over other cultures.
    E. Location is the key to a culture's success.

15. According to Passage 3, "global voices" are being silenced because of

    A. technology.
    B. loss of cultural diversity.
    C. indifference.
    D. cultural conflict.
    E. economic failure.

16. The author uses the phrase "old-growth forest of the mind" to refer to

    A. languages.
    B. mortality.
    C. knowledge.
    D. primitive cultures.
    E. diversity.

17. The author is most likely to agree with which of the following statements?

    A. Languages must adapt to a changing world.
    B. When a language disappears, it is replaced by a new language.
    C. Just as some species can become endangered, so can languages.
    D. Most exotic languages disappear because they contribute little to progress.
    E. The written word keeps languages alive more than the spoken word does.

18. The purpose of the third paragraph of Passage 3 is to

    A. present a point of view different from the author's.
    B. ask a question to be answered in the paragraphs that follow.
    C. underline the differences among cultures of the world.
    D. question the importance of linguistic study.
    E. summarize the ideas in the previous two paragraphs.

19. The best definition of "diaspora" in line 50 is

    A. movement of people from their homeland.
    B. rejection of a particular location.
    C. expulsion of a group from its homeland.
    D. discovery.
    E. long voyage by water.

20. According to Passage 3, the Polynesians successfully navigated the Pacific Ocean a thousand years before Christ because they

    A. were genetically programmed to be sailors.
    B. paid attention to the clues presented by nature.
    C. had access to ancient writings.
    D. were expert astronomers.
    E. spent years in training.

21. According to Passage 3, the Barasana people in Colombia are especially notable in today's world for their

    A. unique language.
    B. preservation of the Amazon basin.
    C. utilization of the Amazon River.
    D. complex mythologies.
    E. effective land-management practices.

22. The ancient wisdom of the Barasana people is based on their

    A. belief that everything in the natural world is connected.
    B. belief in the power of their gods.
    C. determination to survive in an inhospitable environment.
    D. love of nature.
    E. adaptability to changing surroundings.

GO ON TO THE NEXT PAGE

23. The author's main argument in Passage 3 is which of the following?

    A. All human beings from all societies come from the same individuals who left Africa many thousands of years ago.

    B. Cultural priorities determine what different populations decide to pursue.

    C. Linguistic diversity is the key to the survival of the human race.

    D. All cultures have something to contribute to humanity's legacy and should not be lost.

    E. People throughout the world have more similarities than differences.

24. Lines 81–87 of Passage 3 suggest that the author

    A. is probably a Buddhist.

    B. thinks Eastern religions have more to offer than Western religions.

    C. believes Tibetan Buddhists contribute to humanity as a whole because of their science of the mind.

    D. disapproves of people who spend their lives pretending that death doesn't exist.

    E. is skeptical about all religion.

25. The best definition of "patrimony" in line 87 is

    A. a father's endowment to his son.

    B. an unwritten will.

    C. a family fortune.

    D. heritage.

    E. lineage.

IF YOU FINISH BEFORE TIME IS CALLED, CHECK YOUR WORK ON THIS SECTION ONLY. DO NOT WORK ON ANY OTHER SECTION IN THE TEST.

Section 4: Mathematics

Time: 25 minutes

18 Questions

Directions: Solve each problem in this section by using the information given and your own mathematical calculations, insights, and problem-solving skills. Then select the one correct answer of the five choices given and mark the corresponding circle on your answer sheet. Use the available space on the page for your scratch work.

For each question, indicate the best answer, using the following notes.

1. All numerical values used are real numbers.
2. Calculators may be used.
3. Some problems may be accompanied by figures or diagrams. These figures are drawn as accurately as possible EXCEPT when it is stated in a specific problem that a figure is not drawn to scale. The figures and diagrams are meant to provide information useful in solving the problem or problems. Unless otherwise stated, all figures and diagrams lie on a plane.

Data that Can Be Used for Reference

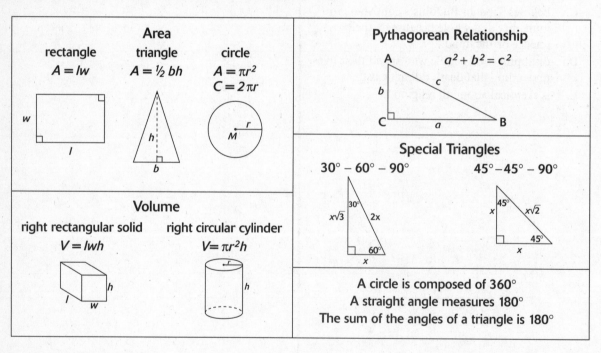

1. If a plane traveled 800 miles in 8 hours and a jet traveled three times as far in half the time, what was the jet's average speed, in miles per hour?

   A. 100
   B. 200
   C. 300
   D. 400
   E. 600

Use the following information for Question 2.

A = The set of prime numbers between 20 and 40.

B = The set of odd numbers between 20 and 40.

GO ON TO THE NEXT PAGE

2. How many numbers do sets A and B have in common?

    A. 4

    B. 5

    C. 6

    D. 7

    E. 10

3. If $3x^2 - 2y^2 = 12$ and $xy = -8$, then $(x + y)(3x - 2y) =$

    A. −96

    B. −20

    C. −4

    D. 4

    E. 20

4. If $\dfrac{a+5}{4}$ is an integer, then a must be

    A. a positive integer

    B. an even integer

    C. an odd integer

    D. a multiple of 4

    E. a multiple of 5

5. A box contains 8 red cards, 7 blue cards, and 6 white cards. How many selections of 3 cards can be made so that all 3 cards are red?

    A. 5

    B. 8

    C. 24

    D. 56

    E. 336

6. Which of the following represents the perimeter of a rectangle if one side is 5 feet longer than twice the other side?

    A. $2x + 5$

    B. $3x + 5$

    C. $6x + 10$

    D. $x^2 + 5$

    E. $x^2 + 5x$

7. $\dfrac{10^{15} - 10^{16}}{10^{15}} =$

    A. -10^{16}

    B. −10

    C. −9

    D. 9

    E. 10

8. Which of the following shows the stated relationship of:

Twice the sum of $5y$ and 3 is equal to the product of y and −3.

    A. $10y + 3 = -3y$

    B. $10y + 6 = -3y$

    C. $10y = -3y + 3$

    D. $10y = -3y + 6$

    E. $10y + 6 = 3y$

GO ON TO THE NEXT PAGE

Directions for Student-Produced Response Questions (Grid-ins): Questions 9–18 require you to solve the problem and enter your answer by carefully marking the circles on the special grid. Examples of the appropriate way to mark the grid follow.

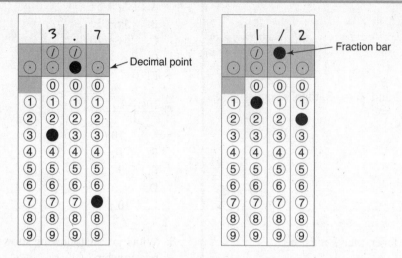

Do not grid in mixed numbers in the form of mixed numbers. Always change mixed numbers to improper fractions or decimals. Here's an example of how to grid when your answer is a mixed number such as $1\frac{1}{2}$.

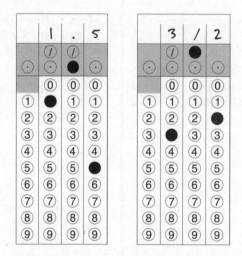

Space permitting, answers can start in any column. Each grid-in answer that follows is correct.

Note: Circles must be filled in correctly to receive credit. Mark only one circle in each column. No credit will be given if more than one circle in a column is marked.

Example:

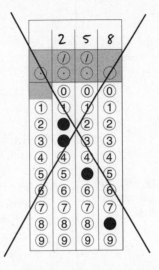

Accuracy of decimals: Always enter the most accurate decimal value that the grid will accommodate. For example: An answer such as .8888 . . . can be gridded as .888 or .889. Gridding this value as .8, .88, or .89 is considered inaccurate and therefore not acceptable. The acceptable grid-ins of $\frac{8}{9}$ are

Be sure to write your answers in the boxes at the top of the circles before filling in the circles. Although writing out the answers above the columns is not required, it is very important to ensure accuracy. Even though some problems may have more than one correct answer, only grid in one answer. Grid-in questions contain no negative answers.

9. If $4x + 2y = 5$ and $5x - 3y = -2$, what is the value of y?

10. If $5^x + 5^x + 5^x + 5^x + 5^x = 5^{10}$, what is the value of x?

11. If $\otimes$ is a binary operation defined as $a \otimes b = a^2 + b^2 - b$, what is the value of $(1 \otimes 2) \otimes 3$?

12. If x, y, and z are positive and x is $\frac{1}{3}$ of y and y is $\frac{5}{6}$ of z, then x is what fraction of z?

GO ON TO THE NEXT PAGE

13. If $5(z + 7) = 9(z - 5)$, what is the value of z?

14. In the figure below, T, W, and Z lie on the same line. What is the value of a?

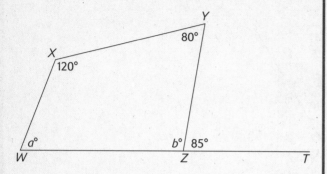

15. In a math class at Southern University, the ratio of females to males is 5 to 3. How many males are in the math class if the total enrollment is 64 students?

16. In the figure below, $MNPQ$ is a square and $PX = 18$. What is the area of $MNPQ$?

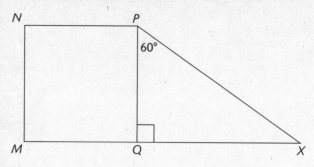

17. If the product of 0.6 and some number is equal to 5, what is the number?

18. The first term of a sequence is 1 and the second term is 3. Each subsequent term of the sequence is 1 less than the product of the preceding 2 terms. What is the seventh term of the sequence?

IF YOU FINISH BEFORE TIME IS CALLED, CHECK YOUR WORK ON THIS SECTION ONLY. DO NOT WORK ON ANY OTHER SECTION IN THE TEST.

Section 5: Writing—Multiple Choice

Time: 25 minutes

35 Questions

Directions: In this section, choose the best answer for each question and fill in the corresponding circle on the answer sheet.

The following questions test correctness and effective expression. In selecting the answer, pay attention to grammar, diction, sentence structure, and punctuation. In the following questions, part or all of each sentence is underlined. Answer Choice A repeats the underlined portion of the original sentence, while the next four choices offer alternatives. Choose the answer that best expresses the meaning of the original sentence and at the same time is grammatically correct and stylistically superior. The correct choice should be clear, unambiguous, and concise.

EXAMPLE:

The forecaster predicted <u>rain and the sky was clear.</u>

    A. rain and the sky was clear.
    B. rain but the sky was clear.
    C. rain the sky was clear.
    D. rain, but the sky was clear.
    E. rain being as the sky was clear.

The correct answer is **D.**

---

1. <u>As a teenager, Robert's grandmother promised him</u> that she would pay his college tuition.

    A. As a teenager, Robert's grandmother promised him
    B. When a teenager, Robert's grandmother promised him
    C. When Roger was a teenager, his grandmother promised him
    D. Roger was promised by his grandmother, when he was a teenager,
    E. As a teenager, Roger was promised by his grandmother

2. The committee decided not to proceed with plans for restructuring, <u>being as how most of the committee members</u> seemed opposed to the idea.

    A. being as how most of the committee members
    B. because of the fact that most of the committee members
    C. on account of most of the committee members
    D. because most of the committee members
    E. the reason being that most of the committee members

GO ON TO THE NEXT PAGE

3. I.M. Pei, the famous <u>architect who designed, among other things, the pyramid addition to the Louvre Museum</u> and the John F. Kennedy Library in Boston.

   A. architect who designed, among other things, the pyramid addition to the Louvre Museum

   B. architect, designed, among other things, the pyramid addition to the Louvre Museum

   C. architect, who designed, as well as other buildings, the pyramid addition to the Louvre Museum

   D. architect, and who designed the pyramid addition to the Louvre Museum, among other things, and

   E. who was the designer, among other things, of the pyramid addition to the Louvre Museum

4. The flood waters engulfed the streets<u>, and the pedestrians run quickly into nearby shops for refuge.</u>

   A. , and the pedestrians run quickly into nearby shops for refuge.

   B. , and the pedestrians ran quickly into nearby shops in order to find refuge.

   C. . And the pedestrians are running quickly into nearby shops to find refuge.

   D. , and the pedestrians ran quickly into nearby shops for refuge.

   E. ; and the pedestrians, they were running quickly into nearby shops hoping to find refuge.

5. Drive carefully on the snow-covered road <u>and you should be ready to pull over to the side if visibility is poor.</u>

   A. and you should be ready to pull over to the side if visibility is poor.

   B. and then, if visibility is poor, you should pull over to the side.

   C. and you will want to pull over to the side in case of poor visibility.

   D. and you will pull over to the side when the visibility becomes poor.

   E. and pull over to the side if visibility is poor.

6. <u>The cause of the interruption during last night's lecture was due to the fact that the smoke alarm went off.</u>

   A. The cause of the interruption during last night's lecture was due to the fact that the smoke alarm went off.

   B. The cause of the interruption during last night's lecture was the smoke alarm.

   C. Last night's lecture was interrupted due to the fact that the smoke alarm went off.

   D. Last night's lecture was interrupted by the smoke alarm, which went off.

   E. The smoke alarm interrupted last night's lecture.

7. The animosity grew <u>between Henderson and I after we both bid on the same painting.</u>

   A. between Henderson and I after we both bid on the same painting.

   B. between Henderson and me after we had both bidden on the same painting.

   C. between Henderson and I after the both of us had bid on the same painting.

   D. between me and Henderson after both of us have bid on the same painting.

   E. between Henderson and me after we both bid on the same painting.

8. <u>While Matthew and Suzanne were tutoring the students after school, they asked</u> dozens of questions about the exam.

   A. While Matthew and Suzanne were tutoring the students after school, they asked

   B. During the tutoring session after school given by Matthew and Suzanne, the students asked

   C. After school, Matthew and Suzanne tutored the students, who asked

   D. Matthew and Suzanne were tutoring the students after school, and they asked

   E. After school while being tutored by Matthew and Suzanne, the students they asked

GO ON TO THE NEXT PAGE

9. Far in the distance, beyond the grove of oak trees and the dark, motionless <u>lake, rose the peaks of the majestic mountain range.</u>

   A. lake, rose the peaks of the majestic mountain range.
   B. lake; rose the peaks of the majestic mountain range.
   C. lake, there rose the peaks of the majestic mountain range.
   D. lake was rising the peaks of the majestic mountain range.
   E. lake. The peaks of the majestic mountain range rose.

10. Factors that have influenced the loss of subscriptions to newspapers include <u>the growing presence of the internet, that television news is watched by so many people, and the economy which has been sluggish.</u>

    A. the growing presence of the internet, that television news is watched by so many people, and the economy which has been sluggish.
    B. the growing presence of the internet, television, and that the economy has been sluggish.
    C. the growing presence of the internet, the popularity of television news, and the sluggish economy.
    D. the fact that the internet has been growing, people are watching television news more, and that the economy has been sluggish.
    E. The growing presence of the internet, the increasing viewership of television news, and the fact that the economy is sluggish.

11. <u>Because of their interest in alternative forms of energy, the new wind machines are being studied closely by environmental engineers.</u>

    A. Because of their interest in alternative forms of energy, the new wind machines are being studied closely by environmental engineers.
    B. Because of their interest in alternative forms of energy, environmental engineers are closely studying the new wind machines.
    C. The new wind machines, which are being closely studied by environmental engineers because they are interested in alternative forms of energy.
    D. Environmental engineers are closely studying the new wind machines because they are interested in alternative forms of energy.
    E. Being interested in alternative forms of energy, the new wind machines are being closely studied by environmental engineers.

GO ON TO THE NEXT PAGE

Directions: The following sentences may contain one error of grammar, usage, diction, or idiom. No sentence contains more than one error, and some have no error. If there is an error, it will be underlined and have a letter beneath it. If there is an error, choose the one underlined part that must be changed to correct the sentence. If there is no error, choose E. Sections of the sentence that are not underlined cannot be changed. In selecting your answer, observe the requirements of standard written English.

12. <u>Riding</u> across the country, George and <u>him</u>
    A   B
    became good friends and <u>decided that</u> they
                              C
    would be <u>roommates</u> at the university.
              D
    <u>No error</u>
     E

13. Audiences <u>enjoyed</u> the <u>actor's</u> antics on the
              A   B
    stage tonight, but <u>very few</u> people saw the
                        C
    trouble he <u>causes</u> before the performance.
                D
    <u>No error</u>
     E

14. Because the misunderstanding <u>was caused by</u>
                                  A
    mistakes in the business letter, the secretary

    <u>blamed herself</u> for the tension between the two
     B
    men and <u>was believing</u> she should explain what
              C
    <u>had happened.</u> <u>No error</u>
     D   E

15. <u>In spite of</u> their parents' advice, neither
     A
    Cameron <u>or</u> Hank <u>signed up</u> for the tutorial
             B   C
    session <u>being offered</u> by their physics teacher.
             D
    <u>No error</u>
     E

16. One topic that hadn't been <u>thoroughly</u>
                                A
    discussed when the <u>guest speaker</u> <u>has been</u>
                        B   C
    invited <u>was</u> the travel arrangements. <u>No error</u>
             D   E

17. Believing that the new law was a questionable

    one, Maxwell <u>decided that</u> he <u>shouldn't of</u>
                  A   B
    agreed to attend the party, <u>which</u> was being
                                 C
    held to thank the volunteers for <u>its</u> passage.
                                       D
    <u>No error</u>
     E

18. When the captain <u>was studying</u> the revised
                      A
    flight plan, he was <u>concerned about</u> whether
                         B
    the planner had taken into consideration <u>it's</u>
                                              C
    <u>likelihood</u> of encountering a hurricane.
     D
    <u>No error</u>
     E

19. Political pressure is growing <u>to achieve</u> energy
                                   A
    independence from <u>overseas</u> suppliers and
                       B
    <u>to use</u> sources such as natural gas <u>to create</u>
     C   D
    electricity. <u>No error</u>
                  E

20. Although history <u>has proved</u> <u>that once</u> a
                     A   B
    weapon is <u>made available</u>, someone will
               C
    use it, governments continue to resist the

    <u>moratorium.</u> <u>No error</u>
     D   E

21. The report stated <u>flatly</u> that a combination of
                       A
    <u>oversight</u> and <u>being consistent</u> would prevent
     B   C
    <u>such behavior.</u> <u>No error</u>
     D   E

GO ON TO THE NEXT PAGE

22. Heathcliff and Cathy, the <u>protagonists</u> of
  A
  Wuthering Heights, are characters who have
  captivated readers since the novel <u>was written</u>,
  B
  and they have <u>inspired</u> both movies and
  C
  romantic novels, also <u>using</u> them as models.
  D
  <u>No error</u>
  E

23. John Steinbeck's novels <u>are memorable</u> not
  A
  only for their characters and plots <u>but also for</u>
  B
  <u>their settings</u>, which are <u>generally</u> in the Salinas
  C
  area, <u>and which</u> Steinbeck makes come alive
  D
  for the reader. <u>No error</u>
  E

24. As the piano teacher told his <u>parents, Martin</u>
  A
  did <u>good enough</u> on the first two pieces at the
  B
  recital, but he couldn't <u>seem to manage</u> the
  C
  more difficult <u>ones</u> that followed the
  D
  intermission. <u>No error</u>
  E

25. In the past, people read reviews of art shows
  with the same <u>keen interest</u> <u>in which</u> they now
  AB
  read movie reviews, and <u>the movie reviews</u>
  C
  aren't <u>any more</u> informative. <u>No error</u>
  DE

26. At the convention last year, the group <u>could of</u>
  A
  stood up for changing the rule <u>requiring</u> a
  B
  <u>two-year residency</u> for new members, but <u>it</u>
  CD
  chose to remain quiet instead. <u>No error</u>
  E

27. Some psychologists <u>believe that</u> children can
  A
  be so <u>affected</u> by the monsters in movies that
  B
  <u>they</u> may resist going to bed without a parent
  C
  checking underneath it and staying with
  <u>him until he falls</u> asleep. <u>No error</u>
  DE

28. The manager, <u>whom</u> the staff admired for his
  A
  fairness and <u>who</u> had never <u>expected</u> them to
  BC
  split shifts before, was surprised when his
  announcement was greeted <u>without hardly</u> a
  D
  murmur. <u>No error</u>
  E

29. The team members were <u>laying</u> on the grass
  A
  instead of <u>beginning</u> practice, and the coach,
  B
  <u>who</u> seldom lost his temper, <u>began</u> yelling at
  CD
  them. <u>No error</u>
  E

GO ON TO THE NEXT PAGE

Directions: The following passage is an early draft of a student essay. Some parts of the essay need to be revised.

Read the selection carefully and answer the questions that follow. There will be questions about sentence structure, diction, and usage in individual sentences or parts of sentences. Other questions will deal with the whole essay or paragraphs in it and ask you to decide about the organization, development, and appropriate language. Choose the answer that follows the requirements of standard written English and most effectively expresses the intended meanings.

Questions 30–35 are based on the following passage.

(1) By any standards, Benjamin Franklin was a remarkable man, not only as a statesman, diplomat, and one of our founding fathers but he was also in fact a scientist and inventor.

(2) According to one of his biographers, Franklin's greatest virtue was an insatiable curiosity. (3) That curiosity would lead him to study nature and be doing experiments. (4) On the basis of his experiments with electricity, in 1753 the Royal Society presented him with the Copley Medal for contributions to the knowledge of lightning and electricity. (5) Perhaps the most famous image of Benjamin Franklin is of a man out on a stormy night flying a kite. (6) What he was doing was that he was attempting to show the electrical nature of lightning and also demonstrating his theory of positive and negative electrical charges. (7) Franklin was always interested in the practical applications of his experiments and research. (8) For example, based on his experiments with lightning, he invented a lightning rod, a tall grounded wire with a pointed end. (9) He invented other useful things as well, such as bifocals and the Franklin stove. (10) He is reported to have said that the bifocals were especially useful at dinner, where he could see the food he was eating, and his Franklin stove became so popular that the essay explaining it was frequently reprinted and translated into several foreign languages. (11) Based on his achievements as a scientist and inventor, Franklin holds a unique place among those who helped form the nation.

30. Which of the following is the best version of the underlined portion of sentence 1 (reproduced below)?

By any standards, Benjamin Franklin was a remarkable man, not only as a statesman, diplomat, and one of our founding fathers <u>but he was also in fact</u> a scientist and inventor.

A. No error
B. but in addition he was also
C. but, in fact, he was also
D. but also as
E. and, additionally, in fact,

31. Which of the following is the best combination of sentences 2 and 3 (reproduced below)?

According to one of his biographers, Franklin's greatest virtue was an insatiable curiosity. That curiosity would lead him to study nature and do experiments.

A. According to one of his biographers, Franklin's greatest virtue was an insatiable curiosity, and that curiosity would lead him to study nature and do experiments.
B. According to one of his biographers, Franklin's greatest virtue leading him to study nature and do experiments, was an insatiable curiosity.
C. According to one of his biographers, Franklin's greatest virtue was an insatiable curiosity, which led him to study nature and do experiments.
D. According to one of his biographers, Franklin's greatest virtue was an insatiable curiosity, studying nature at every opportunity and doing experiments.
E. According to one of his biographers, his greatest virtue was an insatiable curiosity, therefore studying nature and doing experiments.

32. Which of the following is the best version of sentence 3 in the passage?

A. That curiosity would lead him to study nature and conduct experiments.
B. That curiosity would lead him to study nature and also it would lead him to be doing experiments.
C. That curiosity, in addition to studying nature, would lead him to be conducting experiments.
D. In addition to studying nature, that curiosity would lead him to the performance of experiments.
E. As a result of his curiosity, he would be studying nature and would be doing experiments.

GO ON TO THE NEXT PAGE

33. Which of the following is the best version of the underlined portion of sentence 5 (reproduced below)?

    <u>What he was doing was that he was</u> showing the electrical nature of lightning and demonstrating his theory of positive and negative electrical charges.

    A. No error
    B. The thing that he was doing was
    C. What Franklin was doing was that he was
    D. Franklin was
    E. What he was doing, was that Franklin was

34. The best position for sentence 4 would be

    A. where it is now.
    B. after sentence 5.
    C. after sentence 6.
    D. after sentence 7.
    E. at the end of the passage.

35. The best place to begin a second paragraph would be after

    A. sentence 2.
    B. sentence 4.
    C. sentence 5.
    D. sentence 6.
    E. sentence 7.

IF YOU FINISH BEFORE TIME IS CALLED, CHECK YOUR WORK ON THIS SECTION ONLY. DO NOT WORK ON ANY OTHER SECTION IN THE TEST.

Section 6: Critical Reading

Time: 25 minutes
24 Questions

Directions: In this section, choose the best answer for each question and fill in the corresponding circle on the answer sheet.

Each blank in the following sentences indicates that something has been omitted. Consider the lettered words beneath the sentence and choose the word or set of words that *best* fits the whole sentence.

EXAMPLE:

> With a million more people than any other African nation, Nigeria is the most _____ country on the continent.
>
> A. impoverished
> B. successful
> C. populous
> D. developed
> E. militant

The correct answer is **C.**

1. Because Mr. Broderick recited his litany of complaints endlessly, I didn't hesitate to _____ myself from the conversation.

   A. extricate
   B. dismiss
   C. rescind
   D. wean
   E. relocate

2. In the distance we could see a _____ scene of a green pasture with grazing sheep, a grove of willows, a trickling stream, and a simple farmhouse.

   A. bucolic
   B. suburban
   C. populated
   D. surrealistic
   E. joyful

3. Although the _____ girl burst into his office without knocking and demanded to speak to him, the head of the department had no _____ about asking her to leave.

   A. recalcitrant . . . patience
   B. brazen . . . compunction
   C. loquacious . . . inclination
   D. sulky . . . choice
   E. winsome . . . hesitation

4. In spite of the government's threat of _____, the band of _____ rebels proceeded to burn the council buildings.

   A. boycotts . . . spurious
   B. penalties . . . tiresome
   C. reprisals . . . intransigent
   D. retreat . . . litigious
   E. excommunication . . . voracious

5. We hadn't been sure that Mother would like the painting we bought for her, but she not only thanked us over and over and insisted it was the best gift she'd ever received, she also _____ about it to her book club.

   A. remonstrated
   B. lectured
   C. expostulated
   D. mused
   E. rhapsodized

GO ON TO THE NEXT PAGE

Directions: Questions follow each of the passages below. Using only the stated or implied information in each passage and in its introduction, if any, answer the questions.

Questions 6–7 are based on the following passage.

Johann Gutenberg, we learn in school, invented the printing press. But did he? Evidence suggests that a Dutchman, Laurens Janszoon Koster, actually invented movable type and that
(5) Gutenberg learned about it from an apprentice of Koster's, who had come to Germany with some of Koster's blocks and who became a friend of Gutenberg's. That the printing press was basically Koster's idea makes sense, given
(10) that Gutenberg—about whom little is known— had spent most of his life as a stonemason and mirror polisher. That he should suddenly invent a printing press from a wine press and some blocks of wood strains credibility. What we know
(15) for sure is that the use of the printing press grew quickly, and between 1455, when Gutenberg's first Bible was published, and 1500 more than 35,000 books were published in Europe.

6. The purpose of the passage is to

   A. prove that Gutenberg lied about inventing the printing press.

   B. explain the principle behind the printing press.

   C. show the immediate success of the printing press.

   D. suggest that Koster might be responsible for the invention of the printing press.

   E. show that invention of the printing press was most likely a collaborative effort between Koster and his apprentice.

7. The author cites which of the following reasons for doubting that Gutenberg invented the printing press?

   A. a poor education

   B. the friendship with Koster

   C. Gutenberg's work experience

   D. Koster's reputation as an inventor

   E. the findings of recent historical research

Questions 8–9 are based on the following passage.

The author Bill Bryson, in *A Short History of Nearly Everything*, explains Einstein's famous equation ($E = mc^2$) in a simple way. At its most basic, the equation says that mass and energy
(5) have an equivalence, or, in Bryson's phrase, "energy is liberated matter, and matter is energy waiting to happen." c^2 refers to the speed of light squared—a "truly huge number." This means, according to Bryson, that there is an enormous
(10) amount of energy in every material thing.

Among other things, Einstein's theory explains how a star could burn for billions of years and not use up its fuel. Perhaps more significantly to our lives, it explains how radiation
(15) works. A small lump of uranium can throw out streams of energy "without melting away like an ice cube." The most energetic thing we have produced so far is a uranium bomb, and it releases one percent of the energy it could if we
(20) could successfully "liberate" it.

8. The main purpose of the passage is to

   A. explain how radiation led to the uranium bomb.

   B. provide a simplified explanation of Einstein's equation.

   C. emphasize Einstein's pivotal role in physics.

   D. explain how stars can burn for billions of years.

   E. detail the relationship of mass and energy.

9. According to the passage, the c^2 in Einstein's equation indicates the

   A. speed of energy.

   B. connection between light and radiation.

   C. amount of energy in all material things.

   D. speed at which radiation is transmitted.

   E. necessary conditions required for the production of radiation.

GO ON TO THE NEXT PAGE

Questions 10–15 are based on the following passage.

This passage is from an essay written in 1956.

After the lions had returned to their cages, creeping angrily through the chutes, a little bunch of us drifted away and into an open doorway nearby, where we stood for awhile in
(5) semidarkness, watching a big brown circus horse go harrumphing around the practice ring. His trainer was a woman of about forty, and the two of them, horse and woman, seemed caught up in one of those desultory treadmills of afternoon
(10) from which there is no apparent escape. The day was hot, and we kibitzers were grateful to be briefly out of the sun's glare. The long rein, or tape, by which the woman guided her charge counterclockwise in his dull career formed the
(15) radius of their private circle, of which she was the revolving center; and she, too, stepped a tiny circumference of her own, in order to accommodate the horse and allow him his maximum scope. She had on a short-skirted
(20) costume and a conical straw hat. Her legs were bare and she wore high heels, which probed deep into the loose tanbark and kept her ankles in a state of constant turmoil. The great size and meekness of the horse, the repetitious exercise,
(25) the heat of the afternoon, all exerted a hypnotic charm that invited boredom; we spectators were experiencing a languor—we neither expected relief nor felt entitled to any. We had paid a dollar to get into the grounds, to be sure, but we
(30) had got our dollar's worth a few minutes before, when the trainer's whiplash had got caught around a toe of one of the lions. What more did we want for a dollar?

Behind me I heard someone say, "Excuse me,
(35) please," in a low voice. She was halfway into the building when I turned and saw her—a girl of sixteen or seventeen, politely threading her way through us onlookers who blocked the entrance. As she emerged in front of us, I saw that she was
(40) barefoot, her dirty little feet fighting the uneven ground. In most respects she was like any of two or three dozen showgirls you encounter if you wander about the winter quarters of Mr. John Ringling North's circus in Sarasota—cleverly
(45) proportioned, deeply browned by the sun, dusty, eager, and almost naked. But her grave face and the naturalness of her manner gave her a sort of quick distinction and brought a new note into the gloomy octagonal building where we had all cast
(50) our lot for a few moments. As soon as she had squeezed through the crowd, she spoke a word or two to the older woman, whom I took to be her mother, stepped to the ring, and waited while the horse coasted to a stop in front of her. She gave
(55) the animal a couple of affectionate swipes on his enormous neck and then swung herself aboard. The horse immediately resumed his rocking canter, the woman goading him on, chanting something that sounded like "Hop! Hop!"

(60) In attempting to recapture this mild spectacle, I am merely acting as a recording secretary for one of the oldest of societies—the society of those who, at one time or another, have surrendered, without even a show of resistance,
(65) to the bedazzlement of a circus rider. As a writing man, or secretary, I have always felt charged with the safekeeping of all unexpected items of worldly or unworldly enchantment, as though I might be held personally responsible if
(70) even a small one were to be lost. But it is not easy to communicate anything of this nature. The circus comes as close to being the world in microcosm as anything I know; in a way, it puts all the rest of show business in the shade. Its
(75) magic is universal and complex. Out of its wild disorder comes order; from its rank smell rises the good aroma of courage and daring; out of its preliminary shabbiness comes the final splendor. And buried in the familiar boasts of its advance
(80) agents lies the modesty of most of its people. For me the circus is at its best before it has been put together. It is at its best at certain moments when it comes to a point, as through a burning glass, in the activity and destiny of a single performer out
(85) of so many. One ring is always bigger than three. One rider, one aerialist, is always greater than six. In short, a man has to catch the circus unawares to experience its full impact and share its gaudy dream.

10. Which of the following is the best definition of *desultory* (line 9)?

A. ponderous
B. lacking rhythm
C. regimented
D. lacking purpose
E. resistant

GO ON TO THE NEXT PAGE

11. The first two paragraphs of the passage

   A. vividly describe a scene at the circus.
   B. emphasize the tedium of the circus.
   C. show the writer's negative impressions of the circus.
   D. present an objective view of circus performers.
   E. undercut the traditional view of circuses.

12. Which of the following best describes the mood of the first two paragraphs?

   A. childlike anticipation
   B. enthusiasm
   C. pleasant boredom
   D. controlled frustration
   E. nostalgia

13. The main idea the writer expresses in lines 28–33 is that

   A. the circus is an inexpensive entertainment.
   B. sometimes circus performers have not thoroughly rehearsed their acts.
   C. unexpected events are sometimes more entertaining than expected ones.
   D. spectators enjoy seeing performers in danger.
   E. circus animals are not particularly well treated.

14. In the third paragraph the author describes himself as

   A. an avid fan.
   B. a bored observer.
   C. an objective critic.
   D. a recording secretary.
   E. an amused onlooker.

15. According to the passage, the author says he sees himself as

   A. responsible for preserving small, magical moments in life.
   B. "bedazzled" by the mood of the circus.
   C. ultimately incapable of conveying the experience at the circus.
   D. both bored and fascinated by circus performers.
   E. an outsider longing to be part of the magic of the circus.

Questions 16–24 are based on the following passage.

In the classic nightmare scenario of dystopian science fiction, machines become smart enough to challenge humans—and they have no moral qualms about harming, or even destroying us.
(5) Today's robots, of course, are usually developed to help people. But it turns out that they face a host of ethical quandaries that push the boundaries of artificial intelligence, or AI, even in ordinary situations.

(10) Imagine being a resident in an assisted-living facility—a setting where robots will probably become commonplace soon. It is almost 11 o'clock one morning, and you ask the robot assistant in the dayroom for the remote so you
(15) can turn on the TV and watch *The View*. But another resident also wants the remote because she wants to watch *The Price Is Right*. The robot decides to hand the remote to her. At first, you are upset. But the decision, the robot explains,
(20) was fair because you got to watch your favorite morning show the day before. This anecdote is an example of an ordinary act of ethical decision making, but for a machine, it is a surprisingly tough feat to pull off.

(25) The scenario we just described is still theoretical, but we already have created a first demonstration of a robot able to make similar decisions. We have endowed our machine with an ethical principle that it uses to determine how
(30) often to remind a patient to take a medication. Our robot's programming so far is capable of choosing among only a few possible options, such as whether to keep reminding a patient to take medicine, and when to do so, or to accept
(35) the patient's decision not to take the medication. But to our knowledge, it is the first robot to rely on an ethical principle to determine its actions.

It would be extremely difficult, if not impossible, to anticipate every decision a robot might ever face
(40) and program it so that it will behave in the desired manner in each conceivable situation. On the other hand, preventing robots from taking absolutely any action that might raise ethical concern could unnecessarily limit opportunities for robots to
(45) perform tasks that would greatly improve human lives. We believe that the solution is to design robots able to apply ethical principles to new and unanticipated situations—say, to determining who gets to read a new book, rather than who gets
(50) control of the remote. This approach has the additional benefit of enabling robots to refer to

GO ON TO THE NEXT PAGE

those principles if asked to justify their behavior, which is essential if humans are to feel comfortable interacting with them. As a side benefit, efforts to
(55) design ethical robots could also lead to progress in the field of ethics itself, by forcing philosophers to examine real-life situations. As Tufts University philosopher Daniel C. Dennett recently put it, "AI makes philosophy honest."

(60)   Autonomous robots are likely to soon be part of our daily lives. Some airplanes are already capable of flying themselves, and self-driving cars are at the development stage. Even "smart homes," with computers controlling everything
(65) from lighting to the A/C, can be thought of as robots whose body is the entire home—just as HAL 90000, the computer in Stanley Kubrick's classic *2001: A Space Odyssey,* was the brains of a robot spaceship. And several companies have
(70) been developing robots that can assist the elderly with everyday tasks, either to supplement the staff of an assisted living facility or to help the aged live at home by themselves. Although most of these robots do not have to make life-or-death
(75) decisions, for them to be welcome among us their actions should be perceived as fair, correct, or simply kind. Their inventors, then, had better take the ethical ramification of their programming into account.

(80)   If one agrees that embodying ethical principles in autonomous machines is key to their success in interacting with humans, then the first question becomes, "Which principles should go in them?" Fans of science-fiction literature may
(85) believe that Isaac Asimov already provided the answer some time ago, with his original Three Laws of Robotics:

    1. A robot may not injure a human being, or through inaction, allow a human being to come
(90) to harm.

    2. A robot must obey the orders given it by human beings except when such orders would conflict with the First Law.

    3. A robot must protect its own existence as
(95) long as such protection does not conflict with the First or Second Law. But some have discovered inconsistencies when thinking through the implications of these laws, which Asimov first articulated in a short story in 1942. And Asimov
(100) himself illustrated how unsuitable they were in his 1976 story *The Bicentennial Man*, in which human bullies order a robot to dismantle himself. The robot has to obey the bullies because of the Second Law, and he cannot defend himself
(105) without harming them, which would be a violation of the First Law.

---

16. Which of the following is the best definition of the word *dystopian*?

    A. futuristic

    B. angry

    C. anti-human

    D. pessimistic

    E. anti-utopian

17. The function of the second paragraph of the passage is to

    A. provide an example of a dystopian view of robots.

    B. emphasize the negative reaction a person might have to a robot.

    C. illustrate a simple ethical dilemma that a robot might face.

    D. dramatize a way in which robots can help people.

    E. show the dramatic advance made recently in designing robots.

18. The ethical decision that the robot in paragraph 3 has been programmed to make is

    A. whether a medication is appropriate to a patient's condition.

    B. how many times a patient should receive a medication.

    C. when a medication should be discontinued for a patient.

    D. how many times a patient should be reminded to take a medication.

    E. when a physician should be notified of a patient's decisions regarding medication.

19. According to the author, a robot endowed with the ability to make an ethical decision is

    A. being considered.

    B. probably impossible.

    C. possible but dangerous.

    D. opposed by most philosophers and psychologists.

    E. already a reality.

GO ON TO THE NEXT PAGE

20. According to the author, robots designed to make ethical decisions should be

   A. able to justify their behavior if called on.
   B. used primarily in medical situations.
   C. government-regulated and controlled.
   D. programmed by people with strong moral codes.
   E. able to cooperate fully with humans.

21. By saying that "AI makes philosophy honest" (lines 58–59), philosopher Daniel C. Dennett is suggesting that

   A. artificial intelligence will be equipped to make better ethical decisions than philosophers make.
   B. the study of philosophy and ethics in its present state is not honest.
   C. artificial intelligence being involved in ethics is an idea worthy of satire.
   D. designing ethical robots could make philosophers reexamine ethical decisions in real-life situations.
   E. artificial intelligence could provide an employment opportunity for philosophers in the field of ethics.

22. One of the author's main points in paragraph 4 is that robots should be designed so that they

   A. can anticipate the needs of humans who use them.
   B. are able to apply ethical principles to new situations.
   C. will take over mechanical, repetitive tasks.
   D. are unable to cause harm.
   E. will provide methods to improve human behavior.

23. From information in the passage, it can be inferred that the author most likely

   A. is involved in robot design.
   B. is a reporter.
   C. works for a government agency.
   D. is a critic of artificial intelligence.
   E. is a philosopher.

24. The purpose of the last paragraph of the passage is to

   A. recognize the prophetic talents of Isaac Asimov.
   B. contradict Asimov's Three Laws of Robotics.
   C. address the difficulty of deciding which ethical principles should be programmed into robots.
   D. provide an example of the use of artificial intelligence in real-life decisions.
   E. summarize the points made in the passage.

IF YOU FINISH BEFORE TIME IS CALLED, CHECK YOUR WORK ON THIS SECTION ONLY. DO NOT WORK ON ANY OTHER SECTION IN THE TEST.

STOP

Section 7: Mathematics

Time: 20 minutes

16 Questions

Directions: Solve each problem in this section by using the information given and your own mathematical calculations, insights, and problem-solving skills. Then select the one correct answer of the five choices given and mark the corresponding circle on your answer sheet. Use the available space on the page for your scratch work.

For each question, indicate the best answer, using the following notes.

1. All numerical values used are real numbers.
2. Calculators may be used.
3. Some problems may be accompanied by figures or diagrams. These figures are drawn as accurately as possible EXCEPT when it is stated in a specific problem that a figure is not drawn to scale. The figures and diagrams are meant to provide information useful in solving the problem or problems. Unless otherwise stated, all figures and diagrams lie on a plane.

Data that Can Be Used for Reference

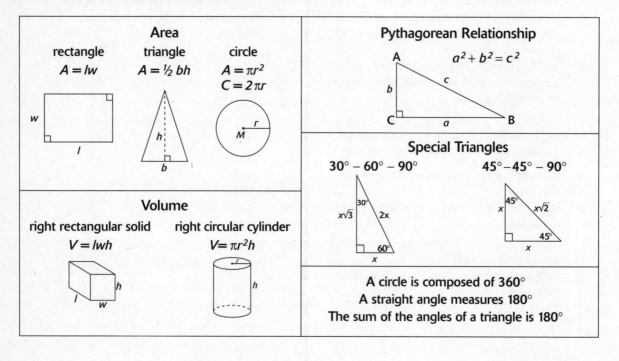

Area

rectangle
$A = lw$

triangle
$A = \frac{1}{2} bh$

circle
$A = \pi r^2$
$C = 2\pi r$

Volume

right rectangular solid
$V = lwh$

right circular cylinder
$V = \pi r^2 h$

Pythagorean Relationship

$a^2 + b^2 = c^2$

Special Triangles

$30° - 60° - 90°$

$45° - 45° - 90°$

A circle is composed of 360°
A straight angle measures 180°
The sum of the angles of a triangle is 180°

GO ON TO THE NEXT PAGE

1. How many different soup, salad, and sandwich combinations are possible from a choice of 4 soups, 3 salads, and 10 sandwiches?

   A. 120
   B. 82
   C. 70
   D. 22
   E. 17

2. $\triangle ABC$ is similar to $\triangle XYZ$ and the perimeter of $\triangle XYZ$ is 60 units. If $\overline{BC}$ has a length of 9 units and $\overline{YZ}$ has a length of 15 units, what is the perimeter of $\triangle ABC$?

   A. 15
   B. 17
   C. 24
   D. 36
   E. It cannot be determined from the information given.

3. If $5(a^2 - b^2) = 100$ and $a + b = 4$, what is the value of $a - b$?

   A. 4
   B. 5
   C. 16
   D. 20
   E. 25

4. The average (arithmetic mean) of 8 test scores is $z\%$. What is the total of all 8 test scores?

   A. $z + 8$
   B. $z - 8$
   C. $\frac{z}{8}$
   D. $\frac{8}{z}$
   E. $8z$

5. What is the area of a circle that has a circumference of π?

   A. $\frac{1}{4}\pi$
   B. $\frac{1}{2}\pi$
   C. 1
   D. π
   E. π^2

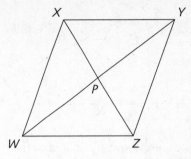

6. In the figure above, $WXYZ$ is a rhombus with $XZ = XY = 8$. What is the length of $\overline{WY}$?

   A. $4\sqrt{3}$
   B. 6
   C. 8
   D. $8\sqrt{3}$
   E. 16

7. If z is directly proportional to y^3 and $z = \frac{1}{9}$ when $y = \frac{1}{3}$, what is the value of y when $z = 24$?

   A. $\frac{1}{4}$
   B. $\frac{1}{2}$
   C. 2
   D. 3
   E. 4

8. How many different 4-digit numbers can be formed if the digits 6, 7, 8, and 9 must all be used in each of the numbers?

   A. 4
   B. 8
   C. 16
   D. 24
   E. 256

9. If $A\,(-3, 8)$ and $B\,(11, 4)$ are the end points of the diameter of a circle, what are the coordinates of O, where O is the center of the circle?

   A. $(8, 12)$
   B. $(-14, 4)$
   C. $(-7, 2)$
   D. $(14, -4)$
   E. $(4, 6)$

GO ON TO THE NEXT PAGE

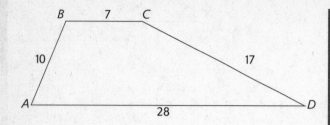

10. In the figure above, if the area of the trapezoid *ABCD* is 140, what is the height of the trapezoid?

A. $2\frac{8}{31}$

B. 4

C. 8

D. 9

E. 10

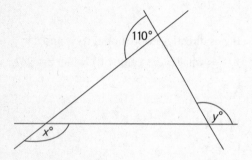

11. In the figure above, *x* + *y* =

A. 180°

B. 220°

C. 230°

D. 240°

E. 250°

12. If *a* is divisible by 5 and *b* is divisible by 7, which of the following must be divisible by 35?

   I. *ab*

   II. 7*a* + 5*b*

   III. 5*a* + 7*b*

A. I only

B. II only

C. I and II only

D. I and III only

E. I, II, and III

13. If *x* represents the smallest of three consecutive odd integers whose sum is 549, which of the following equations can be used to find the integer?

A. 3*x* + 2 = 549

B. 3*x* + 3 = 549

C. 3*x* + 4 = 549

D. 3*x* + 6 = 549

E. 3*x* + 9 = 549

14. If $y = -\frac{1}{2}$ and *a* > 0, which of the following has the largest value?

A. $8ay^2$

B. $8ay^3$

C. $8a^4$

D. $8ay^5$

E. $8ay^6$

15. If each boy enrolled in Period 1 math class weighs more than 130 pounds, which of the following statements must be true?

A. All boys who weigh more than 130 pounds are enrolled in Period 1 math.

B. No boys who weigh less than 130 pounds are enrolled in Period 1 math.

C. There is one boy enrolled in Period 1 math who weighs less than 130 pounds.

D. Every student in Period 1 math who weighs more than 130 pounds is a boy.

E. All boys who are not enrolled in Period 1 math weigh less than 130 pounds.

16. The first term of a sequence is 2 and each successive number is obtained by subtracting 1 from the preceding number and then squaring the result. What is the seventh number in the sequence?

A. −1

B. 0

C. 1

D. 2

E. 64

IF YOU FINISH BEFORE TIME IS CALLED, CHECK YOUR WORK ON THIS SECTION ONLY. DO NOT WORK ON ANY OTHER SECTION IN THE TEST.

Section 8: Critical Reading

Time: 20 minutes
20 Questions

Directions: In this section, choose the best answer for each question and fill in the corresponding circle on the answer sheet.

Each blank in the following sentences indicates that something has been omitted. Consider the lettered words beneath the sentence and choose the word or set of words that *best* fits the whole sentence.

EXAMPLE:

With a million more people than any other African nation, Nigeria is the most _____ country on the continent.

- **A.** impoverished
- **B.** successful
- **C.** populous
- **D.** developed
- **E.** militant

The correct answer is **C**.

---

1. The _____ of the empire resulted in a number of sects that were hoping to take advantage of the power vacuum.

   - **A.** recognition
   - **B.** dissolution
   - **C.** resurgence
   - **D.** calamities
   - **E.** deployment

2. The accusation that the new leader of the committee is not serious about her position is _____ in view of her excellent reputation and _____ dedication to the cause.

   - **A.** spurious . . . unequivocal
   - **B.** villainous . . . reluctant
   - **C.** premature . . . adequate
   - **D.** illicit . . . frenetic
   - **E.** innocuous . . . intemperate

3. The _____ effect of all the new technology Randall introduced at the office was to completely baffle the older secretaries and make them _____ the old-fashioned electric typewriters and copy machines.

   - **A.** hostile . . . amicable toward
   - **B.** underlying . . . averse to
   - **C.** cumulative . . . revert to
   - **D.** disseminating . . . susceptible to
   - **E.** beneficial . . . repulsed by

4. Although I used my best arguments and most ingratiating manner when talking to Benjamin, he was utterly _____ when it came to approving the plan.

   - **A.** intractable
   - **B.** unimpeachable
   - **C.** ambivalent
   - **D.** polemical
   - **E.** irresolute

GO ON TO THE NEXT PAGE

5. The groom's family felt the wedding had been purposely scheduled at a(n) _____ time so that very few of his relatives would _____ to attend.

   A. extraneous . . . refuse
   B. inopportune . . . deign
   C. drastic . . . hesitate
   D. spontaneous . . . guarantee
   E. prohibitive . . . promise

6. His strong _____ for traveling rather than staying in one place would make it difficult for him to perform the duties of the job.

   A. compassion
   B. empathy
   C. support
   D. predilection
   E. commitment

GO ON TO THE NEXT PAGE

Directions: Questions follow each of the passages below. Using only the stated or implied information in each passage and in its introduction, if any, to answer the questions.

Questions 7–20 are based on the following pair of passages.

Passage 1:

Bilingual educators say today that children lose a degree of "individuality" by becoming assimilated into public society. (Bilingual schooling is a program popularized in the seventies, that
(5) decade when middle-class "ethnics" began to resist the process of assimilation—the "American melting pot.") But the bilingualists oversimplify when they scorn the value and necessity of assimilation. They do not seem to realize that a
(10) person is individualized in two ways. So they do not realize that, while one suffers a diminished sense of *private* individuality by being assimilated into public society, such assimilation makes possible the achievement of *public* individuality.
(15) Simplistically again, the bilingualists insist that a student should be reminded of his difference from others in mass society, of his "heritage." But they equate mere separateness with individuality. The fact is that only in private—with intimates—
(20) is separateness from the crowd a prerequisite for individuality; an intimate "tells" me that I am unique, unlike all others, apart from the crowd. Thus it happened for me. Only when I was able to think of myself as an American, no longer an
(25) alien in gringo society, could I seek the rights and opportunities necessary for full public individuality. The social and political advantages I enjoy as a man began on the day I came to believe that my name is indeed *Richard Road-ree-guess*. It
(30) is true that my public society today is often impersonal; in fact, my public society is usually mass society. But despite the anonymity of the crowd, and despite the fact that the individuality I achieve in public is often tenuous—because it
(35) depends on my being one in a crowd—I celebrate the day I acquired my new name. Those middle-class ethnics who scorn assimilation seem to me filled with decadent self-pity, obsessed by the burden of public life. Dangerously, they
(40) romanticize public separateness and trivialize the dilemma of those who are truly socially disadvantaged.

If I rehearse here the changes in my private life after my Americanization, it is finally to
(45) emphasize a public gain. The loss implies the gain. The house I returned to each afternoon was quiet. Intimate sounds no longer greeted me at the door. Inside there were other noises. The telephone rang. Neighborhood kids ran past the
(50) door of the bedroom where I was reading my schoolbooks—covered with brown shopping bag paper. Once I learned the public language, it would never again be easy for me to hear intimate family voices. More and more of my day was
(55) spent hearing words, not sounds. But that may only be a way of saying that on the day I raised my hand in class and spoke loudly to an entire roomful of faces, my childhood started to end.

Passage 2:

In a 1998 *Washington Post* article, a Mexican woman living in Omaha, Nebraska—proud of her Mexican heritage—is quoted as saying, "When my skin turns white and my hair turns
(5) blonde, then I'll be an American." She and her family, like other Mexicans in her neighborhood, are an example of those immigrants who are wary of being assimilated. They don't wholeheartedly reject American culture, of
(10) course; her 11-year-old son is bilingual, is a fan of the San Francisco 49ers, and has a paper route. She herself has become a U.S. citizen. She and her family are here to stay. But she says she doesn't feel like an American. "It is difficult to
(15) adapt to the culture here. In the Hispanic tradition, the family comes first, not money. It's important for our children not to be influenced too much by the *gueros*. I don't want my children to be influenced by immoral things." (*Gueros*
(20) means "blondies," but she uses it in reference to Americans in general.)

This woman and her family are not atypical. The idea of America as a "melting pot" has changed over time because the demographics of
(25) the country have changed. In many communities immigrant populations are transforming American society rather than being transformed by it.

Some sociologists argue that assimilation isn't
(30) always a positive experience—for either society or the immigrants themselves. According to some commentators, assimilation sometimes

GO ON TO THE NEXT PAGE

means "Anglo conformity." Ruben G. Rumbaut, a
sociology professor at Michigan State University,
(35) says, "If assimilation is a learning process, it
involves learning good things and bad things."

In a development referred to as "segmented
assimilation," immigrants follow different paths
into American society. At one end, many follow
(40) the classic American ideal of blending into the
middle class, while at the other end some become
part of an adversarial underclass. In the middle
are those who form "immigrant enclaves"—
living together and maintaining their ethnic
(45) heritage while also adopting many aspects of
mainstream American culture.

7. The author of Passage 1 and of the woman
   described in Passage 2 differ in that

   A. the author of Passage 1 is ashamed of his
      ethnic heritage whereas the woman in
      Passage 2 celebrates hers.

   B. in Passage 1 the author disapproves of
      bilingual education whereas in Passage 2
      the woman is grateful for the opportunities
      it offers.

   C. the author of Passage 1 is well-educated
      while the woman in Passage 2 has a limited
      education.

   D. in Passage 1 the author focuses on
      opportunities that assimilation offers, while
      in Passage 2 the woman focuses on its
      dangers to her values.

   E. the author of Passage 1 is fluent in English
      while the woman in Passage 2 speaks only
      Spanish.

8. In Passage 1, the author's use of the phrase
   "middle-class ethnics" is similar to the woman's
   use of the term *gueros* in Passage 2 because both
   are examples of

   A. name-calling.
   B. generalizations.
   C. ignorance.
   D. exaggeration.
   E. irony.

9. Which of the following best describes a difference
   between the concerns of the author of Passage 1
   and the concerns of the woman in Passage 2?

   A. The author in Passage 1 is concerned with
      bilingual education, while the author of
      Passage 2 is concerned with financial
      security.

   B. In Passage 1, the author is concerned with
      eliminating immigrant communities, and in
      Passage 2 the woman is concerned with
      preserving them.

   C. The author of Passage 1 is concerned with
      a person finding a place in public society,
      while the woman in Passage 2 is concerned
      with maintaining the values of her culture
      and family.

   D. In Passage 1, the author is concerned with
      business success whereas the woman in
      Passage 2 is concerned with spiritual
      growth.

   E. In Passage 1, the author is concerned with
      overcoming the educational disadvantages
      that immigrant children confront, while in
      Passage 2 the woman is concerned with
      overcoming prejudice against her children.

10. In the first paragraph of Passage 1, the author's
    main point is that

    A. bilingual education makes assimilation
       impossible.

    B. *private* individuality is ultimately
       dangerous.

    C. most non-English-speaking people fear the
       dangers of assimilation.

    D. *public* individuality depends on
       assimilation.

    E. bilingual schooling has proved to be
       unsuccessful.

11. According to the author of Passage 1, the
    concept of America as "a melting pot" is

    A. condescending.
    B. unfair.
    C. unpopular with those who resist
       assimilation.
    D. less true today than in the early part of the
       twentieth century.
    E. irrelevant to the majority of immigrants in
       America.

GO ON TO THE NEXT PAGE

12. The author of Passage 1 believes that the "bilingualists" are simplistic because they

   A. associate speaking English with people who are in power.
   B. believe that a person's individuality is based on being separate from the crowd.
   C. are willing to sacrifice a person's success to his maintaining his ethnic heritage.
   D. don't understand the importance of learning English.
   E. regard learning English as too difficult for most children.

13. In Passage 1, the author's attitude toward "middle-class ethnics" can best be described as

   A. indifference.
   B. annoyance.
   C. tolerance.
   D. pity.
   E. ambivalence.

14. In Passage 1, the author describes "public individuality" as all of the following EXCEPT

   A. counterproductive.
   B. presenting opportunities.
   C. tenuous.
   D. offering rights.
   E. impersonal.

15. In the last paragraph of Passage 1, the author describes

   A. how he felt in his family home after he learned English.
   B. his rejection by his family because he was no longer part of their lives.
   C. the frustration of not being able to communicate with his family.
   D. the beginning of his negative feelings about his heritage.
   E. his nostalgic longing for his childhood.

16. In Passage 1, the "loss" referred to in line 45 most directly refers to

   A. "public individuality."
   B. "the anonymity of the crowd."
   C. "decadent self-pity."
   D. "a diminished sense of private individuality."
   E. "social and political advantages."

17. The author of Passage 1 believes that those opposing assimilation (lines 36–42)

   A. believe they should have more power in the public sector.
   B. have ulterior motives in promoting ethnic divisions.
   C. romanticize their Hispanic heritage.
   D. are bitter toward most Anglos.
   E. downplay the plight of the socially and financially disadvantaged.

18. When the woman in Passage 2 says, "When my skin turns white and my hair turns blonde, then I'll be an American," her main point is that

   A. Americans despise immigrants from Mexico.
   B. she will always see herself as Mexican rather than American.
   C. appearance is more important than inner qualities.
   D. being considered an American is overrated.
   E. skin-color determines success in America.

19. Passage 2 uses the term "segmented assimilation" (lines 37–38) to describe

   A. unsuccessful attempts to assimilate.
   B. gradual assimilation.
   C. different routes to assimilation.
   D. rejection of assimilation.
   E. successful assimilation.

20. Compared to the point of view in Passage 1, the point of view in Passage 2 is

   A. defensive.
   B. objective.
   C. argumentative.
   D. subjective.
   E. scholarly.

IF YOU FINISH BEFORE TIME IS CALLED, CHECK YOUR WORK ON THIS SECTION ONLY. DO NOT WORK ON ANY OTHER SECTION IN THE TEST.

STOP

Section 9: Writing—Multiple Choice

Time: 10 minutes
14 Questions

Directions: In this section, choose the best answer for each question and fill in the corresponding circle on the answer sheet.

The following questions test correctness and effective expression. In selecting the answer, pay attention to grammar, diction, sentence structure, and punctuation. In the following questions, part or all of each sentence is underlined. Answer Choice A repeats the underlined portion of the original sentence, while the next four offer alternatives. Choose the answer that best expresses the meaning of the original sentence and at the same time is grammatically correct and stylistically superior. The correct choice should be clear, unambiguous, and concise.

EXAMPLE:

> The forecaster predicted <u>rain and the sky was clear.</u>
>
> **A.** rain and the sky was clear.
> **B.** rain but the sky was clear.
> **C.** rain the sky was clear.
> **D.** rain, but the sky was clear.
> **E.** rain being as the sky was clear.

The correct answer is **D.**

1. The Roman playwright Terrence was born a slave in one of Rome's African colonies and was brought up in a great Roman house <u>where the masters will recognize his talents, educate, and free him.</u>

   A. where the masters will recognize his talents, educate, and free him.
   B. in which he is recognized by the masters for his talents, educated, and becomes a free man.
   C. and the masters, they recognize his talents, give him an education, and then they free him.
   D. where his talents are being recognized by the masters, who will then educate and free him.
   E. where the masters recognized his talents, educated, and freed him.

2. The county is also home to a large community of people whose interest is in agriculture and <u>small-town life, they oppose the plans</u> for a multimillion dollar shopping mall and condominiums on land that was once devoted to citrus orchards.

   A. small-town life, they oppose the plans
   B. small-town life, but they oppose the plans
   C. small-town life; which is the reason that they oppose the plans
   D. small-town life, and therefore they oppose the plans
   E. small-town life, opposing the plans

GO ON TO THE NEXT PAGE

3. <u>A chef whose culinary skills are recognized throughout Europe, dishes created by Giovanni D'Angelo are served to some of the most famous people in the world.</u>

   A. A chef whose culinary skills are recognized throughout Europe, dishes created by Giovanni D'Angelo are served to some of the most famous people in the world.
   B. Dishes are served to some of the most famous people in world, created by Giovanni D'Angelo, a chef whose culinary skills are recognized throughout Europe.
   C. A chef whose culinary skills are recognized throughout Europe, Giovanni D'Angelo creates dishes that are served to some of the most famous people in the world.
   D. Some of the most famous people in the world are served dishes that have been created by a chef whose culinary skills are recognized throughout Europe, Giovanni D'Angelo.
   E. A chef whose culinary skills are recognized throughout Europe, some of the most famous people in the world are served dishes created by Giovanni D'Angelo.

4. According to historians, the most important factor <u>was the link between the rise in population density and the rise in food production.</u>

   A. was the link between the rise in population density and the rise in food production.
   B. were the link between the rise in population density along with the rise in food production.
   C. was the link between the rise in population density and the rising food production.
   D. was the link of rising population density and the rise of food production.
   E. were links between the rises in population density as well as the rises in food production.

5. The promotion, <u>which had went to the man whom we all thought was most deserving,</u> was announced at the Friday staff meeting.

   A. which had went to the man whom we all thought was most deserving,
   B. which had gone to the man who we all thought was most deserving,
   C. which was to go to the man whom we all thought was most deserving,
   D. which would have went to the man who we all thought deserved it most,
   E. which was going to the man who we all thought was the most deserving of it,

6. The reason that the jury members were unable to reach a verdict <u>is because the prosecuting attorney's case was being too weak.</u>

   A. is because the prosecuting attorney's case was being too weak.
   B. is that the prosecuting attorney's case was too weak.
   C. is because the case presented by the prosecuting attorney has been too weak.
   D. is on account of the weakness of the prosecuting attorney's case.
   E. is because the prosecuting attorney's case is too weak.

7. The raw <u>substances, that were available to ancient peoples, were natural materials such as stone, wood, bone, skin, fiber, clay, sand, limestone, and minerals in addition.</u>

   A. substances, that were available to ancient peoples, were natural materials such as stone, wood bone, skin, fiber, clay, sand, limestone, and minerals in addition.
   B. substances, that were available to ancient peoples, were natural materials; among them stone, wood, bone, skin, fiber, clay, sand, limestone, and minerals.
   C. substances, which were available to ancient peoples, were such natural materials as stone, wood, bone, skin, fiber, clay, sand, limestone, and, in addition, minerals.
   D. substances that were available to ancient peoples were; stone, wood, bone, skin, fiber, clay, sand, limestone, and minerals.
   E. substances available to ancient peoples were natural materials such as stone, wood, bone, skin, fiber, clay, sand, limestone, and minerals.

GO ON TO THE NEXT PAGE

8. Some of the changes in the English language since Shakespeare's <u>time, they are obvious, like for example</u> the decline of *thee* and *thou*.

    A. time, they are obvious, like for example

    B. time are obvious, such as for example

    C. time are obvious, such as

    D. time seem to be obvious, such as the example of

    E. time are obvious. For example,

9. English can be a difficult language to spell correctly, <u>although some people contend that computer programs have eliminated the need for teaching spelling at school.</u>

    A. although some people contend that computer programs have eliminated the need for teaching spelling at school.

    B. and some people contend that computer programs which eliminate the need for teaching spelling at school.

    C. although some people, who contend that it is no longer necessary to teach spelling at school, and say that computer programs will take care of the problem.

    D. although some people will have contended that computer programs have eliminated the need for teaching spelling at school.

    E. although there are those people, who contend that it is no longer necessary to teach spelling at school, because of the existence of computer programs.

10. During the trip to Europe, the group <u>expects to visit the wine country in France, to dine out in Paris, cruise along the Rhine, swimming in the Adriatic, and skiing the Alps.</u>

    A. expects to visit the wine country in France, to dine out in Paris, cruise along the Rhine, swimming in the Adriatic, and skiing the Alps.

    B. expects to visit the wine country in France, dine out in Paris, cruise along the Rhine, swim in the Adriatic, and ski the Alps.

    C. expect to visit the wine country in France, to dine out in Paris, to cruise along the Rhine, to swim in the Adriatic, and, of course, skiing the Alps.

    D. expect to visit the wine country in France, dining out in Paris, cruising along the Rhine, swimming in the Adriatic, and skiing the Alps.

    E. expects to visit the wine country in France, to dine out in Paris, and then to cruise along the Rhine, and swimming in the Adriatic, and finally to ski in the Alps.

11. John Milton, the seventeenth-century poet, is probably most famous for his poem *Paradise Lost*<u>, and writing also many excellent prose pieces and lyrics.</u>

    A. , and writing also many excellent prose pieces and lyrics.

    B. , and he also was writing many excellent prose pieces and lyrics.

    C. , and he, in addition, is famous for having wrote his excellent prose pieces and lyrics.

    D. , although he also wrote many excellent prose pieces and lyrics.

    E. , however, he also wrote many excellent prose pieces and lyrics.

GO ON TO THE NEXT PAGE

12. Citing the ongoing controversy between those who wanted the new arena and those who didn't, it was decided by the council to postpone a vote until more facts could be presented.

   A. Citing the ongoing controversy between those who wanted the new arena and those who didn't, it was decided by the council to postpone a vote until more facts could be presented.

   B. It was decided by the council to postpone a vote until more facts could be presented because of the ongoing controversy between those who wanted the new arena and those who didn't.

   C. Citing the ongoing controversy between those who wanted the new arena and those who didn't, the council decided to postpone a vote until more facts could be presented.

   D. Citing the ongoing controversy, the council decided, between those who wanted the new arena and those who didn't, to postpone the vote until more facts could be presented.

   E. The council decided to postpone a vote until more facts could be presented, sighting the controversy between those who wanted it and those who didn't.

13. The experiments conducted by the scientists neither proved nor did they disprove the theory which had been set forth in Bingham's paper.

   A. neither proved nor did they disprove the theory which had been set forth in Bingham's paper.

   B. neither proved nor had they disproved the theory, which Bingham set forth is his paper.

   C. neither did they prove nor were they disproving the theory which Bingham set forth in his paper.

   D. neither proved nor disproved the theory set forth in Bingham's paper.

   E. neither is proving nor are they disproving Bingham's theory, which he set forth in his paper.

14. Dr. Colliers invited us students to attend the lecture he was giving to the faculty next Friday, regardless of whether or not we planned to continue with our studies.

   A. invited us students to attend the lecture he was giving to the faculty next Friday, regardless of whether

   B. invited we students to attend the lecture, that he was giving to the faculty next Friday, irregardless of whether

   C. invited us students to attend the lecture which he was giving to the faculty next Friday irregardless of whether

   D. invited we students to attend the lecture he was to give the faculty next Friday, irregardless of whether

   E. invited us students to attend his lecture to the faculty next Friday, regardless of whether

IF YOU FINISH BEFORE TIME IS CALLED, CHECK YOUR WORK ON THIS SECTION ONLY. DO NOT WORK ON ANY OTHER SECTION IN THE TEST.

Scoring Practice Exam 1

Answer Key for Practice Exam 1

Section 2: Mathematics

1. B	6. B	11. D	16. E
2. C	7. B	12. A	17. D
3. C	8. C	13. B	18. D
4. A	9. E	14. B	19. E
5. D	10. D	15. C	20. A

Section 3: Critical Reading

1. B	8. E	15. B	22. A
2. C	9. C	16. A	23. D
3. A	10. D	17. C	24. C
4. B	11. B	18. B	25. D
5. C	12. A	19. A	
6. B	13. C	20. B	
7. A	14. C	21. E	

Section 4: Mathematics

1. E	6. C	11. 15	16. 81
2. A	7. C	12. $\frac{5}{18}$	17. 8.33
3. D	8. B	13. 20	18. 395
4. C	9. $\frac{3}{2}$ or 1.5	14. 65	
5. D	10. 9	15. 24	

Section 5: Writing—Multiple Choice

1. C	10. C	19. E	28. D
2. D	11. B	20. E	29. A
3. B	12. B	21. C	30. D
4. D	13. D	22. D	31. C
5. E	14. C	23. E	32. A
6. E	15. B	24. B	33. D
7. E	16. C	25. B	34. C
8. C	17. B	26. A	35. D
9. A	18. C	27. D	

Section 6: Critical Reading

1. A	7. C	13. C	19. E
2. A	8. B	14. D	20. A
3. B	9. C	15. A	21. D
4. C	10. D	16. E	22. B
5. E	11. A	17. C	23. A
6. D	12. C	18. D	24. C

Section 7: Mathematics

1. A	5. A	9. E	13. D
2. D	6. D	10. C	14. A
3. B	7. C	11. E	15. B
4. E	8. D	12. C	16. B

Section 8: Critical Reading

1. B	6. D	11. C	16. D
2. A	7. D	12. B	17. E
3. C	8. B	13. B	18. B
4. A	9. C	14. A	19. C
5. B	10. D	15. A	20. B

Section 9: Writing—Multiple Choice

1. E	5. B	9. A	13. D
2. D	6. B	10. B	14. E
3. C	7. E	11. D	
4. A	8. C	12. C	

Charting and Analyzing Your Exam Results

The first step in analyzing your results is to chart your answers. Use the charts on the following pages to identify your strengths and areas that need improvement. Complete the process of evaluating your essays and analyzing problems in each area. Reevaluate your results as you look for trends in the types of errors (repeated errors), and look for low scores in *specific* topic areas. This reexamination and analysis is a tremendous asset to help you maximize your best-possible score. The answers and explanations following these charts will help you solve these types of problems in the future.

Reviewing the Essay

Refer to the sample essay on page 304 as a reference guide. Have an English teacher, tutor, or someone else with good writing skills read and evaluate your essay using the Essay Checklist below. Have your reader evaluate the complete essay as good, average, or marginal. Note that your paper would actually be scored from 1 to 6 by two trained readers (actual total score 2–12). Since you are trying only for a rough approximation, a strong, average, or weak overall evaluation will give you a general feeling for your score range.

Essay Checklist

Questions	Strong Response Score 5 or 6	Average Response Score 3 or 4	Weak Response Score 1 or 2
1. Does the essay focus on the topic and respond to the assigned task?			
2. Is the essay organized and well developed?			
3. Does the essay use specific supporting details and examples?			
4. Does the writing use correct grammar, usage, punctuation, and spelling?			
5. Is the handwriting legible?			

Critical Reading Analysis Sheet

Section 3	Possible	Completed	Right	Wrong
Sentence Completions	8			
Paired Reading Passages	5			
Long Reading Passage	12			
Section 3 Subtotal	**25**			
Section 6	**Possible**	**Completed**	**Right**	**Wrong**
Sentence Completions	5			
Short Reading Passages	4			
Long Reading Passages	15			
Section 6 Subtotal	**24**			
Section 8	**Possible**	**Completed**	**Right**	**Wrong**
Sentence Completions	6			
Paired Passages	14			
Section 8 Subtotal	**20**			
Overall Critical Reading Totals	**69**			

Note: Only 3 Critical Reading sections (approximately 70 questions) count toward your actual score on the SAT.

Mathematics Analysis Sheet

Section 2	Possible	Completed	Right	Wrong
Multiple Choice	20			
Section 2 Subtotal	**20**			
Section 4	**Possible**	**Completed**	**Right**	**Wrong**
Multiple Choice	8			
Grid-Ins	10			
Section 4 Subtotal	**18**			
Section 7	**Possible**	**Completed**	**Right**	**Wrong**
Multiple Choice	16			
Section 7 Subtotal	**16**			
Overall Math Totals	**54**			

Writing—Multiple-Choice Analysis Sheet				
Section 5	**Possible**	**Completed**	**Right**	**Wrong**
Improving Sentences	11			
Identifying Sentence Errors	18			
Improving Paragraphs	6			
Section 5 Subtotal	**35**			
Section 9	**Possible**	**Completed**	**Right**	**Wrong**
Improving Sentences	14			
Section 9 Subtotal	**14**			
Overall Writing—Multiple-Choice Totals	**49**			

Analysis/Tally Sheet for Problems Missed

One of the most important parts of exam preparation is analyzing why you missed a problem so that you can reduce the number of mistakes. Now that you have taken the practice exam and checked your answers, carefully tally your mistakes by marking them in the proper column

Reason for Mistakes						
	Total Possible	**Total Missed**	**Simple Mistake**	**Misread Problem**	**Lack of Knowledge**	**Lack of Time**
Section 3: Critical Reading	25					
Section 6: Critical Reading	24					
Section 8: Critical Reading	20					
Subtotal	**69**					
Section 2: Mathematics	20					
Section 4: Mathematics	18					
Section 7: Mathematics	16					
Subtotal	**54**					
Section 5: Writing—Multiple-Choice	35					
Section 9: Writing—Multiple-Choice	14					
Subtotal	**49**					
Total Critical Reading, Math, and Writing	**172**					

Reviewing the preceding data should help you determine why you are missing certain problems. Now that you've pinpointed the type of error, compare it to other practice tests to spot other common mistakes.

Practice Exam 1: Answers and Explanations

Section 1: Writing—Essay

"Work experience is the best teacher," say many sociologists. With this in mind, some parents encourage their high school-age children to get an after-school or weekend job. Other parents cite the importance of getting good grades to discourage their high school-age children from getting an after-school or weekend job.

Assignment: Do you agree with the parents who are for or against having a job while in school? Use an example or examples from your reading, personal experiences, or observations to write an essay to support your position.

Sample Essay

Some parents want their high school aged children to work part-time, while other parents prefer their children not to work and instead concentrate on studies. I agree with the parents who want their children to get good grades, although I believe that after school work, sports or other activities are helpful in establishing good study habits and creating a well-rounded, successful student.

Life is not all study any more than it is all play. Students need to learn how to manage their time wisely. They need to learn the organizational skills necessary to perform many different tasks in a timely manner. Work, sports, and other activities are necessary to provide a break from continual studying. Activities also provide real-life experiences that are essential to practical educational opportunities, and, therefore, can improve grades.

Since my older brother was responsible for paying the tuition for his own college education, it was necessary for him to work part-time throughout his college years. He had to organize his employment hours around class and study hours. He found a job in a grocery store to provide him the greatest flexibility. He organized his time so that he was able to work, attend classes, and maintain a high grade point average.

He told me that many of his college classmates came from economically wealthier backgrounds. Many of his classmates didn't have to work and were able to concentrate full-time on their studies and their grades. Most of his college friends had time for frequent study breaks, to meet others for coffee or beers, but many of them didn't organize their time well. Some did quite poorly in school even though their parents did all they could to help them focus on grades.

From my own observations and experience I do not feel that after-school or weekend jobs obstruct a student from getting good grades. I feel that these activities can be more helpful than harmful by providing the student with the opportunity to organize their life activities. Whether in high school or in college, a student should be encouraged to engage in many activities and to organize their time so they can succeed in all they do. I plan to get a part-time job during my senior year in high school.

Note: Since the question is "what is your opinion," it is quite permissible to write in the first person (I) and give your opinion without saying "in my opinion" or "I believe" or "my viewpoint is." Be personal and invent supporting examples!

Section 2: Mathematics

1. **B.** Since 4 markers cost $6.40, the cost for one marker is $6.40 ÷ 4 = $1.60. If 10 or more markers are purchased, the cost per marker for the whole order decreases to $1.60 − $0.25 = $1.35. The 12 markers will cost $12 \times \$1.35 = \$16.20$.

2. **C.** The only equation that yields a true statement for all 4 ordered pairs is $2x + 3y = 12$.

3. C. If y is inversely proportional to x, then $y = \dfrac{k}{x}$ where k is a constant.

Since $y = 12$ when $x = 5$,

$$12 = \frac{k}{5}$$

$$12 \cdot 5 = \frac{k}{5} \cdot 5$$

$$60 = k \text{ and } y = \frac{60}{x}$$

If $y = 15$,

$$15 = \frac{60}{x}$$

$$15 \cdot x = \frac{60}{x} \cdot x$$

$$15x = 60$$

$$\frac{15x}{15} = \frac{60}{15}$$

$$x = 4$$

4. A.

$$\text{Since } 3a + c = 5b$$

$$3a + 5b + c = (3a + c) + 5b$$

$$= 5b + 5b$$

$$= 10b$$

$$\text{Since } 3a + 5b + c = 80$$

$$10b = 80$$

$$\frac{10b}{10} = \frac{80}{10}$$

$$b = 8$$

5. D.

$$\text{If } \frac{z-2}{z+4} = \frac{13}{15}, \text{ cross-multiplying yields}$$

$$15(z-2) = 13(z+4)$$

$$15z - 30 = 13z + 52$$

$$15z - 30 - 13z = 13z + 52 - 13z$$

$$2z - 30 = 52$$

$$2z - 30 + 30 = 52 + 30$$

$$2z = 82$$

$$\frac{2z}{2} = \frac{82}{2}$$

$$z = 41$$

6. B.

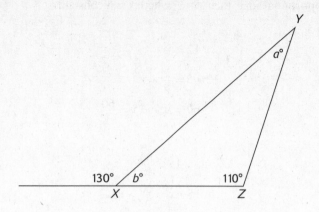

(Note: Figure not drawn to scale.)

In the figure $b + 130 = 180$ since the angles are supplementary, and

$$b + 130 - 130 = 180 - 130$$

$$b = 50$$

Since the sum of the interior angles in any triangle is $180°$,

$$a + b + 110 = 180$$
$$a + 50 + 110 = 180$$
$$a + 160 = 180$$
$$a + 160 - 160 = 180 - 160$$
$$a = 20$$

7. B. Since the average of three numbers is determined by dividing their sum by 3,

$$\frac{x + 2x + 1 + 2x + 7}{3} = 16$$

$$\frac{5x + 8}{3} = 16$$

$$\frac{5x + 8}{3} \cdot 3 = 16 \cdot 3$$

$$5x + 8 = 48$$

$$5x + 8 - 8 = 48 - 8$$

$$5x = 40$$

$$\frac{5x}{5} = \frac{40}{5}$$

$$x = 8$$

8. C. The perimeter of the square is 4 times the perimeter of the triangle, or $4 \cdot 13 = 52$. Since all 4 sides of the square are equal in length, one side has a length of $52 \div 4 = 13$.

9. E.

$$\text{Since } y^2 + 5y + k = y^2 - 3$$
$$y^2 + 5y + k - y^2 = y^2 - 3 - y^2$$
$$5y + k = -3$$
$$5y + k - 5y = -3 - 5y$$
$$k = -3 - 5y \text{ or } -5y - 3$$

10. **D.** For any integer to be a multiple of 3, but not a multiple of 6, it cannot be an even integer. The integers between 10 and 50 that are not even, but are divisible by 3 are 15, 21, 27, 33, 39, and 45.

11. **D.** The smallest positive integer x that makes the expression an integer, must make $\sqrt{\dfrac{6x}{5}}$ a perfect square number. When $x = 30$, the answer appears as follows:

$$\sqrt{\frac{6x}{5}} = \sqrt{\frac{6 \cdot 30}{5}} = \sqrt{36} = 6$$

12. **A.** The square of an odd integer is another odd integer and m^2 is odd since m is odd. The other answer choices will all be even integers.

13. **B.**

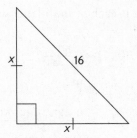

Since the hypotenuse of an isosceles right triangle is equal to $\sqrt{2}$ times the length of one leg,

$$x\sqrt{2} = 16$$
$$\frac{x\sqrt{2}}{\sqrt{2}} = \frac{16}{\sqrt{2}}$$
$$x = \frac{16}{\sqrt{2}} \cdot \frac{\sqrt{2}}{\sqrt{2}} = \frac{16\sqrt{2}}{2} = 8\sqrt{2}$$

The area of the triangle is

$$A = \frac{1}{2}bh$$
$$= \frac{1}{2}\left(8\sqrt{2}\right)\left(8\sqrt{2}\right)$$
$$= \frac{1}{2}\left(64\sqrt{4}\right)$$
$$= 64$$

14. **B.** The graph of $y = x^2 + 5x - 24$ will intersect the x-axis when $y = 0$.

$$x^2 + 5x - 24 = 0$$
$$(x+8)(x-3) = 0$$

$$x + 8 = 0 \qquad\qquad x - 3 = 0$$
$$x + 8 - 8 = 0 - 8 \qquad\qquad x - 3 + 3 = 0 + 3$$
$$x = -8 \qquad \text{or} \qquad x = 3$$

15. **C.** The graph of $f(x - c)$, where $c > 0$, is the same as the graph of $f(x)$ shifted horizontally c units to the right. Hence,

$$g(x) = f(x - 5)$$
$$g(x) = (x - 5)^2$$

16. E. Since $16 = 2^4$ and $32 = 2^5$,

$$16^{x+1} = 32^{x-3}$$
$$\left(2^4\right)^{x+1} = \left(2^5\right)^{x-3}$$
$$4(x+1) = 5(x-3)$$
$$4x + 4 = 5x - 15$$
$$4x + 4 - 4x = 5x - 15 - 4x$$
$$4 = x - 15$$
$$4 + 15 = x - 15 + 15$$
$$x = 19$$

17. D. Since the order of the letters matter in each of the 4-letter words, this is a permutation of 9 letters taken 4 at a time.

$$P(9,4) = \frac{9!}{(9-4)!}$$
$$= \frac{9!}{5!}$$
$$= \frac{9 \cdot 8 \cdot 7 \cdot 6 \cdot 5!}{5!}$$
$$= 9 \cdot 8 \cdot 7 \cdot 6$$
$$= 3024$$

18. D. Since $x^2 + bx + 18 = (x + 1)(x + c)$, $1 \times c = 18$ and $c = 18$.

Hence $x^2 + bx + 18 = (x + 1)(x + 18)$

$$= x^2 + 19x + 18$$

19. E. The triangle inequality property states that for any triangle, the sum of any two sides must be greater than the third side of the triangle.

For the triangle given with sides of length 5, 12, and z,

$$12 - 5 < z < 12 + 5$$
$$7 < z < 17$$

20. A. Since a circle is an arc with a measure of 360°, $\frac{1}{5}$ of a circle is $\frac{1}{5}(360°) = 72°$, and $\frac{1}{8}$ of a circle is $\frac{1}{8}(360°) = 45°$, the difference is $72° - 45° = 27°$.

Section 3: Critical Reading

Sentence Completions

1. **B.** Innovative means "new," and an attentive audience would be expecting to hear new approaches. For the second word, "but," "subjected," and "well-worn" indicate that the audience was disappointed, and therefore the best choice is "platitudes," which are stale, trite remarks. None of the other choices sets up this contrast.

2. **C.** One of the meanings of "maverick" is an independent individual who doesn't go along with the group. The word "although" suggests the governor is staying in line when it comes to the inauguration; "protocol" (meaning a set of conventions) is therefore the best choice for the second word. Of the other answers, D might seem a good choice for the first word, but "composure" isn't as appropriate for the second.

3. **A.** "Amenities" are things conducive to comfort or enjoyment. This hotel has been chosen because of its location and low rates, despite offering few other advantages. The word "plaudits" means enthusiastic approval, which does not fit the context. The other choices are also clearly wrong, given the rest of the sentence.

4. **B.** "Apathy," meaning a lack of interest, cannot be "between" the groups. Because "enmity" means hatred or mutual ill-will between people, it would probably be impossible for them to carry on a fruitful discussion. Often the second word can be determined based on the first word's meaning, or vice versa.

5. **C.** "Commensurate" means equal. The context indicates that Elizabeth is suing her employer, who as a result is going to assign her to a position in line with her education and skills. D doesn't make sense, and her employer wouldn't provide a position superior to her education and skills, Choice A. B and E can be eliminated based on the second word.

6. **B.** A "diatribe" is a bitter and abusive speech and "pernicious" means destructive. Because the context is the commentator insisting that she didn't intend to affect the young man's career, B is a better choice than D ("felicitous" means pleasant or delightful). The other choices do not fit with "off-camera."

7. **A.** "Equivocation" means avoiding commitment to what one is saying. Since the context is that the listeners are annoyed at the spokesperson, this is a better choice than B, C, D, or E.

8. **E.** "Little" and "because he was an honest, good-hearted man" are the clues here. "Little" doesn't fit with A (a harangue is a ranting speech); C and D are not compatible with the idea that Mr. Doolittle was an honest man.

Paired Passages

9. **C.** In Passage 1, see lines 17–24 and 52–60. In Passage 2, see lines 31–33. Both passages make the point that after the wars, women returned to their traditional roles. A and B aren't supported in either passage, and Passage 2 indicates that women didn't play a minor role (D). E is not a point made in either passage.

10. **D.** The author of Passage 1 makes several general statements about the role of women but, unlike Passage 2, specific examples aren't given. Passage 2 presents several examples: lines 6–9, 14–16, 23–30, 46–49, and 50–58, Choices A, C, and E are simply inaccurate. B is also inaccurate; the tone of Passage 2 does not indicate that the author is "poking fun" at women in the examples presented, and the author of Passage 1 doesn't "elevate" women.

11. **B.** See lines 15–23. Although the passage states that male politicians adopted "a powerful new ideology of republican motherhood" in which women's work was seen as rearing good citizens, E, the effect on women themselves was to engage them in political struggles. There is no evidence for A or D, nor is C suggested by the passage (nor would it be likely during the Revolutionary War).

12. **A.** "Homemaker" is a euphemism for "housekeeper," and its intention is to elevate a woman's domestic role. It does not suggest that women "were ashamed," E. There is no evidence in the passage for B, nor does the use of the term indicate that women are being "unfavorably" compared, D, or "ridiculed," C.

13. **C.** The only point that is not made is that women worked for less pay (though this may well have been true). The passage makes all of the other points. Be sure to read questions carefully; this one asks for all the points made "EXCEPT."

Long Reading Passage

14. **C.** See lines 6–9. A and B, while perhaps true, are not assumptions made in the paragraph. Remember to choose an answer that is supported by the passage, not necessarily an answer that may be true. Although in lines 10–11 the passage refers to the West's "stunning works of technological innovation," it does not conclude that this shows intellectual superiority, D. E is irrelevant to the passage.

15. **B.** Although the key indicator of global voices being silenced is the loss of languages, it is the loss of cultural diversity itself that the author is mainly concerned with. Answer C is the second-best choice because the third paragraph of the passage suggests that people don't think the loss of cultural diversity is significant, which suggests indifference. None of the other choices is addressed.

16. **A.** See lines 28–29. B and D are simply irrelevant in the passage. While C and E are addressed, neither is the antecedent of "Each one."

17. **C.** Although the passage does not specifically compare the loss of languages to the loss of animal species, in lines 29–35 it describes the death of a language as similar to the end of a species: When the last member dies, the species is extinct. Note the word "endangered."

18. **B.** The question in the third paragraph is basically, "Why does it matter that cultures are lost?" The rest of the passage gives examples of why the author sees all cultures as important to humanity as a whole. A is the second-best answer, but presenting this opposing point of view is not the purpose of the paragraph. Rather, it introduces the author's specific examples of the main point. C is a minor point. D is irrelevant, and E is inaccurate.

19. **A.** A diaspora in not a "rejection" (B), nor an "expulsion" (C), nor a "discovery" (D) nor a "voyage" (E).

20. **B.** The passage refers to the Polynesians as paying attention to natural cues, such as the location of stars and ocean currents. D and E are subpoints of B. A and C are not addressed in the passage.

21. **E.** The people of Barasana, according to the passage, see all the elements of the natural world as connected, and as a result, they developed land-management policies that are a model today. B, C, and D are all indicated in the passage, but the question asks for the reason the Barasana people are especially important in the modern world. A is not addressed in the passage.

22. **A.** See lines 73–77. D is the second-best answer, although "love of nature" is not indicated. B, C, and E, while they may or may not be true, are not covered in the passage.

23. **D.** Throughout the passage, the author argues that all cultures contribute to humanity. A and B are secondary points. While the passage stresses the importance of keeping languages alive, C, it does not say it is the key to survival. E is irrelevant to the passage.

24. **C.** Nothing in these lines supports A, B, or E. It is the Tibetan Buddhists' science of the mind that is cited in the passage as a meaningful contribution to humanity. D is mentioned, but the author is making a point, not expressing disapproval.

25. **D.** In context, D is the only definition that makes sense. E means descent in a line from a common ancestor.

Section 4: Mathematics

1. **E.** The jet traveled three times as far, or $3 \cdot 800 = 2400$ miles in half the time, or $\frac{1}{2} \cdot 8 = 4$ hours. Since

$$d = r \cdot t$$

$$r = \frac{d}{t}$$

$$r = \frac{2400 \text{ miles}}{4 \text{ hours}}$$

$$r = 600 \text{ miles per hour}$$

2. **A.** Since A is the set of prime numbers between 20 and 40, $A = \{23, 29, 31, 37\}$ and B is the set of odd numbers between 20 and 40, $B = \{21, 23, 25, 27, 29, 31, 33, 35, 37, 39\}$, the sets have 4 numbers in common: 23, 29, 31, and 37.

3. **D.**
$$(x+y)(3x-2y) = 3x^2 - 2xy + 3xy - 2y^2$$
$$= 3x^2 + xy - 2y^2$$

Since $xy = -8$, and $3x^2 - 2y^2 = 12$, then

$$3x^2 + xy - 2y^2 = 3x^2 - 2y^2 + xy$$
$$= 12 - 8$$
$$= 4$$

4. **C.** If $\frac{a+5}{4}$ is an integer, $a + 5$ is divisible by 4 and $a + 5$ must be an even integer. Since $a + 5$ is an even integer, a must be an odd integer.

5. **D.** Since there are 3 red cards selected from a total of 8 red cards in any order, this is a combination of 8 red cards taken 3 at a time.

$$C(8,3) = \frac{8!}{3!(8-3)!}$$
$$= \frac{8!}{3! \cdot 5!}$$
$$= \frac{8 \cdot 7 \cdot 6 \cdot 5!}{3! \cdot 5!}$$
$$= \frac{8 \cdot 7 \cdot 6}{3 \cdot 2 \cdot 1}$$
$$= 8 \cdot 7$$
$$= 56$$

6. **C.** Let x = one side of the rectangle and $2x + 5$ = the longer side of the rectangle.

The perimeter P of the rectangle is:

$P = x + (2x + 5) + x + (2x + 5)$

$P = 6x + 10$

7. **C.**

$$\frac{10^{15} - 10^{16}}{10^{15}} = \frac{10^{15}(1 - 10)}{10^{15}}$$
$$= 1 - 10$$
$$= -9$$

8. **B.** Twice the sum of $5y$ and $3 = 2(5y + 3)$

The product of y and $-3 = -3y$

$2(5y + 3) = -3y$

$10y + 6 = -3y$

Grid-in Questions

9. $\frac{3}{2}$ or 1.5.

$$5 \cdot (4x + 2y = 5)$$
$$\underline{-4 \cdot (5x - 3y = -2)}$$
$$20x + 10y = 25$$
$$\underline{-20x + 12y = 8}$$
$$22y = 33$$
$$\frac{22y}{22} = \frac{33}{22}$$
$$y = \frac{3}{2} \text{ or } 1.5$$

10. **9.**

$$5^x + 5^x + 5^x + 5^x + 5^x = 5^{10}$$
$$5(5^x) = 5^{10}$$
$$5^{x+1} = 5^{10}$$
$$x + 1 = 10$$
$$x + 1 - 1 = 10 - 1$$
$$x = 9$$

11. 15.

Since $a \otimes b = a^2 + b^2 - b,$

$$
\begin{aligned}
1 \otimes 2 &= 1^2 + 2^2 - 2 \\
&= 1 + 4 - 2 \\
&= 3
\end{aligned}
$$

$$
\begin{aligned}
\text{And, } 1 \otimes 2 \otimes 3 &= 3 \otimes 3 \\
&= 3^2 + 3^2 - 3 \\
&= 9 + 9 - 3 \\
&= 15
\end{aligned}
$$

12. $\dfrac{5}{18}$.

Since $x = \dfrac{1}{3} y$ and $y = \dfrac{5}{6} z,$

$$
\begin{aligned}
x &= \frac{1}{3}\left(\frac{5}{6} z\right) \\
x &= \frac{5}{18} z
\end{aligned}
$$

13. 20.

$$
\begin{aligned}
5(z + 7) &= 9(z - 5) \\
5z + 35 &= 9z - 45 \\
5z + 35 - 9z &= 9z - 45 - 9z \\
-4z + 35 &= -45 \\
-4z + 35 - 35 &= -45 - 35 \\
-4z &= -80 \\
\frac{-4z}{-4} &= \frac{-80}{-4} \\
z &= 20
\end{aligned}
$$

14. 65.

Since $\angle WZY$ and $\angle YZT$ are supplementary angles,

$$
\begin{aligned}
b + 85 &= 180 \\
b + 85 - 85 &= 180 - 85 \\
b &= 95
\end{aligned}
$$

Since the sum of the interior angles of a quadrilateral is 360°,

$$
\begin{aligned}
a + b + 120 + 80 &= 360 \\
a + 95 + 120 + 80 &= 360 \\
a + 295 &= 360 \\
a + 295 - 295 &= 360 - 295 \\
a &= 65
\end{aligned}
$$

15. 24.

Let x = the number of male students

and $64 - x$ = the number of female students.

The ratio of female students to male students is

$$\frac{64 - x}{x} = \frac{5}{3}$$
$$3(64 - x) = 5x$$
$$192 - 3x = 5x$$
$$192 - 3x + 3x = 5x + 3x$$
$$192 = 8x$$
$$\frac{192}{8} = \frac{8x}{8}$$
$$x = 24$$

16. 81.

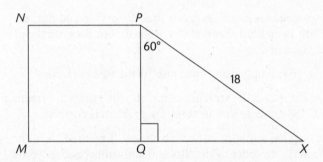

Since $\angle PQX$ is a right angle and $\triangle PQX$ is a right triangle with one acute angle of 60°, the measure of the other acute angle $\angle X$ must be 30°. In a 30° – 60° – 90° right triangle, the side opposite the 30° angle, $\overline{PQ}$ is $\frac{1}{2}$ the length of the hypotenuse $\overline{PX}$. Hence, $PQ = \frac{1}{2}(18) = 9$. $\overline{PQ}$ is also one of the four equal sides of the square. The area A of the square is

$A = S^2$

$A = 9^2$

$A = 81$

17. 8.33.

Let x = some number and

$$0.6x = 5$$
$$\frac{0.6x}{0.6} = \frac{5}{0.6}$$
$$x = \frac{50}{6}$$
$$x = 8.3$$

Since this is a grid-in question, the most accurate answer is $x = 8.33$

18. **395.**

Let $S_n = n$th term of the sequence.

$S_1 = 1$

$S_2 = 3$

$S_3 = 1 \cdot 3 - 1 = 3 - 1 = 2$

$S_4 = 2 \cdot 3 - 1 = 6 - 1 = 5$

$S_5 = 5 \cdot 2 - 1 = 10 - 1 = 9$

$S_6 = 9 \cdot 5 - 1 = 45 - 1 = 44$

$S_7 = 44 \cdot 9 - 1 = 396 - 1 = 395$

Section 5: Writing—Multiple Choice

Improving Sentences

1. **C.** Choice A has a misplaced modifier; it suggests that Robert's grandmother is a teenager. B doesn't correct the problem. Both D and E do correct the problem, but they use the passive voice, which is not as good here as the active voice in C.

2. **D.** A, B, C, and E are wordy; simply using "because" is the best correction.

3. **B.** B is the only choice that makes the sentence complete; the others are fragments. By omitting "who" and thus making "designed" the sentence's main verb, the problem is corrected.

4. **D.** The problem in the original sentence is the verb tenses. "Engulfed" is in the past tense and "run" should consistent with that ("ran"). "In order to" in choice B adds unnecessary words.

5. **E.** The first part of the sentence is imperative; it gives a command or makes a request. The second part of the sentence is not parallel to the first. E is the only choice that corrects the problem and avoids wordiness.

6. **E.** The solution given in Choice E removes the wordiness of the original sentence—a task that is not accomplished by any of the other choices. "Cause of" and "due to the fact" add nothing to the meaning. E makes the point succinctly.

7. **E.** "Between" should be followed by the objective pronoun "me," not the subjective "I." ("Between you and I" is a common mistake made in writing and speech.) B is incorrect; "bidden" is not the past tense of "bid." D is also inaccurate: "Me" should be the second element, not the first; the verb tense is also incorrect.

8. **C.** In the original sentence, the antecedent of the pronoun "they" is unclear. Does the pronoun refer to Matthew and Suzanne or to the students? C changes the structure of the sentence, avoids wordiness, and corrects the problem.

9. **A.** The sentence is best as it is. B is a misuse of the semicolon, C adds an unnecessary word, D is the wrong form and the wrong number of the verb, and E creates a sentence fragment.

10. **C.** The underlined elements in this sentence should be parallel in construction. When ideas in a sentence are parallel, as they are in this sentence, they should be expressed in the same grammatical form: the *presence,* the *popularity,* and the *economy.* A, B, and D are not parallel, and E is wordy.

11. **B.** The problem in the original sentence is a misplaced phrase, which makes it appear that the new wind machines are interested in alternative forms of energy. That problem is not corrected in Choice E. B corrects the problem and also avoids the passive voice. C is a fragment, and the pronoun antecedent in D is unclear.

Identifying Sentence Errors

12. **B.** "Him" should be "he," the subjective form of the pronoun, because it is part of the subject of the sentence. The participial phrase ("Riding . . .") is not misplaced (A).

13. **D.** For consistency, the verb should be in the past tense.

14. **C.** Again, verb tenses should be consistent: "blamed" and "believed."

15. **B.** The correct construction is "neither . . . nor."

16. **C.** The past participle of the verb ("had been") is appropriate here to match the past participle "hadn't been discussed." "Was" (D), the singular form of the verb, is correct because its subject ("one topic") is singular even though the object ("travel arrangements") is plural.

17. **B.** The correct construction is "shouldn't have." The possessive form "its," D, is correct; there is no apostrophe.

18. **C.** As noted in the previous question, the possessive of "it" is "its."

19. **E.** "No error" is the best choice. The infinitive forms of the verbs in the sentence are correct.

20. **E.** "No error" is the best choice. "Has proved" is the correct form of the verb.

21. **C.** Parallel elements in a sentence should be written in parallel form. "Being consistent" should be "consistency" to parallel "oversight." A, the adverbial form of "flat," correctly modifies "stated."

22. **D.** "Using" should be "which use." "Was written" (B) is the correct tense of the verb, and A ("protagonists") is the correct word choice.

23. **E.** "No error" is the best choice. The construction of "not only for . . . but also for" is parallel, "generally" is correctly used (C), and "and which" (D) correctly introduces the dependent clause that follows.

24. **B.** An adverbial form ("well") rather than "good" is needed because the word modifies a verb ("did").

25. **B.** The idiom is "with which," not "in which."

26. **A.** "Could of" is incorrect and should be "could have." B and C are both correct. The pronoun "it" (D) is singular and correctly refers to the singular noun "group." (Words such as "group" and "team" are called *collective nouns* and usually take a singular verb and pronoun.)

27. **D.** The antecedent of the pronouns is "children" and therefore requires a plural pronoun. B ("affected") is the correct verb here. "Effected" and "affected" are frequently confused.

28. **D.** "Without hardly" is a double negative; the correct phrase is "with hardly." A is correct; "whom" is the object of "admired." B is also correct because "who" is the subject of "had expected."

29. **A.** "Lie" and "lay" are frequently confused. Here, the word should be "lying" because the verb does not take an object; "laying" is used when the verb does take an object, as in, for example, "The team members were laying their books on the grass." C ("who") is correct in the sentence; it is the subject of "lost."

Improving Paragraphs

30. **D.** This is the most succinct version of the underlined section of the sentence. In B, "in addition" and "also" mean the same thing. The phrase "in fact" (A, C, and E) adds nothing to the meaning of the sentence.

31. **C.** Using the dependent clause "which led him to study . . . " is the most effective way to combine the two sentences. A is wordy, B is awkward, and D and E are not correct sentences.

32. **A.** Choice A is both grammatically correct and the most succinct version of the sentence. The other choices are not as appropriate.

33. **D.** A, B, C, and E are all wordy. In most cases, the most direct, succinct expression is the correct one as long as the original meaning isn't lost.

34. **C.** Because sentence 4 concerns an award Franklin won for his experiments with electricity, the most logical place for it is after sentence 6, which briefly describes those experiments.

35. **D.** Sentence 7 begins a discussion of Franklin's interest in the practical applications of his inventions. Therefore, the best place to begin a new paragraph would be after sentence 6.

Section 6—Critical Reading

Sentence Completions

1. **A.** To "extricate" is to remove from an entanglement or difficulty, and one can extricate himself from an unpleasant situation. Choice B is not as effective because it does not connote removing oneself from an entanglement or difficulty. C also means to remove or take away, but "rescind myself" is not standard usage; generally, "rescind" is used in the sense of to cancel or make void. The other choices are also not appropriate.

2. **A.** One of the meanings of "bucolic" is pastoral (relating to a rural life), which is an appropriate description of this scene. The correct answer here can be determined by the process of elimination; the other choices do not describe the scene well.

3. **B.** "Brazen" means disregarding the rules, overly bold, which describes the girl's bursting in without knocking. The second word—"compunction"— can mean a twinge of misgiving or guilt, which fits the context here: The head of the department would feel no compunction in asking the girl to leave. In none of the other choices are both words appropriate.

4. **C.** "Reprisals" are actions that use force in retaliation for damage that has been inflicted. "Intransigent" means not unwilling to compromise. Both words are appropriate to the context. None of the other choices are appropriate for both words.

5. **E.** The first part of the sentence makes it clear that Mother was extremely appreciative of the painting. She would be most likely to rhapsodize about it to others. ("Rhapsodize" means to speak in an extremely emotional, glowing way.) Choice D, "mused," does not suggest such enthusiasm. Choice E contains the more appropriate word in this context.

Short Passages

6. **D.** Lines 3–8 present the topic of the paragraph. The passage doesn't "prove" anything, A, and although it mentions the principle behind the printing press, it doesn't explain it, B. Choice C is a secondary point, and there is no evidence for Choice E.

7. **C.** See lines 8–12. While the other choices may or may not be true, they are not indicated in the passage.

8. **B.** The first sentence of the passage provides a statement of its purpose. A, D, and E are secondary points. The passage does not emphasize Einstein's pivotal role in physics, C.

9. **C.** See lines 8–10. The speed of light is c^2, not energy, A, or radiation, D. Choices B and E are irrelevant in the passage.

Long Passages

10. **D.** "Desultory" means lacking purpose or direction, which fits in the context of the passage: "desultory treadmills of afternoon."

11. **A.** C is inaccurate; the passage does not present a "negative impression" but rather a "vivid description" with many details. The author's reactions to the scene are not objective but subjective, D. Although the author says the scene "exerted a hypnotic charm that invited boredom," he does not emphasize tedium, B, nor does he "undercut" a traditional view, E.

12. **C.** C is the best choice of those given. There is no sense of "childlike anticipation" (A), "enthusiasm" (B), or "nostalgia" (E), and nothing indicates "frustration" (D). Throughout the passage, both in word choice and selection of details, the mood is closest to being "pleasant boredom."

13. **C.** In these lines, the author says he got his money's worth by seeing the trainer's whiplash catch around a lion's toe. The comment indicates that this unexpected event was more entertaining than watching the horse trainer lead her horse around the ring. The other choices are opinions, and they are not presented in the passage.

14. **D.** This is how the author explicitly describes himself. See lines 60–65. A and E may be true of the author, but they are not his self-description.

15. **A.** See lines 65–70. In this view of his responsibilities, the author explains the reason for the essay itself. None of the other choices, while perhaps true, explain the author's comment that he has "always felt charged with the safekeeping of all unexpected items" of enchantment.

16. **E.** Since a utopia is an ideal world, from the context it should be evident that the passage is referring to the opposite of an ideal world ("classic nightmare scenario"). C is the second-best answer, but the prefix "dys" indicates that the word is an opposite.

17. **C.** See lines 21–24. This paragraph presents a hypothetical situation in which a robot makes a decision based on an ethical principle. A is simply inaccurate. The other choices may be true, but the function of the paragraph is expressed in C.

18. **D.** Lines 28–30 explicitly state that the robot in paragraph 3 has already been created, and that its only function is to determine how many times to remind a patient to take medication. Don't be confused by B; the robot has not been programmed to make the decision as to how many times to take the medication.

19. **E.** See lines 25–28. Although the robot is intended to make only a simple ethical decision, according to the passage it has already been created.

20. **A.** See lines 50–54. The passage suggests that robots should be able to refer to their programmed ethical principles for justification if humans are to be comfortable with the machines. The second-best choice is E. While the other choices may or may not be good ideas, they are not considered in the passage.

21. **D.** The quotation is from a philosopher, who is suggesting that designing robots to make ethical decisions could, as a side effect, benefit philosophy by making philosophers look more carefully at real-life ethical situations. The quotation does not support A or C. Also, Dennett is not implying that philosophy is currently dishonest, only that artificial intelligence may help philosophers rethink ethics. E is irrelevant to the passage.

22. **B.** See lines 46–48. Neither A nor E is suggested in the passage. C and D, while they are considerations in the design of robots, are not main points in this paragraph.

23. **A.** A is the best choice of those given. In the third paragraph, the author uses the pronouns "we" and "our," which implies that he/she is part of the design process. None of the other choices is implied.

24. **C.** The question, "If one agrees . . . Which [ethical] principles should go in them?" (lines 80–84) is the core of the last paragraph (lines 94–106). D and E are inaccurate, and — although Asimov is cited in the paragraph, and his Three Laws of Robotics are key to the issue (A, B) — the main purpose is to focus on the difficulty in determining which ethical principles should be programmed into robots.

Section 7: Mathematics

1. **A.** Each of the 4 soups can be paired with each of the 3 salads for $4 \cdot 3 = 12$ combinations. Each of the 12 soup-salad combinations can be paired with each of the 10 sandwiches for $12 \cdot 10 = 120$ soup, salad, and sandwich combinations.

2. **D.** Since $\triangle ABC$ is similar to $\triangle XYZ$, their corresponding sides are proportional and the ratio of their perimeters is equal to the ratios of their corresponding sides.

$$\frac{\text{perimeter of } \triangle ABC}{\text{perimeter of } \triangle XYZ} = \frac{AB}{XY} = \frac{BC}{YZ} = \frac{AC}{XZ}$$

Given that $BC = 9$, $YZ = 15$, and the perimeter of $\triangle XYZ$ is 60,

$$\frac{\text{perimeter of } \triangle ABC}{\text{perimeter of } \triangle XYZ} = \frac{BC}{YZ}$$

$$\frac{P(\triangle ABC)}{60} = \frac{9}{15} = \frac{3}{5}$$

$$5 \cdot P(\triangle ABC) = 3 \cdot 60$$

$$5 \cdot P(\triangle ABC) = 180$$

$$P(\triangle ABC) = \frac{180}{5}$$

$$P(\triangle ABC) = 36$$

3. B. Since $a^2 - b^2 = (a + b)(a - b)$ and $a + b = 4$,

$$5(a^2 - b^2) = 5(a+b)(a-b) = 100$$

$$5(4)(a-b) = 100$$

$$20(a-b) = 100$$

$$\frac{20(a-b)}{20} = \frac{100}{20}$$

$$a - b = 5$$

4. E. Since the average of 8 test scores is determined by dividing the sum of the 8 scores by the number of tests,

$$\frac{\text{sum of 8 tests}}{8} = z$$

$$8 \cdot \frac{\text{sum of 8 tests}}{8} = 8 \cdot z$$

$$\text{sum of 8 tests} = 8z$$

5. A. The circumference C of a circle with a diameter d is $C = \pi d$. Since the circumference of the circle is π,

$$\pi = \pi d$$

$$\frac{\pi}{\pi} = \frac{\pi d}{\pi}$$

$$d = 1$$

The area A of a circle where the radius r is $A = \pi r^2$. Since the diameter is 1, and the radius is $\frac{1}{2}$ the diameter,

$$r = \frac{1}{2}d = \frac{1}{2}(1) = \frac{1}{2}$$

Hence the area of the circle is

$$A = \pi \left(\frac{1}{2}\right)^2$$

$$A = \frac{1}{4}\pi$$

6. D.

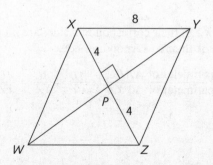

Since the diagonals of a rhombus are perpendicular and bisect each other, $\overline{XZ} \perp \overline{WY}$, $XP = ZP = 4$, and $WP = YP$. $\triangle XYP$ is a right triangle with one leg length of 4 and a hypotenuse with a length of 8. Using the Pythagorean Theorem, in any right triangle with legs a and b and hypotenuse c,

$$c^2 = a^2 + b^2$$
$$(XY)^2 = (XP)^2 + (YP)^2$$
$$8^2 = 4^2 + (YP)^2$$
$$64 = 16 + (YP)^2$$
$$64 - 16 = 16 + (YP)^2 - 16$$
$$48 = (YP)^2$$
$$YP = \sqrt{48} = \sqrt{16 \cdot 3}$$
$$YP = 4\sqrt{3}$$

Since $YP = WP = 4\sqrt{3}$
$$WY = YP + WP$$
$$= 4\sqrt{3} + 4\sqrt{3}$$
$$= 8\sqrt{3}$$

7. C. Since z is directly proportional to y^3, $z = ky^3$, where k is a constant. If $z = \frac{1}{9}$ when $y = \frac{1}{3}$,

$$z = ky^3$$
$$\frac{1}{9} = k\left(\frac{1}{3}\right)^3$$
$$\frac{1}{9} = \frac{1}{27}k$$
$$\frac{1}{27}k \cdot 27 = \frac{1}{9} \cdot 27$$
$$k = 3 \quad \text{and} \quad z = 3y^3$$

When $z = 24$,

$$z = 3y^3$$
$$24 = 3y^3$$
$$\frac{3y^3}{3} = \frac{24}{3}$$
$$y^3 = 8$$
$$y = \sqrt[3]{8}$$
$$y = 2$$

8. D. Any one of the 4 numbers can be used in the thousands place value with any of the 3 remaining numbers used in the hundreds place. The tens place can be filled with either of the 2 remaining numbers and the 1 remaining number must be used in the units place. Hence, the number of 4-digit numbers that can be formed is $4 \cdot 3 \cdot 2 \cdot 1 = 24$.

9. E. The center of the circle O is the midpoint of any diameter of the circle. The midpoint M of any two points (x_1, y_1) and (x_2, y_2) is

$$M = \left(\frac{x_1 + x_2}{2}, \frac{y_1 + y_2}{2}\right)$$

For the diameter endpoints $A(-3, 8)$ and $B(11, 4)$, the coordinates of the center of the circle O are

$$O = \left(\frac{-3+11}{2}, \frac{8+4}{2}\right)$$

$$O = \left(\frac{8}{2}, \frac{12}{2}\right)$$

$$O = (4, 6)$$

10. **C.**

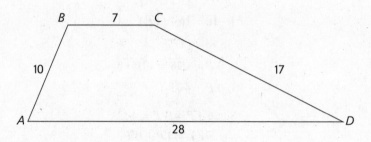

The area of a trapezoid with bases B and b and altitude/height h is

$$A = \tfrac{1}{2}h(B+b)$$

Since the area of the trapezoid is 140,

$$140 = \tfrac{1}{2}h(28+7)$$

$$= \tfrac{1}{2}h(35)$$

$$140 = 17.5h$$

$$\frac{140}{17.5} = \frac{17.5h}{17.5}$$

$$h = 8$$

11. **E.**

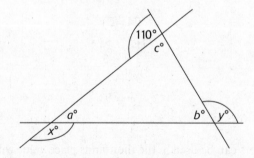

In the figure, $c + 110 = 180$ or $c = 70$

$a + x = 180$

$b + y = 180$

The angles are supplementary. And since the sum of the interior angles in a triangle is 180°,

$a + b + c = 180$

$a + b + 70 = 180$

$a + b + 70 - 70 = 180 - 70$

$a + b = 110$

Since $a + x = 180$ and $b + y = 180$,

$$(a + x) + (b + y) = 360$$
$$(a + b) + (x + y) = 360$$
$$110 + x + y = 360$$
$$110 + x + y - 110 = 360 - 110$$
$$x + y = 250$$

12. **C.** If a is divisible by 5 and b is divisible by 7, ab is divisible by 35. Also, $7a$ and $5b$ are each divisible by 35 and their sum, $7a + 5b$, is divisible by 35. However, $5a$ and $7b$ *are not necessarily* divisible by 35 nor would their sum, $5a + 7b$, necessarily be divisible by 35. For example, if $a = 5$ and $b = 7$:

$$5a + 7b = 5 \cdot 5 + 7 \cdot 7$$
$$= 25 + 49$$
$$= 74, \text{ which is not divisible by 35.}$$

13. **D.**

   Let x = 1st odd integer

   $x + 2$ = 2nd odd integer

   $x + 4$ = 3rd odd integer

   The sum of the 3 consecutive odd integers is

   $$x + (x + 2) + (x + 4) = 549$$
   $$3x + 6 = 549$$

14. **A.** If $y = -\frac{1}{2}$ and $a > 0$, then $8ay^2$ has the largest value. Since $y = -\frac{1}{2}$ $8ay^3 < 0$ and $8ay^5 < 0$. Also, for $y = -\frac{1}{2}$, $y^2 > y^4 > y^6$ and $8ay^2 > 8ay^4 > 8ay^6$.

15. **B.** Since all boys enrolled in Period 1 math weigh more than 130 pounds, no boys who weigh less than 130 pounds are enrolled in the Period 1 math class.

16. **B.**

   Let S_n = nth term of the sequence

   $S_1 = 2$

   $S_2 = (2 - 1)^2 = 1^2 = 1$

   $S_3 = (1 - 1)^2 = 0^2 = 0$

   $S_4 = (0 - 1)^2 = (-1)^2 = 1$

   $S_5 = (1 - 1)^2 = 0^2 = 0$

   $S_6 = (0 - 1)^2 = (-1)^2 = 1$

   $S_7 = (1 - 1)^2 = 0^2 = 0$

Section 8—Critical Reading

Sentence Completions

1. **B.** "Power vacuum" is the context clue. Choice B means decay or disintegration, which would allow "a number of sects" to move in to take power. D is the second-best answer, but it doesn't describe the situation as well as B.

2. **A.** The second part of the sentence indicates that the accusation is questionable; "spurious" means false, or of erroneous origin. B is the second-best answer but is more extreme, and the second word in B should rule it out; reluctant dedication is not a good fit with "excellent reputation." On the other hand, the second word in A, unequivocal, means unquestionable or leaving no doubt, which fits well here. None of the other choices fits either the first or second blank.

3. **C.** "Cumulative" means increasing by successive additions; but the best context clue is for the second word. The new technology "completely baffled" the older secretaries, which would lead them to revert to (turn back to) the old office equipment. None of the other choices fits well here.

4. **A.** The context clue is "although." The speaker used his/her most ingratiating manner and best arguments, but Benjamin still remained "utterly" unmoved. The only choice that conveys his reaction is "intractable," which means not easily managed or manipulated. Since the other choices don't convey Benjamin's "utter" refusal, the correct answer can be determined by the process of elimination.

5. **B.** "Inopportune" means inconvenient or unreasonable. The other choices for the first word are not appropriate. The second word is "deign," which means condescend reluctantly or stoop to do something. The inconvenient scheduling of the wedding, and the clue that "very few relatives" would come, make B the best choice.

6. **D.** The word must mean something that would indicate why he would find it difficult to perform the duties of the job. "For traveling" is a clue; it should rule out choices A, B, and C, none of which fit well with "for traveling." "Predilection" means a strong preference or liking for something, and that word is a good fit. D is incorrect because the phrase would be "commitment to," not "commitment for."

Paired Passages

7. **D.** The author of Passage 1 sees assimilation as positive (lines 43–46), whereas the woman in Passage 2 sees it as a threat to her values (lines 14–19). Nothing suggests that the author of Passage 1 is "shamed" by his heritage, A; he feels, however, that assimilation is necessary for his success in public life. There is no evidence for C. There is also no evidence that the woman in Passage 2 is "grateful" for bilingual education, B. E is also inaccurate. In the last paragraph of the first passage, the author refers to his loss of family intimacy after his mastery of English.

8. **B.** The author of Passage 1 generalizes about middle class Hispanics who resist assimilation, while the woman in Passage 2 uses the term *gueros* (literally meaning "blondies") as a generalization about all Americans. A is too strong, and there is no evidence for C. D is not as appropriate here, and in neither passage are the terms used ironically, E.

9. **C.** C is the best description of the different concerns of the two passages. The author of Passage 1 is emphasizing that through learning English and assimilating into the American culture, a person can find a place in public society—a public individuality. The main concern of the woman in Passage 2 is maintaining the values of her culture and family. None of the other choices illustrates their different concerns as precisely.

10. **D.** See lines 10–14. A overstates his point, and there is no evidence that private individuality is "dangerous," nor that "most" non-English speakers fear assimilation (B, C). The author's main point is not that bilingual education has been unsuccessful, E; he is bothered by those bilingual educators who believe that individuality depends on refraining from assimilation.

11. **C.** See lines 3–8. The author does not refer to the idea of America as a "melting pot" except in these lines. The passage indicates he would probably not agree with A or B, and there is no evidence for D or E.

12. **B.** The second paragraph of the passage clearly identifies "bilingualists" as simplistic because they equate "mere separateness with individuality." D is the second-best answer, but the author uses the term "simplistic" specifically in reference to the "bilingualists" linking individuality to a person's difference in mass society.

13. **B.** B is the best answer of those provided. The author shows his annoyance in lines 35–42 when he refers to the "middle-class ethnics" as "filled with decadent self-pity" and "obsessed by the burden of public life"; he accuses them of "dangerously romanticizing" public separateness and "trivializing" the plight of those who are "truly socially disadvantaged." These comments rule out the other choices.

14. **A.** "Counterproductive" means hindering desired progress. This is the only point that the author does not make about "public individuality." Watch out for the word EXCEPT in questions. He does use the terms "tenuous," C, and "impersonal," E, (lines 34 and 31).

15. **A.** Lines 45–55 describe the author's feelings in his home after learning to speak English. Neither his family's rejection (B) nor his frustration (C) is mentioned. D is also not indicated; the author displays no "negative feelings" about his heritage. He may be nostalgic for his childhood (E), but he does not state this specifically. A is a more general and accurate description of the last paragraph.

16. **D.** The author describes the public individuality he gained by learning English and not by resisting assimilation. In lines 45–46, he mentions the loss that accompanied that gain. Lines 10–13 express the loss.

17. **E.** See lines 39–42. The author believes that "middle-class ethnics," because they can afford to, trivialize the plight of those who are truly disadvantaged. The author believes that the best chance for non-English speakers to increase their possibilities in America is to learn English and become part of public society. A, B, and D are not shown in the passage. The middle-class Hispanics that oppose assimilation may romanticize their heritage (C), but the author's point is that in opposing assimilation, they downplay the plight of other Hispanics who are financially and socially disadvantaged.

18. **B.** The point of her comment is that nothing will make her feel like an American. She may or may not believe A, D, and E, but the point of her comment is that her identity as Mexican is permanent and unchangeable. C is not a good choice; no reference is made to inner qualities.

19. **C.** See lines 37–46. The passage refers to the point that there are now different routes to assimilation, including blending into the middle or becoming an "adversarial underclass." (Passage 1 does not consider these "different routes.") None of the other choices is specifically defined by the term.

20. **B.** Passage 2 is an objective report; the writer presents facts and quotes sources. Passage 1 is autobiographical, and the author presents his own opinions based on his experiences; the point of view is subjective, and the tone is sometimes argumentative.

Section 9: Writing—Multiple Choice

Improving Sentences

1. **E.** The verbs should be in the past tense. B uses the present tense and the passive voice. C is an incorrect structure; "they" should be eliminated. The last phrase is also not parallel because it includes "then." D also has a tense problem and uses the passive voice.

2. **D.** As written, the sentence is a run-on or comma splice. B uses the coordinating conjunction "but," which doesn't make sense with the meaning of the first clause. C is wordy, and E seems to be an incomplete thought. The phrase "and therefore" makes the most sense in this sentence.

3. **C.** A and E include misplaced modifiers, and the placement of elements in B suggests that the chef created the world. D puts the name of the chef at the end of the sentence; it would be better to follow "created by" with his name, and follow his name with the appositive ("a chef whose culinary skills are recognized throughout Europe"). An appositive is a noun or pronoun that explains or identifies the noun or pronoun that precedes it (e.g. Mr. Evans, the lawyer). An appositive phrase is an appositive with its modifiers (e.g. Mr. Evans, the most experienced lawyer in the firm, . . .).

4. **A.** The sentence is correct as written, and none of the other choices is correct, either because of the lack of agreement between subject and verb ("factor was," not "factor were") or faulty parallelism.

5. **B.** First, the proper verb is "had gone" not "had went," A and D, and second, the correct pronoun is "who," not "whom." The pronoun is the subject of "was most deserving," not the object of "we all thought," C. In situations like this one, the subjective case takes precedence over the objective case. The verb tense is incorrect in E; the event was concluded in the past.

6. **B.** "Reason is because" is an incorrect phrase; it should be "reason is that." This is a common mistake. Also, the verb tense is incorrect in A, C, and E. D ("on account of") is wordy.

7. **E.** In A, B, and C the clause following "substances" is offset with commas. This a restrictive clause, which means that it is necessary to the noun it modifies and shouldn't be set off with commas. In D, a semicolon follows "were." This is not a correct use of the semicolon. E is both succinct and uses the proper punctuation.

8. **C.** In A, "they" should be eliminated. In B, "such as for example" is wordy. In D, "seem to be" and "such as the example of" are also wordy. E creates a sentence fragment.

9. **A.** The sentence is correct as written. B and C are sentence fragments. The verb tense is incorrect in D, and E is wordy. Also, there should be no comma before "because."

10. **B.** In this version of the sentence, all of the elements are parallel: "visit," "dine," "cruise," "swim," and "ski." This is not true of A, C, D, or E. Also, "group" is a collective noun and should in most cases take the singular verb: "expects."

11. **D.** A and B use the wrong verb. In C, "having wrote" should be "having written." "Although" in D makes the point better than "and" or "and, in addition." E creates a run-on sentence, or comma splice. "However" should be preceded by a period or semicolon; a comma is not a strong-enough punctuation mark.

12. **C.** A uses the passive voice (which creates a dangling participle) and is wordy. B and D are both awkward and wordy. E uses the wrong word; "sighting" should be "citing."

13. **D.** "Neither proved nor disproved" maintains parallel structure. The other choices do not maintain parallelism with "neither...nor." In B and C, verb tenses are inconsistent.

14. **E.** Although A is not incorrect, E becomes more succint by eliminating "he was giving." B has two problems: The correct pronoun here is "us" (the object of "invited"), and the correct word is "regardless." "Irregardless" is not a word. D also includes these errors, and C, while using the correct pronoun, also uses "irregardless." The use of "irregardless" in place of "regardless" is a common error.

Chapter 10

Practice Exam 2

Section 2	Section 3	Section 4	Section 5	Section 6
1 Ⓐ Ⓑ Ⓒ Ⓓ Ⓔ	1 Ⓐ Ⓑ Ⓒ Ⓓ Ⓔ	1 Ⓐ Ⓑ Ⓒ Ⓓ Ⓔ	1 Ⓐ Ⓑ Ⓒ Ⓓ Ⓔ	1 Ⓐ Ⓑ Ⓒ Ⓓ Ⓔ
2 Ⓐ Ⓑ Ⓒ Ⓓ Ⓔ	2 Ⓐ Ⓑ Ⓒ Ⓓ Ⓔ	2 Ⓐ Ⓑ Ⓒ Ⓓ Ⓔ	2 Ⓐ Ⓑ Ⓒ Ⓓ Ⓔ	2 Ⓐ Ⓑ Ⓒ Ⓓ Ⓔ
3 Ⓐ Ⓑ Ⓒ Ⓓ Ⓔ	3 Ⓐ Ⓑ Ⓒ Ⓓ Ⓔ	3 Ⓐ Ⓑ Ⓒ Ⓓ Ⓔ	3 Ⓐ Ⓑ Ⓒ Ⓓ Ⓔ	3 Ⓐ Ⓑ Ⓒ Ⓓ Ⓔ
4 Ⓐ Ⓑ Ⓒ Ⓓ Ⓔ	4 Ⓐ Ⓑ Ⓒ Ⓓ Ⓔ	4 Ⓐ Ⓑ Ⓒ Ⓓ Ⓔ	4 Ⓐ Ⓑ Ⓒ Ⓓ Ⓔ	4 Ⓐ Ⓑ Ⓒ Ⓓ Ⓔ
5 Ⓐ Ⓑ Ⓒ Ⓓ Ⓔ	5 Ⓐ Ⓑ Ⓒ Ⓓ Ⓔ	5 Ⓐ Ⓑ Ⓒ Ⓓ Ⓔ	5 Ⓐ Ⓑ Ⓒ Ⓓ Ⓔ	5 Ⓐ Ⓑ Ⓒ Ⓓ Ⓔ
6 Ⓐ Ⓑ Ⓒ Ⓓ Ⓔ	6 Ⓐ Ⓑ Ⓒ Ⓓ Ⓔ	6 Ⓐ Ⓑ Ⓒ Ⓓ Ⓔ	6 Ⓐ Ⓑ Ⓒ Ⓓ Ⓔ	6 Ⓐ Ⓑ Ⓒ Ⓓ Ⓔ
7 Ⓐ Ⓑ Ⓒ Ⓓ Ⓔ	7 Ⓐ Ⓑ Ⓒ Ⓓ Ⓔ	7 Ⓐ Ⓑ Ⓒ Ⓓ Ⓔ	7 Ⓐ Ⓑ Ⓒ Ⓓ Ⓔ	7 Ⓐ Ⓑ Ⓒ Ⓓ Ⓔ
8 Ⓐ Ⓑ Ⓒ Ⓓ Ⓔ	8 Ⓐ Ⓑ Ⓒ Ⓓ Ⓔ	8 Ⓐ Ⓑ Ⓒ Ⓓ Ⓔ	8 Ⓐ Ⓑ Ⓒ Ⓓ Ⓔ	8 Ⓐ Ⓑ Ⓒ Ⓓ Ⓔ
9 Ⓐ Ⓑ Ⓒ Ⓓ Ⓔ	9 Ⓐ Ⓑ Ⓒ Ⓓ Ⓔ	9 Ⓐ Ⓑ Ⓒ Ⓓ Ⓔ	9 Ⓐ Ⓑ Ⓒ Ⓓ Ⓔ	
10 Ⓐ Ⓑ Ⓒ Ⓓ Ⓔ	10 Ⓐ Ⓑ Ⓒ Ⓓ Ⓔ	10 Ⓐ Ⓑ Ⓒ Ⓓ Ⓔ	10 Ⓐ Ⓑ Ⓒ Ⓓ Ⓔ	
11 Ⓐ Ⓑ Ⓒ Ⓓ Ⓔ	11 Ⓐ Ⓑ Ⓒ Ⓓ Ⓔ	11 Ⓐ Ⓑ Ⓒ Ⓓ Ⓔ	11 Ⓐ Ⓑ Ⓒ Ⓓ Ⓔ	
12 Ⓐ Ⓑ Ⓒ Ⓓ Ⓔ	12 Ⓐ Ⓑ Ⓒ Ⓓ Ⓔ	12 Ⓐ Ⓑ Ⓒ Ⓓ Ⓔ	12 Ⓐ Ⓑ Ⓒ Ⓓ Ⓔ	
13 Ⓐ Ⓑ Ⓒ Ⓓ Ⓔ	13 Ⓐ Ⓑ Ⓒ Ⓓ Ⓔ	13 Ⓐ Ⓑ Ⓒ Ⓓ Ⓔ	13 Ⓐ Ⓑ Ⓒ Ⓓ Ⓔ	
14 Ⓐ Ⓑ Ⓒ Ⓓ Ⓔ	14 Ⓐ Ⓑ Ⓒ Ⓓ Ⓔ	14 Ⓐ Ⓑ Ⓒ Ⓓ Ⓔ	14 Ⓐ Ⓑ Ⓒ Ⓓ Ⓔ	
15 Ⓐ Ⓑ Ⓒ Ⓓ Ⓔ	15 Ⓐ Ⓑ Ⓒ Ⓓ Ⓔ	15 Ⓐ Ⓑ Ⓒ Ⓓ Ⓔ	15 Ⓐ Ⓑ Ⓒ Ⓓ Ⓔ	
16 Ⓐ Ⓑ Ⓒ Ⓓ Ⓔ	16 Ⓐ Ⓑ Ⓒ Ⓓ Ⓔ	16 Ⓐ Ⓑ Ⓒ Ⓓ Ⓔ	16 Ⓐ Ⓑ Ⓒ Ⓓ Ⓔ	
17 Ⓐ Ⓑ Ⓒ Ⓓ Ⓔ	17 Ⓐ Ⓑ Ⓒ Ⓓ Ⓔ	17 Ⓐ Ⓑ Ⓒ Ⓓ Ⓔ	17 Ⓐ Ⓑ Ⓒ Ⓓ Ⓔ	
18 Ⓐ Ⓑ Ⓒ Ⓓ Ⓔ	18 Ⓐ Ⓑ Ⓒ Ⓓ Ⓔ	18 Ⓐ Ⓑ Ⓒ Ⓓ Ⓔ	18 Ⓐ Ⓑ Ⓒ Ⓓ Ⓔ	
19 Ⓐ Ⓑ Ⓒ Ⓓ Ⓔ	19 Ⓐ Ⓑ Ⓒ Ⓓ Ⓔ	19 Ⓐ Ⓑ Ⓒ Ⓓ Ⓔ	19 Ⓐ Ⓑ Ⓒ Ⓓ Ⓔ	
20 Ⓐ Ⓑ Ⓒ Ⓓ Ⓔ	20 Ⓐ Ⓑ Ⓒ Ⓓ Ⓔ	20 Ⓐ Ⓑ Ⓒ Ⓓ Ⓔ	20 Ⓐ Ⓑ Ⓒ Ⓓ Ⓔ	
21 Ⓐ Ⓑ Ⓒ Ⓓ Ⓔ		21 Ⓐ Ⓑ Ⓒ Ⓓ Ⓔ	21 Ⓐ Ⓑ Ⓒ Ⓓ Ⓔ	
22 Ⓐ Ⓑ Ⓒ Ⓓ Ⓔ		22 Ⓐ Ⓑ Ⓒ Ⓓ Ⓔ	22 Ⓐ Ⓑ Ⓒ Ⓓ Ⓔ	
23 Ⓐ Ⓑ Ⓒ Ⓓ Ⓔ		23 Ⓐ Ⓑ Ⓒ Ⓓ Ⓔ	23 Ⓐ Ⓑ Ⓒ Ⓓ Ⓔ	
24 Ⓐ Ⓑ Ⓒ Ⓓ Ⓔ		24 Ⓐ Ⓑ Ⓒ Ⓓ Ⓔ	24 Ⓐ Ⓑ Ⓒ Ⓓ Ⓔ	
25 Ⓐ Ⓑ Ⓒ Ⓓ Ⓔ		25 Ⓐ Ⓑ Ⓒ Ⓓ Ⓔ	25 Ⓐ Ⓑ Ⓒ Ⓓ Ⓔ	
26 Ⓐ Ⓑ Ⓒ Ⓓ Ⓔ			26 Ⓐ Ⓑ Ⓒ Ⓓ Ⓔ	
			27 Ⓐ Ⓑ Ⓒ Ⓓ Ⓔ	
			28 Ⓐ Ⓑ Ⓒ Ⓓ Ⓔ	
			29 Ⓐ Ⓑ Ⓒ Ⓓ Ⓔ	
			30 Ⓐ Ⓑ Ⓒ Ⓓ Ⓔ	
			31 Ⓐ Ⓑ Ⓒ Ⓓ Ⓔ	
			32 Ⓐ Ⓑ Ⓒ Ⓓ Ⓔ	
			33 Ⓐ Ⓑ Ⓒ Ⓓ Ⓔ	
			34 Ⓐ Ⓑ Ⓒ Ⓓ Ⓔ	
			35 Ⓐ Ⓑ Ⓒ Ⓓ Ⓔ	

9.

10.

11.

CUT HERE

12.

13.

14.

15.

16.

17.

18.

Section 7

1 Ⓐ Ⓑ Ⓒ Ⓓ Ⓔ
2 Ⓐ Ⓑ Ⓒ Ⓓ Ⓔ
3 Ⓐ Ⓑ Ⓒ Ⓓ Ⓔ
4 Ⓐ Ⓑ Ⓒ Ⓓ Ⓔ
5 Ⓐ Ⓑ Ⓒ Ⓓ Ⓔ
6 Ⓐ Ⓑ Ⓒ Ⓓ Ⓔ
7 Ⓐ Ⓑ Ⓒ Ⓓ Ⓔ
8 Ⓐ Ⓑ Ⓒ Ⓓ Ⓔ
9 Ⓐ Ⓑ Ⓒ Ⓓ Ⓔ
10 Ⓐ Ⓑ Ⓒ Ⓓ Ⓔ
11 Ⓐ Ⓑ Ⓒ Ⓓ Ⓔ
12 Ⓐ Ⓑ Ⓒ Ⓓ Ⓔ
13 Ⓐ Ⓑ Ⓒ Ⓓ Ⓔ
14 Ⓐ Ⓑ Ⓒ Ⓓ Ⓔ
15 Ⓐ Ⓑ Ⓒ Ⓓ Ⓔ
16 Ⓐ Ⓑ Ⓒ Ⓓ Ⓔ

Section 8

1 Ⓐ Ⓑ Ⓒ Ⓓ Ⓔ
2 Ⓐ Ⓑ Ⓒ Ⓓ Ⓔ
3 Ⓐ Ⓑ Ⓒ Ⓓ Ⓔ
4 Ⓐ Ⓑ Ⓒ Ⓓ Ⓔ
5 Ⓐ Ⓑ Ⓒ Ⓓ Ⓔ
6 Ⓐ Ⓑ Ⓒ Ⓓ Ⓔ
7 Ⓐ Ⓑ Ⓒ Ⓓ Ⓔ
8 Ⓐ Ⓑ Ⓒ Ⓓ Ⓔ
9 Ⓐ Ⓑ Ⓒ Ⓓ Ⓔ
10 Ⓐ Ⓑ Ⓒ Ⓓ Ⓔ
11 Ⓐ Ⓑ Ⓒ Ⓓ Ⓔ
12 Ⓐ Ⓑ Ⓒ Ⓓ Ⓔ
13 Ⓐ Ⓑ Ⓒ Ⓓ Ⓔ
14 Ⓐ Ⓑ Ⓒ Ⓓ Ⓔ

Section 9

1 Ⓐ Ⓑ Ⓒ Ⓓ Ⓔ
2 Ⓐ Ⓑ Ⓒ Ⓓ Ⓔ
3 Ⓐ Ⓑ Ⓒ Ⓓ Ⓔ
4 Ⓐ Ⓑ Ⓒ Ⓓ Ⓔ
5 Ⓐ Ⓑ Ⓒ Ⓓ Ⓔ
6 Ⓐ Ⓑ Ⓒ Ⓓ Ⓔ
7 Ⓐ Ⓑ Ⓒ Ⓓ Ⓔ
8 Ⓐ Ⓑ Ⓒ Ⓓ Ⓔ
9 Ⓐ Ⓑ Ⓒ Ⓓ Ⓔ
10 Ⓐ Ⓑ Ⓒ Ⓓ Ⓔ
11 Ⓐ Ⓑ Ⓒ Ⓓ Ⓔ
12 Ⓐ Ⓑ Ⓒ Ⓓ Ⓔ
13 Ⓐ Ⓑ Ⓒ Ⓓ Ⓔ
14 Ⓐ Ⓑ Ⓒ Ⓓ Ⓔ
15 Ⓐ Ⓑ Ⓒ Ⓓ Ⓔ
16 Ⓐ Ⓑ Ⓒ Ⓓ Ⓔ
17 Ⓐ Ⓑ Ⓒ Ⓓ Ⓔ
18 Ⓐ Ⓑ Ⓒ Ⓓ Ⓔ
19 Ⓐ Ⓑ Ⓒ Ⓓ Ⓔ

Section 1: Writing—Essay

Time: 25 minutes
1 Essay Question

You have 25 minutes to plan and write an essay on the topic below. DO NOT WRITE ON ANOTHER TOPIC. AN ESSAY ON ANOTHER TOPIC WILL NOT BE SCORED.

The essay is intended to give you the chance to show your writing skills. Be sure to express your ideas on the topic clearly and effectively. The quality of your writing is much more important than the quantity, but to cover the topic adequately, you may want to write more than one paragraph. Be specific.

Your essay must be written on two lined pages. Two pages should be enough if you write on every line, avoid wide margins, and keep your handwriting a reasonable size. You will not be given any additional paper. On the actual SAT you must

- Only use a pencil. You will receive a score of zero if you use ink.
- Only write on your answer sheet. You will not receive credit for material written in the test book.
- Only write on the topic presented below. An essay that is off-topic will receive a score of zero.
- Write an essay that reflects original work.

Directions: Read the following paragraph and assignment carefully. Then prepare and write a persuasive essay. Be sure to support your reasons with specific examples that will make your essay more effective.

> Some public schools in the United States have removed the "A" to "F" grading system and substituted "Pass-Fail" grading, with the instructor adding a written statement about the student's progress.

> **Assignment:** What are the pros and cons, and do you agree or disagree with public schools that use a "Pass-Fail" grading system? Using an example or examples from your reading, personal experiences, or observations, write an essay to support your position.

ON THE ACTUAL EXAM, THE PROCTOR WILL ANNOUNCE WHEN 25 MINUTES HAVE PASSED. IF YOU FINISH YOUR ESSAY BEFORE 25 MINUTES HAVE PASSED, YOU MAY NOT GO ON TO ANY OTHER SECTION OF THE EXAM. THE PROCTOR WILL ANNOUNCE WHEN TO START THE NEXT SECTION.

Section 2: Critical Reading

Time: 25 minutes
26 Questions

Directions: In this section, choose the best answer for each question and fill in the corresponding circle on the answer sheet.

Each blank in the following sentences indicates that something has been omitted. Consider the lettered words beneath the sentence and choose the word or set of words that best fits the whole sentence.

EXAMPLE:

With a million more people than any other African nation, Nigeria is the most _____ country on the continent.

    A.   impoverished
    B.   successful
    C.   populous
    D.   developed
    E.   militant

The correct answer is **C.**

1. Although many mortgage companies are requiring condominium owners to carry insurance, it is still considered _____.

    A.   expensive
    B.   optional
    C.   extraordinary
    D.   economical
    E.   superfluous

2. As happens every year, the elected representatives in the state capital face the _____ and _____ dilemma in deciding which programs to cut.

    A.   terminal . . . questionable
    B.   illogical . . . imprecise
    C.   unprecedented . . . futile
    D.   persistent . . . difficult
    E.   solemn . . . controversial

3. After the severe flooding that destroyed their home and farmland, the McMullens impressed everyone with their _____ and _____ in rebuilding.

    A.   tenacity . . . fortitude
    B.   fatalism . . . intelligence
    C.   temerity . . . acumen
    D.   prudence . . . sensitivity
    E.   modesty . . . deference

4. Because Maxim Gorky was both a writer and a social _____, he used his talent to describe the lives of Russia's impoverished and _____ peasants.

    A.   instigator . . . archaic
    B.   dilettante . . . miserable
    C.   apologist . . . ignorant
    D.   activist . . . disenfranchised
    E.   recluse . . . hostile

5. Some _____ populations became so reduced in numbers by foreign disease and genocide that they are now outnumbered by the descendants of early invaders.

    A.   inept
    B.   genetic
    C.   indigenous
    D.   infantile
    E.   adaptable

GO ON TO THE NEXT PAGE

Directions: Questions follow each of the passages below. Answer the questions using only the stated or implied information in each passage and in its introduction, if any.

Questions 6–7 are based on the following passage.

Passage 1:

The term *meteorology* has been around since the seventeenth century, but meteorology as we know it today didn't actually exist until instruments that could accurately measure temperatures were
(5) developed. This wasn't an easy task; an accurate reading depended on putting a very even bore in a glass tube. Daniel Gabriel Fahrenheit solved the problem and produced an accurate thermometer in 1717, but for some unknown reason, he calibrated
(10) it so that freezing was put at 32 degrees and boiling at 212 degrees. This seemed odd to many people, among them astronomer Anders Celsius, who in 1748 came up with a competing scale that he felt made more sense: zero would be the boiling point
(15) and 100 the freezing point. However, that certainly wasn't the end of the story. Celsius's scale was soon reversed, and zero became freezing and 100 the boiling point. Both the Fahrenheit and Celsius scales are used today, confusing many people who
(20) simply want to know how cold or warm the weather is going to be.

6. The main purpose of the passage is to

   A. explain meteorology to a layman.
   B. demonstrate how scientists and inventors don't always agree.
   C. summarize the origins of the Fahrenheit and Celsius temperature scales.
   D. describe the technical difficulties of producing an accurate thermometer.
   E. compare and contrast Fahrenheit and Celsius as scientists.

7. The author of the paragraph would agree with which of the following statements?

   A. The Celsius temperature scale is more accurate than the Fahrenheit scale.
   B. The designation of freezing in both scales is arbitrary.
   C. Anders Celsius questioned the methods of Daniel Gabriel Fahrenheit.
   D. Having two different temperature scales leads to serious problems.
   E. Fahrenheit's thermometer, though accurate, was inefficient.

Questions 8–10 are based on the following passage.

Passage 2:

American faith in democracy, like that in nationalism, is partially traceable to the frontier heritage. That either democratic theory or practice originated in the backwoods is
(5) demonstrably untrue; both were well advanced when the conquest of the West began and both continued to receive stimulation from Europe during the eighteenth and nineteenth centuries. Yet frontier conditions tended to modify
(10) imported institutions along more democratic lines. In primitive communities the wide diffusion of land ownership created a natural demand that those with a stake in society should have a voice in society, while the common level of social and
(15) economic status and the absence of any prior leadership structure encouraged universal participation in government. With self-rule a brutal necessity due to the nonexistence of external controls, and with men and women
(20) accustomed to widespread participation in group affairs through cabin raising, corn husking bees, and the like, it was natural that they should think in terms of political equality. Democratic practices came naturally to frontier groups, and
(25) with them an unswerving faith in democracy as a panacea for all the ills of the nation or the world.

8. According to the author, one important reason democratic institutions in American frontier society differed from European models was that

   A. Americans distrusted Europeans in general and therefore didn't want to imitate their institutions.
   B. unlike in Europe, the American frontier lacked a history of leadership.
   C. Americans in the westward movement were fierce nationalists, whereas Europeans were not.
   D. Americans had a tradition of strong individualism while Europe relied more on conformity.
   E. on the frontier in America, stronger restrictions were required than the European institutions allowed.

GO ON TO THE NEXT PAGE

Practice Exam 2

9. Which of the following best characterizes the principal method the author uses in this passage?

    A. a series of generalizations

    B. metaphorical language

    C. contrast

    D. paradox

    E. irony and understatement

10. In the last sentence of the passage, the best definition for *panacea* is

    A. bandage.

    B. medicine.

    C. cure-all.

    D. elixir.

    E. inspiration.

Questions 11–16 are based on the following passage.

This passage is from a twentieth-century American short story.

Passage 3:

Next morning Grandma came with them to the orchard. She was quite calm, and for five minutes at a time her lips, instead of trembling in a stream of soundless words, were quiet, a little

(5) puckered; her eyes followed the preparation for picking with what seemed to Janet interest. Tom set up the ladders and laid out a string of lugs in the shade, and Grandma watched the four of them climb into the foliage among the bright

(10) globes of fruit.

Oliver picked a ripe apricot and stood on the ladder ready to toss it. "Here, Grandma," he said, "have an apricot."

He held it out, but the old lady made no move

(15) to come near and get it. "Just help yourself off the trees anywhere, Grandma," Janet said, and gave Oliver a sign to go on picking. When they were all up on ladders and busy, Grandma stooped quickly and snatched up a windfall

(20) apricot from the ground. "No, Grandma," Janet said. "From the trees. Pick all you want. Those on the ground may be spoiled." Grandma dropped the windfall and wiped her fingers on her dress. After a moment, she started at her

(25) hurrying, shoulder-forward walk down the orchard toward the lower fence.

"Do you want her taking off cross country?" Tom said.

"Who do you think you are, a jailer?" Janet

(30) said. "Let her feel free for once."

"I haven't got time to go out every half hour and round her up."

"You won't have to. She'll come back."

"Sure?"

(35) "Absolutely sure," Janet said. "Wait and see."

Thrust up among leaves and branches, they looked down to where Grandma's figure had stopped at the fence. The old lady looked around furtively, then stooped, picked up something

(40) from the ground, and popped it into her mouth.

"You've got a ways to go," Tom said, and his voice from the other tree was so impersonal and dry that she was angry with him.

"Give her a little time!" she said. "Give her a

(45) chance!" She was confident, yet when Grandma had not returned at eleven her faith began to waver. She did not want Tom to catch her anxiously looking down the orchard, but every time she dumped a pail in the lug she snatched

(50) quick looks all around, and she was almost at the point of sending the boys out searching when she saw the gingham figure marching homeward along the upper fence. She threw an apricot into the tree where Tom was picking. "See?" she said.

(55) "What did I tell you?"

Every morning thereafter, Grandma took a walk through the orchards and along the lanes. Every afternoon she settled down in the wicker rocker on the porch, and rocked and talked and

(60) told herself things. Janet, working around the house, heard the steady voice going, and sometimes she heard what it said. It said that Simms, the drayman, had his eye on Grandma's house and was trying to get her moved out so

(65) that he could move his daughter and her husband in. It said that the minister was angry at her, ever since she sided with the evangelicals, and wanted the Ladies Aid to leave her out of things. It said that George's wife was trying everything to get

(70) George to send Grandma away. Just the other day Grandma had overheard George's wife talking to the cleaning woman, plotting to leave Grandma's room dirty and then blame her in front of George. There were things Grandma

(75) knew, and she proved them with great vehemence and circumstantiality. Sometimes Janet came and sat beside Grandma. When she did, the talk went underground; the lips moved, sometimes fervidly, and the little brown eyes snapped, but

(80) there was no conversation between them. Janet might comment on how the air cooled down

GO ON TO THE NEXT PAGE

when fog rolled over the crest of the coast hills, or might point out a hummingbird working the flower beds, but she did not expect replies. She (85) took it as a hopeful sign that her presence did not drive Grandma away or stop her enthusiastic rocking, and sometimes it seemed to her that the rhythmic motion erased the strain from the old lady's face and smoothed the wrinkle between (90) her eyes. Then one afternoon Janet came quietly on the porch and found Grandma rocking like a child in the big chair, pushing with her toes, lifting off the floor, rocking back down to push with her toes again. She was not talking at all, (95) but was humming a tuneless little song to herself.

It was early August, and dense heat lay over the valley. The apricots were long gone; in the upper orchard the prunes were purple among the leaves, the limbs of the trees propped against the (100) weight of fruit. The unirrigated pasture was split by cracks three inches wide, and even in the shade one felt the dry panting of the earth for the rain that would not come for another three months. Looking out over the heat-hazed valley, (105) Grandma pushed with her toes, rocking and humming. Her face was mild and soft, and Janet slipped into the next chair, almost holding her breath for fear of breaking the moment. It was so easy to make a mistake. Weeks of improvement (110) could be canceled by one false move that the sick mind could seize on as it had seized on a harmless conversation between George's wife and her cleaning woman. It was Grandma herself who spoke first. She looked over at Janet brightly and (115) said, "Tom's a handsome man."

"Yes," Janet said. "He's filled out," Grandma said. "He was a skinny boy." She went back to her humming. For ten minutes Janet sat still, wishing that Tom was there to see his mother as (120) she had once been, speculating on how the moment might be stretched, wondering if possibly this was a turning point. If Grandma had come out of the twilight where she lived and would from now on shake off the suspicions and (125) the fears.

11. The point of view in the passage is

   A.   limited to Janet's.
   B.   an all-knowing narrator's.
   C.   both Janet's and Tom's.
   D.   Grandma's.
   E.   limited to Tom's.

12. The phrase "trembling in a stream of soundless words" (lines 3–4) suggests that Grandma

   A.   doesn't speak English well.
   B.   is shy.
   C.   has been agitated.
   D.   is illiterate.
   E.   is antisocial.

13. In lines 11–13, Oliver is most likely

   A.   showing great compassion for his grandmother.
   B.   making a friendly gesture toward his grandmother.
   C.   obeying his mother's request.
   D.   trying to influence his grandmother.
   E.   trying to overcome his fear of his grandmother.

14. In the context of the passage, Grandma's reaction to Janet (lines 22–26 and 38–40) is most likely based on

   A.   mistrust.
   B.   hatred.
   C.   affection.
   D.   distaste.
   E.   humility.

15. Which of the following best describes Tom and Janet's relationship?

   A.   Tom refuses to listen to Janet and insists on making the decisions in the family.
   B.   Janet is bitterly unhappy in the relationship and wants her freedom.
   C.   Tom and Janet disagree about how Grandma should be treated.
   D.   Although Janet doesn't realize it, Grandma is trying to manipulate Tom so that he will leave his wife.
   E.   Janet is afraid of Tom's anger.

16. In lines 60–76, Grandma's words indicate that she

   A.   has been treated cruelly and unfairly by others.
   B.   believes that others are persecuting her.
   C.   has lost her memory.
   D.   is holding a grudge against her family.
   E.   loves her family but doesn't know how to relate to them.

GO ON TO THE NEXT PAGE

331

Questions 17–26 are based on Passage 4 and Passage 5.

The following two passages are both concerned with the concept of biodiversity.

Passage 4:

The term "biodiversity" has become widely used largely because of the growing concern about nature and conservation. The concern is warranted because of accelerating rates of (5) habitat degradation and loss, which result in entire species becoming extinct.

What does the term mean? It is a contracted version of "biological diversity," and a summary of the definition created by the Convention on (10) Biological Diversity is "the variability among living organisms from all sources," including diversity within species and between species, and the diversity of ecosystems themselves. Scientists and other experts in the field agree that biological (15) diversity is essential to the functioning of all natural and human-engineered ecosystems and by extension to the ecosystem services that nature provides to all of us. Living organisms play a fundamental role in the cycles of major (20) elements, such as carbon and nitrogen, and in the water of our environment. Diversity of species is specifically important in that these cycles require a large number of species to interact. A single species can't do it alone.

(25) Estimates of how many species currently live on earth vary widely, largely because most living species are microorganisms and tiny invertebrates. To suggest the guesswork involved, estimates of the number of species range from five to 30 (30) million. Of these, roughly a million and a quarter have been formally described and given official names.

Passage 5:

In the history of the earth, there have been five major mass extinction events. The one that occurred in the Late Devonian period (378 to 375 million years ago) was different from the (5) others, however. The number of species lost wasn't higher in this period, but very few new species arose. Alycia Stigall, a scientist at Ohio University says, "We refer to the Late Devonian as a massive extinction, but it was actually a (10) biodiversity crisis." The natural process of new species formation was affected. The typical method by which new species originate is called "vicariance," which occurs when a population becomes geographically divided by a natural, (15) long-term event, such as formation of a mountain range. Research suggests that vicariance was absent during this ancient phase of earth's history and could be to blame for mass extinction. Of the species that Stigall studied, (20) most lost substantial diversity during the late Devonian. The entire marine ecosystem suffered a major collapse. For example, reef-forming corals were decimated, and reefs didn't appear again for 100 million years. Her study of the Late (25) Devonian is relevant to the current biodiversity crisis, she says, because an influx of invasive species can stop the dominant natural process of new species formation.

Human activity has introduced many invasive (30) species into new ecosystems. In addition, the modern extinction rate exceeds the rate of ancient extinction events, including the one that wiped out dinosaurs 65 million years ago. "Even if you can stop habitat loss, the fact that we've (35) moved all these invasive species around the planet will take a long time to recover from." The high level of invasions has suppressed new species formation substantially. Maintaining earth's ecosystems would be helped, according to (40) Stigall, if we focused efforts on protecting the generation of new species. "The more we know about this process, the more we will understand how to best preserve biodiversity."

17. The two passages are most similar in that both

   A. define biodiversity.

   B. believe the central issue is protecting the generation of new species.

   C. discuss the effect of vicariance.

   D. present an approach to habitat preservation.

   E. consider the effects of biodiversity loss.

18. One way in which the passages differ is that

   A. Passage 4 is objective and Passage 5 is argumentative.

   B. while Passage 5 cites the danger of invasive species, Passage 4 does not.

   C. Passage 4 is written by a scientist and Passage 5 is not.

   D. Passage 4 cites habitat degradation as important, while Passage 5 does not.

   E. Passage 5 describes the results of the massive loss of species, while Passage 4 describes the causes.

GO ON TO THE NEXT PAGE

19. In Passage 4, which of the following is an example of an "ecosystem service"?

   A. creation of new species
   B. regeneration of species
   C. cycle of nitrogen
   D. human engineering
   E. accelerated degradation

20. According to Passage 4, no one knows the exact number of species on earth because

   A. some species are too small to count.
   B. scientists disagree on the exact definition of "species."
   C. the number of species increases continually.
   D. the number of species decreases continually.
   E. species are too widely dispersed.

21. All of the following are true about the definition of *biodiversity* in the first passage EXCEPT that it

   A. was created by the Convention of Biological Diversity.
   B. is not accepted by all scientists because it is too inclusive.
   C. includes diversity of ecosystems.
   D. does not specify the reasons for habitat degradation.
   E. can refer to diversity within a particular species.

22. According to Passage 5, the mass extinction occurring in the Late Devonian period was unusual because

   A. the number of species that was lost was greater than in other extinction events.
   B. its primary effect was on the marine ecosystem.
   C. it took place over a longer period than other extinctions.
   D. the cause was the creation of new mountain ranges.
   E. few new species arose during the period.

23. In Passage 5, line 13, *vicariance* refers to the

   A. rate at which new species form.
   B. formation of mountain ranges and new river channels.
   C. typical method by which new species are formed.
   D. predictable method of invasive species interfering with new species.
   E. failure to preserve new species.

24. In Passage 5, Alycia Stigall refers to the Late Devonian period as a "biodiversity crisis" rather than a mass extinction because

   A. only marine species became extinct.
   B. few new species formed during the period.
   C. habitat degradation grew more common.
   D. those species that became extinct were crucial.
   E. whole ecosystems were destroyed.

25. Stigall says in Passage 5 that in today's world

   A. vicariance is a danger, as it was in the Late Devonian.
   B. scientists are not addressing the primary cause of species loss.
   C. the loss of reef-forming corals is a warning sign of mass extinction.
   D. the formation of new species is endangered by invasive species.
   E. habitat loss is not a cause of species becoming extinct.

26. It can be inferred from Passage 5 that

   A. Stigall believes too much emphasis is given to habitat preservation.
   B. Stigall's research of the Devonian period included studying marine species.
   C. many scientists disagree that invasive species hinder the formation of new species.
   D. reef-forming corals never recovered from extinction in the Late Devonian.
   E. the rate of extinction events has decreased since the extinction of dinosaurs.

IF YOU FINISH BEFORE TIME IS CALLED, CHECK YOUR WORK ON THIS SECTION ONLY. DO NOT WORK ON ANY OTHER SECTION IN THE TEST.

Section 3: Mathematics

Time: 25 minutes

20 Questions

Directions: Solve each problem in this section by using the information given and your own mathematical calculations, insights, and problem-solving skills. Then select the one correct answer of the five choices given and mark the corresponding circle on your answer sheet. Use the available space on the page for your scratch work.

For each question, indicate the best answer, using the following notes.

1. All numerical values used are real numbers.
2. Calculators may be used.
3. Some problems may be accompanied by figures or diagrams. These figures are drawn as accurately as possible EXCEPT when it is stated in a specific problem that a figure is not drawn to scale. The figures and diagrams are meant to provide information useful in solving the problem or problems. Unless otherwise stated, all figures and diagrams lie on a plane.

Data that Can Be Used for Reference

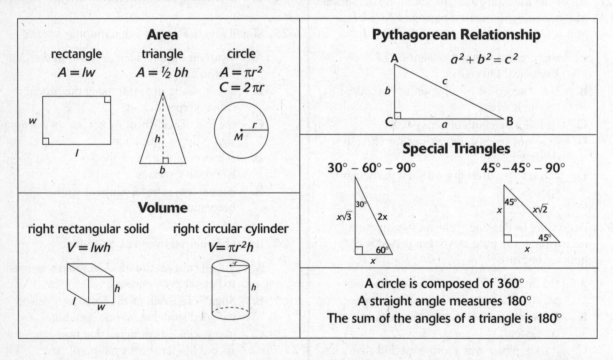

1. If $\frac{1}{5}$ of a number is 2, what is $\frac{1}{2}$ of the number?

   A. 10
   B. 5
   C. 3
   D. 2
   E. 1

2. If a store purchases several items for $1.80 per dozen and sells them at 3 for $0.85, what is the store's profit on 6 dozen of these items?

   A. $4.20
   B. $5.70
   C. $9.60
   D. $10.60
   E. $20.40

GO ON TO THE NEXT PAGE

3. If $x = -1$, then $x^4 + x^3 + x^2 + x - 3 =$

   A. -13

   B. -7

   C. -3

   D. -2

   E. 1

4. If P is the set of prime numbers less than 10 and Q is the set of odd integers between 2 and 8, what is the union of set P and Q?

   A. $\{3, 5, 7\}$

   B. $\{2, 3, 5, 7\}$

   C. $\{3, 5, 7, 9\}$

   D. $\{2, 3, 5, 7, 9\}$

   E. $\{1, 2, 3, 5, 7\}$

5. If $f(x) = 3^x + 5x$, then $f(3) =$

   A. 17

   B. 24

   C. 42

   D. 80

   E. 96

6. The symbol $\otimes$ represents a binary operation defined as $a \otimes b = a^3 + b^2$. What is the value of $(-2) \otimes (-3)$?

   A. 17

   B. 1

   C. 0

   D. -1

   E. -17

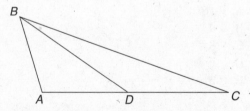

Note: Figure not drawn to scale.

7. In the preceding figure, $AB = AD$ and $BD = CD$. If $\angle C$ measures $19°$, what is the measure of $\angle A$ in degrees?

   A. $75°$

   B. $94°$

   C. $104°$

   D. $114°$

   E. $142°$

8. Angela has nickels and dimes in her pocket. She has twice as many dimes as nickels. What is the best expression of the amount of money she has in cents if x equals the number of nickels she has?

   A. $25x$

   B. $10x + 5(2x)$

   C. $x + 2x$

   D. $5(3x)$

   E. $20(x + 5)$

9. If $x - 4 = y$, what must $(y - x)^3$ equal?

   A. -64

   B. -12

   C. 12

   D. 64

   E. 128

10. In the above figure, the length of a rectangle is $3x$, and its perimeter is $10x + 8$. What is the width of the rectangle?

   A. $2x + 4$

   B. $2x + 8$

   C. $4x + 8$

   D. $4x + 4$

   E. $5x + 4$

11. If $\dfrac{2}{3x - 1} = \dfrac{5}{5x - 2}$, then $x =$

   A. $-\dfrac{9}{5}$

   B. $-\dfrac{1}{5}$

   C. $\dfrac{1}{2}$

   D. $\dfrac{1}{5}$

   E. $\dfrac{9}{5}$

GO ON TO THE NEXT PAGE

Practice Exam 2

12. A car travels 140 miles in 4 hours, while the return trip takes $3\frac{1}{2}$ hours. What is the average speed in miles per hour for the entire trip?

A. 35
B. $37\frac{1}{3}$
C. $37\frac{1}{2}$
D. 40
E. 75

13. If $a > b$, and $ab > 0$, which of the following must be true?

I. $a > 0$
II. $b > 0$
III. $\frac{a}{b} > 0$

A. I only
B. II only
C. III only
D. I and II only
E. I and III only

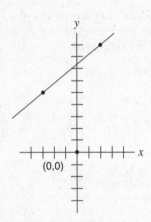

14. What is the slope of the line passing through the points $(-3, 5)$ and $(2, 9)$?

A. -4
B. $-\frac{5}{4}$
C. $-\frac{4}{5}$
D. $\frac{4}{5}$
E. $\frac{5}{4}$

15. Which of the following is equal to $\left(\dfrac{x^{-5}y^2}{x^{-2}y^{-3}}\right)^{-2}$?

A. $x^6 y^2$
B. $x^6 y^{10}$
C. $\dfrac{x^6}{y^2}$
D. $\dfrac{x^6}{y^{10}}$
E. $\dfrac{x^3}{y^5}$

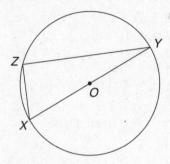

16. In circle O above, $\overline{XY}$ is a diameter, $\overline{OX} = 8.5$, and $\overline{YZ} = 15$. What is the area of $\triangle XYZ$ in square units?

A. 40
B. 60
C. 120
D. 127.5
E. 180

17. A bag contains 20 gumballs. If there are 8 red, 7 white, and 5 green, what is the minimum number of gumballs one must pick from the bag to be assured of getting 1 of each color?

A. 16
B. 9
C. 8
D. 6
E. 3

18. If the five vowels are repeated continuously in the pattern $a, e, i, o, u, a, e, i, o, u$, and so on, what vowel will the 327th letter be?

A. a
B. e
C. i
D. o
E. u

GO ON TO THE NEXT PAGE

19. The base of an isosceles triangle exceeds each of the equal sides by 8 feet. If the perimeter is 89 feet, what is the length of the base in feet?

   A. 27
   B. $29\frac{2}{3}$
   C. 35
   D. 54
   E. 70

20. What is the area of a rhombus with a perimeter of 40 and a diagonal of 10?

   A. $50\sqrt{3}$
   B. 100
   C. $100\sqrt{5}$
   D. 200
   E. 400

IF YOU FINISH BEFORE TIME IS CALLED, CHECK YOUR WORK ON THIS SECTION ONLY. DO NOT WORK ON ANY OTHER SECTION IN THE TEST.

Section 4: Critical Reading

Time: 25 minutes
25 Questions

Directions: In this section, choose the best answer for each question and fill in the corresponding circle on the answer sheet.

Each blank in the following sentences indicates that something has been omitted. Consider the lettered words beneath the sentence and choose the word or set of words that *best* fits the whole sentence.

EXAMPLE:

With a million more people than any other African nation, Nigeria is the most _____ country on the continent.

A. impoverished
B. successful
C. populous
D. developed
E. militant

The correct answer is **C.**

1. Although most of the reviews were _____, one critic praised the artist for her _____ in rejecting conventions.

   A. vague . . . negativity
   B. negative . . . audacity
   C. cursory . . . immaturity
   D. uninteresting . . . humility
   E. positive . . . conservatism

2. President Eisenhower was a _____ editor who refined many of his major speeches as many as 12 times.

   A. timorous
   B. reluctant
   C. nonchalant
   D. prescient
   E. rigorous

3. For a researcher who spends his life moving from one research outpost to another, his social skills are as important as his scientific _____.

   A. liabilities.
   B. assimilation.
   C. prowess.
   D. platitudes.
   E. imagination.

4. Compared to the _____ pace of human evolution, viruses mutate rapidly, and what might be _____ one day could be deadly the next.

   A. glacial . . . benign
   B. frantic . . . beneficial
   C. moderate . . . toxic
   D. tranquil . . . trivial
   E. placid . . . nebulous

5. When the group members learned of the _____ meetings held by the fiscal committee, they demanded that all financial issues be discussed openly at a general meeting.

   A. progressive
   B. lackluster
   C. desultory
   D. tumultuous
   E. clandestine

GO ON TO THE NEXT PAGE

338

6. Although I knew that Templeton despised his boss, his _____ behavior whenever the man appeared was evidence of his hypocrisy.

    A. neurotic
    B. obsequious
    C. garish
    D. incompatible
    E. censorious

7. When he learned of the cheating plot, the professor _____ the culprits and expelled them from the class.

    A. castigated
    B. mollified
    C. rescinded
    D. persecuted
    E. cajoled

8. In trying to improve American eating habits, nutritionists would have to _____ the notion that healthful food is both bland and unsatisfying.

    A. support
    B. reconsider
    C. dispel
    D. reiterate
    E. nullify

GO ON TO THE NEXT PAGE

Practice Exam 2

Directions: Questions follow each of the passages below. Answer the questions using only the stated or implied information in each passage and in its introduction, if any.

Questions 9–18 are based on the following pair of passages.

The subject of both passages is the Brontë family (Charlotte, Emily, Anne, and Branwell), their home, and their legacy. Charlotte is the author of Jane Eyre and Emily is the author of Wuthering Heights, two well-known nineteenth-century novels.

Passage 1:

The house of the Brontës at Haworth Parsonage in Yorkshire was a two-story gray millstone grit house with four rooms on each floor, standing at the top of a steep hill behind the
(5) town. Built in 1799, along the simple and stately lines dictated by Georgian architecture, its sturdy foundations and heavily flagged roof resisted the harsh winter winds and snows, and the mists and rains of other seasons. Together with the church
(10) and the schoolhouse, the Brontë home formed a triangle, a fourth side opening onto sweeping wild moors. These wastelands of black rock, grasses, and heather altered seasonally in color from a tantalizing purple in August and September to
(15) dark brown at other periods. The moors represented joy and liberation for the Brontë children and particularly for Emily, who withered physically and emotionally when away from them.

Not without significance for the Brontës, and
(20) perhaps an omen, was the graveyard that surrounded the house and garden. Since sanitary conditions were primitive in the early 1900s and the mortality rate high, one wonders whether, as has been suggested, the decaying bodies buried
(25) in the earth polluted the Brontës' water supply, thus paving the way for disease. The graveyard may also be viewed as both a real and symbolic reminder of the virtually continuous presence of Death in their lives.

Passage 2:

In the last century and a half, Haworth has thus become firmly established on the tourist trail. As the working mills and factories disappeared from the surrounding area, tourism
(5) became more and more important to the local economy and is now the biggest employer in Haworth. The travel sections of today's newspapers continue in the tradition of the turn-of-the-century guidebooks encouraging
(10) readers to wear their wellies to Brontëland. In the 1990s, one finds a tourist board official quoted as comparing "Brontë" as a brand to "Coca-Cola," and local businesses use the name unsparingly, often for its recognition value alone.
(15) A taxi company or a hairdresser's named after the Brontës has little to do with Haworth's most famous family, though one wonders about the cabinetmaker-cum-undertaker who, among other items, advertised coffins under the banner
(20) "Brontë Product" in the 1950s.

Much of the imagery popularly associated with the Brontës today postdates the Victorian cult of Charlotte. In the twentieth century, Emily toppled her elder sister from her preeminent
(25) position and became enshrined as the free spirit of the moors. It was through the cult of Emily that the myth of the Brontës as forces of nature rising ineluctably out of the Wuthering landscape gained currency. Images of storm-tossed passion
(30) associated with her—or with the Hollywoodization of *Wuthering Heights*—are now part and parcel of the Brontë brand. Yet if you visit the souvenir shops (with names like "Brontësaurus") which crowd up Haworth's steep Main Street, you can
(35) still detect the lingering presence of the domestic saint originally created by Elizabeth Gaskell.[1]

Tea towels printed with the Brontës' faces or miniature brass warming pans send debased messages of homely nostalgia connected at some
(40) vestigial level to Gaskell's image of Charlotte the housewife rolling up her sleeves to peel Tabby's potatoes. Brontë Original Unique Liqueur (surely not a reference to Branwell's[2] drinking problem?) comes in an olde worlde stoneware flagon straight
(45) from the kitchen of yesteryear. The former apothecary's shop, which supplied Branwell with laudanum, is now a sort of novelty chemist's selling colored bath salts in Victorian-style packaging (the Emily Brontë soap has "the elusive fragrance of the
(50) wild moors"). During a visit in 1994, it was depressing to discover from the proprietor that the premises had previously been a bookshop which had closed due to lack of demand.

---

[1] Elizabeth Gaskell (1810–1865) wrote the first and most celebrated biography of Charlotte Brontë.

[2] Branwell Brontë was Charlotte, Emily, and Anne's brother. When his own ambitions as a painter and writer were frustrated, he became an alcoholic and took opium.

GO ON TO THE NEXT PAGE

9. One aspect of the Brontë sisters that the authors of both passages address is

   A. the quality of their novels.
   B. the quality of their home life.
   C. Haworth and its surroundings.
   D. the differences between Charlotte and Emily.
   E. factors that influenced their work.

10. In Passage 2, the author's primary purpose is to

    A. show how the Industrial Revolution changed the countryside around Haworth.
    B. criticize the Brontës for their melodramatic fiction.
    C. criticize early biographies of Charlotte Brontë.
    D. explain why the "cult of Emily" replaced the "cult of Charlotte."
    E. show examples of the myth of the Brontës in popular culture.

11. A primary contrast between the passages is the

    A. use of personification in Passage 1 but not in Passage 2.
    B. different time frames.
    C. authors' judgments of the Brontë novels.
    D. lack of detail in Passage 2 compared to Passage 1.
    E. complex language in Passage 2 as opposed to the language in Passage 1.

12. The best example of irony in the passages is found in

    A. Passage 1, lines 5–6: "Built in 1799, along the simple and stately lines . . ."
    B. Passage 1, lines 19–21: "Not without significance for the Brontës, . . ."
    C. Passage 2, lines 1–3: "In the last century and a half, Haworth . . . "
    D. Passage 2, lines 23–24: "In the twentieth century, Emily toppled her elder sister . . ."
    E. Passage 2, lines 42–43: "Brontë Original Unique Liqueur (surely not a reference . . ."

13. Lines 17–20 (in Passage 2) most closely mirror which of the following lines in Passage 1?

    A. lines 9–12: "Together with the church and the schoolhouse . . ."
    B. lines 12–15: "These wastelands of black rock, . . . "
    C. lines 15–18: "The moors represented joy and liberation . . ."
    D. lines 21–25: "Since sanitary conditions were primitive . . ."
    E. lines 26–29: "The graveyard may also be viewed as . . ."

14. In Passage 2, all of the following are examples of the author's dry humor EXCEPT

    A. lines 3–5: "As the working mills and factories disappeared . . ."
    B. lines 7–10: "The travel sections of today's newspapers . . . "
    C. lines 32–33: "Yet if you visit the souvenir shops . . ."
    D. lines 37–39: "Tea towels printed with the Brontës' faces . . ."
    E. lines 47–48: " . . . chemist's selling colored bath salts . . ."

15. In lines 50–53 of Passage 2, the author most clearly

    A. regrets that the commercialism of tourism has replaced an interest in books.
    B. is disdainful of the myth surrounding the Brontë sisters.
    C. shows appreciation for the talents of Charlotte and Emily Brontë.
    D. is discouraged by the decline of literacy in Great Britain.
    E. argues for greater emphasis on teaching literature in the schools.

16. The best definition in context for the word *ineluctably* in line 28 of Passage 2 is

    A. timidly
    B. awkwardly
    C. inevitably
    D. joyfully
    E. nostalgically

GO ON TO THE NEXT PAGE

Practice Exam 2

17. In lines 38–39 of Passage 2, the phrase "debased messages of homely nostalgia" conveys the author's

    A. sorrow at the decline of language.
    B. anger at those who visit Haworth.
    C. disappointment with the Brontës.
    D. distaste for trivial souvenirs.
    E. belief in commercialization.

18. In can be inferred that the author of Passage 2

    A. prefers Emily Brontë to Charlotte Brontë.
    B. would like to see Haworth restored by the British government.
    C. believes Elizabeth Gaskell's biography paints an idealized picture of Charlotte.
    D. fears that books have become obsolete.
    E. sees Branwell Brontë as the most misunderstood member of the family.

Questions 19–25 are based on the following passage.

Passage 3:

A few years ago the city council of Monza, Italy, barred pet owners from keeping goldfish in curved fishbowls. The sponsors of the measure explained that it is cruel to keep a fish in a bowl
(5) because the curved sides give the fish a distorted view of reality. Aside from the measure's significance to the poor goldfish, the story raises an interesting philosophical question: How do we know that the reality we perceive is true?
(10) The idea of alternative realities is a mainstay of today's popular culture. For example, in the science-fiction film *The Matrix* the human race is unknowingly living in a simulated virtual reality created by intelligent computers to keep
(15) them pacified and content while the computers suck their bioelectrical energy (whatever that is). How do we know we are not just computer-generated characters living in a *Matrix*-like world? If we lived in a synthetic, imaginary
(20) world, events would not necessarily have any logic or consistency or obey any laws. The aliens in control might find it more interesting or amusing to see our reactions, for example, if everyone in the world suddenly decided that
(25) chocolate was repulsive or that war was not an option, but that has never happened. If the aliens did enforce consistent laws, we would have no way to tell that another reality stood behind the simulated one. It is easy to call the world the
(30) aliens live in the "real" one and

the computer-generated world a false one. But if—like us—the beings in the simulated world could not gaze into their universe from the outside, they would have no reason to doubt
(35) their own pictures of reality.

The goldfish are in a similar situation. Their view is not the same as ours from outside their curved bowl, but they could still formulate scientific laws governing the motion of the objects
(40) they observe on the outside. For instance, because light bends as it travels from air to water, a freely moving object that we would observe to move in a straight line would be observed by the goldfish to move along a curved path. The goldfish could
(45) formulate scientific laws from their distorted frame of reference that would always hold true and that would enable them to make predictions about the future motion of objects outside the bowl. Their laws would be more complicated than
(50) the laws in our frame, but simplicity is a matter of taste. If the goldfish formulated such a theory, we would have to admit the goldfish's view as a valid picture of reality.

19. The most accurate way to describe the point of the opening paragraph of Passage 3 is that it

    A. emphasizes a humorous view of reality.
    B. compares humans to goldfish.
    C. introduces the idea that reality is subjective.
    D. satirizes animal rights legislation.
    E. questions the importance of philosophy.

20. The authors refer to *The Matrix* in line 12 to

    A. show how sophisticated special effects can be in modern science fiction films.
    B. demonstrate that current science fiction films are primarily philosophical in nature.
    C. prove that we could be living in a simulated reality.
    D. show the popularity of alternative realities as a subject of today's culture.
    E. counteract the humor of the example of goldfish in the first paragraph.

GO ON TO THE NEXT PAGE

21. The authors use the parenthetical phrase in line 16 to

    A. gently poke fun at the "scientific" term "bioelectrical energy."
    B. belittle the scientific knowledge of the makers of *The Matrix*.
    C. undercut the subject of alternative realities.
    D. show the creativity of the filmmakers.
    E. show their superiority to the writers of science fiction films.

22. According to the authors, if we lived in a simulated world with no consistent laws,

    A. there would be no war.
    B. we would be unable to form relationships.
    C. events would be haphazard, governed by no logic.
    D. life wouldn't have any meaning.
    E. robots would replace humans.

23. In theory, according to the authors, the main reason the goldfish in paragraph 1 are in a situation similar to the one of humans in a world created by aliens is that

    A. each can't see his world from the outside.
    B. both are powerless to make their own laws.
    C. neither is able to understand how light travels in space.
    D. both know nothing about power.
    E. neither is willing to see the world from a different point of view.

24. The primary purpose of Passage 3 is to

    A. indicate how prevalent the idea of alternative realities is in today's popular culture.
    B. suggest that what we believe is objective reality based on our perceptions.
    C. question the formulation of scientific laws.
    D. compare our ideas of reality with those of goldfish.
    E. examine the difference between alternative realities and our reality.

25. In lines 40–44, the authors suggest that goldfish would observe light to move in a curved path rather than a straight one because

    A. the bowl the goldfish are in is curved.
    B. of the location of their eyes.
    C. movements in the water distort lines.
    D. a glass bowl distorts the path of light.
    E. light bends when it travels from air to water.

Practice Exam 2

IF YOU FINISH BEFORE TIME IS CALLED, CHECK YOUR WORK ON THIS SECTION ONLY. DO NOT WORK ON ANY OTHER SECTION IN THE TEST.

STOP

Section 5: Writing—Multiple Choice

Time: 25 minutes
35 Questions

Directions: In this section, choose the best answer for each question and fill in the corresponding circle on the answer sheet.

The following questions test correctness and effective expression. In selecting the answer, pay attention to grammar, diction, sentence structure, and punctuation. In the following questions, part or all of each sentence is underlined. Answer Choice A repeats the underlined portion of the original sentence, while the next four offer alternatives. Choose the answer that best expresses the meaning of the original sentence and at the same time is grammatically correct and stylistically superior. The correct choice should be clear, unambiguous, and concise.

EXAMPLE:

The forecaster predicted <u>rain and the sky was clear</u>.

- **A.** rain and the sky was clear
- **B.** rain but the sky was clear
- **C.** rain the sky was clear
- **D.** rain, but the sky was clear
- **E.** rain being as the sky was clear

The correct answer is **D.**

---

1. The summer concerts usually begin at 8:00 p.m., <u>and this week's concert will begin earlier.</u>

   - **A.** , and this week's concert will begin earlier.
   - **B.** but this weeks will begin earlier.
   - **C.** and this weeks will be beginning earlier.
   - **D.** , but this week's will begin earlier.
   - **E.** ; but this weeks concert will be beginning at an earlier time.

2. One way <u>of expanding the money supply and to raise prices</u> was to coin unlimited amounts of silver.

   - **A.** of expanding the money supply and to raise prices
   - **B.** to expand the money supply and raise prices
   - **C.** of the expansion of the money supply and the raising of prices
   - **D.** to expand the money supply and raising prices
   - **E.** of expanding the money supply and in addition to raise prices

3. <u>Forgetting to notify the neighborhood of the toxic chemical spill</u> may cost the company millions of dollars.

   - **A.** Forgetting to notify the neighborhood of the toxic chemical spill
   - **B.** To forget the notification of the neighborhood of the toxic chemical spill
   - **C.** The forgetting the notification of the neighborhood of the toxic chemical spill
   - **D.** Notification of the neighborhood of the toxic spill being forgotten
   - **E.** Having forgotten notification of the neighborhood of the toxic chemical spill

GO ON TO THE NEXT PAGE

4. Mark Twain's books, which are a staple of American literature even <u>today, but have frequently been the subject of controversy</u> since the beginning.

    A. today, but have frequently been the subject of controversy

    B. today, except for the fact they have frequently been the subject of controversy

    C. today; but have frequently been the subject of controversy

    D. today, have frequently been the subject of controversy

    E. today, with the exception that they have frequently been the subject of controversy

5. <u>During the Industrial Revolution occurred one of the most important transportation improvements in the United States, which was the Central Pacific Railroad.</u>

    A. During the Industrial Revolution occurred one of the most important transportation improvements in the United States, which was the Central Pacific Railroad.

    B. During the Industrial Revolution, the Central Pacific Railroad was one of the most important improvements in transportation in the United States.

    C. In the United States there occurred, during the Industrial Revolution, one of its most important transportation improvements: the Central Pacific Railroad.

    D. The Central Pacific Railroad, coming to be in the United States during the Industrial Revolution, was one of the most important improvements in transportation.

    E. In the United States the most important transportation improvement was the Central Pacific Railroad, during the Industrial Revolution.

6. At this point <u>the President reads a prepared statement but refused to answer questions</u> despite the shouts from the angry reporters.

    A. the President reads a prepared statement but refused to answer questions

    B. the President, who is reading a prepared statement but refusing to answer questions

    C. the President read a prepared statement but refused to answer questions

    D. the President, after he reads a prepared statement, continued to refuse to answer questions

    E. the President, reading a prepared statement but refusing to answer questions

7. <u>While watching television, the doorbell rang, and Robert decided</u> to ignore it.

    A. While watching television, the doorbell rang, and Robert decided

    B. Watching television, the doorbell rang, and Robert decided

    C. Robert decided, when the doorbell rang while watching television,

    D. While he was watching television, the doorbell rang, and Robert decided

    E. While watching television, the doorbell was ringing, and Robert decided

8. <u>Passing the written test is usually more difficult than to pass the hands-on driving test,</u> according to many teenagers.

    A. Passing the written test is usually more difficult than to pass the hands-on driving test

    B. Passing the written test is usually more difficult than passing the hands-on driving test

    C. To pass the written test is usually more difficult than passing the hands-on driving test

    D. The passing of the written test can be usually more difficult than the passing of the hands-on driving test

    E. Passing the written test is usually more difficult than the passing of the hands-on driving test

GO ON TO THE NEXT PAGE

9. <u>One of the nation's most serious concerns are the health and financial security of all of its citizens, irregardless of</u> their ethnic backgrounds.

   A. One of the nation's most serious concerns are the health and financial security of all of its citizens, irregardless of
   B. One of the nation's most serious concerns is the health and financial security of all of its citizens, irregardless of
   C. One of the nation's most serious concerns are the health and financial security of all of its citizens, regardless of
   D. One of the nation's most serious concerns is the health and financial security of all of its citizens, regardless of
   E. One of the nation's most serious concerns were the health and financial security of all of its citizens; regardless of

10. The new administrator <u>could of chosen whomever he wanted</u> to run the computer lab, but instead he let Carter make the selection, because Carter was more familiar with the staff.

    A. could of chosen whomever he wanted
    B. could of chosen whomever he was wanting
    C. could have chosen whoever he wanted
    D. could have chosen whomever he wanted
    E. could have chose whoever he wanted

11. Ancient Greeks were so accustomed to using the names of the winds to indicate the directions <u>from which they came that "wind" became</u> a synonym for direction.

    A. from which they came that "wind" became
    B. wherever they came that from that "wind" becomes
    C. from which they came from that "wind" would have become
    D. whichever they came from that "wind" was becoming
    E. from which they came and "wind" will become

GO ON TO THE NEXT PAGE

Directions: The following sentences may contain one error of grammar, usage, diction, or idiom. No sentence contains more than one error, and some have no error. If there is an error, it will be underlined and have a letter beneath it. If there is an error, choose the one underlined part that must be changed to correct the sentence. If there is no error, choose E. Sections of the sentence that are not underlined cannot be changed. In selecting your answer, observe the requirements of standard written English.

EXAMPLE:

The film <u>tell the story</u> of a army captain and <u>his wife</u> who <u>try to</u> <u>rebuild their lives</u> after the Iraq War.
      A   B   C   D

<u>No error</u>
  E

The correct answer is **A.**

---

12. Among the dignitaries <u>who were attending</u> the
                  A

conference <u>was</u> the governor and the assistant
           B

governor, who <u>had flown in</u> from the capital
               C

and were expecting to meet with <u>him and me</u>
                             D

after the introductory session. <u>No error</u>
                          E

13. <u>Reading the newspaper at breakfast, the article</u>
                     A

about the hurricane in Florida made me

wonder <u>whether</u> Walter and <u>I</u> should cancel
       B   C

our trip or <u>should perhaps</u> choose another
            D

destination. <u>No error</u>
         E

14. A growing body of research <u>suggest</u> that
                 A

spaces <u>that are</u> filled with leafy vegetation <u>filter</u>
       B   C

pollution and <u>trap</u> tiny particles of dirt and
          D

soot. <u>No error</u>
      E

15. When one <u>wishes</u> to apply for <u>admission to</u> the
         A   B

advanced class, <u>you</u> should submit at <u>least</u> four
          C   D

samples of scientific prose. <u>No error</u>
               E

16. The doctor spoke so <u>soft</u> that <u>no one</u> in the
              A   B

room <u>was able</u> to understand <u>what he was</u>
      C   D

<u>saying</u> about her condition. <u>No error</u>
                    E

17. <u>According to</u> the speaker, the university <u>is failing</u>
     A   B

to <u>instill in</u> future teachers a sense of urgency
     C

about how <u>bad</u> the situation is in many of the
         D

nation's classrooms. <u>No error</u>
              E

18. Richardson's plan will pay its own way because

it <u>will specify</u> that anyone who <u>wants</u> to use the
     A   B

new service <u>will be required</u> to pay a fee, and if
          C

someone <u>refused</u> to pay, he will be excluded.
        D

<u>No error</u>
  E

19. The football game was a perfect chance for Bill

Stevens and <u>myself</u> to <u>prove to</u> the coach that
        A   B

we <u>were very serious</u> about playing, not just
        C

on the team because we wanted to meet the

<u>most popular</u> girls. <u>No error</u>
  D   E

GO ON TO THE NEXT PAGE

20. Brown told us <u>that</u> the owner of the building
    A
    <u>could of decided</u> to waive the fees for the
    B
    nonprofit organization, but he <u>not only</u>
    C
    demanded the entire rent <u>but also</u> required a
    D
    large security deposit. <u>No error</u>
    E

21. Folic acid <u>appears to</u> exert a protective <u>affect;</u>
    A   B
    for example, when a large group of expectant
    mothers <u>was given</u> folic acid supplements, the
    C
    number of neural defects found in their babies
    <u>was</u> much lower than had been predicted.
    D
    <u>No error</u>
    E

22. <u>While lying asleep in the tall prairie grass and</u>
    A
    <u>dreaming</u> of a hot shower, the snake slithered
    <u>quietly past</u> my older brother, <u>who was</u>
    B   C
    <u>supposed to be</u> keeping an eye on me, and
    drove its <u>deadly</u> fangs into my ankle. <u>No error</u>
    D   E

23. The Harrisons and <u>them</u>, <u>regardless</u> of how
    A   B
    many attempts have been made to negotiate a
    settlement, continue to fight <u>mercilessly</u> over
    C
    the small patch of land that <u>lies</u> between their
    D
    garages. <u>No error</u>
    E

24. The trip to Italy had been planned for several
    months, and my <u>brother and I</u> <u>had arranged</u>
    A   B
    accommodations in each city, so we <u>felt badly</u>
    C
    when Mother and Father, <u>who</u> wanted to visit
    D
    their homeland, were simply too ill to make the
    journey. <u>No error</u>
    E

25. The <u>better plan</u> of the two was to raise money
    A
    by having a concert, which <u>almost everyone</u>
    B
    wanted to do, and <u>to delay</u> raising membership
    C
    dues until the regional chairperson contacted
    <u>he and I</u> with further information. <u>No error</u>
    D   E

26. The area right <u>beside</u> the stream smelled
    A
    so <u>bad</u> because many people had picnicked
    B
    there without <u>cleaning up</u> after they <u>had ate</u>.
    C   D
    <u>No error</u>
    E

27. The author of the new book, a man <u>whom</u>
    A
    was respected <u>both for his writing</u> and for
    B
    his <u>understanding of the issues</u>, agreed to
    C
    <u>appear briefly</u> at the council meeting to support
    D
    our request for a community garden. <u>No error</u>
    E

28. <u>In the opinion</u> of some critics, Marlon Brando
    A
    <u>was</u> the <u>most unique</u> actor in Hollywood films
    B   C
    of the <u>twentieth century</u>. <u>No error</u>
    D   E

29. As I told <u>them</u>, the argument between David
    A
    and <u>I</u> earlier that day <u>had begun</u> over an issue
    B   C
    that neither <u>he</u> nor I cared much about.
    D
    <u>No error</u>
    E

GO ON TO THE NEXT PAGE

Directions: The following passage is an early draft of a student essay. Some parts need to be revised.

Read the selection carefully and answer the questions that follow. There will be questions about sentence structure, diction, and usage in individual sentences or parts of sentences. Other questions will deal with the whole essay or paragraphs and ask you to decide about the organization, development, and appropriate language. Choose the answer that follows the requirements of standard written English and most effectively expresses the intended meanings.

Questions 30–35 are based on the following passage.

(1) Since its beginning America was basically a rural society, with most people living on farms or in villages. (2) They made their living off the land or from small businesses. (3) In the nineteenth century, however, the economy underwent major changes, and these changes were often disruptive due to the fact that they disturbed people. (4) The Industrial Revolution brought factories and mass production, which meant that many people had to move to larger towns and cities in order to support themselves. (5) In addition to creating a large working class of people who had to endure low wages, long hours, and sometimes dangerous conditions, an upper class of wealthy individuals who owned the new factories and businesses, were created. (6) For example, men like John D. Rockefeller and Andrew <u>Carnegie, who became major figures</u>. (7) In 1894 Henry Demarest Lloyd wrote a vicious attack on John D. Rockefeller and Standard Oil Company. (8) For the working class, the slower pace and simpler pleasures of the countryside vanished. (9) In the 1890s and early 1900s, vocal critics worried that individual democracy was in danger. (10) Some of them lashed out in articles and books at the new industrialists for introducing corruption and exploitation into the American economy. (11) Theodore Roosevelt coined the term "muckrakers" to describe many of the writers who he believed were "wallowing in the mud" and exaggerating their stories.

30. In context, which of the following is the best way to revise sentence 3 (*reproduced below*)?

    In the nineteenth century, however, the economy underwent major changes, and these changes were often disruptive due to the fact that they disturbed people.

    A. The economy underwent major changes during the nineteenth century, however, and these changes were often disruptive.

    B. With the advent of the nineteenth century, however, the economy underwent major changes, and these changes were oftentimes disruptive and disturbing to people.

    C. Disruptions which disturbed people occurred during the nineteenth century, however, because the economy underwent major changes.

    D. In the nineteenth century, however, the economy underwent major changes which caused disruption and made people disturbed.

    E. The major changes that occurred in the nineteenth century with the economy, however, not only disrupted people but also disturbed them.

GO ON TO THE NEXT PAGE

31. Which of the following is the best version of sentence 5 (*reproduced below*)?

In addition to creating a large working class of people who had to endure low wages, long hours, and sometimes dangerous conditions, an upper class of wealthy individuals who owned the new factories and businesses, were created.

A. A large working class of people who had to endure low wages, long hours and sometimes dangerous conditions was created by the Industrial Revolution; as well as a new upper class of wealthy individuals many of whom owned the new factories and businesses.

B. In addition to creating a large working class of people who had to endure low wages, long hours, and sometimes dangerous conditions, the Industrial Revolution gave rise to a new upper class of wealthy factory and business owners.

C. The Industrial Revolution created a large working class of people who had to endure low wages, long hours, and sometimes dangerous conditions, and also created a new upper class of wealthy individuals who owned the factories and businesses.

D. Both a large working class of people who had to endure low wages, long hours, and sometimes dangerous conditions and a wealthy upper class made up of individuals who owned factories and businesses was created by the Industrial Revolution.

E. In addition to creating a large working class of people who had to work for low wages, long hours, and sometimes dangerous conditions, an upper class of wealthy individuals who owned factories and businesses came into being at the time of the Industrial Revolution.

32. The underlined part of sentence 6 should be rewritten in which of the following ways?

A. Carnegie became
B. Carnegie, both of whom became
C. Carnegie, both of who became
D. Carnegie, and they both became
E. Carnegie, who will become

33. Where is the best place for sentence 7 (*reproduced below*)?

In 1894 Henry Demarest Lloyd wrote a vicious attack of John D. Rockefeller and Standard Oil Company.

A. between sentences 5 and 6
B. after sentence 11
C. between sentences 10 and 11
D. between sentences 8 and 9
E. between sentences 4 and 5

34. Where is the best place for sentence 8 (*reproduced below*)?

For the working class, the slower pace and simpler pleasures of the countryside vanished.

A. where it is now
B. after sentence 2
C. after sentence 6
D. after sentence 4
E. after sentence 10

35. Which of the following would be the best concluding sentence for this paragraph?

A. The term "muckraker" is used today to describe social reformers, showing the profound effect that Theodore Roosevelt had on the American people.

B. Thus, the Industrial Revolution affected many people in America.

C. The average citizen at the time of the Industrial Revolution wanted nothing more than to return to the simpler, rural existence that had been left behind.

D. The changes in America society were beneficial to its diverse citizenry, as both workers and owners thrived during the nineteenth and twentieth centuries.

E. Whether the "muckraker" stories were exaggerated or not, the changes in society triggered by the Industrial Revolution created a widening gap between the industrialists and factory owners and the people who worked for them.

IF YOU FINISH BEFORE TIME IS CALLED, CHECK YOUR WORK ON THIS SECTION ONLY. DO NOT WORK ON ANY OTHER SECTION IN THE TEST.

Section 6: Mathematics

Time: 25 minutes

18 Questions

Directions: Solve each problem in this section by using the information given and your own mathematical calculations, insights, and problem-solving skills. Then select the one correct answer of the five choices given and mark the corresponding circle on your answer sheet. Use the available space on the page for your scratch work.

For each question, indicate the best answer, using the following notes.

1. All numerical values used are real numbers.
2. Calculators may be used.
3. Some problems may be accompanied by figures or diagrams. These figures are drawn as accurately as possible EXCEPT when it is stated in a specific problem that a figure is not drawn to scale. The figures and diagrams are meant to provide information that is useful in solving the problem or problems. Unless otherwise stated, all figures and diagrams lie on a plane.

Data that Can Be Used for Reference

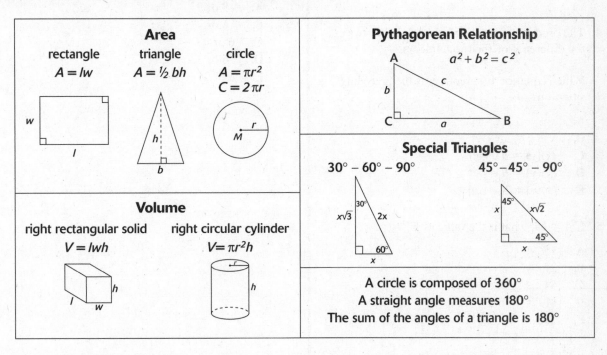

Area

rectangle
$A = lw$

triangle
$A = \frac{1}{2}bh$

circle
$A = \pi r^2$
$C = 2\pi r$

Volume

right rectangular solid
$V = lwh$

right circular cylinder
$V = \pi r^2 h$

Pythagorean Relationship

$a^2 + b^2 = c^2$

Special Triangles

$30° - 60° - 90°$

$45° - 45° - 90°$

A circle is composed of 360°
A straight angle measures 180°
The sum of the angles of a triangle is 180°

8, 9, 12, 17, 24, . . .

1. In the preceding sequence, a certain pattern determines each of the subsequent numbers. What is the next number in the sequence?

   A. 41
   B. 35
   C. 33
   D. 30
   E. 29

2. What is $\frac{1}{4}$ of 0.03%?

   A. 0.75
   B. 0.075
   C. 0.0075
   D. 0.00075
   E. 0.000075

GO ON TO THE NEXT PAGE

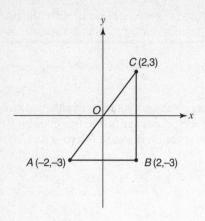

3. What is the area of $\triangle ABC$ in the figure above?

   A. 3
   B. 6
   C. 12
   D. 18
   E. 24

4. The product of two numbers is equal to twice the difference of the two numbers.

   Which equation best represents the preceding situation?

   A. $x + y = 2(x - y)$
   B. $x + y = 2(x \div y)$
   C. $(x)(y) = 2(x \div y)$
   D. $(x)(y) = 2(x - y)$
   E. $(x)(y) = 2(x + y)$

5. If $4^n = 64$, what is the value of 3^{n+2}?

   A. 15
   B. 27
   C. 54
   D. 81
   E. 243

6. For what values of z is $f(z) = \dfrac{3z^3 + z - 7}{z^2 - 25}$ undefined?

   A. 25
   B. 5
   C. 0
   D. −5
   E. −5, 5

7. If D is between A and B on $\overleftrightarrow{AB}$, then which of the following must be true?

   A. $AD = DB$
   B. $BD = AB - AD$
   C. $AD = AB + DB$
   D. $DB = AD + AB$
   E. $AB = AD - BD$

8. If $x - 3 = \dfrac{18}{x}$, then $x =$

   A. −9 or 9
   B. −6 or −3
   C. 6 or −3
   D. −6 or 3
   E. 6 or 3

GO ON TO THE NEXT PAGE

Directions for Student-Produced Response Questions (Grid-ins): Questions 9–18 require you to solve the problem and enter your answer by carefully marking the circles on the special grid. Examples of the appropriate way to mark the grid follow.

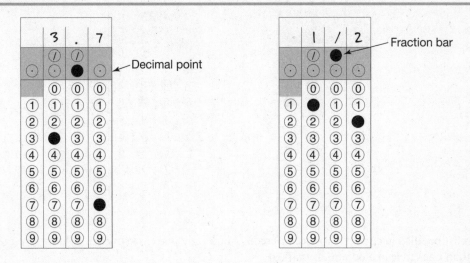

Do not grid in mixed numbers in the form of mixed numbers. Always change mixed numbers to improper fractions or decimals. Here's an example of how to grid when your answer is a mixed number such as $1\frac{1}{2}$.

Change to 1.5   or   Change to $\frac{3}{2}$

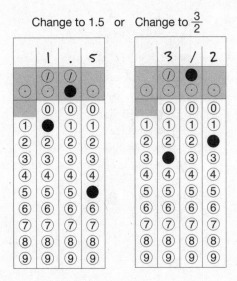

Space permitting, answers can start in any column. Each grid-in answer that follows is correct.

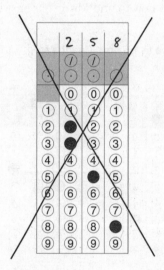

Note: Circles must be filled in correctly to receive credit. Mark only one circle in each column. No credit will be given if more than one circle in a column is marked.

Example:

Accuracy of decimals: Always enter the most accurate decimal value that the grid will accommodate. For example: An answer such as .8888 . . . can be gridded as .888 or .889. Gridding this value as .8, .88, or .89 is considered inaccurate and therefore not acceptable. The acceptable grid-ins of $\frac{8}{9}$ are

Be sure to write your answers in the boxes at the top of the circles before doing your gridding. Although writing out the answers above the columns is not required, it is very important to ensure accuracy. Even though some problems may have more than one correct answer, only grid in one answer. Grid-in questions contain no negative answers.

9. What is the value of $5x^2 - 3x + 2$ when $x = -4$?

10. A long-distance telephone call costs $2.45 for the first three minutes and $.32 per minute for each additional minute. What is the cost in dollars and cents for a 25-minute call? (Disregard the $ sign when gridding your answer.)

11. A jacket sold for $56, which was 80% of the original price. What was the original price in dollars and cents? (Disregard the $ sign when gridding your answer.)

12. How many different 5-person committees can be formed from a group of 5 females and 7 males, if each committee must have 2 female and 3 male members?

GO ON TO THE NEXT PAGE

Bill for Purchase	
Science Textbooks	$840
Lab Equipment	$460
Formaldehyde	$320
Teacher's Manuals	$120
TOTAL	$2,220

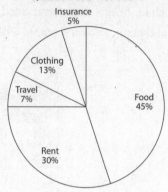

$8000 Total Per Year

13. Scholastic Supplies, Inc., sends the above bill to Martin Luther King High School. Although the bill's total includes the cost of science lab workbooks, Scholastic Supplies forgot to list them on the bill. How much did the science lab workbooks cost Martin Luther King High School? (Disregard the $ sign when gridding your answer.)

14. If the numerator of a fraction is tripled, and the denominator of a fraction is doubled, the resulting fraction will reflect an increase of what percent? (Disregard the % sign when gridding your answer.)

16. Based on the chart above, how much more money was spent on clothing than on insurance? (Disregard the $ sign when gridding your answer.)

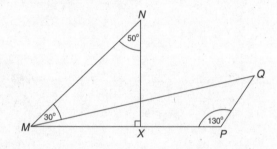

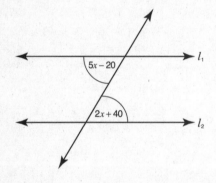

15. In the figure above $l_1 \parallel l_2$, what is the value of x?

17. In the figure above, what is the ratio of the degree measure of $\angle MQP$ to the degree measure of $\angle PXN$?

18. A bus leaves from Albuquerque at 9:00 a.m. traveling east at 50 mph. At 1:00 p.m., a plane leaves Albuquerque traveling east at 300 mph. How many minutes will it take for the plane to overtake the bus?

IF YOU FINISH BEFORE TIME IS CALLED, CHECK YOUR WORK ON THIS SECTION ONLY. DO NOT WORK ON ANY OTHER SECTION IN THE TEST.

Section 7: Mathematics

Time: 20 minutes

16 Questions

Directions: Solve each problem in this section by using the information given and your own mathematical calculations, insights, and problem-solving skills. Then select the one correct answer of the five choices given and mark the corresponding circle on your answer sheet. Use the available space on the page for your scratch work.

For each question, indicate the best answer, using the following notes.

1. All numerical values used are real numbers.

2. Calculators may be used.

3. Some problems may be accompanied by figures or diagrams. These figures are drawn as accurately as possible EXCEPT when it is stated in a specific problem that a figure is not drawn to scale. The figures and diagrams are meant to provide information useful in solving the problem or problems. Unless otherwise stated, all figures and diagrams lie on a plane.

Data that Can Be Used for Reference

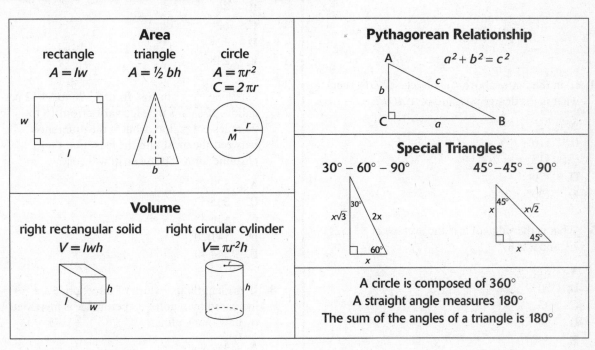

1. If $2x + 13$ represents an odd number, what must the next consecutive odd number be?

   A. $2x + 15$
   B. $2x + 14$
   C. $3x + 13$
   D. $3x + 15$
   E. $4x + 1$

2. A suit that originally sold for $120 was on sale for $90. What was the rate of discount?

   A. 75%
   B. $33\frac{1}{3}\%$
   C. 30%
   D. 25%
   E. 20%

GO ON TO THE NEXT PAGE

3. If $\sqrt{\dfrac{81}{x}} = \dfrac{9}{5}$, then $x =$

 A. 5
 B. 9
 C. 25
 D. 50
 E. 53

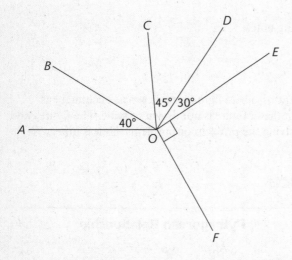

4. If, in the figure above, $\overline{CO}$ bisects $\angle BOD$, then what is the degree measure of $\angle AOF$?

 A. 95°
 B. 110°
 C. 115°
 D. 120°
 E. 130°

5. What is the value of x if the average of 93, 82, 79, and x is 87?

 A. 87
 B. 90
 C. 93
 D. 94
 E. 348

Schoolwide Eye Color Survey

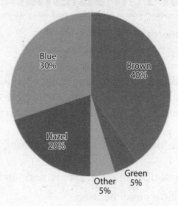

6. Annette does a schoolwide survey and publishes her results in the preceding circle graph. If 62 people at Annette's school have hazel eyes, how many have brown eyes?

 A. 20
 B. 40
 C. 62
 D. 124
 E. 248

7. Gasoline varies in cost from $3.96 to $4.12 per gallon. If a car's mileage varies from 16 to 24 miles per gallon, what is the difference between the most and the least that the gasoline for a 480-mile trip will cost?

 A. $29.12
 B. $35.52
 C. $36.40
 D. $41.20
 E. $44.40

8. If the length and width of a rectangle are increased by x units, its perimeter is increased by how many units?

 A. $4x$
 B. $2x$
 C. x^2
 D. x
 E. $x + 4$

GO ON TO THE NEXT PAGE

9. If $\dfrac{x^2-5x+7}{x^2-4x+10}=1$, then $x=$

   A. -3

   B. $\dfrac{1}{3}$

   C. $\dfrac{7}{10}$

   D. $\dfrac{17}{9}$

   E. 3

10. Nicole planned to complete a certain task on Wednesday, January 1, but because of illness, the completion date was postponed 48 days. On which day of the week in February was the task completed?

    A. Monday
    B. Tuesday
    C. Wednesday
    D. Thursday
    E. Friday

11. One angle of a triangle is 68°. The other two angles are in the ratio of 3:4. Which of the following is the number of degrees in the smallest angle of the triangle?

    A. 16
    B. 34
    C. 48
    D. 64
    E. 68

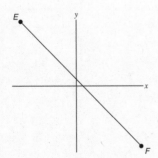

12. If, in the preceding graph, point E has coordinates $(-3, 5)$ and point F has coordinates $(6, -7)$, then the length of $EF =$

    A. 21
    B. 15
    C. 7
    D. 5
    E. 3

13. A random poll of 2,500 moviegoers throughout New York found that 1,500 preferred comedies, 500 preferred adventure films, and 500 preferred dramas. Of the 8,000,000 moviegoers in New York, which of the following is (are) the most reasonable estimate(s) drawn from the poll?

    I.   1,500,000 prefer comedies
    II.   500,000 prefer dramas
    III. 1,600,000 prefer dramas

    A. I only
    B. II only
    C. III only
    D. I and II only
    E. I and III only

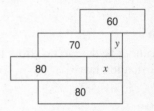

14. The horizontal length of each rectangle above is marked within. What is the total horizontal length of $x + y$?

    A. 40
    B. 50
    C. 80
    D. 90
    E. It cannot be determined from the information given.

15. How will the graph of $g(x) = (x + 5)^2$ differ from the graph of $f(x) = x^2$?

    A. $g(x)$ will be 5 units above $f(x)$.
    B. $g(x)$ will be 5 units below $f(x)$.
    C. $g(x)$ will be 5 units to the right of $f(x)$.
    D. $g(x)$ will be 5 units to the left of $f(x)$.
    E. $g(x)$ will be 25 units above $f(x)$.

GO ON TO THE NEXT PAGE

Practice Exam 2

359

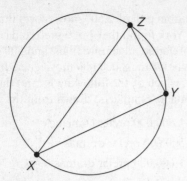

Note: Figure not drawn to scale

16. What is the length of the diameter $\overline{XZ}$ of the circle above if $\overline{XY} = 15$ and $\overline{YZ} = 8$?

   A. 17
   B. 23
   C. 46
   D. 289
   E. It cannot be determined from the information given.

IF YOU FINISH BEFORE TIME IS CALLED, CHECK YOUR WORK ON THIS SECTION ONLY. DO NOT WORK ON ANY OTHER SECTION IN THE TEST.

360

Section 8: Writing—Multiple Choice

Time: 10 minutes

14 Questions

Directions: In this section, choose the best answer for each question and fill in the corresponding circle on the answer sheet.

The following questions test correctness and effective expression. In selecting the answer, pay attention to grammar, diction, sentence structure, and punctuation. In the following questions, part or all of each sentence is underlined. Answer Choice A repeats the underlined portion of the original sentence, while the next four offer alternatives. Choose the answer that best expresses the meaning of the original sentence and at the same time is grammatically correct and stylistically superior. The correct choice should be clear, unambiguous, and concise.

EXAMPLE:

The forecaster predicted rain and the sky was clear.

A.   rain and the sky was clear
B.   rain but the sky was clear
C.   rain the sky was clear
D.   rain, but the sky was clear
E.   rain being as the sky was clear

The correct answer is **D**.

1. After Norm and Bradley left the theater, he realized he had left his jacket on the back of the seat, and they hurried back inside to find it.

    A.   he realized he had left his jacket on the back of the seat
    B.   he realizes he has left his jacket on the back of the seat
    C.   Norm has realized he left his jacket on the back of the seat
    D.   Norm realized he had left his jacket on the back of the seat
    E.   Norm, he realized he had his jacket on the back of the seat

2. Removing the books from the library shelves and boxing them for storage is the first steps in the renovation process.

    A.   Removing the books from the library shelves and boxing them for storage is the first steps
    B.   To remove the books from the library shelves and to box them for storage is the first steps
    C.   Removing the books from the library shelves and boxing them for storage are the first steps
    D.   Removing the books from the library shelves and then to put them in boxes for storage is the first step
    E.   Removing the books from the library shelves and boxing them for storage, those are the first steps

GO ON TO THE NEXT PAGE

3. While sitting in the front row of the classroom, the teacher's voice could be heard clearly, but in the back row no one knew what he was saying.

    A. While sitting in the front row of the classroom, the teacher's voice could be heard clearly

    B. The teacher's voice could be heard clearly in the front row of the classroom

    C. The teacher's voice, while sitting in the front row of the classroom, could be heard clearly

    D. Having sat in the front row of the classroom the teacher's voice could be heard clearly

    E. If sitting in the front row of the classroom, the teacher's voice could be heard clearly

4. Edward Witten, who was one of the pioneers and leading experts in string theory and who summarized the situation by saying that "string theory is a part of twenty-first century physics that fell by chance into the twentieth century."

    A. Edward Witten, who was one of the pioneers and leading experts in string theory and who summarized the situation by saying

    B. Edward Witten, who was one of the pioneers and also one of the leading experts in string theory, and whom summarized the situation by saying

    C. Edward Witten, a pioneer and leading expert in string theory, who summarized the situation by saying

    D. One of the pioneers and leading experts in string theory, Edward Witten, who summarized the situation by saying

    E. Edward Witten, one of the pioneers and leading experts in string theory, summarized the situation by saying

5. Although the hikers couldn't remember exactly when they had last seen Robert and her, they were sure it had been before noon.

    A. Although the hikers couldn't remember exactly when they had last seen Robert and her, they were sure

    B. Although the hikers couldn't remember exactly when they had last seen she and Robert, they were sure

    C. The hikers couldn't remember exactly when they had last seen Robert and her, they were sure

    D. Not remembering exactly when they had last seen her and Robert, the hikers were sure

    E. Although the hikers couldn't remember exactly when her and Robert had been seen by them, they were sure

6. Because proof of his accusations was unable to be offered by Stevens, the prosecution dismissed the case against Murphy.

    A. Because proof of his accusations was unable to be offered by Stevens,

    B. Because the accusations made by Stevens hadn't been offered proof,

    C. Because the accusations, which had been made by Stevens, were unable to be offered proof,

    D. Because Stevens wasn't able to offer proof of his accusations,

    E. Because Stevens, who had made accusations, was not able to offer proof of them,

7. The importance of thinking quickly, clearly, and to act with determination cannot hardly be overestimated when dealing with an emergency.

    A. The importance of thinking quickly, clearly, and to act with determination cannot hardly be overestimated

    B. The importance of thinking quickly, with clarity, and to act with determination cannot hardly be

    C. The importance of thinking quickly, thinking clearly, and acting with determination can hardly be overestimated

    D. To think quickly, to think clearly, and acting with determination is important, and cannot be overestimated

    E. You cannot hardly overestimate the importance of thinking quickly, then thinking clearly, and then to act with determination in an emergency.

GO ON TO THE NEXT PAGE

8. Although the woman could not have fell more than 6 feet, her ankle was broke and she had to be carried to the car.

   A. Although the woman could not have fell more than 6 feet, her ankle was broke

   B. Although the woman could not have fell more than 6 feet, her ankle was broken

   C. The woman's ankle was broke, even though she had fallen only 6 feet

   D. Although the woman had fell no more than 6 feet, her ankle broke

   E. Although the woman could not have fallen more than 6 feet, her ankle was broken

9. The disagreement between the President and him was based on their different views of the forefathers' original intentions.

   A. The disagreement between the President and him was based on their different views of the forefathers' original intentions.

   B. The disagreement between the President and he was based on their different view of what the original intentions of the forefathers were.

   C. The disagreement between he and the President was that they had different views of what the forefathers originally intended.

   D. The disagreement that existed between the President and he was based on their different views of the forefather's original intentions.

   E. Because the President and him had different views of what the forefather's had originally intended, there was a disagreement between them.

10. Everyone in the car and everyone waiting on the sidewalk were injured when the delivery truck went out of control, crashing into the car and then jumped the curb and mowed down the crowd.

    A. Everyone in the car and everyone waiting on the sidewalk were injured when the delivery truck went out of control, crashing into the car and then jumped the curb and mowed down the crowd.

    B. Everyone in the car and everyone waiting on the sidewalk was injured when the delivery truck went out of control, it crashed into the car and then jumped the curb and mowed down the crowd.

    C. Everyone in the car and everyone waiting on the sidewalk were injured when the delivery truck went out of control, crashing into the car and then jumping the curb and mowing down the crowd.

    D. Everyone in the car and everyone waiting on the sidewalk was injured when the delivery truck went out of control, crashed into the car, jumped the curb. and mowed down the crowd.

    E. Everyone in the car and everyone waiting on the sidewalk was injured; when the delivery truck went out of control, crashing into the car, and then jumping the curb resulting in the mowing down of the crowd.

11. Believing that family ties were more important than financial gain and political power, the campaign was abandoned by the candidate even before the primary election.

    A. Believing that family ties were more important than financial gain and political power, the campaign was abandoned by the candidate

    B. The campaign, believing that family ties were more important than financial gain and power, was abandoned by the candidate

    C. Believing that family ties were more important than financial gain and political power, the candidate abandoned the campaign

    D. The candidate believed that family ties were more important than financial gain and power, therefore he abandoned the campaign

    E. Because he believed that family ties were more important than financial gain and political power, the campaign was abandoned by the candidate

GO ON TO THE NEXT PAGE

12. <u>The descent down to the underground cave took several minutes and during which the guide tells us about the large amount of people who have visited</u> it over the years.

    A. The descent down to the underground cave took several minutes and during which the guide tells us about the large amount of people who have visited

    B. The descent down to the underground cave took several minutes, during which the guide told us about the large number of people who had visited

    C. The descent to the underground cave took several minutes, during which the guide told us about the many people who had visited

    D. During the descent down to the underground cave, which takes several minutes, the guide told us about the large multitude of people who visited

    E. The guide told us about the large amount of people who had visited the underground cave over the years during the descent down

13. <u>If the student didn't eat breakfast that morning, he could of arrived</u> at the meeting on time.

    A. If the student didn't eat breakfast that morning, he could of arrived

    B. If the student does not eat breakfast that morning, he can have arrived

    C. If the student was not eating breakfast that morning, he will have arrived

    D. If the student is not eating breakfast that morning, he could of arrived

    E. If the student had not eaten breakfast that morning, he could have arrived

14. <u>Surrealism was a major international style that affected developments in both the fine arts and literature</u> in the 1920s and 1930s.

    A. Surrealism was a major international style that affected developments in both the fine arts and literature

    B. Surrealism was a major international style that effected developments in both the fine arts and literature

    C. Surrealism was to have been a major international style, which affected developments in both the fine arts and literature

    D. Surrealism was a major international style that affected developments in both the fine arts and also affected them in literature

    E. Surrealism being a major international style that effected developments in both the fine arts and also literature

IF YOU FINISH BEFORE TIME IS CALLED, CHECK YOUR WORK ON THIS SECTION ONLY. DO NOT WORK ON ANY OTHER SECTION IN THE TEST.

Section 9: Critical Reading

Time: 20 minutes

19 Questions

Directions: In this section, choose the best answer for each question and fill in the corresponding circle on the answer sheet.

Each blank in the following sentences indicates that something has been omitted. Consider the lettered words beneath the sentence and choose the word or set of words that *best* fits the whole sentence.

EXAMPLE:

With a million more people than any other African nation, Nigeria is the most _____ country on the continent.

- A. impoverished
- B. successful
- C. populous
- D. developed
- E. militant

The correct answer is **C**.

1. The editorial was fairly _____, but the councilwoman reacted to it with fury, and the mayor couldn't do much to _____ her.

- A. heinous . . . ameliorate
- B. innocuous . . . placate
- C. captious . . . disarm
- D. vociferous . . . pacify
- E. contemptible . . . importune

2. The spokesperson's _____ handling of the reporter's pointed questions impressed the committee and improved his chances of becoming campaign manager.

- A. adroit
- B. pretentious
- C. capricious
- D. cynical
- E. bombastic

3. During the church service, the group of girls giggled continually, and afterward the older woman who had been sitting behind them scolded them for their _____.

- A. licentiousness
- B. mayhem
- C. levity
- D. heresy
- E. calumny

4. Leaving the office two hours early may be the _____ of an executive in the company, but it was certainly not _____ for a new employee.

- A. prerogative . . . appropriate
- B. intention . . . credible
- C. sinecure . . . practical
- D. propensity . . . indicative
- E. requirement . . . optimal

GO ON TO THE NEXT PAGE

5. The _____ reason for deciding to travel to Italy was to visit his brother, but the real reason was to check on his villa in Tuscany.

    A. overpowering
    B. problematic
    C. discreet
    D. transparent
    E. ostensible

6. Unfortunately, the young girl's happiness proved to be _____ because the next day her father _____ his promise to support her marriage to the struggling artist.

    A. nebulous . . . nullified
    B. hedonistic . . . negated
    C. ephemeral . . . rescinded
    D. apocryphal . . . reiterated
    E. cursory . . . elicited

GO ON TO THE NEXT PAGE

Directions: Questions follow the passage below. Answer the questions using only the stated or implied information in the passage and in its introduction, if any.

Questions 7–19 are based on the following passage.

This passage is from a 1970s memoir of childhood by a Chinese-American woman.

When we Chinese girls listened to the adults' talk-story, we learned that we failed if we grew up to be but wives or slaves. We could be heroines, swordswomen. Even if she had to rage across all
(5) China, a swordswoman got even with anybody who hurt her family. Perhaps women were once so dangerous that they had to have their feet bound. It was a woman who invented white crane boxing only two hundred years ago. She
(10) was already an expert pole fighter, daughter of a teacher trained at the Shao-lin temple, where there lived an order of fighting monks. She was combing her hair one morning when a white crane alighted outside her window. She teased it
(15) with her pole, which it pushed aside with a soft brush of its wing. Amazed, she dashed outside and tried to knock the crane off its perch. It snapped her pole in two. Recognizing the presence of great power, she asked the spirit of
(20) the white crane if it would teach her to fight. It answered with a cry that white crane boxers imitate today. Later the bird returned as an old man, and he guided her boxing for many years. Thus she gave the world a new martial art.

(25) This was one of the tamer, more modern stories, mere introduction. My mother told others that followed swordswomen through woods and palaces for years. Night after night my mother would talk-story until we fell asleep. I couldn't
(30) tell where the stories left off and the dreams began, her voice the voice of the heroines in my sleep. And on Sunday, from noon to midnight, we went to the movies at the Confucius Church. We saw swordswomen jump over houses from a
(35) standstill; they didn't even need a running start.

At last I saw that I too had been in the presence of great power, my mother talking-story. After I grew up, I heard the chant of Fa Mu Lan, the girl who took her father's place in
(40) battle. Instantly I remembered that as a child I had followed my mother about the house, the two of us singing about how Fa Mu Lan fought gloriously and returned alive from war to settle in the village. I had forgotten this chant that was
(45) once mine, given me by my mother, who may not

have known its power to remind. She said I would grow up a wife and a slave, but she taught me the song of the warrior woman. I would have to grow up a warrior woman.

(50) The call would come from a bird that flew over our roof. In the brush drawings it looks like the ideograph for "human," two black wings. The bird would cross the sun and lift into the mountains (which look like the ideograph
(55) "mountain"), there parting the mist briefly that swirled opaque again. I would be a little girl of seven the day I followed the bird away into the mountains. The brambles would tear off my shoes and the rocks cut my feet and fingers, but I
(60) would keep climbing, eyes upward to follow the bird. We would go around and around the tallest mountain, climbing ever upward. I would drink from the river, which I could meet again and again. We would go so high the plants would
(65) change, and the river that flows past the village would become a waterfall. At the height where the bird used to disappear, the clouds would gray the world like an ink wash.

Even when I got used to that gray, I would only
(70) see peaks as if shaded in pencil, rocks like charcoal rubbings, everything so murky. There would be just two black strokes—the bird. Inside the clouds—inside the dragon's breath—I would not know how many hours or days passed. Suddenly,
(75) without noise, I would break clear into a yellow, warm world. New trees would lean toward me at mountain angles, but when I looked for the village, it would have vanished under the clouds.

The bird, now gold so close to the sun, would
(80) come to rest on the thatch of a hut, which until the bird's two feet touched it, was camouflaged as part of the mountainside.

The door opened, and an old man and an old woman came out carrying bowls of rice and
(85) soup and a leafy branch of peaches.

"Have you eaten rice today, little girl?" they greeted me.

"Yes, I have," I said out of politeness. "Thank you."

(90) ("No, I haven't," I would have said in real life, mad at the Chinese for lying so much. "I'm starved. Do you have any cookies? I like chocolate chip cookies.")

GO ON TO THE NEXT PAGE

7. The first paragraph of the passage primarily serves to

   A. introduce the character of the speaker's mother.
   B. provide an example of a talk-story.
   C. explain the origin of white crane boxing.
   D. indicate that the speaker is naive.
   E. show the rebellious nature of the speaker.

8. The story of the white crane boxer "explains" which of the following?

   A. Why the speaker's mother wanted her daughter to be a woman warrior.
   B. Why Chinese women had their feet bound.
   C. How a particular martial art originated.
   D. The symbolic importance of cranes in China.
   E. How women were able to gain stature in China.

9. From lines 29–30, it can be inferred that the speaker

   A. admired her mother more than her father.
   B. wanted to be a swordswoman.
   C. sometimes confused reality and dreams.
   D. got many of her ideas from the movies.
   E. was of limited intelligence.

10. The best definition of "ideograph" in line 52 is

   A. an illustration of a general idea.
   B. a painting of something in the natural world.
   C. a mental picture formed during a conversation.
   D. an ancient engraving representing a myth.
   E. a picture or symbol used in a system of writing.

11. According to the passage, a warrior woman would

   A. always surpass a man in physical combat.
   B. take revenge on anyone who hurt her family.
   C. always return to her village after a quest.
   D. overturn tyrannical leaders.
   E. never marry or have children.

12. The movies that the speaker watched at the Confucius Church

   A. frightened her with their violent subjects.
   B. were more powerful than her mother's talk-stories.
   C. increased her desire to see the world.
   D. fed her imagination about the powers of swordswomen.
   E. made her doubtful about the existence of real swordswomen.

13. In lines 40–49, as an adult the speaker realized which of the following?

   A. Her mother thought she'd grow up to be a woman warrior.
   B. Her mother idealized Fa Mu Lan.
   C. She had exaggerated the powers of Fa Mu Lan.
   D. The words of her mother, although well-meaning, couldn't be trusted.
   E. Her mother's talk-stories gave her the power to become a woman warrior.

14. According to the passage, Ma Fu Lan

   A. could fly over houses.
   B. invented a new martial art.
   C. took her father's place in battle.
   D. was the first woman warrior.
   E. was an expert pole fighter.

15. Lines 50–68 represent a change in the passage because they

   A. move from the speaker's childhood narrative to a child's fantasy.
   B. introduce action into a straightforward autobiography.
   C. indicate that the speaker's mother is responsible for her daughter's unrealistic picture of the world.
   D. satirize the picture of the talk-story presented previously in the passage.
   E. cast doubt on the speaker's reliability as an autobiographer.

GO ON TO THE NEXT PAGE

16. From lines 51–56 ("In the brush drawings . . . ideograph 'mountain'") we can infer that the

    A. speaker is an artist.
    B. speaker's mother was an artist.
    C. child was devoted to learning.
    D. child's fantasy was influenced by a drawing.
    E. child recorded her adventures in detail.

17. Which of the following most obviously interrupts the mood of the passage beginning on line 56 until the end?

    A. " . . . brambles would tear off my shoes. . . ." (lines 58–59)
    B. " . . . clouds would gray the world like an ink wash." (lines 67–68)
    C. " . . . everything so murky . . ." (line 71)
    D. "Do you have any cookies?" (line 92)
    E. "The door opened, and an old man and woman came out. . . ." (lines 83–84)

18. The author uses all of the following in the passage EXCEPT

    A. dialogue.
    B. sarcasm.
    C. imagery.
    D. myth.
    E. simile.

19. When the speaker says she was "mad at the Chinese for lying so much" (line 91), she is most likely referring to

    A. her lie about not being hungry.
    B. the old man and woman (lines 83–84).
    C. talk-stories.
    D. the story of Ma Fu Lan.
    E. her mother's prediction about the speaker's future.

IF YOU FINISH BEFORE TIME IS CALLED, CHECK YOUR WORK ON THIS SECTION ONLY. DO NOT WORK ON ANY OTHER SECTION IN THE TEST.

STOP

Scoring Practice Exam 2

The following section will assist you in scoring and analyzing your practice test results. Use the answer key below to score your results, and then carefully review the analysis charts to identify your strengths and weaknesses. Finally, read through the answer explanations starting on page 374 to clarify the solutions to the problems.

Answer Key for Practice Exam 2

Section 2: Critical Reading

1. B	8. B	15. C	22. E
2. D	9. A	16. B	23. C
3. A	10. C	17. E	24. B
4. D	11. A	18. B	25. D
5. C	12. C	19. C	26. B
6. C	13. B	20. A	
7. B	14. A	21. B	

Section 3: Mathematics

1. B	6. B	11. D	16. B
2. C	7. C	12. B	17. A
3. C	8. A	13. C	18. B
4. B	9. A	14. D	19. C
5. C	10. A	15. D	20. A

Section 4: Critical Reading

1. B	8. C	15. A	22. C
2. E	9. C	16. C	23. A
3. C	10. E	17. D	24. B
4. A	11. B	18. C	25. E
5. E	12. E	19. C	
6. B	13. E	20. D	
7. A	14. A	21. A	

Section 5: Writing—Multiple Choice

1. D	10. D	19. A	28. C
2. B	11. A	20. B	29. B
3. A	12. B	21. B	30. A
4. D	13. A	22. A	31. B
5. B	14. A	23. A	32. A
6. C	15. C	24. C	33. C
7. D	16. A	25. D	34. D
8. B	17. E	26. D	35. E
9. D	18. D	27. A	

Section 6: Mathematics

1. C	6. E	11. 70	16. 640
2. E	7. B	12. 350	17. $\frac{4}{9}$
3. C	8. C	13. 480	18. 48
4. D	9. 94	14. 50	
5. E	10. 9.49	15. 20	

Section 7: Mathematics

1. A	5. D	9. A	13. C
2. D	6. D	10. B	14. E
3. C	7. E	11. C	15. D
4. B	8. A	12. B	16. A

Section 8: Writing—Multiple Choice

1. D	5. A	9. A	13. E
2. C	6. D	10. D	14. A
3. B	7. C	11. C	
4. E	8. E	12. C	

Section 9: Critical Reading

1. B	6. C	11. B	16. D
2. A	7. B	12. D	17. D
3. C	8. C	13. E	18. B
4. A	9. C	14. C	19. A
5. E	10. E	15. A	

Charting and Analyzing Your Exam Results

The first step in analyzing your results is to chart your answers. Use the charts on the following pages to identify your strengths and areas of improvement. Complete the process of evaluating your essays and analyzing problems in each area. Reevaluate your results as you look for trends in the types of errors (repeated errors), and look for low scores in results in specific topic areas. This reexamination and analysis is a tremendous asset to help you maximize your best-possible score. The answers and explanations following these charts will provide you clarification to help you solve these types of problems in the future.

Reviewing the Essay

Refer to the sample essay on page 374 as a reference guide. Have an English teacher, tutor, or someone else with good writing skills read and evaluate your essay using the Essay Checklist given below. Have your reader evaluate the complete essay as good, average, or marginal. Note that your paper would actually be scored from 1 to 6 by two trained readers (actual total score 2–12). Since we are trying only for a rough approximation, a strong, average, or weak overall evaluation will give you a general feeling for your score range.

Essay Checklist			
Questions	Strong Response Score 5 or 6	Average Response Score 3 or 4	Weak Response Score 1 or 2
1. Does the essay focus on the topic and respond to the assigned task?			
2. Is the essay organized and well developed?			
3. Does the essay use specific supporting details and examples?			
4. Does the writing use correct grammar, usage, punctuation, and spelling?			
5. Is the handwriting legible?			

Critical Reading Analysis Sheet				
Section 2	Possible	Completed	Right	Wrong
Sentence Completions	5			
Short Reading Passages	5			
Long Reading Passage	6			
Paired Passages	10			
Section 2 Subtotal	26			
Section 4	Possible	Completed	Right	Wrong
Sentence Completions	8			
Paired Reading Passages	10			
Short Reading Passages	7			
Section 4 Subtotal	25			

Section 9	Possible	Completed	Right	Wrong
Sentence Completions	6			
Paired Passages	13			
Section 9 Subtotal	**19**			
Overall Critical Reading Totals	**70**			

Note: Only 3 Critical Reading sections (approximately 70 questions) count toward your actual score on the SAT.

Mathematics Analysis Sheet				
Section 3	**Possible**	**Completed**	**Right**	**Wrong**
Multiple Choice	20			
Section 3 Subtotal	**20**			
Section 6	**Possible**	**Completed**	**Right**	**Wrong**
Multiple Choice	8			
Grid-Ins	10			
Section 6 Subtotal	**18**			
Section 7	**Possible**	**Completed**	**Right**	**Wrong**
Multiple Choice	16			
Section 7 Subtotal	**16**			
Overall Math Totals	**54**			

Writing—Multiple-Choice Analysis Sheet				
Section 5	**Possible**	**Completed**	**Right**	**Wrong**
Improving Sentences	11			
Identifying Sentence Errors	18			
Improving Paragraphs	6			
Section 5 Subtotal	**35**			
Section 8	**Possible**	**Completed**	**Right**	**Wrong**
Improving Sentences	14			
Section 8 Subtotal	**14**			
Overall Writing Totals	**49**			

Analysis/Tally Sheet for Problems Missed

One of the most important parts of test preparation is analyzing why you missed a problem so that you can reduce the number of mistakes. Now that you have taken the practice test and checked your answers, carefully tally your mistakes by marking them in the proper column.

Reason for Mistakes						
	Total Possible	Total Missed	Simple Mistake	Misread Problem	Lack of Knowledge	Lack of Time
Section 2: Critical Reading	26					
Section 4: Critical Reading	25					
Section 9: Critical Reading	19					
Subtotal	**70**					
Section 3: Mathematics	20					
Section 6: Mathematics	18					
Section 7: Mathematics	16					
Subtotal	**54**					
Section 5: Writing—Multiple Choice	35					
Section 8: Writing—Multiple Choice	14					
Subtotal	**49**					
Total Critical Reading, Math and Writing	**173**					

Reviewing the preceding data should help you determine why you are missing certain problems. Now that you've pinpointed the type of error, compare it to other practice tests to spot other common mistakes.

Practice Exam 2: Answers and Explanations

Section 1: Writing—Essay

To help you evaluate your essay-writing skills, below is an example of a high-scoring, strong essay response for the essay topic in this test. Compare your essay to this sample essay and the analysis of a strong essay, an average essay, and a poorly written essay. Use the suggested checklist to evaluate your essay, and to help you take a closer look and understand your scoring range.

Sample Essay

Although it would be nice to say that a grade "doesn't matter" as much as the student's experience in a class, that simply isn't true. Most students want some validation and a way to measure how well they are doing. Traditional schools provide students with a letter grade that validates their progress and provides encouragement to succeed.

Using a letter grade is better than the "pass-fail" option. If a student receives a "C," the student knows that he is ranked as average in a class. If he receives an "A," he knows he is among the top students. And if he receives a "D," he knows that he is behind his fellow students and perhaps in danger of failing a class. The "pass-fail" system, on the other hand, is always open to question. If he passes, the student doesn't know precisely where he falls in terms of the other students. Even a teacher's comment may not make it clear. A student may choose to interpret a teacher's comment as positive when the teacher actually meant that the student's progress was simply adequate. Letter grades are also commonly understood by schools, so that when a student with a strong "B" average is applying to a university or moving to a different school, the school knows where that student stands in compared to others.

On the other hand, letter grades are not as clear cut as they may seem. One of the problems might be that different teachers and different schools often have different standards for certain grades. For example, a teacher in my high school was known for giving nothing higher than a B, no matter how exceptional a student might perform. This means that students can be ranked differently by different teachers for the same subject.

Another problem might be that students who receive letter grades may not have a clear idea about his performance which can influence his attitude. With a "pass-fail" system, however, students may have a clearer picture of their strengths and weaknesses. A teacher's statement, along with the pass-fail mark, can be very helpful in motivating a student. Another advantage of the pass-fail system is that students are more likely to focus on the material being taught than the letter grade they will receive. Many students may struggle more to get a certain grade than to understand what is being taught. This may be the best argument for a "pass-fail" system. The focus is on learning, not on "getting an 'A.'" The best argument against it is that it can be too vague and some students will not try to push themselves to succeed because it is difficult to understand where he stands in compared to other students. Also, many colleges do not accept the "pass-fail" for admission.

Each system has its good points and its bad points. What may occur is that a student, or an school, may simply translate what is said in a "pass-fail" statement to an equivalent letter grade. In my opinion, the better option might be a combination of the letter grade system with a written statement like the one that is used in the "pass-fail" system.

Section 2: Critical Reading

Sentence Completions

1. **B.** Of the choices, it is the one most clearly opposite in meaning to "requiring." When answering sentence completion questions, look carefully at clues in the introductory phrase or clause. Although Choice A is possibly true, it isn't the opposite of "requiring." Choice D is incorrect because it does not fit with the meaning of the rest of the sentence. Choice C is irrelevant, and Choice E is a less-satisfactory contrast to "requiring."

2. **D.** Choices A and C can be ruled out immediately based on the first words of those choices; how can the dilemma be considered unprecedented or terminal if it happens every year? Choice B is incorrect; it is not clear how a dilemma can be imprecise. "Solemn," Choice E, isn't as effective with the opening phrase, "As happens every year."

3. **A.** Both words fit well in the context of the sentence. Choice B is incorrect based on the first word in the pair; if they were fatalistic, the McMullens would feel they were powerless to change events. Choice D can be ruled out based on the second word; "sensitivity" doesn't describe their determination. Neither word in Choice E is appropriate in context; "deference" means regard for another's wishes. In Choice C, "temerity" means a foolish disregard of danger; it does not fit well with "acumen," which means keenness and depth of perception.

4. **D.** As a social activist and writer, Gorky could describe the disenfranchised (not given the right to vote) peasants. Choices B and C can be ruled out on the basis of the first word; a dilettante (a dabbler in the arts) wouldn't be concerned with the peasants, and an apologist would defend the system. Choice E is also incorrect; a recluse is cut off from social issues. Choice A can also be ruled out; "archaic" means characteristic of an earlier time.

5. **C.** "Indigenous" means having originated and grown in a particular environment. The context of the sentence makes this the best choice. The sentence says that some indigenous populations are now outnumbered by invaders—or outsiders—and their descendants. None of the other choices clearly differentiates between native and invading populations.

Short Reading Passages

6. **C.** Choices B and D might seem possible answers, but not enough details are given in the passage to make either a main point. The passage doesn't explain meteorology, Choice A, nor does it compare Fahrenheit and Celsius, Choice E.

7. **B.** The two scientists arbitrarily designated their freezing points, and they were different. In addition, the Celsius freezing point was later changed. Choice A is incorrect because the author makes no judgment. Choice D is also incorrect because although the author says two scales might be confusing, there is no indication that this causes serious problems. There is no evidence in the passage that Celsius questioned Fahrenheit's methods, Choice C, even though he chose a different freezing point. Choice E is not addressed in the passage.

8. **B.** See lines 15 and 16. The other choices, while they might be true, are not addressed in the passage.

9. **A.** The passage consists of a number of general statements about frontier life and the reasons democratic institutions were modified. Although contrast, choice C, is implied, it is not the author's principal method. Choices B, D, and E are not used in the passage.

10. **C.** A "panacea" is a remedy for all ills, a cure-all. Choice B is too general. Choices A, D, and E aren't synonyms for "panacea" and are not appropriate in the context of the passage.

Long Reading Passage

11. **A.** The passage is told from Janet's point of view. Notice that in line 43 Janet is angry, and lines 45–55 make it even clearer that the action is described through Janet's eyes. Although Choice B may seem a good choice, it is only through Janet that the reader sees Grandma's, Tom's, and Oliver's behaviors.

12. **C.** When the family is going to the orchard, Grandma is calm and her lips are quiet, as opposed to "trembling in a stream of soundless words" as they were previously. The phrase suggests the opposite of calmness, that is, agitation. Choices A and D are not indicated, and choices B and E do not suggest the opposite of calmness.

13. **B.** Although we are not told Oliver's feelings, his words and his holding out the apricot probably indicate a friendly gesture. Nothing suggests that he is obeying his mother here, Choice C, or that he is either trying to influence his grandmother or overcome his fear, choices D and E. "Great compassion," Choice A, overstates the meaning of such a gesture.

14. **A.** This is a difficult question, but in the context of the passage, Grandma's behavior shows mistrust of everyone. Here, she refuses to accept Janet's suggestion to pick an apricot from the trees but instead hurries away, and then looks around "furtively" before picking up something (a windfall apricot?) from the ground and popping it in her mouth. Later, in lines 62–86, her talking to herself reveals that she is suspicious of everyone. Choices B and D are not as accurate a description of her behavior as Choice A. Choices C and E are clearly wrong.

15. **C.** Although they disagree about Grandma, the relationship doesn't suggest that Tom makes all the decisions, Choice A; in fact, he goes along with Janet's advice to wait and see if Grandma comes back. The only anger that is mentioned is Janet's, not Tom's, Choice E, and nothing suggests that Janet is bitterly unhappy, Choice B. Choice D is simply inaccurate.

16. **B.** Grandma's words in these lines show that she believes others are persecuting her. This is a better choice than Choice A because throughout the passage Grandma has shown mistrust even when it seems unwarranted. She has not lost her memory, Choice C; she seems to remember "injustices" quite well. Choices D and E are not substantiated by events described in the passage.

Paired Reading Passages

17. **E.** In Passage 4, see lines 13–16, 21–24; in Passage 5, lines 21–24. Passage 5 doesn't define biodiversity, Choice A, and Passage 4 doesn't discuss protecting the generation of new species, Choice B. Only Passage 5 discusses vicariance, Choice C, and neither passage includes an approach to preventing habitat degradation, Choice D.

18. **B.** Passage 5 is concerned with the process of new species generation and the dangers presented by invasive species; Passage 4 does not deal with that issue. Both passages cite habitat degradation, Choice D. Neither passage is argumentative in approach, Choice A, and there is no indication that a scientist wrote either passage, Choice C. Neither passage discusses the causes of habitat degradation, Choice E.

19. **C.** Lines 18–24 specifically cite biodiversity as essential for the cycles of major elements such as nitrogen, which the passage refers to as "ecosystem services." None of the other answers refer to an ecosystem service.

20. **A.** See lines 25–27. The implication is that estimates of the number of species are not exact because most are too small to count. Choice B is not supported in the passage, and choices C, D, and E are not mentioned.

21. **B.** Notice the word EXCEPT in the question. Choices A, C, D, and E are all true of the definition of biodiversity. Choice B, however, is not pertinent; no mention is made of whether scientists accept or do not accept the definition.

22. **E.** According to Passage 5, the number of species lost in the Late Devonian was not higher than in other mass extinctions, Choice A; the difference was that in the Late Devonian few new species arose. The entire marine ecosystem was affected, but the passage does not compare that effect to other mass extinctions, Choice B. Neither choices C nor D is supported by information in the passage.

23. **C.** The method, not the rate (Choice A) of new species creation is vicariance. According to the passage, Choice B is a way that vicariance can occur, but it is not the process itself. Choices D and E are both irrelevant to vicariance.

24. **B.** Stigall states that because the process of new species formation was affected, the Late Devonian extinction resulted in a loss of biodiversity. Choice A is not supported in the passage; although the marine ecosystem was devastated, it was not only marine species that became extinct. Choice D is also not a good choice; no distinction is made between crucial and noncrucial species. Choice E is also inaccurate because although whole ecosystems were destroyed, it was the failure of new species to emerge that was key in the Late Devonian. Choice C is irrelevant; habitat degradation is not cited in Stigall's comments about the Late Devonian.

25. **D.** See lines 24–28. She does not suggest that vicariance is a danger, Choice A, nor that the loss of reef-forming corals is a warning sign, Choice C. Although she emphasizes the importance of focusing on new species formation, she does not state that scientists are not addressing the primary cause of species loss, Choice B, nor does she deny that habitat loss is a cause of species extinction, choice E. She merely urges that we focus efforts on protecting the generation of new species.

26. **B.** See lines 21–24. Although Stigall stresses the importance of new species formation, she does not imply that there is too much emphasis on habitat preservation, Choice A, nor can it be inferred that many scientists disagree with her about invasive species, Choice C. Choices D and E are inaccurate. Reefs appeared after 100 million years, and the modern extinction rate surpasses ancient extinction rates.

Section 3: Mathematics

1. **B.** Setting up an equation gives $\frac{1}{5}x = 2$. Multiplying both sides by 5,

$$(5)\frac{1}{5}x = 2(5)$$

Then $x = 10$, and $\frac{1}{2}$ of 10 is 5.

2. **C.** The selling price for 1 dozen at 3 for $0.85 is $3 \times 4 = 12 = 1$ dozen $= \$0.85 \times 4 = \$3.40$.

Therefore, 6 dozen will yield $\$3.40 \times 6 = \$20.40$. The store's cost for 6 dozen at $1.80 per dozen is $\$1.80 \times 6 = \$10.80$. The profit on 6 dozen of these items will be $\$20.40 - \$10.80$, or $\$9.60$.

3. C.

$$\text{If } x = -1,$$
$$x^4 + x^3 + x^2 + x - 3$$
$$= (-1)^4 + (-1)^3 + (-1)^2 + (-1) - 3$$
$$= 1 + (-1) + 1 + (-1) - 3$$
$$= 0 + 1 + (-1) - 3$$
$$= 1 + (-1) - 3$$
$$= 0 - 3$$
$$= -3$$

4. B. The union of two sets is the set of elements belonging to set P or to set Q or to both sets P and Q.

$$P = \{2,3,5,7\} \text{ and } Q = \{3,5,7\}$$
$$P \cup Q = \{2,3,5,7\}$$

5. C. Substitute 3 for x

$$f(x) = 3^x + 5x$$
$$f(x) = 3^3 + 5(3)$$
$$= 27 + 15$$
$$= 42$$

6. B. Since $a \otimes b = a^3 + b^2$,

$$(-2) \otimes (-3) = (-2)^3 + (-3)^2$$
$$= (-8) + 9$$
$$= 1$$

7. C.

Since $BD = CD, \angle CBD = \angle C = 19° \longrightarrow$ Then, $\angle BDA = 180° - \angle BDC$

Therefore, $\angle BDC = 180° - (\angle CBD + \angle C)$ $\qquad = 180° - 142°$

$$= 180° - (19° + 19°) \qquad\qquad = 38°$$
$$= 180° - 38°$$
$$= 142°$$

Since $AB = AD,\ \angle ABD = \angle BDA = 38°$

Therefore, $\angle A = 180° - (\angle BDA + \angle ABD)$

$$= 180° - (38° + 38°)$$
$$= 180° - 76°$$
$$= 104°$$

8. A. The number of nickels that Angela has is x. Therefore, the total value of those nickels (in cents) is $5x$. Angela also has twice as many dimes as nickels, or $2x$. The total in cents of those dimes is $2x$ (10), or $20x$. Adding together the value of the nickels and the dimes gives $5x + 20x$, or $25x$.

9. A. If $x - 4 = y$, then $y - x = -4$. Therefore, $(y - x)^3 = (-4)^3 = -64$.

10. **A.** The perimeter of a rectangle with length l and width w is $2l + 2w$. Because the perimeter of the triangle is $10x + 8$ and its length is $3x$,

$$perimeter = 2l + 2w$$
$$10x + 8 = 2(3x) + 2w$$
$$10x + 8 = 6x + 2w$$
$$10x + 8 - 6x = 6x + 2w - 6x$$
$$4x + 8 = 2w$$
$$2x + 4 = w$$

Therefore, the width of the rectangle is $2x + 4$.

11. **D.** If $\dfrac{2}{3x-1} = \dfrac{5}{5x-2}$, then cross-multiplying yields

$$2(5x - 2) = 5(3x - 1)$$
$$10x - 4 = 15x - 5$$
$$10x - 4 - 15x = 15x - 5 - 15x$$
$$-5x - 4 = -5$$
$$-5x - 4 + 4 = -5 + 4$$
$$-5x = -1$$
$$\frac{-5x}{-5} = \frac{-1}{-5}$$
$$x = \frac{1}{5}$$

12. **B.** The car travels a total distance of 280 miles in $7\frac{1}{2}$ hours for the round trip. Its average speed in miles per hour is

$$280 \div 7\frac{1}{2} = \frac{280}{1} \div \frac{15}{2}$$
$$= \frac{280}{1} \times \frac{2}{15} = \frac{560}{15} = \frac{112}{3}$$
$$= 37\frac{1}{3}$$

13. **C.** Because a and b must both be positive or both be negative, Choice C, III only, is the only answer that *must* be true.

14. **D.** The slope (m) of a line passing through the points (x_1, y_1) and (x_2, y_2) is

$$m = \frac{y_2 - y_1}{x_2 - x_1}$$

The line passes through $(-3, 5)$ and $(2, 9)$, so

$$m = \frac{9 - 5}{2 - (-3)} = \frac{4}{5}$$

Note that you could eliminate choices A, B, and C because they are all negative slopes, and the diagram shows a line with a positive slope.

15. D.

$$\left(\frac{x^{-5}y^2}{x^{-2}y^{-3}}\right)^{-2} = \frac{x^{10}y^{-4}}{x^4 y^6}$$

$$= x^{10-4} y^{-4-6}$$

$$= x^6 y^{-10}$$

$$= \frac{x^6}{y^{10}}$$

16. B. $\angle XYZ$ is inscribed in a semicircle and is therefore a right angle. Therefore, $\triangle XYZ$ is a right triangle and the Pythagorean Theorem states

$$(XY)^2 = (XZ)^2 + (YZ)^2$$

$$(17)^2 = (XZ)^2 + (15)^2 \ (XY \text{ is a diameter})$$

$$289 = (XZ)^2 + 225$$

$$289 - 225 = (XZ)^2$$

$$(XZ)^2 = 64$$

$$XZ = \sqrt{64}$$

$$XZ = 8$$

$$\text{Area of } \triangle XYZ = \frac{1}{2}bh$$

$$= \frac{1}{2}(XZ)(YZ)$$

$$= \frac{1}{2}(8)(15)$$

$$= (4)(15)$$

$$= 60$$

17. A. If 15 gumballs were picked from the bag, it is possible that 8 of them are red and 7 are white. On the next (16th) pick however, one is assured of having 1 gumball of each color.

18. B. Because each letter repeats after every five vowels, divide 327 by 5, and the remainder will determine the vowel in that place of the pattern. Since $327 \div 5 = 65$ with a remainder of 2, the remainder of 2 indicates that the second vowel (e) will be the 327th letter.

19. C. Let x = length of equal sides in feet and $x + 8$ = length of base in feet, as shown below.

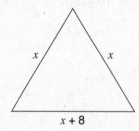

Since the perimeter is 89 feet,

$$x + x + x + 8 = 89$$
$$3x + 8 = 89$$
$$3x + 8 - 8 = 89 - 8$$
$$3x = 81$$
$$\frac{3x}{3} = \frac{81}{3}$$
$$x = 27$$

Therefore, the length of the base is $x + 8$, or 35 feet.

20. **A.** Because the perimeter of the rhombus is 40, each side has length 10. Because the diagonals of a rhombus are perpendicular and bisect each other,

$$x^2 + 5^2 = 10^2$$
$$x^2 + 25 = 100$$
$$x^2 = 75$$
$$x = \sqrt{75}$$
$$x = 5\sqrt{3}$$

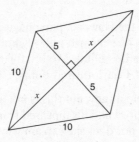

The area of a quadrilateral with perpendicular diagonals d_1 and d_2 is

$$\text{area} = \frac{1}{2} d_1 \cdot d_2$$
$$= \frac{1}{2} (10)(10\sqrt{3})$$
$$= 50\sqrt{3}$$

Section 4: Critical Reading

Sentence Completions

1. **B.** If only one critic offered praise, then most of the reviews must have been poor ("negative," Choice B). Reviews are generally not "vague," Choice A, and Choice E is the opposite of what the context suggests. The second word is "audacity," which means bold or daring, a trait that would be required to reject conventions. "Immaturity," Choice C, and "humility," Choice D, do not fit well here.

2. **E.** A rigorous editor would refine his speeches over and over. A timorous (Choice A), reluctant (Choice B), or nonchalant (Choice C) editor would not. "Prescient," Choice D, means the ability to anticipate future events, which does not apply here.

3. **C.** The sentence is stating that social skills are as important as scientific ability for a researcher who moves from place to place. "Prowess" means extraordinary ability. Choice A is the opposite of what is meant in the sentence, and Choice B does not fit with "scientific." Choice E is the second-best answer, but "prowess" is a better choice in context. "Platitudes" (Choice D) are dull or trite statements.

4. **A.** "Glacial" suggests very slow movement, which is appropriate here in describing evolution, and "benign" is the opposite of deadly. None of the other answers is appropriate in context.

5. **E.** "Clandestine" means secret, which contrasts with the demand that financial issues be discussed openly. Choices A and D don't provide the necessary contrast, nor do Choice C ("desultory" means not conducted with a plan) and Choice B ("lackluster" means lacking in vitality or dull).

6. **B.** The word "obsequious," which means a fawning attentiveness, is evidence of Templeton's hypocrisy. None of the other choices indicates hypocrisy.

7. **A.** "Castigated" means subjected to severe punishment. Choice D is the only other possible choice, and it is doubtful that the professor would persecute his students. Choice B (meaning "soothed"), and choices C and E do not suggest actions the professor would take if students cheated.

8. **C.** To convince people to eat well, nutritionists would have to counteract the notion that healthful food is bland, not support it (Choice A), reconsider it (Choice B), reiterate it (state it again, Choice D), or nullify it (Choice E).

Paired Passages

9. **C.** Passage 1 provides a description of the Haworth parsonage at the time of the Brontës, and Passage 2 describes what has become of the town of Haworth today. Choices B and E are touched upon in the first passage but not the second, and Choice D is alluded to briefly in the second passage but not the first. Neither passage addresses the novels of Charlotte and Emily, Choice A.

10. **E.** The author alludes to the Gaskell biography, but this is not a main point, Choice C. Choice A is not mentioned; the working mills and factories had disappeared from the Haworth area. The author does not criticize the Brontës' fiction, Choice B, nor does she explain why Emily replaced Charlotte as the preeminent figure of the myth, Choice D.

11. **B.** Obviously, Passage 1 is describing Haworth as it was for the Brontë sisters, while Passage 2 focuses on how the Brontë myth has created tourist trade today. Neither passage includes personification, Choice A, and neither author judges the Brontës' novels, Choice C. Both authors use details, Choice D. The language in both passages is not particularly complex or difficult, Choice E.

12. **E.** The author is using humor, being ironic in suggesting that the liqueur sold in "olde worlde" flagons couldn't *possibly* be related to Branwell Brontë's drinking problem. She is poking fun at the Brontë myth souvenirs. The second-best answer is Choice D, but it isn't as clearly ironic. None of the other choices is ironic.

13. **E.** The lines in Passage 2 refer to a "cabinetmaker-cum-undertaker" advertising coffins as a "Brontë Product." This is mirrored in lines 26–28 of the first passage: "The graveyard may also be viewed as both a real and symbolic reminder of the virtually continuous presence of Death in their lives." None of the other answers cite lines clearly related to death.

14. **A.** Of the answers, this is the only one that doesn't suggest the author's dry humor but is rather a straightforward observation. Be sure to note the use of the word EXCEPT in the question.

15. **A.** Note the word "depressing" in line 51 of Passage 2. The comment follows descriptions of tourist souvenir and novelty shops that cater to the Brontë myth. These lines do not show disdain for the myth itself, Choice B, as clearly as they show regret for the triumph of commercialism. Choice C is irrelevant, and choices D and E are generalizations not supported anywhere in the passage.

16. **C.** By the process of elimination, one can see that none of the other definitions is appropriate in the context of Passage 2.

17. **D.** Choice E can be immediately ruled out because the author clearly dislikes commercialization of the Brontë legacy, and Choice C is incorrect because the Brontës are not responsible for souvenirs created long after their deaths. Both "anger," Choice B, and "sorrow," Choice A, are words too strong to suggest the author's viewpoint.

18. **C.** See lines 35–36, 40–42 of Passage 2. The reference to Gaskell's Charlotte as a "domestic saint" implies the author's belief that Gaskell's book idealized Charlotte. Choices A, B, and E are not implied anywhere in the passage, and although the author regrets the loss of the book store, there is no indication that she fears that books have become obsolete, Choice D.

Short Reading Passage

19. **C.** The goldfish would interpret reality from their point of view, making it subjective. In fact, Passage 3 suggests that no one can be sure that a view of reality is anything but subjective, based on perception. Goldfish aren't being compared to humans here, Choice B, nor is the view of reality humorous, Choice A. Choice D is simply incorrect; although the council of Monza's action may seem extreme, it is not being satirized. The opening paragraph is also not questioning the importance of anything, Choice E.

20. **D.** See lines 10–12. Choices A and B are irrelevant to the passage, which is not concerned with science fiction films.. The *Matrix* example does not "prove" anything about our living in a simulated reality, Choice C, and rather than counteracting the example of goldfish, it is linking it to the idea of the film's alternative reality.

21. **A.** The parenthetical phrase is gently poking fun at the filmmaker's use of a pseudo-scientific term. "Belittle," Choice B, and "undercut," Choice C, are too strong to describe the author's intent. The passage isn't concerned with filmmakers, making D and E inaccurate choices.

22. **C.** The point the authors are making is that a simulated world with no consistent laws would mean that events would be haphazard, and therefore no assertions could be counted on; that eliminates choices A, B, and D. Choice E is irrelevant to the passage.

23. **A.** Choice A is precisely the point the author makes in lines 8–9. Choice B is inaccurate; according to the author, the goldfish, and humans in a simulated reality could make their own laws based on their perceptions. The laws could simply not be called "true." Choices C and D are simply irrelevant, and willingness is not an issue, Choice E.

24. **B.** Choice A is a minor point in Passage 3, and Choice D is wrong; the authors use the goldfish model not as a comparison but as lead-in to the idea that we cannot know if our reality is real. Choice C is not an issue in the passage. Choice E is incorrect; the author makes no comparison between our reality (which may not be truth at all) and alternative realities.

25. **E.** See lines 40–44. Choice A is a tempting choice; in paragraph 1 the city council bars curved fishbowls because they distort the fish's reality. However, it is not the curved bowl that bends light but the movement of the light from air to water. The location of the fish's eyes is not mentioned in the passage, Choice B, nor are the glass bowl or movements in the water, choices D, C, cited as reasons that the light moves in a curved path.

Section 5: Writing—Multiple Choice

Improving Sentences

1. **D.** The second part of the sentence is an exception to the information in the first part. Therefore, "but," not "and," is the best conjunction to use. The other choices change the form of the verb for no good reason. Choice B is not correct because the apostrophe is missing from the possessive "week's." Choice E also adds unnecessary words.

2. **B.** The problem here is parallel structure. Choice B corrects this by using "to" for both phrases. Parallel elements in a sentence should be presented in parallel constructions: to expand and [to] raise. None of the other choices is parallel, and, in addition, they are wordy.

3. **A.** The sentence is correct as it is written. The participial (or gerund) phrase "Forgetting to notify" acts as the subject of the sentence. The other choices are wordy or awkward.

4. **D.** The original sentence is a fragment. There is no main verb. By eliminating "but," as in Choice D, the sentence is correct. Adding a semicolon, Choice C, does not correct the fragment, and choices B and E are wordy, but still fragments. The phrase "which are a staple of American literature even today" must be followed by a main verb.

5. **B.** The sentence as it exists is wordy and awkward, The best version, Choice B, corrects this by restructuring, making "Central Pacific Railroad" the subject. None of the other choices restructures the sentence to avoid awkwardness. Notice the poor placement of the phrase "during the Industrial Revolution" in Choice E.

6. **C.** Verb tense is not consistent in the original sentence: "reads" and "refused" (present and past tenses). Choice D adds words, but doesn't correct the inconsistent tenses. Choices B and E are fragments.

7. **D.** In the original sentence, the doorbell is watching television. This is a dangling participle. By adding "he" to the phrase, the sentence is corrected. Choices B, C, and E do not correct the dangling participle.

8. **B.** The two parts of the sentence are not parallel in structure: "passing" and "to pass." Choice B corrects this, while Choice C does not. Choice D is wordy, and Choice E adds "the" before the second "passing," again making the elements not parallel.

9. **D.** There are two problems with the original sentence: first, subject-verb agreement; and second, the use of "irregardless." The subject of the sentence is "one," and therefore the verb should be singular ("is," not "are"). "Irregardless" is not a word, though it is used frequently. The correct word is "regardless." Choice B corrects the first problem but not the second, and Choice C corrects the second but not the first. Choice E changes the tense, but not the number, of the verb.

10. **D.** "Could have," not "could of," is correct. "Whomever" is also correct. It is the objective case of "whoever," which is appropriate here because "whomever" is the object of "he wanted." Choice C uses the subjective case. Choices B and E use incorrect forms of the verb.

11. **A.** The sentence is correct as is. Choices B and D are wordy and awkward, and choices C, D, and E use inappropriate forms of the verb "become" in the context of the sentence.

Identifying Sentence Errors

12. **B.** The subject is plural (the governor and the assistant governor) and therefore the verb must be plural ("were," not "was"). Choices A and C are the correct verb tense and Choice D correctly uses the objective forms of the pronouns because they are the objects of the preposition "with."

13. **A.** This is a misplaced participle, suggesting that the article is reading the newspaper. Choice C is correct; "I" is the right pronoun because it is part of the compound subject of "should cancel." The other choices are also correct.

14. **A.** The verb should be singular ("suggests") because the subject ("body") is singular. Choices B, C, and D are correct; the subject of the verb is "spaces," which requires plural verbs.

15. **C.** "You" is a change of person; it should be "one," as in the first clause. The other choices are correct.

16. **A.** The adverb "softly" is needed here because it describes an action ("spoke"). Choices B and C are correct; "no one" is singular, as is the verb "was." Choice D is also correct.

17. **E.** The sentence is correct as it is. Note that in Choice D, the adjective "bad" is the correct modifier; adjectives are used with linking verbs such as "is."

18. **D.** The verb should be in the present tense ("refuses") to match "wants." The other verbs are in the future tense, which is correct.

19. **A.** The pronoun here should be "me," the object of the preposition "for." "Myself" is a reflexive pronoun: "I hurt myself." Choices B, C, and D are correct.

20. **B.** The correct verb is "could have," not "could of." The combination "not only . . . but also" is correct (choices C and D).

21. **B.** The right word here is "effect," not "affect." Choice C is correct; "was given" is singular, and the subject is also singular ("group"). Choice D is also correct; "was" is singular, and the subject number is also singular.

22. **A.** This is a dangling or misplaced participle; it is not the snake that is lying asleep and dreaming of a hot shower. Choice B is correct; "quietly" is an adverb modifying the verb "slithered." Choice C correctly uses the pronoun "who"; it is the subject of the verb "was." Choice D is the correct modifier here.

23. **A.** The pronoun should be "they," not "them." It is part of the compound subject of the verb "continue." Choice B ("regardless") is correct. Choice C is an adverb modifying the verb "fight." Choice D is also correct; "lies" means rests or resides.

24. **C.** "Felt" is a linking verb here and should be followed by an adjective ("bad"), not the adverb "badly." Linking verbs are words such as "is," "smells," "tastes," and "feels": "I feel good today"; "it smells good"; "it tastes bad." Unlike action verbs (such as "jump," "run," "live," and "think") that take adverbs as modifiers, linking verbs are modified by adjectives. The other choices in this sentence are correct.

25. **D.** "He and I" should be in the objective case ("him and me") as objects of the verb "contacted." Choice A is used correctly; "better" distinguishes between two things. Choice B is also correct: "almost" (not "most") is the correct word here.

26. **D.** The past participle of "eat" is "have eaten," not "ate." The other choices are correct as they are.

27. **A.** "Who," not "whom," is correct here; it is the subject of "was respected." Choices B and C are parallel, and choice D is correct in using the adverb "briefly" to describe the action "appear."

28. **C.** "Unique" should not be used comparatively; it means one of a kind. This misuse of "unique" is common. Choices A, B, and D are correct.

29. **B.** "I" is incorrect. "Me" is the object of the preposition "between." "Between you and I" is a frequent mistake in both speaking and writing. The preposition always takes an objective pronoun ("me" instead of "I"). Choices A, C, and D are correct.

Improving Paragraphs

30. **A.** The sentence is wordy as it is. To say that the changes were disruptive because they disturbed people is redundant; the word "disruptive" indicates that the changes disturbed people. "Due to the fact" is also wordy. The other choices do not address the redundancy problem.

31. **B.** In addition to an agreement problem between subject and verb ("class was created," not "class were created"), the original sentence is in the passive voice ("were created"), which is less effective than the active voice ("gave rise to") in Choice B. Choice C, although it does use the active voice for both subjects, is awkward. Choice D has a subject-verb agreement problem and also uses the passive voice. Choice E has a dangling participle.

32. **A.** Choice A is the only choice that corrects the sentence fragment by removing "who." Choice D's structure, however, still makes it a fragment.

33. **C.** This sentence is an example of the statement made in sentence 10, and therefore it is best placed following the statement. The only other possible placement would be after sentence 11, but the sentence more naturally follows sentence 10.

34. **D.** Sentence 4 states that people had to move to larger towns and cities, which indicates that for them the simpler pleasures of the country vanished. Choice B is incorrect; the effect of the Industrial Revolution has not yet been stated. Choices C and E, as well as A, are not good locations for the sentence because it deals with the working class, while those locations are in a section dealing with the industrialists and factory owners.

35. **E.** Although none of these sentences may be ideal as a conclusion, this is the best choice because it provides a link to the previous sentence as well as addresses the content of the passage as a whole. Choice B is flat and mechanical. Choice C is not connected to the previous sentence, and Choice A focuses on Roosevelt, not the subject of the passage. Choice D is simply inaccurate in terms of the rest of the paragraph.

Section 6: Mathematics

1. **C.** In the series 8, 9, 12, 17, 24, . . .

$$9 - 8 = 1$$
$$12 - 9 = 3$$
$$17 - 12 = 5$$
$$24 - 17 = 7$$

Therefore, the difference between the next term and 24 must be 9, or $x - 24 = 9$, $x = 33$.

Therefore, the next term in the series must be 33.

2. **E.**

$$\frac{1}{4} \text{ of } 0.03\% =$$

Change $\frac{1}{4}$ to .25 and 0.03% to 0.0003.

$$(.25)(0.0003) = 0.000075$$

3. **C.** The area of a triangle is $\frac{1}{2} \times$ base $\times$ height

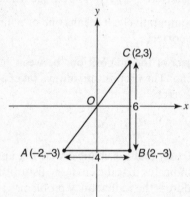

Base AB of a triangle is 4 units (because from A to the y-axis is 2 units, and from the y-axis to B is 2 units). Height BC of the triangle is 6 units (3 units from B to the x-axis, and another 3 units to C). Note that $\angle B$ is a right angle. So,

$$\text{Area of triangle} = \frac{1}{2} \times 4 \times 6$$
$$= \frac{1}{2} \times 24$$
$$= 12$$

4. **D.** You should have a working knowledge of these expressions:

Sum: The result of addition

Difference: The result of subtraction

Product: The result of multiplication

Quotient: The result of division

Therefore, the *product* of two numbers may be represented as $(x)(y)$. The *difference* of the two numbers may be either $x - y$ or $y - x$. The term "twice" indicates that the expression is to be multiplied by 2. Therefore, the entire expression breaks down as follows.

$$The\ product\ of\ two\ numbers\quad is\ equal\ to\quad twice\ the\quad difference\ of\ the\ two\ numbers$$
$$(x)(y) \qquad\qquad = \qquad\qquad 2 \qquad\qquad (x - y)$$

$$(x)(y) = 2(x - y)$$

5. E.

If $4^n = 64$, then $n = 3$ (since $4 \times 4 \times 4 = 64$)

Now substitute 3 for n.

$3^{n+2} = 3^{3+2} = 3^5 = 243$

6. E.

$f(z) = \dfrac{3z^3 + z - 7}{z^2 - 25}$ is undefined when $z^2 - 25 = 0$, since the denominator of a fraction cannot be equal to 0.

So set $z^2 - 25$ equal to 0 and solve.

$$z^2 - 25 = (z + 5)(z - 5) = 0$$
$$z + 5 = 0 \quad \text{or} \quad z - 5 = 0$$
$$z = -5 \quad \text{or} \quad z = 5$$

7. B. Because D is between A and B on $\overleftrightarrow{AB}$, you know that the sum of the lengths of the smaller segments AD and DB is equal to the length of the larger segment AB.

$$\longleftarrow \quad \underset{A}{\bullet} \quad \underset{D}{\bullet} \quad\quad\quad \underset{B}{\bullet} \quad \longrightarrow$$

Therefore,

$$AB = AD + DB$$
$$AB - AD = AD + DB - AD$$
$$AB - AD = DB$$

8. C. Solve the equation as follows:

$$x - 3 = \frac{18}{x}$$
$$x(x - 3) = x \cdot \frac{18}{x}$$
$$x(x - 3) = 18$$
$$x^2 - 3x = 18$$
$$x^2 - 3x - 18 = 0$$
$$(x - 6)(x + 3) = 0$$
$$x - 6 = 0 \quad \text{or} \quad x + 3 = 0$$
$$x = 6 \quad \text{or} \quad x = -3$$

Grid-In Questions

9. 94 Since $x = -4$,

$$5x^2 - 3x + 2 = 5(-4)^2 - 3(-4) + 2$$
$$= 5(16) + 12 + 2$$
$$= 80 + 12 + 2$$
$$= 94$$

10. 9.49 For a 25-minute call, the first 3 minutes will cost $2.45, and the additional 22 minutes will cost $.32 per minute. The cost (C) for the call will be

$$C = \$2.45 + (22)(\$.32)$$
$$= \$2.45 + \$7.04$$
$$= \$9.49$$

11. 70 Let n = the original price of the jacket. 80% of n is $56.

$$(0.80) \cdot n = \$56$$
$$n = \$56 \div 0.80$$
$$n = \$70$$

12. 350 The committee is formed by a combination of 2 females from a group of 5 females and a combination of 3 males from a group of 7 males. The number of different groups of 2 females is

$$_5C_2 = C(5,2) = \frac{5!}{2!(5-2)!} = \frac{5!}{2! \cdot 3!} = \frac{5 \cdot 4}{2 \cdot 1} = 10$$

The number of different groups of 3 males is

$$_7C_3 = C(7,3) = \frac{7!}{3!(7-3)!} = \frac{7!}{3! \cdot 4!} = \frac{7 \cdot 5 \cdot 6}{3 \cdot 2 \cdot 1} = 35$$

Hence, the total number of 2-female and 3-male groups is $_5C_2 \cdot {}_7C_3 = 10 \cdot 35 = 350$ groups

13. 480 You can quickly solve this problem by using your calculator. Total the four listed items: $840 + $460 + $320 + $120 = $1,740. Subtract $1,740 from the given total:

$2,220 – $1,740 = $480. The lab workbooks cost $480.

14. 50 Begin by choosing a simple fraction, $\frac{100}{100}$, for example. If the numerator is tripled and the denominator is doubled, the resulting fraction is $\frac{300}{200}$, or $1\frac{1}{2}$. So the new fraction represents a 50% increase over the original fraction.

15. 20 Since $l_1 \parallel l_2$, the alternate interior angles have the same measure and

$$5x - 20 = 2x + 40$$
$$3x - 20 = 40$$
$$3x = 60$$
$$x = 20$$

16. 640 The phrase "how much" more indicates subtraction. Clothing was 13% of the total. Insurance was 5% of the total. So 13% – 5%, or 8%, more of the total of $8,000 was spent on clothing than on insurance.

$$.08 \times \$8,000 = \$640$$

17. $\frac{4}{9}$

In $\triangle MXN$, $\angle MNX = 50°$, $\angle MXN = 90°$, and $\angle NMQ = 30°$

$$\angle NMQ + \angle QMX = \angle NMX$$

$$\text{So,} \quad 50° + 90° + 30° + \angle QMX = 180°$$
$$170° + \angle QMX = 180°$$
$$\angle QMX = 10°$$

In $\triangle MPQ$,

$$\angle QMP + \angle MPQ + \angle MQP = 180°$$
$$10° + 130° + \angle MQP = 180°$$
$$140° + \angle MQP = 180°$$
$$\angle MQP = 40°$$

Angle PXN is 90°, so the ratio of $\angle MQP$ to $\angle PXN$ is $\frac{40}{90}$, or $\frac{4}{9}$, or .444.

18. **48** Set up the equation as follows: Let t be the length of time it will take the plane to overtake the bus. Then $t + 4$ is the number of hours the bus has traveled before the plane starts. The distance the bus has traveled by 1:00 p.m. is $50(t + 4)$ because distance equals rate times time ($d = rt$). The distance the plane will travel is $300t$. Now, equate these two (they will have to travel the same distance for one to overtake the other), giving you $50(t + 4) = 300t$.

Solve the equation as follows:

$$50(t + 4) = 300t$$
$$50t + 200 = 300t$$
$$200 = 250t$$

Therefore, $\frac{4}{5} = t$

Four-fifths of an hour $\left(\frac{4}{5} \times 60\right)$ is 48 minutes. Therefore, it will take 48 minutes for the plane to overtake the bus.

Section 7: Mathematics

1. **A.** Since the difference between any two consecutive odd numbers is 2, the next odd number after $2x + 13$ would be

$$2x + 13 + 2 = 2x + 15$$

2. **D.** The amount of discount was $120 – $90 = $30. The rate of discount is a percent, so

$$\frac{\text{percent}}{100} = \frac{\text{is number}}{\text{of number}}$$
$$\frac{x}{100} = \frac{30}{120}$$

Cross-multiplying

$$120x = 3000$$
$$\frac{120x}{120} = \frac{3000}{120}$$
$$x = 25$$

Therefore, the rate of discount was 25%

3. **C.**

$$\sqrt{\frac{81}{x}} = \frac{9}{5}$$

Squaring both sides,

$$\frac{81}{x} = \frac{81}{25}$$

Therefore, $x = 25$

4. **B.** Since $\overline{CO}$ bisects $\angle BOD$, then $\angle BOC = \angle COD = 45°$.

Since the sum of the angles in the figure is $360°$,

$40° + 45° + 45° + 30° + 90° + \angle AOF = 360°$.

$250° + \angle AOF = 360°$

$\angle AOF = 360° - 250°$

$\angle AOF = 110°$

5. **D.**

$$\text{Average} \quad \frac{93 + 82 + 79 + x}{4} = 87$$
$$93 + 82 + 79 + x = 87 \cdot 4$$
$$254 + x = 348$$
$$x = 94$$

6. **D.** According to the graph, 20% have hazel eyes and 40% have brown eyes. This means there are twice as many brown-eyed people as there are hazel-eyed people.

$62 = $ people with hazel eyes

$2 \times 62 = 124$ people with brown eyes

7. **E.** The highest cost for the 480-mile trip would result from the poorest mileage and the highest gas price. At 16 mpg, the trip would require $480 \div 16 = 30$ gallons of gas at \$4.12 per gallon, or a cost of $\$4.12 \times 30 = \$123.60$.

The lowest cost for the 480-mile trip would result from the best mileage and the lowest gas price. At 24 mpg, the trip would require $480 \div 24 = 20$ gallons of gas at \$3.96 per gallon, or a cost of $\$3.96 \times 20 = \$79.20$. The difference between the two costs is $\$123.60 - \$79.20 = \$44.40$.

8. **A.** The perimeter of a rectangle equals $2l + 2w$, where l is the length and w is the width. If the length and width are increased by x, the perimeter will be

$$2(l + x) + 2(w + x)$$
$$= 2l + 2x + 2w + 2x$$
$$= 2l + 2w + 4x$$

which is an increase of $4x$ units.

9. **A.** Since $\frac{x^2 - 5x + 7}{x^2 - 4x + 10} = 1 = \frac{1}{1}$, cross-multiply to get

$$x^2 - 5x + 7 = x^2 - 4x + 10$$
$$x^2 - 5x + 7 - x^2 = x^2 - 4x + 10 - x^2$$
$$-5x + 7 = -4x + 10$$
$$-5x + 7 + 4x = -4x + 10 + 4x$$
$$-x + 7 = 10$$
$$-x + 7 - 7 = 10 - 7$$
$$-x = 3$$
$$x = -3$$

10. **B.** Forty-eight days late is one day shy of exactly 7 weeks (7 weeks = 7×7 = 49 days). If the job were finished in 49 days, then it would have been completed on the same day, Wednesday. Because 48 is one day less than 7 weeks, however, the job was completed one day earlier than Wednesday–Tuesday.

11. **C.** Let $3x$ = one angle and $4x$ = other angle.

$$3x + 4x + 68 = 180$$
$$7x + 68 = 180$$
$$7x = 112$$
$$x = 16$$
$$3x = 48$$
$$4x = 64$$

Therefore, the smallest angle of the triangle is 48°.

12. **B.** If two points have coordinates (x_1, y_1) and (x_2, y_2), the distance d between these points is defined as

$$d = \sqrt{(x_1 - x_2)^2 + (y_1 - y_2)^2}$$

Since E has coordinates (–3, 5) and F has coordinates (6, –7), the distance between E and F is

$$EF = \sqrt{(-3 - 6)^2 + \left[5 - (-7)\right]^2}$$
$$= \sqrt{(-9)^2 + (12)^2}$$
$$= \sqrt{81 + 144}$$
$$= \sqrt{225}$$
$$= 15$$

13. **C.** The random sample indicates that 1,500 out of 2,500 New York moviegoers prefer comedies, or 60% of those polled prefer comedies. Of those polled, 500 out of 2,500, or 20%, prefer dramas. Therefore, out of 8,000,000 total New York moviegoers, 60% should be found to prefer comedies (4,800,000), and 20% (1,600,000) should be found to prefer dramas. Only Choice III reflects either of these estimates.

14. **E.** The horizontal length of x cannot be determined because there is no indication of the overlapping length of the rectangle to the left of x. If x cannot be determined, then $x + y$ cannot be determined.

15. **D.** Adding a positive number to the domain variable shifts the graph of a function to the left. Hence, $g(x)$ will be five units to the left of $f(x)$.

16. **A.** Since $\angle Y$ is inscribed in a semicircle, $\angle Y$ is a right angle. So using the Pythagorean Theorem you get

$$(XY)^2 + (YZ)^2 = (XZ)^2$$
$$15^2 + 8^2 = (XZ)^2$$
$$225 + 64 = (XZ)^2$$
$$289 = (XZ)^2$$
$$\sqrt{289} = XZ$$
$$XZ = 17$$

Section 8: Writing—Multiple Choice

Improving Sentences

1. **D.** The problem with the original sentence is an unclear pronoun reference. Choice D makes it clear that Norm is the person who left his jacket. Choice C also corrects the problem but uses the wrong verb tense, and Choice E unnecessarily adds "he" after "Norm."

2. **C.** Two steps in the renovation are mentioned, and therefore the verb should be plural ("are"). Faulty parallel structure, as well as a singular verb, is the problem with Choice D, and "those" should be omitted from Choice E.

3. **B.** This is the only choice that corrects the problem of a misplaced modifying phrase. The teacher's voice is *not* sitting in the front row of the classroom. Choice B is also the most succinct and direct version of the sentence.

4. **E.** Of all the choices, E is the only one that corrects the basic problem, which is that the original is a sentence fragment. All the other choices are also fragments. Choice E also improves the original by eliminating unnecessary words.

5. **A.** The original version of the sentence is correct. "Her" is the object of "seen," and is therefore the correct case of the pronoun.

6. **D.** This is the best choice. It replaces the passive voice with the active voice of the verb and is less wordy than Choice E.

7. **C.** Of the choices, C is best. It corrects the faulty parallelism of choices A, B, D, and E, and it also eliminates the double negative "cannot hardly." "Can hardly" is correct.

8. **E.** In the original sentence, both verb forms are incorrect. "Have fell" should be "had fallen," and "was broke" should be "was broken." One tense is wrong in each of the other choices.

9. **A.** The original version is correct. The objective case of the pronoun ("him") is appropriate; it is an object of the preposition "between." None of the other choices uses the correct case.

10. **D.** The original version is incorrect because the verb should be "was injured," not "were injured." "Everyone" takes a singular verb. The original sentence also includes a faulty parallel structure: "crashing," "jumped," and "mowed." Choice D corrects both problems. Choice B is a run-on sentence (comma splice). The semicolon in Choice E creates a sentence fragment.

11. **C.** The original version, and choices B and E have dangling (or misplaced) participles; it is not the campaign that believes family ties are more important but the candidate. Choice D is a run-on sentence (comma splice).

12. **C.** Of the choices, C is best. It eliminates the redundancy of "descent down," corrects the verb tense ("told" rather than "tells"), and changes "large amount of people" to the more succinct "many people." "Large amount of people" is not only wordy but also incorrect; "large number of people" is the right phrase.

13. **E.** Verb tense with "if" is the problem in the original sentence and in all the choices except Choice E; "had not eaten" is the correct verb. Also, "could of arrived" is incorrect. The correct phrase is "could have arrived." The use of "of" rather than "have" is a common error with "could," "would," and "should."

14. **A.** The original version is the best choice. The correct verb is "affected," not "effected," Choice B. The verb tense is incorrect in Choice C. Choice D has faulty parallel structure, and Choice E is a fragment, in addition to using "effected" rather than "affected."

Section 9: Critical Reading

Sentence Completions

1. **B.** "But" is the word that suggests a difference between the woman's fury and the content of the editorial. The woman's reaction is surprising because the editorial is fairly innocuous. "Innocuous" means harmless. None of the other choices suggests such a difference.

2. **A.** Choice A is the best answer; "adroit" means skillful. Choices B, C, D, and E are not favorable adjectives in this context and would not impress the committee.

3. **C.** Choices A, B, D, and E are condemnations that are too strong for the girls' giggling, whereas "levity" (excessive frivolity) would be more likely to deserve a scolding from the woman.

4. **A.** "Prerogative" is a special privilege or right. Leaving early would be the right of an executive but not appropriate for a new employee. None of the other choices fits the context.

5. **E.** A visit to his brother is his apparent reason for a trip to Italy, but his real reason is to check on his villa. Again, "but" is the clue. Choice E, "ostensible," which means apparent, is the contrast to "real." The other choices do not provide this contrast.

6. **C.** Remember that both words must be appropriate for the context. In this sentence, "ephemeral" means fleeting, not lasting. This word fits best with the father's rescinding his promise the next day. None of the other choices for the first word is appropriate.

Long Reading Passage

7. **B.** Although most of the first paragraph tells the story of the woman who invented white crane boxing, the purpose of the paragraph is to introduce the kind of talk-story that influenced the speaker. The speaker's mother, Choice A, isn't introduced until the second paragraph. Choice D is a detail, not the primary purpose of the paragraph. And Choice E—while a tempting choice—is not the best one because in the first paragraph the speaker is repeating a story that has been told to her.

8. **C.** See lines 20–24. Choice B is a comment made by the speaker, but it is not directly connected to the white crane boxer. Choice A is not indicated, and Choice D is irrelevant to the passage. Choice E is also incorrect; nothing suggests that women gained stature in China because of the white crane boxer.

9. **C.** Although it is clear that the girl wanted to be a swordswoman, Choice B, these particular lines emphasize her confusion of dreams and reality. Choice A is not implied. Choice D is accurate but is not indicated in these lines. Choice E is simply incorrect; there is no such implication.

10. **E.** An ideograph is a picture or symbol used in writing. This is clear from lines 51–52.

11. **B.** See lines 5–6. Choice A is not implied, and choices C, D, and E, while perhaps true in stories of warrior women, are not mentioned in the passage.

12. **D.** The swordswomen in the movies "jumped over houses from a standstill; they didn't even need a running start." Nothing indicates that they frightened the speaker, Choice A, or made her doubtful that real swordswomen existed, Choice E. Although the movies affected her, there is no suggestion that they were as powerful as her mother's stories, Choice B, or that they made her wish to see the world, Choice C.

13. **E.** In lines 46–49, the speaker says that although her mother thought the speaker would grow up to be a wife and a slave, her mother actually taught her the song of the warrior women, making the girl realize she would have to be one herself. Choice A is contradicted in lines 46–47. Nothing suggests that the speaker's mother idealized Fa Mu Lan, Choice B, or that the speaker exaggerated the story, Choice C. Choice D is not suggested.

14. **C.** The only thing that is directly stated is that Ma Fu Lan took her father's place in battle. Choices A and D, while they could be true, are not suggested. Choices B and E apply to the white crane boxer, not Ma Fu Lan.

15. **A.** At this point in the passage the speaker creates a childhood fantasy that has her following a bird into the mountains. The other two possible choices would be B and E, but the passage is never a straightforward autobiography because of the warrior women stories, and the speaker's reliability is not truly in question since she is recounting her thoughts as a child. There is no satire in these lines, and her mother's influence is not an issue here.

16. **D.** The fantasy begins with the speaker referring to "the brush drawings," which suggests she is looking at a painting. Other lines also suggest a drawing (lines 68, 69, and 70). None of the other choices is implied in the passage.

17. **D.** This line is most clearly the utterance of a child, not a warrior woman, and it breaks the mood of the fantasy. All of the other choices maintain the child's fantasy.

18. **B.** The author does not use sarcasm, but uses dialogue (lines 86–89), imagery (for example, lines 50–68), myth (the talk-stories), and similes (for example, lines 67–68).

19. **A.** The comment immediately follows her lie to the old man and woman that she has eaten that day. The speaker does not see the talk-stories as lies, choices C and D. She also would not characterize her mother's prediction as a lie, Choice E.

Chapter 11

Practice Exam 3

Section 2

1 Ⓐ Ⓑ Ⓒ Ⓓ Ⓔ	21 Ⓐ Ⓑ Ⓒ Ⓓ Ⓔ
2 Ⓐ Ⓑ Ⓒ Ⓓ Ⓔ	22 Ⓐ Ⓑ Ⓒ Ⓓ Ⓔ
3 Ⓐ Ⓑ Ⓒ Ⓓ Ⓔ	23 Ⓐ Ⓑ Ⓒ Ⓓ Ⓔ
4 Ⓐ Ⓑ Ⓒ Ⓓ Ⓔ	24 Ⓐ Ⓑ Ⓒ Ⓓ Ⓔ
5 Ⓐ Ⓑ Ⓒ Ⓓ Ⓔ	25 Ⓐ Ⓑ Ⓒ Ⓓ Ⓔ
6 Ⓐ Ⓑ Ⓒ Ⓓ Ⓔ	26 Ⓐ Ⓑ Ⓒ Ⓓ Ⓔ
7 Ⓐ Ⓑ Ⓒ Ⓓ Ⓔ	27 Ⓐ Ⓑ Ⓒ Ⓓ Ⓔ
8 Ⓐ Ⓑ Ⓒ Ⓓ Ⓔ	28 Ⓐ Ⓑ Ⓒ Ⓓ Ⓔ
9 Ⓐ Ⓑ Ⓒ Ⓓ Ⓔ	29 Ⓐ Ⓑ Ⓒ Ⓓ Ⓔ
10 Ⓐ Ⓑ Ⓒ Ⓓ Ⓔ	30 Ⓐ Ⓑ Ⓒ Ⓓ Ⓔ
11 Ⓐ Ⓑ Ⓒ Ⓓ Ⓔ	31 Ⓐ Ⓑ Ⓒ Ⓓ Ⓔ
12 Ⓐ Ⓑ Ⓒ Ⓓ Ⓔ	32 Ⓐ Ⓑ Ⓒ Ⓓ Ⓔ
13 Ⓐ Ⓑ Ⓒ Ⓓ Ⓔ	33 Ⓐ Ⓑ Ⓒ Ⓓ Ⓔ
14 Ⓐ Ⓑ Ⓒ Ⓓ Ⓔ	34 Ⓐ Ⓑ Ⓒ Ⓓ Ⓔ
15 Ⓐ Ⓑ Ⓒ Ⓓ Ⓔ	35 Ⓐ Ⓑ Ⓒ Ⓓ Ⓔ
16 Ⓐ Ⓑ Ⓒ Ⓓ Ⓔ	36 Ⓐ Ⓑ Ⓒ Ⓓ Ⓔ
17 Ⓐ Ⓑ Ⓒ Ⓓ Ⓔ	
18 Ⓐ Ⓑ Ⓒ Ⓓ Ⓔ	
19 Ⓐ Ⓑ Ⓒ Ⓓ Ⓔ	
20 Ⓐ Ⓑ Ⓒ Ⓓ Ⓔ	

Section 3

1 Ⓐ Ⓑ Ⓒ Ⓓ Ⓔ	21 Ⓐ Ⓑ Ⓒ Ⓓ Ⓔ
2 Ⓐ Ⓑ Ⓒ Ⓓ Ⓔ	22 Ⓐ Ⓑ Ⓒ Ⓓ Ⓔ
3 Ⓐ Ⓑ Ⓒ Ⓓ Ⓔ	23 Ⓐ Ⓑ Ⓒ Ⓓ Ⓔ
4 Ⓐ Ⓑ Ⓒ Ⓓ Ⓔ	24 Ⓐ Ⓑ Ⓒ Ⓓ Ⓔ
5 Ⓐ Ⓑ Ⓒ Ⓓ Ⓔ	25 Ⓐ Ⓑ Ⓒ Ⓓ Ⓔ
6 Ⓐ Ⓑ Ⓒ Ⓓ Ⓔ	26 Ⓐ Ⓑ Ⓒ Ⓓ Ⓔ
7 Ⓐ Ⓑ Ⓒ Ⓓ Ⓔ	27 Ⓐ Ⓑ Ⓒ Ⓓ Ⓔ
8 Ⓐ Ⓑ Ⓒ Ⓓ Ⓔ	28 Ⓐ Ⓑ Ⓒ Ⓓ Ⓔ
9 Ⓐ Ⓑ Ⓒ Ⓓ Ⓔ	
10 Ⓐ Ⓑ Ⓒ Ⓓ Ⓔ	
11 Ⓐ Ⓑ Ⓒ Ⓓ Ⓔ	
12 Ⓐ Ⓑ Ⓒ Ⓓ Ⓔ	
13 Ⓐ Ⓑ Ⓒ Ⓓ Ⓔ	
14 Ⓐ Ⓑ Ⓒ Ⓓ Ⓔ	
15 Ⓐ Ⓑ Ⓒ Ⓓ Ⓔ	
16 Ⓐ Ⓑ Ⓒ Ⓓ Ⓔ	
17 Ⓐ Ⓑ Ⓒ Ⓓ Ⓔ	
18 Ⓐ Ⓑ Ⓒ Ⓓ Ⓔ	
19 Ⓐ Ⓑ Ⓒ Ⓓ Ⓔ	
20 Ⓐ Ⓑ Ⓒ Ⓓ Ⓔ	

CUT HERE

Section 4

1 Ⓐ Ⓑ Ⓒ Ⓓ Ⓔ
2 Ⓐ Ⓑ Ⓒ Ⓓ Ⓔ
3 Ⓐ Ⓑ Ⓒ Ⓓ Ⓔ
4 Ⓐ Ⓑ Ⓒ Ⓓ Ⓔ
5 Ⓐ Ⓑ Ⓒ Ⓓ Ⓔ
6 Ⓐ Ⓑ Ⓒ Ⓓ Ⓔ
7 Ⓐ Ⓑ Ⓒ Ⓓ Ⓔ
8 Ⓐ Ⓑ Ⓒ Ⓓ Ⓔ
9 Ⓐ Ⓑ Ⓒ Ⓓ Ⓔ
10 Ⓐ Ⓑ Ⓒ Ⓓ Ⓔ
11 Ⓐ Ⓑ Ⓒ Ⓓ Ⓔ
12 Ⓐ Ⓑ Ⓒ Ⓓ Ⓔ
13 Ⓐ Ⓑ Ⓒ Ⓓ Ⓔ
14 Ⓐ Ⓑ Ⓒ Ⓓ Ⓔ
15 Ⓐ Ⓑ Ⓒ Ⓓ Ⓔ
16 Ⓐ Ⓑ Ⓒ Ⓓ Ⓔ
17 Ⓐ Ⓑ Ⓒ Ⓓ Ⓔ
18 Ⓐ Ⓑ Ⓒ Ⓓ Ⓔ
19 Ⓐ Ⓑ Ⓒ Ⓓ Ⓔ
20 Ⓐ Ⓑ Ⓒ Ⓓ Ⓔ

Section 5

1 Ⓐ Ⓑ Ⓒ Ⓓ Ⓔ	21 Ⓐ Ⓑ Ⓒ Ⓓ Ⓔ
2 Ⓐ Ⓑ Ⓒ Ⓓ Ⓔ	22 Ⓐ Ⓑ Ⓒ Ⓓ Ⓔ
3 Ⓐ Ⓑ Ⓒ Ⓓ Ⓔ	23 Ⓐ Ⓑ Ⓒ Ⓓ Ⓔ
4 Ⓐ Ⓑ Ⓒ Ⓓ Ⓔ	24 Ⓐ Ⓑ Ⓒ Ⓓ Ⓔ
5 Ⓐ Ⓑ Ⓒ Ⓓ Ⓔ	25 Ⓐ Ⓑ Ⓒ Ⓓ Ⓔ
6 Ⓐ Ⓑ Ⓒ Ⓓ Ⓔ	26 Ⓐ Ⓑ Ⓒ Ⓓ Ⓔ
7 Ⓐ Ⓑ Ⓒ Ⓓ Ⓔ	27 Ⓐ Ⓑ Ⓒ Ⓓ Ⓔ
8 Ⓐ Ⓑ Ⓒ Ⓓ Ⓔ	28 Ⓐ Ⓑ Ⓒ Ⓓ Ⓔ
9 Ⓐ Ⓑ Ⓒ Ⓓ Ⓔ	
10 Ⓐ Ⓑ Ⓒ Ⓓ Ⓔ	
11 Ⓐ Ⓑ Ⓒ Ⓓ Ⓔ	
12 Ⓐ Ⓑ Ⓒ Ⓓ Ⓔ	
13 Ⓐ Ⓑ Ⓒ Ⓓ Ⓔ	
14 Ⓐ Ⓑ Ⓒ Ⓓ Ⓔ	
15 Ⓐ Ⓑ Ⓒ Ⓓ Ⓔ	
16 Ⓐ Ⓑ Ⓒ Ⓓ Ⓔ	
17 Ⓐ Ⓑ Ⓒ Ⓓ Ⓔ	
18 Ⓐ Ⓑ Ⓒ Ⓓ Ⓔ	
19 Ⓐ Ⓑ Ⓒ Ⓓ Ⓔ	
20 Ⓐ Ⓑ Ⓒ Ⓓ Ⓔ	

Section 6

1 Ⓐ Ⓑ Ⓒ Ⓓ Ⓔ
2 Ⓐ Ⓑ Ⓒ Ⓓ Ⓔ
3 Ⓐ Ⓑ Ⓒ Ⓓ Ⓔ
4 Ⓐ Ⓑ Ⓒ Ⓓ Ⓔ
5 Ⓐ Ⓑ Ⓒ Ⓓ Ⓔ
6 Ⓐ Ⓑ Ⓒ Ⓓ Ⓔ
7 Ⓐ Ⓑ Ⓒ Ⓓ Ⓔ
8 Ⓐ Ⓑ Ⓒ Ⓓ Ⓔ

9. **10.** **11.** **12.**

13. **14.** **15.** **16.**

CUT HERE

17. **18.**

Section 7

1 Ⓐ Ⓑ Ⓒ Ⓓ Ⓔ
2 Ⓐ Ⓑ Ⓒ Ⓓ Ⓔ
3 Ⓐ Ⓑ Ⓒ Ⓓ Ⓔ
4 Ⓐ Ⓑ Ⓒ Ⓓ Ⓔ
5 Ⓐ Ⓑ Ⓒ Ⓓ Ⓔ
6 Ⓐ Ⓑ Ⓒ Ⓓ Ⓔ
7 Ⓐ Ⓑ Ⓒ Ⓓ Ⓔ
8 Ⓐ Ⓑ Ⓒ Ⓓ Ⓔ
9 Ⓐ Ⓑ Ⓒ Ⓓ Ⓔ
10 Ⓐ Ⓑ Ⓒ Ⓓ Ⓔ
11 Ⓐ Ⓑ Ⓒ Ⓓ Ⓔ
12 Ⓐ Ⓑ Ⓒ Ⓓ Ⓔ
13 Ⓐ Ⓑ Ⓒ Ⓓ Ⓔ
14 Ⓐ Ⓑ Ⓒ Ⓓ Ⓔ
15 Ⓐ Ⓑ Ⓒ Ⓓ Ⓔ

Section 8

1 Ⓐ Ⓑ Ⓒ Ⓓ Ⓔ
2 Ⓐ Ⓑ Ⓒ Ⓓ Ⓔ
3 Ⓐ Ⓑ Ⓒ Ⓓ Ⓔ
4 Ⓐ Ⓑ Ⓒ Ⓓ Ⓔ
5 Ⓐ Ⓑ Ⓒ Ⓓ Ⓔ
6 Ⓐ Ⓑ Ⓒ Ⓓ Ⓔ
7 Ⓐ Ⓑ Ⓒ Ⓓ Ⓔ
8 Ⓐ Ⓑ Ⓒ Ⓓ Ⓔ
9 Ⓐ Ⓑ Ⓒ Ⓓ Ⓔ
10 Ⓐ Ⓑ Ⓒ Ⓓ Ⓔ
11 Ⓐ Ⓑ Ⓒ Ⓓ Ⓔ
12 Ⓐ Ⓑ Ⓒ Ⓓ Ⓔ
13 Ⓐ Ⓑ Ⓒ Ⓓ Ⓔ
14 Ⓐ Ⓑ Ⓒ Ⓓ Ⓔ
15 Ⓐ Ⓑ Ⓒ Ⓓ Ⓔ
16 Ⓐ Ⓑ Ⓒ Ⓓ Ⓔ

Section 9

1 Ⓐ Ⓑ Ⓒ Ⓓ Ⓔ
2 Ⓐ Ⓑ Ⓒ Ⓓ Ⓔ
3 Ⓐ Ⓑ Ⓒ Ⓓ Ⓔ
4 Ⓐ Ⓑ Ⓒ Ⓓ Ⓔ
5 Ⓐ Ⓑ Ⓒ Ⓓ Ⓔ
6 Ⓐ Ⓑ Ⓒ Ⓓ Ⓔ
7 Ⓐ Ⓑ Ⓒ Ⓓ Ⓔ
8 Ⓐ Ⓑ Ⓒ Ⓓ Ⓔ
9 Ⓐ Ⓑ Ⓒ Ⓓ Ⓔ
10 Ⓐ Ⓑ Ⓒ Ⓓ Ⓔ
11 Ⓐ Ⓑ Ⓒ Ⓓ Ⓔ
12 Ⓐ Ⓑ Ⓒ Ⓓ Ⓔ
13 Ⓐ Ⓑ Ⓒ Ⓓ Ⓔ
14 Ⓐ Ⓑ Ⓒ Ⓓ Ⓔ
15 Ⓐ Ⓑ Ⓒ Ⓓ Ⓔ

Section 1: Writing—Essay

Time: 25 minutes
1 Essay Question

You have 25 minutes to plan and write an essay on the topic below. DO NOT WRITE ON ANOTHER TOPIC. AN ESSAY ON ANOTHER TOPIC WILL NOT BE SCORED.

The essay is intended to give you the chance to show your writing skills. Be sure to express your ideas on the topic clearly and effectively. The quality of your writing is much more important than the quantity, but to cover the topic adequately you may want to write more than one paragraph. Be specific.

Your essay must be written on two lined pages. Two pages should be enough if you write on every line, avoid wide margins, and keep your handwriting a reasonable size. You will not be given any additional paper. On the actual SAT you must

- Only use a pencil. You will receive a score of zero if you use ink.
- Only write on your answer sheet. You will not receive credit for material written in the test book.
- Only write on the topic presented below. An essay that is off-topic will receive a score of zero.
- Write an essay that reflects original work.

Directions: Read the following paragraph and assignment carefully. Then prepare and write a *persuasive* essay. Be sure to support your reasons with specific examples that will make your essay more effective.

"We learn, as we say, by 'trial and error.' Why do we always say that? Why not 'trial and rightness' or 'trial and triumph'? The old phrase puts it that way because that is, in real life, the way it is done."

—Lewis Thomas

> **Assignment:** Thomas suggests that learning is a result of making mistakes rather than doing things correctly. Do you agree or disagree with Thomas? Using an example or examples from your reading or your personal observations, write an essay to support your position.

ON THE ACTUAL EXAM, THE PROCTOR WILL ANNOUNCE WHEN 25 MINUTES HAVE PASSED. IF YOU FINISH YOUR ESSAY BEFORE 25 MINUTES HAVE PASSED, YOU MAY NOT GO ON TO ANY OTHER SECTION OF THE EXAM. THE PROCTOR WILL ANNOUNCE WHEN TO START THE NEXT SECTION.

Section 2: Writing—Multiple Choice

Time: 25 minutes

36 Questions

Directions: In this section, choose the best answer for each question and fill in the corresponding circle on the answer sheet.

The following questions test correctness and effective expression. In selecting the answer, pay attention to grammar, diction, sentence structure, and punctuation. In the following questions, part or all of each sentence is underlined. Answer Choice A repeats the underlined portion of the original sentence, while the next four choices offer alternatives. Choose the answer that best expresses the meaning of the original sentence and at the same time is grammatically correct and stylistically superior. The correct choice should be clear, unambiguous, and concise.

EXAMPLE:

The forecaster predicted <u>rain and the sky was clear.</u>

    A. rain and the sky was clear

    B. rain but the sky was clear.

    C. rain the sky was clear.

    D. rain, but the sky was clear.

    E. rain being as the sky was clear.

The correct answer is **D.**

1. The melting of Antarctic ice affects ocean <u>currents, and the sunlight's penetration of the water and the growth of microorganisms are also affected.</u>

    A. currents, and the sunlight's penetration of the water and the growth of microorganisms are also affected.

    B. currents; also affected are the sunlight's penetration of the water and the growth of microorganisms.

    C. currents, and it also affects the sunlight's penetration of the water and the growth of microorganisms.

    D. currents, the sunlight's penetration of the water and the growth of microorganisms.

    E. currents, with the sunlight's penetration of the water and the growth of microorganisms also being affected.

2. Coffee drinking may protect against cancer of the colon, <u>which is surprising since coffee drinking increases</u> the risk of heart attack.

    A. which is surprising since coffee drinking increases

    B. and this is surprising since coffee drinking increases

    C. surprising, since coffee drinking increases

    D. and this surprises us because coffee drinking increases

    E. which surprises since coffee drinking increases

GO ON TO THE NEXT PAGE

3. The excavations at Ceren reveal <u>the prosperity of the rural Mayans, the staples of their diet, and</u> the architecture of their homes.

   A. the prosperity of the rural Mayans, the staples of their diet, and

   B. the prosperity of the rural Mayan; the staples of their diets; and

   C. the prosperity of the rural Mayans, and the staples of their diet, and

   D. the rural Mayans, the prosperity and the diet they ate, as well as

   E. how prosperous the rural Mayans were, what their diet was, and

4. Human cells grown in a test tube can reproduce as many as sixty <u>times then they die</u> from old age.

   A. times then they die
   B. times but then they die
   C. times and then they die
   D. times; then they die
   E. times; before dying

5. <u>In the official portrait of Richard III, it shows an attractive and healthy man, and does not present</u> the deformed demon of Shakespeare's play.

   A. In the official portrait of Richard III, it shows an attractive and healthy man, and does not present

   B. In the official portrait of Richard III, an attractive, healthy man is shown; it does not present

   C. The official portrait of Richard III shows an attractive and healthy man, not

   D. The official portrait of Richard III shows a man who is attractive and healthy, and does not present

   E. Richard III, in the official portrait, is a man who is attractive and healthy, and he is not

6. <u>George Eliot was an ardent and knowledgeable lover of music, and she had</u> little skill in composing melodious verse.

   A. George Eliot was an ardent and knowledgeable lover of music, and she had

   B. George Eliot loved music ardently and knowledgeably, and she

   C. George Eliot was ardent and knowledgeable in her love of music, and she had

   D. George Eliot was an ardent, knowledgeable music lover, having

   E. Although George Eliot was an ardent, knowledgeable lover of music, she had

7. Nestled in the mountains of southwestern Colorado, <u>the extinction of the town of Silverton is imminent</u> with the closing of its silver mine.

   A. the extinction of the town of Silverton is imminent

   B. the extinction of Silverton as a town is imminent

   C. the imminent extinction of the town of Silverton is likely

   D. the town of Silverton faces imminent extinction

   E. the town of Silverton will become extinct imminently

GO ON TO THE NEXT PAGE

Practice Exam 3

Directions: The following sentences may contain one error of grammar, usage, diction, or idiom. No sentence contains more than one error, and some have no error. If there is an error, it will be underlined and have a letter beneath it. If there is an error, choose the one underlined part that must be changed to correct the sentence. If there is no error, choose E. Sections of the sentence that are not underlined cannot be changed. In selecting your answer, observe the requirements of standard written English.

EXAMPLE:

The film <u>tell the story</u> of a army captain and <u>his wife</u> who <u>try to</u> <u>rebuild their lives</u> after the Iraq War.
       A   B   C   D

<u>No error</u>
E
The correct answer is **A**.

---

8. <u>Strange as it now seems</u>, Japan and Italy once
     A
<u>agreed to limit</u> car imports because Japan
     B
<u>fears</u> <u>competition from Italian cars</u>. <u>No error</u>
  C   D   E

9. In December, 2011, <u>there were</u> darkness
               A
at noon <u>in Mexico City</u>, as the moon
       B
<u>passed between</u> the sun <u>and the Earth</u>.
    C   D
<u>No error</u>
E

10. The advertisement for the Broadway musical

    Wicked <u>features</u> two <u>witch hats</u> <u>who appear</u>
           A   B   C
    <u>to be whispering</u> to each other. <u>No error</u>
       D   E

11. You can grow a number of spring-flowering

    bulbs <u>indoors, but</u> if the plants <u>are to blossom,</u>
         A   B
    one must carefully <u>control the light</u>. <u>No error</u>
     C   D   E

12. <u>Despite lagging productivity</u> by its work force,
         A
    the Cuban government <u>has continued</u> to
                 B
    <u>provide</u> a <u>first-rate health-care</u> program.
      C   D
    <u>No error</u>
    E

13. <u>Nowadays most medical authorities agree</u> that
             A
    <u>huge doses</u> of <u>just about any substance</u> is
       B   C
    <u>likely to be dangerous</u>. <u>No error</u>
        D   E

14. <u>As a resulting of overgrazing</u>, firewood
         A
    cutting, and <u>increased cultivation</u> the Sahara
             B
    Desert has <u>steadily grown</u> <u>larger</u> in this decade.
           C   D
    <u>No error</u>
    E

15. <u>To safeguard wildlife,</u> the state of Florida will
        A
    <u>line its highways</u> with high fencing, <u>forcing</u>
        B   C
    panthers <u>to scoot</u> beneath the roads through
           D
    specially designed animal underpasses.

    <u>No error</u>
    E

16. Hypnotism, chewing gum, and <u>nicotine-releasing</u>
                         A
    <u>skin patches</u> are <u>probably</u> the <u>most used method</u>
                 B   C
    to break the <u>cigarette smoking habit</u>. <u>No error</u>
            D   E

GO ON TO THE NEXT PAGE

17. The <u>decline in</u> the Dow Jones Industrial
        A
    Average (DJIA) in 2008 was much smaller

    <u>compared</u> <u>to the 1929 decline</u> because the Dow
      B   C
    Index <u>stands with</u> a much higher level today.
          D
    <u>No error</u>
     E

18. <u>Missing the forehand volley</u>, a <u>relative easy shot</u>,
          A   B
    Andres fell behind <u>early in the match</u>, and
                C
    <u>he never recovered</u>. <u>No error</u>
      D   E

19. <u>In an area of</u> <u>the Pacific Ring of Fire</u> of
       A   B
    <u>special interest to</u> volcanologists <u>lie</u> the western
       C   D
    Siberian Kamchatka Peninsula. <u>No error</u>
                    E

20. Bears, mountain lions, beavers, <u>deer</u>, squirrels,
                    A
    and coyotes <u>inhabit</u> Sequoia Park, and <u>they</u>
            B   C
    may be <u>dangerous to campers</u>. <u>No error</u>
         D   E

21. <u>No Latin American matador</u> <u>can become</u>
          A   B
    famous <u>without he succeeds</u> in Spain where
            C
    bullfighting <u>was invented</u>. <u>No error</u>
          D   E

22. The discovery of the existence of a fifth force

    <u>could have</u> enormous <u>impact on</u> theoretical
     A   B
    physicists who <u>are trying to develop</u> a unified
              C
    theory <u>to explain the interactions of matter</u>.
            D
    <u>No error</u>
     E

23. When it is five o'clock in New York, <u>it is</u>
                        A
    <u>only three</u> in Texas, and <u>it will be</u> two o'clock
      B   C
    in California <u>or Oregon</u>. <u>No error</u>
            D   E

24. New Englanders seem to believe that <u>us Texans</u>
                        A
    talk <u>oddly</u>, but we think <u>they are the ones</u> who
       B   C
    <u>have strange ways of speaking</u>. <u>No error</u>
         D   E

25. <u>To encourage better reading skills</u>, teachers in
            A
    the public schools <u>now requisite</u> students to
            B
    submit weekly journals <u>listing the books</u>,
            C
    magazines, and newspapers <u>they have read</u>.
            D
    <u>No error</u>
     E

26. The best <u>examples of plays</u> that can
           A
    <u>be produced</u> with a minimum of <u>expense for</u>
       B   C
    settings and costumes <u>must be</u> Wilder's *Our*
               D
    Town. <u>No error</u>
         E

GO ON TO THE NEXT PAGE

Directions: The following passages are early drafts of student essays. Some parts of them need to be revised.

Read the selections carefully and answer the questions that follow. There will be questions about sentence structure, diction, and usage in individual sentences or parts of sentences. Other questions will deal with the whole essay or paragraphs in it and ask you to decide about the organization, development, and appropriate language. Choose the answer that follows the requirements of standard written English and most effectively expresses the intended meanings.

Questions 27-32 are based on the following passage.

(1) In 2011, the Iowa Writers' Workshop celebrated its 75th anniversary. (2) There are probably many Americans who have never heard of the workshop, however its students over the
(5) years have produced and sent into the world more than 3500 books, many of which have won or have been nominated for prestigious literary awards. (3) Poetry and fiction from the workshop has won 28 Pulitzer Prizes. (4) Actually winning
(10) nine in the 1990s alone. (5) Today there are more than 800 similar writers' workshops across the country, but Iowa was the first.

(6) The way the Iowa Writers' Workshop got started was that a writer named Wilbur Schramm
(15) proposed to the university that the writing workshop be created, although many academics were against it because they didn't think degrees should be awarded to people for creative writing rather than for academic achievement. (7)
(20) Schramm convinced the university, however, and the idea became a reality in 1936. (8) Since then the Iowa Writers' Workshop students have released a flood of notable stories, poems, novels, and nonfiction works into the world. (9) Some
(25) critics of the writing workshop idea even today, they say that the workshops teach the craft of writing rather than insisting that students learn about the literary tradition.

(10) Writers who attend the various writing
(30) workshops often praise them for offering time to work on creative projects, as well as providing an audience of other writers and accomplished writing teachers.

27. Which of the following is the best version of sentence 2, reproduced below?

There are probably many Americans who have never heard of the workshop, however its students over the years have produced and sent into the world more than 3500 books, many of which have won or been nominated for prestigious literary awards.

A. There are probably many Americans, who have never heard of the workshop, however its students over the years have produced and sent into the world more than 3500 books, many of which have won or been nominated for prestigious literary awards.

B. Many American have never heard of the workshop, and will not have realized that students from the workshop have produced and sent into the world more than 3500 books, and many of these have won or nominated for prestigious literary awards.

C. Although not realizing that many of its students have produced 3500 books, many of which have won prestigious awards or been nominated for them, many Americans have probably never heard of the workshop.

D. The workshop is probably unheard of by many Americans, however its students have produced and sent into the world over 3500 books, of which many have been nominated for or won prestigious literary awards.

E. Many Americans have probably never heard of the workshop; however, over the years its students have produced more than 3500 books, including works that have won or been nominated for prestigious literary awards.

28. Which of the following choices is the best combination of sentences 3 and 4, reproduced below?

Poetry and fiction from the workshop has won 28 Pulitzer Prizes. Actually winning nine in the 1990s alone.

A. Poetry and fiction from the workshop have won 28 Pulitzer Prizes, nine of these in the 1990s alone.

B. Poetry and fiction from the workshop have won 28 Pulitzer Prizes, and they won nine of these alone in the 1990s.

GO ON TO THE NEXT PAGE

C.   Of the 28 Pulitzer Prizes won by poetry and fiction produced by the workshop, there were nine of these alone that were won in the 1990s.

D.   Poetry and fiction that has been produced by students of the workshop have been awarded 28 Pulizer Prizes, and in the 1990s nine of the 28 were awarded.

E.   Poetry and fiction from the workshop have won 28 Pulitzer Prizes, they actually won nine of these in the 1990s.

29. Which of the following is the best version of sentence 6, reproduced below.

The way the Iowa Writers' Workshop got started was that a writer named Wilbur Schramm proposed to the university that the writing workshop be created, although many academics were against it because they didn't think degrees should be awarded to people for creative writing rather than for academic achievement.

A.   The way the Iowa Writers' Workshop got started was that Wilbur Schramm told the university it should be created, although many academics were against it in that they thought degrees shouldn't be awarded to creative writers but to academic achievement.

B.   A writer, whose name was Wilbur Schramm, he proposed that the writing workshop should be created at the University of Iowa, although there were a number of academics that opposed the idea because they didn't think creative writing should get you a degree instead of academic achievement.

C.   Wilbur Schramm, a writer, proposed to the University of Iowa that a writing workshop be created, although many academics argued that degrees shouldn't be awarded for creative writing but should be reserved for academic achievement.

D.   The Iowa Writers' Workshop came into being because of a man named Wilbur Schramm, who was a writer, and because he proposed the idea to the university although many academics said it was wrong to give degrees to creative writing instead of academic achievement.

E.   In spite of the fact that many academics didn't think a degree should be awarded for creative writing but should be awarded only for academic achievement; a man named Wilbur Schramm proposed to the university that they create a writers' workshop.

30. Which of the following is the best placement of sentence 10?

A.   after sentence 5
B.   after sentence 4
C.   in its present position
D.   after sentence 1
E.   after sentence 6

31. Which of the following is the best version of sentence 9, reproduced below?

Some critics of the writing workshop idea even today, they say that the workshops teach the craft of writing rather than insisting that students learn about the literary tradition.

A.   Some critics of the writing workshop idea even today say that the workshops are teaching only the craft of writing and that they are not studying the literary tradition.

B.   Even today some critics say that writing workshops teach the craft of writing without also insisting that students learn about the literary tradition.

C.   Some critics say that writing workshops even today are not teaching students about the literary tradition but that they are teaching the craft of writing.

D.   It is said by some critics, even today, that while the writing workshops are teaching students the craft of writing, they are not teaching them about the literary tradition.

E.   Writing workshops even today, some critics say, shouldn't be teaching students about the craft of writing but they should also be teaching them about the literary tradition.

32. Which of the following would most improve the passage?

    A. Details about Wilbur Schramm's life

    B. Information on how to apply for the Iowa workshop

    C. A list of the other writing workshops in the country

    D. Details about how the Iowa workshop is conducted

    E. Details about writers who won Pulitzer Prizes in the 1990s

Questions 33–36 are based on the following passage.

(1) I had not looked forward to going to my cousin's wedding in Idaho. (2) I did not want to go because it was on the last weekend of the summer, and I would rather have spent it with my friends at home. (3) I never had wanted to visit Idaho, even though my cousins lived there. (4) My family and I only had stand-by airline tickets, and we missed two flights, so we ended up waiting at the airport for three hours before we even left. (5) <u>Finally having arrived there after nine at night, the weather</u> was cold and rainy. (6) <u>It made me feel like this would be the worst weekend of my life.</u>

(7) When we woke up the next morning at the motel, I looked out the window, and it <u>looked dismal, the sky was gray, and you could see</u> small patches of rain falling. (8) My family and I ate a light breakfast and left for the wedding. (9) It was a half hour drive to the wedding. (10) My cousin was getting married in a park. (11) By the time we got there it was starting to clear up. (12) The wedding was outdoors in the woods, and just when the bride came in, the sun came out. (13) You could feel everybody's spirits lift.

(14) After that everything seemed to go right. (15) The food at the wedding party was great. (16) There was a good band. (17) The friends of my cousin who were my age were fun. (18) When the time came to go home the next day, I was sorry to leave. (19) Next year I may go to college in Idaho.

33. Which of the following is the best version of the underlined part of sentence 5 (reproduced below)?

<u>Finally having arrived there after nine at night, the weather</u> was cold and rainy.

    A. No error

    B. Having finally arrived there after nine at night, the weather

    C. Arrived there finally, after nine at night, the weather

    D. Not getting there until after nine at night, the weather

    E. When we finally got there, after nine at night, the weather

34. Which of the following is the best version of sentence 6 (reproduced below)?

<u>It made me feel like this would be the worst weekend of my life.</u>

    A. No error

    B. I felt like this would be the worst weekend of my life.

    C. I thought that this would be the worst weekend of my life.

    D. It felt like this would be the worst weekend of my life.

    E. It seemed like this would be the worst weekend of my life.

35. Which of the following is the best version of the underlined portion of sentence 7 (reproduced below)?

When we woke up the next morning at the motel, I looked out the window, and <u>it looked dismal, the sky was gray, and you could see</u> small patches of rain falling.

    A. No error

    B. looked dismal; the sky was gray, and you could see

    C. looked dismal, the sky was gray; and you could see

    D. looked dismal, and the sky was gray, and you could see

    E. looked dismal. The sky was gray, you could see

36. All of the following strategies are used by the writer of the passage EXCEPT

    A. frequent reliance on figurative language.

    B. chronological arrangement of events.

    C. connecting the first and last sentence of the passage.

    D. use of a first person speaker.

    E. use of details of weather to convey mood.

IF YOU FINISH BEFORE TIME IS CALLED, CHECK YOUR WORK ON THIS SECTION ONLY. DO NOT WORK ON ANY OTHER SECTION IN THE TEST.

Section 3: Critical Reading

Time: 25 minutes
28 Questions

Directions: Each blank in the following sentences indicates that something has been omitted. Consider the lettered words beneath the sentence and choose the word or set of words that *best* fits the whole sentence.

1. As the turbulent storm blew the boat closer and closer toward the rocks, the people in the lighthouse became increasingly _____ about its safety.

   A. cowardly
   B. intrepid
   C. apprehensive
   D. eager
   E. receptive

2. If only a native can understand the dialect of this region, even the best foreign linguist will be _____ by the indigenous speakers.

   A. mistaken
   B. baffled
   C. misrepresented
   D. addressed
   E. translated

3. Adam described the changes he had made in the story as merely _____, not censorship, because the alterations were made with the writer's prior knowledge and _____.

   A. editing . . . permission
   B. revising . . . prohibition
   C. expurgation . . . warrant
   D. corrections . . . disapproval
   E. decimation . . . connivance

4. The thousand-mile trek across the wilderness was a severe test of the children's _____ and their capacity to adapt.

   A. proportion
   B. immaturity
   C. openness
   D. weakness
   E. resilience

5. A change in fashion to a very thin look is not just an innocent _____ or trend; it is a serious _____ for many women who may suffer from dangerous eating disorders.

   A. victim . . . peril
   B. prank . . . challenge
   C. whim . . . undertaking
   D. fad . . . hazard
   E. idea . . . response

6. The public was _____ by the use of human bones and teeth in the jewelry and made their disapproval clear by refusing to buy any of the _____ items.

   A. enthralled . . . unusual
   B. fascinated . . . remarkable
   C. horrified . . . ghoulish
   D. repulsed . . . amiable
   E. hypnotized . . . grisly

7. In the unsuccessful conference, none of the speakers _____ much response from the audience, but Dr. Borum's address reached the _____ in tediousness.

   A. aggrandized . . . pinnacle
   B. elicited . . . nadir
   C. attributed . . . record
   D. raised . . . ebb
   E. induced . . . medley

8. In a landscape so calm and beautiful, it was hard to believe that anything _____ could occur.

   A. untoward
   B. temperate
   C. halcyon
   D. seemly
   E. refined

GO ON TO THE NEXT PAGE

Directions: Questions follow each of the passages below. Using only the stated or implied information in each passage and in its introduction, if any, answer the questions.

Questions 9–10 are based on the following passage.

As a child in Victorian England, Florence Nightingale used to sew up the wounds her sister had inflicted upon her dolls and put splints on her dog's injured paws. Nightingale was a
(5) member of a wealthy and socially prominent family and, as a female, barred from the formal study of the sciences. Nevertheless, as she grew up she pored over the reports of medical commissions and hospitals. She visited hospitals
(10) in England and throughout Europe. In the end, she convinced her conservative family to allow her to become the superintendent of a charitable nursing home in London. Then, in 1854, during the Crimean War, she took a team of nurses to
(15) Scutari in Turkey. The hospital death rate fell from 42 to 2 percent.

9 The passage suggests that Florence Nightingale became a nurse because

   A. nursing was a highly respected profession in the early nineteenth century.
   B. her parents were wealthy enough to sponsor her studies and recognized her strong interest in medicine.
   C. her religious feelings could find no other appropriate outlet.
   D. from childhood, nursing was a primary interest.
   E. the conventions of the time would not allow her to become a veterinarian.

10. The primary function of the last sentence of the paragraph is to

   A. act as a transition to a new idea that will be presented in the next paragraph.
   B. suggest the importance of Florence Nightingale's nurses in the Crimean War.
   C. refute the nineteenth-century idea that women were incapable of becoming physicians.
   D. dramatize the terrible conditions in military hospitals during the nineteenth century.
   E. provide a factual detail to support the main idea of the paragraph.

Questions 11–12 are based on the following passage.

An under-recognized and unfortunate consequence of the piracy of digitized music, with its negative impact on record sales, is the decline of the professional songwriter. In genres such as
(5) country, pop, and R&B, many songs traditionally have been written by professional songwriters to be performed by the artists, whose vocal talents often outshone their writing gifts. Songwriters received a few cents in royalties each time one of
(10) their songs was played on the radio (performance royalties), in addition to a few cents per song each time an album or CD was sold containing one of their songs (mechanical royalties). Artists received no performance royalties for songs they did not
(15) write, but received mechanical royalties for every song on every album or CD they sold. However, the virtual disappearance of album sales because of the digitization of music has resulted in more artists writing all of their own material instead of
(20) relying on professional songwriters.

11. The main topic of the paragraph is

   A. to describe how the decline of the record album industry has changed the way songs are written.
   B. to argue for the return of the professional songwriter to the music industry.
   C. to trace the recent decline in the quality of songwriting.
   D. to call for reforms in the royalty structure for singers and songwriters.
   E. to point out that performers of music typically can't write it.

GO ON TO THE NEXT PAGE

12. What statement(s) can be inferred from the passage about the difference between mechanical royalties and performance royalties?

   I.   Mechanical royalties are paid based on album sales.

   II. Performance royalties are paid based on air time.

   III. Mechanical royalties are paid only to songwriters.

   A. I only
   B. I and II only
   C. I and III only
   D. II and III only
   E. I, II, and III

Questions 13–14 are based on the following passage.

   Even oil industry leaders have been forced to pay attention to global warming in Alaska since their exploration season on the North Slope has dropped from 200 to 100 days in only three
(5) decades. The reason for this is what scientists call the "feedback processes." When the region's abundant snow and ice melt away, more areas of water and earth are exposed to the sun. Those darker surfaces absorb much higher amounts of
(10) solar radiation, and, as they expand in size, they take in more heat. Basically, this means that the warming builds upon itself; the more surfaces that are exposed to the sun, the faster global warming occurs.

13. The effect of the phrase "Even oil industry leaders" in the first sentence is to show that

   A. global warming has economic consequences that are not fully understood by the layperson.
   B. people in states other than Alaska have reasons to be concerned about the pace of global warming.
   C. productivity decreases in warmer climates.
   D. the problem in Alaska must be serious if those not usually sensitive to environmental problems are taking notice.
   E. the price of gasoline may be directly related to global warming.

14. Which of the following best describes "feedback processes"?

   A. recurring cycles of solar radiation
   B. a vicious circle of warming causing more warming
   C. melting snow and ice absorbing solar radiation
   D. exposure to the sun causing increased heat absorption
   E. lighter surfaces becoming darker surfaces

Questions 15–21 are based on the following passage.

   The rabies virus, which can cause disease in any mammal, is spread by the bite of an infected animal. It is lethal once symptoms develop but can be blocked by timely administration of a
(5) series of vaccine injections soon after an attack. The vaccine, which today may be given in an arm rather than the abdomen, is derived from a killed rabies virus. The inactivated virus prods the immune system to destroy active virus, especially
(10) when the injections are combined with application of rabies-specific antibodies to the wound area.

   Unfortunately, in any year thousands of people who are probably uninfected undergo
(15) treatment because they do not know whether the animal that bit them had rabies. These high numbers are disturbing because therapy is costly and because vaccination of any kind carries a risk of side effects. (The expense is a major
(20) reason veterinarians and others who are very likely to encounter rabid animals are generally the only people immunized prophylactically.) Even more distressing, most people who die of rabies are lost simply because they live in
(25) impoverished nations. Those who are attacked by infected animals often lack access to therapy or cannot pay for it. Routine immunization of the animal species most likely to transmit the virus to humans would be a more efficient,
(30) health-conscious way to save human lives and, not incidentally, to spare animals from suffering. To an extent, such inoculation is already a reality.

   In many wealthy nations, including the U.S., periodic injection of pet dogs with vaccine has
(35) all but stopped canine transmission to humans. Disease caused by cats can be limited in the same way. According to the Centers for Disease Control and Prevention (2011), over the 100 years, rabies in the United States has changed

GO ON TO THE NEXT PAGE

(40) dramatically, and 90 percent of all cases reported to the CDC now occur in wildlife. Prior to 1960 the majority were in domestic animals. The principal rabies hosts today are wild carnivores and bats. In developing countries, however,
(45) obtaining veterinary care can be extremely difficult, which is one reason why dogs continue to account for at least 90 percent of all human deaths from rabies. Another problem in developing countries is that even where pet rabies
(50) is under good control, wild animals—not being very amenable to collection and carting to the local veterinarian—pose a threat.

For these unattended groups, distribution of vaccine-laced baits for animals to eat in the field
(55) is showing particular promise. This approach is already halting the spread of rabies by foxes in many parts of Western Europe and Canada. More preliminary work suggests rabies in other species can be controlled as well. Indeed, a
(60) vaccine-filled bait for raccoons is now being tested in the U.S. If the results are good, the bait method might finally check an epidemic of raccoon rabies that has been spreading up the East Coast from Florida. If baiting can be
(65) perfected for distribution to dogs in developing countries, then the goal of sharply curtailing human cases worldwide would finally seem feasible.

This encouraging state of affairs stands in
(70) marked contrast to the situation in the 1960s, when research into vaccinating wild animals started in earnest. By then immunization had already reduced the incidence of dog rabies in the U.S. But infection by foxes, skunks, raccoons,
(75) and bats, the other significant rabies reservoirs in this country, was a continuing concern. Compared with dogs, those groups have less direct contact with humans, but collectively they are more abundant.
(80) To control rabies in free-ranging animals, health officials in the 1950s had depended on thinning populations that harbored the offending virus. They tried gassing of dens, poisoning, trapping, and shooting, among other tactics. The
(85) workers reasoned that destruction of enough animals would so reduce a population that any infected individuals would die without tangling with another animal. When diseased creatures disappeared, only healthy ones would remain.
(90) Yet the strategy halted the spread of the malady in target groups only some of the time.

15. All of the following could be infected with rabies EXCEPT

   A. raccoons.
   B. cats.
   C. humans.
   D. skunks.
   E. carrion birds.

16. The passage suggests that a human infected with rabies by a dog bite who did nothing for a long period of time would

   A. be unable to spread the disease to another human
   B. probably never be aware of having been infected.
   C. die.
   D. be cured by a vaccine injection.
   E. be cured by applying rabies-specific antibodies in the area of the bite.

17. The passage suggests that throughout the world the largest cause of human exposure to the rabies virus is from

   A. dogs that have not been immunized.
   B. dogs that have been immunized.
   C. cats that have not been immunized.
   D. cats that have been immunized.
   E. wild animals such as raccoons, foxes, or skunks.

18. It can be inferred that the number of fatalities from rabies in the United States is small because

   I. most dogs have been immunized by injections.
   II. people exposed to the virus have access to immediate treatment.
   III. the rabies virus is rare in the wild-animal populations of the United States.

   A. I only
   B. I and II only
   C. I and III only
   D. II and III only
   E. I, II, and III

GO ON TO THE NEXT PAGE

19. As it is used in line 68, the word "feasible" means

   A. unpredictable.
   B. inexpensive.
   C. hygienic.
   D. practicable.
   E. endurable.

20. At present, humans infected with rabies virus can be treated by

   I. a vaccine injection in the abdomen.
   II. a vaccine injection in the arm.
   III. an oral recombinant vaccine.

   A. I only
   B. II only
   C. I and II only
   D. II and III only
   E. I, II, and III

21 Vaccine-laced baits would be most effective in preventing rabies among

   I. wild-animal populations susceptible to rabies.
   II. domestic animals in areas where injections are impossible.
   III. wild or domestic animals already infected with disease.

   A. III only
   B. I and II only
   C. I and III only
   D. II and III only
   E. I, II, and III

Questions 22–28 are based on the following passage.

The following passage is from the autobiography of a young black woman who was among the first women to attend the New England prep school, St. Paul's.

Outside my personal circle, the school that term seemed to buzz, buzz. Class officers, it seemed, were often called upon to talk. We talked day and evening, in club activities and rehearsals,
(5) in the houses, in the hallways, in our rooms, in the bathrooms, and in meetings after meetings. We gossiped. We criticized. We whined. We analyzed. We talked trash. We talked race

relations, spiritual life, male-female relations,
(10) teacher-student trust. We talked confidentially. We broke confidences and talked about the results. We talked discipline and community. We talked Watergate and social-fabric stuff.

I did not follow the Watergate hearings. I did
(15) not rush to the third floor of the Schoolhouse for the ten-thirty *New York Times* delivery to read about it; nor did I crowd around the common-room TV to watch the proceedings. I could not bother to worry about which rich and powerful
(20) white people had hoodwinked which other rich and powerful white people. It seemed of a piece with their obsession with fairness.

I was unprepared, therefore, to dine at the Rectory with Mr. Archibald Cox, the St. Paul's
(25) alumnus whom President Nixon had fired when, as U.S. Special Prosecutor, Mr. Cox began to reveal the Watergate break-in and cover-up. Seated around him were the Rector and a handful of faculty members and student leaders. I said as
(30) little as possible in order to conceal my ignorance. Mr. Cox was acute. He referred to the Watergate players and the major events in witty shorthand. I couldn't quite follow, so I ate and smiled and made periodic conversation noises.
(35) Then he wanted to hear about St. Paul's School. There had been so many changes since his time. I found myself saying, in answer to his question, or the Rector's signal, that I was more aware of being black at St. Paul's than I was of
(40) being a girl. I used a clever phrase that I stole from somewhere and hoped he hadn't already heard: "Actually, we're still more like . . . a boys' school with girls in it. But black people's concerns—diversifying the curriculum and that
(45) sort of thing—the truth is that that's more important to me than whether the boys have the better locker room." Pompous it was, and I knew it, but better to be pompous in the company of educated and well-off white folk, better even to
(50) be stone wrong, than to have no opinion at all.

Mr. Cox thought a moment. God forbid he should go for the cross-examination. I added more. "Black concerns here at school may look different, but are not really, from the concerns
(55) that my parents have taught me all my life at home." I put that one in just so he'd know that I had a family. "And believe me, Sir, my mama and daddy did not put President Nixon into the White House. *We* didn't do that!"

(60)   Mr. Cox wrinkled his lean, Yankee face into a mischievous smile. His voice whispered mock conspiracy. He leaned toward me. "Do you know who Nixon hates worst of all?"

          I shook my head no. I had no idea.

(65)   "Our kind of people."

          My ears felt hot. I wanted to jump on the table. I wanted to go back home and forget that I'd ever come. I wanted to take him to West Philly and drop him off at the corner of Fifty-second

(70)   and Locust, outside Foo-Foo's steak emporium, right by the drug dealers, and leave him there without a map or a bow tie. Then tell me about our kind of people.

          The Rector gave me a look that urged caution.

(75)   I fixed my face. "What kind of people are those?" I asked.

          "Why, the educated Northeastern establishment," he said. The Rector smiled as if relieved.

22. The speaker's lack of interest in the Watergate hearings is chiefly due to her

    A. feeling alienated from the others at her school.

    B. concern with issues of gender rather than politics.

    C. belief that it was just another rich white person's problem.

    D. eagerness to be accepted by her peers at school.

    E. fear that it would separate her from her family's values.

23. In line 21, the phrase "of a piece" means

    A. consistent with.

    B. a small part of.

    C. indifferent to.

    D. partly to blame for.

    E. inconsistent with.

24. The word "acute" in line 31 means

    A. sharp-pointed.

    B. shrewd.

    C. critical.

    D. angular.

    E. severe.

25. The speaker in line 52 uses the phrase "cross-examination" because

    A. she wishes to amuse the others in the discussion.

    B. she feels she has committed a serious crime.

    C. she prefers to be wrong than to have no opinion at all.

    D. Archibald Cox is a lawyer.

    E. she has misunderstood Cox's questions.

26. When the speaker responds with the thoughts expressed in lines 66–73 ("My ears felt hot . . . our kind of people."), she is responding especially to what single word in the dialogue before?

    A. "Nixon" (line 63)

    B. "hates" (line 63)

    C. "worst" (line 63)

    D. "Our" (line 65)

    E. "people" (line 65)

27. It can be inferred from the passage that the "Rector smiled as if relieved" (line 78) because he

    A. has been afraid the speaker would say something shocking.

    B. disapproves of political arguments.

    C. has not understood what the speaker has been thinking.

    D. is too conventional to imagine a violent difference in opinion or in background.

    E. is amused by Archibald Cox's witty remark.

28. The passage as a whole is characterized by the speaker's

    A. lack of feeling and self-discipline.

    B. candor and self-awareness.

    C. bitterness and sense of unfairness.

    D. hypocrisy and self-deception.

    E. naiveté and charm.

IF YOU FINISH BEFORE TIME IS CALLED, CHECK YOUR WORK ON THIS SECTION ONLY. DO NOT WORK ON ANY OTHER SECTION IN THE TEST.

Section 4: Mathematics

Time: 25 minutes
20 Questions

Directions: Solve each problem in this section by using the information given and your own mathematical calculations, insights, and problem-solving skills. Then select the one correct answer of the five choices given and mark the corresponding circle on your answer sheet. Use the available space on the page for your scratch work.

For each question, indicate the best answer, using the following notes.

1. All numerical values used are real numbers.
2. Calculators may be used.
3. Some problems may be accompanied by figures or diagrams. These figures are drawn as accurately as possible EXCEPT when it is stated in a specific problem that a figure is not drawn to scale. The figures and diagrams are meant to provide information useful in solving the problem or problems. Unless otherwise stated, all figures and diagrams lie on a plane.

Data that Can Be Used for Reference

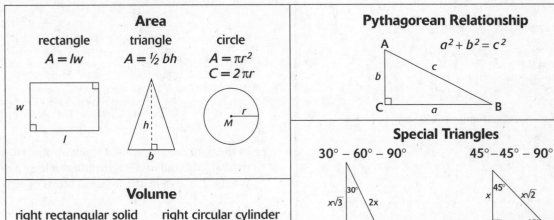

---

1. A man purchased 4 pounds of steak priced at $3.89 per pound. How much change did he receive from a $20 bill?

   A. $44.66
   B. $15.56
   C. $4.46
   D. $4.44
   E. $4.34

2. If a number is divisible by 7 but is not divisible by 21, then the number cannot be divisible by

   A. 2
   B. 3
   C. 5
   D. 8
   E. 10

GO ON TO THE NEXT PAGE

3. If $.0039y = 39$, then $y =$

   A. 10
   B. 100
   C. 1000
   D. 10,000
   E. 100,000

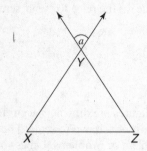

Note: Figure not drawn to scale

4. In the above figure $\triangle XYZ$, $XY = 10$, $YZ = 10$, and $\angle a = 84°$. What is the degree measure of $\angle Z$?

   A. 96°
   B. 84°
   C. 48°
   D. 42°
   E. 24°

5. If $|3x - 4| = 20$, then $x =$

   A. −8
   B. 8
   C. −8, 8
   D. $-\frac{16}{3}, 8$
   E. $-8, \frac{16}{3}$

6″	2″	10″	2″	5″

6. In the above box are the measures of rainfall for 5 consecutive days during the winter. For these 5 days, which of the following is true?

   I.   The median equals the mode.
   II. The median equals the arithmetic mean.
   III. The range equals the median.

   A. I only
   B. II only
   C. III only
   D. I and II only
   E. I and III only

7. Three-fifths of a geometry class is made up of female students. What is the ratio of male students to female students?

   A. $\frac{2}{5}$
   B. $\frac{3}{5}$
   C. $\frac{2}{3}$
   D. $\frac{5}{3}$
   E. $\frac{3}{2}$

8. What is the slope of the line for the equation $6x + y = 3$?

   A. 6
   B. 3
   C. −2
   D. −6
   E. −9

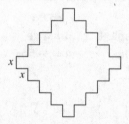

9. In the figure above, all line segments meet at right angles, and each segment has a length of x. What is the area of the figure in terms of x?

   A. $25x$
   B. $36x$
   C. $36x^2$
   D. $41x^2$
   E. $41x^3$

10. If $x - y = 15$ and $3x + y = 13$, then $y =$

    A. −8
    B. −7
    C. 7
    D. 8
    E. 15

GO ON TO THE NEXT PAGE

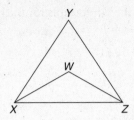

11. $\overline{WX}$ and $\overline{WZ}$ are angle bisectors of the base angles of isosceles triangle XYZ above. If $\angle Y = 80°$, what is the degree measure of $\angle XWZ$?

- **A.** 65°
- **B.** 80°
- **C.** 100°
- **D.** 130°
- **E.** 160°

12. If $m^2 + n^2 = 12$ and $mn = 9$, then $(m + n)^2 =$

- **A.** 12
- **B.** 24
- **C.** 30
- **D.** 42
- **E.** 48

13. If x, y, and z are consecutive positive integers greater than 1, not necessarily in that order, which of the following is (are) true?

- I. $x > z$
- II. $x + y > z$
- III. $yz < xz$
- IV. $xy < y + z$

- **A.** I only
- **B.** II only
- **C.** II and III only
- **D.** II and IV only
- **E.** III and IV only

14. The area of a square is 72 square feet. What is the length of a diagonal of the square?

- **A.** 36 feet
- **B.** $18\sqrt{2}$ feet
- **C.** 12 feet
- **D.** $6\sqrt{2}$ feet
- **E.** 6 feet

15. In a triangle, the ratio of two angles is 5:2, and the third angle is equal to the difference between the other two. What is the number of degrees in the smallest angle?

- **A.** 36
- **B.** $25\frac{5}{7}$
- **C.** $25\frac{2}{7}$
- **D.** 18
- **E.** 9

16. If $(a,b) \oplus (c,d) = (ac - bd,\ ad)$, then $(-2,3) \oplus (4,-1) =$

- **A.** $(-5,\ 2)$
- **B.** $(-5,\ -2)$
- **C.** $(-11,\ 2)$
- **D.** $(-11,\ -2)$
- **E.** $(-5,\ -3)$

17. A collection of 25 coins consists of nickels, dimes, and quarters. There are 3 times as many dimes as nickels and 3 more dimes than quarters. What is the total value of the collection in dollars and cents?

- **A.** $3.65
- **B.** $3.25
- **C.** $2.25
- **D.** $1.65
- **E.** $1.25

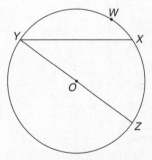

Note: Figure not drawn to scale

18. On the circle above with center O, arc YWX equals 100°. Which of the following is the degree measure of $\angle XYZ$?

- **A.** 130°
- **B.** 100°
- **C.** 80°
- **D.** 50°
- **E.** 40°

GO ON TO THE NEXT PAGE

19. If m and n are integers and $\sqrt{mn} = 10$, which of the following CANNOT be a value of $m + n$?

    A. 25
    B. 29
    C. 50
    D. 52
    E. 101

20. What are the y-intercepts for the hyperbola $2y^2 - 5x^2 = 50$?

    A. $\left(0, \pm 5\sqrt{2}\right)$
    B. $\left(0, \pm\sqrt{10}\right)$
    C. $\left(0, \pm\sqrt{5}\right)$
    D. $(0, \pm 25)$
    E. $(0, \pm 5)$

IF YOU FINISH BEFORE TIME IS CALLED, CHECK YOUR WORK ON THIS SECTION ONLY. DO NOT WORK ON ANY OTHER SECTION IN THE TEST.

Section 5: Critical Reading

Time: 25 minutes

28 Questions

Directions: Each blank in the following sentences indicates that something has been omitted. Consider the lettered words beneath the sentence and choose the word or set of words that *best* fits the whole sentence.

1. By banning cameras from the courtroom, the judge has _____ the public access to the most important civil-rights trial.

   A. belied
   B. denied
   C. defied
   D. afforded
   E. disowned

2. The grocer reluctantly admitted that, despite his care, shoplifting was still _____.

   A. exceptional
   B. sporadic
   C. commonplace
   D. redundant
   E. hackneyed

3. The work that once took two men one week might well, one year later, take the same two men three weeks, since as Parkinson's law _____, "Work _____ so as to fill the time for its completion."

   A. urges . . . grows easier
   B. explains . . . becomes familiar
   C. states . . . decreases
   D. forbids . . . increases
   E. asserts . . . expands

4. Although they loudly cheered the news of the renewed contract, the _____ of many workers was _____ by a fear that this would be the last year of government support.

   A. sorrow . . . tempered
   B. happiness . . . augmented
   C. gladness . . . enervated
   D. euphoria . . . moderated
   E. buoyancy . . . debilitated

5. The local conversation was nothing if not _____ for no sentence was ever more than four words long.

   A. ambiguous
   B. timely
   C. vague
   D. terse
   E. cordial

6. If both political parties can abandon _____ positions in the face of economic realities, a _____ may be achieved that will permit the government to function.

   A. sensible . . . compromise
   B. dogmatic . . . consensus
   C. incisive . . . schism
   D. irrational . . . dichotomy
   E. reasoned . . . division

7. The universal Victorian preference of the more conventional morality of Charlotte Brontë to that of her sister is indicative of the nineteenth-century reader's _____ conformity.

   A. impolitic
   B. genteel
   C. discordant
   D. iconoclastic
   E. individualistic

8. Though the first thirty pages are interesting and lively, chapter after chapter about obscure musicians grows _____, and the book never recovers the _____ of its opening chapter.

   A. unmanageable . . . pace
   B. tedious . . . verve
   C. repetitive . . . torpor
   D. dull . . . lethargy
   E. boring . . . challenge

GO ON TO THE NEXT PAGE

9. Some of the dangerous dishes on the menu are _____, but most are made without peppers or other spices and are as mild as most American restaurant food.

    A. bland
    B. palatable
    C. torrid
    D. insipid
    E. piquant

10. As a young man, he regarded France as _____, but in his malcontent maturity, he considered visiting any place outside of Ireland to be _____.

    A. hostile . . . irritating
    B. perfect . . . jocund
    C. irksome . . . drab
    D. edenic . . . perplexing
    E. ideal . . . painful

Directions: Questions follow each of the passages below. Answer the questions using only the stated or implied information in each passage and in its introduction, if any.

Questions 11–12 are based on the following passage.

At many times in our planet's history, north has become south and south has become north. Paleogeologists have discovered this phenomenon by investigating rocks. When rocks are being
(5) formed from magmas, atoms within their crystals respond to the earth's magnetic field by "pointing" toward the magnetic north pole. By age dating the rocks and noting their magnetic alignment, scientists can determine where on
(10) earth the north pole was located at that time because as the rocks solidified, they trapped that information within them. The study of ancient lava flows has revealed that at certain periods in history magnetic north was directly opposite its
(15) present location. In fact, it has been determined that magnetic reversal has occurred on average every 500,000 years.

11. "Magnetic reversal" refers to

    A. the atoms in rock crystals pointed toward the magnetic north pole.
    B. north becoming south and south becoming north.
    C. the reversal of direction in ancient lava flows.
    D. a reversal of the direction of convection currents in the earth's outer core.
    E. a disturbance in the regular 500,000-year cycle of the magnetic field.

12. According to the paragraph, which of the following was crucial to the discovery of magnetic reversal?

    A. change in direction of lava flows
    B. extinction of certain species 500,000 years ago
    C. the rapid change from "normal" to "reversed" polarity
    D. solidification of rocks formed from magma
    E. reversal in the direction of convection currents 500,000 years ago

Questions 13–16 are based on the following pair of passages.

Passage 1:

The poet Emily Dickinson was an eccentric, almost reclusive woman who never married. In the town of Amherst, Massachusetts, where she lived, people knew she could write verse, but of
(5) what real use was that, except for writing a condolence note or a compliment to accompany a gift. During her lifetime, her writing was treated as not very significant.

Of course, there wasn't much of it, at least
(10) that people knew about. Only a few of her many poems were published while she was alive. Now, in our own time, she is one of America's most celebrated poets. In some ways, Emily Dickinson's life is a variation on the Cinderella story. She was
(15) transformed from a rather drab spinster to a fascinating woman—not by a fairy godmother but by the poetry she wrote.

GO ON TO THE NEXT PAGE

Passage 2:

The ideas in Emily Dickinson's poems are provocative, and she is skillful with metaphors, rhythm, and euphony. But it is Dickinson's attention to the individual word that distinguishes
(5) her style. From extant manuscripts it is obvious that she weighed each word of her poems and was meticulous in choosing the right one. In some manuscripts she would write down nine or ten different words for the same idea so that she
(10) could study which one would best suit her purpose in a poem. One reason her poems are so economical is that she respected the importance of every word she chose.

13. The author of Passage 1 emphasizes which of the following about Emily Dickinson?

    A.   the contrast between her quiet life and her talent

    B.   her inability to be taken seriously as a writer during her lifetime

    C.   the isolated life she led

    D.   her reputation as a poet today

    E.   the psychological motivations for her poetry

14. In Passage 1, line 2, the word "reclusive" means

    A.   snobbish.

    B.   ill-natured.

    C.   uninteresting.

    D.   solitary.

    E.   unconventional.

15. The author of Passage 2 is most impressed by Emily Dickinson's

    A.   provocative ideas.

    B.   ability to choose vivid imagery.

    C.   precision with language.

    D.   diligence in revising her work.

    E.   skill with poetic meters.

16. Which of the following best describes the attitudes of both authors toward Emily Dickinson?

    A.   The author of Passage 1 feels her life is more interesting than her poetry, while the opposite is true for the author of Passage 2.

    B.   Both authors consider her an important poet.

    C.   Both authors express surprise that a sheltered woman could write such great poetry.

    D.   The author of Passage 1 feels Dickinson's life was pathetic, while the author of Passage 2 does not.

    E.   The author of Passage 1 is more interested in the ideas in Dickinson's poems than is the author of Passage 2.

Questions 17–28 are based on the following passage.

We know a good deal about the Spanish Armada as it waited to sortie from Lisbon harbor in 1588 to attack England. Medina Sidonia, Spain's "Captain General of the Ocean
(5) Sea," had an elaborate report drawn up, with not just the order of battle by squadrons, but the name of each ship in every squadron, its estimated tonnage, the number of its guns, its sails, its soldiers. For good measure he added the
(10) principal gentlemen-adventurers on each ship, listed by name, with the number of their combatant servants, also the gunners, the medical corps, the friars and regular priests (one hundred and eighty of these), the organization
(15) of the *tercios* with a list of their officers and the strength of every company, the siege train, the field guns, the small arms of all kinds, the total supply of powder (all fine-corned arquebus powder, he noted proudly), the number of
(20) cannon balls of all weights (123,790), the lead for bullets, the match. The report also listed provisions, biscuit, bacon, fish, cheese, rice, beans, wine, oil, vinegar, water, in so many thousands or tens of thousands of
(25) hundredweights, or in so many pipes and tuns and casks. Even if the figures are not all accurate (and they certainly were not), the quantity of detailed information is greater than we have about any other fleet of the sixteenth century,
(30) and even if the total strength adds up to less than half the fleet . . . it still looks . . . like a very formidable force indeed. In the official

GO ON TO THE NEXT PAGE

publication embodying all these figures, the fleet is called *La felicissima armada*—the most
(35) fortunate fleet—but popular parlance at once substituted "invincible" in tribute to its awesome strength [and this is how the "Invincible Armada" entered history].

It seems odd that Medina Sidonia's detailed
(40) report should have been published. Today such a document would be classified "Top Secret" until long after its last item was well known to the enemy, and even in those days Walsingham's agents, spies for the English, had been working
(45) hard to collect some scraps of its wealth of information. But published it was, with relatively few changes, all exaggerations of its strength, at Lisbon, only ten days after it was drawn up, and while the invasion fleet still lay in the Tagus
(50) River. Hence the document spread to Rome, to Paris, to Delft, to Cologne, so rapidly that copies were for sale in Amsterdam before the *San Martin* (flag ship of the invading fleet) had raised the Lizard and reached the western entrance to
(55) the English Channel. Even the least accurate copies of the report still gave a fair idea of the information supplied to King Philip II and the Council of War and printed with official approval at Madrid. We can only conclude that
(60) the Council of War at Madrid believed that the propaganda value of their show of strength would do more good than the disclosure of the information could do harm.

Perhaps what counted most was simply that
(65) this fleet Duke Medina Sidonia commanded was ready at last to meet the enemy, its new-built fighting castles glistening with fresh paint, its banners snapping from the mastheads, its decks thronged with handsome cavaliers. As soon as
(70) the weather moderated enough to make it feasible, therefore, the duke began to work his way out of Lisbon River. On May 28th, his flagship, the *San Martin*, in the lead, the royal galleons of Portugal passed Castle St. Julian,
(75) replying in turn to the fort's salutes. By May 30th, in spite of fitful and contrary winds, the whole Armada (130 ships) was standing out to sea, close hauled to a north-northwest breeze.

17. It can be inferred from the passage that historians value the Spanish war council's publication because

   I. it provides a wealth of information about the Spanish fleet.
   II. it establishes the motive for Spain's attack on England at the time.
   III. it suggests the strongly international nature of sixteenth century warfare.

   A. I only
   B. I and II only
   C. I and III only
   D. II and III only
   E. I, II, and III

18. Medina Sidonia's report seemed excessive or exaggerated for all the following reasons EXCEPT

   A. it identified the servants of gentlemen-adventurers.
   B. it itemized combatants and noncombatants by name.
   C. it listed provisions each ship carried.
   D. it included the supply of matches for lighting the powder.
   E. it drew up the order of battle and named each ship.

19. It is clear from context that "hundredweights," "pipes," "tuns," and "casks" are all

   A. containers.
   B. units of measure.
   C. types of provisions.
   D. companies of marines.
   E. gunners' supplies.

20. According to the historian, the Invincible Armada got its name from

   A. the Captain General of the Ocean Sea.
   B. the Council of War in Madrid.
   C. Walsingham's agents.
   D. a popular play on words.
   E. Medina Sidonia at Lisbon.

GO ON TO THE NEXT PAGE

21. Aside from the level of detail of information on the Spanish Armada, what else do historians regard as unusual about Medina Sidonia's report?

    A. It was top secret.
    B. It was for sale in Amsterdam.
    C. It was published prior to the invasion.
    D. It took only ten days to print.
    E. It contained inaccuracies and exaggerations.

22. In which of the following sentences does the historian most directly link past to present?

    A. Medina Sidonia, Spain's "Captain General of the Ocean Sea," had an elaborate report drawn up. . . .
    B. Today such a document would be classified "Top Secret". . . .
    C. . . . the quantity of detailed information is greater than we have about any other fleet of the sixteenth century. . . .
    D. Hence the document spread to Rome, to Paris, to Delft, to Cologne, . . . It seems odd that Medina Sidonia's detailed report should have been published.
    E. We know a good deal about the Spanish Armada. . . .

23. From context, Lisbon harbor, the Tagus, and the Lizard were most likely names for

    A. nautical locations.
    B. fortifications.
    C. moorings.
    D. geographical features.
    E. bodies of water.

24. Medina Sidonia's report included a tally of pikes, lances, corselets, and mail. Where would these items most likely be listed?

    A. the organization of the *tercios*
    B. siege trains and field guns
    C. small arms and armor
    D. friars and regular priests
    E. lead for bullets and powder

25. If the report on *"La felicissima armada"* included salt, pepper, sassafras, and cloves, where would these items most likely be listed?

    A. squadrons
    B. gentlemen-adventurers
    C. pipes, tuns and casks
    D. provisions
    E. medical supplies

26. The historian suggests that the report on the Spanish Armada was leaked for all the following reasons EXCEPT

    A. it had propaganda value.
    B. it was an impressive show of strength.
    C. it had official approval from the king and Council of War in Madrid.
    D. English spies already had much of the information.
    E. it disclosed information to the enemy that could turn the tide of battle.

27. The number of ships in the Spanish Armada was

    A. 180
    B. 130
    C. 123,790
    D. 10
    E. 28

28. The author seeks to make this passage thrilling for readers through which of the following visually stimulating descriptions?

    I.   fighting castles glistening with fresh paint
    II. banners snapping from the masthead
    III. decks thronged with handsome cavaliers

    A. I only
    B. I and II only
    C. I and III only
    D. II and III only
    E. I, II, and III

IF YOU FINISH BEFORE TIME IS CALLED, CHECK YOUR WORK ON THIS SECTION ONLY. DO NOT WORK ON ANY OTHER SECTION IN THE TEST.

Section 6: Mathematics

Time: 25 minutes

18 Questions

Directions: Solve each problem in this section by using the information given and your own mathematical calculations, insights, and problem-solving skills. Then select the one correct answer of the five choices given and mark the corresponding circle on your answer sheet. Use the available space on the page for your scratch work.

For each question, indicate the best answer, using the following notes.

1. All numerical values used are real numbers.
2. Calculators may be used.
3. Some problems may be accompanied by figures or diagrams. These figures are drawn as accurately as possible EXCEPT when it is stated in a specific problem that a figure is not drawn to scale. The figures and diagrams are meant to provide information useful in solving the problem or problems. Unless otherwise stated, all figures and diagrams lie on a plane.

Data that Can Be Used for Reference

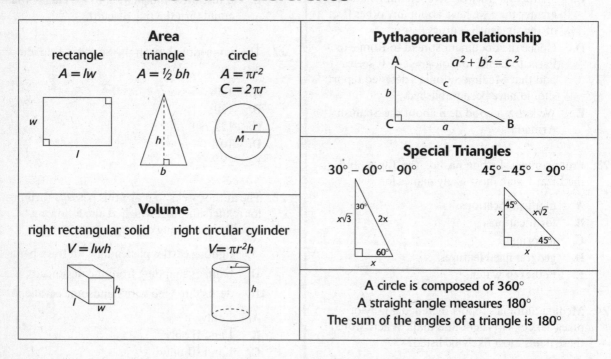

1. If $x^4 = z^{16}$, what is x in terms of z ?

 A. $\sqrt{z}$
 B. z^2
 C. z^4
 D. z^8
 E. z^{16}

2. In the arithmetic sequence 4, 8, 12, 16, 20, . . . , which of the following could not be a term in the sequence?

 A. 760
 B. 656
 C. 512
 D. 438
 E. 392

GO ON TO THE NEXT PAGE

3. A plumber charges $45 for the first hour of work and $20 per hour for each additional hour of work after the first. What would be the total bill for labor if the plumber worked 6 consecutive hours?

   A. $ 65
   B. $120
   C. $145
   D. $165
   E. $180

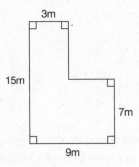

4. What is the perimeter, in meters, of the figure above?

   A. 40
   B. 42
   C. 48
   D. 58
   E. It cannot be determined from the given information.

5. If $a = p + prt$, then $r =$

   A. $\dfrac{a-1}{t}$
   B. $\dfrac{a-p}{pt}$
   C. $a - p - pt$
   D. $\dfrac{a}{t}$
   E. $\dfrac{a+p}{pt}$

6. Rajiv will be y years old x years from now. How old will he be z years from now?

   A. $y - x + z$
   B. $y + x + z$
   C. $y + x - z$
   D. $y - x - z$
   E. $x + z - y$

7. The average of 3 numbers is 55. The second is one number more than twice the first, and the third is 4 less than 3 times the first. What is the largest number?

   A. 165
   B. 88
   C. 80
   D. 57
   E. 28

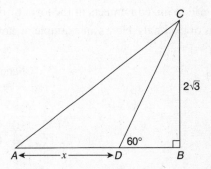

8. In the figure above, the area of $\triangle ABC = 6\sqrt{3}$. What is the value of x?

   A. 2
   B. $2\sqrt{3}$
   C. 4
   D. $4\sqrt{2}$
   E. 6

GO ON TO THE NEXT PAGE

Directions for Student-Produced Response Questions (Grid-ins): Questions 9–18 require you to solve the problem and enter your answer by carefully marking the circles on the special grid. Examples of the appropriate way to mark the grid follow.

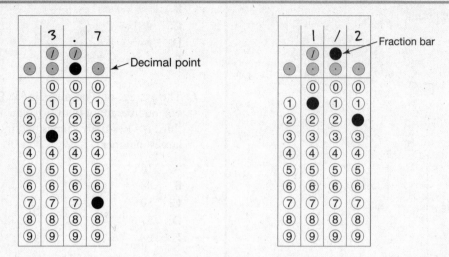

Do not grid in mixed numbers in the form of mixed numbers. Always change mixed numbers to improper fractions or decimals. Here's an example of how to grid when your answer is a mixed number such as $1\frac{1}{2}$.

Change to 1.5   or   Change to $\frac{3}{2}$

Space permitting, answers can start in any column. Each grid-in answer that follows is correct.

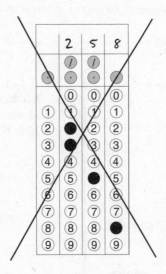

Note: Circles must be filled in correctly to receive credit. Mark only one circle in each column. No credit will be given if more than one circle in a column is marked.

Example:

Accuracy of decimals: Always enter the most accurate decimal value that the grid will accommodate. For example: An answer such as .8888 . . . can be gridded as .888 or .889. Gridding this value as .8, .88, or .89 is considered inaccurate and therefore not acceptable. The acceptable grid-ins of $\frac{8}{9}$ are

Be sure to write your answers in the boxes at the top of the circles before filling in the circles. Although writing out the answers above the columns is not required, it is very important to ensure accuracy. Even though some problems may have more than one correct answer, only grid in one answer. Grid-in questions contain no negative answers.

9. If $x + \frac{3}{5}x = 1$, then $x =$

10. In a class of 35 students, 60% are girls. How many boys are in the class?

11. What is the average of $\frac{1}{4}, \frac{1}{6}$, and $\frac{1}{12}$?

12. If a car averages 317.9 miles on 17 gallons of gas, how many miles will it travel on 5 gallons of gas?

	Math	Critical Reading	Writing
2008	520	540	512
2009	515	532	560
2010	518	528	519
2011	510	525	537
2012	507	510	540

13. What was the mean (average) of the Critical Reading SAT scores for the five-year period 2008 through 2012?

14. The ratio of the measures of the angles in a quadrilateral is 3:5:7:9. What is the degree measure of the smallest angle?

15. If Jim takes 6 days to paint a house alone and Mike takes 8 days to paint the same house alone, what part of the job will be completed if both boys work for 2 days?

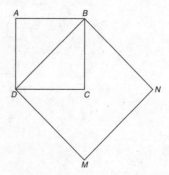

16. In square $ABCD$ in the figure above, $AB = 5$. What is the area of square $BDMN$?

GO ON TO THE NEXT PAGE

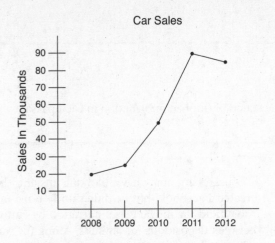

Car Sales

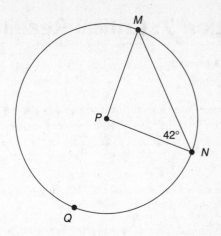

17. In the graph above, if each point aligns exactly with a grid mark or aligns halfway between 2 grid marks, what was the greatest percentage increase between two consecutive years? (Disregard the % sign when you are gridding your answer.)

18. What is the measure in degrees of arc *MQN* in the circle above with center *P*?

IF YOU FINISH BEFORE TIME IS CALLED, CHECK YOUR WORK ON THIS SECTION ONLY. DO NOT WORK ON ANY OTHER SECTION IN THE TEST.

Section 7: Critical Reading

Time: 15 minutes

15 Questions

Directions: Questions follow the passages below. Using only the stated or implied information in each passage and in the introduction, if any, answer the questions.

Questions 1–13 are based on the following pair of passages.

The following critical commentaries were written by two American film reviewers about the 2010 blockbuster film The Social Network.

Passage 1:

The Social Network is about a young man who possessed an uncanny ability to look into a system of unlimited possibilities and sense a winning move. His name is Mark Zuckerberg, he
(5) created Facebook, he became a billionaire in his early 20s, and he reminds me of the chess prodigy Bobby Fischer. There may be a touch of Asperger's syndrome in both: They possess genius but are tone-deaf in social situations.
(10) Example: It is inefficient to seek romance by using strict logic to demonstrate your intellectual arrogance. David Fincher's film has the rare quality of being not only as smart as its brilliant hero, but in the same way. It is cocksure,
(15) impatient, cold, exciting, and instinctively perceptive. It hurtles through two hours of spellbinding dialogue. It makes an untellable story clear and fascinating.

The Social Network begins with Erica's date
(20) with Zuckerberg. He nervously sips a beer and speed-talks through an aggressive interrogation. It's an exercise in sadistic conversational gamesmanship. Erica (a fictional character) gets fed up and walks out. Zuckerberg goes home,
(25) has more beers and starts hacking into the "facebooks" of Harvard dorms to collect the headshots of campus women. He programs a page where they can be rated for their beauty. This is sexist and illegal, and proves so popular,
(30) it crashes the campus servers. Zuckerberg grows it into Facebook.

Zuckerberg may have had the insight that created Facebook, but he didn't do it alone in a room, and the movie gets a narration by cutting
(35) between depositions for lawsuits. Along the way, we get insights into the pecking order at Harvard, a campus where ability joins wealth and family as success factors. We meet the twins Cameron and Tyler Winklevoss (both played by Armie
(40) Hammer), rich kids who believe Zuckerberg stole their "Harvard Connection" in making Facebook. We meet Eduardo Saverin (Andrew Garfield), Zuckerberg's roommate and best (only) friend, who was made CFO of the
(45) company, lent it the money that it needed to get started, and was frozen out. And we meet Sean Parker (Justin Timberlake), the founder of two legendary web startups, Napster and Plaxo.

It is the mercurial Parker who grabbed
(50) Zuckerberg by the ears and pulled him into the big time. He explained why Facebook needed to move to Silicon Valley. Why more money would come from venture capitalists than Eduardo would ever raise with his hat-in-hand visits to
(55) wealthy New Yorkers. And he tried, not successfully, to introduce Zuckerberg into the fast lane: big offices, wild parties, women. Zuckerberg was not seduced by his lifestyle. He was uninterested in money, stayed in modest
(60) houses, didn't fall into drugs. Zuckerberg doesn't have much of a social life onscreen, misses parties, would rather work. He has such tunnel vision he doesn't even register when Sean redrafts the financial arrangements to write himself in
(65) and Eduardo out.

The testimony in the depositions makes it clear there is a case to be made against Zuckerberg, many of them sins of omission. It's left to the final crawl to explain how they turned
(70) out. The point is to show an interaction of

GO ON TO THE NEXT PAGE

undergraduate chaos, enormous amounts of money, and manic energy. *The Social Network* is a great film not because of its dazzling style or visual cleverness, but because it is splendidly
(75) well-made. Despite the baffling complications of computer programming, web strategy, and big finance, Aaron Sorkin's screenplay makes it all clear, and we don't follow the story so much as get dragged along behind it.

Passage 2:

From the first sentence, the first word, the first nervily in-drawn breath, this compulsively watchable picture announces itself as the unmistakable work of Aaron Sorkin. He's found
(5) an almost perfect subject: the creation of the networking web site Facebook, and the backstabbing legal row among the various nerds, geeks, brainiacs, and maniacs about who gets the credit and the cash.
(10) Part boardroom drama, part conspiracy thriller, the story is adapted from Ben Mezrich's non-fiction *The Accidental Billionaires*. There appears, however, to be nothing accidental about it. The film version perfectly displays Sorkin's
(15) gift for creating instantly believable sympathetic-yet-irritating characters, and the chief of these is Facebook's driving force, Mark Zuckerberg, played with exemplary intuition by Jesse Eisenberg. He is a borderline sociopath, never
(20) smiling, never raising his voice, never conceding an argument, driven to create his masterpiece through the unforgettable pain of being dumped in the movie's opening scene. Sorkin gives everyone great lines. It's pretty much a non-stop
(25) fusillade of put-downs, insights, and zingers.
David Fincher's direction creates just the right intensity and claustrophobia for a story that takes place largely in a stupefyingly male environment at Harvard University in 2003,
(30) shown in flashback from various acrimonious legal proceedings. Here, computer-science student Zuckerberg has the same sense of entitlement and self-congratulation as everyone else, but combined with social resentment about
(35) being barred from snobby fraternities and clubs. When his girlfriend Erica (Rooney Mara) breaks up with him, the director shows how the emotionally wounded Zuckerberg embarks on a retaliatory campaign. He blogs vengefully about
(40) Erica and, in an evil-genius frenzy, creates

Facemash, a spiteful and misogynistic site that invites the guys to rate campus girls against each other. It is from this beginning that the smilier, friendlier Facebook emerges. But we have been
(45) cleverly shown the site's nastier, more paranoid origins: a clue to its unspoken world of friend-number envy, cyber-stalking, and anxiety about having no friends at all.
Zuckerberg gets investment from fellow geek
(50) Eduardo Saverin, played by Andrew Garfield, of whose marginally superior social success he is jealous and whom he later betrays by cutting him out of the action in favor of web entrepreneur Sean Parker, smoothly played by Justin
(55) Timberlake. Wealthy alpha-male twin brothers Cameron and Tyler Winklevoss (both played by Armie Hammer) plan to launch their own site, called The Harvard Connection, and try to recruit Mark as their tame techie-nerd; initially
(60) dazzled by their cachet, Zuckerberg plays them along, fatally delaying their launch while secretly getting his own up and running. Shrewdly, Sorkin and Fincher show how the Winklevosses are afraid to sue, because that's not the action of
(65) an effortlessly superior Harvard man.
The success of *The Social Network* lies in capturing the fever of Facebook's startup, while subversively implying that it created money and ephemeral buzz, but not a whole lot else; there is
(70) very little about the interconnectivity and creativity that its evangelizers often claim. At the end, all is loneliness. This is an exhilaratingly hyperactive, hyperventilating portrait of an age when Web 2.0 became sexier and more important
(75) than politics, art, books—everything. Sorkin and Fincher combine the excitement with a dark, insistent kind of pessimism. Smart work.

1. In the first paragraph the author of Passage 1 compares the subject of the movie, Mark Zuckerberg, with

I. the director of the film, David Fincher.

II. the chess prodigy, Bobby Fischer.

III. someone with Asperger's Syndrome.

A. I only
B. II only
C. I and II only
D. II and III only
E. I, II, and III

GO ON TO THE NEXT PAGE

2. In Passage 1, which of the following sentences best expresses the reviewer's explanation of the main reason *The Social Network* is a good movie?

   A. It is cocksure, impatient, cold, exciting, and instinctively perceptive.
   B. It makes an untellable story clear and fascinating.
   C. It hurtles through two hours of spellbinding dialogue.
   D. We don't follow the story so much as get dragged along behind it.
   E. It has a dazzling style and visual cleverness.

3. In Passage 1 the plot sequence begins with Erica's rejection of Zuckerberg, following which he

   A. is hired by the Winklevoss twins to develop The Harvard Connection.
   B. moves to Silicon Valley to seek venture capital.
   C. hacks Harvard's dorms' facebooks for headshots of women.
   D. is sued by his only friend, Eduardo Saverin.
   E. meets Napster genius Sean Parker.

4. The author of Passage 1 believes that Zuckerberg's initial development of Facebook was

   A. sexist and illegal.
   B. unstable and unpopular.
   C. sketchy and underfunded.
   D. technically clever and brilliant.
   E. unoriginal and sophomoric.

5. As used in Passage 1, in the first sentence of the fourth paragraph the word "mercurial" means

   A. hot.
   B. god-like.
   C. able to act quickly.
   D. fast.
   E. prone to rapid rise or fall.

6. According to the reviewer in Passage 1, the "interaction of undergraduate chaos, enormous amounts of money, and manic energy" were responsible for

   A. the success of the movie *The Social Network*.
   B. Zuckerberg's decision to drop out of Harvard.
   C. Saverin's decision to sue Zuckerberg.
   D. the origins of Facebook.
   E. the dialogue in Aaron Sorkin's screenplay.

7. In the opinion of the author of Passage 1, the legal depositions against Zuckerberg

   A. are mainly unfounded.
   B. show how a case can be made against him.
   C. probably stem from peer jealousy and rivalry.
   D. cast doubts on the real motives of elite universities.
   E. are destructive and unfair.

8. The main purpose of the first two paragraphs of Passage 2 is

   A. to introduce the main characters in the movie.
   B. to identify the subject as "nerds, geeks, brainiacs, and maniacs."
   C. to credit the book on which the movie was based.
   D. to compare the movie with a combination boardroom drama and conspiracy thriller.
   E. to credit the movie's screenwriter for a "compulsively watchable picture."

9. The author of Passage 2 describes Mark Zuckerberg as

   A. exhilaratingly hyperactive.
   B. claustrophobic.
   C. an accidental billionaire
   D. a borderline sociopath.
   E. backstabbing and paranoid.

10. In the second paragraph of Passage 2, in the sentence, "It's pretty much a non-stop fusillade of put-downs, insights and zingers," the meaning of the word "fusillade" is

    A. a sustained burst, as gunfire.
    B. an assortment or hodgepodge.
    C. a tirade or harangue.
    D. continuous blasphemy, as a curse.
    E. a train of insults.

GO ON TO THE NEXT PAGE

11. On which of the following points would both reviewers likely agree?

    I. Zuckerberg's Harvard was a stupefying male environment.

    II. Zuckerberg's blogs about Erica were spiteful and misogynistic.

    III. *The Social Network* is ultimately about friendship and betrayal.

    A. I only
    B. I and II only
    C. III only
    D. II and III only
    E. I, II, and III

12. Based on context clues in Passage 2, "misogyny" means

    A. rule by women.
    B. men's hatred of women.
    C. women's fear of men.
    D. peer envy.
    E. cyberstalking of woman by men.

13. In the fourth paragraph, the author of Passage 2 says of Zuckerberg's relationship with the Winklevoss twins that Zuckerberg was "initially dazzled by their cachet." In the context of the passage, "cachet" means

    A. official seal of approval.
    B. lack of charm or appeal.
    C. printed logo.
    D. quality of distinction.
    E. phoniness.

Questions 14–15 are based on the following passage.

    A person experiencing synesthesia may "see" green when hearing a particular musical note, or taste sweetness when touching a circular object. Rather than remaining separate, the senses get
(5) mixed up. Francis Galton, Charles Darwin's cousin, published a paper on synesthesia in 1880, but many people dismissed the phenomenon, attributing it to the effects of drug use or perhaps childhood memories. In recent years, however,
(10) research suggests that synesthesia results from a kind of cross-wiring in the brain—that is, two normally separate areas of the brain elicit activity in each other. In studying synesthesia, scientists are learning how the brain processes
(15) sensory information and uses it to make connections between seemingly unrelated inputs. An interesting finding, according to one study, is that synesthesia is much more common in creative people than in the general population.

14. The author of the passage cites the article by Francis Galton primarily to

    A. show the importance of synesthesia to the scientific community.
    B. explain how the phenomenon received its name.
    C. suggest that Charles Darwin was interested in the phenomenon.
    D. dismiss the idea that synesthesia is merely the result of childhood memories.
    E. indicate that the phenomenon of synesthesia was recognized in the nineteenth century.

15. Which of the following statements is suggested by the last sentence of the paragraph?

    A. The brain processes of creative people are identical to the brain processes of people who experience synesthesia.
    B. People unable to experience synesthesia will be inclined to prefer professions requiring logical thinking.
    C. Creativity may be related to the ability to make connections between seemingly unrelated inputs.
    D. Because of cross-wiring in the brain, creative people are often unstable and erratic.
    E. The frequent occurrence of synesthesia among creative people is probably related to drug use.

IF YOU FINISH BEFORE TIME IS CALLED, CHECK YOUR WORK ON THIS SECTION ONLY. DO NOT WORK ON ANY OTHER SECTION IN THE TEST.

STOP

Section 8: Mathematics

Time: 20 minutes
16 Questions

Directions: Solve each problem in this section by using the information given and your own mathematical calculations, insights, and problem-solving skills. Then select the one correct answer of the five choices given and mark the corresponding circle on your answer sheet. Use the available space on the page for your scratch work.

For each question, indicate the best answer, using the following notes.

1. All numerical values used are real numbers.
2. Calculators may be used.
3. Some problems may be accompanied by figures or diagrams. These figures are drawn as accurately as possible EXCEPT when it is stated in a specific problem that a figure is not drawn to scale. The figures and diagrams are meant to provide information useful in solving the problem or problems. Unless otherwise stated, all figures and diagrams lie on a plane.

Data that Can Be Used for Reference

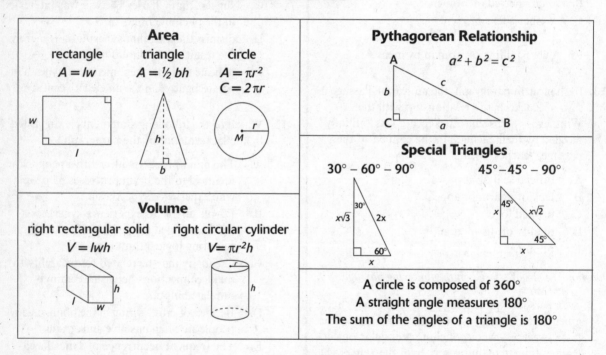

1. What is .25% of 12?

   A. $\frac{3}{100}$

   B. $\frac{3}{10}$

   C. $\frac{1}{3}$

   D. 3

   E. 300

2. How many integers between 0 and 90 are NOT the square of an integer?

   A. 9
   B. 79
   C. 80
   D. 81
   E. 82

GO ON TO THE NEXT PAGE

3. If a book costs $5.70 after a 40% discount, what was its original price?

   A. $2.28
   B. $6.10
   C. $7.98
   D. $9.12
   E. $9.50

4. $\dfrac{\dfrac{2}{3} - \dfrac{1}{2}}{\dfrac{1}{6} + \dfrac{1}{4} + \dfrac{2}{3}} =$

   A. $\dfrac{2}{13}$

   B. $\dfrac{2}{9}$

   C. $\dfrac{13}{20}$

   D. $1\dfrac{1}{13}$

   E. $3\dfrac{1}{4}$

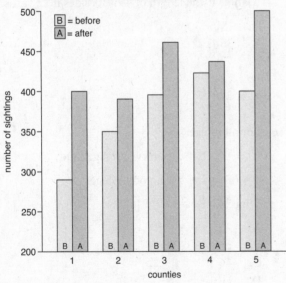

Number of Wild Bear Sightings Before and After Conservation Measures in Five Different Counties

5. According to the graph above, which county had the most bear sightings before the conservation measures?

   A. 1
   B. 2
   C. 3
   D. 4
   E. 5

6. If x is an integer and $(x + 1)$ times $(2x + 1)$ is an odd integer, then x must be

   A. an odd integer
   B. an even integer
   C. a prime number
   D. a composite number
   E. a negative number

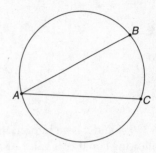

7. If $\angle A = 40°$ and $\overarc{AC} = 130°$, then $\overarc{AB} =$

   A. 60°
   B. 80°
   C. 150°
   D. 190°
   E. It cannot be determined from the given information.

8. A certain geometry class has 36 students. If two-thirds of the students are boys and three-fourths of the boys are under 6 feet tall, how many boys in the class are under 6 feet tall?

   A. 6
   B. 12
   C. 18
   D. 24
   E. 27

9. If $|3x + 6| = 15$, then $x =$

   A. 3
   B. −3
   C. −3, 3
   D. −7, 3
   E. −7, 7

GO ON TO THE NEXT PAGE

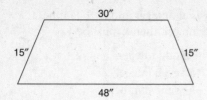

10. What is the area of the trapezoid above in square inches?

    A. 108
    B. 234
    C. 368
    D. 468
    E. 585

11. If $f(x) = 3^x + 4$ and x is an integer, then which of the following could be a value of $f(x)$?

    A. 3
    B. 4
    C. $4\frac{1}{9}$
    D. $5\frac{1}{3}$
    E. 9

12. If $y = \dfrac{1-x}{x}$, then $x =$

    A. $\dfrac{1}{y+1}$

    B. $\dfrac{1-y}{y}$

    C. $\dfrac{y}{1-y}$

    D. $y + 1$

    E. $\dfrac{1}{y-1}$

13. Three factories of Conglomerate Corporation are capable of manufacturing skateboards. Two of the factories can each produce 100,000 skateboards in 15 days. The third factory can produce skateboards 30% faster. Approximately how many days would it take to produce 1 million skateboards with all 3 factories working simultaneously?

    A. 38
    B. 42
    C. 44
    D. 46
    E. 50

14. If $4\sqrt{y+3} + 14 = 50$, then $y =$

    A. 81
    B. 78
    C. −9
    D. −81
    E. −84

15. What is the area in square yards of an equilateral triangle if the length of 1 of its sides is 12 yards?

    A. $18\sqrt{3}$
    B. $36\sqrt{3}$
    C. 72
    D. $72\sqrt{3}$
    E. 216

16. For all integers z,

    $\boxed{z} = z^2 - 1$, if z is an even integer and

    $\boxed{z} = z^2 + 1$, if z is an odd integer.

    What is the value $\boxed{7} - \boxed{6}$?

    A. −2
    B. 2
    C. 4
    D. 11
    E. 15

IF YOU FINISH BEFORE TIME IS CALLED, CHECK YOUR WORK ON THIS SECTION ONLY. DO NOT WORK ON ANY OTHER SECTION IN THE TEST.

Section 9: Writing—Multiple Choice

Time: 10 Minutes
15 Questions

Directions: In this section, choose the best answer for each question and fill in the corresponding circle on the answer sheet.

The following questions test correctness and effective expression. In selecting the answer, pay attention to grammar, diction, sentence structure, and punctuation. In the following questions, part or all of each sentence is underlined. The A answer repeats the underlined portion of the original sentence, while the next four offer alternatives. Choose the answer that best expresses the meaning of the original sentence, and at the same time is grammatically correct and stylistically superior. The correct choice should be clear, unambiguous, and concise.

EXAMPLE:

The forecaster predicted <u>rain and the sky was clear</u>.

- **A.** rain and the sky was clear
- **B.** rain but the sky was clear
- **C.** rain the sky was clear
- **D.** rain, but the sky was clear
- **E.** rain being as the sky was clear

The correct answer is **D.**

1. Alexander Frater was educated in Australia, <u>when he emigrated to England</u>, and eventually became a correspondent for a London newspaper.

- **A.** when he emigrated to England,
- **B.** emigrated to England,
- **C.** while he emigrated to England,
- **D.** emigrating to England,
- **E.** from whence he emigrated to England,

2. In Hawaii, they <u>are emphasizing the Hawaiian language as a part of</u> a renaissance in the native culture, including music and dance.

- **A.** they are emphasizing the Hawaiian language as a part of
- **B.** the emphasis on the Hawaiian language is part of
- **C.** they are putting emphasis on Hawaiian as a language as part of
- **D.** by emphasizing the Hawaiian language, they are creating a part of
- **E.** the emphasis on the Hawaiian language is to them a part of

3. Women are starting small businesses <u>twice as fast as men; 1 of</u> 20 working women is now self-employed.

- **A.** twice as fast as men; one of
- **B.** twice as fast as men one of
- **C.** twice as fast as men, one of
- **D.** two times as fast as men, one of
- **E.** two times as fast as men one of

GO ON TO THE NEXT PAGE

4. Illiteracy costs more than 5 billion dollars in unemployment and welfare benefits yearly, affecting one-fifth of the adult population.

   A. Illiteracy costs more than 5 billion dollars in unemployment and welfare benefits yearly, affecting one-fifth of the adult population.

   B. Yearly, illiteracy costs more than 5 billion dollars in unemployment and welfare benefits, affecting one-fifth of the adult population.

   C. Affecting one-fifth of the adult population, illiteracy costs more than 5 billion dollars in unemployment and welfare benefits yearly.

   D. Yearly affecting one-fifth of the adult population, illiteracy costs more than 5 billion dollars in unemployment and welfare benefits.

   E. Costing more than 5 billion dollars in unemployment and welfare benefits, illiteracy affects one-fifth of the adult population yearly.

5. Luis Jimenez's fiberglass sculpture *Fiesta Jarabe* depicting a traditional hat dance, and placed just north of the Mexican border.

   A. depicting a traditional hat dance, and placed

   B. depicting a traditional hat dance, and is placed

   C. depicting a traditional hat dance

   D. depicts a traditional hat dance, placed

   E. depicts a traditional hat dance and is placed

6. At one time, nearly all of Kuwait's 700 oil wells were on fire the crippled refineries were closed.

   A. fire the crippled

   B. fire but the crippled

   C. fire, crippled, the

   D. fire; the crippled

   E. fire, crippled

7. The skydiver compared his feelings of elation to winning a lottery, scoring a touchdown, or beating the odds in Las Vegas.

   A. to winning a lottery, scoring a touchdown, or beating

   B. to when one wins a lottery, scores a touchdown, or beating

   C. to winning a lottery, to scoring a touchdown, or beating

   D. to winning a lottery, to scoring a touchdown, or to beating

   E. to a win in a lottery, scoring a touchdown, or beating

8. In 2011, Stanley Plummer exposed a multi-million-dollar scandal that involved the Governor's son, and he lost his job as a newspaper editor.

   A. In 2011, Stanley Plummer exposed a multi-million-dollar scandal that involved the governor's son, and he

   B. Stanley Plummer, exposing in 2011 a multi-million-dollar scandal that involved the governor's son,

   C. In 2011, having exposed a multi-million-dollar scandal that involved the governor's son, Stanley Plummer

   D. It was 2011 when Stanley Plummer exposed a multi-million-dollar scandal involving the governor's son, and he

   E. In 2001, Stanley Plummer exposed a multi-million-dollar scandal that involved the governor's son, and consequently he

9. The population of beluga whales in the Gulf of St. Lawrence has failed to increase, and this worries many marine biologists.

   A. increase, and this

   B. increase; and this

   C. increase; this

   D. increase, which

   E. increase, a fact that

GO ON TO THE NEXT PAGE

10. The developer plans to dismantle and move a fourteenth-century English church to Nevada <u>which will give it</u> the oldest church in the western hemisphere.

   A.   which will give it
   B.   and this will give it
   C.   which will give the state
   D.   and this will give the state
   E.   to give the state

11. Banking regulators have seized a Georgia savings bank and charged that the institution <u>both used deceptive lending and business practices and it misled</u> its stockholders.

   A.   both used deceptive lending and business practices and it misled
   B.   both used deceptive business lending practices and it misled
   C.   used deceptive lending and business practices and misled
   D.   both used lending and business practices that were deceptive, misleading
   E.   used both deceptive and misleading business and lending practices, and it misled

12. For three years, the group called White Flag <u>has virtually ignored Chicago, the city where they started in.</u>

   A.   as virtually ignored Chicago, the city where they started in.
   B.   have virtually ignored Chicago, the city where they started in.
   C.   has virtually ignored Chicago, the city where it started.
   D.   has virtually ignored Chicago, where they started.
   E.   have virtually ignored the city where they started, Chicago.

13. Readers admire Margaret Fuller's <u>eagerness to succeed, that she is willing to work hard, and her refusal to give up.</u>

   A.   eagerness to succeed, that she is willing to work hard, and her refusal to give up.
   B.   eagerness for success, willingness to work hard, and that she refuses to give up.
   C.   being eager to succeed, willing to work hard, and her refusal to give up.
   D.   eagerness to succeed, willingness to work hard, and refusal to give up.
   E.   being eager to succeed, being willing to work hard, and refusing to give up.

14. Understanding why a sentence or a paragraph is awkward is essentially no different <u>from when you see</u> why a mathematical proof is unconvincing.

   A.   from when you see
   B.   from if you see
   C.   from seeing
   D.   than when you see
   E.   than if you see

15. <u>Where the main purpose of the greenhouse is</u> to raise half-hardy plants for planting out in the garden or to grow flowering plants in pots for cut flowers and for bringing into the house.

   A.   Where the main purpose of the greenhouse is
   B.   When the main purpose of the greenhouse is
   C.   The main purpose of the greenhouse is
   D.   If the main purpose of the greenhouse were
   E.   While the main purpose of the greenhouse is

IF YOU FINISH BEFORE TIME IS CALLED, CHECK YOUR WORK ON THIS SECTION ONLY. DO NOT WORK ON ANY OTHER SECTION IN THE TEST.

Scoring Practice Exam 3

The following section will assist you in scoring and analyzing your practice test results. Use the answer key below to score your results, and then carefully review the analysis charts to identify your strengths and weakness. Finally, read through the answer explanations starting on page 441 to clarify the solutions to the problems.

Answer Key for Practice Exam 3

Section 2: Writing—Multiple Choice

1. D	10. C	19. D	28. A
2. C	11. C	20. C	29. C
3. A	12. E	21. C	30. A
4. D	13. B	22. E	31. B
5. C	14. A	23. C	32. D
6. E	15. E	24. A	33. E
7. D	16. C	25. B	34. C
8. C	17. D	26. A	35. B
9. A	18. B	27. E	36. A

Section 3: Critical Reading

1. C	8. A	15. E	22. C
2. B	9. D	16. C	23. A
3. A	10. B	17. A	24. B
4. E	11. A	18. B	25. D
5. D	12. B	19. D	26. D
6. C	13. D	20. C	27. A
7. B	14. B	21. B	28. B

Section 4: Mathematics

1. D	6. B	11. D	16. A
2. B	7. C	12. C	17. A
3. D	8. D	13. B	18. E
4. C	9. D	14. C	19. C
5. D	10. A	15. A	20. E

Section 5: Critical Reading

1. B	8. B	15. C	22. B
2. C	9. C	16. B	23. A
3. E	10. E	17. A	24. C
4. D	11. B	18. E	25. D
5. D	12. D	19. B	26. E
6. B	13. A	20. D	27. B
7. B	14. D	21. C	28. E

Section 6: Mathematics

1. C	6. A	11. $\frac{1}{6}$	15. $\frac{7}{12}$
2. D	7. C	12. 93.5	16. 50
3. C	8. C	13. 527	17. 100
4. C	9. $\frac{5}{8}$	14. 45	18. 264
5. B	10. 14		

Section 7: Critical Reading

1. E	5. E	9. D	13. D
2. B	6. D	10. A	14. E
3. C	7. B	11. E	15. C
4. A	8. E	12. B	

Section 8: Mathematics

1. A	5. D	9. D	13. D
2. C	6. B	10. D	14. B
3. E	7. C	11. C	15. B
4. A	8. C	12. A	16. E

Section 9: Writing—Multiple Choice

1. B	5. E	9. E	13. D
2. B	6. D	10. E	14. C
3. A	7. A	11. C	15. C
4. C	8. C	12. C	

Charting and Analyzing Your Exam Results

The first step in analyzing your results is to chart your answers. Use the charts on the following pages to identify your strengths and areas of improvement. Complete the process of evaluating your essays and analyzing problems in each area. Reevaluate your results as you look for trends in the types of errors (repeated errors), and look for low scores in results in *specific* topic areas. This reexamination and analysis is a tremendous asset to help you maximize your best possible score. The answers and explanations following these charts will provide you clarification to help you solve these types of problems in the future.

Reviewing the Essay

Refer to the sample essay on page 440 as a reference guide. Have an English teacher, tutor, or someone else with good writing skills read and evaluate your essay using the Essay Checklist given below. Have your reader evaluate the complete essay as good, average, or marginal. Note that your paper would actually be scored from 1 to 6 by two trained readers (actual total score 2–12). Since we are trying only for a rough approximation, a strong, average, or weak overall evaluation will give you a general feeling for your score range.

Essay Checklist			
Questions	**Strong Response Score 5 or 6**	**Average Response Score 3 or 4**	**Weak Response Score 1 or 2**
1. Does the essay focus on the topic and respond to the assigned task?			
2. Is the essay organized and well developed?			
2. Does the essay use specific supporting details and examples?			
4. Does the writing use correct grammar, usage, punctuation, and spelling?			
5. Is the handwriting legible?			

Critical Reading Analysis Sheet				
Section 3	**Possible**	**Completed**	**Right**	**Wrong**
Sentence Completions	8			
Short Reading Passages	6			
Long Reading Passage	14			
Section 3 Subtotal	**28**			
Section 5	**Possible**	**Completed**	**Right**	**Wrong**
Sentence Completions	10			
Short Reading Passages	2			
Paired Reading Passages	4			
Long Reading Passages	12			
Section 5 Subtotal	**28**			
Section 7	**Possible**	**Completed**	**Right**	**Wrong**
Paired Reading Passages	13			
Short Reading Passage	2			
Section 7 Subtotal	**15**			
Overall Critical Reading Totals	**71**			

Note: Only 3 Critical Reading sections (approximately 70 questions) count toward your actual score on the SAT.

Mathematics Analysis Sheet

Section 4	Possible	Completed	Right	Wrong
Multiple Choice	20			
Section 4 Subtotal	**20**			
Section 6	Possible	Completed	Right	Wrong
Multiple Choice	8			
Grid-Ins	10			
Section 6 Subtotal	**18**			
Section 8	Possible	Completed	Right	Wrong
Multiple Choice	16			
Section 8 Subtotal	**16**			
Overall Math Totals	**54**			

Writing—Multiple-Choice Analysis Sheet

Section 2	Possible	Completed	Right	Wrong
Improving Sentences	7			
Identifying Sentence Errors	19			
Improving Paragraphs	10			
Section 2 Subtotal	**36**			
Section 9	Possible	Completed	Right	Wrong
Improving Sentences	15			
Section 9 Subtotal	**15**			
Overall Writing—Multiple-Choice Totals	**51**			

Analysis/Tally Sheet for Problems Missed

One of the most important parts of test preparation is analyzing why you missed a problem so that you can reduce the number of mistakes. Now that you have taken the practice exam and checked your answers, carefully tally your mistakes by marking them in the proper column.

Reason for Mistakes

	Total Possible	Total Missed	Simple Mistake	Misread Problem	Lack of Knowledge	Lack of Time
Section 3: Critical Reading	28					
Section 5: Critical Reading	28					
Section 7: Critical Reading	15					
Subtotal	**71**					
Section 4: Mathematics	20					
Section 6: Mathematics	18					
Section 8: Mathematics	16					
Subtotal	**54**					

	Total Possible	Total Missed	Simple Mistake	Misread Problem	Lack of Knowledge	Lack of Time
Section 2: Writing—Multiple Choice	36					
Section 9: Writing—Multiple Choice	15					
Subtotal	**51**					
Total Critical Reading, Math and Writing	**176**					

Reviewing the preceding data should help you determine why you are missing certain problems. Now that you've pinpointed the type of error, compare it to other practice tests to spot other common mistakes.

Practice Exam 3: Answers and Explanations

Section 1: Writing—Essay

To help you evaluate your essay writing skills, listed below is an example of a high-scoring strong essay response for essay topic. Compare your essay to this sample essay and the analysis of a strong essay, an average essay, and a poorly written essay. Use the above suggested checklist to evaluate your essays, and to help you take a closer look and understand your scoring range.

Sample Essay

Fortunately or otherwise, we learn from our mistakes. And when things go right, we take for granted that we're on track, even if this success is more because of luck than skill.

The failure of the American manufacturing 1980's provides a good example: Propelled by past successes, this reckless and overfed industry believed that a market for their products would always be available. This led to a general reduction in quality American cars. For a few years, few customers noticed: American cars were known to be the best in the world, just as the words "made in Japan" stood for shoddy workmanship. But evidence to the contrary continued to accumulate and people eventually began to catch on. Their American cars were breaking down more frequently (and more expensively), just as Japan—not to mention Germany and South Korea—began producing quality cars for less. For the auto industry, it was a painful lesson: A huge share of the market for automobiles disappeared overseas.

This lesson is clear, yet paradoxical: Success can breed arrogance, while failure can inspire humility and the ability to look at life in a new way.

In my own life, I have been forced to learn this lesson often. What may work one day, or even over a period of months or years, suddenly breaks down in the face of a changing world—or changes in myself. As a scientific person, I was often resistant to a spiritual perspective on the world. I am skeptical of organized religion, which I took to mean any belief possibility that meaning exists beyond what the eyes can observe and the mind can understand scientifically. While this provided me with many benefits, it also left me with a burden of the world on my shoulders. If I couldn't understand life, then perhaps life was truly meaningless.

My own personal breakthrough came as a result of the failure rather than the success of this outlook. This mindset was purely mechanistic, with no room for love, kindness, and connection with my fellow humans. Only when I became unhappy enough with this way of perceiving the world was I ready to consider alternatives. And when I did so, a new and warmer world was ready to greet me. My personal failure of understanding, once accepted, allow me to open to my own human frailties and capacities.

To sum up, success is never a permanent state of affairs—nor should it be. And while nobody welcomes failure, in most cases failure is the only means by which people learn. With this perspective, perhaps we can greet failure with a bit more patience and self-compassion. We all make mistakes; how we react in response to them may well be what sets us up for future success.

Section 2: Writing—Multiple Choice

Improving Sentences

1. **D.** The original version has faulty parallelism and is verbose. Choice B is not so wordy, but it shifts from the active verb ("affects") to "affected are." "Also being affected" in Choice E is no better. The best choice is D, which is the most concise of the five and a parallel construction of the series.

2. **C.** This is another of those sentences in which the pronouns have no specific antecedents, but refer to a general idea or the entire first clause. Changing pronouns (from "which" to "this," as in choices B and D) does no good. To repair a sentence like this, you must either supply a specific antecedent (you might say "a fact which is surprising"), or get rid of the pronoun. Choice C eliminates the pronoun.

3. **A.** This sentence is a series; the original version here is the best of the five—it is parallel, correctly punctuated with commas, and concise. The semicolons of Choice B are incorrect; Choice C has an extra "and." Choices D and E break up the parallel construction.

4. **D.** The original is a run on of two sentences without any punctuation or connective words between them. Here the semicolon is the best choice to connect the two independent clauses. It won't work in Choice E because the second clause is no longer independent; it is now a sentence fragment.

5. **C.** Compare C with A and you see that four words ("in," "it," "and," and "does") can be cut with no change of meaning. None of the four other versions of the sentence is as economical as Choice C, though they are all grammatical, except Choice A, which has the vague pronoun "it."

6. **E.** The original sentence here is not really wrong, but it is less effective because it treats all the elements as equal, while the superior version, Choice E, subordinates the first clause, clarifying the meaning of the relationship between the parts of the sentence. Here Choice D is a shorter sentence than Choice E, but the gain in clarity is worth more than the gain in economy.

7. **D.** The sentence begins with the past participle "nestled," and the opening participial phrase dangles. The town, not its extinction, is nestled, so we can eliminate choices A, B, and C. Choice D is more concise than Choice E.

Identifying Sentence Errors

8. **C.** The verb "agreed" and the opening phrase "strange as it now seems" place the action of this sentence in the past. The verb "fears" ought to be "feared," since the point of the sentence is that although Japan once feared Italian competition, it no longer does.

9. **A.** The singular subject "darkness" does not agree with the plural verb "were"; the verb should be "was."

10. **C.** It is the pronoun "who" not the verb "appear" that is in error here. The pronoun refers to the witch hats, which are garments, not human beings, so the correct pronoun is "that."

11. **C.** The sentence changes from a second person subject ("you") to a third person ("one"). It should be either "you can . . . you must" or " one can . . . one must."

12. **E.** There is no error in this sentence.

13. **B.** The subject and verb in this sentence are separated and do not agree. Since the singular verb "is" is not underlined and cannot be changed, "huge doses" must be changed to "a huge dose" to correct the grammar.

14. **A.** The opening phrase is not idiomatic. We say "as a result of" or "resulting from."

15. **E.** There is no error in the sentence.

16. **C.** Since the first part of the sentence lists three, the singular "method" should be the plural "methods."

17. **D.** The error in this sentence is the unidiomatic use of the preposition "with." The usual expression to denote the Dow Index level is "stands at."

18. **B.** The error is the confusion of an adjective and an adverb. The right word to modify the adjective "easy" here is the adverb "relatively."

19. **D.** The subject of the sentence, the singular "Peninsula," follows the plural verb "lie." It should be the singular "lies."

20. **C.** The "they" in this sentence is an ambiguous pronoun. It could refer to any of the animals including the deer, beavers, and squirrels, which are not, as a rule, dangerous.

21. **C.** The problem is the phrase "without he succeeds." A better one would be "unless he suceeds," "without success," or "without succeeding."

22. **E.** The sentence is grammatical and idiomatic.

23. **C.** The sequence of tenses here is inconsistent. The first and second verbs use the present tense ("is," "is") but the third uses the future tense instead of another present tense verb.

24. **A.** If you ignore the word "Texans," the error is easy to find: "that us talk oddly." It is an error of pronoun case, using the objective "us" rather than the subjective "we" as the subject of a clause.

25. **B.** This is a diction error. The word "requisite" is a noun or an adjective meaning something that is necessary in the circumstances. But the context calls for a verb. The right word is the verb "require."

26. **A.** There is an agreement problem here. The sentence gives only one example, Wilder's *Our Town*. To be consistent, the sentence has to say "example of a play."

Improving Paragraphs

27. **E.** Of the choices given, E corrects the run-on sentence and is concise. "However" should be preceded by a period or semicolon. Choice B corrects the run-on, but incorrectly uses a future tense ("will not have realized") and is wordy. The order of information in Choice C doesn't make sense. D is a run-on and replaces the active verb ("never heard of") with a passive one ("unheard of by").

28. **A.** Choice A eliminates the sentence fragment *Actually winning nine in the 1990s alone* by making it a dependent phrase. This choice also uses the plural verb *have* rather than *has* because the subject is plural (*Poetry and fiction*). Choice B, which—although not grammatically incorrect—creates two independent clauses joined by *and*. Subordinating the fragment, as in Choice A, is better. Choice C changes the emphasis of the sentence. Choice D is wordy and uses a singular verb (*has*) with a plural subject. Choice E is a run-on sentence.

29. **C.** Choice C is succinct and makes the point most clearly. Choice A is wordy, and Choice B uses the pronoun *he* after *Schramm*, which is incorrect; the sentence already has a subject: *A writer*. Choice D is both wordy and awkward, and E creates a sentence fragment.

30. **A.** Choice A is the most logical placement because sentence 5 states that there are more than 800 workshops across the country, and sentence 10 refers to writers who attend *them*, not just the Iowa workshop.

31. **B.** This choice alone retains the meaning of the original sentence and eliminates the *they* that incorrectly repeats the subject of the sentence (critics). Choice A includes an unclear pronoun; to whom does the *they* refer? Choices C and E do not retain the meaning of the original sentence, and Choice D includes unnecessary words (*It is said by some critics*).

32. **D.** Of the choices, D would be most effective. The focus of the passage is on the workshop itself, and choices A, C, and E do not maintain this focus. The passage is not intended as a "how to" piece, ruling out B.

33. **E.** The only version here that avoids a dangling participle is E, which supplies a subject and a verb ("we . . . got"). In choices A, B, C, and D, it is the weather that arrives after nine, not the wedding guests.

34. **C.** The trouble here is the use of "like" as a conjunction in the phrase "feel like this would be." The error is minor, but given a chance to revise the sentence, you are better off with C, which eliminates "like." All the other choices use "like" as a conjunction, though the verbs are different.

35. **B.** The issue here is the comma splice. Since "the sky was gray" is a complete sentence, it should be separated from "dismal" by either a semicolon or a period. Choice E corrects the original error, but introduces another comma splice after "gray."

36. **A.** The passage does not rely on figurative language such as metaphor and simile. It does arrange events chronologically, connecting the first and last sentences (by repeating "Idaho"), uses a first person speaker ("I"), and uses details of the weather to convey mood (sentences 5–7 and 12–13).

Section 3: Critical Reading

Sentence Completions

1. **C.** The adjective needed here will describe the growing fear of those who watched the endangered boat. Choice B, "intrepid," means fearless, and "cowardly," Choice A, although it describes a fearful person, means those who fear for themselves, not others. The best choice is "apprehensive," meaning uneasy, anxious, or troubled by fears.

2. **B.** "Native" and "indigenous" here mean the same thing. Since even the best language students who are foreign will not understand the native speaker, the missing word must mean something like puzzled or bewildered. The best choice, then, is "baffled."

3. **A.** With the use of "merely" and "not censorship," the sentence implies that the missing first word describes some minor changes in a text, something like "editing," or "revising," or "corrections," but not so serious as "expurgation" or "decimation." The phrase "with the writer's prior knowledge and" suggests that the last word must mean something like approval. In Choice B the use of "prohibition" and in Choice C the use of "disapproval" won't work. so the correct answer must be Choice A, "permission."

4. **E.** The missing noun probably describes a strength, since it is being tested and is parallel to the phrase "capacity to adapt." The best choice is "resilience," that is, the capacity to bounce back, to recover strength or good spirits.

5. **D.** The first noun is probably a synonym for "trend," and although Choice D, "fad," looks like the best choice, "prank" or "whim" might work. The second noun describes a serious threat (*not* an innocent or harmless challenge or undertaking). Either "peril" (danger, Choice A), or "hazard" (risk, Choice D), will do, but since Choice D has the better first word, it is the better answer.

6. **C.** Since the second half of the sentence tells us of the public's disapproval, the missing adverb must reflect this attitude. Either "horrified," Choice C, or "repulsed," Choice D, will fit. Only "ghoulish" continues the expression of condemnation. A repulsed public would not find the jewelry amiable.

7. **B.** The first missing word, a verb, has "response" as its object; choices A and C do not fit this context. The second word, a noun, describes a point that can be reached. Only choices A, B, and C might fit here. Thus, the correct choice is B. "Elicited" means evoked or drew, while "nadir" means the lowest point.

8. **A.** Since the missing word must be surprising in an atmosphere of calm and beauty, choices B, C, D, and E are all unsuitable. But "untoward," that is perverse, unseemly, unexpected, fits well.

Short Reading Passages

9. **D.** Nightingale showed an early interest in taking care of animals and dolls. Later, she "pored" over medical reports. She convinced her family to allow her to do something that was considered off-limits for a woman of her class. They did not sponsor her studies, Choice B. Nothing in the passage supports Choice A, and Nightingale's religious feelings are not addressed at all, Choice C. In spite of her putting splints on her dog's paws, there is no indication in the rest of the paragraph that she wanted to be a veterinarian, Choice E.

10. **B.** The author cites the reduction in the hospital death rate immediately after stating that Nightingale took a team of nurses to Turkey. Choice D might seem correct, but the emphasis is on the reduction in the death rate, not on the horrible conditions in hospitals. Choice E might also seem possible, but this detail is used specifically to dramatize the effect of the nurses, which is not the main idea of the paragraph. Choice C is

irrelevant because the passage deals with Nightingale's becoming a nurse, not a physician. Finally, the reader has no way of determining whether Choice A is true.

11. **A.** The paragraph is not descriptive and does not attempt to argue a point or persuade others to action. Therefore, answer choices B and D are incorrect. The paragraph also does not aim to criticize singers or songwriters, who are equally affected by changes in the music industry caused by the digitization of music, which makes answer choices C and E incorrect. Choice A is correct because the paragraph describes the relationships between industry changes and songwriting.

12. **B.** Statement III is false. Mechanical royalties, the sum paid for album or CD sales, are paid to both the songwriter and the artist. Statements I and II are true, making Choice B correct.

13. **D.** By using the phrase "Even oil industry leaders," the author of the paragraph is suggesting that global warming is of concern not only to environmentalists but also to people whose primary interest is in making a profit, not in preserving the environment. Choices A and B are perhaps true, but the phrase doesn't pertain to them. Choices C and E are points not even considered in the paragraph.

14. **B.** The passage explains that when warming causes snow and ice to melt, more areas are exposed to the sun. These areas then take in more solar radiation and heat, thus increasing the speed of warming.

Long Reading Passages

15. **E.** The passage mentions raccoons, cats, humans, and skunks as rabies victims. Since the first paragraph explicitly limits the disease to any "mammal," carrion birds are not susceptible to the virus.

16. **C.** Unless rabies is treated by "timely" injections of vaccine, it is a fatal disease (lines 3–5).

17. **A.** Although dogs are no longer the major carriers in countries with good veterinary services and laws requiring inoculation, they still account for "90 percent of all human deaths from rabies," chiefly in developing nations.

18. **B.** The number of fatalities from the disease is small in the United States because most dogs have been immunized, people are aware of the danger of the disease, and those at risk of having been infected are treated before the symptoms of the disease can develop. The virus is not rare in wild-animal populations. In lines 62–64, the passage refers to an epidemic among raccoons in America.

19. **D.** The word "feasible" means practicable or possible.

20. **C.** The treatment of humans can now include vaccine injections (in the abdomen or arm) and application of rabies-specific antibodies in the wound area. The passage makes no mention of an oral recombinant vaccine.

21. **B.** The vaccine-laced bait could be useful in dealing with wild populations and with dogs in countries where large-scale inoculation is impossible. The vaccine would not be useful in animals already infected, since once the symptoms of the disease develop, it is too late to save the victim.

22. **C.** In lines 18–21, the speaker says she did not follow the Watergate proceedings because it was just a case of one set of rich white people hoodwinking another set.

23. **A.** "Of a piece" means part of, consistent with, or in keeping with.

24. **B.** In this context, "acute" means shrewd or clever. Although some of the other meanings can apply in other contexts, here it is opposed to the word "ignorance" and associated with wit.

25. **D.** The words here are the thoughts of the speaker, not what she says. Throughout the passage, the reader knows both what she says and also what she thinks but does not say. Aware here of the pompous remarks she had just made, she is not eager to elaborate on these second-hand ideas, and remembering that Cox is a lawyer, she hopes to herself that he will not cross-examine her further.

26. **D.** The comic scene she imagines—Cox left in West Philly "without a map or a bow tie"—is her response to his inclusive "our." The speaker does not feel with a part the white New England establishment, and it is this pronoun that inspires her thoughts.

27. A. The Rector, a shrewd observer throughout the passage, has some idea of what is going on in the speaker's mind. For a moment, he is afraid she will blurt out something that will embarrass the school. He is relieved that the moment has passed without incident.

28. B. Because the passage was written some time after the events and allows the reader to know the thoughts of the speaker, the selection as a whole is very frank, even self-critical. The author understands herself and reveals this understanding very candidly. None of the other choices is appropriate.

Section 4: Mathematics

1. D. The 4 pounds of steak will cost

$4 \times \$3.89 = \$15.56$

The change from a $20 bill would be

$$\begin{array}{r} \$20.00 \\ -15.56 \\ \hline \$\ 4.44 \end{array}$$

2. B. For a number to be divisible by 21, it must be divisible by 3 and by 7 because $21 = 3 \times 7$. Therefore, if a number is divisible by 7 but not by 21, it cannot be divisible by 3.

3. D.

$$.0039y = 39$$
$$\frac{39}{10,000}y = 39$$
$$y = \frac{10,000}{39} \times 39$$
$$y = 10,000$$

Or, using your calculator, divide 39 by .0039.

4. C. Since $XY = YZ = 10$, $\triangle XYZ$ is an isosceles triangle and $\angle X \cong \angle Z$. $\angle Y = 84°$ because it forms a vertical angle with the given angle.

$$\angle X + \angle Y + \angle Z = 180°$$
$$\angle X + 84° + \angle Z = 180°$$
$$2(\angle Z) + 84° = 180°$$
$$2(\angle Z) = 96°$$
$$\angle Z = 48°$$

5. D. If $|3x - 4| = 20$ then

$$\begin{array}{ccc} 3x - 4 = 20 & \text{or} & 3x - 4 = -20 \\ 3x - 4 + 4 = 20 + 4 & & 3x - 4 + 4 = -20 + 4 \\ 3x = 24 & & 3x = -16 \\ \dfrac{3x}{3} = \dfrac{24}{3} & & \dfrac{3x}{3} = \dfrac{-16}{3} \\ x = 8 & \text{or} & x = -\dfrac{16}{3} \end{array}$$

6. **B.** II only. The arithmetic mean is the average (sum divided by number of items), or $6 + 2 + 10 + 2 + 5 = 25 \div 5 = 5$.

   The median is the middle number after the numbers have been ordered: 2, 2, 5, 6, 10. The median is 5.

   The mode is the most frequently appearing number: 2.

   The range is the highest minus the lowest, or $10 - 2 = 8$.

   Therefore, only II is true: The median (5) equals the mean (5).

7. **C.** Since three-fifths of the class are females, two-fifths of the class are males. Therefore, the ratio of males to females is

$$\frac{2}{5} \text{ to } \frac{3}{5} = \frac{\frac{2}{5}}{\frac{3}{5}}$$

$$= \frac{2}{5} \div \frac{3}{5}$$

$$= \frac{2}{\cancel{5}} \cdot \frac{\cancel{5}}{3}$$

$$= \frac{2}{3}$$

8. **D.** First change the equation to slope-intercept form $y = mx + b$, where m is the slope and b is the y intercept.

$$6x + y = 3$$
$$\underline{-6x \qquad\quad -6x}$$
$$y = 3 - 6x \quad \text{or} \quad y = -6x + 3$$

   Next, you can see that in the equation $y = -6x + 3$, -6 is in the m position and is therefore the slope.

9. **D.** Breaking the figure into squares of side x by adding the lines gives

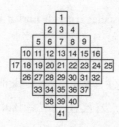

   Remember that each square has area x^2. Then the total area is $41x^2$.

10. A. Adding the two equations,

$$x - y = 15$$
$$\underline{3x + y = 13}$$
$$4x \quad\;\; = 28$$
$$\frac{4x}{4} \quad = \frac{28}{4}$$
$$x \quad\;\; = 7$$

Since $x = 7$	or	Since $x = 7$
and $x - y = 15$		and $3x + y = 13$
$7 - y = 15$		$3(7) + y = 13$
$7 - 7 - y = 15 - 7$		$21 + y = 13$
$-y = 8$		$21 - 21 + y = 13 - 21$
$y = -8$		$y = -8$

Therefore, $x = 7$ and $y = -8$.

11. D. In isosceles $\triangle XYZ$, $\angle X \cong \angle Z$

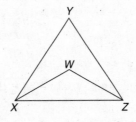

In $\triangle XYZ$,

$$\angle X + \angle Y + \angle Z = 180°$$
$$\angle X + 80° + \angle Z = 180°$$
$$\angle X + \angle Z = 100°$$
$$\angle X = \angle Z = 50°$$

Since $\overline{WX}$ bisects $\angle YXZ$ and $\overline{WZ}$ bisects $\angle YZX$,

$\angle YXW = \angle WXZ = \angle YZW = \angle WZX = 25°$

Therefore, on $\triangle XWZ$,

$$\angle XWZ + \angle WXZ + \angle WZX = 180°$$
$$\angle XWZ + 25° + 25° = 180°$$
$$\angle XWZ + 50° = 180°$$
$$\angle XWZ = 130°$$

12. **C.**

$$(m+n)^2 = (m+n)(m+n)$$
$$= m^2 + mn + mn + n^2$$
$$= m^2 + 2mn + n^2$$
$$= (m^2 + n^2) + (2mn)$$

Since $m^2 + n^2 = 12$ and $mn = 9$,
$$(m^2 + n^2) + (2mn) = 12 + 2(9)$$
$$= 12 + 18$$
$$= 30$$

13. **B.** Adding any two of three consecutive positive integers greater than 1 will always have a result greater than the other integer. Therefore, II is true. The others cannot be determined because they depend on values and/or the order of x, y, and z.

14. **C.** Area of the square

$= \frac{1}{2} \times$ product of diagonals

$= \frac{1}{2} d_1 d_2$

$= \frac{1}{2} d^2$ (because $d_1 = d_2$ in a square)

Therefore, $\frac{1}{2} d^2 = 72$

$d^2 = 144$

$d = 12$ feet

15. **A.** Let $5x$ = first angle, $2x$ = second angle, and $5x - 2x = 3x$ = third angle. Since the sum of the angles in any triangle is 180°,

$5x + 2x + 3x = 180°$

$10x = 180°$

$\frac{10x}{10} = \frac{180°}{10}$

$x = 18°$

Therefore,

$5x = 90°$

$2x = 90°$

$3x = 54°$

The smallest angle will have a measure of 36°.

16. **A.**

$$(-2,3) \oplus (4,-1) = [(-2)(4) - (3)(-1), (-2)(-1)]$$
$$= [(-8) - (-3), (2)]$$
$$= (-5, 2)$$

17. **A.** Let n = number of nickels, $3n$ = number of dimes, and $3n - 3$ = numbers of quarters. Since 25 coins are in the collection,

$$n + 3n + (3n - 3) = 25$$
$$7n - 3 = 25$$
$$7n = 28$$
$$n = 4 \text{ nickels} = \$0.20$$
$$3n = 12 \text{ dimes} = \$1.20$$
$$3n - 3 = 9 \text{ quarters} = \$2.25$$

Therefore, the total value of the collection is $0.20 + $1.20 + $2.25 = $3.65.

18. E. Since arc YXZ is a semicircle, its measure is 180°,

$$\widehat{XZ} = \widehat{YXZ} - \widehat{YWX}$$
$$= 180° - 100°$$
$$= 80°$$

Since an inscribed angle $= \frac{1}{2}$ (intercepted arc),

$$\angle XYZ = \frac{1}{2}\left(\widehat{XZ}\right)$$
$$= \frac{1}{2}\left(80°\right)$$
$$= 40°$$

Therefore, $\angle XYZ$ has a measure of 40°.

19. C. Since $\sqrt{mn} = 10$, $mn = 100$, and the possible values or m and n would be

1 and 100   5 and 20

2 and 50   10 and 10

4 and 25

Since none of these combinations yields $m + n = 50$, Choice C is correct.

20. E. To find the y-intercepts, set $x = 0$ and solve for y.

$$2y^2 - 5\left(0^2\right) = 50$$
$$2y^2 = 50$$
$$\frac{2y^2}{2} = \frac{50}{2}$$
$$y^2 = 25$$
$$y = \pm\sqrt{25}$$
$$y = \pm 5$$

Therefore, the y-intercepts are at $(0, \pm 5)$

Section 5: Critical Reading

Sentence Completions

1. **B.** The clue in the sentence is "banning." If cameras have been banned, the public will not see the whole story, so their access (right to approach), has been curtailed. The best word here is "denied," Choice B. "Belied" means lied about.

2. **C.** The adverb "reluctantly" and the phrase "despite his care" suggest that the adjective that modifies "shoplifting" here is one that distresses the grocer, and so you can infer a word that means frequent. The only word that is close is "commonplace"; that is, common or ordinary.

3. **E.** The sentence presents an example of Parkinson's law as the same number of workers taking more time for the same job. The missing word in the law itself must explain this phenomenon. If work does something to fill the time for its completion, and the time for its completion has increased, then work must grow larger to fill the longer time. The missing word cannot be "decreases" or "grows easier." The right answer must be choices D or E, and "expands," Choice E, goes better with "fill." The missing verb must be a synonym for "states" or "says." Choices B, C, and E would work, but E also has the best answer for the second blank.

4. **D.** The noun must reflect the mood of loud cheering or something happy, such as "happiness" (Choice B), "gladness" (Choice C), "euphoria," (Choice D), or "buoyancy," (Choice E). The second word must qualify this mood, however, because the first clause begins with "although." A proper word here could be "tempered" (Choice A) or "moderated" (Choice D). The words "enervated" and "debilitated," although they can mean weaken, cannot be used in this context. They refer to physical weakness. Only Choice D has two good choices; "euphoria" is a feeling of well-being.

5. **D.** The clues in the sentence tell you that the missing word must describe a conversation with no sentence longer than four words. The correct answer is "terse"; that is, brief or to the point. None of the other choices makes sense.

6. **B.** The second term, a noun, must be a word that suggests a functioning government, so you can eliminate "schism," "dichotomy," and "division." Either "compromise" or "consensus" (agreement) will fit. The first term, an adjective, describes a position that should be abandoned. Therefore, "dogmatic" is a much better choice than "sensible."

7. **B.** The words "conventional morality" and "conformity" suggest that the missing adjective to modify "conformity" will express the correctness of the Victorian reader. Choice B, "genteel," means polite, refined, well-bred—just what would be expected. The incorrect answers are all adjectives describing the opposite of what is suggested by "conventional morality."

8. **B.** "Though" at the beginning of the sentence suggests that the missing adjective will be the opposite of "lively" and "interesting." The second missing word refers to the "lively" first chapter, so it must be a noun synonym for liveliness. "Tedious," Choice B; "repetitive," Choice C; "dull," Choice D; or "boring," Choice E, would do for the first blank, but only "pace," Choice A, or "verve," Choice B, are possible for the second. The right response must be Choice B. Words like "torpor" and "lethargy" are the opposite of what is needed for the second noun, and "verve" means vigor or energy.

9. **C.** The useful clues here are "dangerous," "without peppers or other spices," and "mild," with the last two set in opposition to the missing adjective by the word "but." Choices A, B, and D are just what you don't want. Both Choice C, "torrid" (that is, fiery or very hot), or Choice E, "piquant," are possible, but because "piquant" suggests an agreeable tartness and these dishes are dangerous, "torrid" is better.

10. **E.** The second adjective, expressing the response of a malcontent (a dissatisfied or rebellious person), must be disparaging, and the first adjective, coming before the "but," must be opposite in effect. The favorable first adjectives are Choice B, "perfect"; Choice D, "edenic"; and Choice E, "ideal"; the pejorative second words are Choice A "irritating," Choice C "drab," and Choice E "painful." The correct answer must therefore be E.

Short Reading Passages

11. **B.** Choice A might seem tempting, but which way atoms are pointing in rock crystals was only the means by which magnetic reversal was shown to have occurred. The passage does not consider a change in the direction of lava flows, Choice C, or convection currents, Choice D. The paragraph does state that it appears that magnetic reversal occurs on average every 500,000 years; however, magnetic reversal is not a disturbance in some other undefined 500,000-year cycle of the magnetic field, Choice E.

12. **D.** The solidified rocks can be age dated, and the alignment of atoms in the rocks reveals magnetic reversal. The speed with which the reversal takes place is not indicated in the paragraph, Choice C, nor is species extinction, Choice B, mentioned. The study of lava flows is important, Choice E, but only because the lava flows produce magma, not because their direction shifts.

13. **A.** The final sentence of the paragraph clearly makes a contrast between the "drab spinster" and the poet. B, C, and D are secondary points, and E is not addressed in the passage.

14. **D.** The sense of Dickinson in the paragraph is that she was a solitary person. None of the other definitions makes sense in context. Nowhere is Dickinson described as snobbish or ill-natured, choices A and B, and the word "eccentric," which precedes "reclusive," means Choice E and is the opposite of Choice C, making these poor choices for "reclusive."

15. **C.** The details in Passage 2 emphasize Dickinson's insistence on choosing the right word (see lines 5–7). The author mentions Choice A, and refers to her metaphors and rhythm, choices B and E, but it is her precision with language that is emphasized. Choice D is indicated in the passage, but it is not what impresses the author; rather, it is the means to an end—that is, Dickinson's precision.

16. **B.** See lines 11–13 in Passage 1 and lines 3–5 in Passage 2. The author of Passage 1 focuses on her life, but doesn't indicate he finds her life more interesting than her work, Choice A. He also doesn't describe her as "pathetic," even though she lived a secluded life, Choice D. The author of Passage 2 doesn't address Dickinson's life at all, Choice C, and the author of Passage 1 doesn't address the ideas in her poems, Choice E.

Long Reading Passages

17. **A.** The reasons for Spain's attack (II) are not addressed in the passage, and other countries (III) are mentioned only in the context of where the report about the Spanish fleet was circulated after it was published. Thus I only, Choice A, is the correct answer.

18. **E.** The historian's list identifies the order of battle and ships' names as basic information that may be expected in such a report, making Choice E correct in this context. According to the historian, all the other items, choices A, B, C, and D, represent increasingly detailed (and exaggerated or less accurate) information.

19. **B.** Although some of the terms refer to containers, Choice A, the report associates them all with quantities or weights of provisions such as biscuits, beans, vinegar, and water, making Choice B the correct answer.

20. **D.** According to the historian, the Spanish people substituted the word "invincible" for the original "most fortunate," making Choice D the correct answer.

21. **C.** The historian remarks that the document probably should have been kept secret but was not, thus Choice A is incorrect. That the report was for sale in Amsterdam and was printed in ten days, choices B and D, were not surprising for the times, and that it contained inaccuracies and exaggerations, Choice E, had already been established. What was most surprising was the timing of the publication, Choice C, which warned the English of what to expect.

22. **B.** The historian's reference to the classification of documents "today" as "Top Secret" is the most direct link between past and present in the passage.

23. **A.** The names refer to places where ships were. Because this included ships under sail as well as ships at anchor, Choice C is excluded, making nautical locations, Choice A, the best answer. Choices B and D are incorrect as they refer to locations on land. Choice E is incorrect because the Lizard is a location in the English Channel and not a body of water, and while rivers may be referred to as bodies of water, harbors normally are not.

24. **C.** Even not knowing the precise meaning of pikes and corselets, they most logically fit in the category of small arms and armor.

25. **D.** Even not knowing the precise nature of pepper and cloves, one would most logically classify them with foodstuffs as provisions.

26. **E.** Choices A, B, C, and D were all good reasons for leaking the report, making these incorrect answers in this context. However, the report was not leaked to give the enemy an advantage. Therefore, Choice E is the correct answer.

27. **B.** The number of ships was 130, Choice B. The number of friars and priests was 180, Choice A, while 123,790, Choice C, was the number of cannon balls. Ten, Choice D, was the number of days before publication of the report, and 28, Choice E, was the date the royal flag ship sailed out of Lisbon harbor to begin an invasion of England.

28. **E.** The author uses all three phrases to help readers visualize and feel thrilled by the event described.

Section 6: Mathematics

1. **C.** If $x^4 = z^{16}$ then $\sqrt[4]{x^4} = \sqrt[4]{z^{16}}$

   or $\left(x^4\right)^{\frac{1}{4}} = \left(z^{16}\right)^{\frac{1}{4}}$

   and $x = z^4$

2. **D.** Each term in the sequence must be divisible by 4, and 438 is not divisible by 4.

3. **C.** If the plumber works 6 consecutive hours, the charge is $45 for the first hour plus $20 for each of the five additional hours: $45 + 5($20) = $45 + $100 = $145

4. **C.** Notice how drawing some line segments can assist you in finding the necessary lengths.

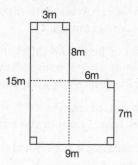

Note: Figure not drawn to scale

The perimeter is the sum of the length of the sides.

$P = 15 + 3 + 8 + 6 + 7 + 9 = 48\text{m}$

5. **B.** Since $a = p + prt$,

$$a - p = p + prt - p$$
$$a - p = prt$$
$$\frac{a - p}{pt} = \frac{prt}{pt}$$
$$\frac{a - p}{pt} = r$$

Therefore,

$$r = \frac{a - p}{pt}$$

6. **A.** Since Rajiv will be y years old x years from now, he is $y - x$ years old now. Therefore, z years from now he will be $y - x + z$ years old.

7. C. Let x = first number, $2x + 1$ = second number, and $3x - 4$ = third number. Since the average of the 3 numbers is 55,

$$\frac{x + (2x + 1) + (3x - 4)}{3} = 55$$

Multiplying both sides of the equation by 3,

$$x + (2x + 1) + (3x - 4) = 165$$
$$6x - 3 = 165$$
$$6x - 3 + 3 = 165 + 3$$
$$6x = 168$$
$$\frac{6x}{6} = \frac{168}{6}$$
$$x = \frac{168}{6}$$
$$x = 28 = \text{first number}$$
$$2x + 1 = 57 = \text{second number}$$
$$3x - 4 = 80 = \text{third number}$$

Therefore, the largest number is 80.

8. C. $\triangle DBC$ is a 30-60-90 triangle, which means the sides DB, CD, and CB are in the ratio $1 : 2 : \sqrt{3}$, respectively.

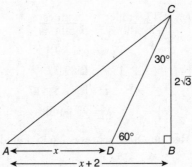

You're given $BC = 2\sqrt{3}$, which means the common factor for all three sides is 2. The side BD is $2 \times 1 = 2$. If $BD = 2$, then $AB = x + 2$. The area of $\triangle ABC$ is given as $6\sqrt{3}$. So you can solve as follows:

$$\text{Area} = \frac{1}{2} \times \text{base} \times \text{height}$$
$$6\sqrt{3} = \frac{1}{2}(AB)(BC)$$
$$6\sqrt{3} = \frac{1}{2}(x + 2)(2\sqrt{3})$$
$$6\sqrt{3} = (x + 2)\sqrt{3}$$
$$6 = x + 2$$
$$6 - 2 = x$$
$$4 = x$$

Grid-In Questions

9. $\frac{5}{8}$. Multiplying both sides of the equation by the LCD of 5,

$$5\left(x+\frac{3}{5}x\right)=5(1)$$
$$5x+3x=5$$
$$8x=5$$
$$x=\frac{5}{8}\quad\text{or }.625$$

10. **14.** Since 60% of the students are girls, 40% of the students are boys. Hence, 40% of 35 = (.40)(35) = 14 boys.

11. $\frac{1}{6}$. The average of any 3 numbers is equal to the sum of the numbers divided by 3,

$$\frac{1}{4}+\frac{1}{6}+\frac{1}{12}=\frac{3}{12}+\frac{2}{12}+\frac{1}{12}$$
$$\text{The sum}=\frac{6}{12}$$
$$=\frac{1}{2}$$

The average of the numbers is $\frac{1}{2}\div3=\frac{1}{2}\cdot\frac{1}{3}=\frac{1}{6}$ or .166 or .167.

12. **93.5.**

$$\frac{317.9\text{ miles}}{17\text{ gallons}}=\frac{x\text{ miles}}{5\text{ gallons}}$$
$$17x=(317.9)(5)$$
$$17x=1589.5$$
$$x=1589.5\div17$$
$$x=93.5\text{ miles}$$

13. **527.** The total of the five Critical Reading SAT scores is 2,635. Dividing that total by 5 (the number of scores) gives 527 as the average.

14. **45.** Since the sum of the measures of the angles of a quadrilateral is 360 and the ratio of the measure angle is 3:5:7:9,

$$3x+5x+7x+9x=360$$
$$24x=360$$
$$x=360\div24$$
$$x=15$$

The smallest angle is $3x=(3)(15)=45$.

15. $\frac{7}{12}$. If Jim works for 2 days, he will complete $\frac{2}{6}$, or $\frac{1}{3}$, of the job. If Mike works for 2 days, he will complete $\frac{2}{8}$, or $\frac{1}{4}$, of the job. Together they will complete $\frac{1}{3}+\frac{1}{4}=\frac{4}{12}+\frac{3}{12}=\frac{7}{12}$ (or .583) of the job.

16. 50. Since BD is a diagonal of square $ABCD$, $BD = 5\sqrt{2}$

The area of square $BDMN = (BD)^2$

$$= \left(5\sqrt{2}\right)^2$$
$$= 25 \times 2$$
$$= 50$$

17. 100.

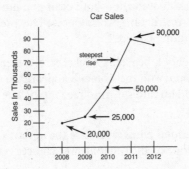

The greatest increase is indicated by the steepest rise in the graph lines, between 2010 and 2011. But you are looking for the greatest *percentage* increase, which means the increase as compared to the starting point. To find percentage increase

$$\frac{\text{amount of increase}}{\text{starting point}} = \text{percentage increase}$$

2008–2009	20 to 25	$\frac{5}{20} = 25\%$ increase
2009–2010	25 to 50	$\frac{25}{25} = 100\%$ increase
2010–2011	50 to 90	$\frac{40}{50} = 80\%$ increase
2011–2012	decrease	

18. 264. In $\triangle MNP$, $PM = PN$ and $\angle PMN = \angle PNM = 42°$. Also, in $\triangle MNP$,

$$\angle PMN + \angle PNM + \angle MPN = 180°$$
$$42° + 42° + \angle MPN = 180°$$
$$84° + \angle MPN = 180°$$
$$\angle MPN = 96°$$

Since $\angle MPN$ is a central angle, arc $MN = 96°$

Also, arc MN + arc $MQN = 360°$

$$96° + \text{arc } MQN = 360°$$
$$\text{arc } MQN = 264°$$

Section 7: Critical Reading

Paired Passages

1. **E.** In the first paragraph the author compares Mark Zuckerberg with Bobby Fischer and with a person with Asperger's Syndrome, and also compares David Fincher's moviemaking style with Zuckerberg's personality.

2. **B.** The author's main point is that the movie makes its difficult subject—an unsocial computer prodigy and his development of a social networking web site—both clear and interesting to a general audience, Choice B. Choices A and C express supporting details, while Choice D expresses the author's response to viewing the film. Lines 72–75 directly contradict Choice E.

3. **C.** Passage 1 makes clear that Facebook began as Zuckerberg's revenge against Erica and other women through a web site inviting commentary on the women's appearance and sex appeal. To get pictures of women for this purpose, he hacked Harvard's dorms' facebooks. The events in choices A, B, D, and E occur at other times in the plot sequence.

4. **A.** The last two sentences of the second paragraph state the author's view that the start of Zuckerberg's Facebook was sexist and illegal. None of the other answer choices is expressed in the passage.

5. **E.** "Mercurial" modifies Sean Parker, an internet entrepreneur who, like mercury in a thermometer, rose and fell with Napster and Plaxo. Choice A alludes to Mercury the planet, while Choice B alludes to Mercury the Roman god. Choices C and D refer to Mercury's characteristic of speed (which applies to both the planet and the god). However, those choices do not define "mercurial" in the context of Passage 1.

6. **D.** The last paragraph of Passage 1 clarifies that the outcomes of the events shown in *The Social Network* are not the point of the movie, which is to show how the "interaction of undergraduate chaos, enormous amounts of money, and manic energy" shape Facebook's origins.

7. **B.** The last paragraph supports the author's claim that a case can be made against Zuckerman. None of the other answer choices apply.

8. **E.** In the first two paragraphs the reviewer focuses mainly on the contribution of screenwriter Aaron Sorkin, whose script makes the characters and story accessible. The main characters, Choice A, are introduced in subsequent paragraphs. Choices B, C, and D are supporting details mentioned briefly in the first two paragraphs but cannot be inferred as their main purpose.

9. **D.** In the second paragraph the author of Passage 2 describes Zuckerberg as "a borderline sociopath." Choices A, B, and E describe situations or settings rather than the person, and Choice C is the title of the book on which the movie was based.

10. **A.** A "fusillade" is continuous gunfire.

11. **E.** Both reviewers likely would agree on all three points. Both passages imply that Harvard's was a male culture (I) and that Zuckerberg's activities were spiteful and sexist or misogynistic (II). Both reviews also point out the betrayals of friendships and agreements during Facebook's startup (III), such as Zuckerberg's calculating secret competition against the Winklevoss brothers and callous disregard of his original friend and business partner, Eduardo Saverin.

12. **B.** "Misogyny" means hatred of women by men. Rule by women, Choice A, is "gynecocracy." Fear and hatred of men and boys, Choice C, is "misandry," and of all people, "misanthropy." Answer choices D and E do not apply.

13. **D.** "Cachet" in this context means a special characteristic or quality of distinction or authenticity. It comes from a French word that referred to a stamped or printed official logo or seal of approval, choices A and C. Choices B and E do not apply.

Short Reading Passages

14. E. By referring to an article written in 1880, the author of the passage suggests that recognition of synesthesia is not recent. However, the article cited doesn't show the importance of the concept, Choice A. Also, nothing indicates that Galton's article deals with the origin of the word "synesthesia," Choice B. Although the passage identifies Galton as Darwin's cousin, nothing suggests that Darwin himself was interested in the phenomenon, Choice C.

15. C. Choice A is an overstatement. (Beware of words like "identical" in multiple-choice questions.) Similarly, choices B and D are unwarranted generalizations and Choice E is a hypothesis not touched upon in the passage.

Section 8: Mathematics

1. A.

$$\frac{\text{percent}}{100} = \frac{\text{is number}}{\text{of number}}$$
$$\frac{.25}{100} = \frac{x}{12}$$

Cross-multiplying,

$$100x = 3.00$$
$$\frac{100x}{100} = \frac{3.00}{100}$$
$$x = .03 \text{ or } \frac{3}{100}$$

2. C. There are 9 perfect squares between 0 and 90: 1, 4, 9, 16, 25, 36, 49, 64, and 81. Since there are 89 integers between 0 and 90, there are 80 integers that are not a square of an integer.

3. E. Let x = original price. Then

$$x - .40x = 5.70$$
$$.60x = 5.70$$
$$\frac{.60x}{.60} = \frac{5.70}{.60}$$
$$x = 9.50$$

Hence, the book originally cost $9.50.

4. A. Multiply the numerator and denominator by 12 (LCD).

$$\frac{12\left(\frac{2}{3} - \frac{1}{2}\right)}{12\left(\frac{1}{6} + \frac{1}{4} + \frac{2}{3}\right)} = \frac{8-6}{2+3+8} = \frac{2}{13}$$

5. D. According to the graph, the tallest "B" (before) bar is County 4.

6. B Solve this problem by substituting in simple numbers. Start with 1, an odd integer.

$$(1+1)\cdot(2\cdot1+1)$$
$$=(2)\cdot(2+1)$$
$$=2\cdot3$$
$$=6 \quad (\text{not odd})$$

Now, try 2, an even integer; Choice B.

$$(2+1)\cdot(2\cdot2+1)$$
$$=(3)\cdot(4+1)$$
$$=3\cdot5$$
$$=15 \quad (\text{an odd integer})$$

7. C.

$$\text{Since } \angle A = 40°, \quad \widehat{BC} = 80°$$

Since the measure of a circle is 360°, then

$$\widehat{AB} = 360° - \left(\widehat{AC} + \widehat{BC}\right)$$
$$= 360° - \left(130° + 80°\right)$$
$$= 360° - 210°$$
$$= 150°$$

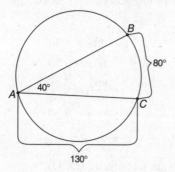

8. C. Since two-thirds of the students are boys, $\frac{2}{3}(36) = 24$ boys in the class. Out of the 24 boys in the class, three-fourths of them are under 6 feet tall, or $\frac{3}{4}(24) = 18$ boys under 6 feet tall.

9. D. Since $|3x + 6| = 15$

$$
\begin{array}{ccc}
3x + 6 = 15 & \text{or} & 3x + 6 = -15 \\
3x + 6 - 6 = 15 - 6 & \text{or} & 3x + 6 - 6 = -15 - 6 \\
3x = 9 & & 3x = -21 \\
\dfrac{3x}{3} = \dfrac{9}{3} & & \dfrac{3x}{3} = \dfrac{-21}{3} \\
x = 3 & \text{or} & x = -7
\end{array}
$$

10. D. Since the area of a trapezoid $= \frac{1}{2} \cdot h \cdot (b_1 + b_2)$, we need to find the altitude, h. Draw altitudes in the figure as follows:

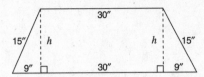

Since the triangles formed are right angles, use the Pythagorean Theorem, which says,

$$c^2 = a^2 + b^2$$
$$15^2 = 9^2 + h^2$$
$$225 = 81 + h^2$$
$$h^2 = 225 - 81$$
$$h^2 = 144$$
$$h = \sqrt{144} = 12 \text{ inches}$$

Hence, the area of the trapezoid will be

$$\frac{1}{2} \cdot h \cdot (b_1 + b_2) = \frac{1}{2} \cdot 12 \cdot (30 + 48)$$
$$= (6)(78)$$
$$= 468 \text{ square inches}$$

11. C. Since x is an integer, x could be a negative, zero, or a positive whole number. If you substitute in some integers for x you can see that 3^x cannot be a negative number or zero, so $f(x)$ could not be 3 or 4. Eliminate choices A and B.

If x is -2, and then $f(x)$ could be $4\frac{1}{9}$ as follows:

$$f(x) = 3^x + 4$$
$$= 3^{-2} + 4$$
$$= \frac{1}{9} + 4$$
$$= 4\frac{1}{9}$$

At this point, select Choice C and go on to the next problem. If you try some other integers you'll notice that $5\frac{1}{3}$ and 9 are not possible values for $f(x)$.

12. **A.**

$$y = \frac{1-x}{x}$$

$$y = \frac{1}{x} - \frac{x}{x}$$

$$y = \frac{1}{x} - 1$$

$$y + 1 = \frac{1}{x} - 1 + 1$$

$$y + 1 = \frac{1}{x}$$

Taking the reciprocal of both sides of the equation,

$$\frac{1}{y+1} = x$$

An alternative solution would be,

$$\frac{y}{1} = \frac{1-x}{x} \ \left(\text{cross-multiply}\right)$$

$$xy = 1 - x$$

$$xy + x = 1 \ \left(\text{factor out } x\right)$$

$$x(y+1) = 1 \ \left(\text{divide by } y+1\right)$$

$$x = \frac{1}{y+1}$$

13. **D.** To be 30% faster means to produce 30% more in the same amount of time. Therefore, the third plant makes 100,000 + (.30)(100,000) = 100,000 + 30,000 = 130,000 skateboards in 15 days. With all three plants working together, they produce 330,000 skateboards every 15 days. To produce 1,000,000 skateboards, they would need $\frac{1,000,000}{330,000} \times \frac{15}{1}$ days ≈ 45.45 days. Therefore, with all three plants working together, they would need approximately 46 days to produce 1 million skateboards.

14. **B.** Solve as follows:

$$4\sqrt{y+3} + 14 = 50$$

$$4\sqrt{y+3} = 36$$

$$\frac{4\sqrt{y+3}}{4} = \frac{36}{4}$$

$$\sqrt{y+3} = 9$$

$$\left(\sqrt{y+3}\right)^2 = (9)^2$$

$$y + 3 = 81$$

$$y + 3 - 3 = 81 - 3$$

$$y = 78$$

Any time you square both sides of an equation, you must check for extraneous roots. So check $y = 78$.

$$4\sqrt{y+3} + 14 = 4\sqrt{78+3} + 14$$

$$= 4\sqrt{81} + 14$$

$$= 4 \cdot 9 + 14$$

$$= 36 + 14$$

$$= 50$$

15. B.

$$\text{Area} = \frac{1}{2} \times \text{base} \times \text{height}$$

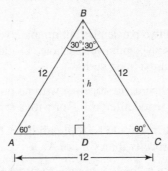

Since $\triangle ABC$ is equilateral, each of its angles measures 60°. Drawing altitude $\overline{BD}$ creates a 30-60-90 right triangle with *CD, BC,* and *BD* in the ratio of $1:2:\sqrt{3}$.

Since $BC = 12$, the scale factor is 6, thus $BD = 6\sqrt{3}$.

Hence, the area of $\triangle ABC$ is

$$\begin{aligned} &= \frac{1}{2}(AC)(BD) \\ &= \frac{1}{2}(12)(6\sqrt{3}) \\ &= (6)(6\sqrt{3}) \\ &= 36\sqrt{3} \text{ square yards} \end{aligned}$$

16. E. Since 6 is even, $\boxed{6} = 6^2 - 1 = 36 - 1 = 35$

Since 7 is odd, $\boxed{7} = 7^2 + 1 = 49 + 1 = 50$

$$\begin{aligned} \text{So, } \boxed{7} - \boxed{6} &= \left(7^2 + 1\right) - \left(6^2 - 1\right) \\ &= 50 - 35 \\ &= 15 \end{aligned}$$

Section 9: Writing—Multiple Choice

Improving Sentences

1. **B.** The sentence presents a series of three parts in chronological order. The first and third parts of the series use indicative verbs in the past tense, but the second element is subordinated in choices A, C, D, and E. To keep the three parts parallel, there should be no "when," "while," or "whence," and the verb should be in the past tense to maintain the parallel ("was educated," "emigrated," "became").

2. **B.** All four of the incorrect versions of this sentence have a vague pronoun ("they," or "them" in E). Who are "they"? Choice B is the clearest and the briefest sentence.

3. **A.** The original sentence is correct. The two independent clauses are separated by the semicolon. A period would also work here, but a comma or no punctuation at all will produce a comma splice or run-on sentence.

4. **C.** In this section of the exam, when all of a long sentence is underlined, there is a good chance that the problem being tested is the placement of a modifier. Here the phrase "affecting one-fifth of the adult population" modifies "illiteracy." The best answer will find a way to keep the two together. Choice D keeps the two together, but misplaces "yearly" so that it appears to modify "affecting" rather than "costs." Choice E also misplaces "yearly."

5. **E.** This is a sentence fragment, with two participles but no main verb. Choices A, B, and C retain the participle "depicting" but do not supply a main verb. Choice D adds a verb but the participle "placed" now modifies "dance." E has the two required main verbs.

6. **D.** There are two complete sentences here, run together with no punctuation between them. They should be punctuated as two sentences with a period after "fire," or with a semicolon, as in Choice D.

7. **A.** The three elements of the series here should be kept parallel. Choice A uses three gerunds. Choices B, C, and E are not parallel; Choice D is wordier than Choice A.

8. **C.** In choices A, D, and E, the pronoun "he" could refer to either Stanley Plummer or the governor's son. Choices B and C avoid this ambiguity. The sequence of verb tenses is clearer in Choice C; by placing the exposure of the scandal before the job loss, Choice B suggests that the first action was the cause of the second.

9. **E.** The pronouns ("this" and "which") in choices A, B, C, and D have no specific antecedent; Choice E avoids this vagueness by adding the noun "fact."

10. **E.** This sentence uses a pronoun with no specific antecedent, and tries to correct the error by changing the pronoun; neither "which" nor "this" will work, but eliminating the pronoun eliminates the error.

11. **C.** With the correlatives "both . . . and," the same structure should follow each conjunction. Since choices A and B begin with "both used," the "and" should be followed by a verb, not the pronoun "it." Choice D never completes the "both" with an "and." Choice E uses "both . . .and" correctly (to introduce adjectives that are parallel), but it is a very wordy sentence—four words longer than Choice C. Choice C avoids a lot of trouble simply by not using "both . . . and."

12. **C.** The issues in this sentence are the agreement of the verb and the pronoun with the subject "group," and the phrase "where . . . in." Since "group" refers to a single unit, we should take it to be singular and use the singular "has ignored" and "it." In the phrase "the city where they started in," the "in" is unnecessary.

13. **D.** The sentence is testing parallel elements in a series. The series could use three nouns or three clauses beginning with "that" or three gerunds to keep the parallelism, although the "that" clauses would be wordy. None of the wrong answers uses all three consistently, but Choice D uses three nouns ("eagerness," "willingness," and "refusal").

14. **C.** The phrase "is no different from" is another way of saying "is like." Comparisons, whether negative ("not different") or not, should be kept as parallel as possible. Here we need a parallel to the gerund "understanding." The addition of a subject ("you") and verbs in choices A, B, D, or E is unnecessary. The parallel is the most concise choice, which is the gerund "seeing."

15. **C.** This is a sentence fragment. Introduced by "where," it is a dependent clause. The change to "when," or "if," or "while" does not make the clause independent. Choice C rightly drops the subordinating conjunction, and the sentence is now complete.

Section 2

1 (A) (B) (C) (D) (E)
2 (A) (B) (C) (D) (E)
3 (A) (B) (C) (D) (E)
4 (A) (B) (C) (D) (E)
5 (A) (B) (C) (D) (E)
6 (A) (B) (C) (D) (E)
7 (A) (B) (C) (D) (E)
8 (A) (B) (C) (D) (E)
9 (A) (B) (C) (D) (E)
10 (A) (B) (C) (D) (E)
11 (A) (B) (C) (D) (E)
12 (A) (B) (C) (D) (E)
13 (A) (B) (C) (D) (E)
14 (A) (B) (C) (D) (E)
15 (A) (B) (C) (D) (E)
16 (A) (B) (C) (D) (E)
17 (A) (B) (C) (D) (E)
18 (A) (B) (C) (D) (E)
19 (A) (B) (C) (D) (E)
20 (A) (B) (C) (D) (E)
21 (A) (B) (C) (D) (E)
22 (A) (B) (C) (D) (E)
23 (A) (B) (C) (D) (E)
24 (A) (B) (C) (D) (E)
25 (A) (B) (C) (D) (E)
26 (A) (B) (C) (D) (E)
27 (A) (B) (C) (D) (E)
28 (A) (B) (C) (D) (E)

Section 3

1 (A) (B) (C) (D) (E)
2 (A) (B) (C) (D) (E)
3 (A) (B) (C) (D) (E)
4 (A) (B) (C) (D) (E)
5 (A) (B) (C) (D) (E)
6 (A) (B) (C) (D) (E)
7 (A) (B) (C) (D) (E)
8 (A) (B) (C) (D) (E)
9 (A) (B) (C) (D) (E)
10 (A) (B) (C) (D) (E)
11 (A) (B) (C) (D) (E)
12 (A) (B) (C) (D) (E)
13 (A) (B) (C) (D) (E)
14 (A) (B) (C) (D) (E)
15 (A) (B) (C) (D) (E)
16 (A) (B) (C) (D) (E)
17 (A) (B) (C) (D) (E)
18 (A) (B) (C) (D) (E)
19 (A) (B) (C) (D) (E)
20 (A) (B) (C) (D) (E)

Section 4

1 (A) (B) (C) (D) (E)
2 (A) (B) (C) (D) (E)
3 (A) (B) (C) (D) (E)
4 (A) (B) (C) (D) (E)
5 (A) (B) (C) (D) (E)
6 (A) (B) (C) (D) (E)
7 (A) (B) (C) (D) (E)
8 (A) (B) (C) (D) (E)
9 (A) (B) (C) (D) (E)
10 (A) (B) (C) (D) (E)
11 (A) (B) (C) (D) (E)
12 (A) (B) (C) (D) (E)
13 (A) (B) (C) (D) (E)
14 (A) (B) (C) (D) (E)
15 (A) (B) (C) (D) (E)
16 (A) (B) (C) (D) (E)
17 (A) (B) (C) (D) (E)
18 (A) (B) (C) (D) (E)
19 (A) (B) (C) (D) (E)
20 (A) (B) (C) (D) (E)
21 (A) (B) (C) (D) (E)
22 (A) (B) (C) (D) (E)
23 (A) (B) (C) (D) (E)
24 (A) (B) (C) (D) (E)
25 (A) (B) (C) (D) (E)
26 (A) (B) (C) (D) (E)
27 (A) (B) (C) (D) (E)
28 (A) (B) (C) (D) (E)
29 (A) (B) (C) (D) (E)
30 (A) (B) (C) (D) (E)
31 (A) (B) (C) (D) (E)
32 (A) (B) (C) (D) (E)
33 (A) (B) (C) (D) (E)
34 (A) (B) (C) (D) (E)
35 (A) (B) (C) (D) (E)

Section 5

1 (A) (B) (C) (D) (E)
2 (A) (B) (C) (D) (E)
3 (A) (B) (C) (D) (E)
4 (A) (B) (C) (D) (E)
5 (A) (B) (C) (D) (E)
6 (A) (B) (C) (D) (E)
7 (A) (B) (C) (D) (E)
8 (A) (B) (C) (D) (E)
9 (A) (B) (C) (D) (E)
10 (A) (B) (C) (D) (E)
11 (A) (B) (C) (D) (E)
12 (A) (B) (C) (D) (E)
13 (A) (B) (C) (D) (E)
14 (A) (B) (C) (D) (E)
15 (A) (B) (C) (D) (E)
16 (A) (B) (C) (D) (E)
17 (A) (B) (C) (D) (E)
18 (A) (B) (C) (D) (E)
19 (A) (B) (C) (D) (E)
20 (A) (B) (C) (D) (E)
21 (A) (B) (C) (D) (E)
22 (A) (B) (C) (D) (E)
23 (A) (B) (C) (D) (E)
24 (A) (B) (C) (D) (E)
25 (A) (B) (C) (D) (E)
26 (A) (B) (C) (D) (E)
27 (A) (B) (C) (D) (E)

Section 6

1 (A) (B) (C) (D) (E)
2 (A) (B) (C) (D) (E)
3 (A) (B) (C) (D) (E)
4 (A) (B) (C) (D) (E)
5 (A) (B) (C) (D) (E)
6 (A) (B) (C) (D) (E)
7 (A) (B) (C) (D) (E)
8 (A) (B) (C) (D) (E)

9.

10.

11.

12.

13.

14.

15.

16.

17.

18.

Section 7

1	Ⓐ	Ⓑ	Ⓒ	Ⓓ	Ⓔ
2	Ⓐ	Ⓑ	Ⓒ	Ⓓ	Ⓔ
3	Ⓐ	Ⓑ	Ⓒ	Ⓓ	Ⓔ
4	Ⓐ	Ⓑ	Ⓒ	Ⓓ	Ⓔ
5	Ⓐ	Ⓑ	Ⓒ	Ⓓ	Ⓔ
6	Ⓐ	Ⓑ	Ⓒ	Ⓓ	Ⓔ
7	Ⓐ	Ⓑ	Ⓒ	Ⓓ	Ⓔ
8	Ⓐ	Ⓑ	Ⓒ	Ⓓ	Ⓔ
9	Ⓐ	Ⓑ	Ⓒ	Ⓓ	Ⓔ
10	Ⓐ	Ⓑ	Ⓒ	Ⓓ	Ⓔ
11	Ⓐ	Ⓑ	Ⓒ	Ⓓ	Ⓔ
12	Ⓐ	Ⓑ	Ⓒ	Ⓓ	Ⓔ
13	Ⓐ	Ⓑ	Ⓒ	Ⓓ	Ⓔ
14	Ⓐ	Ⓑ	Ⓒ	Ⓓ	Ⓔ
15	Ⓐ	Ⓑ	Ⓒ	Ⓓ	Ⓔ

Section 8

1	Ⓐ	Ⓑ	Ⓒ	Ⓓ	Ⓔ
2	Ⓐ	Ⓑ	Ⓒ	Ⓓ	Ⓔ
3	Ⓐ	Ⓑ	Ⓒ	Ⓓ	Ⓔ
4	Ⓐ	Ⓑ	Ⓒ	Ⓓ	Ⓔ
5	Ⓐ	Ⓑ	Ⓒ	Ⓓ	Ⓔ
6	Ⓐ	Ⓑ	Ⓒ	Ⓓ	Ⓔ
7	Ⓐ	Ⓑ	Ⓒ	Ⓓ	Ⓔ
8	Ⓐ	Ⓑ	Ⓒ	Ⓓ	Ⓔ
9	Ⓐ	Ⓑ	Ⓒ	Ⓓ	Ⓔ
10	Ⓐ	Ⓑ	Ⓒ	Ⓓ	Ⓔ
11	Ⓐ	Ⓑ	Ⓒ	Ⓓ	Ⓔ
12	Ⓐ	Ⓑ	Ⓒ	Ⓓ	Ⓔ
13	Ⓐ	Ⓑ	Ⓒ	Ⓓ	Ⓔ
14	Ⓐ	Ⓑ	Ⓒ	Ⓓ	Ⓔ
15	Ⓐ	Ⓑ	Ⓒ	Ⓓ	Ⓔ
16	Ⓐ	Ⓑ	Ⓒ	Ⓓ	Ⓔ

Section 9

1	Ⓐ	Ⓑ	Ⓒ	Ⓓ	Ⓔ
2	Ⓐ	Ⓑ	Ⓒ	Ⓓ	Ⓔ
3	Ⓐ	Ⓑ	Ⓒ	Ⓓ	Ⓔ
4	Ⓐ	Ⓑ	Ⓒ	Ⓓ	Ⓔ
5	Ⓐ	Ⓑ	Ⓒ	Ⓓ	Ⓔ
6	Ⓐ	Ⓑ	Ⓒ	Ⓓ	Ⓔ
7	Ⓐ	Ⓑ	Ⓒ	Ⓓ	Ⓔ
8	Ⓐ	Ⓑ	Ⓒ	Ⓓ	Ⓔ
9	Ⓐ	Ⓑ	Ⓒ	Ⓓ	Ⓔ
10	Ⓐ	Ⓑ	Ⓒ	Ⓓ	Ⓔ
11	Ⓐ	Ⓑ	Ⓒ	Ⓓ	Ⓔ
12	Ⓐ	Ⓑ	Ⓒ	Ⓓ	Ⓔ
13	Ⓐ	Ⓑ	Ⓒ	Ⓓ	Ⓔ
14	Ⓐ	Ⓑ	Ⓒ	Ⓓ	Ⓔ
15	Ⓐ	Ⓑ	Ⓒ	Ⓓ	Ⓔ

CUT HERE

Section 1: Writing—Essay

Time: 25 minutes
1 Essay Question

You have 25 minutes to plan and write an essay on the topic below. DO NOT WRITE ON ANOTHER TOPIC. AN ESSAY ON ANOTHER TOPIC WILL NOT BE SCORED.

The essay is intended to give you the chance to show your writing skills. Be sure to express your ideas on the topic clearly and effectively. The quality of your writing is much more important than the quantity, but to cover the topic adequately you may want to write more than one paragraph. Be specific.

Your essay must be written on two lined pages. Two pages should be enough if you write on every line, avoid wide margins, and keep your handwriting a reasonable size. You will not be given any additional paper. On the actual SAT you must

- Only use a pencil. You will receive a score of zero if you use ink.
- Only write on your answer sheet. You will not receive credit for material written in the test book.
- Only write on the topic presented below. An essay that is off-topic will receive a score of zero.
- Write an essay that reflects original work.

Directions: Read the following paragraph and assignment carefully. Then prepare and write a persuasive essay. Be sure to support your reasons with specific examples that will make your essay more effective.

> Be neither a conformist or a rebel, for they are really the same thing. Find your own path, and stay on it.

Assignment: How accurate do you find this statement? Explain your reasoning using specific examples and reasons from your experience, your reading, or observations.

ON THE ACTUAL EXAM, THE PROCTOR WILL ANNOUNCE WHEN 25 MINUTES HAVE PASSED. IF YOU FINISH YOUR ESSAY BEFORE 25 MINUTES HAVE PASSED, YOU MAY NOT GO ON TO ANY OTHER SECTION OF THE EXAM. THE PROCTOR WILL ANNOUNCE WHEN TO START THE NEXT SECTION.

STOP

Section 2: Critical Reading

Time: 25 minutes
28 Questions

Directions: In this section, choose the best answer for each question and fill in the corresponding circle on the answer sheet.

Each blank in the following sentences indicates that something has been omitted. Consider the lettered words beneath the sentence and choose the word or set of words that best fits the whole sentence.

EXAMPLE:

With a million more people than any other African nation, Nigeria is the most _____ country on the continent.

A. impoverished
B. successful
C. populous
D. developed
E. militant

The correct answer is **C**.

---

1. Loved and hated by thousands, Dr. Joyce Elders may well be the most _____ physician ever to become surgeon general.

   A. controversial
   B. popular
   C. extreme
   D. unconventional
   E. professional

2. Over thousands of years, organisms have _____ many strategies to conserve water.

   A. administered
   B. evolved
   C. organized
   D. transformed
   E. transferred

3. My cat is a creature of contradictions: _____ yet affectionate, _____ yet alert.

   A. aloof . . . dreamy
   B. cruel . . . shrewd
   C. quiet . . . lively
   D. selfish . . . nimble
   E. loving . . . sly

4. _____ for talking too much, the teacher _____ his reputation by keeping the class 30 minutes longer than the scheduled class time.

   A. Famous . . . evinced
   B. Renowned . . . overturned
   C. Notorious . . . solidified
   D. Illustrious . . . rebutted
   E. Eminent . . . established

GO ON TO THE NEXT PAGE

5. If our senator runs for reelection in the U.S. Senate race next year, she will have the money-raising advantage of the _____.

   A. veteran
   B. favorite
   C. underdog
   D. incumbent
   E. candidate

6. Using his own home as _____, Jose obtained a private loan that enabled him to _____ his financial obligations to the other partners and emerge free of debt.

   A. pledge . . . increase
   B. surety . . . augment
   C. collateral . . . discharge
   D. profit . . . eliminate
   E. deposit . . . endorse

7. The absurdist as opposed to the heroic treatment of war reached maturity in *Catch-22*, and the Iraq War made this approach, which seemed so _____ and shocking, the only way to write about that conflict.

   A. banal
   B. radical
   C. plausible
   D. disjointed
   E. familiar

8. Because the issue is so insignificant, it was surprising that the disagreement among city council members was so _____.

   A. tepid
   B. slovenly
   C. trivial
   D. acrimonious
   E. genial

9. The musicians in the band were young and avant-garde, but the lead singer crooned _____ ballads.

   A. atonal
   B. unique
   C. familiar
   D. jarring
   E. ludicrous

10. Hoping to escape detection, Cara _____ placed an ace in her sleeve while John shuffled the cards.

    A. brazenly
    B. overtly
    C. furtively
    D. hopefully
    E. eagerly

GO ON TO THE NEXT PAGE

Directions: Questions follow each of the passages below. Answer the questions using only the stated or implied information in each passage and in its introduction, if any.

Questions 11–12 are based on the following passage.

The doctrine of association has been the basis for explaining how one idea leads to another. Aristotle provided the basic law: association by contiguity. Seeing a shotgun may remind you of
(5) a murder, or it may remind you of a hunting experience in Wyoming, depending on your history. When you hear the word "table" you think of chair (or bench or wood or something else in your history), carrots make you think of
(10) rabbits, and so on. In each case, you experienced the two items contiguously in the same place or at the same time, or both, and they became linked in your mind. In psychology, word association tests are based on contiguity, the idea
(15) being that your response to a particular word is based on your personal history.

11. The author of the paragraph would agree with which of the following statements?

   A. No one thing is necessarily associated with any other particular thing.

   B. Aristotle posited associations that have become part of the modern experience.

   C. Some associations are fixed and unchangeable.

   D. Culture determines what associations a person makes.

   E. Word association is a poor test because people's associations vary so much.

12. Which of the following examples most strengthens the main point of the paragraph?

   A. Some people are able to experience more than two items contiguously.

   B. The smell of coffee makes everyone think of breakfast.

   C. Aristotle's writing is full of unexplained associations.

   D. People who make uncommon associations are often mentally disturbed, whereas people who make overly predictable associations lack creativity.

   E. Some Londoners who endured German bombings in World War II are still frightened by loud noises.

Questions 13–14 are based on the following passage.

Like many birds, the monarch butterfly is migratory. Each year, more than 100 million of the insects fly from their summer homes in the north to areas in the south. Unlike migratory
(5) animals who learn their routes from their parents or other members of the species, the life span of monarchs is 90 days or less; an older generation cannot instruct a younger one. Not one of the insects that flew north in the spring is alive to fly
(10) south in the fall. Insect ecologists have recently established that monarchs use the position of the sun to determine their direction. It may also be that the butterflies can sense the force lines of the earth's magnetic field to use as a navigational
(15) aid, or that they find directional clues in the changing length of the days.

13. According to the information in the passage, which of the following do butterflies use to help them find their way when they migrate?

   A. the prevailing winds

   B. one generation's teaching the next

   C. the position of the sun

   D. force lines of the earth's magnetic field

   E. the changing length of days and nights

14. Of the following general statements, which is best supported by the passage?

   A. Scientists have been unable to explain completely how monarch butterflies migrate successfully.

   B. Butterflies and other insects would be unable to navigate on cloudy days.

   C. Smaller animals like insects depend more on instincts than larger animals.

   D. Scientists know more about larger land and sea animals than they do about insects like the monarch butterfly.

   E. Scientists will never be able to explain how butterflies can find their way over long distances.

GO ON TO THE NEXT PAGE

Questions 15–20 are based on the following passage.

The following passage is from a book about Paul Gauguin, the late nineteenth-century artist who left France to live and paint on the Pacific island of Tahiti.

Gauguin decided to settle in Mataiea, some forty-five kilometers from Papeete, probably on the advice of a Tahitian chief whom he had befriended. There he rented a native-style oval
(5) bamboo hut, roofed with pandanu leaves. Once settled, he was in a position to begin work in earnest and to tackle serious figure studies. It was probably soon after this that he painted *Vahine no te tiare*, his first portrait of a Tahitian model.
(10) By the late summer of 1892 the completed canvas was back in Paris, hanging in the Goupil gallery. From the many subsequent references to this image in his correspondence, it is clear that Gauguin set considerable store by his
(15) "Tahitienne" and, by sending her on ahead to Paris, wanted her to serve as an ambassadress for the further images of Tahitian women he would be bringing back with him on his return. He pressed his male friends for their reactions to the
(20) girl, rather than to the picture, anxious to know whether they, like him, would be responsive to the beauty of her face: "And her forehead," he later wrote, "with the majesty of upsweeping lines, reminded me of that saying of Poe's, 'There
(25) is no perfect beauty without a certain singularity in the proportions.'" No one, it seems, was quite attuned to his emotional perception: while Aurier was enthusiastic, excited by the picture's rarity value, Schuffenecker was somewhat taken aback
(30) by the painting's lack of Symbolist character. Indeed, apart from the imaginary floral background which harked back to Gauguin's 1888 *Self-Portrait*, the image is a relatively straightforward one. Recent anthropological
(35) work, backed by the use of photography, had scientifically characterized the physical distinctions between the different races, distinctions that in the past had been imperfectly understood. Generally speaking, artists before
(40) Gauguin's time had represented Tahitians as idealized types, adjusting their features and proportions to accord with European taste. This meant that hitherto the Tahitian in Western art could scarcely be distinguished from his African
(45) or Asian counterpart.

Unfortunately, Charles Giraud's paintings have disappeared, so we cannot compare them with Gauguin's, but this first image by Gauguin suggests a desire to portray the Tahitian
(50) physiognomy naturalistically, without the blinkers of preconceived rules of beauty laid down by a classical culture. Naturalism as an artistic creed, though, was anathema to Gauguin; it made the artist a lackey of science and knowledge rather
(55) than a god-like creator. He wanted to go beyond empirical observation of this kind, to find a way of painting Tahiti that would accord with his Symbolist aspirations, that would embody the feelings he had about the place and the poetic
(60) image he carried with him of the island's mysterious past.

15. In line 13, the word "correspondence" means

A. correlation.
B. agreement.
C. conformity.
D. similarity.
E. letters.

16. Gauguin found the faces of Tahitian women beautiful because of their

A. elegant coloration.
B. unusual proportions.
C. refusal to wear makeup.
D. dark hair covering the forehead.
E. openness and innocence.

17. The passage suggests that a painter depicting a Tahitian in a period sometime before Gauguin would probably

A. rely on photographs for models.
B. make an image that was not in accord with European ideals of female beauty.
C. paint a picture that uses a symbolic landscape as background.
D. fail to differentiate a Tahitian from the inhabitants of Asian countries.
E. paint only models who were fully clothed in Western-style costume.

GO ON TO THE NEXT PAGE

18. It can be inferred that the author would like to see the lost paintings of Charles Giraud in order to

  A. determine whether they presented the Tahitians realistically.

  B. determine whether they were better paintings than Gauguin's.

  C. determine whether they deserve their high reputation.

  D. compare the symbolism of these paintings with that of Gauguin's.

  E. discover what subjects Giraud chose to paint.

19. Of the following phrases, which does the author use to refer to the aspect of Gauguin's art that attempts to depict the real world accurately?

  I. "the image is a relatively straightforward one" (lines 33–34)

  II. "desire to portray the Tahitian physiognomy naturalistically" (lines 49–50)

  III. "a way of painting Tahiti that would accord with his Symbolist aspirations" (lines 56–58)

  A. II only
  B. III only
  C. I and II only
  D. I and III only
  E. I, II and III

20. The passage suggests that an important problem Gauguin would have to deal with in his paintings of Tahiti was how to

  A. reconcile his Naturalistic and Symbolistic impulses.

  B. make Europeans understand the beauty of Tahiti.

  C. find the necessary supplies in a remote location.

  D. earn enough money to support himself by selling his paintings in Paris.

  E. make artistic use of the new advances in photography.

Questions 21–28 are based on the following passage.

Global warming is at the forefront of international environmental research and debate. As the warming continues, many scientists place the blame on the buildup of greenhouse gases (5) in the Earth's atmosphere caused by the contributions of humankind. Jim Hansen, head of the NASA Goddard Institute for Space Studies and an environmental activist, argues that the International Panel on Climate Change's (10) (IPCC's) conservative tendencies grossly underestimate the risk posed by rising sea-levels, and that the rise makes vulnerable many low-lying regions, such as those in the southeastern United States, most notably those in Louisiana, (15) Mississippi, and the southernmost part of Florida. Unconvinced skeptics, however, argue that the IPCC overstates the likelihood of global warming and that there is a need for a secure consensus among scientific and government (20) representatives before major policy shifts and billions of taxpayer dollars are appropriated to address the problem. Skeptics doubt that the warming will be great enough to produce a serious threat and fear that measures to reduce (25) the emissions would throw a wrench into the gears that drive the United States' economy.

The stakes in this debate are extremely high, for it pits society's short-term well-being against the future of all the planet's inhabitants. Our (30) past transgressions have altered major portions of the earth's surface, but the effects of our past transgressions have been limited and/or grossly misunderstood. Now we can foresee the possibility that to satisfy the energy needs of an (35) expanding human population, we will rapidly change the climate of the entire planet, with consequences for even the most remote and unspoiled regions of the globe.

The notion that certain gases could warm the (40) planet is not new. In 1896 Svante Arrhenius, a Swedish chemist, resolved the longstanding question of how the earth's atmosphere could maintain the planet's relatively warm temperature when the oxygen and nitrogen that make up 99 (45) percent of the atmosphere do not absorb any of

GO ON TO THE NEXT PAGE

the heat escaping as infrared radiation from the earth's surface into space. He discovered that even the small amounts of carbon dioxide in the atmosphere could absorb large amounts of heat.
(50) Furthermore, he reasoned that the burning of coal, oil, and natural gas could eventually release enough carbon dioxide to warm the earth. Hansen and most other climatologists agree that enough greenhouse gases have accumulated in
(55) the atmosphere to make Arrhenius's prediction come true. Burning fossil fuels is not the only problem; a fifth of global emissions of carbon dioxide now come from clearing and burning forests. Scientists are also tracking a host of
(60) other greenhouse gases that emanate from a variety of human activities; the warming effect of methane, chlorofluorocarbons, and nitrous oxide combined equals that of carbon dioxide.

Although the current warming from these
(65) gases may be difficult to detect against the background noise of natural climate variation, most climatologists are certain that as the gases continue to accumulate, increases in the earth's temperature will become evident even to skeptics.
(70) Those with concerns about global warming point to the 2007 IPCC report that finds it is "unequivocal" that Earth's climate is warming, and that it is very likely that "emissions of heat-trapping gases from human activities have caused
(75) most of the observed increase in globally averaged temperatures since the mid-20th century."

S. Fred Singer, author of *Climate Change Reconsidered* (2009), is one of many notable scientists who state there is no proof that the
(80) current warming is caused by the rise of greenhouse gases from human activity and that temperature trends were heading downwards from natural variations, even as greenhouse gases like CO_2 were increasing in the atmosphere.
(85) If the reality of global warming were put on trial, each side would have trouble making its case. Jim Hansen's side could not prove beyond a reasonable doubt that carbon dioxide and the other greenhouse gases have warmed the planet.
(90) But neither could skeptics prove beyond a reasonable doubt that the warming expected from greenhouse gases has not occurred.

21. The purpose of the first paragraph (lines 1–26) of the passage is to

A. argue for the reduction of greenhouse gases in the atmosphere.
B. defend on economic grounds the reduction of greenhouse gases.
C. present two opposing positions on the subject of the earth's rising temperature.
D. lessen the concern of the public about the alleged buildup of greenhouse gases.
E. introduce the two most important spokesmen for and against ecological reforms.

22. In the second paragraph in line 28, the word "pits" means

A. removes the core of.
B. sets in competition.
C. depresses.
D. marks with small scars.
E. hardens.

23. From the information in the third paragraph of the passage, you can infer that a planet

A. whose atmosphere was made up entirely of oxygen would be warmer than a planet equally distant from the sun with an atmosphere made up entirely of nitrogen.
B. whose atmosphere was made up entirely of nitrogen would be warmer than a planet equally distant from the sun with an atmosphere made up entirely of oxygen.
C. with a larger amount of carbon dioxide in its atmosphere, other factors being equal, will be warmer than a planet with less carbon dioxide.
D. with a small amount of carbon dioxide in its atmosphere cannot increase this amount.
E. with little infrared radiation escaping from its surface is likely to be extremely cold.

GO ON TO THE NEXT PAGE

24. The passage implies that a greenhouse gas is one that

   I.   forms a large part of the earth's atmosphere.
   II. absorbs heat escaping from the earth's surface.
   III. can be formed by the clearing and burning of forests.

   A. III only
   B. I and II only
   C. I and III only
   D. II and III only
   E. I, II, and III

25. From the passage, it can be inferred that all the following are greenhouse gases EXCEPT

   A. nitrogen.
   B. carbon dioxide.
   C. methane.
   D. chlorofluorocarbons.
   E. nitrous oxide.

26. Which of the following statements, if true, would call into question the argument of the Intergovernmental Plan on Climate Change (IPCC) report?

   A. Mounting evidence suggests that Earth's temperature trends are naturally occurring earth-based and atmospheric variations.
   B. Sea level rise as a consequence of global warming is a growing threat that cannot be ignored.
   C. Most climatologists agree that heat-trapping gases in the atmosphere can trigger the kinds of changes Arrhenius predicted.
   D. Compared to potential benefits, the costs of preventing further global warming should not be regarded as prohibitive.
   E. The temperature of the earth is found to be affected by the presence of carbon dioxide, methane, chlorofluorocarbons, and nitrous oxide in the earth's atmosphere.

27. The phrase "emanate from" in line 60 most nearly means

   A. are opposed by
   B. are illustrated by
   C. are leaked by
   D. are emitted by
   E. are made significant by

28. With which of the following conclusions would the author most likely agree?

   A. Fluctuations in the earth's climate that cause periods of cooling prove that human activity is not a significant factor in the earth's temperature.
   B. Deforestation and the burning of fossil fuels have not been proven to affect levels of gases in the earth's atmosphere.
   C. Because of contradictory evidence, no conclusions about global warming can be drawn at this time.
   D. Fiscal conservatism alone motivates IPCC critics to deny the existence of global warming.
   E. Global warming is a reality even if scientists cannot yet determine the relative impacts of human and natural causes.

IF YOU FINISH BEFORE TIME IS CALLED, CHECK YOUR WORK ON THIS SECTION ONLY. DO NOT WORK ON ANY OTHER SECTION IN THE TEST.

Section 3: Mathematics

Time: 25 minutes

20 Questions

Directions: Solve each problem in this section by using the information given and your own mathematical calculations, insights, and problem-solving skills. Then select the one correct answer of the five choices given and mark the corresponding circle on your answer sheet. Use the available space on the page for your scratch work.

For each question, indicate the best answer, using the following notes.

1. All numerical values used are real numbers.

2. Calculators may be used.

3. Some problems may be accompanied by figures or diagrams. These figures are drawn as accurately as possible EXCEPT when it is stated in a specific problem that a figure is not drawn to scale. The figures and diagrams are meant to provide information useful in solving the problem or problems. Unless otherwise stated, all figures and diagrams lie on a plane.

Data that Can Be Used for Reference

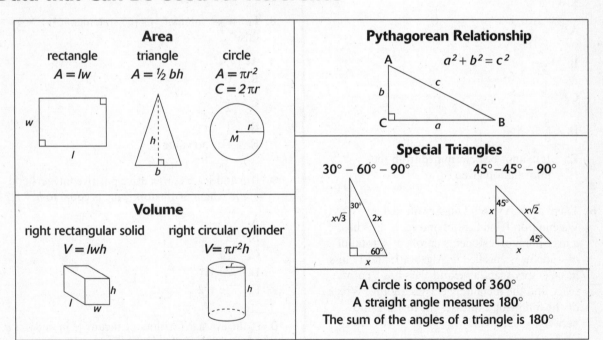

1. The first 4 terms of a sequence are 3, 7, 19, and 55. Each term after the first is obtained by multiplying the preceding term by a and then subtracting b. What is the value of b?

   A. 1
   B. 2
   C. 3
   D. 4
   E. 5

2. If $5y - 12 = 7y + 12$, what is the value of y?

   A. −12
   B. −1
   C. 0
   D. 1
   E. 12

GO ON TO THE NEXT PAGE

3. For which of the following functions is
   $h(5) < h(-5)$?

   A. $h(x) = -5$
   B. $h(x) = -5x^2$
   C. $h(x) = 5 - x^2$
   D. $h(x) = 5 - x^3$
   E. $h(x) = x^3 + 5$

4. How many different shirt and tie combinations
   are possible with 3 different colors of shirts and
   5 different colors of ties?

   A. 8
   B. 9
   C. 15
   D. 25
   E. 35

5. If $12y = 7x$ and $20z = 7x$, what is the ratio of
   z to y?

   A. $\dfrac{49}{240}$

   B. $\dfrac{7}{32}$

   C. $\dfrac{3}{5}$

   D. $\dfrac{5}{3}$

   E. It cannot be determined from the
      information given.

6. There are x Algebra I classes offered at
   Washington High School and each class has
   a maximum of s students enrolled. A total of
   m students is enrolled in Algebra I, and 1 class
   has 4 empty seats, a second class has 3 empty
   seats, and the remaining classes are full. Which
   of the following expresses the relationship
   between x, s, and m?

   A. $m = x \times s + 7$
   B. $m = x \times s - 7$
   C. $x + s + 7$
   D. $x + s - 7$
   E. $s = m \times x + 7$

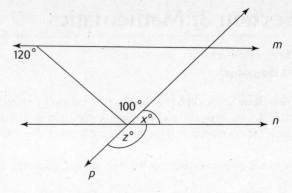

7. In the figure above, line m is parallel to line n.
   What is the value of z?

   A. 160
   B. 150
   C. 140
   D. 120
   E. 100

8. For what value of y is the statement $(4y)^2 > 4y^2$
   false?

   A. -4
   B. 0
   C. $\dfrac{1}{4}$
   D. 1
   E. For no value of y

9. If a and b are consecutive positive integers and
   $b > a$, which of the following is equal to $b^2 - a^2$?

   A. 1
   B. a
   C. $2a$
   D. $2a + 1$
   E. $2a + 2$

10. If the average (arithmetic mean) of m and n is a,
    which of the following is the average of m, n,
    and p?

    A. $\dfrac{a + p}{3}$

    B. $\dfrac{a + p}{2}$

    C. $\dfrac{2a + p}{2}$

    D. $\dfrac{2(a + p)}{3}$

    E. $\dfrac{2a + p}{3}$

GO ON TO THE NEXT PAGE

11. When 19 is divided by a positive integer x, the remainder is 1. For how many different values of x is this true?

   A. 1
   B. 2
   C. 3
   D. 4
   E. 5

12. A set of numbers consists of x even numbers and z odd numbers. If a number is chosen at random from the set, the probability that the number is odd is $\frac{5}{12}$. What is the value of $\frac{x}{z}$?

   A. $\frac{17}{5}$

   B. $\frac{17}{12}$

   C. $\frac{7}{5}$

   D. $\frac{5}{7}$

   E. $\frac{5}{17}$

13. For how many ordered pairs of positive integers (x, y) is $5x + 2y < 10$?

   A. 2
   B. 3
   C. 4
   D. 5
   E. 6

14. If $x = \frac{1}{3}$, what is the value of $\frac{1}{x-1} + \frac{1}{x}$?

   A. $\frac{-3}{2}$

   B. $-\frac{1}{3}$

   C. 0

   D. $\frac{1}{3}$

   E. $\frac{3}{2}$

15. X, Y, and Z are points on a line in that order. If $XY = 65$ and XZ is 30 more than XY, what does YZ equal?

   A. 30
   B. 35
   C. 55
   D. 65
   E. 95

16. If $a + 5 = x$, then $5a + 11 =$

   A. $x - 14$
   B. $x + 16$
   C. $5x + 6$
   D. $5x - 14$
   E. $5x + 36$

17. How old will a person be 3 years from now if y years ago the person was x years old?

   A. $x - y - 3$
   B. $x + y - 3$
   C. $x - y + 3$
   D. $x + y + 3$
   E. $y - x + 3$

18. If w, x, y, and z are 4 nonzero numbers, then all of the following proportions are equivalent EXCEPT

   A. $\frac{w}{x} = \frac{y}{z}$

   B. $\frac{w}{z} = \frac{y}{x}$

   C. $\frac{w}{y} = \frac{x}{z}$

   D. $\frac{x}{w} = \frac{z}{y}$

   E. $\frac{xy}{wz} = \frac{1}{1}$

x	−1	0	2	5
$h(x)$	0	−1	3	24

19. The table above gives values of the quadratic function h for selected values of x. Which of the following defines h?

   A. $h(x) = x^2 + 1$
   B. $h(x) = x^2 - 1$
   C. $h(x) = 2x^2 - 2$
   D. $h(x) = 2x^2 - 1$
   E. $h(x) = 3x^2 - 3$

GO ON TO THE NEXT PAGE

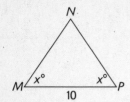 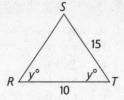

20. If $x = 60$ in $\triangle MNP$ above, how much greater is the perimeter of $\triangle RST$ than the perimeter of $\triangle MNP$?

    A. The perimeters are equal.

    B. 5

    C. 10

    D. 15

    E. It cannot be determined from the information given.

IF YOU FINISH BEFORE TIME IS CALLED, CHECK YOUR WORK ON THIS SECTION ONLY. DO NOT WORK ON ANY OTHER SECTION IN THE TEST.

Section 4: Writing—Multiple Choice

Time: 25 Minutes

35 Questions

Directions: In this section, choose the best answer for each question and fill in the corresponding circle on the answer sheet.

The following questions test correctness and effective expression. In selecting the answer, pay attention to grammar, diction, sentence structure, and punctuation. In the following questions, part or all of each sentence is underlined. Answer Choice A repeats the underlined portion of the original sentence, while the next four choices offer alternatives. Choose the answer that best expresses the meaning of the original sentence and at the same time is grammatically correct and stylistically superior. The correct choice should be clear, unambiguous, and concise.

EXAMPLE:

The forecaster predicted <u>rain and the sky was clear</u>.

   A.   rain and the sky was clear
   B.   rain but the sky was clear
   C.   rain the sky was clear
   D.   rain, but the sky was clear
   E.   rain being as the sky was clear

The correct answer is **D.**

1. Some players have no trouble seeing the weaknesses <u>in other people's game and they</u> are quite unable to see faults of their own.

   A.   in other people's game and they
   B.   in other games and they
   C.   in other players' games, and they
   D.   in other people's game, but they
   E.   in other games, but they

2. The conservative Tea Party Republicans are now powerful enough to worry the more moderate governing Republicans and liberal Democrats, <u>and they may win</u> 50 seats in the next election.

   A.   and they may win
   B.   and they might win
   C.   and the Tea Party candidates may win
   D.   and the party
   E.   winning

3. The Medical Board is supposed to protect consumers from <u>incompetent, grossly negligent, unlicensed, and unethical practitioners.</u>

   A.   incompetent, grossly negligent, unlicensed, and unethical practitioners.
   B.   incompetent, grossly negligent practitioners who are unlicensed or unethical.
   C.   the incompetent and grossly negligent who practice without ethics or a license.
   D.   incompetent practitioners, gross and negligent, unlicensed and unethical.
   E.   those practitioners who are incompetent, grossly negligent, unlicensed, and unethical.

4. The wall is a continually evolving work of <u>art, it is a</u> forum for messages against violence, war, and cruelty.

   A.   art, it is a
   B.   art; it is a
   C.   art, in that it is a
   D.   art it is a
   E.   art a forum

GO ON TO THE NEXT PAGE

5. Many years ago, Australia had a strong tradition of private <u>medical care, but even conservatives now accepting</u> the national health care plan.

   A. medical care, but even conservatives now accepting

   B. medical care; but even conservatives now accepting

   C. medical care, but now with even conservatives accepting

   D. medical care, conservatives now accepting

   E. medical care, but now even conservatives accept

6. In the play, <u>great care is given to present the workers' oppression, and the author is uninterested</u> in the psychology of his characters.

   A. great care is given to present the workers' oppression, and the author is uninterested

   B. great care is given to present the workers' oppression, but the author is uninterested

   C. great care is given to the presentation of the workers' oppression, but the author is uninterested

   D. the author takes great care to present the workers' oppression, but is uninterested

   E. the author is very careful to present the workers' oppression, and he is uninterested

7. <u>Twenty-five thousand troops went to Somalia, and they failed to disarm the warring clans and failed</u> to create a secure environment.

   A. Twenty-five thousand troops went to Somalia, and they failed to disarm the warring clans and failed

   B. Twenty-five thousand troops went to Somalia, but they failed to disarm the warring clans and so they failed

   C. Twenty-five thousand troops went to Somalia, but they failed to disarm the warring clans and

   D. Twenty-five thousand troops went to Somalia, failing to disarm the warring clans and failing

   E. There were twenty-five thousand troops who went to Somalia, and they failed to disarm the warring clans, also failing

GO ON TO THE NEXT PAGE

Directions: The following sentences may contain one error of grammar, usage, diction, or idiom. No sentence contains more than one error, and some have no error. If there is an error, it will be underlined and have a letter beneath it. If there is an error, choose the one underlined part that must be changed to correct the sentence. If there is no error, choose E. Sections of the sentence that are not underlined cannot be changed. In selecting your answer, observe the requirements of standard written English.

EXAMPLE:

The film <u>tell the story</u> of a army captain and <u>his wife</u> who <u>try to</u> <u>rebuild their lives</u> after the Iraq War.
     A   B   C   D

<u>No error</u>
  E

The correct answer is **A.**

---

8. The owners hired <u>my husband and I</u> to <u>manage</u>
               A   B

   the inn because <u>we had</u> more experience
               C

   <u>than the other applicants</u>. <u>No error</u>
        D   E

9. Pistachios <u>imported from Asia</u> <u>cost more than</u>
                A   B

   <u>the orchards of</u> California but <u>they are</u> larger
      C   D

   and have more flavor. <u>No error</u>
                 E

10. <u>There are</u> in the House and Senate general
    A

   agreement <u>about the energy bill</u>, but <u>they are</u>
             B   C

   far <u>from agreeing about</u> the budget. <u>No error</u>
        D   E

11. Early tomorrow morning, <u>weather permitting</u>,
                           A

   he <u>departed on</u> an <u>around-the-state run</u> to
        B   C

   <u>raise money</u> for the disabled. <u>No error</u>
     D   E

12. When they <u>had completed</u> the layout of the
          A

   <u>paper's front page</u>, the editors <u>considered the</u>
      B   C

   problems of the <u>sports page</u>. <u>No error</u>
            D   E

13. The volleyball players <u>which arrived</u> for the
                   A

   team picture <u>in the uniforms</u> that they <u>had</u>
            B

   <u>worn to practice</u> were <u>irritable and tired</u>.
      C   D

   <u>No error</u>
    E

14. The soil conditions <u>beneath structures</u> may
               A

   cause <u>more worse</u> damage <u>in an earthquake</u>
         B   C

   than the temblor <u>itself.</u> <u>No error</u>
            D   E

15. The debate <u>appeared to be stalemated</u>, since
           A

   <u>there was</u> no possibility of the conservatives'
    B

   <u>conceding with</u> their opponents' offer
     C

   to compromise. <u>No error</u>
     D   E

16. The region is <u>so dry</u> that <u>there are</u> <u>hardly any</u>
           A   B   C

   animals, and <u>scarcely no</u> plant life in the dunes.
             D

   <u>No error</u>
    E

17. Either <u>the allied bombing</u> or the subsequent
         A

   Iraqi attempt <u>to quell</u> the Shiite uprising
           B

   <u>are responsible for</u> the <u>damage to the shrines</u>.
     C   D

   <u>No error</u>
    E

18. Japanese defense policy <u>was changed</u>
                     A

   <u>completely</u> when the Socialist Party <u>scrapped</u>
                                  B

   <u>its age-old</u> insistence <u>to dismantle</u> the armed
      C   D

   forces. <u>No error</u>
       E

GO ON TO THE NEXT PAGE

19. The election of a <u>separatist-dominated</u>
                        A
    Parliament <u>has alarmed</u> those <u>who will believe</u>
                  B   C
    Quebec <u>must not secede</u> from Canada.
                  D
    <u>No error</u>
       E

20. The engineers <u>have designed</u> an offshore
                     A
    drilling platform <u>strong enough</u> <u>to withstand</u>
                         B   C
    <u>not only</u> Atlantic storms <u>but also the</u>
       D   D
    occasional iceberg. <u>No error</u>
                           E

21. In Britain, <u>a nationwide</u> business <u>in buying</u>
                   A   B
    <u>and selling</u> special license plates <u>have</u>
       C   C
    <u>developed</u>, and <u>prices rise</u> each year. <u>No error</u>
       D   D   E

22. If <u>we plan carefully</u> and waste no time <u>on</u>
          A   A
    <u>irrelevant topics</u>, you should <u>be able</u> to <u>finish</u>
       B   C   D
    <u>the essay</u> in 20 minutes. <u>No error</u>
       E   E

23. <u>Desperately trying</u> <u>to lead</u> the cat away from
       A   B
    the nest, the bird <u>had flew</u> within inches of <u>its</u>
                          C   D
    claw. <u>No error</u>
             E

24. The citizens of Berlin <u>bid</u> a <u>fondly good-bye</u> to
                             A   B
    the American troops <u>who had occupied</u> much
                           C
    of the city <u>since WWII ended</u>. <u>No error</u>
                   D   E

25. When the new ambassador <u>first arrived</u> <u>in the</u>
                              A   B
    <u>capital</u>, though <u>late in May</u>, <u>they found</u> that the
       B   C   D
    larger lakes were still frozen. <u>No error</u>
                                       E

26. <u>Encouraged by</u> the success of <u>its</u> weekly
       A   B
    Spanish-language programs, MTV <u>will launch</u>
                                      C
    a <u>24-hour</u> Spanish language cable network.
        D
    <u>No error</u>
       E

Directions: The following passages are early drafts of student essays. Some parts of them need to be revised.

Read the selections carefully and answer the questions that follow. There will be questions about sentence structure, diction, and usage in individual sentences or parts of sentences. Other questions will deal with the whole essay or paragraphs in it and ask you to decide about organization, development, and appropriate language. Choose the answer that follows the requirements of standard written English, and most effectively expresses the intended meanings.

Questions 27–31 are based on the following passage.

(1)Attachment and the natural ability to separate from one another are important determinants of healthy interpersonal relationships. (2) As human beings move from one stage of life to another, the ability to attach and separate in relationships plays a vital role in how an individual views and relates to the world.

(3) Attachment is an instinctual force that drives behaviors and regulates emotions. (4) Learning attachment and a natural separation begins with early bonding between infants and their primary caregivers. (5) Some infants have a stronger need for attachment and others have a stronger need for independence, but beginning in infancy, individuals struggle with separation anxiety when their need for attachment outweighs their need for separation. (6) In their earliest stages of life, infants forge an emotional connection through attachment with their primary caregivers that anchors their personality and affects how they relate to others and their surrounding world.

(7) A mature adult experiences separation in many areas of life, but without a secure early attachment, what seems like a normal separation or loss can awaken irrational emotions. (8) For example, separation from a job, school, or marriage partner may be devastating if unplanned or unwanted. (9) The loss and change may bring about a certain amount of anxiety, anger, and an inability to regulate tension and stress. (10) Although feelings may appear irrational, they are real and have a basis in personal history.

(11) We never lose the need to be connected to another. (12) The need for attachment is often the primary motivator that can inhibit or help interpersonal relationships. (13) Recognizing the link between the templates of our early infant attachment to our primary caretakers can bring about an awareness that helps us to freely experience positive health in relationships.

27. Which of the following is the best revision of the underlined portions of sentences 3 and 4 (reproduced below)?

Attachment is an instinctual force that drives behaviors and regulates emotions. Learning attachment and a natural separation begins with early bonding between infants and their primary caregivers.

A. is both an instinctual and learned force that drives behaviors and regulates emotions. Learning attachment and separation begins with early bonding between infants and their primary caretakers.

B. is a force of behavior and emotional regulation that is learned early in life.

C. is to behavior and emotions in the same way as separation is related to behavior and emotions.

D. is an instinctual force learned through early bonding between infants and adults.

E. and natural separation are learned in infancy.

28. Which of the following is the best revision for sentence 13 (reproduced below)?

Recognizing the link between the templates of our early infant attachment to our primary caretakers can bring about an awareness that helps us to freely experience positive health in relationships.

A. Recognizing templates in our attachment in early infancy can help us have healthy relationships.

B. Awareness of the link between the template of our attachment to primary caregivers in infancy and our need for attachment as adults can help us have positive and healthy relationships.

C. Being aware of links between early infant attachment templates and primary caretakers gives us freedom to experience positive health in our relationships.

D. Positive health in relationships requires awareness of our attachment templates to primary caretakers in infancy.

E. Recognition of links between templates, starting with our attachment to our primary caretakers in infancy, can result in an awareness that helps us experience positive relationships.

29. Which of the following statements best describes the writer's thesis statement (theme or central message) for the whole passage?

A. We never lose the need to be connected to another.

B. Attachment is an instinctual force that drives behaviors and regulates emotions.

C. Attachment and the natural ability to separate from one another are important determinants of healthy interpersonal relationships.

D. Although feelings may appear irrational, they are real and have a basis in personal history.

E. All infants struggle with separation anxiety when their need for attachment outweighs their need for separation.

30. Which of the sentences from the passage would best support the following statement?

Children typically experience separation anxiety at the start and end of the school year, for example, and at and the start and end of summer camp.

A. sentence 2
B. sentence 12
C. sentence 5
D. sentence 4
E. sentence 7

31. Which of the sentences from the passage would best support the following statement?

For example, insecurely attached infants may be more fearful of others or resistant to change.

A. sentence 2
B. sentence 12
C. sentence 5
D. sentence 4
E. sentence 7

Questions 32–35 are based on the following passage.

(1) Almost every week I am guilty of procrastination. (2) The dictionary definition of "procrastination" is "habitually putting off doing something that should be done." (3) For me, the act of procrastinating is a series of excuses for avoiding assigned tasks. (4) I can't say exactly why I go through the agony of waiting till the very last moment of all to begin my chore. (5) But though I always ask, "Why do you wait so long?" I keep putting things off to the last minute.

(6) The reasons for procrastinating vary and I am not always sure which category of reasons the enterprise falls into. (7) The easiest reason of all to recognize is that of simply trying to avoid an unpleasant chore. (8) It is not surprising that I would want to put off doing something that would cause emotional distress. (9) Another reason for procrastinating is facing a task that seems insurmountable. (10) "It's too much," I tell myself. (11) Sometimes it is the unfamiliarity that causes this behavior. (12) After all, the fear of the unknown requires taking a risk. (13) Taking a risk requires the possibility of failure—could that be the real reason for procrastinating?

GO ON TO THE NEXT PAGE

(14) Whatever the reasons, the result is the same: a sleepless night filled with guilt and anxiety. (15) Guilt and its by-product, anxiety, become the major components of the effects of procrastination. (16) I know that I can avoid all the psychological imbalances associated with procrastination. (17) Logically, I can take out my planning calendar and schedule my time to accommodate any task, any chores, or any assignment. (18) And once again, procrastination overpowers logic and the last minute rush begins.

32. Which of the following is the best version of sentence 6 (reproduced below)?

The reasons for procrastinating vary and I am not always sure which category of reasons the enterprise falls into.

A. Leave it as it is.
B. The reasons for procrastination vary, and into which category of reasons the enterprise falls is not always sure.
C. The reasons for procrastinating are varied and which category fits the enterprise is uncertain.
D. The reasons vary, and I am not always sure why I procrastinate.
E. The categories of reasons for procrastination vary, and which fits an enterprise is not always sure.

33. Sentence 7 (reproduced below) could be made more concise by deleting all of the following words EXCEPT

The easiest reason of all to recognize is that of simply trying to avoid an unpleasant chore.

A. reason
B. of all
C. that of
D. simply
E. to avoid

34. Which of the following best describes the writer's intention in the second paragraph?

A. to suggest reasons that explain behavior
B. to summarize evidence of irrational behavior
C. to give specific details
D. to point to a moral conclusion
E. to evaluate evidence of irrational behavior

35. Which of the following sentences could be eliminated from the third paragraph without seriously affecting its meaning or coherence?

A. sentence 14
B. sentence 15
C. sentence 16
D. sentence 17
E. sentence 18

IF YOU FINISH BEFORE TIME IS CALLED, CHECK YOUR WORK ON THIS SECTION ONLY. DO NOT WORK ON ANY OTHER SECTION IN THE TEST.

STOP

Section 5: Critical Reading

Time: 25 Minutes

27 Questions

Directions: In this section, choose the best answer for each question and fill in the corresponding circle on the answer sheet.

Each blank in the following sentences indicates that something has been omitted. Consider the lettered words beneath the sentence and choose the word or set of words that *best* fits the whole sentence.

EXAMPLE:

With a million more people than any other African nation, Nigeria is the most _____ country on the continent.

- A. impoverished
- B. successful
- C. populous
- D. developed
- E. militant

The correct answer is **C**.

---

1. It is _____ to assume that if aspirin can prevent second heart attacks, it can also _____ an attack in the first place.

   - A. fanciful . . . eliminate
   - B. logical . . . ward off
   - C. sensible . . . encourage
   - D. reasonable . . . foment
   - E. idle . . . defend against

2. Cigars are not a safe _____ to cigarettes because, though cigar smokers do not inhale, they are still _____ higher rates of lung and mouth cancers than nonsmokers.

   - A. answer . . . responsible for
   - B. preference . . . free from
   - C. alternative . . . subject to
   - D. rejoinder . . . involved in
   - E. accent . . . victimized by

3. Evidence supports the fact that many capital punishment cases have failed to _____ crimes, and that far more murders per capita were committed in states or countries with capital punishment than in those without it.

   - A. explain
   - B. augment
   - C. foster
   - D. deter
   - E. exculpate

4. After the smoke and _____ of the city, Mr. Gilmore was glad to return to the _____ air and peace of the mountains.

   - A. hubbub . . . turbid
   - B. grime . . . murky
   - C. tranquility . . . effulgent
   - D. composure . . . brisk
   - E. hustle-bustle . . . exhilarating

GO ON TO THE NEXT PAGE

5. A strike by Ford workers in Mexico poses a(n) _____ for the ruling party, which must choose between alienating its union ally or undermining its fight against inflation.

   A. enigma

   B. dilemma

   C. aberration

   D. opportunity

   E. regret

6. By combining an American cartoon character with Japanese traditions, the popular comic by Stan Sakai presents as a hero a samurai rabbit, a unique _____ of East and West.

   A. fusion

   B. division

   C. aberration

   D. opportunity

   E. regret

7. A _____ that allowed voters to decide on the legality of casino gambling was passed by a(n) _____ 9-to-1 margin.

   A. statute . . . meager

   B. referendum . . . overwhelming

   C. prohibition . . . huge

   D. bill . . . narrow

   E. ban . . . sizable

8. The _____ upon which this fine novel is developed with great _____ and intelligence is that no males live beyond the age of 18.

   A. theory . . . fatuity

   B. plot . . . understanding

   C. idea . . . recalcitrance

   D. premise . . . subtlety

   E. solution . . . cleverness

9. The _____ use of washing machines and automobiles in the Middle Ages is part of the comedy of this high-spirited film.

   A. untimely

   B. anachronistic

   C. unconvincing

   D. archaic

   E. supposed

GO ON TO THE NEXT PAGE

Directions: Questions follow each of the passages below. Using only the stated or implied information in each passage and in its introduction, if any, answer the questions.

Questions 10–11 are based on the following passage.

Latex, the milky-colored extract from the *Hevea brasiliensis* species of tree, is commonly used in the medical appliance and consumables markets. The use of latex-based appliances and
(5) products, especially latex gloves by healthcare and other services-sector workers, has grown substantially since the early 1980s, largely due to concerns about exposure to and infection from blood-borne pathogens.

(10) This explosive growth in the latex-based products market is not, however, a unilateral success for producers, medical service employers, health insurance companies, or patients. Along with the success of latex gloves, a proven
(15) prophylactic against exposure to blood-borne pathogens and other germs and viruses, has come a substantial increase in the symptoms of latex allergy.

Research indicates that 5 to 17 percent of
(20) healthcare workers worldwide report latex-related allergies. Although symptoms are usually mild and not life threatening, the impact on healthcare workers and patients is cause for concern. This concern raises demands for a
(25) market-based latex alternative or a rethinking of current healthcare practices to reduce risk of exposure to both blood-borne pathogens and allergic reactions to latex. Some reports indicate that individuals with latex allergies tend to
(30) change their workplace or leave their profession.

According to some alarmists opposed to latex-based products, high employee turnover will severely undermine the delivery of quality care to patients. They argue further that
(35) continued use of the substance can disrupt local, state, national, and global economies and healthcare delivery systems. The solution, they say, is for the private sector to create safe alternatives, even at the expense of diluting
(40) corporate profits for existing products. Otherwise, corporate greed may pave the way for a regional or even a global healthcare crisis.

10. The author's main purpose in writing this passage is to:

A. Examine the myriad ways latex-based medical products grow the economy.

B. Survey the differences between latex-based and non-latex-based products.

C. Present the main pros and cons of using latex-based medical products.

D. Argue that latex-based medical products are more harmful than helpful.

E. Advocate the continued use of latex-based medical products.

11. Which of the following statements, if true, most seriously weakens the position of the anti-latex alarmists?

A. High turnover rates in the medical and healthcare fields have increased since latex-based allergies have been reported and tracked.

B. In surveys, healthcare workers cited reasons other than their allergies to latex as reasons for leaving their jobs or professions.

C. Latex allergies costs employers billions of dollars in lost productivity, workers compensation, leaves of absence, and illness benefits.

D. Latex-based allergies are projected to increase in direct proportion to the growth of healthcare products markets worldwide.

E. Alternatives to latex-based medical appliances are currently under development, with business and government working collaboratively to maintain prophylactic effectiveness while reducing risk of allergic reactions.

GO ON TO THE NEXT PAGE

Questions 12–15 are based on the following pair of passages.

Passage 1:

The television "tube" hasn't done much for national elections. Political ads are sound bites, and televised debates have become less and less informative. Generally, candidates are elliptical
(5) in expressing their convictions. In the 2004 Bush-Gore debates both candidates were relatively forthright. Both candidates, however, were hesitant to agree to raise taxes in the interest of national defense, something politicians talk
(10) about more frequently in spite of theirs fears that an opponent would focus on the statement in a negative campaign commercial. The amount of time each candidate spends making a point and answering questions has decreased from election
(15) to election. Is this because the audience's attention span is getting shorter or is it because neither candidate wants to be too specific about issues on the chance that someone's feathers might get ruffled?

Passage 2:

Television has become an integral part of the political process in America. In 2008 the audience for the vice-presidential debate between Biden and Palin and the presidential debate between
(5) Obama and McCain brought in a combined audience of more than 100 million viewers. Many people regard television debates as the most effective way we have of choosing a leader, and the popularity of the town-hall style of
(10) television debates may signal Americans' desire to enter the political process and become more active in making their choices. Because of television, candidates are less dependent on party infrastructure to disseminate their messages.
(15) They can appeal to people directly. A good example is the 1992 independent candidacy of Ross Perot. Although losing the election, Perot garnered 19 percent of the popular vote, and for much of this, he had television to thank.

12. According to the author of Passage 1, television debates

   A. have improved since the Bush-Gore debates in 2004.
   B. are of little interest to most Americans.
   C. provide valuable information to the electorate.
   D. encourage the candidates to be forthright in their responses.
   E. give candidates less time to speak than they did in 2004.

13. In Passage 1, the word "elliptical" (line 4) most nearly means

   A. redundant.
   B. sincerely felt.
   C. deliberately obscure.
   D. terse and to the point.
   E. circumspect.

14. According to the author of Passage 2, all of the following are positive results of televised debates EXCEPT

   A. greater voter turnout at the polls.
   B. greater interest in taking an active role in elections.
   C. greater availability of information for voters.
   D. less importance of political party infrastructure.
   E. greater visibility for independent candidates.

15. Which of the following best characterizes the difference between Passage 1 and Passage 2?

   A. Passage 1 is lighthearted and Passage 2 is philosophical.
   B. The two passages are alike in tone but different in point of view.
   C. Passage 1 is colloquial and sarcastic and Passage 2 is straightforward.
   D. While Passage 2 is literary and pompous, Passage 1 is objective and journalistic.
   E. Passage 1 focuses on facts, whereas Passage 2 focuses on ideas.

GO ON TO THE NEXT PAGE

Questions 16–27 are based on the following passage.

Early in the day Dorothea had returned from the infant school which she had set going in the village, and was taking her usual place in the pretty sitting-room which divided the bedrooms
(5) of the sisters, bent on finishing a plan for some buildings (a kind of work which she delighted in), when Celia, who had been watching her with a hesitating desire to propose something, said, "Dorothea dear, if you don't mind—if you are
(10) not very busy—suppose we looked at mamma's jewels today, and divided them? It is exactly six months today since uncle gave them to you, and you have not looked at them yet."

Celia's face had the shadow of a pouting
(15) expression in it, the full presence of the pout being kept back by an habitual awe of Dorothea and principle; two associated facts which might show a mysterious electricity if you touched them incautiously. To her relief, Dorothea's eyes
(20) were full of laughter as she looked up.

"What a wonderful little almanac you are, Celia! Is it six calendar or six lunar months?" "It is the last day of September now, and it was the first of April when uncle gave them to you. You
(25) know, he said that he had forgotten them till then. I believe you have never thought of them since you locked them up in the cabinet here."

"Well, dear, we should never wear them, you know." Dorothea spoke in a full cordial tone,
(30) half caressing, half explanatory. She had her pencil in her hand, and was making tiny side-plans on a margin.

Celia colored, and looked very grave. "I think, dear, we are wanting in respect to mamma's
(35) memory, to put them by and take no notice of them. And," she added, after hesitating a little, with a rising sob of mortification, "necklaces are quite usual now; and Madame Poinçon, who was stricter in some things even than you are, used to
(40) wear ornaments. And Christians generally—surely there are women in heaven now who wore jewels." Celia was conscious of some mental strength when she really applied herself to argument.

"You would like to wear them?" exclaimed
(45) Dorothea, an air of astonished discovery animating her whole person with a dramatic action which she had caught from that very Madame Poinçon who wore the ornaments. "Of course, then, let us have them out. Why did you
(50) not tell me before? But the keys, the keys!" She pressed her hands against the sides of her head and seemed to despair of her memory.

"They are here," said Celia, with whom this explanation had been long meditated and
(55) prearranged.

"Pray open the large drawer of the cabinet and get out the jewel-box." The casket was soon open before them, and the various jewels spread out, making a bright parterre on the table. It was
(60) no great collection, but a few of the ornaments were really of remarkable beauty, the finest that was obvious at first being a necklace of purple amethysts set in exquisite gold-work, and a pearl cross with five brilliants in it. Dorothea
(65) immediately took up the necklace and fastened it round her sister's neck, where it fitted almost as closely as a bracelet; but the circle suited the Henrietta-Maria style of Celia's head and neck, and she could see that it did, in the pier-glass
(70) opposite.

"There, Celia! You can wear that with your Indian muslin. But this cross you must wear with your dark dresses."

Celia was trying not to smile with pleasure.
(75) "O, Dodo, you must keep the cross yourself."

"No, no, dear, no," said Dorothea, putting up her hand with careless deprecation.

"Yes, indeed you must; it would suit you–in your black dress, now," said Celia, insistingly.
(80) "You *might* wear that."

"Not for the world, not for the world. A cross is the last thing I would wear as a trinket." Dorothea shuddered slightly.

"Then you will think it wicked in me to wear
(85) it," said Celia, uneasily.

"No, dear, no," said Dorothea, stroking her sister's cheek. "Souls have complexions too: what will suit one will not suit another."

"But you might like to keep it for mamma's
(90) sake."

"No, I have other things of mamma's—her sandal-wood box, which I am so fond of—plenty of things. In fact, they are all yours, dear. We need discuss them no longer. There—take away
(95) your property."

Celia felt a little hurt. There was a strong assumption of superiority in this Puritanic toleration, hardly less trying to the blond flesh of an unenthusiastic sister than a Puritanic
(100) persecution.

GO ON TO THE NEXT PAGE

16. From the details of the passage, it can be learned or inferred that

    I.   Dorothea and Celia are sisters.
    II. Dorothea and Celia may be orphans.
    III. Dorothea and Celia are temperamentally very alike.

    A. III only
    B. I and II only
    C. I and III only
    D. II and III only
    E. I, II, and III

17. The first paragraph of the passage refers to the "infant school" and "plan for some buildings" to suggest that Dorothea is

    A. prying and interfering.
    B. rich and idle.
    C. self-centered and ambitious.
    D. active and unselfish.
    E. philanthropic and ineffectual.

18. In line 22, Dorothea asks Celia whether it is "six calendar or six lunar months" because she

    A. wants to know exactly how many days have passed.
    B. is good-humoredly teasing Celia.
    C. had hoped to keep the jewels from Celia.
    D. wants to demonstrate the scientific precision of her mind.
    E. has forgotten what the current month is.

19. In line 34, the phrase "wanting in respect" can be best understood to mean

    A. obliged to be more differential.
    B. desirous to esteem.
    C. lewd in regard.
    D. deficient in regard.
    E. eager for consideration.

20. The "argument" to which Celia has "really applied herself" (line 43) is intended to convince Dorothea to

    A. show greater respect for their dead mother.
    B. give all the jewels to her.
    C. give the most valuable of the jewels to her.
    D. agree to sharing and wearing the jewels.
    E. examine the jewels and lock them up again.

21. Although in lines 28–29 Dorothea has said, "we should never wear them, you know," she changes her opinion because she

    A. is moved by Celia's appeal to the memory of their mother.
    B. is convinced by Celia's reference to Madame Poinçon.
    C. realizes that Celia wants to wear the jewels.
    D. sees how becoming the jewels are to Celia.
    E. can appear superior to Celia by refusing to wear them herself.

22. In line 77, the word "deprecation" means

    A. protest.
    B. lessening.
    C. indifference.
    D. removal.
    E. agreement.

23. The word "trying" in line 98 means

    A. irksome.
    B. attempting.
    C. effortful.
    D. experimental.
    E. determining.

24. In lines 97–98, "Puritanic toleration" is a reference to

    A. Celia's awe of Dorothea.
    B. Celia's acceptance of Dorothea's foibles.
    C. Celia's love of jewels and finery.
    D. Dorothea's hypocritical indifference to finery.
    E. Dorothea's self-denial and generosity.

25. In the last sentence of the passage, the word "unenthusiastic" refers to

    A. Dorothea's refusal to wear jewels.
    B. Dorothea giving her permission for Celia to wear jewels.
    C. Celia's attitude toward self-denial.
    D. Celia's attitude toward wearing jewels.
    E. the author's attitude toward Dorothea.

GO ON TO THE NEXT PAGE

26. The inconsistency in Dorothea's reasoning that the passage reveals is her

    A. forgetting about when the jewels were given to her.
    B. losing the keys to the cabinet holding the jewels.
    C. insistence that Christians cannot wear jewels.
    D. wanting Celia to wear jewels but refusing to wear them herself.
    E. deceitful claim that she honors the memory of her mother.

27. The purpose of the passage as a whole is to

    A. reveal the likeness of Celia and Dorothea.
    B. expose the submerged ill feelings between Celia and Dorothea.
    C. reveal the differences in the natures of Celia and Dorothea.
    D. demonstrate the dangers of materialism.
    E. satirize the hypocrisy of the two young women.

IF YOU FINISH BEFORE TIME IS CALLED, CHECK YOUR WORK ON THIS SECTION ONLY. DO NOT WORK ON ANY OTHER SECTION IN THE TEST.

Section 6: Mathematics

Time: 25 minutes

18 Questions

Directions: Solve each problem in this section by using the information given and your own mathematical calculations, insights, and problem-solving skills. Then select the one correct answer of the five choices given and mark the corresponding circle on your answer sheet. Use the available space on the page for your scratch work.

For each question, indicate the best answer, using the following notes.

1. All numerical values used are real numbers.
2. Calculators may be used.
3. Some problems may be accompanied by figures or diagrams. These figures are drawn as accurately as possible EXCEPT when it is stated in a specific problem that a figure is not drawn to scale. The figures and diagrams are meant to provide information useful in solving the problem or problems. Unless otherwise stated, all figures and diagrams lie on a plane.

Data that Can Be Used for Reference

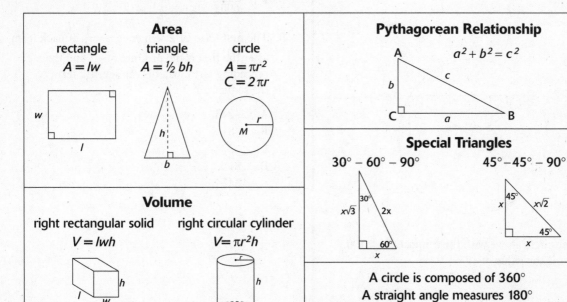

1. If $a + b = 12$, what is the value of $a + b - 30$?

   A.   42
   B.   –18
   C.   –8
   D.   18
   E.   42

2. The numerator of a fraction is 6 more than the denominator. If the fraction is equal to $\frac{3}{2}$, what is the numerator of the fraction?

   A.   8
   B.   9
   C.   12
   D.   18
   E.   24

GO ON TO THE NEXT PAGE

3. Mario weighs more than Eric and less than Hector. If m, e, and h represent the weight, in pounds, of Mario, Eric, and Hector, respectively, which of the following is true?

   A. $m < e < h$
   B. $m < h < e$
   C. $e < m < h$
   D. $h < e < m$
   E. $h < m < e$

4. If the areas of 2 triangles are equal and the sum of the areas of the triangles is 25, what is the average (arithmetic mean) of the areas of the 2 triangles?

   A. $\dfrac{25}{2}$
   B. $\dfrac{25}{4}$
   C. 5
   D. 25
   E. 50

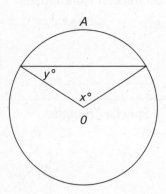

5. In the circle above with the center O, $x = 100$. What is the value of y?

   A. 20
   B. 30
   C. 40
   D. 50
   E. 60

6. A "simple square" is any integer greater than 1 that has exactly 3 positive integer factors: the integer itself, its square root, and 1. Which of the following is a simple square?

   A. 64
   B. 81
   C. 100
   D. 144
   E. 169

7. If x and z are positive and $\dfrac{25x^4}{z} = 625x^3$, what is $\dfrac{1}{x}$ in terms of z?

   A. $\dfrac{z}{25}$
   B. $25z$
   C. $\dfrac{25}{z}$
   D. $\dfrac{1}{25z}$
   E. $\dfrac{1}{600z}$

8. The first term of a sequence is $-\dfrac{1}{9}$. If each term after the first is the product of -3 and the preceding term, what is the seventh term of the sequence?

   A. -243
   B. -81
   C. -27
   D. 81
   E. 243

GO ON TO THE NEXT PAGE

Directions for Student-Produced Response Questions (Grid-ins): Questions 9–18 require you to solve the problem and enter your answer by carefully marking the circles on the special grid. Examples of the appropriate way to mark the grid follow.

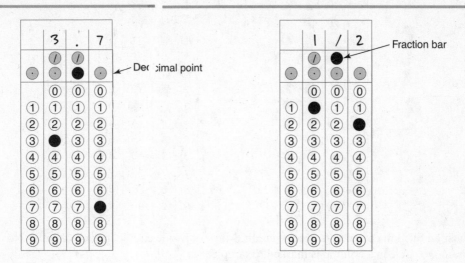

Do not grid in mixed numbers in the form of mixed numbers. Always change mixed numbers to improper fractions or decimals. Here's an example of how to grid when your answer is a mixed number such as $1\frac{1}{2}$.

Change to 1.5   or   Change to $\frac{3}{2}$

GO ON TO THE NEXT PAGE

Space permitting, answers can start in any column. Each grid-in answer that follows is correct.

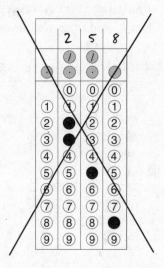

Note: Circles must be filled in correctly to receive credit. Mark only one circle in each column. No credit will be given if more than one circle in a column is marked. Example:

Accuracy of decimals: Always enter the most accurate decimal value that the grid will accommodate. For example: An answer such as .8888 . . . can be gridded as .888 or .889. Gridding this value as .8, .88, or .89 is considered inaccurate and therefore not acceptable. The acceptable grid-ins of $\frac{8}{9}$ are

Be sure to write your answers in the boxes at the top of the circles before filling in the circles. Although writing out the answers above the columns is not required, it is very important to ensure accuracy. Even though some problems may have more than one correct answer, only grid in one answer. Grid-in questions contain no negative answers.

9. The median of a set of 7 consecutive even integers is 84. What is the smallest of these 7 integers?

10. If $x + 4y$ is equal to 120% of $10y$, what is the value of $\frac{x}{y}$?

GO ON TO THE NEXT PAGE

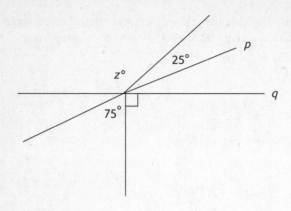

11. In the figure above, what is the value of z?

12. If $h(x) = x - 3$ and if $3\,h(a) = 15$, what is the value of $h(2a)$?

13. The center of a circle has coordinates (6, 8) and the circle intersects the y-axis at 1 point only. What is the radius of the circle?

14. A landscaper purchased $1,000 worth of plants for his business. Some of the plants cost $3 each and the others cost $4 each. If twice as many $3 plants as $4 plants were purchased, what was the total number of plants purchased?

15. If $9a^2 - 9b^2 = 90$ and $a + b = 30$, what is the value of $a - b$?

16. The perimeter of a rectangular plot of land is 200 yards. If the length of 1 side of the plot is 60 yards, what is the area of the plot in square yards?

17. If $\boxtimes$ is a binary operation and $a \boxtimes b$ is defined as $\dfrac{2a + b}{a + 2b}$, what is the value of $1 \boxtimes 4$?

18. In $\triangle XYZ$, 2 of its angles have the same measure and the lengths of 2 of the sides of the triangle are 25 and 15. What is the smallest possible value for the perimeter of the triangle?

IF YOU FINISH BEFORE TIME IS CALLED, CHECK YOUR WORK ON THIS SECTION ONLY. DO NOT WORK ON ANY OTHER SECTION IN THE TEST.

Section 7: Critical Reading

Time: 20 minutes

15 Questions

Directions: In this section, choose the best answer for each question and fill in the corresponding circle on the answer sheet.

Questions follow the two passages below. Using only the stated or implied information in each passage and in its introduction, if any, answer the questions.

Questions 1–15 are based on the following pair of passages.

The two passages that follow are taken from recent articles on human impact on the environment.

Passage 1:

A team of geologists from Baylor University recently concluded a study that indicates Native American pre-colonial land-use practices, such as deforestation, plowing, and damming, resulted
(5) in major changes to the topography and hydrological systems of eastern North America. Previous research had suggested that Native Americans' land use in eastern North America caused notable changes prior to contact, but
(10) little evidence existed until recently to support this conclusion.

Evidence now shows that pre-European natural floodplains have a history of prehistoric indigenous land use that pre-dates colonial-era
(15) Europeans. The presence and practices of European colonists have long been associated with usurpation, exploitation, and destruction of land, peoples, and resources, but that view may now change. Colonial-era Europeans were not
(20) the first to have an adverse impact on the hydrologic systems, for example. Researchers discovered that prehistoric agricultural societies caused widespread ecological change and increased sedimentation in hydrologic systems
(25) during the Little Ice Age, about 700 to 1,000 years ago. In one case, through their agricultural practices Native Americans increased soil erosion and sediment yields in the Delaware River basin.

The team also discovered evidence that
(30) prehistoric Native Americans decreased forest acreage to establish or re-establish settlements and to increase corn yields, their staple crop. Their contribution to increased sedimentation in valley bottoms 700 years ago was earlier than

(35) previously thought. That land use was the initial cause of increased sedimentation in valley bottoms, which later accelerated through greater precipitation in the region.

To conduct the study, geologists took samples
(40) from several locations along the Delaware River. They mapped landforms at elevations relative to the Delaware River base flow and conducted archaeological excavations to assess the presence and impacts of human habitation. The team
(45) then analyzed the data in relation to their hypothesis that the indigenous population had a significant impact on terrestrial sedimentation. Their analysis supported the hypothesis, confirming widespread pre-colonial-era effects
(50) of native people on sedimentation rates and the practices that caused it.

Passage 2:

Genghis Khan and his Mongol hordes had an impact on the global carbon cycle as big as today's annual demand for gasoline. The Black Death, on the other hand, came and went too
(5) quickly to cause much of a blip in the global carbon budget. Dwarfing both these events, however, has been the historical trend toward deforestation, which over centuries has released vast amounts of carbon dioxide into the
(10) atmosphere, as crop and pasture lands expanded to feed growing human populations.

"It's a common misconception that the human impact on climate began with the large-scale burning of coal and oil in the industrial era,"
(15) says Julia Pongratz of the Carnegie Institution's Department of Global Ecology, lead author of a new study on the impact of historical events on global climate (2011). "Actually, humans started to influence the environment thousands of years ago
(20) by changing the vegetation cover of the Earth's landscapes when we cleared forests for agriculture."

GO ON TO THE NEXT PAGE

Clearing forests releases carbon dioxide into the atmosphere when the trees and other vegetation are burned or when they decay. The
(25) rise in atmospheric carbon dioxide resulting from deforestation is recognizable in ice cores from Greenland and Antarctica before the fossil-fuel era. But deforestation has had its ups and downs during human history. During high-
(30) mortality events, such as wars and plagues, large areas of croplands and pastures have been abandoned and forests have re-grown, absorbing carbon dioxide from the atmosphere.

Pongratz decided to see how much effect these
(35) events could have had on the overall trend of rising carbon dioxide levels. Working with colleagues at the Max Planck Institute for Meteorology in Germany and with global ecologist Ken Caldeira at Carnegie, she compiled
(40) a detailed reconstruction of global land cover from 800 C.E. to the present and used a global climate-carbon cycle model to track the impact of land use changes on global climate. Pongratz was particularly interested in four major events
(45) in which large regions were depopulated: the Mongol invasions in Asia (1200–1380), the Black Death in Europe (1347–1400), the conquest of the Americas (1519–1700), and the fall of the Ming Dynasty in China (1600–1650).
(50) "We found that during the short events such as the Black Death and the Ming Dynasty collapse, the forest re-growth wasn't enough to overcome the emissions from decaying material in the soil," says Pongratz. "But during the
(55) longer-lasting ones like the Mongol invasion and the conquest of the Americas there was enough time for the forests to re-grow and absorb significant amounts of carbon."

The global impact of forest re-growth in even
(60) the long-lasting events was diminished, however, by the continued clearing of forests elsewhere in the world. In the case of the Mongol invasions, which had the biggest impact of the four events studied, re-growth on depopulated lands
(65) stockpiled nearly 700 million tons of carbon absorbed from the atmosphere. This is equivalent to the world's total annual demand for gasoline today.

Pongratz points out the relevance of the study
(70) to current climate issues. "Today about a quarter of the net primary production on the Earth's land surface is used by humans in some way, mostly through agriculture," she says. "So there is a large potential for our land-use choices to
(75) alter the global carbon cycle. In the past we have had a substantial impact on global climate and the carbon cycle, but it was all unintentional. Based on the knowledge we have gained from the past, we are now in a position to make land-use
(80) decisions that will diminish our impact on climate and the carbon cycle. We cannot ignore the knowledge we have gained."

1. All the following factors are cited in Passage 1 as contributing to major changes in the present-day topography and hydrological systems of eastern North America EXCEPT:

A. deforestation.
B. plowing.
C. river-damming practices.
D. greater regional precipitation.
E. archaeological excavations.

2. In Passage 1 in the second paragraph, the word "indigenous" means

A. impoverished.
B. foreign.
C. excavated.
D. native.
E. insignificant.

3. In Passage 1, the terms "hydrologic" and "hydrological" mean of or pertaining to

A. geology and geography.
B. soils and sediments.
C. water systems.
D. landforms.
E. rivers and estuaries.

GO ON TO THE NEXT PAGE

4. Which of the following sentences in Passage 1 most directly challenges the widely held view that colonial-era Europeans were solely responsible for altering the environment of eastern North America?

   A. Previous research had suggested that Native Americans' land use in eastern North America caused notable changes prior to contact, but little evidence existed until recently to support this conclusion.

   B. The presence and practices of European colonists have long been associated with usurpation, exploitation, and destruction of land, peoples, and resources, but that view may now change.

   C. The team then analyzed the data in relation to their hypothesis that the indigenous population had a significant impact on terrestrial sedimentation.

   D. Evidence now shows that pre-European natural floodplains have a history of prehistoric indigenous land use that pre-dates colonial-era Europeans.

   E. Colonial-era Europeans were not the first to have an adverse impact on the hydrologic systems, for example.

5. The major purpose of Passage 1 is to

   A. praise the work of the Baylor University geologists for their groundbreaking study.

   B. criticize precolonial Native Americans for their land use practices.

   C. recast the debate over who actually caused more widespread damage to the environment of eastern North America.

   D. advocate a new dialogue over whose land use practices resulted in greater changes to present-day topography and hydrology in eastern North America.

   E. present information confirming the impact of Native American land-use practices on river valley sedimentation in eastern North America.

6. With which of the following conclusions would the author of Passage 1 most likely agree?

   A. The Baylor study shows that Native Americans were just as destructive to the environment as colonial-era Europeans, whose damaging practices are better documented.

   B. The Baylor study suggests we should modify what we teach about the impacts of Native Americans and European colonists on environmental change.

   C. The sedimentation of the Delaware River basin had to have been repeated in the other river valleys of eastern North America.

   D. The Little Ice Age was the period of greatest agricultural activity among indigenous people of eastern North America.

   E. Topography and hydrology were the geographic features most impacted by Native American and Colonial European land use.

7. The reference to Genghis Khan and his Mongol hordes in the first sentence of Passage 2 serves chiefly to

   A. gain the reader's attention through reference to a cult figure.

   B. connect a well-known historical figure to a present-day environmental problem.

   C. introduce Genghis Khan as a major contributor to global warming.

   D. suggest that Genghis Khan's impact on the carbon cycle was as significant as the Black Death's.

   E. identify deforestation as the principal cause of carbon dioxide build-up.

8. To determine if periods of reforestation could reduce the rate of rising atmospheric carbon dioxide caused by agricultural activities, the scientist in Passage 2 chose to study

   A. the environmental impacts of high-mortality events.

   B. ice cores from Greenland and Antarctica from before the fossil fuel era.

   C. the effects of the bubonic plague on the global carbon budget.

   D. a predictive model of the global carbon cycle.

   E. the historical trend toward deforestation.

GO ON TO THE NEXT PAGE

9. Which of the following ideas in Passage 2 does the author identify as a common misconception about the problem of carbon dioxide accumulation in the atmosphere?

   A. Historical events had an impact on the global carbon cycle.

   B. Some events passed too quickly to cause changes in the global carbon budget.

   C. The need to feed growing human populations led to deforestation.

   D. Carbon dioxide accumulation began with the large-scale burning of coal and oil in the industrial era.

   E. Periods of depopulation can result in the reabsorption of carbon dioxide from the atmosphere.

10. In Passage 2, examples of events that caused land use changes affecting the global climate include all the following EXCEPT the

   A. Mongol invasions in Eurasia.

   B. Black Death in Europe.

   C. conquest of the Americas.

   D. fall of the Ming Dynasty in China.

   E. genocides in sub-Saharan Africa.

11. The general conclusion that is drawn from the study described in Passage 2 is that

   A. human choices about land and energy use could reduce atmospheric carbon dioxide.

   B. at this point in history only mass extinctions could correct the global carbon budget.

   C. human population factors have no significant lasting impact on the global climate.

   D. deforestation and reforestation of the earth tend to cancel each other out.

   E. the only way to reduce atmospheric carbon dioxide is to stop practicing agriculture.

12. According to the passage, which of the following high-mortality events were sufficiently long-term to affect the global climate?

   I. the Black Death in Europe

   II. the fall of the Ming Dynasty in China

   III. the conquest of the Americas

   IV. the Mongol invasions in Asia

   A. I only

   B. I and III

   C. I and II

   D. III and IV

   E. IV only

13. The two passages, although they describe different scientific studies, share a common goal. Which of the following statements best expresses that common goal?

   A. Correct misconceptions about human environmental impacts.

   B. Influence future legislation for greater environmental protection.

   C. Test new methods of historical reconstruction and analysis.

   D. Prove that deforestation ultimately is the cause of global warming.

   E. Explain how accumulations of atmospheric carbon dioxide harm the planet.

14. Based on information in both passages, which of the following inferences can be made about potentially harmful effects of removing vegetation from the earth's surface?

   I. Without vegetation to absorb it, water runs off the land, causing erosion and sedimentation of waterways.

   II. Without vegetation to absorb it, carbon dioxide is trapped in the atmosphere, which makes the earth hotter.

   III. Without vegetation to absorb it, Earth's heat melts glaciers, raising sea levels, which disrupts ecosystems and habitation patterns.

   A. I only

   B. I and II only

   C. II and III only

   D. II only

   E. I, II, and III

GO ON TO THE NEXT PAGE

15. Both passages imply or state that the harmful effects of deforestation were unintentional in the past—the unintended consequences of human activities as population levels rose. With which of the following measures would the researchers in both passages most conservatively agree as an application of our knowledge today?

A. We should invest in alternatives to agriculture to feed the world's people.

B. We should preserve undeveloped lands to permit the regrowth of forests.

C. We should restore environments to their original conditions.

D. We should reduce population growth and prevent overpopulation.

E. We should invent technology to scrub carbon dioxide from the atmosphere.

IF YOU FINISH BEFORE TIME IS CALLED, CHECK YOUR WORK ON THIS SECTION ONLY. DO NOT WORK ON ANY OTHER SECTION IN THE TEST.

STOP

Section 8: Mathematics

Time: 20 minutes

16 Questions

Directions: Solve each problem in this section by using the information given and your own mathematical calculations, insights, and problem-solving skills. Then select the one correct answer of the five choices given and mark the corresponding circle on your answer sheet. Use the available space on the page for your scratch work.

For each question, indicate the best answer, using the following notes.

1. All numerical values used are real numbers.

2. Calculators may be used.

3. Some problems may be accompanied by figures or diagrams. These figures are drawn as accurately as possible EXCEPT when it is stated in a specific problem that a figure is not drawn to scale. The figures and diagrams are meant to provide information useful in solving the problem or problems. Unless otherwise stated, all figures and diagrams lie on a plane.

Data that Can Be Used for Reference

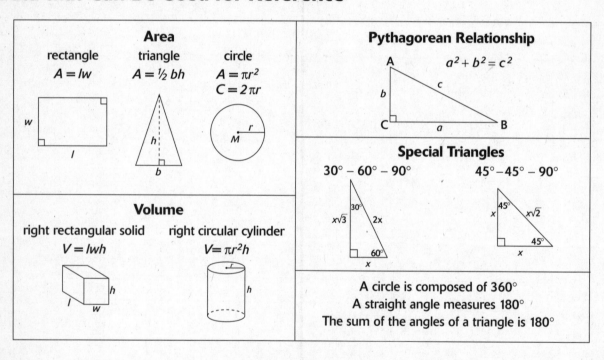

1. If $\sqrt{z} - 14 = -5$, then $z =$

   A. 3
   B. 9
   C. 19
   D. 81
   E. 361

2. If $4(3x - 1) = 20$, what is the value of x?

   A. $\dfrac{7}{4}$
   B. 2
   C. 5
   D. $\dfrac{17}{3}$
   E. 27

GO ON TO THE NEXT PAGE

3. When purchasing a sports car, a buyer can choose from 5 exterior colors and 3 interior colors. How many color combinations are possible?

  A. 4
  B. 6
  C. 8
  D. 11
  E. 15

4. In a poll, 84 voters favored candidate x, 65 voters favored candidate y, and 11 voters were undecided. What fraction of those polled favored candidate x?

  A. $\frac{13}{32}$

  B. $\frac{19}{40}$

  C. $\frac{21}{40}$

  D. $\frac{85}{149}$

  E. $\frac{19}{32}$

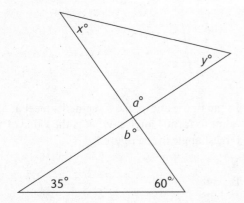

5. In the figure above, what is the value of $x + y$?

  A. 75
  B. 85
  C. 95
  D. 105
  E. It cannot be determined from the information given.

6. If $\frac{25}{y} = \frac{5n}{3y}$, what is the value of n?

  A. 15
  B. 5
  C. $\frac{5}{3}$
  D. $\frac{1}{5}$
  E. $\frac{1}{15}$

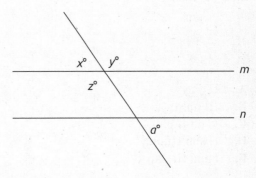

7. In the figure above $m \parallel n$ and $a = 40$. What is the value of $x + y + z$?

  A. 220
  B. 260
  C. 280
  D. 300
  E. 320

8. In the xy-coordinate plane, if a line is perpendicular to the x-axis and passes through the point $(-8, 5)$, which of the following is an equation of the line?

  A. $y = 0$
  B. $y = 5$
  C. $x = -8$
  D. $-8x = 5y$
  E. $y - 5 = x + 8$

9. The volume of a right circular cylinder with radius r and height h is V. In terms of V, what is the volume of a right circular cylinder with the same height if the radius is tripled?

  A. $\frac{V}{9}$

  B. $\frac{V}{3}$

  C. $3V$
  D. $9V$
  E. $27V$

GO ON TO THE NEXT PAGE

10. If 30% of a equals 75% of b, which of the following expresses b in terms of a?

    A. $b = 40\%$ of a
    B. $b = 45\%$ of a
    C. $b = 60\%$ of a
    D. $b = 105\%$ of a
    E. $b = 250\%$ of a

11. If $0 < x < 1$, which of the following statements must be true?

    I. $x^2 > 1$
    II. $x^3 > x^2$
    III. $x > \dfrac{x}{3}$

    A. II only
    B. III only
    C. I and II only
    D. II and III only
    E. I and III only

12. Which of the following is an expression for the statement: The product of $7x$ and the square root of y is equal to the square of the difference between x and y.

    A. $\sqrt{7xy} = (x - y)^2$
    B. $7x\sqrt{y} = (x - y)^2$
    C. $7x\sqrt{y} = x^2 - y^2$
    D. $7x\sqrt{y} = \sqrt{x - y}$
    E. $7\sqrt{xy} = (x - y)^2$

13. The square of an integer cannot end in which of the following digits?

    A. 1
    B. 4
    C. 5
    D. 6
    E. 7

14. In a sequence, each term after the first term is 5 more than $\dfrac{1}{4}$ of the preceding term. If a is the first term of the sequence and $a \neq 0$, what is the ratio of the second term to the first term?

    A. $\dfrac{a + 5}{4}$
    B. $\dfrac{a + 5}{4a}$
    C. $\dfrac{a + 20}{4}$
    D. $\dfrac{a + 20}{4a}$
    E. $\dfrac{a + 20}{a}$

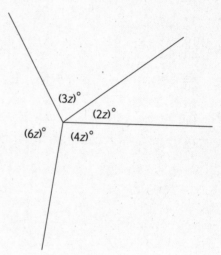

15. In the figure above, the 4 segments meet at a point to form 4 angles. What is the value of the largest angle in the figure?

    A. 24
    B. 48
    C. 72
    D. 96
    E. 144

GO ON TO THE NEXT PAGE

16. The lengths of the sides of a right triangle are consecutive integers and the length of the longest side is x. Which of the following equations expresses the relationship between the sides of the triangle?

   A. $(x-2) + (x-1) = x$
   B. $(x-4) + (x-1) = x$
   C. $(x-2)^2 + (x-1)^2 = x^2$
   D. $(x-4)^2 + (x-2)^2 = x^2$
   E. $(x-2)(x-1) = x$

IF YOU FINISH BEFORE TIME IS CALLED, CHECK YOUR WORK ON THIS SECTION ONLY. DO NOT WORK ON ANY OTHER SECTION IN THE TEST.

STOP

Section 9: Writing—Multiple Choice

Time: 10 minutes

15 Questions

Directions: In this section, choose the best answer for each question and fill in the corresponding circle on the answer sheet.

The following questions test correctness and effective expression. In selecting the answer, pay attention to grammar, diction, sentence structure, and punctuation. In the following questions, part or all of each sentence is underlined. The A answer repeats the underlined portion of the original sentence, while the next four offer alternatives. Choose the answer that best expresses the meaning of the original sentence, and at the same time is grammatically correct, and stylistically superior. The correct choice should be clear, unambiguous, and concise.

EXAMPLE:

The forecaster predicted <u>rain and the sky was clear</u>.

- **A.** rain and the sky was clear
- **B.** rain but the sky was clear
- **C.** rain the sky was clear
- **D.** rain, but the sky was clear
- **E.** rain being as the sky was clear

The correct answer is **D.**

1. <u>Nikisha saw that novels had ceased to paint idealized figures of romance, reviewing Jane Austen's *Emma*, and would henceforth copy real life.</u>

- **A.** Nikisha saw that novels had ceased to paint idealized figures of romance, reviewing Jane Austen's *Emma*, and would henceforth copy real life.
- **B.** Nikisha saw that novels had ceased to paint idealized figures of romance and would henceforth copy real life, reviewing Jane Austen's *Emma*.
- **C.** Nikisha saw that by copying real life novels had ceased to paint idealized figures of romance, reviewing Jane Austen's *Emma*.
- **D.** Reviewing Jane Austen's *Emma*, Nikisha saw that novels had ceased to paint idealized figures of romance, and would henceforth copy real life.
- **E.** Reviewing Jane Austen's *Emma*, that the novel had ceased to paint idealized figures of romance and would henceforth copy real life was seen by Nikisha.

2. Immobilizing animals through anesthesia is not a new <u>technique zoos</u> have used this procedure for decades.

- **A.** technique zoos
- **B.** technique; zoos
- **C.** technique, zoos
- **D.** technique although zoos
- **E.** technique for the reason that zoos

GO ON TO THE NEXT PAGE

3. Many small seed companies were privately owned, but they have been taken over by chemical giants and they depend on large pesticide sales.

   A. Many small seed companies were privately owned, but they have been taken over by chemical giants and they depend on large pesticide sales.

   B. Many small seed companies were privately owned, have been taken over by chemical giants, and they depend on large pesticide sales.

   C. Many small seed companies are privately owned, and they have been taken over by chemical giants that depend on large pesticide sales.

   D. Many small privately owned seed companies depending on large sales of pesticides have been taken over by chemical giants.

   E. Chemical giants that depend on large pesticide sales have taken over many small privately owned seed companies.

4. Drawing on resources that include unpublished letters and manuscripts, Anne Atkinson has written a thorough and original biography of Emily Dickinson.

   A. Drawing on resources that include unpublished letters and manuscripts,

   B. Drawn on resources that include unpublished letters and manuscripts,

   C. She has drawn on resources that include unpublished letters and manuscripts, and so

   D. Unpublished letters and manuscripts are the resources used, and

   E. Drawing on unpublished letters and manuscripts as her resources,

5. The rites of how an adolescent female is initiated becoming a member of adult society have never been photographed.

   A. of how an adolescent female is initiated becoming

   B. initiating an adolescent female so that she becomes

   C. of the adolescent female's initiation becoming

   D. which initiate an adolescent female and she becomes

   E. by which the adolescent female is initiated and becomes

6. Manning's book on *Nicholas Nickleby* is the most dependable guide to this difficult novel, and it is also the wittiest account.

   A. guide to this difficult novel, and it is also the wittiest account.

   B. guide, and it is also the wittiest account of this difficult novel.

   C. guide to this difficult novel, and the wittiest.

   D. guide and also the wittiest account of this difficult novel.

   E. and wittiest guide to this difficult novel.

7. To lose weight rapidly, one must weigh every food portion carefully, exercise regularly, and you should only drink water, black coffee, or diet soda.

   A. and you should only drink

   B. and you should drink only

   C. only drinking

   D. and drink only

   E. and one should drink only

8. Different from any other designs in the show, *Project Runway* exhibited a collection made entirely of nylon.

   A. Different from any other designs in the show,

   B. Different from any designs in the show,

   C. With designs different from any others in the show,

   D. Designed differently from others in the show,

   E. Different from other designs in the show,

9. As Daniel's army advanced farther into the interior, and its supply line from the coast became more and more vulnerable.

   A. and its supply line from the coast became more and more vulnerable.

   B. its supply line from the coast became more and more vulnerable.

   C. its supply line from the coast becoming more and more vulnerable.

   D. while its supply line from the coast became more and more vulnerable.

   E. and its supply line from the coast becoming more and more vulnerable.

GO ON TO THE NEXT PAGE

10. The crowned crane lives in the marshlands and meadows of West Africa, <u>and you can find them in the open grasslands as well.</u>

    A. and you can find them in the open grasslands as well.
    B. and they also live in the open grasslands.
    C. and they also can be found in the open grasslands.
    D. and in the open grasslands, as well.
    E. and they live also in the open grasslands.

11. The banking system is stronger now than it has been in many <u>years; which may encourage bankers</u> to reduce their reserves.

    A. years; which may encourage bankers
    B. years; and this may encourage bankers
    C. years, a condition that may encourage bankers
    D. years, and because of this fact, bankers may be encouraged
    E. years, this may encourage bankers

12. This summer, Las Vegas will see a record number of visitors, <u>and a very high percentage of them will be children.</u>

    A. and a very high percentage of them will be children.
    B. being children in a very high percentage.
    C. and children will be among them in a very high percentage.
    D. among whom a very high percentage of them will be children.
    E. and among them will be children in a very high percentage.

13. <u>Nature has provided so that nearly every plant-eating insect has a natural enemy, but</u> most insecticides kill both.

    A. Nature has provided so that nearly every plant-eating insect has a natural enemy, but
    B. Nature has seen to it that nearly every plant-eating insect has a natural enemy, and
    C. Nature provides that nearly every plant-eating insect has a natural enemy, but
    D. Nearly every plant-eating insect has a natural enemy, but
    E. Natural enemies of nearly every plant-eating insect have been provided by nature, but

14. By mid-October, black oaks, dogwood, and big-leaf <u>maples which form splashes</u> of yellow, red, and orange.

    A. maples which form splashes
    B. maples form splashes
    C. maples which are forming splashes
    D. maples forming splashes
    E. maples that form splashes

15. <u>Throughout the entire work, Huxley is constantly repeating</u> that we have become the slaves of machines.

    A. Throughout the entire work, Huxley is constantly repeating
    B. Throughout the entire work, Huxley states repeatedly
    C. Constantly throughout the entire work, Huxley states
    D. Throughout, Huxley repeatedly states
    E. Huxley states

IF YOU FINISH BEFORE TIME IS CALLED, CHECK YOUR WORK ON THIS SECTION ONLY. DO NOT WORK ON ANY OTHER SECTION IN THE TEST.

Scoring Practice Exam 4

The following section will assist you in scoring and analyzing your practice exam results. Use the answer key below to score your results, and then carefully review the analysis charts to identify your strengths and weaknesses. Finally, read through the answer explanations starting on page 514 to clarify the solutions to the problems.

Answer Key for Practice Exam 4

Section 2: Critical Reading

1. A	8. D	15. E	22. B
2. B	9. C	16. B	23. C
3. A	10. C	17. D	24. D
4. C	11. A	18. A	25. A
5. D	12. E	19. C	26. A
6. C	13. C	20. A	27. D
7. B	14. A	21. C	28. E

Section 3: Mathematics

1. B	6. B	11. E	16. D
2. A	7. A	12. C	17. D
3. D	8. B	13. A	18. B
4. C	9. D	14. E	19. B
5. C	10. E	15. A	20. C

Section 4: Writing—Multiple Choice

1. D	10. A	19. C	28. B
2. C	11. B	20. E	29. C
3. A	12. E	21. C	30. C
4. B	13. A	22. A	31. A
5. E	14. B	23. C	32. D
6. D	15. C	24. B	33. E
7. C	16. D	25. D	34. A
8. A	17. C	26. E	35. B
9. C	18. D	27. A	

Section 5: Critical Reading

1. B	8. D	15. C	22. A
2. C	9. B	16. B	23. A
3. D	10. C	17. D	24. E
4. E	11. B	18. B	25. C
5. B	12. E	19. D	26. D
6. A	13. C	20. D	27. C
7. B	14. A	21. C	

Section 6: Mathematics

1. B	6. E	11. 140	16. 2,400
2. D	7. D	12. 13	17. $\frac{2}{3}$
3. C	8. B	13. 6	18. 55
4. A	9. 78	14. 300	
5. C	10. 8	15. $\frac{1}{3}$	

Section 7: Critical Reading

1. E	5. E	9. D	13. A
2. D	6. B	10. E	14. E
3. C	7. B	11. A	15. B
4. D	8. A	12. D	

Section 8: Mathematics

1. D	5. C	9. D	13. E
2. B	6. A	10. A	14. D
3. E	7. E	11. B	15. E
4. C	8. C	12. B	16. C

Section 9: Writing—Multiple Choice

1. D	5. E	9. B	13. D
2. B	6. E	10. D	14. B
3. E	7. D	11. C	15. D
4. A	8. C	12. A	

Charting and Analyzing Your Test Results

The first step in analyzing your results is to chart your answers. Use the charts on the following pages to identify your strengths and areas of improvement. Complete the process of evaluating your essays and analyzing problems in each area. Reevaluate your results as you look for trends in the types of errors (repeated errors), and look for low scores in results in *specific* topic areas. This reexamination and analysis is a tremendous asset to help you maximize your best-possible score. The answers and explanations following these charts will provide you clarification to help you solve these types of problems in the future.

Reviewing the Essay

Refer to the sample essay on page 514 as a reference guide. Have an English teacher, tutor, or someone else with good writing skills read and evaluate your essay using the Essay Checklist given below. Have your reader evaluate the complete essay as good, average, or marginal. Note that your paper would actually be scored from 1 to 6 by two trained readers (actual total score 2–12). Since we are trying only for a rough approximation, a strong, average, or weak overall evaluation will give you a general feeling for your score range.

Essay Checklist			
Questions	Strong Response Score 5 or 6	Average Response Score 3 or 4	Weak Response Score 1 or 2
1. Does the essay focus on the topic and respond to the assigned task?			
2. Is the essay organized and well developed?			
2. Does the essay use specific supporting details and examples?			
4. Does the writing use correct grammar, usage, punctuation, and spelling?			
5. Is the handwriting legible?			

Critical Reading Analysis Sheet				
Section 2	Possible	Completed	Right	Wrong
Sentence Completions	10			
Short Reading Passages	4			
Long Reading Passages	14			
Section 2 Subtotal	28			
Section 5	Possible	Completed	Right	Wrong
Sentence Completions	9			
Short Reading Passages	2			
Paired Reading Passages	4			
Long Reading Passages	12			
Section 5 Subtotal	27			
Section 7	Possible	Completed	Right	Wrong
Paired Passages	15			
Section 7 Subtotal	15			
Overall Critical Reading Totals	70			

Note: Only 3 Critical Reading sections (approximately 70 questions) count toward your actual score on the SAT.

Mathematics Analysis Sheet

Section 3	Possible	Completed	Right	Wrong
Multiple Choice	20			
Section 3 Subtotal	**20**			
Section 6	**Possible**	**Completed**	**Right**	**Wrong**
Multiple Choice	8			
Grid-Ins	10			
Section 6 Subtotal	**18**			
Section 8	**Possible**	**Completed**	**Right**	**Wrong**
Multiple Choice	16			
Section 8 Subtotal	**16**			
Overall Math Totals	**54**			

Writing—Multiple-Choice Analysis Sheet

Section 4	Possible	Completed	Right	Wrong
Improving Sentences	7			
Identifying Sentence Errors	19			
Improving Paragraphs	9			
Section 4 Subtotal	**35**			
Section 9	**Possible**	**Completed**	**Right**	**Wrong**
Improving Sentences	15			
Section 9 Subtotal	**15**			
Overall Writing—Multiple-Choice Totals	**50**			

Analysis/Tally Sheet for Problems Missed

One of the most important parts of test preparation is analyzing why you missed a problem so that you can reduce the number of mistakes. Now that you have taken the practice exam and checked your answers, carefully tally your mistakes by marking them in the proper column.

Reason for Mistakes						
	Total Possible	Total Missed	Simple Mistake	Misread Problem	Lack of Knowledge	Lack of Time
Section 2: Critical Reading	28					
Section 5: Critical Reading	27					
Section 7: Critical Reading	15					
Subtotal	**70**					
Section 3: Mathematics	20					
Section 6: Mathematics	18					
Section 8: Mathematics	16					
Subtotal	**54**					
Section 4: Writing—Multiple Choice	35					
Section 9: Writing—Multiple Choice	15					
Subtotal	**50**					
Total Critical Reading, Math and Writing	**174**					

Reviewing the preceding data should help you determine why you are missing certain problems. Now that you've pinpointed the type of error, compare it to other practice tests to spot other common mistakes.

Practice Exam 4 Answers and Explanations

Section 1: Writing—Essay

To help you evaluate your essay writing skills, listed below is an example of a high-scoring strong essay response for the essay topic. Compare your essay to this sample essay and the analysis of a strong essay, an average essay, and a poorly written essay. Use the suggested checklist to evaluate your essays, and to help you take a closer look and understand your scoring range.

Sample Essay

Rebellion, paradoxically, is in itself a form of conformity. And it is the classic teen response to powerlessness. Even so, it is a necessary step between childhood and maturity, by which a young person finds his or her path and, as such, cannot be discarded lightly. That said, teenagers can, with proper guidance and a lot of luck, find ways to curb a few excesses.

To take an example from my own life: When I was a child, my parents would read to me, and I enjoyed it. Later, in school, I found myself falling behind in reading because I didn't enjoy or understand the books that were being assigned. They didn't seem to apply to my life. On my own, I began reading science fiction, which I liked better than books assigned in my English classes. This was not only my own form of rebellion, but also I felt I was embracing writers who were, themselves, rebels. Genre fiction may not be accepted for the same level of quality as more mainstream fiction, but still these writers kept at it.

As I progressed in reading these books, I found myself becoming less satisfied with them. I began to see in what ways quality was lacking in their characters, their prose style, even the writing itself. But I also became interested in other types of fiction that seemed to straddle the border between science fiction and literature. The authors I found most interesting were Kurt Vonnegut, John Barth, and Thomas Pynchon. They, themselves, were rebels, but to me it seemed that they were working inside the form of mainstream literature to change it.

In time, I wondered where these works had come from. I heard of writers like Flannery O'Connor, Shirley Jackson, and Grace Paley, who were rebellious in their own ways. I enjoyed their work, but wondered whether my tastes were becoming more mainstream—and, if so, was that really so bad? I even became curious about earlier writers such as Nathaniel West and Evelyn Waugh, who were light years away from the science fiction where I'd begun my journey.

Surprisingly, I began to see that all writers are in some sense rebels and, beyond this, that every step on the way is a combination of conformity and rebellion. Writing itself requires a certain amount of conformity, even if this is only a willingness to meet a reader halfway in his or her expectations of a good story and engaging characters. And yet, the writer has to surprise, engage, perhaps enlighten— the job of the rebel. Merging these two contradictory requirements—conformity and rebellion—is an essential part of the path to originality: a path I hope to find for myself, in my own way.

Section 2: Critical Reading

Sentence Completions

1. **A.** The adjective here should pick up the implications of "loved" and "hated," not just one or the other. The word "controversial," Choice A, accounts for both. The other choices are not specifically related in any way to the rest of the sentence.

2. **B.** You need a verb here describing the action of organisms, with a meaning like "developed" or "discovered." The best choice is B, "evolved," developed gradually, which also fits well with the detail of "thousands of years." The wrong answers describe too conscious an action.

3. **A.** Here you need words that are contradictory to the two words given: "affectionate" and "alert." "Aloof," Choice A, "cruel," Choice B, or "selfish," Choice D, are possible first words, but "shrewd," Choice B, "lively," Choice C, and "nimble," Choice D, are not contradictions of "alert," so the only possible right answer is Choice A.

4. **C.** Any of the five adjective choices would fit the first phrase. Because this fame is for an unfavorably regarded trait (talking too much), however, the best choice is "notorious." A hero is "famous," "renowned," "illustrious," or "eminent," but a man who talks too much is "notorious." Because the action described confirms the reputation for long-windedness, "solidified" is the only possible choice for the verb.

5. **D.** You know that the subject already is a senator who may run for reelection. Therefore, she is the incumbent, the holder of an office. The details of the sentence support this choice. Although the other nouns are not wholly unsuitable, none of them has any real connection with the details in the rest of the sentence.

6. **C.** The first noun must be a term that refers to what is pledged to obtain a loan—a word like "pledge," or "surety," or "collateral," or "deposit." Only "profit," Choice D, can be eliminated. The verb must mean liquidate or get rid of, because he emerges free of debt. That means you must eliminate choices A, B, and E. Only "discharge," Choice C, is left. This confirms the sense of "collateral" being the best of the four available nouns.

7. **B.** The missing word describes absurdist fiction and is parallel to the word "shocking." Clearly, "banal," Choice A; "plausible," Choice C; "disjointed," Choice D; and "familiar," Choice E, will not do. The adjective "radical" here means "marked by a considerable departure from the usual or traditional."

8. **D.** The sense of the sentence calls for an adjective expressing strong feelings, because the writer is surprised by this response to an insignificant issue. D is the only logical answer. "Acrimonious" means angry and bitter.

9. **C.** The sentence describes a band of avant-garde instrumentalists and a singer who croons ballads. The adjective "familiar," Choice C, is the best contrast to "avant garde."

10. **C.** Because she hoped to be undetected, she had to hide the card "furtively," that is, stealthily or surreptitiously. The words "brazenly," Choice A, and "overtly," Choice B, contradict the opening phrase.

Short Reading Passages

11. **A.** The fact that associations vary from person to person, depending on personal history, is the point of the paragraph. Choice C contradicts this point, and Choice D, while a tempting answer, is incorrect. Your culture may help determine your associations, but it is your own history that is the prime determiner, according to the passage. Choice B is meaningless here. The reverse of Choice E is true; word association tests are valuable because people's associations vary and can therefore provide clues to their personal history.

12. **E.** This example should illustrate how personal history creates associations. Choice B may seem correct, but to some people, coffee might be associated with a cigarette, inability to sleep, or something else. "Everyone" is the problem word here. Choices A and C are irrelevant. Choice D draws a conclusion that is not warranted, nor does it strengthen the main point of the paragraph.

13. **C.** Lines 10–12 state that this fact has been "recently established." Choices D and E are presented as possibilities, not certainties. Nothing in the passage suggests Choice A, and, according to the passage, Choice B is simply untrue because of the butterfly's short life span.

14. **A.** The point of the paragraph is that scientists cannot yet fully explain how the migrating butterfly finds its way. They don't know enough about how the butterfly navigates to know whether Choice B is correct. Nothing in the passage either supports or refutes choices C and D, and Choice E may or may not be true. (Beware of words like "never" and "always" in answer choices.)

Long Reading Passages

15. **E.** Although "correspondence" can mean correlation, agreement, or similarity, here it means communication by letters. Gauguin's "correspondence" refers to the letters he wrote to France from the South Pacific.

16. **B.** Gauguin's letter refers to the quotation from Poe that perfect beauty must possess "singularity" (oddness, uniqueness, strangeness), and he is reminded of these lines by the beauty of his first Tahitian model.

17. **D.** The passage points out that most of the artists before Gauguin had not painted Tahitians realistically, but as idealized types, altered to fit European tastes—just the opposite of Choice B. The passage goes on to point out that the Tahitian could "scarcely be distinguished from his African or Asian counterpart."

18. **A.** The reader can infer that Charles Giraud painted Tahitians before Gauguin did, but because the paintings have not survived, the author cannot know whether Giraud followed other artists and painted to suit European ideas of beauty or if, like Gauguin, he painted the Tahitians as they really were. It is for this reason the author would like to see Giraud's work.

19. **C.** The passage opposes the terms "Naturalism" and "Symbolism." The naturalistic or realistic in Gauguin is alluded to in lines 33–34 ("straightforward") and lines 49–50 ("naturalistically"), while lines 55–58 refer to the nonrealistic "Symbolist aspirations."

20. **A.** The two impulses in Gauguin that appear to be at odds are his wish to render the Tahitians as they really are and at the same time to reveal a "poetic image" of the "island's mysterious past." The problem is discussed in the last lines of the passage.

21. **C.** The first paragraph is introductory and presents the opposing positions on global warming and greenhouse gases represented by the climatologist Jim Hansen and the skeptics.

22. **B.** Although "pit" (the verb) can mean to scar or remove the core of, the meaning here is sets in opposition or sets in competition.

23. **C.** Because neither oxygen nor nitrogen absorbs heat, neither choices A nor B is likely. The amount of carbon dioxide in the atmosphere can be increased by burning fossil fuels, making Choice D untrue. In Choice E, the opposite is more likely to be true because heat escapes as infrared radiation. Because carbon dioxide absorbs heat, a planet with more in its atmosphere would be warmer.

24. **D.** Because oxygen and nitrogen, which are not greenhouse gases, form 99 percent of the atmosphere according to the second paragraph, the passage does not imply that greenhouse gases make up a large part of the atmosphere. The second paragraph also tells us that carbon dioxide absorbs large amounts of heat and that the release of carbon dioxide can lead to warming. The third paragraph adds that clearing and burning forests create carbon dioxide.

25. **A.** If greenhouse gases absorb heat and nitrogen does not absorb heat (paragraph 2), then nitrogen is not a greenhouse gas. The other four are mentioned in the second and third paragraphs of the passage.

26. **A** The first statement directly contradicts the main argument of the IPCC report that earth's climate is "unequivocally" getting warmer as a result of heat-trapping greenhouse gases produced by human activity. All the other statements of fact and opinion directly or indirectly support the IPCC argument.

27. **D.** The phrase "emanates from" means "are emitted by." Choices C and E are less precise.

28. **E.** The author would most likely disagree with all the statements except the last. The passage clearly supports the views that human activity is a significant factor despite natural fluctuations, Choice A, and that deforestation and burning of fossil fuels are examples of human activity, Choice B. The author likely would not accept the conclusion that no conclusion can be made, Choice C, or that the issue is merely political, Choice D. The author would agree, however, that global warming is a reality in which both human and natural causes play a role, Choice E.

Section 3: Mathematics

1. B. The second term of the sequence is $3a - b = 7$ and the third term is $7a - b = 19$.

$$3a - b = 7$$
$$-1 \cdot \underline{(7a - b = 19)}$$
$$3a - b = 7$$
$$-\ \underline{7a + b = -19}$$
$$-\ 4a \quad = -12$$
$$\frac{-4a}{-4} = \frac{-12}{-4}$$
$$a = 3$$

Since $a = 3$ and $3a - b = 7$,

$$3(3) - b = 7$$
$$9 - b = 7$$
$$9 - b - 9 = 7 - 9$$
$$-b = -2$$
$$-1 \cdot (-b) = -1 \cdot (-2)$$
$$b = 2$$

2. A.

$$\text{If } 5y - 12 = 7y + 12$$
$$5y - 12 - 7y = 7y + 12 - 7y$$
$$-2y - 12 = 12$$
$$-2y - 12 + 12 = 12 + 12$$
$$-2y = 24$$
$$\frac{-2y}{-2} = \frac{24}{-2}$$
$$y = -12$$

3. D.

If $h(x) = 5 - x^3$ then

$$h(5) = 5 - (5)^3 \quad \text{and} \quad h(-5) = 5 - (-5)^3$$
$$= 5 - 125 \qquad\qquad = 5 - (-125)$$
$$h(5) = -120 \quad \text{and} \quad h(-5) = 130$$

Hence $h(5) < h(-5)$. For choices A, B, and C, $h(5) = h(-5)$ and for Choice E, $h(5) > h(-5)$.

4. C. Since each of the 3 shirts may be worn with each of the 5 ties, there are $3 \times 5 = 15$ different shirt and tie combinations.

5. C. Since $12y = 7x$ and $20z = 7x$, $12y = 20z$.

$$\frac{12y}{20y} = \frac{20z}{20y}$$

$$\frac{12}{20} = \frac{z}{y}$$

$$\frac{3}{5} = \frac{z}{y}$$

6. B. Since there are x Algebra I classes with a maximum of s students per class, the total number of students that could be enrolled in Algebra I is $x \times s$. However, there are a total of 7 empty seats in 2 of the classes, which means the total number of students m enrolled in Algebra I is $m = x \times s - 7$.

7. A. Since $m \parallel n$, alternate interior angles are equal and

$$x + 100 = 120$$
$$x + 100 - 100 = 120 - 100$$
$$x = 20$$

Since p is a straight line,

$$x + z = 180$$
$$20 + z = 180$$
$$20 + z - 20 = 180 - 20$$
$$z = 160$$

8. B.

If $y = 0$, then

$(4y)^2 = (4 \times 0)^2 = 0^2 = 0$

and

$4y^2 = 4(0^2) = 4 \times 0 = 0$. Hence $(4y)^2 = 4y^2$.

For $y = -4$, $y = \frac{1}{4}$, and $y = 1$, $(4y)^2 > 4y^2$.

9. D. Since a and b are consecutive positive integers with $b > a$, then $b = a + 1$ and

$$b^2 - a^2 = (a+1)^2 - a^2$$
$$= a^2 + 2a + 1 - a^2$$
$$= 2a + 1$$

10. E. The average of 2 numbers m and n is

$$\frac{m+n}{2} = a$$

$$\frac{m+2}{2} \cdot 2 = a \cdot 2$$

$$m + n = 2a$$

The average of 3 numbers m, n, and p is

$$\frac{m+n+p}{3} = \frac{2a+p}{3}$$

11. E. The remainder will be 1 when 19 is divided by 2, 3, 6, 9, and 18.

12. C. The probability P that a number chosen at random is odd is

$$P = \frac{\text{number of odd numbers}}{\text{total number of numbers}}$$

Since there are z odd numbers and $x + z$ numbers in the set

$$\frac{z}{x+z} = \frac{5}{12}$$
$$12 \cdot z = 5 \cdot (x+z)$$
$$12z = 5x + 5z$$
$$12z - 5z = 5x$$
$$7z = 5x$$
$$\frac{7z}{5z} = \frac{5x}{5z}$$
$$P = \frac{7}{5} = \frac{x}{z}$$

13. A. Since x and y are positive integers, and $5x + 2y < 10$, then $0 < x < 2$ and $0 < y < 2$. There are 2 ordered pairs (x, y) for which $5x + 2y < 10$: $(1, 1)$ and $(1, 2)$.

14. E. If $x = \frac{1}{3}$,

$$\frac{1}{x-1} + \frac{1}{x} = \frac{1}{\frac{1}{3}-1} + \frac{1}{\frac{1}{3}}$$
$$= \frac{1}{\frac{-2}{3}} + 3$$
$$= \frac{-3}{2} + 3$$
$$= \frac{-3}{2} + \frac{6}{2}$$
$$= \frac{3}{2}$$

15. A. Since X, Y, and Z are points on a line in that order, $XY + YZ = XZ$.

Since $XY = 65$ and XZ is 30 more than XY,

$$XZ = XY + 30$$
$$= 65 + 30$$
$$= 95$$

Hence $XY + YZ = XZ$
$$65 + YZ = 95$$
$$65 + YZ - 65 = 95 - 65$$
$$YZ = 30$$

16. D. If $a + 5 = x$,

$$a + 5 - 5 = x - 5$$
$$a = x - 5$$

$$\text{Hence } 5a + 11 = 5(x - 5) + 11$$
$$= 5x - 25 + 11$$
$$= 5x - 14$$

17. D. If y years ago a person was x years old, then that person is $x + y$ years old today. In 3 years, the person will be $x + y + 3$ years old.

18. B. The cross-product for Choice B is $wx = yz$, while the cross-products for the other 4 choices are the same, $wz = xy$.

19. B. The four values of x and $h(x)$ are true for $h(x) = x^2 - 1$ since

$$h(-1) = (-1)^2 - 1 = 1 - 1 = 0$$
$$h(0) = (0)^2 - 1 = 0 - 1 = -1$$
$$h(2) = (2)^2 - 1 = 4 - 1 = 3$$
$$h(5) = (5)^2 - 1 = 25 - 1 = 24$$

20. B. In $\triangle MNP$, since $x = 60°$, the triangle is equilateral and $MN = NP = MP = 10$ and the perimeter of $\triangle MNP$ is $10 + 10 + 10 = 30$. Since $\angle R = \angle T$ in $\triangle RST$, the sides opposite these angles are equal, $RS = ST = 15$. Hence the perimeter of $\triangle RST$ is $15 + 15 + 10 = 40$ and the perimeter of $\triangle RST$ is 10 greater than the perimeter of $\triangle MNP$.

Section 4: Writing—Multiple Choice

Improving Sentences

1. **D.** The correct version should include either "people's" or "players'" to avoid changing the meaning. Since the word "players" has already been used in the sentence, "people's" is the better choice. The second part of the sentence specifically contrasts the two behaviors, so "but" is a better choice of conjunction than "and." The sentence contains two independent clauses that should be separated by a conjunction *and* a comma.

2. **C.** The problem in this sentence is the ambiguous "they." To which group does it refer? Choice C uses more words, but makes clear which group will win the election. Choices D and E are also ambiguous.

3. **A.** The original version is correct. It consists of a series of four adjectives, with one adverbial modifier ("grossly"). It is also the most concise of the five versions of the sentence. There is no need to break up the series of adjectives, and the other versions add unnecessary words. Choice D, by changing "grossly" to "gross," changes the meaning of the sentence.

4. **B.** The error in the original sentence is a comma splice, the use of a comma to join two complete sentences. Choice D, omitting the comma, is even worse. Choice B's use of a semicolon corrects the sentence. Remember that the semicolon is usually the equivalent of a period, not a comma. Choice E needs a comma to be correct; Choice C is wordy and awkward, though the punctuation is not wrong.

5. **E.** Up to the comma, this is a complete sentence, but the second half has a subject but no main verb. Choices A, B, C, and D have only the participle "accepting" (a verbal adjective, not a verb). Choice E has a main verb, "accept," and is the only version that is not a sentence fragment.

6. **D.** The conjunction "but" is a better choice than the "and." Although Choice B is not grammatically wrong, it is wordier than Choice D, the most concise of the five choices.

7. **C.** Again, "but" is a better conjunction choice than "and." Although Choice B is not grammatically wrong, it is wordier than Choice C.

Identifying Sentence Errors

8. **A.** There is an error in the case of the pronoun "I." It is the object of the verb "hired" and should be "me." "The owners hired I," would be easy to spot as an error. Don't let words between related parts of a sentence distract you.

9. **C.** As it stands, two unlike objects are compared. The sentence should say that imported pistachios cost more than California pistachios.

10. **A.** The verb "are" (a plural) does not agree with the singular "agreement." Again, the error would be easy to see if the two words were together. The plural "they" is correct, as it refers to both House and Senate.

11. **B.** The verb tense is wrong here. The use of "tomorrow" tells us the action is to take place in the future, but "departed" is past tense. It should be "will depart."

12. **E.** The sentence has no errors. The verb tense sequence using the past perfect "had completed" followed by the past "considered" is correct.

13. **A.** The pronoun "who" should replace the pronoun "which." To refer to persons, use "who"; to refer to things, use "which" or "that."

14. **B.** The comparative here repeats itself, since "worse" already means "more bad." You could say something like "more harmful" or "worse," but not "more worse."

15. **C.** The choice of preposition here is not idiomatic. We say "concede to," not "concede with."

16. **D.** The error is a double negative. The "hardly any" avoids the error, but "scarcely no" has two negatives. A sentence testing this error will probably use either "hardly" or "scarcely" as one of the negatives. A "not" and a "no" (I don't have no money) is too easy.

17. **C.** This is an agreement error, common in constructions using "either/or." Here the subject of the plural verb "are" is the singular "attempt," or the singular "bombing." It cannot be both, since the point of the sentence is that one or the other is responsible.

18. **D.** An often-tested idiom error is the interchange of an infinitive ("to dismantle") and a prepositional phrase with a gerund ("on dismantling"). Here, the noun "insistence" requires the prepositional phrase, "on dismantling."

19. **C.** The use of the future tense of the verb ("will believe") makes no sense in this context. The present tense, "believe," should have been used.

20. **E.** The sentence uses the correlative "not only . . . but also," which often introduces errors of parallelism, but here there are no errors.

21. **C.** This is another agreement error; the singular subject "business" requires the singular verb "has developed."

22. **A.** The subject of the second half of the sentence is "you," and since it is not underlined, it cannot be changed. To keep the pronouns consistent, the "we" at the beginning must also be "you."

23. **C** The verb form "had flew" is the error here. Either the past tense "flew" or the past perfect "had flown" would be correct.

24. **B.** There is adverb-adjective confusion here. The adjective "fond" should be used to modify the noun "good-bye."

25. **D.** The sentence begins with a singular "ambassador," but changes to an unspecified plural "they" in the main clause. They who?

26. **E.** The sentence is correct. The singular "its" refers to the singular MTV and the verb tense is reasonable.

Improving Paragraphs

27. **A.** Sentences 3 and 4 are contradictory. Sentence 3 states that attachment is instinctual, while sentence 4 implies that it is learned. Choice A corrects this error by adding both to the sentence. Choice B omits any reference to natural separation and is therefore incomplete as a choice. Choice C is a general analogy, but is not the best way to revise the sentences. Choice D omits any reference to natural separation or to the relationship between infants and their primary caregivers, not just any adults. Choice E lacks details.

28. **B.** Choice B is the most direct and inclusive revision of the last sentence. The conjunction "between" in the sentence requires a comparison, which the revision in Choice B provides. The comparison is between attachment in infancy and attachment in adulthood. The clarified meaning is that our patterns of attachment and separation as adults are based on the template of our attachment as infants, and understanding the link can help us in our relationships as adults. The other answer choices do not address the comparison and so do not clarify the sentence meaning.

29. **C.** Choices A and B are topic sentences of paragraphs but do not make good thesis statements for the entire passage. Choices D and E present details or examples and so do not make good thesis statements. Choice C, the first sentence, is the thesis statement to which all three paragraphs refer.

30. **C.** The example does not refer to relationships, making choices A and B incorrect. Choice C is the best alternative because the sentence is about separation anxiety, which the example illustrates. Choice D in incorrect between the example does not illustrate bonding in infancy, and Choice E is incorrect because the example does not illustrate irrational emotions.

31. **A.** The example shows a relationship between quality of attachment and responses to others and the world, making A the best answer choice. The example does not address attachment needs, Choice B, separation anxiety, Choice C, or bonding, Choice D. The example could support Choice E but not as well, because Choice E focuses on feelings about a separation or loss, while the example focuses on feelings about other people and change.

32. **D.** A good revision of this sentence will eliminate the repetition of "reasons" as well as the vague and pompous "category of reasons" and "enterprise." Choice D keeps the meaning intact, and does so with the greatest clarity and fewest words.

33. **E.** The sentence could do without choices A, B, C, and D, and the word "trying" as well. The slimmed-down sentence would read: The easiest to recognize is to avoid an unpleasant chore.

34. **A.** The paragraph offers three plausible reasons to explain why the writer procrastinates.

35. **B.** The paragraph still reads smoothly without sentence 15, which does little more than repeat the content of sentence 14: that procrastination produces guilt and anxiety.

Section 5: Critical Reading

Sentence Completions

1. **B.** The "also" in the second half of the sentence signals that the verb is parallel to "prevent" in the first half. You can eliminate choices C and D. The first adjective must mean something like reasonable or sensible, so Choice B, "logical," is a better option than Choice A, "fanciful," or E, "idle," which mean just the opposite.

2. **C.** The first noun must mean something like "substitute" but be a word that will fit with the preposition "to." Choice A, "answer," is possible, Choice C "alternative" is a good answer, and Choice D is awkward. For the second blank, the phrase "subject to" is clearly the best of the three, and Choice C the best of the five choices.

3. **D.** The logic of the sentence suggests that the missing verb must mean something like prevent or decrease. Choice B, "augment" (increase), and Choice C, "foster," are the opposite of what is needed. Neither "explain," Choice A, nor "exculpate" (excuse), Choice E, makes much more sense, although "deter" (discourage, keep from doing), Choice D, fits well.

4. **E.** The sentence opposes the unpleasant "smoke and _____ of the city," with the "_____ air and peace of the mountains," so the first blank must be a noun similar in effect to "smoke," and the second blank requires an adjective with pleasant connotations. In A and B the nouns are possible, but the adjectives are not. In choices C and D, the noun choices cannot fit. Choice E correctly has the bad "hustle-bustle" and the good "exhilarating."

5. **B.** A situation requiring the choice between two unpleasant alternatives is the definition of the word "dilemma," and that is what this sentence describes.

6. **A.** The word "combining" should alert you to look for a noun here that means a coming together of East and West. Choices B, C, and D are clearly wrong. Choice A, "fusion," the union of different things, fits well.

7. **B.** The noun referring to what "allowed voters to decide" on an issue could be "statute," Choice A, "referendum," Choice B (the most precise word), or "bill," Choice D. The missing adverb that describes the 9-to-1 win must denote a very resounding margin of victory. Neither "meager," Choice A, nor "narrow," Choice D, will do. Again, the best answer uses the most specific noun as well as the most suitable adverb.

8. **D.** The first blank requires a noun describing something a novel is based on. Choices A, C, and D are possible. Choices B and E are eliminated by the use of "upon which." The second word must praise the book because it is parallel with "intelligence" and the novel has been called "fine." Choices A and C must be eliminated, and only Choice D remains.

9. **B.** The adjective "anachronistic" means representing something as existing at other than its proper time, such as a washing machine in the Middle Ages or a knight in armor at a football game. Choice A is a possibility, although B is more exact.

Short Reading Passages

10. **C.** The author does not list or examine the myriad ways latex-based medical products grow the economy, so Choice A is not the answer. Neither is Choice B, because the author does not survey differences between latex-based and nonlatex-based products. The author neither makes an argument that latex-based products are more harmful than helpful, Choice D, nor advocates continued use of latex-based products, Choice E. Choice C is correct. By drawing attention to latex as a prophylactic (preventive) and as an allergen, the author is identifying the main pros and cons of latex applications in medicine.

11. **B.** The alarmists' position is that latex allergies are responsible for high turnover in the healthcare field and if unchecked, will cause disruptions to quality healthcare delivery and to the economy. Choice B, which indicates that high turnover may exist for reasons other than latex allergies, most seriously weakens that position. Choices A, C, and D, in contrast, strengthen or support the alarmists' position. Choice E suggests that the solution the alarmists want is already under way.

Paired Passages

12. **E.** In Passage 1, see lines 12–15. The author believes the opposite of choices A, C, and D, and does not express an opinion on Choice B. The point of the passage is that debates have become less and less informative and the candidates less and less forthright.

13. **C.** Even without knowing the definition of the word, you can determine that this is the only choice that makes sense in context. Choices B, D, and E all contradict the picture the author gives of candidates who are less than forthright and who are afraid of saying anything that might ruffle feathers. Choice A is completely unrelated to "elliptical."

14. **A.** The author of Passage 2 cites B (lines 10–12), C (lines 5–6), D (lines 12–14), and E (lines 15–17). The author does NOT, however, cite any evidence that these positive effects have increased voter turnout.

15. **C.** For example, Passage 1 uses words like "tube" and "sound bites" and asks a sarcastic rhetorical question at the end of the passage. Passage 2, on the other hand, presents points in a straightforward fashion. Choice A is not accurate because "philosophical" is an inappropriate characterization of Passage 2. The tone used in Passage 1 is not like the tone in Passage 2; Choice B and Choice D aren't accurate characterizations of either passage. Choice E is simply too vague.

Long Reading Passages

16. **B.** The passage explicitly refers to Celia and Dorothea as sisters. Although it does not mention their father's death, you know that the jewels belonged to their mother, and because an uncle, not her father, gave them to Dorothea, it may be that the father is dead and they are in the uncle's care.

17. **D.** That Dorothea has started an "infant school" in the village and is busy with plans for some buildings tells you at once that she is active and generous. No details in the passage suggest that she is prying, idle, ambitious, or ineffectual, although she may be rich or philanthropic.

18. **B.** The preceding sentence tells you that Dorothea's eyes are "full of laughter," and her tone when she speaks again is "full" and "cordial." She is teasing Celia good-naturedly, making fun of her sister's remark that it is exactly "six months today." In this dialogue, it is Celia who has planned what she will say, and Dorothea speaks spontaneously. Dorothea has probably forgotten all about the jewels, and Celia has probably been thinking about them for some time.

19. **D.** The phrase means disrespectful or lacking in respect. The reader must recognize that the verb "want" here means to lack, not the more common to wish for. Choice C confuses "wanting" and "wanton."

20. **D.** Celia does not wish to have all the jewels, although she does want a share, and she expects to wear them. Unlike Dorothea, she is not at all Puritanical. She correctly anticipates that Dorothea might object to wearing jewelry, so she has prepared this defense on the moral grounds that she thinks will best convince Dorothea.

21. **C.** Dorothea, who does not care about the jewels herself, has simply not realized that Celia really wants to wear them. In lines 45–46, the reader is told that this "discovery" is astonishing to her, and the moment she realizes Celia's true feeling, she rushes to open the cabinet. Celia's arguments would have been more effective if she had simply told Dorothea of her real wishes because Dorothea loves her sister and is eager to make her happy. Notice that Dorothea said the jewels would not be worn only before she realized what Celia really wishes.

22. **A.** "Deprecation" is disapproval, or protest, as is suggested in this sentence by Dorothea's saying no. A lessening is a depreciation, and a removal is a deprivation.

23. **A** The adjective in this context comes from the verb meaning to annoy, to irk, as in to try one's p.atience. In some contexts, "trying" might mean attempting or determining, but here, irksome is the best definition.

24. **E.** The "Puritanic toleration" is Dorothea's. She has given up all the jewels to Celia and even encouraged her to wear them. Although this is in one way pleasing to Celia, it does put Dorothea in a position of moral superiority, which Celia finds annoying.

25. **C.** Dorothea is the Puritan, and Celia is the "unenthusiastic sister"; that is, one who has not adopted the religious extremes of self-denial, such as wearing jewels.

26. **D.** Although some answers here describe Dorothea accurately, only Choice D points to an inconsistency. Dorothea regards wearing jewelry as somehow immoral, and yet, because she sees that Celia really wants to wear the jewels, she encourages her to do so. She believes what is right for her sister would not be right for her.

27. **C.** The passage is centrally concerned with delineating the two sisters. Although there is some mild comedy at the expense of both, the passage is not satiric, and it reveals as much love as friction between the sisters. They are not alike, and though Celia may take pleasure in jewels, the passage is not about the dangers of materialism. The author, the reader senses, is amused by and fond of both of these young women.

Section 6: Mathematics

1. B. If $a + b = 12$, then $a + b - 30 = 12 - 30 = -18$.

2. D. Let x = denominator of the fraction and $x + 6$ = numerator of the fraction. Then,

$$\frac{x+6}{x} = \frac{3}{2}$$
$$2 \cdot (x+6) = 3 \cdot x$$
$$2x + 12 = 3x$$
$$2x + 12 - 2x = 3x - 2x$$
$$12 = x = \text{denominator}$$
$$x + 6 = 12 + 6 = 18 = \text{numerator}$$

3. C. Since Mario weighs more than Eric, $m > e$, and since Mario weighs less than Hector, $h > m$. Hence, $h > m > e$ or $e < m < h$.

4. A. The average (arithmetic mean) is determined by dividing the sum of the numbers in the data by the number of items in the data. Hence, the average of the areas of the 2 triangles is

$$\frac{\text{sum of the areas}}{\text{number of triangles}} = \frac{25}{2}$$

5. C. Since the radii in a circle are equal, the angles opposite the radii are equal and the third angle of the triangle has a measure of $y°$. The sum of the interior angles of a triangle is $180°$ and

$$x + y + y = 180$$
$$x + 2y = 180$$
$$100 + 2y = 180$$
$$100 + 2y - 100 = 180 - 100$$
$$2y = 80$$
$$\frac{2y}{2} = \frac{80}{2}$$
$$y = 40$$

6. E. The only positive integer factors of 169 are 1, 13, and 169. Each of the other answer choices have more than 3 factors.

7. D.

$$\frac{25x^4}{z} = 625x^3$$
$$\frac{25x^4}{z} \cdot z = 625x^3 \cdot z$$
$$25x^4 = 625x^3 z$$
$$\frac{25x^4}{25x^3} = \frac{625x^3}{25x^3} z$$
$$x = 25z$$

Hence $\dfrac{1}{x} = \dfrac{1}{25z}$

8. B. Let S_n represent the nth term of the sequence. Then,

$$S_1 = -\frac{1}{9}$$

$$S_2 = -\frac{1}{9}(-3) = \frac{1}{3}$$

$$S_3 = \frac{1}{3}(-3) = -1$$

$$S_4 = -1(-3) = 3$$

$$S_5 = 3(-3) = -9$$

$$S_6 = -9(-3) = 27$$

$$S_7 = 27(-3) = -81$$

Grid-in Questions

9. 78. The median of a set of numbers is the middle number, which in this problem is the fourth number of the set. Since the numbers of the set are consecutive even integers and the fourth number is 84, the third number is 82, the second number is 80, and the first number is 78, which would be the smallest of the 7 numbers.

10. 8.

$$\text{Since } 120\% = 1.20 = 1\frac{1}{5} = \frac{6}{5},$$

$$x + 4y = \frac{6}{5} \cdot (10y)$$

$$x + 4y = 12y$$

$$x + 4y - 4y = 12y - 4y$$

$$x = 8y$$

If $x = 8y$, then $\frac{x}{y} = \frac{8y}{y} = 8$.

11. 140.

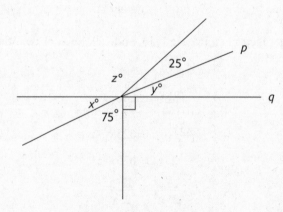

In the figure, $x + 75 = 90$

$$x + 75 - 75 = 90 - 75$$

$$x = 15$$

Since vertical angles are equal, $x = y = 15$ and q is a straight line,

$$y + 25 + z = 180$$
$$15 + 25 + z = 180$$
$$40 + z = 180$$
$$40 + z - 40 = 180 - 40$$
$$z = 140$$

12. 13.

Since $3h(a) = 15,$
$$3(a - 3) = 15$$
$$\frac{3(a - 3)}{3} = \frac{15}{3}$$
$$a - 3 + 3 = 5 + 3$$
$$a = 8$$

Hence $h(2a) = h(16) = 16 - 3 = 13$

13. 6.

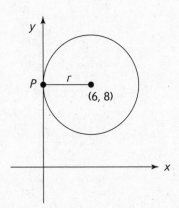

Since the circle intersects the y-axis at 1 point only, the point of tangency P has coordinates $(0, 8)$.

The length of the radius r is

$$r = \sqrt{(x_1 - x_2)^2 + (y_1 - y_2)^2}$$
$$= \sqrt{(6 - 0)^2 + (8 - 8)^2}$$
$$= \sqrt{6^2 + 0^2}$$
$$= \sqrt{36}$$
$$= 6$$

14. **300.**

Let x = the number of $4 plants and $2x$ = the number of $3 plants.

Since $1,000 worth of plants were purchased,

$$4x + 3(2x) = 1,000$$
$$4x + 6x = 1,000$$
$$10x = 1,000$$
$$\frac{10x}{10} = \frac{1,000}{10}$$
$$x = 100 = \text{the number of \$4 plants.}$$
$$2x = 200 = \text{the number of \$3 plants.}$$

Hence, the total number of plants purchased was $100 + 200 = 300$ plants.

15. $\frac{1}{3}$.

$$\text{Since} \quad 9a^2 - 9b^2 = 90$$
$$9(a^2 - b^2) = 90$$
$$\frac{9(a^2 - b^2)}{9} = \frac{90}{9}$$
$$a^2 - b^2 = 10$$
$$(a - b)(a + b) = 10$$

Since $a + b = 30$ and $(a - b)(a + b) = 10$

$$(a - b)(30) = 10$$
$$\frac{(a - b)(30)}{30} = \frac{10}{30}$$
$$a - b = \frac{1}{3}$$

16. **2400.** The perimeter P of a rectangle with base b and height h is $P = 2b + 2h$. Since the perimeter of the plot is 200 yards and one side is 60 yards,

$$P = 2b + 2h$$
$$200 = 2(60) + 2h$$
$$200 = 120 + 2h$$
$$200 - 120 = 120 + 2h - 120$$
$$80 = 2h$$
$$\frac{80}{2} = \frac{2h}{2}$$
$$40 = h$$

The area A of a rectangle with base b and height h is

$$A = bh$$
$$= (60)(40)$$
$$= 2400$$

17. $\frac{2}{3}$.

Since $a \boxtimes b = \frac{2a+b}{a+2b}$,

$$1 \boxtimes 4 = \frac{2(1)+4}{1+2(4)}$$

$$= \frac{2+4}{1+8}$$

$$= \frac{6}{9}$$

$$= \frac{2}{3}$$

18. **55.** Since $\triangle XYZ$ has 2 equal angles, the sides opposite these angles are equal in length. The only possible lengths for the 3 sides of the triangle are 25, 25, and 15 or 15, 15, and 25. Hence, the smallest possible value for the perimeter P of the triangle is

$$P = 15 + 15 + 25 = 55$$

Section 7: Critical Reading

Paired Passages

1. **E.** Choices A, B, C, and D are directly stated or implied in the passage as having contributed to major changes in the present-day topography and hydrology of eastern North America. Although the Baylor team conducted archaeological research, its excavations were not a factor in the sedimentation of valley basins, making Choice E the correct answer.

2. **D.** "Indigenous" means originating in and characteristic of a particular region or country, or native. All the other answer choices are incorrect.

3. **C.** The prefix "hydro" means water, and the word "hydrologic" means of or pertaining to the movement of water above, on, and below the earth. The water cycle of condensation and precipitation is one example. Choices A, B, D, and E are incorrect.

4. **D.** While all the sentences contain information that helps challenge the widely held view that colonial-era Europeans were solely responsible for altering our environmental and climate, the most direct challenge is stated in Choice D.

5. **E.** The author does not purport to praise, criticize, recast, or advocate anything, as suggested by the first words of answer choices A, B, C, and D. Only Choice E correctly characterizes the author's neutral tone and objective voice.

6. **B.** The author's interest is in correcting misconceptions about the causes of environmental change, which to date have been attributed to European colonists alone, and thus would most likely agree with Choice B. The author does not seek to spread blame, Choice A, and as a scientist would hesitate to claim choices C, D, or E, all of which make generalizations that are not directly supported by the Baylor study data.

7. **B.** The author relates Genghis Khan's impact on the earth to a present-day equivalent, making Choice B the correct answer. The first sentence is not a mere attention-getting device, Choice A, and the passage is not about Genghis Khan, Choice C. The author compares the impacts of four historical events or periods in terms of how much time depopulated lands had for reforestation, making Choice D too narrow as a purpose of the first sentence. Choice E is incorrect because the author does not make that claim in the first sentence or elsewhere in the passage.

8. **A.** The passage states that the environmental impacts of four high-mortality historical events were the units of study, Choice A. During high-mortality events such as wars, conquests, cultural collapses, and epidemics, there are fewer people, hence less agricultural activity, hence less deforestation. The study used a predictive model, Choice D, rather than ice cores, Choice B, but they represent research methods rather than the subject of study and so are incorrect. By referring to only one of the four high-mortality events, Choice C is too narrow and therefore incorrect. Choice E is incorrect because it states an underlying fact on which the research was based and was not the subject of study.

9. **D.** The first sentence of the second paragraph identifies as a common misconception the idea that the human impact on climate began with large-scale burning of coal and oil in the industrial era. The problem began, instead, with the advent of agriculture, which led to deforestation. Choices A, B, C, and E, while true, are not identified as commonly held misconceptions.

10. **E.** All except answer Choice E are given as examples of land use changes affecting the global climate. It is likely that historical changes in population in parts of Africa could be shown to have affected regional or global climate, but the example is not cited in the passage.

11. **A.** The passage ends with the conclusion that "we are now in a position to make land-use decisions that will diminish our impact on climate and the carbon cycle." Choice A is therefore correct. Choices B and C are contradicted in the passage, and choices D and E cannot be inferred or concluded from the information given. The point was made that reforestation in some areas at certain times did not make up for aggressive continuous deforestation overall, and no one could reasonably conclude from the passage that people should not grow crops.

12. **D.** Passage 2 (paragraph 5) states that in "short events such as the Black Death and the Ming Dynasty collapse, the forest re-growth wasn't enough to overcome the emissions from decaying material in the soil. . . . But during the longer-lasting ones like the Mongol invasion and the conquest of the Americas there was enough time for the forests to re-grow and absorb significant amounts of carbon." The correct answer, referring to both the Americas and the Mongol invasions, is Choice D.

13. **A.** Choice B is incorrect because neither passage refers to legislation or appeals to political leadership. Choice C is incorrect because although both studies used new methods as research tools, testing those methods was not the goal of the research. Choice D is incorrect because although both studies were concerned with causes and effects of deforestation, neither passage referred to global warming. Choice E is incorrect because although the second passage referred to atmospheric carbon dioxide, neither passage had as a goal explaining how that harms the planet. The best answer is Choice A. Passage 1 sought to correct the misperception that European colonists were the source of environmental degradation in the Americas, because Native Americans practicing agriculture had already caused significant deforestation. Passage 2 sought to correct the misperception that the Industrial Revolution caused harmful climate change, because deforestation caused by people practicing agriculture had already changed the climate.

14. **E.** All three statements can be inferred from the passages, with deforestation (removal of vegetation from the earth's surface) as the concept common to both passages.

15. **B.** Choices A and E, while perhaps not impossible, represent somewhat radical or futuristic solutions to the problem. Choice C the authors of both passages would likely acknowledge is not possible, as environmental change is a constant in the planet's history. What environment would we identify as an original condition? Choice D is a popular sentiment but difficult to do. The most conservative answer to which the authors of both passages would agree is Choice B, saving forests and conserving the land.

Section 8: Mathematics

1. **D.**

$$\sqrt{z} - 14 = -5$$
$$\sqrt{z} - 14 + 14 = -5 + 14$$
$$\sqrt{z} = 9$$
$$\left(\sqrt{z}\right)^2 = (9)^2$$
$$z = 81$$

2. **B.**

$$4(3x - 1) = 20$$
$$\frac{4(3x - 1)}{4} = \frac{20}{4}$$
$$3x - 1 = 5$$
$$3x - 1 + 1 = 5 + 1$$
$$3x = 6$$
$$\frac{3x}{3} = \frac{6}{3}$$
$$x = 2$$

3. **E.** Since each of the 5 exterior colors can be paired with each of the 3 interior colors, there are $5 \times 3 = 15$ possible color combinations.

4. **C.** Since there are a total of 160 voters polled, with 84 voters favoring candidate x, the fraction of those polled who favored candidate x is

$$\frac{84}{160} = \frac{21}{40}$$

5. **C.**

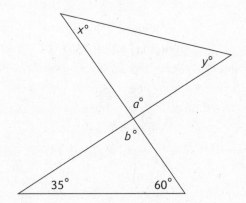

Since the sum of the interior angles of a triangle is 180°, $a + x + y = b + 35 + 60 = 180$, and since vertical angles are equal in measure, $a = b$. Hence, $x + y = 35 + 60 = 95$.

6. A.

$$\text{Since } \frac{25}{y} = \frac{5n}{3y}$$

$$(25)\cdot(3y)=(y)\cdot(5n)$$

$$75y=5ny$$

$$\frac{75y}{5y}=\frac{5ny}{5y}$$

$$15=n$$

7. E. If 2 lines are parallel, their alternate exterior angles are equal in measure and $a = x = 40$. Since 2 adjacent angles along a straight line are supplementary,

$$
\begin{array}{lll}
x+y=180 & \text{and} & x+z=180 \\
40+y=180 & & 40+z=180 \\
40+y-40=180-40 & & 40+z-40=180-40 \\
y=140 & \text{and} & z=140
\end{array}
$$

Hence, $x + y + z = 40 + 140 + 140 = 320$.

8. C. Since the line is perpendicular to the x-axis, the x value for all points (x, y) on the line is constant and the equation of the line is of the form $x = $ constant. Since the given line is perpendicular to the x-axis and passes through the point $(–8, 5)$, the equation of the line is $x = –8$.

9. D. The volume V of a right circular cylinder with radius r and height h is $V = \pi r^2 h$. If the height is the same and the radius is tripled, the volume is

$$\pi(3r)^2 h = \pi\left(9r^2\right)h$$

$$= 9\pi r^2 h$$

$$= 9V$$

10. A.

If 30% of a equals 75% of b,

$$.30a = .75b$$

$$100(.30a)=100(.75b)$$

$$30a=75b$$

$$\frac{30a}{75}=\frac{75b}{75}$$

$$\frac{30}{75}a=b$$

$$b=\frac{2}{5}a=.4a$$

Hence $b = 40\%$ of a.

11. B. If $0 > x > 1$, as an example, let $x = \frac{1}{2}$ and insert it into each answer choice.

I. $x^2 = \left(\frac{1}{2}\right)^2 = \frac{1}{4} < 1$, x^2 is not > 1

II. $x^3 = \left(\frac{1}{2}\right)^3 = \frac{1}{8} < 1$, $\frac{1}{8} < \frac{1}{4}$ and $x^3 < x^2$, x^3 is not $> x^2$

III. $x = \frac{1}{2}$ and $\frac{x}{3} = \frac{\frac{1}{2}}{3} = \frac{1}{6}$ and $\frac{1}{2} > \frac{1}{6}$ and x is $> \frac{x}{3}$

12. **B.** The expression for the product of $7x$ and the square root of y is $7x\sqrt{y}$. The expression for the square of the difference between x and y is $(x-y)^2$. Hence the expression for the statement: "The product of $7x$ and the square root of y is equal to the square of the difference between x and y" is

$$7x\sqrt{y} = (x-y)^2$$

13. **E.** The square of an integer cannot end in 3, 7, or 8.

14. **D.** If the first term of the sequence is a, then the second term of the sequence is $\frac{1}{4}a + 5$. Hence the ratio of the second term to the first term is

$$\frac{\frac{1}{4}a + 5}{a} = \frac{\frac{1}{4}a + 5}{a} \cdot \frac{4}{4}$$

$$= \frac{4 \cdot \frac{1}{4}a + 4 \cdot 5}{4a}$$

$$= \frac{a + 20}{4a}$$

15. **E.** Since the sum of the 4 angles in the figure is 360°,

$$2z + 3z + 4z + 6z = 360$$

$$15z = 360$$

$$\frac{15z}{15} = \frac{360}{15}$$

$$z = 24$$

Hence, the largest angle in the figure is $6z = 6 \times 24 = 144$.

16. **C.** Let x = the largest integer, $x - 1$ = the second integer, and $x - 2$ = the smallest integer.

The Pythagorean Theorem states that the square of the hypotenuse in a right triangle is equal to the sum of the squares of the 2 legs of the triangle. Since the hypotenuse is the longest side in a right triangle, $x^2 = (x-2)^2 + (x-1)^2$.

Section 9: Writing-Multiple Choice

Improving Sentences

1. **D.** The problem here is a misplaced modifier. The participial phrase "reviewing Jane Austen's *Emma*" modifies "Nikisha" and should appear as close to the noun it modifies as possible. The solution is Choice D, which puts the modifying phrase at the beginning of the sentence, immediately followed by the word it modifies.

2. **B.** There are two complete sentences here, but no conjunction or punctuation to join them. The run-on sentences can be corrected by putting a period or semicolon at the end of the first sentence (after "technique"). Choices D and E change the meaning of the sentence, and need a comma.

3. **E.** The original version has an ambiguous pronoun (does the second "they" refer to the seed or the chemical companies?), is wordy ("they" is used twice), and shifts from active to passive voice. Choice B has the ambiguous pronoun and the active-passive shift. Choice C is wordy and has the active-passive shift. Choice D corrects these problems but distorts the meaning. Choice E solves all the problems.

4. **A.** Though the sentence begins with a participle, "drawing" does not dangle, but modifies Ann Atkinson, which immediately follows. The original version is the best of the five, avoiding the verbosity of Choice C, the passive voice of Choice D, the awkward tense change of Choice B, and the slight change of meaning in Choice E.

5. **E.** Choice C is attractively concise, but is so shortened that it doesn't quite make sense. The two verbs here, "initiate" and "become," are equally important, and can be made parallel as in Choice E; choices A and B subordinate one or the other.

6. **E.** All of these sentences are grammatical, but Choice E is the most concise in normal word order. Choice C uses the same words, but the word order is unconventional, making "wittiest" an afterthought.

7. **D.** We can eliminate choices A and B because they use "you," but the sentence began with the pronoun "one" (the third, not the second person) as the subject. Choice E corrects this error, but repetition of the "one should" breaks the parallel verbs without a repeated subject. Choice D keeps the parallel use of active verbs, while Choice C replaces the verb with a participle.

8. **C.** Choices A, B, D, and E are adjectival phrases that modify the designs or collection, not the television fashion project. The designs, not the fashion project, are "different." By adding "with designs" to the beginning, the phrase now logically refers to *Project Runway*, which follows it.

9. **B.** The sentence is a fragment in all four versions except Choice B. Here the first clause is dependent, and the main clause has a subject ("supply line") and a main verb ("became"). Though both choices A and D also use "became," the clauses are still dependent because the conjunctions ("and" and "while") join them to the initial dependent clause. The word "becoming" is a participle, not a verb.

10. **D.** The original version needlessly shifts from third person subject ("the crane") to a second person ("you"). Choice C shifts from an active to a passive verb. Using the prepositional phrase, as in Choice D, eliminates the need for "they."

11. **C.** Choice A creates a fragment. In Choice B, "this" has a vague antecedent. Choice D is a run-on sentence.

12. **A.** The original version is the best choice here. Choice B is the only one that is shorter, but it is too short to make sense. The other choices are not bad, but they are wordier than Choice A. As long as you can be sure the meaning is the same and the grammar is right, choose the version with the fewest words.

13. **D.** The issue here is does the omission of a phrase like "nature has provided" or its equivalent change the meaning of the sentence. Clearly Choice D is the most concise, and "but" is preferable to "and." Since the clause also uses the adjective "natural," the "nature has provided" phrase is redundant.

14. **B.** As it stands, this is a sentence fragment; it has no main verb, since "form" is in a dependent clause. The same problem exists in choices C and E, while Choice D is a participle and not a verb. In B, "form" is the main verb of a sentence with "maples" the subject.

15. **D.** This is another verbose sentence. If you say "throughout," there is no need to also say "the entire work," since "throughout" means "all the way through." Choice E pares too much from the sentence, losing the sense of both "throughout" (where) and "constantly" (how often).

Final Preparation

One Week Before the Exam

1. **Clear your schedule** one week before the exam. Try to avoid scheduling events during this week so that you can focus on your preparation.

2. **Review the SAT website** at sat.collegeboard.org for updated exam information.

3. **Review your notes** from this study guide and make sure you know the question types, basic skills, strategies, and directions for each section on the test.

4. **Review the practice tests.** Allow yourself enough time to review the practice problems you have already completed from this study guide and the accompanying CD-ROM. If you haven't yet taken all of the practice tests, take the practice tests during this week. Be sure to time yourself as you practice.

5. **Know the testing center.** Make sure you are familiar with the driving directions and where the parking facilities near the testing center are located.

6. **Relax the night before the exam.** Try to get a good night's sleep. Trying to cram a year's worth of reading and studying into one night can cause you to feel emotionally and physically exhausted. Save your energy for exam day.

Exam Day

1. **Arrive early.** Arrive at the exam location in plenty of time (at least 30 minutes early).

2. **Dress appropriately** to adapt to any room temperature. If you dress in layers, you can always take off clothing to adjust to warmer temperatures.

3. **Bring identification.** Remember to bring the required identification documents: valid photo ID and your authorization voucher.

4. **Leave your electronic devices.** Leave all electronic devices at home or in your car (cell phone, smartphone, PDA, etc.) with the exception of an acceptable calculator (see below). You may also be asked to remove your watch during the exam.

5. **Bring an acceptable calculator** to perform math calculations; also bring extra batteries. For more information about calculator requirements, visit the SAT College Board website. Type "acceptable calculators" in the search menu.

6. **Answer easy questions first.** Start off crisply, working the questions you know first, and then go back and try to answer the others within the section. Use the elimination strategy to determine if a problem is possibly solvable or too difficult to solve.

7. **Don't get stuck on any one question.** Never spend more than about 1 to 1½ minutes on a multiple-choice question.

8. **Guess** only if you can narrow down your choices because there is a penalty for guessing.

9. **Writing in the test booklet (not the answer sheet)** is a test-taking advantage. Write notes in the margins to perform calculations, redraw diagrams, note eliminated choices, or simply make helpful notes to jog your memory.

Sources

Sincere appreciation is extended to the following authors and publishers for allowing the use of excerpts for reading passages.

Anderson, Michael and Susan Leigh Anderson, "Robot be Good," *Scientific American* (October 2010), 74. (Test 1)

Bach, Richard. *The Bridge Across Forever*. Harper Collins, 1989. (Diagnostic Test)

Bernstein, Leonard. *The Joy of Music*. Amadeus Press, 2004. (Test 7)

Billington, Ray Allen. *The Westward Movement in the United States*. Van Nostrand Reinhold Company, 1959. (Test 2)

Bradshaw, Peter, "The Social Network—Review," *The Guardian,* 14 October, 2010. www.guardian.co.uk/film/2010/oct/14/the-social-network-review (Test 3)

Broecker, Wallace S, "Global Warming on Trial," *Natural History Magazine* (April 1992), 6. (Test 4)

Bronson, Po and Ashley Merryman. *NurtureShock*. Twelve Publishers, 2009. (Diagnostic Test)

Cary, Lorene. *Black Ice*. Alfred A. Knopf, 1991. (Test 3)

Chaisson, Eric, "Early Results from the Hubble Space Telescope," *Scientific American* (June 1992), 44–46. (Test 7)

Davis, Wade, "Last of Their Kind," *Scientific American* (Sept. 2010), 62. (Test 1)

Diamond, Jared. *Guns, Germs and Steel: The Fates of Human Societies*. W. W. Norton & Company, 1997. (Test 5)

Ebert, Roger, "The Social Network," *Chicago Sun-Times,* 29 September 2010. (Test 3)

Eliot, George. *Middlemarch: A Study of Provincial Life,* 1874. (Test 4)

Evans, Sara M. *Born for Liberty: A History of Women in America.* The Free Press, Simon & Schuster, 1989. (Test 1)

Fraser, Antonia. *The Warrior Queens*. Alfred A. Knopf, 1988. (Test 6)

Greenblatt, Stephen. *Shakespeare's Freedom*. University of Chicago Press, 2010. (Test 5)

Herman, Judith. *Trauma and Recovery*. Basic Books, 1997. (Diagnostic Test)

Karl, Thomas R, Neville Nicholls and Jonathan Gregory, "Coming Climate," *Scientific American* (May 1997), 79–83. (Chapter 2)

Kingston, Maxine Hong. *The Woman Warrior*. Alfred A. Knopf, 1976. (Test 2)

Knapp, Bettina L. *The Brontes: Branwell, Anne, Emily, Charlotte*. Continuum Publishing, 1991. (Test 2)

Lee, Chang-Rae. *Native Speaker*. Penguin Group, 1995. (Test 5)

Manhard, Stephen J. *The Goof Proofer*. Scribner, 1987. (Chapter 2)

Mattingly, Garrett. *The Armada*. Houghton Mifflin Harcourt Publishing, 1987. (Test 3)

Mazonowicz, Douglas. *Voices from the Stone Age: A Search for Cave and Canyon Art*. Gallery of Prehistoric Art, 1974. (Test 5)

Miller, Lucasta. *The Bronte Myth*. Alfred A. Knopf, 2001. (Test 2)

Mlodinow, Leonard, and Stephen Hawking, *"The (Elusive) Theory of Everything,"* *Scientific American,* (October 2010), 70. (Test 2)

O'Connor, Flannery. "Good Country People" from *A Good Man is Hard to Find and Other Stories*. Houghton Mifflin Harcourt Publishing, 1983. (Diagnostic Test)

Parker, Dorothy. "Writing About Hemingway" from *A Book of Great Short Stories*. New Yorker, 1927. (Diagnostic Test)

Powell, James Lawrence. *Mysteries of Terra Firma*. The Free Press, Simon & Schuster, 2001. (Test 6)

Rodriguez, Richard. Aria: "A Memoir of a Bilingual Childhood" from *Hunger of Memory: The Education of Richard Rodriguez.* David R. Godine Publisher, 1983. (Test 1)

Rogers, Carl. *On Becoming a Person*. Houghton Mifflin Harcourt Publishing, 1961. (Diagnostic Test)

Roszak, Theodore. *The Voice of the Earth*. Simon & Schuster, 1992. (Test 7)

Shields, Carol. "Marriage" from *The Stone Diaries*. Viking, Penguin, 1993. (Test 6)

Slatkin, Wendy. "Women Artists in History" from *Antiquity to the 20th Century*. Prentice Hall, 2000 (Test 6)

Stegner, Wallace. "The Double Corner" from *Collected Stories of Wallace Stegner*. Random House, 2006. (Test 2)

Stinchcomb, Gary, and Steve Driese. *Native Americans Modified American Landscape Years Prior to the Arrival of Europeans*. Baylor University, 2011. (Test 4)

Stravinsky, Igor and Robert Craft. *Themes and Episodes*. Alfred A. Knopf, 1966. (Test 7)

Thomson, Belinda. *Gauguin*. Thames & Hudson Ltd., London, 1987. (Test 4)

Vermeiji, Geerat J. *The Evolutionary World: How Adaptation Explains Everything from Seashells to Civilization.* Thomas Dunne Books, 2010. (Test 6)

"War, Plague No Match for Deforestation in Driving CO_2 Buildup," *Carnegie Institute for Science* (20 January, 2011), carnegiescience.edu/news/war_plague_no_match_deforestation_driving_co2_buildup (Test 4)

White, E. B. "The Ring of Time" from *Essays of E.B. White*. International Creative Management, Inc., 1979. (Test 1)

Willingham, Daniel, "Trust Me, I'm a Scientist," *Scientific American* (May 2011), 13. (Test 6)

Winkler, William, and Konrad Bogel, "Control of Rabies in Wildlife," *Scientific American* (June 1992) 86. (Test 3)